Margaret of Anjou and the men around her

Portrait medallion of Margaret of Anjou, by Piero da Milano, 1463.

Margaret of Anjou and the men around her

*History to the defeated
May say alas
But cannot help
Or pardon.*

W. H. Auden

B. M. CRON

History & Heritage
Publishing

Copyright © 2021 B. M. Cron

All rights reserved. No part of this publication may be reproduced or transmitted in any form or by any means, electronic or mechanical including photocopying, recording or any information storage or retrieval system, without prior permission in writing from the publishers.

The right of B. M. Cron to be identified as the author of this work has been asserted by her in accordance with the Copyright, Designs and Patents Act 1988

First published in the United Kingdom in 2021 by
History and Heritage Publishing

ISBN 978-1-914280-01-6

Front cover image: This image is reproduced under a creative commons licence by courtesy of https://commons.wikimedia.org/wiki/User:Sodacan

Contents

Young Margaret

1 Woe to Thee, O Land	2
2 The House of Anjou	10
3 The Truce of Tours	20
4 England's Queen	31

The Suffolk Years

5 The Quest for Peace	48
6 Destruction of a Duke	60
7 Ceding Maine	70
8 The King's Lieutenant in France	82
9 Losing Normandy	94
10 Suffolk Disgraced	107

Power Strugle

11 Aftermath	120
12 Somerset or York	134
13 Strife	148
14 Triumph and Disaster	160
15 Queen in Waiting	172
16 My Lord Protector	185
17 Fortune's Wheel	198

Contents

Lancastrian Queen

18	Queen Consort	214
19	Royal Court in the Midlands	227
20	Loveday	242
21	An Uneasy Interlude	254

The Yorkists' Challenge

22	The Earl of Warwick's War	268
23	The Defence of the Realm	282
24	The Yorkists' Revenge	296
25	The Westminster Accord	309
26	Embattled Queen	320

Queen in Exile

27	Victory into Defeat	338
28	The Search for Allies	353
29	Into Exile	367
30	Margaret in Exile	379
31	Years of Exile	392

The Last Years

32	Warwick's Apostasy	406
33	The Queen and the Earl	419
34	The Final Throw	432
35	Captive Queen	447

Appendix: Finances and Dower Lands	461
Abbreviations	471
Notes	476
Bibliography	591
Index	609

Young Margaret

1
Woe to Thee, O Land

War was the Great Game in fifteenth-century Europe. It was played at all levels of political society with territorial acquisition as its raison d'être. Its savagery was disguised under the twin cloaks of 'chivalry' and 'just cause', punctuated by periods of truce to allow the exhausted combatants time to recover and regroup for the next round. The principal protagonists were the Kings of France and England, who had been at war intermittently for as long as anyone could remember in a conflict now known as the Hundred Years' War. The Duke of Burgundy, a monarch in all but name, was the third protagonist in the struggle. He was the most powerful political and military force in France.

The French royal family was singularly unlucky. King Charles VI was subject to bouts of insanity often for long periods. His two eldest sons died in 1415 and 1417 respectively and his last surviving son, Charles, became the Dauphin at the age of fourteen. Until his coronation as King Charles VII in 1429, when he was twenty-six, Charles remained a weak-willed, ineffectual creature, who gave no indication of the formidable monarch he would become. The French magnates acknowledged him only when it suited them; they were far more independent of the crown than their counterparts in England.

Henry V, the Lancastrian King of England, revived his great grandfather Edward III's claim to the crown of France and his victory at the Battle of Agincourt in 1415 decimated the ranks of the French nobility. In 1419 King Henry had a tremendous stroke of luck: John the Fearless, Duke of Burgundy, was assassinated in the presence of the Dauphin Charles. John's son Philip, the new Duke of Burgundy, swore never to forgive his father's murder and he recognised Henry V's right to the French crown.[1] Henry continued his conquest of Normandy and other parts of France in alliance with Burgundy. In 1420 he forced King Charles VI, who was little more than a cipher, and Queen Isabelle to sign the Treaty of Troyes repudiating the Dauphin Charles and making Henry their heir. Henry would act as Regent for his father-in-law until Charles VI died, when he would become King of France. Henry married Charles VI's daughter, Katherine, and to all intents and purposes her dowry was the Kingdom of France. After he was disinherited, the Dauphin Charles had set up a separate kingdom centred on the city of Bourges.[2]

Henry V died of dysentery at Vincennes in August 1422, at the age of thirty-six, after a spectacularly successful reign of nine and a half years. He left a son less than a year old to become King Henry VI of England. Charles VI died two months later, and the baby king inherited the dual monarchy. He was crowned in England in 1429 at the age of eight and taken to France at vast expense in 1430 to be crowned in Paris in 1431 as King Henri II. It was the only time Henry VI ever set foot in France.

On his deathbed Henry V had named his brother John, Duke of Bedford, as Regent of France and his youngest brother, Humphrey, Duke of Gloucester, as Regent of England. Bedford was a brilliant administrator and a military commander only slightly less talented than Henry V. From his headquarters in Rouen, Bedford set about completing the mammoth task of making good his baby nephew's claim to be King of France.

The English Council mistrusted the Duke of Gloucester and they refused to make him Regent of England. Instead they allotted him the lesser title and status of Protector and Defender of the Realm. Gloucester bitterly resented the slight and he blamed Henry VI's great uncle, Cardinal Henry Beaufort, Bishop of Winchester, for the opposition to his regency. During the fourteen years until Henry VI came of age the Council was divided by faction as Gloucester and the Cardinal struggled for mastery. Beaufort was older, shrewder, more experienced, and far less abrasive than Gloucester, and he had the advantage of being the richest man in England. English military efforts in France were sustained throughout Henry VI's minority and beyond largely by Beaufort's financial backing.[3]

The first blow to English rule in France was struck in 1429 when Joan of Arc raised the siege of Orleans and opened the way for the Dauphin Charles to be crowned King Charles VII at Rheims. A double disaster in 1435 sounded the death knell for the English: John, Duke of Bedford died in Rouen and the Duke of Burgundy abandoned his alliance with England. Bedford was worn out by the demands made on him as Regent and the growing realisation that Henry V's dream of a dual monarchy would never come true. He died on 14 September 1435, exactly one week before the Duke of Burgundy, whose dedication to the English cause had been waning for years, repudiated the English alliance that Bedford had worked so hard to maintain.

Burgundy convened a conference at Arras ostensibly to broker a peace between England and France but in fact to mask his more sinister intentions.[4] Charles VII's ambassadors were not at Arras to make peace but to detach a willing Burgundy from his English allies. The English delegation was barely listened to and as soon as they left Arras Burgundy happily changed sides. King Henry, now fourteen years old, was so upset that he remembered Burgundy's desertion for the rest of his life. Many years later he would tell a French envoy that if he had to fight anyone, he would far rather fight Burgundy than France.[5]

In England war weariness replaced the enthusiasm of Henry V's reign and the upkeep of garrisons in Normandy imposed an ever-increasing burden on an already overstrained Exchequer. The expectation that Henry VI would emulate his father and continue Henry V's conquests was slow to dissipate, but as he grew to manhood it became increasingly clear that he bore no resemblance to his mighty father. He inherited his father's piety but not his ruthlessness or military capabilities. A young man of limited intelligence, Henry was totally unsuited to be a king. His deeply rooted religious beliefs made him loathe bloodshed and shrink from all aspects of war.[6] King Charles VII recovered Paris in 1436 and made steady territorial gains thereafter until only the Duchies of Normandy and Gascony, parts of the County of Maine, and the Pale of Calais, were left in English hands.

The Kings of England were also Dukes of Gascony, an inheritance dating back to the twelfth-century Angevin empire of Henry II, the first Plantagenet King of England and his wife Eleanor, Duchess of Aquitaine. Successive Kings of France maintained that Gascony was a fief, held in liege homage by the Kings of England. The English insisted that their kings held it in full sovereignty, a King of England could never be a vassal of the King of France. Charles VII marched into Gascony in the spring of 1442, calling on the great southern magnates, Armagnac, Foix, and Albret, to join him arrayed for war. These magnates shifted their loyalties as the fortunes of war ebbed and flowed, and they frequently had a foot in both camps with the head of the house allied to the King of England while one of his sons served the King of France.

Unwisely the Count of Armagnac elected to play both ends against the middle. He professed loyalty to King Charles and sent his son to join the French army but he also sent envoys to England to propose an Anglo–Armagnac alliance to be sealed by a marriage between King Henry and one of his three daughters.[7] Henry entertained the proposal enthusiastically and the Council acquiesced. The advantages were not great, but Armagnac's lands bordered Gascony and a reliable neighbour who could offer swift military support was tempting. King Henry commissioned Sir Robert Roos, one of his knights of the body, and Thomas Beckington his secretary, as his emissaries.[8] He sent them instructions signed with his own hand, 'the whiche as ye wote wel we

Young Margaret

be not muche accustomed for to do' and he urged them to cross to Bordeaux immediately. He adjured them not to pre-empt his choice by making any commitment as to which girl would be selected. He wanted portraits of all three 'in their kerttelles simple, and their visages', showing their height, the colour of their skin and their features so that he could make an informed decision.[9] It is one of the few recorded occasions on which Henry ever expressed an interest in the physical appearance of women.

The timing could not have been worse. By one of those coincidences which were consistently fatal to the English and favourable to the French throughout the 1440s, the presence of a French army made it impossible for Roos and Beckington to proceed to Auch, Armagnac's capital, or even to Lectoure, his principal town some seventy miles south-east of Bordeaux. Armagnac naïvely applied to Charles VII for safe conducts for the English, but unsurprisingly they were not forthcoming.

Roos soon discovered that Armagnac was not the powerful ally the English hoped for and he became extremely angry when he learned that Armagnac's son was with the French army. He threatened Armagnac that such bad faith would not go unpunished and he wrathfully declared that the English army, when it arrived, would be sent against Armagnac as well as against Charles VII.[10] Roos had King Henry's word that an English army was on its way. Edward Hull, who had carried the news of Charles VII's campaign in Gascony to England, returned to Bordeaux in October with letters from King Henry announcing that an army would be sent – as soon as it could be assembled. The citizens of Bordeaux began to doubt the King of England's promises; perhaps it would be more advantageous to come to terms with the King of France?

King Henry remained naïvely confident that the negotiations with Armagnac could continue. He sent an artist, one Hans, to Bordeaux to paint the prospective brides' portraits. The conscientious Roos had Hans conveyed through enemy lines and Hans set to work on the portraits of Armagnac's daughters in late November. He completed one portrait but was unable to continue because he could not mix his colours properly owing to the severity of the weather. Henry never received the portraits and the fate of Hans is not known.[11]

Roos and Beckington returned to England early in 1443 empty handed while Armagnac paid dearly for his flirtation with the English. A French army marched into Armagnac territory, confiscated the Count's lands, and arrested Armagnac, who remained in captivity until 1446, four years before his death. The failure of the Armagnac marriage passed into legend to the detriment of Margaret of Anjou. The most closely contemporary version of *The Brut* chronicle describes her marriage to King Henry as 'worthy' with no dire predictions of fatal consequences.[12] A revised version written many years later recorded that Margaret's marriage was the cause of all the subsequent dissensions in England and the calamity of civil war. By breaking faith with Armagnac to marry Margaret, Henry incurred the wrath of God and so brought his troubles upon himself. The country was impoverished because Margaret came dowerless to England whereas a daughter of Armagnac would have brought a substantial dowry.[13] This fictitious supposition was engendered by the emotive word 'Armagnac'. It had nothing to do with the Count of Armagnac, who was neither rich nor powerful, but it was synonymous in English minds with the once great Armagnac/Orleans faction in France.

The reverses suffered in Gascony alarmed the English Council. They appointed Sir William Bonville, who was nearly fifty and had not seen service in France since he was a young man, as Seneschal of Gascony. He would lead an advance contingent of an army that still had to be raised. Bonville sailed in February 1443 with a pitifully small force: some of those who mustered failed to embark, one ship foundered, and Bonville eventually reached Bordeaux with less than 400 men.[14]

The English Council clung to the belief that the best way to achieve a negotiated peace was to bring the French to battle: a second

Young Margaret

Agincourt would allow England to dictate terms. But they could not agree on the size of the army, where it should be sent, or who should take command. King Henry was twenty-two, but no one suggested that he should accompany, let alone command, the army. It was accepted without question that Henry would never fight in France. The Treasurer, Lord Cromwell, warned that raising and maintaining a large army was beyond the means of the Exchequer. Cardinal Beaufort was the only man in England able to underwrite the cost and he was prepared to do so, but only if his nephew, John Beaufort, Earl of Somerset, was given command.[15]

Unfortunately, John Beaufort was not the man for the job. He had been captured at the Battle of Baugé in 1421 when he was only sixteen and he remained in French custody until 1438, giving him the dubious distinction of being a prisoner in France for longer than any other Englishman throughout the Hundred Years' War. He was nearly forty years old and imprisonment had sapped his vitality and undermined his health. He was an inexperienced soldier, but he was willing to go. King Henry created him Duke of Somerset in consideration of their kinship and the great services Somerset was about to perform.

Somerset's initial offer to muster in May 1443, with seven barons, eight knights, 800 men-at-arms, and over 3,000 archers, was wildly over optimistic. He asked to have his muster dates postponed to the end of May and then into June. By mid-June there was still no sign of Somerset or his army; he remained at his home in Corfe Castle into July.[16] The Council lost patience and ordered Somerset to ship by 18 July at the very latest; if necessary, musters could be taken after he reached France. He finally sailed in early August, but no barons and only six knights had indented to serve with him.

Somerset moved through western Normandy towards the Loire valley, not south to Gascony. His expedition diverted precious military resources that the Duke of York, the King's Lieutenant in France, needed to reinforce the English garrisons in Normandy. Money spent to mount Somerset's expedition would be wasted if Somerset failed, and fail he did. Sir William Bonville and the citizens of Bordeaux waited anxiously for the promised army, but John Beaufort never set foot in Gascony. He exhausted his strength campaigning ineffectually on the borders of Anjou, Maine, and Brittany while King Charles maintained a masterly inactivity. Somerset returned home in January 1444, when his resources and his health gave out, with nothing to show for his vaunted expedition except its expense. His reception at court was decidedly frosty; even King Henry was angry and disappointed.[17] Somerset retired to his estates and died in May, a broken man.

King Charles countered Somerset's ineffectual military campaign by a diplomatic masterstroke. He requested Duke Francis of Brittany to send an embassy to England with an offer to open peace negotiations.[18] Francis was eager to oblige, the Dukes of Brittany had an ancient claim to the Earldom of Richmond and a Breton peace mission offered Francis a chance to reclaim the earldom. Adroitly he included his brother Giles in the embassy and authorised him to do homage for the earldom by proxy. Francis and Giles were King Henry's first cousins and Giles had spent two years in England as a boyhood companion to the young Henry, who was delighted to welcome him again.[19] Giles was twenty-three, a year older than Henry, and he had an agenda of his own. He was chronically dissatisfied with his inheritance as a younger son and he offered his allegiance to King Henry. The Council awarded him a pension of 1,000 marks a year, which they deemed sufficient to retain his loyalty. But they short-sightedly rejected Duke's Francis's claim, and the opportunity to secure Brittany's allegiance was lost.[20]

King Henry accepted Charles VII's overture with alacrity. He had been influenced against his better judgement by those who urged a military solution to the war, and they had been proved wrong. The failure of Somerset's expedition meant that peace with France was imperative. The Council did not trust the French, but they agreed to send ambassadors to France to seek for peace and a marriage for King Henry.

2
The House of Anjou

Margaret of Anjou was born in the Duchy of Lorraine on 23 March 1430, the youngest of the four surviving children of René of Anjou and Isabelle of Lorraine.[1] But for the unexpected death of her uncle, Duke Louis III of Anjou, Margaret would have been known to history, if she was known at all, as Margaret of Lorraine. Her mother, Isabelle, was the eldest daughter and heir of Duke Charles II of Lorraine, and through her mother, Margaret of Bavaria, Isabelle could trace her descent from Charlemagne. René of Anjou began life as a younger son, but four deaths in as many years made him Duke of Bar, Duke of Lorraine, Duke of Anjou, and King of Naples.[2]

Margaret came into the world just as her father's inheritances began to drop into his lap like ripe plums, first the Duchy of Bar and then the Duchy of Lorraine. Bar was a fief of the Holy Roman Empire with territorial holdings in France and strong ties to the French court. Louis, Cardinal Duke of Bar, was the last survivor of the ducal line and René's mother, Yolande of Aragon, the Dowager Duchess of Anjou, who had a collateral claim to Bar, coerced the Cardinal into adopting René as his heir. Bar bordered Lorraine, making René an eligible suitor for Isabelle. They were married in 1420 when René was twelve and Isabelle was ten. Cardinal Louis died in 1430 and René became Duke of Bar. Charles of Lorraine died six months later and Isabelle inherited the duchy. Her right was disputed by her cousin, Antoine de Vaudemont, who claimed Lorraine as the closest male heir.[3] With typical impetuosity René ignored the advice of his more experienced

The House of Anjou

war captains and met de Vaudemont in battle at Bulgnéville on 2 July 1431, with disastrous results. De Vaudemont had appealed to Duke Philip of Burgundy for military aid and Burgundian artillery won the day. René was captured and became Burgundy's prisoner.

Isabelle was left to face the daunting task of defending her duchy. She was only twenty-one, but she had a strong sense of duty and an even stronger sense of dynasty. A few years later when she was styled Queen of Naples, she disputed precedence with the Duchess of Burgundy and an eye-witness tells us that 'neither of them was likely to damage their knee-caps in curtsying to each other.'[4] Isabelle dispatched messengers to towns throughout Lorraine ordering them to close their gates against de Vaudemont. She warned Antoine that if he attacked Nancy, she would declare all-out war. He was so impressed by her courageous defiance that despite his victory he agreed to a temporary truce.[5]

René remained in captivity until Burgundy released him on parole in 1432 to raise his ransom, but he had to send his young sons John and Louis to Dijon as hostages. In 1433 Burgundy forced René to betroth his elder daughter Yolande to Antoine de Vaudemont's heir to enhance de Vaudemont's claim to Lorraine. Yolande, still only five years old, was to be brought up in the de Vaudemont household.[6] René needed money desperately to pay his ransom if he was ever to get out of Burgundy's clutches and on his way back to Anjou he visited John of Luxembourg, Count of Ligny. The Luxembourgs were adherents of the Duke of Burgundy and allies of the English. John had conquered René's small patrimony of the Duchy of Guise and René agreed to recognise John's right to it in return for a cash payment. He also gave a vague undertaking to betroth his daughter Margaret, aged three, to John's nephew, Jacques of Luxembourg, the brother of Louis of Luxembourg, Count of St Pol.[7]

René's fortunes appeared to improve dramatically in 1434 when his brother, Duke Louis III of Anjou, died in Naples in November. The Dukes of Anjou had struggled unsuccessfully for three generations to

11

establish their claim to the Kingdom of Naples and René's father, Louis II, had spent much of his life campaigning in Italy. He died there in 1417 and the Angevin claim passed to Louis III.[8] The Queen of Naples, Joanna II, sat none too securely on her throne. The scandals of her sex life were notorious, with her lovers grabbing temporary power through the medium of the bedchamber. Pope Martin V excommunicated her for her sexual exploits and her refusal to acknowledge papal suzerainty over Naples, and he endorsed the young Louis III as the rightful king. Joanna looked around for military aid and thought she had found it in King Alfonso V of Aragon, who was intent on extending Aragon's domination in the Mediterranean. Rashly and unwisely, Joanna invited Alfonso to Naples as her heir, but it was not long before she realised her mistake. Alfonso was not disposed to wait for his inheritance; he acted as though he were already King of Naples and in the ensuring conflict Joanna was forced to flee the city.

Shrewdly Louis III threw in his lot with Joanna and at first luck favoured him: Alfonso was recalled to Aragon by domestic upheavals. Louis recovered Naples and Joanna named Louis as her heir. He was only a young man while she was an ageing and debauched woman thirty-five years his senior, but it was Louis who died first. He had no children and, unpredictable to the last, Joanna followed him to the grave in February 1435 after naming René, whom she had never met, as her successor.[9]

Joanna was styled Queen of Jerusalem, Hungary, the Two Scillies (as the Kingdom of Naples was known) and Countess of Provence. These impressive but empty titles, founded on incessant warfare, were highly prized. René was now far more valuable than he had been when he was captured at Bulgnéville and the Duke of Burgundy ordered him to return to Dijon. René chose to emulate his ancestor King John II of France, whose 'honour' had compelled him (to the amazement of his people) to return to captivity in England in 1363 when he could not raise his ransom.

The House of Anjou

René was twenty-six, an ardent, impulsive, and idealistic young man. All his life through many vicissitudes he remained a fantastic figure, partly medieval in outlook, partly a man of the Renaissance. He was a poet, a painter, a linguist, an indifferent soldier, but a devotee of pageantry, chivalry, and tournaments. René always found it difficult to differentiate between his romantic outlook, his overly optimistic ambitions, and political reality. René's decision to return to Dijon was a hard one: it was imperative for him to go to Naples to secure his inheritance.

Since he could not go, he appointed Isabelle as Lieutenant General to go in his stead. The Duke of Burgundy released René's younger son, Louis, Marquis of Pont, and he accompanied his mother to Naples. They received a rapturous welcome. All the buildings were splendidly decorated, and the Neapolitan women danced in the streets. Whether this joyous reception was heartfelt or merely prudent, it encouraged Isabelle to hope that if only she could hold out until René arrived, he would be welcomed as their king.

Isabelle needed money. She pawned her jewels and sought help wherever she could. Pope Eugenius IV promised her financial aid in return for an acknowledgement of papal suzerainty over Naples. Isabelle flattered the Neapolitans, and the Genoese offered to support her with their splendid navy. As far as Isabelle knew, Alfonso of Aragon posed no immediate threat. He had been captured in a sea battle and was a prisoner of the Visconti Duke of Milan, with whom René had an alliance. The smooth-tongued Alfonso convinced the lethargic Visconti that it was in their mutual interest to suppress French pretensions in Italy. In a characteristic about-face Visconti abandoned his Angevin alliance and in marked contrast to Burgundy's treatment of René, he freed Alfonso without ransom.[10] If Isabelle had not been there Alfonso would have taken Naples in 1436. As it was, she rallied sufficient support to defend the city until René could arrive.[11]

René's biographer represents the second phase of his captivity as '*durance vile*', describing in lurid terms the iron bars on the windows

Young Margaret

of his living quarters. René's freedom was certainly curtailed and access to his person carefully monitored, but he could communicate with the outside world. It was the circumstances not the conditions in which René was held that made a lasting impression on him. He suffered intense frustration at being unable to claim his Italian inheritance in person. A moving and pathetic prayer in his *London Book of Hours* is appended to a list of Biblical figures who had escaped worse perils than his own. It reads: *Libera Renatu de omnibus angustiis. Libera me Renatum.* ('Free René from all straits and confinements! Free René!')[12]

René told a Milanese ambassador that the Duke of Burgundy had offered him his freedom in exchange for the Duchy of Bar, but that René had indignantly refused. Burgundy then suggested that René's daughter, Margaret, should marry Burgundy's only son, the Count of Charolais, with the Duchy of Bar and the Marquisate of Pont as her dowry. The lands were to be turned over to Burgundy immediately and Margaret was to be brought up at the Burgundian court until the children were old enough to marry. Again, René refused. He had sworn allegiance to his brother-in-law, King Charles VII, his sister Marie was Queen of France, and his redoubtable mother, Yolande, would never allow him to enlarge Burgundian territory while the Duke of Burgundy was an ally of England. René declared that he would remain in prison for the rest of his life rather than agree to Burgundy's proposals.[13] Burgundy took his revenge by setting René's ransom at 400,000 gold crowns (*écus*), an impossibly high figure, and he demanded a number of border towns in the Duchy of Bar as security.[14]

René remained in captivity until 1437 when, by the Treaty of Lille, he undertook to pay Burgundy 200,000 crowns unconditionally and a further 200,000 when (and if) he recovered Naples. His eleven-year old son John, styled Duke of Calabria, as the heir to Naples would marry Burgundy's niece, Marie of Bourbon, and Burgundy would contribute two thirds of her dowry towards René's ransom. A later

The House of Anjou

claim that a secret clause in the Treaty of Lille committed René to marry Margaret to King Henry VI is without foundation.[15] Even the mighty Duke of Burgundy would not risk diplomatic humiliation by negotiating a marriage for the King of England without the English Council's knowledge or consent. René had no intention of meeting the terms of the treaty. He accepted his freedom, but he did not give his parole. Once he had chivalrously returned to captivity; he would not do so a second time.

René and John of Calabria were welcomed on their return to Angers, the capital of Anjou, by his mother, Yolande, and his daughter Margaret with all the pageantry due to the homecoming of a Duke of Anjou. John of Calabria and Marie of Bourbon were married in the cathedral at Angers at the beginning of April and René set about raising funds for a military campaign in Italy. He left Anjou for Provence in October, taking the young couple with him.[16]

René finally reached Naples in May 1438. He did not have the means to wage a long campaign; his only hope was to bring Alfonso to battle and defeat him quickly. He failed, despite the loyalty of the Neapolitans, because he was reliant on the notoriously mercenary Italian condottiere and there was never enough money to satisfy their rapacious demands. René's exploits in Italy, which included a dash across the Apennines in bitterly cold weather losing men, horses, and baggage on the way, and his quixotic challenge to Alfonso to meet him in a personal encounter, read like an epic tale of knight errantry. But Alfonso was no knight errant and he could afford to wait. His navy blockaded Naples and provisions brought in by Genoese ships were all that stood between the city and starvation. In the summer of 1440 Alfonso tightened the blockade and René sent Isabelle and Louis back to Provence. Only René could have conceived the fantastic offer he then made to Alfonso: he would quit Naples, leaving it to Alfonso, if Alfonso, who had no legitimate son, agreed to adopt John of Calabria as his heir in Italy. Not surprisingly Alfonso refused.

Young Margaret

René held on for another two years until, in June 1442, Alfonso's army stormed Naples. Romantic accounts claim that they gained entry though the same aqueduct used by the Roman general Belisarius 900 years earlier. René mounted a stout defence, but his situation was hopeless. He did not lack courage and he did not fear death, but he could not face being taken prisoner. His captivity was still fresh in his mind and the thought of another imprisonment was more than he could bear. Alfonso magnanimously granted him a ten-day truce during which René escaped from Naples and abandoned his kingdom.[17] He was back in Provence in October with his Neapolitan adventure at an end.[18] René never entirely relinquished his dream, but in the years ahead it would be John of Calabria who pursued the chimera of an Angevin dynasty on the throne of Naples.

Margaret of Anjou was only five years old when her mother left for Italy. Her early biographers tell the romantic tale that she accompanied Isabelle and grew up 'in the soft air of Naples' but Margaret spent her formative years at her grandmother's court in Anjou.[19] By any standards Yolande of Aragon, Dowager Duchess of Anjou, was a remarkable woman. She was energetic, cultured, and intelligent, with more political foresight and courage than most of her male contemporaries. She was the only woman summoned to the Estates General of France in 1439 to discuss the state of the realm. A daughter of the King of Aragon, Yolande had married Louis II of Anjou in 1400 and she governed Anjou and Provence during his Italian campaigns. When he died Yolande continued to rule in the name of her son Louis III, she retained control of the Duchy of Anjou when Louis left for Italy, and she administered the Angevin lands during René's captivity.

Yolande was one of the few people King Charles VII respected and she retained her influence with him throughout her life. She had arranged his marriage to her daughter Marie when they were children, and until he became the Dauphin she kept him in Anjou away from the dangerous intrigues that beset the French court. She was a strong

The House of Anjou

proponent of resistance to the English invasion of France and in 1421 she sent a thousand Angevin troops to the Battle of Baugé, not far from Angers, where a French and Scots army defeated and killed King Henry V's brother, the Duke of Clarence. There is an apocryphal story that Yolande donned armour at Baugé and directed her troops in person. And it was Yolande who introduced Joan of Arc into King Charles VII's court.[20]

The young Margaret could have had no better preceptor. Few details of her early life survive. There is an unsubstantiated story that she received special care from Tiphanie la Magine, who had been René's nurse, although Tiphanie's epitaph records that she nursed René but not his children.[21] Margaret's daily life was supervised by the mistress of her household, a cross between a mother and a governess, who was responsible for Margaret's deportment, for her diet and dress, and for her education.

There is a glimpse of Margaret in 1442 when an elaborate costume was ordered for her during a visit by the Emperor Frederick's ambassadors.[22] The reception of dignitaries was part of Margaret's training and by the age of twelve she was well versed in the codes of conduct and the 'courtesies' that befitted her rank.

Margaret learned the languages and history of her parents' domains, but probably not English, the language of the enemy. She would have been familiar with the morality tales compiled by the Angevin knight Geoffrey de la Tour Landry for the instruction of his daughters. His stories make it clear that in an age when violence and death were accepted as the natural order of things, there was little that young women did not learn about vice: incest, rape, fornication, and physical brutality were among the themes he expounded to frighten his three daughters into good behaviour.[23] Margaret also read the works of Giovanni Boccaccio, whose *De Mulieribus Claris* recounted the lives of famous women from Eve to Queen Joanna I of Naples.

Christine de Pizan, the only woman of the period to earn a living by her pen, based her account of the lives of great women who had governed as forcefully as men on Boccaccio. In *La Cité des Dames* she cited the Duchess Marie of Anjou, Margaret's great-grandmother, as a 'wise and valiant' lady who ruled while her children were minors and put down a revolt in the County of Provence by a mixture of force and negotiation. Christine's *Le Livre des Trois Vertus* included a programme for the education of a young princess: it stressed that after God her most important duty was to her husband. She must be humble, obedient, and cheerful, no matter what the provocation offered by a less-than-perfect spouse. She must honour her husband's relatives, overlook his moral lapses, and eschew all gossip concerning him. She must be discreet and not antagonise those around her even if they disliked her, but study to be on good terms with everyone. The moral education of her children should be her central concern along with the spiritual wellbeing of her ladies. Finally, she must handle her finances prudently and reward good service. Christine also offered advice to 'powerful women' called upon to take charge in the absence of their lord: 'She should have a man's heart. She must know the laws of arms and all things pertaining to warfare, ever prepared to command her men if there is need of it.'[24] Christine might have been describing the women of the House of Anjou.

Margaret's recreation comprised secular reading, music, dancing, and sewing; noble ladies practised embroidery and tapestry work to combat the sin of idleness. Hunting was a favourite pastime and it was not an exclusively male preserve. A mistress of the hunt could be appointed for a day's outing when a large mixed group of courtiers and servants would set out in a festive atmosphere rather like an extended picnic. Margaret enjoyed hunting and all her life she felt a fondness for her hunting dogs; she kept some with her even in her last years in exile.[25]

Margaret's childhood came to an end when Yolande of Aragon died at Saumur in November 1442 at the age of sixty-two. In her will she made it plain that she had spent her personal wealth on the defence of Anjou and the wars in Italy and she had little to leave. She bequeathed some jewels to Margaret but her principal beneficiary was her youngest son Charles, Count of Maine.[26] Margaret was not reunited with her parents until they returned to Anjou in the summer of 1443 when she was thirteen. They were strangers to her; she had not seen her mother since those far off days in Nancy.

Isabelle spent the winter of 1441/42 in Provence marshalling resources in a vain attempt to sustain René. In the spring she went to home to Lorraine and the Duke of Burgundy sent an envoy to broach certain 'secret matters' to her.[27] He proposed a marriage for her daughter Margaret to his stepson Charles, Count of Nevers.[28] His terms were a variation on the offer he had made to René during his captivity: Margaret and Nevers's children would take precedence in the inheritance of the Duchy of Bar and the County of Provence over Yolande's de Vaudemont children.[29] Margaret's dowry would be 50,000 *livres tournois* (considerably more than would subsequently be offered to the King of England) and Burgundy would transfer 40,600 *écus* of René's ransom to the Count of Nevers.[30] Isabelle met René at Aix in Provence on his return from Naples and put the proposal to him. She argued that with his ransom still unpaid a rapprochement with the Duke of Burgundy was in their best interests and René concurred. Charles of Nevers signed the marriage contract in January 1443 and René signed at Tarascon on 4 February; Burgundy ratified it a month later.

Various theories have been adduced to explain why, with the contract signed and a papal dispensation obtained (Margaret and Nevers were related through their descent from King John of France), the Nevers marriage did not take place. It may be that a better prospect for his daughter made René change his mind. Possibly Nevers decided that he preferred to remain single; he did not marry until 1456 less than ten years before his death.[31] But the real reason was King Charles VII's opposition. He would not permit an alliance between the House of Anjou and the Duke of Burgundy.

3

The Truce of Tours

William de la Pole, Earl of Suffolk and steward of the royal household, was entrusted with the delicate and difficult task of negotiating with King Charles VII. Suffolk was one of the few Englishmen who liked and respected the French. He had been a war captain in France under the Regent Bedford, but he was no soldier. He had been in command of the English army at Orleans in 1429 when Joan of Arc raised the siege. Shortly afterwards he was captured by France's foremost military commander Jean de Dunois, Bastard of Orleans, and a year in custody plus the cost of his ransom had convinced Suffolk of the futility and financial waste of war.[1] He made friends with Dunois and on his return to England Suffolk befriended Dunois's half-brother, Charles, Duke of Orleans, who had been a prisoner in England since the Battle of Agincourt. King Henry released Orleans in 1440 after Orleans promised to do all he could to persuade King Charles to end the war, and Orleans suggested to King Charles that his friend the Earl of Suffolk should be England's ambassador. Pleasing King Charles was of paramount importance, and if Suffolk was the man he wanted, Suffolk he would get.

Suffolk was wary; there were risks as well as potential rewards involved in accepting the commission. He expressed his reservations in an eloquent speech to the Council in which he made no secret of his friendships 'among the parties of your adversaries in France' and said he knew there was concern that he would favour the enemy and make too many concessions. He respectfully begged to be excused but his objections were overruled. Chancellor Stafford assured him that his appointment was at King Henry's expressed wish and promised that he would not be held responsible no matter what the outcome.[2]

Bowing to the inevitable, Suffolk asked to be accompanied by only a small embassy and he chose Adam Moleyns and three others to go with him. Moleyns was a far more experienced diplomat than Suffolk, a churchman and a classical Latin scholar. He had been Cardinal Beaufort's personal envoy to Pope Eugenius, had represented King Henry at the papal court and been part of a delegation to the Emperor Frederick in 1442. Henry made Moleyns Keeper of the Privy Seal to enhance his status. Sir Robert Roos had led the abortive attempt to arrange an Armagnac marriage: he knew King Henry's requirements in the physical appearance of a bride. John Wenlock had first-hand knowledge of the men with whom Suffolk expected to deal: he frequently carried diplomatic correspondence between the English Council and French magnates. Richard Andrew, the King's secretary, would keep a record of the proceedings and Sir Thomas Hoo, the Chancellor of Normandy, was expected to join the embassy at Rouen.[3]

Suffolk landed at Harfleur towards the end of March, before he was expected. He made a brief visit to Rouen to consult the Duke of York, the King's Lieutenant in France, but King Charles was not yet ready to receive him. The Duke of Orleans hastily invited Suffolk to visit him at Blois. The governor of Blois advised Suffolk and his party not to present themselves at Tours until after Easter, as King Charles had been unwell.[4]

And so it was that on the morning of 16 April 1444, Suffolk sailed along the Loire accompanied by Orleans and Dunois. René of Anjou, Charles, Count of Maine, and a host of others were at the gates to welcome Suffolk. King Charles granted him an audience and did him the honour of presenting him to Queen Marie and the Dauphine, Margaret of Scotland. Suffolk was gratified and relieved by his reception and his letter of introduction enhanced the affable mood:

for the first time King Henry addressed King Charles as his 'uncle of France' and not as his 'adversary of France'.

The city of Tours was *en fête*. King Charles had summoned his entire nobility to meet the English ambassadors and the French magnates vied with each other in displays of opulence. When Duke Francis of Brittany rode out to pay his respects to the King his retinue stretched from the gates of Tours to the chateau of Montils-les-Tours, two miles away. On May Day Queen Marie and the Dauphine led a cavalcade of courtiers into the fields around Tours for the Maying festival, the ladies in their colourful high-waisted, full-skirted gowns and heart-shaped headdresses, the men in robes of the King's favourite colour, green, with scarlet hats and doublets of the costly black satin of Lucca. The English longbow men in Suffolk's entourage were challenged to an archery contest, and the prize of a 1,000 *écus* was carried off, to the honour of France, by the Scottish archers of the King's bodyguard.

King Charles appointed the Duke of Orleans and Louis of Bourbon, Count of Vendôme, to conduct the negotiations. The talks revolved around the status of the English-held Duchies of Normandy and Gascony and the Pale of Calais. Suffolk requested that they be recognised as English possessions in full sovereignty. The French countered with an offer of Gascony, the adjacent counties of Quercy and Périgord and the Pale of Calais, to be held as fiefs of the French crown, but they adamantly refused to admit that King Henry had any claim to Normandy.[5] Suffolk was in a quandary, he had come to make peace but not peace at any price. Retaining Gascony and Calais as mere fiefs would outrage English public opinion and impugn King Henry's honour. Gascony had been an inheritance of English kings since the twelfth century, Calais was the seat of England's vital wool trade, but Normandy was the emotive issue. Henry V's military exploits were the glory of England and the conquest of Normandy had been his personal triumph. Suffolk could not abandon Normandy without betraying the great king's memory and dealing a severe blow to English pride.

The Truce of Tours

The negotiations reached a stalemate and King Charles declared that since a peace settlement was proving so elusive he was willing to offer a truce, which had been his intention all along. Suffolk failed to realise, then or later, that Charles would never make peace while English soldiers remained on French soil. But Charles needed a breathing space to prepare for the war he would have to wage to recover Normandy. Even so, his offer came at a price. Suffolk must accept Charles's niece, Margaret of Anjou, as a bride for King Henry. Margaret was the King's niece by marriage, and she fitted his requirements exactly.

Suffolk had expected to be offered Charles's daughter, Jeanne, who was of marriageable age, but Charles would not take the risk. Twice in the past a daughter of France had married an English king with disastrous results. King Edward III had claimed the French throne through his mother, Isabelle of France, and Charles's sister Katherine had married Henry V with France as her dowry. Their son had been crowned King of France in 1431.

The suggestion of Margaret as a bride for King Henry originated in the fertile mind of the Angevin courtier Pierre de Brezé, who had known Margaret since her childhood. Brezé was Captain of Angers; he had been brought to the King's notice by René's brother, Charles of Maine, who was rising in royal favour. Brezé's charm, ready tongue, and resourcefulness appealed to King Charles, who gave him a seat on the royal council and made him Seneschal of Poitou. Brezé had acted as go-between when Margaret's betrothal to the Count of Nevers was broken off.[6] He was an arch-intriguer and it was typical of him to come up with a scheme that advanced the Angevins' standing at court and furthered his own aspirations by foiling a marriage that he knew King Charles would not sanction.

Margaret was just fourteen. She had been destined for marriage with an obscure Burgundian count when suddenly she was faced by the dazzling prospect of becoming Queen of England. To be a queen was the pinnacle of every noble lady's ambition, but Yolande had taught her that the English were the enemy. Now she was being assured by her uncles and her father that her marriage would change all that. No contemporary portrait of Margaret survives. Many years later, in 1458, a Milanese ambassador who had never seen her recorded on the information of an unnamed Englishman that she was 'a most handsome woman though she is somewhat dark [and] not so beautiful as your Serenity.'[7] This cannot be taken literally, as the ambassador was writing to Bianca, Duchess of Milan, who by no stretch of the imagination could be called good looking, and tact required him to add the 'somewhat dark'. In the fifteenth century fair women were deemed beautiful: the ideal woman had 'skin as white as the fleur de lys ... fair hair like fine gold, a high forehead, little eyebrows, grey or green eyes, a straight nose, a round chin, red lips and compact white teeth', while an ugly woman was 'round as an apple and dark as an owl.'[8] Margaret's father was brown haired and light eyed and, coupled with her mother's Germanic heritage, Margaret may have been fair rather than dark, but her appearance remains conjectural.[9] A medal struck in 1463 and thought to be a direct likeness shows a youthful face for a woman of thirty-three, with a high forehead, straight nose, full lips, and a rounded but firm chin.

Pierre de Brezé negotiated Margaret's marriage contract on René's behalf. Her dowry was the paltry sum of 20,000 *écus*, in line with King Charles's determination that the English must accept her on his terms. René made over to her his ephemeral claim, inherited from his mother, to the islands of Majorca and Minorca and Margaret renounced any claims she might have to René's other lands.[10] Suffolk, perforce, accepted Margaret on these terms. He was in no position to argue; he could not afford to return to England empty handed.

The marriage took place at an elaborate ceremony in the church of St Martin on Sunday, 24 May 1444. King Charles and René of Anjou entered the church first, followed by Queen Marie, Queen Isabelle, the Dauphine, and Marie of Bourbon, Duchess of Calabria. The Dauphin Louis escorted Margaret into the church to be presented to King

The Truce of Tours

Charles by the Count of Maine. The King doffed his hat to her as a mark of courtesy before leading her up to the altar where Suffolk, who stood proxy for the absent King Henry, was waiting.[11] Piero da Monte, Bishop of Brescia, performed the service. Da Monte had been a collector of papal taxes in England and he had seen King Henry when Henry was only sixteen. Even at that age, according to da Monte, the pious young man 'was firmly resolved to have intercourse with no woman unless within the bonds of matrimony.'[12]

After the ceremony, a stately procession made its way along the Grande Rue through the centre of Tours to the Abbey of Saint Julien. The route was lined with cheering crowds clapping their hands, thumping one another on the shoulder and shouting the traditional cry of gladness and hope, *Noel! Noel!* Peace had come at last! The banquet and entertainments lasted for hours, as course succeeded course. Margaret was seated at the high table with Queen Marie on her right and the Bishop of Brescia on her left, while Suffolk occupied a lower table with the Dauphine and the Duchess of Calabria. Two 'giants' appeared, carrying 'trees' in their hands, possibly a display of the Scottish art of tossing the caber. A parody of jousting was enacted by mock soldiers armed with lances fighting each other from pavilions strapped onto the backs of two camels and the evening ended with dancing, in which the queens took part.[13]

Suffolk signed the Truce of Tours on 28 May. It was to run from June 1444 to April 1446. The signatories included all the major powers in Europe, even those who were not at Tours. The French comprised the Dauphin Louis, the Dukes of Orleans, Burgundy, Brittany, Bourbon, Alençon, and Charles, Count of Maine. René signed as King of Naples and Sicily; the Kings of Castile and Scotland were included as allies of France. The Kings of Scandinavia and Portugal were claimed as allies of England, while both sides claimed the Emperor Frederick. Suffolk committed the Dukes of Gloucester, York, Exeter, Somerset, and Norfolk, the Earl of Stafford (soon to be made Duke of Buckingham), and Sir Thomas Stanley, Lord of the Isle of Man.[14] King

Young Margaret

Charles undertook to send an embassy to London to treat for a final peace.

Suffolk left Tours for Rouen on the following day. All along his route crowds gathered to cheer him as the man who had ended decades of war. In the years ahead he would be censured for conceding too much and gaining too little, but he succeeded where earlier embassies had failed. The Truce of Tours put an end to hostilities for the first time in thirty years. It afforded England the same breathing space as France to rebuild militarily and to profit from the resumption of trade without the continual drain and strain of war. Suffolk returned to England in June to a hero's welcome.

After the heady excitement of her marriage Margaret went back to Anjou. King Henry was eagerly awaiting her arrival in England. He wrote to her, and to King Charles, that he wished her to be conducted to Pontoise on the Norman border as soon as possible. Charles replied sympathetically that he understood the bridegroom's impatience, but claimed that he had no idea how long it would take to outfit Margaret as became a Queen of England.[15] Charles had made a leisurely journey to Lorraine, reaching Nancy in September and he settled down to spend the winter enjoying René's hospitality. Queen Marie and the Dauphine arrived in November, and it was fortunate that only the physical presence of the Dauphin Louis was required since on reaching Nancy a sulky Louis took to his bed, declaring that he was too ill to take part in the festivities. He had been campaigning in Alsace and would have preferred to remain there; he had no time for the kind of expensive ostentation that delighted René. Margaret was summoned to join her family. They were all there: René and Isabelle, Charles of Maine, John and Marie of Calabria, and her sister Yolande, whom Margaret barely remembered, with her husband Ferry de Vaudemont.[16]

René invited men from far and wide to a joust to celebrate Mardi Gras. Nancy was thronged by a vast concourse of men and horses and the wintry skies reflected a blaze of colour as heralds assembled the combatants and the ladies took their places in the covered boxes on the viewing platform next to the judges. Jousting was socially and politically significant, prowess in the grand *pas d'armes* ranked second only to prowess in war.

A pavilion of white, red, and green silk occupied the central square. Opposite it stood a tall pillar draped in green, with a paper scroll inscribed with the rules of the joust. At exactly ten o'clock trumpets sounded, and René rode out in front of the pavilion. His clothing and horse trappings were of purple velvet, embroidered with the sword points and the golden *croix potencies* of Jerusalem. His twelve gentlemen ushers and six pages were dressed in yellow velvet. The pages wore Turkish turbans instead of hats, each adorned with costly ostrich feathers, adding the exotic touch so dear to René's heart. His six horses were draped in different colours: crimson velvet, embroidered with his motto, black velvet worked with gold threads, blue velvet embroidered with golden teardrops, white cloth of gold, grey velvet with large golden leaves, and yellow velvet embroidered with turbaned heads. René was flanked by Louis of Luxembourg, Ferry de Vaudemont and Pierre de Brezé. A late addition to their ranks was the Burgundian Jacques de Lalain, one of the best-known knights errant of his day. The challengers were Gaston de Foix, John of Clermont, son of the Duke of Bourbon, Jacques of Luxembourg, to whom Margaret had once been briefly promised, and Bertrand de Beauvau.

To the surprise and delight of the spectators, King Charles, not renowned for martial accomplishments, appeared in the challengers' lists, dressed in his favourite green velvet embroidered with small suns. A joust, no matter how well ordered, could be dangerous and Charles's opponents were carefully chosen to show the King to advantage while ensuring that no harm came to him. He broke two lances against René without mishap but Pierre de Brezé had the misfortune to use too heavy a lance, knocking away the King's shield. René re-entered the lists and allowed Charles to break his third lance

Young Margaret

and retire with honour to join the ladies. At the end of the day prizes were awarded to Louis of Luxembourg and Gaston de Foix by Queen Marie of France and Queen Margaret of England.[17]

The festivities continued for eight days and it was in this fairy tale atmosphere that Margaret saw the last of her family. King Henry's herald, Garter King of Arms, arrived in Nancy with a copy of the marriage contract ratified by Henry and assurances that England would honour the Truce of Tours.[18] Once these diplomatic niceties were complete King Charles agreed to let Margaret go and she set out on the first leg of her journey at the beginning of March. The King escorted her to beyond the St Nicolas Gate and René rode with her as far as Bar le Duc.[19] John of Calabria and the Duke of Alençon accompanied her to Paris where she was received by the Duke of Orleans, who had not attended the festivities in Nancy. Nor had Suffolk. While waiting for Margaret to arrive he met with Orleans in Paris to complete negotiations for the ransom and release of Orleans's brother, John Count of Angoulême, who was still a prisoner in England.[20]

Margaret crossed the border into Lancastrian France in March 1445. She was welcomed by the Duke of York at Pontoise, and they sailed down the Seine to Rouen landing beneath the battlements of the Castle de Bouvreuil, a circular stone structure flanked by six towers reminiscent of Margaret's home at Angers. King Henry had stayed at Bouvreuil while waiting to be crowned King of France and he was there when Joan of Arc, abandoned by her 'gentle Dauphin', was burned in the marketplace adjacent to the castle.

Suffolk had left England with an extensive entourage in November 1444 to welcome Margaret. One chronicler estimated that his retinue numbered a thousand men on horseback.[21] They had been kicking their heels in Rouen for five months and the cost was crippling. The Common Council of London had loaned over £1,000, and King Henry had cheerfully requested his more affluent subjects to contribute on the grounds that by investing in his marriage they were investing in peace.[22] Fifty-six ships were required to transport horses, carriages, and personnel to Normandy and to bring the Queen and her household back to England. Eighty-eight men and women were paid above the going rates as the Queen's servants.[23] Gifts from the civic dignitaries of Rouen to the Queen totalled over £2,000, including a set of silver plate that had belonged to the late chancellor of the duchy. His arms had to be removed and Margaret's substituted at her expense.[24]

Margaret's introduction to her new subjects was not auspicious. On 22 March, an impressive procession made its way from the Old Palace along the banks of the Seine towards Rouen's great arched bridge, turning left to the cathedral of Notre Dame where the Regent Bedford was buried. Suffolk and his retinue, arrayed in crimson livery embroidered with his arms, rode in front of a magnificent carriage draped in multi-coloured fabrics and drawn by six white horses, its canopy of cloth of gold emblazoned with the arms of England and France. Margaret should have been seated in this splendid equipage, but she was not there. A combination of excitement and apprehension had made her ill and Suffolk was so anxious to avoid further expensive delays that he elected to manage without her. Alice, Duchess of Suffolk, took Margaret's place, dressed as a bride, with the Countess of Salisbury and the Countess of Shrewsbury seated beside her.[25]

The carriage was flanked by Richard, Duke of York, and John Talbot, Earl of Shrewsbury, England's greatest living soldier, *tenans meniere come se la Royne eust este dedans* (just as if the Queen were riding in it). Behind the carriage came five riderless horses, richly caparisoned in red velvet embroidered with golden roses. They represented *in absentia* the five magnates of England who were signatories to the Truce of Tours. A second carriage conveyed the senior ladies of the Queen's household: Beatrice, Lady Talbot, Emma, Lady Scales, Lady Elizabeth Grey, and Lady Margaret Hull, while her younger ladies followed on horseback.

Richard Neville, Earl of Salisbury, the northern lords, Clifford and

Young Margaret

Greystoke and Sir James Butler, the eldest son of the Earl of Ormond, headed the procession followed by the knights of the Queen's escort: Edward Hull, Robert Hungerford, John Holand, Robert Harcourt, Hugh Cokesay, Richard Roos, and Robert Wingfield. Sir William Bonville, Seneschal of Gascony, represented the southern duchy. Flanking them were 400 archers dressed in sombre grey, emblematic of the fighting forces of England. The officials and clerics of the Queen's household were escorted by 200 archers in the white and blue livery of Lancaster with gold crowns on their sleeves. Six mounted pages dressed in black with silver trimmings led a splendid riding horse, its saddle and harness studded with gold, one of King Henry's gifts to his queen.

Margaret's indisposition may have been no more than nausea, brought on by reaction to unfamiliar surroundings. She had met Suffolk briefly at Tours, but everyone else was a stranger to her and although they addressed her in French, they spoke English among themselves. Having to learn all the new names and new faces was bewildering. Her physician Francisco Panizonus, prescribed for her and she recovered sufficiently in the week before Easter to be able to distribute the customary alms on Maundy Thursday: on 23 March she bestowed fourteen grey hooded dresses, fourteen pairs of shoes and fourteen pence on fourteen poor women to mark what was, in fact, her fifteenth birthday.[26]

4

England's Queen

Margaret embarked for England at Harfleur aboard the *John of Cherbourg*. Her fleet was battered by a severe storm and it was a very sick girl who came ashore at Southampton to a tumultuous welcome as people gathered to get a glimpse of her. *Te Deums* were sung and bells were rung to give thanks for the safe arrival of England's queen.[1] For a second time illness prevented Margaret from enjoying her reception. After enduring agonies of seasickness she broke out in a rash, and King Henry informed Chancellor Stafford that he would be unable to attend the Feast of the Garter at Windsor on St George's Day because his marriage had to be postponed. The Queen was 'seke of the labour and indisposicion of the see, by occasion of which the pokes been broken out upon hir.'[2] He had to wait for five days before he could meet his bride.

Many years later a Milanese ambassador to the French court wrote an entertaining but imaginary account of Margaret's first encounter with the King: Henry and Suffolk disguised themselves as squires and Henry knelt before Margaret and presented her with a letter from himself so that he could observe her while she read it. He then left the chamber and Suffolk asked her what she had made of the squire. Margaret replied that she had not noticed him, whereupon Suffolk revealed that it was the King! Margaret was vexed because she had kept him on his knees. Such behaviour is quite unlike Henry and while Margaret may not have recognised the King, she would certainly have recognised Suffolk.[3]

Young Margaret

Henry and Margaret were married for the second time on 22 April 1445 by Henry's confessor, William Aiscough Bishop of Salisbury, in the Premonstratensian Abbey of St Mary and St John the Evangelist at Titchfield a few miles from Southampton. A gold ring set with a ruby, which had been Henry's coronation ring when, as a boy, he was crowned King of France in Paris in 1431, had been refashioned into a wedding ring for Margaret and the proceedings were enlivened by the gift of a lion, which would have startled the inmates of the abbey.[4] It was a quiet and inexpensive wedding for a King of England.

Margaret knew little about King Henry and he may not have measured up to her expectations, but she had been trained to accept that her first duty was to her husband. She anticipated giving him, and England, an heir as soon as possible. Henry spent five days in Margaret's company after their wedding and presumably the marriage was consummated, although it was later rumoured that Bishop Aiscough forbade Henry to have physical relations with his queen.[5] The story may be a discreet veil to cover Henry's inadequacies, since Margaret did not conceive a child for nearly eight years.

Henry was incapable of deep affection and for this his cloistered childhood was partly to blame. He had a few boyhood friends, his cousin Giles of Brittany, and Henry Beauchamp, the Earl of Warwick's son. Giles returned home in 1434 and Beauchamp died in 1446; after that Henry had his favourites but no close friends. As a child he had lived in his mother, Queen Katherine's, household, but she retired from court when she contracted a serious misalliance by marrying Owen Tudor, a Welsh squire. Whether Henry felt her desertion is unknown, but he appears to have distrusted, if not actually disliked, women, although the affection he expressed for Margaret at the time of their marriage was genuine. He was a lonely man and he looked forward with delight to the prospect of a bride and companion.

He was twenty-three in 1445, a personable, pious young man with none of the flamboyant good looks and charm of his Plantagenet ancestors. He was solemn, earnest, well meaning, and guided by his religious convictions. Uniquely, Henry could not remember a time when he had not been king. His governor, Richard Beauchamp, Earl of Warwick, was a renowned soldier and the epitome of chivalry but he lacked humour and kindliness. Beauchamp had been a close friend and comrade in arms of Henry V, and he tried to shape the boy into a warrior king. Such expectations placed a weight on the young Henry's shoulders that he was psychologically unable to bear. Military exploits appalled him, and his passive nature took refuge in piety. This was not unusual in a violent age, but it was fatal in a king whose duty was to impose justice, defend his subjects' rights, and lead them in war.

Henry meant to be a 'good' king and according to his own lights this is precisely what he was. He began his personal rule when he was barely sixteen, but he was far from self-reliant. The political tug of war between Cardinal Beaufort and the Duke of Gloucester for influence over him had pulled him first one way and then another, and their rivalry inculcated a habit of dependence on the opinion of others that Henry never outgrew. He lacked the dominating personality that kingship required, and his quiescence created a dichotomy that neither he nor those around him could resolve. Routine administration bored him, detailed appraisal of political and fiscal realities was beyond him. He may have suffered from a memory disorder, which would account for his irresponsible habit of granting offices twice over, or perhaps he just could not bring himself to say no. He shirked confrontation and disliked people who hectored him, he ignored unwelcome advice and cold-shouldered anyone who gave it. Henry functioned adequately within his limited capacity and was amenable to suggestion, but he had all the obstinacy and single-mindedness of the weak-willed. At times he acted as he saw fit regardless of possible consequences.

Plans for Margaret's coronation went ahead after their wedding. A dressmaker, Margaret Chamberlain, was summoned to work on Margaret's coronation robes and Henry ordered the nobility and clergy to present themselves in London by 15 May 'al other things left

Young Margaret

and excusacions ceasing.'6 The royal couple visited Cardinal Beaufort at Bishops Waltham and Henry left Margaret in the Cardinal's care while he went on to Westminster. Beaufort kept open house in her honour, entertaining the lords, ladies, and gentlemen who flocked to pay her homage and attract her notice. She then made a leisurely journey through the English countryside, staying for a few days with Chancellor Stafford, the Archbishop of Canterbury, in the Archbishop's eleventh-century palace at Croydon.[7] Henry joined Margaret at the palace of Eltham for the Feast of Pentecost. Eltham had been renovated for her reception with a new hall and kitchen quarters. The parlour in the Queen's apartments had six windows, requiring forty-two feet of stained glass 'flourished' with birds and beasts.[8] It was a pleasant place for Margaret to rest and prepare for her official entry into the capital.

London was far larger and wealthier than any city Margaret had ever seen. Its size, the beauty of its churches, its numerous goldsmiths, and its general air of prosperity impressed foreign visitors. The wharves of foreign merchants lined the banks of the Thames: Galley Key, where the Italian galleys were moored, and the Steelyard, occupied by merchants of the Hanseatic League of Germany. In their midst stood the customs house and the Wool Key, the basis of English wealth and a mainstay of royal finance. To the west of the customs house were the warehouses and homes of London's wealthiest merchants. The population numbered between 30–40,000, but only a small percentage were enfranchised: no more than 4,000 men. Artisans, unskilled labourers, clerks, religious orders, apprentices, foreign traders (called aliens), vagrants, and retainers of the great magnates who had town houses in the City made up the bulk of its inhabitants.[9] Collectively Londoners were volatile, pugnacious, and xenophobic; alarms and affrays were frequent, deaths in brawls were not uncommon, and, on occasion, its mob could turn ugly.

The City was ruled by an oligarchy, members of the twelve principal companies of which the Mercers, Grocers, and Drapers were the most influential. Sir William Estfeld, who had loaned £2,000 towards the cost of bringing Margaret to England, was a Mercer.[10] Stephen Browne and Simon Eyre, who would escort Margaret through London, were Grocers. Harvests had been bad in the late 1430s and Stephen Browne had sent all the way to East Prussia to buy grain to feed the citizens. Simon Eyre financed the building of a new storage granary to avoid the repetition of such a calamity.[11] The munificence of these bequests testified to the wealth of the London merchant community and the King depended on them for substantial loans. These sober-sided men expected the truce with France to restore favourable trade relations and open French markets that had been closed while hostilities continued.

Margaret was met at Blackheath and welcomed into the City by the Mayor, aldermen, sheriffs, and representatives of the merchant companies, wearing their full regalia of scarlet hoods and blue gowns with the insignia of their crafts embroidered on their sleeves. The first of the elaborate pageants prepared for Margaret's reception set the theme: Noah's Ark stood in the middle of London Bridge displaying the dove of peace, and the figures of 'Peace and Plenty' declared that England and France were now united through Margaret's marriage.[12] Margaret and her escort turned east into Thames Street towards the Tower of London, where Margaret would spend the night and where King Henry would perform the traditional ceremony of creating new Knights of the Bath on the eve of a coronation.

On her way to Westminster Abbey on the following day Margaret presented a glittering image of a fairy-tale princess. She was dressed in white cloth of gold with her hair loose about her shoulders and a golden bejewelled coronet on her head. She wore the gold necklace set with four rubies, four sapphires, and thirty-two large pearls, known as the 'Iklyngton Collar' and a girdle of gold studded with precious stones.[13] Her litter, draped with cloth of gold, was slung between two white horses and the canopy above her head was supported on gilded staves decorated with silver bells.

Young Margaret

Heralds, minstrels, and trumpeters bore colourful banners, some of them displaying Margaret's arms.[14] Margaret's chamberlain rode ahead of the litter and gentlemen of the Queen's chair rode beside it. Two gentlemen ushers in mantles and hats of estate represented the Duchies of Normandy and Gascony. Behind them came her esquires in liveries of crimson and blue. Her palfrey, saddled and draped with crimson cloth of gold, was led by her yeoman of horse. Margaret's ladies were mounted on palfreys with gaily decorated saddles while the peeresses, wearing the velvet gowns bestowed on them for the occasion, were jolted over the cobblestones in crimson draped carriages. The principal officers of Margaret's household were followed by the Mayor of London carrying his mace, and the lower ranks of the household brought up the rear. The crowds were dense, pickpockets plied their trade, and rowdy apprentices made the most of their half-day holiday. The Great Conduit, the principal source of water for the City, ran with wine.

Wooden platforms along the route served as stages with large brightly painted backdrops for the enactment of allegorical tableaux. Margaret was well versed in Biblical allegory and she had no difficulty in recognising the figures portrayed, but it is doubtful if she understood much of what was being said. At the top of Grace Church Street Madame Grace, as God's chancellor, attended by four young women representing the popular conception of the four daughters of God – Truth, Mercy, Justice, and Peace – wished the Queen a long and prosperous life.

The procession turned up Cornhill to the highest vantage point in the City in front of the grim Tun prison. Here Saint Margaret hailed her namesake as the symbol of peace. The shops and houses of wealthy townsmen were situated along Poultry and into Cheapside where the wives and daughters of those lucky enough to secure an invitation viewed the proceedings from windows adorned by tapestries, coloured cloth, and flower-wreaths. Cheapside Cross stood three storeys high, carved with statues of the Pope, the Virgin and

Child, and the Apostles, but its stonework was crumbling, and a new cross was to be built at the City's expense. Here the Heavenly City of Jerusalem was on display, an allusion to Margaret as the daughter of the King of Jerusalem. She was assured once again of the universal rejoicing at her coming.

The final pageant was the Last Judgement staged at St Michael in Querne, the quarter of the goldsmiths, where King Henry watched from a window as a guest of the goldsmith William Flour.[15] The Virgin Mary looked down from heaven to pray that the earthly queen might enjoy the crown terrestrial to be followed by the crown celestial. The procession halted at the north gate of St Pauls cathedral with its fire-blackened roof. The spire had been destroyed by lightning earlier in the year. Margaret made an offering at the high altar before resuming her progress to Westminster Palace.

Margaret was crowned Queen of England and France and Lady of Ireland on Sunday 30 May 1445.[16] She walked in stocking feet from the palace along the woollen cloth laid across Palace Yard and into the precincts of Westminster Abbey, with the Wardens of the Cinque Ports holding a canopy over her head. She was escorted by two bishops and followed, in case she needed prompting, by the Abbot of Westminster, who was responsible for the smooth course of the ceremony. Behind her came the peeresses in scarlet velvet robes with ermine surcoats. The baronesses wore miniver surcoats and the knights' ladies were in plain scarlet gowns.

Margaret traversed the choir to the high altar and prostrated herself while the Archbishop of Canterbury prayed over her. She knelt as the circlet was removed from her head, her mantle and kirtle were loosened, and her hair was wrapped in a linen cloth to protect the holy oil with which Archbishop Stafford anointed her. The coronation ring was slipped onto the fourth finger of her right hand and the crown was placed on her head. The Archbishop then presented her with the sceptre and the rod.

A chair of estate draped in costly fabrics and furnished with cushions stood on a high dais in the centre of the abbey, visible to everyone. Two bishops led Margaret up the steps of the dais and presented her to her subjects for the traditional shouts of acclamation. She seated herself, the choir sang the *Agnus Dei,* and the pax was brought for her to kiss. Margaret descended from the dais and walked to the high altar to make her confession, receive absolution, and the Archbishop's blessing. She made the traditional offering of a piece of silk cloth embroidered with gold and the Abbot of Westminster gave her a drink of wine. She was conducted back to the dais by the assembled lords and she remained seated in her chair of estate while a mass was sung.

At the end of the ceremony she walked from the abbey beneath her canopy, escorted by her bishops, while the choir sang a *Te Deum,* and returned to her chamber in Westminster Palace to rest and break her fast.

Margaret entered Westminster Hall in the late afternoon for the coronation banquet. She was seated at the high table with Archbishop Stafford and Jacquetta, Duchess of Bedford and first lady of the land, on her right and the Duke of Gloucester on her left, while two countesses knelt before her. It was their duty to hold up a wide cloth to screen Margaret if she needed privacy while she ate or to allow her a respite by having the crown lifted from her head. The Earl of Oxford, as chamberlain for the feast, and the Earl of Devon, as coronation steward, presented her with a basin and ewer for a ritual washing of her hands.

Four tables stretched the length of the hall to seat everyone who had taken part in the coronation. John Mowbray, Duke of Norfolk, the Earl Marshall of England, and Viscount Beaumont, the Constable of England, patrolled the hall mounted on elaborately caparisoned horses. Minstrels, trumpeters, and the choir of the royal chapel occupied a stage at the far end. René had sent minstrels and members of his household to witness the splendid ceremony. Antoine de la Sale, a soldier, scholar and historian of the House of Anjou was mightily impressed: he described the English as *les plus seremonieuses gens en honnneurs que je ay gaires veu*.[17] (The most ceremonious people in matters of good manners that I have ever met.)

The three courses at the banquet were introduced by a fanfare of trumpets and preceded by a procession of peers. The dishes were served by the newly created Knights of the Bath. Minstrels played, but they were not easily heard amid the noise and bustle. The last course was ushered in by the Earl of Oxford and a company of knights. At the end of the banquet Margaret washed her hands a second time and a spice plate with wafers was offered to her. The cloth at the high table was ritually folded by Margaret's almoner, Henry Trevelian and her chaplain, Michael Tregury. The final act was performed by Henry Frowyk, the Mayor of London, who presented Margaret with the valedictory cup of hypocras in a golden goblet. He would retain the goblet and the ewer as his fee. Everything used in the coronation ceremony and banquet was a hereditary perquisite, either to the abbey or to those who served throughout the day.

Margaret left the Hall with the sceptre and rod carried before her. The long and exhausting ordeal was over: she was tired but elated. She had been welcomed by her new subjects and hailed as the harbinger of peace just as her father and uncle had promised her that she would be. Three days of festivities followed with jousting in Westminster Yard. Margaret's champion was Sir Richard Woodville, the Duchess of Bedford's husband, and the most highly accomplished exponent of the joust in England.

Parliament granted Margaret the Queen's traditional dowry of 10,000 marks, or £6,666 13s 4d a year, made up of King Henry's Duchy of Lancaster estates and cash payments from the Exchequer.[18] Margaret's predecessors had found it inadequate and so did she, especially as payment was usually in arrears. Margaret's dower lands made her a great landowner with the same responsibilities as any other magnate. During her first ten years in England she occupied herself with the management of her household and her estates. She exercised 'good ladyship' towards her servants, her tenants, or indeed anyone who could attract her notice.[19] The social fabric of fifteenth-century England was based on 'good lordship': the concept of reward and protection in return for loyal service.[20] Magnates exercised extensive patronage in their localities and advanced the interests of their clients, tenants, and dependents, who in turn extended a lesser patronage to friends and relations.

Increasingly, as she came to understand what was involved in sound estate management, Margaret appointed experienced men from whom she expected and received efficient attention to her business.[21] Queens of England had their own council, with a chancellor in charge of their great and privy seals. Margaret's council chamber was in a tower at the end of the Great Hall at Westminster, overlooking the courtyard of the Outer Ward and conveniently located adjacent to the Exchequer.[22] William Booth, Bishop of Coventry and Lichfield, was Margaret's chancellor.[23] She issued warrants under her own seals and she employed a team of expert lawyers, headed by her attorney general, Robert Tanfield, to pursue and protect her interests.

The King's patronage was sought by everyone. The royal court encompassed an ever-shifting throng of courtiers, petitioners, place seekers, visitors, and hangers-on. It was a clearing house for gossip, rumour, political speculation, and intrigue, a male-dominated, hierarchical world with men constantly jockeying for grants, pensions, offices, and material gifts. Wine, meat, and wood magnates came to court escorted by their liveried retainers; the higher clergy came with their attendant clerks; gentlemen came from the shires, especially during sessions of Parliament, creating a noisy, often quarrelsome amalgam of men pursuing their own interests. Royal service was a form of investment; wages were usually in arrears, but the work was secure and royal employment carried increased status. A yeoman of the chamber ranked as an esquire, a king's esquire was equivalent to a knight. Many yeomen, grooms and pages were younger sons of knightly families or lesser landowners, not all of them young men. Their kinship and that of their wives and daughters was intertwined, complex and diffuse: everyone was related to or connected with everyone else and the network thus established was influential throughout the country.

The formation of Margaret's household was a major event. She was expected to maintain it, to pay her expenses and to contribute £6 a day to the costs of Henry's establishment during the periods when they were together and the two households merged.[24] It was presided over by her chamberlain and consisted of her ladies, her knights of the body (the Queen's carvers), a confessor, chaplains and clerks, plus the esquires, yeomen, grooms, and pages of the chamber (above stairs). The Queen also had her own yeomen, grooms, and pages of the kitchen, bake house, buttery, cellar, larder, scullery, laundry, scalding-house, poultry, and cattery who accompanied the peripatetic court from one royal residence to the next. They received an annual salary or a daily stipend, plus a gift at New Year. Their perquisites took the form of food, lodging, and clothing, with possibly a small annuity at the end of long service.[25]

A display of munificence was expected of the Queen. Lavish hospitality and gift-giving were manifestations of royal pomp and a magnificent court commanded obedience at home and respect abroad. Margaret liberally rewarded her master cook, David Lloyd; he ranked above the menials in the household, achieving the status of an esquire.[26] From her first Christmas in England Margaret devised entertainments for the festive season and Henry granted her £1,000 'as well for the daily expenses of her chamber as in relief of the great charges which the said Queen incurred on the day of Circumcision of our Lord last past.'[27] Margaret's gift-giving at New Year was on a grand scale. The most expensive gifts naturally went to King Henry and the Duke of Gloucester as the King's uncle, but she also sent gifts to duchesses, magnates, bishops, and the principal officers of state, as well as to favoured members of King Henry's household.[28] She patronised several London goldsmiths to whom she was frequently in debt, but her patronage was well worth having. When the Abbot of St Osyths accused her goldsmith Humphrey Hayford of trespass, Margaret somewhat sententiously suggested to him that as a man of God the Abbot should search his conscience and not bear false witness. Margaret was acting as 'good lady' to Hayford, but it may have been Hayford who was bearing false witness.[29]

Margaret was conventionally pious and she possessed several books of devotion: John Lydgate's *Life of our Lady* and the *Riches Psalter*, illuminated by the court painter William Abel, a gift from John Stafford, the Archbishop of Canterbury.[30] The Book of Hours belonging to René of Anjou, now known as his *London Book of Hours*, was probably one of her bridal gifts.[31] Her prayer roll depicted a wheel with seven spokes inscribed with prayers to the Virgin.[32] Her day began with matins followed by a mass for the Virgin and ended with evensong and the Little Office of Our Lady.[33] She gave alms of 4d a day (a penny more than her yeomen received in wages) and on twenty-one 'special feast days' she made an offering of a gold coin.[34] Only two of her 'special days' were secular: the anniversaries of the deaths of Henry V and Queen Katherine. The festivals marked her religious year, beginning with the Annunciation of the Virgin on 25 March two days after her birthday, and ending with the Purification of the Virgin on 2 February.

The first meal of the day was eaten in public in the Queen's great chamber towards midday. Supper was taken in her private chamber with her ladies unless there were visitors who might be allowed in to watch her eat. After dinner Margaret received petitions and dealt with the business of her household and estates. Recreations in the late afternoon and evening included word games, chess, dice, or cards while music, dancing, and reading aloud featured regularly. The Earl of Shrewsbury had presented Margaret with a sumptuously illustrated anthology to celebrate her marriage and coronation. It contained romances, chronicles, *chansons de geste*, and tales of chivalry, including Christine de Pizan's *Book of Feats of Arms and Chivalry* and the statutes of the Order of the Garter of which Shrewsbury was a member.[35] The dedicatory verse very properly hopes that the book will entertain her but adds the sly wish that since she must now speak English this gift will ensure that she does not forget her native tongue. Margaret also owned an elaborate roll of heraldic devices depicting shields and blazons from all over Europe, probably a gift from René of Anjou, that connoisseur of all aspects of chivalry. A copy of *Les Grandes Chroniques de France* possessed by King Richard III may once have belonged to Margaret. Originally commissioned by a Duke of Anjou, it came into Yorkist hands as part of the royal library.[36]

Margaret's first years in England were spent in King Henry's company at the royal palaces of Windsor, Sheen, and Eltham. In 1447 Henry gave her the manor at Greenwich called Pleasaunce on the banks of the Thames that had belonged to the Duke of Gloucester. It became her favourite residence and the closest thing to a home of her own she was ever to know. Margaret expended time, thought, and money on its improvement – she redesigned the gardens and had a private parlour and a gallery built to overlook them. The great garden was enclosed by an arbour, and a smaller garden was laid out directly under the manor's windows, probably on the sunny south side away from the river. Margaret favoured large windows and the King's glazier set new glass into the windows at Pleasaunce. The chapel was fitted out with a private oratory for King Henry with a window over its altar depicting the crucifixion and supported by the arms of the King, the Queen, and St George.[37]

If Henry had a passion it was for his foundations of Eton College and the College of Our Lady and St Nicholas at Cambridge, known as King's College. Margaret was anxious to establish a college of her own and she was approached by Andrew Dockett, a persuasive individual whose burning ambition was to become president of a Cambridge college no matter how small. King Henry had granted him a charter to found the College of St Bernard for four fellows with himself as president. Margaret requested Henry's permission to enlarge and rename Dockett's college as the Queen's College of St Margaret and St Bernard, a sister college to Henry's foundation, to the 'laud and honneure of sexe feminine'. Cambridge had 'no collage founded by eny queen of Englond hidertoward', and Margaret wanted the honour to be hers.

Henry was not particularly generous; he resumed the lands already granted to the college and bestowed them, with £200, on Margaret.[38] She had no gift of patronage. The president of the college was to be elected by the fellows but she could authorise them to accumulate land to the value of another £200. Margaret issued her charter on 15 April 1448, and she granted the college the right to display her arms, as it does to this day. The college's seal depicted St Margaret and St Bernard above a shield bearing the Angevin arms with Andrew Dockett kneeling to one side and the four fellows to the other.[39] Margaret's chamberlain, Sir John Wenlock, laid the chapel's foundation stone and her chancellor, William Booth, probably drew up its statutes, but the college's records from this period have disappeared. A gift from Marmaduke Lumley, the Treasurer of England and a Cambridge man, allowed the buildings around the main court, the hall, buttery, kitchen chambers, and front court to be completed. Lumley also bequeathed books to the college library in his will. The president's lodgings occupied the western corner of the court and the tower above the main gate housed the treasury. The troubles of the 1450s, and a permanent lack of money, meant that it was left to Margaret's successor, Queen Elizabeth Woodville, to continue what Margaret had started. Elizabeth acknowledged Margaret's involvement with a clever back-handed compliment: she changed the college's name from Queen's College to Queens' College.

Margaret began to perform her duties as Queen within a year of her arrival. In 1446 she acted as arbitrator in a dispute over the appointment of the Dean of Wells Cathedral to sort out one of King Henry's embarrassing administrative muddles. Henry had promised the deanery to his almoner John de la Bere, when the incumbent, John Forest, should die. Forest died in March 1446 and Henry reminded Thomas Beckington, the Bishop of Bath and Wells, of his promise to de la Bere, but the right of election lay with the canons of the cathedral and de la Bere was not their choice. John Stafford, Archbishop of Canterbury, the Bishop of Salisbury, Suffolk, and Beckington himself assured the canons that the King would respect their rights and authorised them to proceed with their election. The canons chose Nicholas Caraunt, a local man who was secretary to Margaret's council. Bishop Beckington confirmed his election, Caraunt made his profession of obedience and was installed, but King Henry ignored the election and confirmed de la Bere's right as dean.[40] De la Bere brought a suit in the papal court at Rome against Beckington, the canons of Wells, and Nicholas Caraunt. Pope Eugenius's appointee to judge the case found in favour of de la Bere, and the Pope ordered the canons to evict Caraunt and install de la Bere forthwith, under pain of excommunication.[41]

Suffolk asked Margaret to intervene. Good ladyship as well as expediency dictated her support for Caraunt.[42] When Pope Eugenius died in February 1447 Margaret petitioned the new pope on Caraunt's behalf and Pope Nicholas graciously confirmed her judgement.[43] Caraunt then claimed in the Archbishop of Canterbury's court that property belonging to the deanery had been damaged and that the repair costs should be borne by Thomas Forest, executor of the late dean's estate. Caraunt was awarded £227 but this satisfied neither party. Caraunt and Forest appealed to the Pope and Margaret wrote to Forest to make it plain that she would not be pleased if her secretary incurred further expense as too much time and money had already been wasted. She requested Pope Nicholas to allow the case to be heard in England.[44] De la Bere had expended more money than he could afford in bribes at the papal court with little to show for it, and he wisely reassessed his options. Possibly at Margaret's behest, de la

Bere was promised a bishopric if he submitted to her arbitration. When the bishop-elect of St David's died in July, King Henry bestowed the bishopric on de la Bere. Caraunt remained Dean of Wells for the rest of his life.

The Suffolk Years

5

The Quest for Peace

As soon as the feasts and jousting to celebrate Margaret's coronation ended, Suffolk reported to Parliament on his mission to Tours and announced the imminent arrival of French ambassadors to continue peace negotiations. He assured the members that no preconditions had been set, but he warned that the outcome was uncertain, and he recommended that additional supplies should be sent to the Duke of York in Normandy and that the garrisons there should be strengthened. His warning fell on deaf ears. In the Commons' opinion Margaret's marriage and the Truce of Tours were the prelude to peace, so there was no need to vote further funds for Normandy. The Speaker, William Burley, thanked Suffolk, and the Duke of Gloucester congratulated him on his achievement.[1] King Henry created him Marquess of Suffolk and for the moment Suffolk was the hero of the hour.

The arrival in July of an impressive French embassy was the major event of the summer; French ambassadors had not been seen in England for over thirty years.[2] William Bruges, Garter King of Arms, rounded up the delegates at Calais and shepherded them across the Channel.[3] Messengers from King Henry caught up with them at Rochester. Henry had received the news of their arrival just as he was going to bed and he requested them to break their journey to allow time for suitable arrangements to be made for their reception. The French did not care for Rochester, they thought it unhealthy and complained that the water was brackish, but they

The Quest for Peace

agreed to await the King's pleasure and hoped the delay would be short.

The Earls of Suffolk, Somerset, Salisbury, and Shrewsbury, with an escort of knights and squires met them several miles outside London. The Dukes of Exeter and Warwick awaited them at London Bridge where the Mayor, aldermen, and guildsmen, in full regalia, welcomed them into the City. The watching crowds were friendly; they cheered as the Frenchmen made their way to their lodgings.

On the following day, the Duke of Buckingham escorted them to Westminster by barge. King Henry waited to receive them, seated in his chair of estate with his magnates and bishops grouped around him. He was sumptuously dressed in a robe of red cloth of gold clasped with a golden girdle and a flat, broad-brimmed hat of purple velvet decorated with a long streamer. As soon as he saw the ambassadors he stood up and moved forward taking each man by the hand and slightly raising his hat to Jacques Juvenal des Ursins, the Archbishop of Rheims. Juvenal des Ursins opened the proceedings in French, announcing that the Count of Vendôme carried letters from King Charles of France to King Henry of England. John Stafford, Archbishop of Canterbury and Chancellor, started to express the King's formal thanks but Henry interrupted him and rebuked him for not displaying a friendlier attitude. Henry approached the delegates once again, raising his hat and slapping them on the back while repeating his favourite affirmative oath, 'Saint Jehan grant mercis.' Such familiar behaviour surprised the French and Suffolk intervened hastily to explain that the King did not think of them as strangers but as members of his own household.

Juvenal des Ursins delivered a long speech, the gist of which was that King Charles welcomed the opportunity to obtain first-hand news of his nephew since, except for the Dauphin Louis, King Henry was his closest male relative and Charles's affection for him was commensurate with their kinship. Henry was plainly delighted but at his side the Duke of Gloucester stiffened. Henry's unfeigned pleasure

The Suffolk Years

at the use of the title 'King of France' for Charles was hard for Gloucester to stomach. Henry saw his movement of distaste and smiled, informing Chancellor Stafford in English that he was glad that words had been heard by someone who would take no pleasure in them. Gloucester and the Count of Vendôme had been present in 1415 when Henry V received an embassy from Charles VI, and they could scarcely help contrasting the cool courtesy of that monarch with the gauche behaviour of his son.[4]

The company gathered for a second meeting on the following day. Gloucester was not present, and Suffolk took the opportunity to discredit him further. He recalled that he had heard a rumour in Tours that Gloucester opposed the peace but that he, Suffolk, had dismissed it, since Gloucester had no influence at court. King Henry added 'Saint Jehan oui.' The King and his minister thus went out of their way to belittle the last surviving brother of Henry V, a living reminder of the days of English conquest. Henry's preference for his French uncle, whom he had never met, over his English uncle and heir, the erstwhile Protector of England, did not go unnoticed. Suffolk confided to the ambassadors that, excepting only Queen Margaret, Henry's 'uncle of France' was closest to the King's heart. He further averred that for his part, saving only King Henry, King Charles was the man above all others whom he wished to serve. Juvenal des Ursins reminded his hearers that the King of France had agreed to a truce at England's behest although he was well able to continue hostilities, and he had promoted Henry's marriage to Margaret and wasted no time in sending her to England. Henry accepted these extraordinary pronouncements with evident pleasure. Louis of Vendôme picked up his cue and opined that with such close family ties there should be no difficulty in reaching a peace settlement. Henry then left Westminster to join Margaret at Windsor.

Discussions began in earnest on 19 July 1445. Humphrey Stafford, Duke of Buckingham, was the royal representative. He was a great grandson of King Edward III and his Stafford inheritance made him

The Quest for Peace

one of the richest men in England. Cardinal John Kemp, Archbishop of York, Suffolk, and Lord Sudeley, the Treasurer of England, opened the negotiations.[5] Kemp had been Chancellor of Normandy during Henry V's second campaign in France and he had negotiated a temporary truce with Yolande of Aragon for Anjou and Maine. He was instrumental in drafting the Treaty of Troyes, making Henry V heir to the French throne, and he had led the English embassy at the abortive peace conference at Arras in 1435.

The negotiations were farcical from the start. Despite Juvenal des Ursins's hyperbole, the French had not come to make peace. Suffolk claimed the Duchies of Normandy and Gascony as English possessions in full sovereignty, as he had at Tours. Juvenal des Ursins threw him completely off balance by reiterating precisely what the French had offered at Tours: Gascony, Quercy, Périgord, and the Pale of Calais in liege homage. But not Normandy. Suffolk was incredulous, he insisted that King Charles must have authorised them to go further. Surely after all their fair words they meant to make an acceptable offer? Cardinal Kemp counter-claimed Normandy, Gascony, Poitou, and Ponthieu, in full sovereignty. The French refused. Kemp expressed his surprise and regret at being offered considerably less than he expected, but Juvenal des Ursins replied that it was a substantial concession and the meeting broke up. The French made their final offer two days later: they would enlarge Gascony to include the whole of Saintonge. Kemp declared that it was too meagre, he could not accept it, and he would have to consult King Henry.[6]

Impending failure was averted by René of Anjou's representative, Bertrand de Beauvau. He suavely suggested that the best way to resolve the impasse was by a conference at the highest level. If King Henry would travel to France and meet his uncle face to face all their differences could be resolved.[7] Suffolk, never at his best in a crisis, clutched at this straw and undertook to put the proposal to the King immediately. He reached Windsor late on that summer evening and broke the news that the talks had collapsed but that all was not lost,

Beauvau had suggested a way forward. Henry was receptive and Margaret was delighted by this unexpected opportunity to visit her family in her husband's company.

Henry was flattered to think he might succeed where his diplomats had failed. At the end of July, he gave a private audience to the French ambassadors attended only by Kemp, Suffolk, and Sudeley. Juvenal des Ursins launched into another of his longwinded speeches and Henry showed the same pleasure as before, raising his hat whenever King Charles's name was mentioned and repeating 'Saint Jehan grant mercis' when the Archbishop touched on his uncle's affection for him. Juvenal des Ursins extended a formal invitation for Henry to visit France and he made a vital concession: if Henry accepted, the truce would be extended from April to November 1446. Suffolk pressed for a longer period but Juvenal des Ursins declared that this was as far as he could go. He suggested that English envoys should accompany him back to France to persuade King Charles to extend the truce.

Cardinal Kemp replied to Juvenal des Ursins's eloquent French in elegant Latin. In measured tones he declared that King Henry was aware of the blessings of peace and the evils of war; to avert the latter he was willing to travel to France, even though he was disappointed by the French offers. It should be clearly understood, however, that such a journey could not be undertaken hurriedly and there must be some guarantee that a lasting peace would result. King Henry would inform King Charles of when, where, and on what terms the visit could take place. It was a statesmanlike reply, making no definite commitment.[8]

The French went home well pleased with themselves. They had fulfilled Charles VII's promise to send an embassy to England without the smallest intention of making peace unless Normandy was surrendered. They had also achieved Charles's underlying aim by convincing King Henry that a visit to his 'uncle of France' was the surest way to promote peace. King Charles did not doubt that he could exploit his nephew's naïveté in a personal meeting.

On his return to Anjou, the resourceful Bertrand de Beauvau

The Quest for Peace

suggested to René that King Henry's susceptibility to protestations of affectionate kinship was well worth exploiting. René should propose a closer relationship between the House of Anjou and the King of England and ask Henry to demonstrate his affection by returning the English-held County of Maine to his bride's family. It was a clever idea. Maine had not figured in the peace negotiations thus far. The Regent Bedford had occupied parts of it after his victory at the Battle of Verneuil in 1424 and Maine was linked in English minds with Anjou, not with Normandy, and was therefore not sacrosanct.[9]

René welcomed Beauvau's suggestion enthusiastically and asked King Charles's permission to raise the question with his daughter and son-in-law. Charles agreed graciously, since it would cost him nothing, and would bring him a step closer to recovering Normandy. The English might be persuaded that ceding Maine would guarantee Normandy's safety, but that was not what René had to offer. He requested 'the surrender of the County of Maine, *or what our dear son holds of it*,' in return for a twenty-year truce with the Angevins.[10]

King Charles sent his representatives, Guillaume Cousinot and Jean Havart to London in November. Cousinot agreed to extend the truce until 1 April 1447 in return for a promise that King Henry would visit France sometime before November 1446.[11] He also presented letters from Charles to Henry and to Margaret, in which the King exhorted them to work for peace and advised them that the best way to achieve it was to agree to René's request. Margaret saw no reason why Henry should not restore Maine to her family: she had been raised to think of her father's brother as Count of Maine. With his customary disregard for military realities, René had bestowed Maine on his younger brother before leaving for Naples in 1437.[12] Margaret did not betray Henry by encouraging Henry to cede Maine – she aligned herself with him. Henry wanted to please his uncle of France and his queen but above all he wanted peace, and he did not consider the risks involved. Blissfully unaware of the consequences, Henry and Margaret accepted a proposal they did not fully understand and

The Suffolk Years

Margaret wrote to King Charles that she had done her utmost to further his wishes 'for no greater pleasure can we have in this world than to see an arrangement for a final peace.'[13] With his mission accomplished, Cousinot returned to France bearing a hunting horn garnished with gold as a gift from Margaret to her father.[14]

On 22 December 1445 King Henry wrote to Charles and undertook 'on his kingly honour' to cede Maine to René and Charles of Anjou by 30 April 1446, only four months away, in return for a formal alliance and truce with the House of Anjou.[15]

The extension of the truce was publicly proclaimed just before Parliament reassembled in January for an unprecedented fourth term.[16] But Henry's promise remained a secret. How best to implement it was something Suffolk needed time to ponder. Parliament rescinded the clause in the Treaty of Troyes of 1420 requiring parliamentary approval for peace with France, but in his closing address Chancellor Stafford made a startling pronouncement: the responsibility for the outcome of a meeting between Henry and King Charles rested solely with King Henry.[17] The Lords disassociated themselves from Henry's determination to visit France without denying his right to make it. They had serious reservations and even Suffolk doubted the wisdom of giving the King a free hand. The thought of their gullible, unworldly, but often disastrously pig-headed king face to face with skillful French diplomats, flattered by his 'uncle of France' and welcomed by those charming Angevins, the Queen's father, brother, and uncle, was enough to give anyone nightmares. Henry was not deterred; he accepted the Lords' caveat and continued to plan his expedition.

The deadline for Maine's surrender passed unnoticed. King Charles ignored it; he hoped to reap even greater advantages if he could entice Henry to France. Margaret wrote to Charles in May naïvely invoking the Holy Spirit to incline both parties to settle their differences and expressing her willingness to do anything in her power to bring this about. Her husband wanted peace and she was sure that 'as a good

The Quest for Peace

Catholic prince' her uncle must feel the same.[18] There was little enthusiasm for the visit to France except from the royal couple, and attempts to raise loans proved disappointing.[19] The best hope of aborting the meeting lay in the empty Treasury.

The Duke of York came home in the autumn of 1445 when his term as the King's Lieutenant in France expired. He was satisfied that he had done all he could to safeguard Normandy. York was not a natural soldier or a brilliant administrator like the Regent Bedford, but he was competent and conscientious, and he had the support of the veteran war captains who had fought under Henry V. Parliament thanked and congratulated him and King Henry instructed the Exchequer to pay York what was due to him, but the total was far in excess of what the Exchequer could raise.[20] The Treasurer assigned tallies for repayment, and York passed them on to his captains for the soldiers' wages. The problem was that there was no actual money to disburse, which naturally caused dissatisfaction among the troops.

Rumours that he had defrauded his men reached York's ears. He was acutely sensitive to criticism and he took umbrage at what he perceived as a reflection on his honour. York was thirty-four years old, a humourless man with an exalted notion of his high estate as a direct descendant of King Edward III. Adam Moleyns had just returned from France and York accused him of reporting that Normandy was in jeopardy because York had rewarded his lieutenants at the expense of the common soldiers. Moleyns refuted the allegation. He pointed out that payment of the soldiers' wages was always in arrears, but that neither York nor anyone else deliberately withheld them; the money was simply not forthcoming. He expressed surprise that York could think Normandy was in danger when, for his part, he believed it to be secure. Moreover, he was not such a fool as to criticise so high and mighty a prince as Richard of York.[21] Until this contretemps Suffolk and York had worked together, urging a strong defence of Normandy, but York's confrontation with Moleyns alienated Suffolk and King Henry. His unfounded charges against one of Suffolk's closest associates and the Keeper of the King's Privy Seal were politically inept and damaging to his prospects. York had negotiated with King Charles for the marriage of his son Edward to one of Charles's daughters and Charles had shown a flattering interest in the proposal.[22] The French king kept himself fully informed of the political climate in England and as the English court's attitude towards York cooled, he quietly allowed the scheme to drop.

Suffolk preferred not to venture abroad again following his success at Tours. The burden of travelling to France fell on Adam Moleyns and King Henry made him Bishop of Chichester. In the summer of 1446 Moleyns and John Sutton, Lord Dudley, a councillor and a diplomat with previous experience of negotiating with the French, went to France to request an indefinite postponement of the proposed meeting of the two kings. Margaret entrusted Dudley with letters of credence to her uncle but she did not mention Maine. She requested Charles to speed up the release of an English prisoner of war.[23] Charles began to suspect that the English Council was looking for a way to renege on Henry's promise. He sent Cousinot and Havart back to England in November 1446 to deliver an ultimatum: any further extension of the truce was now conditional on Maine's surrender.[24] He urged Margaret to use her influence but she had learned to be more circumspect, she was no longer her uncle's impulsive advocate and she side-stepped him neatly by reiterating her husband's desire for peace and identifying her wishes with his.[25]

The Council met at Sheen in December to debate Maine and money – peace or war.[26] King Charles's ultimatum coincided with a financial crisis that was severe even by Lancastrian standards, incurred in part by the expense of bringing Margaret to England. Without drastic retrenchment there would be no money to meet the costs of the royal household let alone a renewal of the war. Solvency depended on a continuation of the truce and Lord Cromwell, a former Treasurer whose view on financial matters was widely respected, declared that war would mean economic disaster. He made a scathing

The Quest for Peace

attack on the incumbent Treasurer, Lord Sudeley, who prudently resigned. Sudeley was replaced by Marmaduke Lumley, Bishop of Carlisle. Lumley was well versed in dealing with administrative insolvency; Carlisle was an impoverished town under constant threat from Scottish depredations and, unusually for a bishop, Lumley had served briefly as Warden of the West March. He could be relied on to curtail expenditure although he was unlikely to make much impression on King Henry.

The Truce of Tours had been Suffolk's supreme achievement and he could not allow it to founder. He believed that he had the numbers to continue his (and King Henry's) peace policy. The Duke of Buckingham was Captain of Calais *in absentia*; he preferred life at court to service abroad. Richard Neville, Earl of Salisbury, and Henry Percy, Earl of Northumberland, as Wardens of the West and East Marches were the military guardians of the Anglo–Scottish border. They had no special interest in Maine whereas war with France inevitably meant an increase in Scottish incursions and possibly war on two fronts.

The bishops knew that war meant demands for money from the church. Archbishop Stafford, like Buckingham, was a peace-loving man. Cardinal Kemp disliked the French, but he accepted that maintaining the truce was essential. Reginald Boulers, Abbot of Gloucester, was a courtier rather than a churchman: he would not jeopardise his career by antagonising Suffolk. Lord Sudeley was King Henry's chamberlain, John Stourton was Treasurer of the Household, and Richard Rolleston was Keeper of the Great Wardrobe. They were bound to the King by loyalty and to Suffolk by self-interest. Adam Moleyns and Lord Dudley were just back from France; they knew better than anyone that King Charles was in no mood to compromise.

No one at the Council table actively favoured a renewal of the war but English pride was at stake. Men who had risked their lives and fortunes fighting in France fiercely resented the demand of a *soi-disant* king that they should cede hard-won English territory. There were,

The Suffolk Years

however, reasons for allowing Suffolk to persuade them. Theoretically, Edmund Beaufort, the English Count of Maine, had the most to lose.[27] King Henry had granted him the title and all the English-held lands there for life, but with the proviso that Maine could be ceded to the French to secure peace.[28] It was an awkward clause that Suffolk would not hesitate to invoke. The income from Maine was not great and Beaufort could ill afford to forfeit the King's favour by opposing Suffolk.

John Holand, Duke of Exeter, had been captured at the Battle of Baugé in 1421. His ransom crippled the family's fortunes and deprived him of his liberty for four years. Exeter and the older members of the Council would think twice about risking their lives, their inheritance, and their heirs to fight a war in which the King would take no part.

The Duke of Gloucester was not at the meeting. He had always resisted making any concessions to the French, but Gloucester disliked Edmund Beaufort almost as much as he hated Cardinal Beaufort. He had protested vehemently in 1438 that resources which should have been sent to Normandy had been wasted by permitting Beaufort to campaign in Maine.[29] The defence of Normandy was far more important than the aggrandisement of the upstart Beauforts, and Gloucester would gladly have sacrificed Beaufort interests to secure the duchy. The Duke of York had no illusions that he or anyone else could complete Henry V's conquest of France, but he held extensive estates in Normandy, and they were his paramount concern. Maine was a small price to pay to extend the truce and guarantee the safety of Normandy.

In the end the Council agreed to honour King Henry's promise and negotiate the surrender of Maine. The truce was due to expire, King Henry was implacably opposed to war, and the Treasury was empty. Adam Moleyns and Lord Dudley returned to France to inform King Charles and Charles agreed to extend the truce to the end of 1447, with a meeting between the two kings to take place before that date.[30] He would send ambassadors to London for further discussions.

The Quest for Peace

The Duke of York believed that he was the King's Lieutenant in France by right, as well as by service, and he expected his tenure to be renewed. It came a shock to him when at the end of December King Henry appointed Edmund Beaufort in his stead. It was an inept move that would have far reaching consequences, but it was Suffolk's insurance policy. If King Charles threatened Normandy, Suffolk could rely on Cardinal Beaufort to contribute handsomely to sustain the position of the King's Lieutenant in France that he had long coveted for his nephew.

6

Destruction of a Duke

At the age of fifty-two William de la Pole, Earl and then Marquess of Suffolk, was at the pinnacle of his career. He had worked hard and patiently for his success. The de la Poles were parvenus; Suffolk's grandfather had been ennobled by Richard II for financial services to the crown and Suffolk had inherited the earldom when his father and older brother died serving Henry V in France. After he returned to England from his own captivity, Suffolk had married Alice Chaucer, the wealthy widow of Thomas Montague, Earl of Salisbury. She had inherited wealth and property from her father, Thomas Chaucer, as well as from Salisbury, and this consideration weighed with Suffolk, but Alice was a woman who inspired affection. Her marriage to Salisbury had been happy and Suffolk was devoted to her.[1] They remained childless for over ten years until their son John was born in 1442, when Alice was in her late thirties. John's birth raised Suffolk's sights from the pursuit of a profitable career in the King's service to a determination to establish a de la Pole dynasty which would rival in wealth and prestige that of the princely families of the Staffords, the Holands, and the Beauforts.

Suffolk was King Henry's favourite minister and Henry trusted him implicitly. Suffolk relieved the King of the irksome day-to-day demands that sovereignty imposed. He kept Henry functioning by taking pressure off him and he made royal government work. King Henry carried the concept of good lordship to great lengths, equating it with Christian charity, and neither Suffolk nor anyone else could curb the King's practise of making indiscriminate grants to anyone who petitioned him. His generosity, or credulity, was exploited by high and low alike. Suffolk took his share, many believed it to be the lion's share, of the King's bounty and his patronage was widely sought.

Continual land-grabs characterised much of society. A common method of obtaining a property was to wrest it by force. The violent seizure of a disputed estate was the accepted, if not the acceptable, method of enforcing a claim to it, although to some extent the threat of violence was part of the ritual, a declaration of war on a small scale. Recovery depended on recourse to law, a slow, expensive, and dubious process, open to abuse. Impartial justice and good lordship were virtually incompatible since the local magnates who enforced the law protected their clients, regardless of the rights of opposing claimants. Lawlessness was rife, landowners great and small were often at loggerheads and local feuds were the norm. Far stronger kings than Henry VI had found it impossible to check the violent propensities and acquisitiveness of their subjects. The acquisition of property by fair means or foul was the pinnacle of every man's ambition. Land and power were synonymous; litigation and lawlessness went hand in hand.[2] Land reflected rank, wealth, and status, and any weak title to landed property was liable to be challenged at any time. Suffolk faced the impossible task of holding a balance between the demands of good lordship and the requirements of impartial royal justice.

Margaret formed a close friendship with Suffolk and Alice based on shared cultural interests. Suffolk was a sophisticated, well-read man, and something of a poet. He wrote elegant French verses in emulation of his friend the Duke of Orleans, who had whiled away the tedium of captivity in England after the Battle of Agincourt by writing poetry.[3] Alice was Geoffrey Chaucer's granddaughter and as befitted a descendant of England's great poet, Alice was a book lover. She instructed one of her servants to move some of her books from a ground floor closet to make sure they did not get damp or damaged.[4] Alice was an intelligent, experienced, and warm-hearted older woman to whom the young queen could turn for advice, and she attended on Margaret for much of the year.[5] Henry and Margaret were guests at Ewelme, Alice's comfortable house in Oxfordshire. A measure of Margaret's friendship is reflected in the value of her gifts to Alice and a rare example of a woman being favoured above her husband.[6]

King Henry had granted Suffolk and his heirs the reversion of the Duke of Gloucester's great Earldom of Pembroke, and Suffolk coveted Gloucester's other prestigious titles and estates.[7] Parliament was to meet in February 1447 and Suffolk set a trap for Gloucester with great care. He advised King Henry to change its venue from Cambridge to Winchester and then to the Abbey of Bury St Edmunds. When a confused Chancellor Stafford asked for an explanation, Henry replied that 'for certaine causes that have be declared unto us sith that time, we be nowe fully deliberated and advised that our said parliament shall be holden at our town of seint Edmunds Bury.'[8] Unusually, the King was escorted to Bury by a large bodyguard and despite the bitterly cold weather the shire levies were ordered out to guard the countryside, although no one knew why.[9] The great Benedictine Abbey of Bury St Edmunds lay in the heart of Suffolk's lands and King Henry had an especial fondness for Bury. He had made a protracted stay there as a boy in 1433-34 and the poet-monk John Lydgate had written a life of St Edmund for him. Henry would handle a confrontation with Gloucester more easily at Bury than in Cambridge or Winchester. The 'certaine causes' comprised a carefully constructed account of the Duke of Gloucester's intended treason, which Suffolk unfolded to the King.

As Protector of England during Henry's minority Gloucester's burning ambition had been to emulate the exploits of his eldest brother, but he lacked the abilities that amounted to genius in Henry V. Gloucester was by turns indolent and impulsive, charming, sullen, wildly enthusiastic, and as easily bored. Curiously, for so militant a man, he was more like his nephew than like any of his brothers, for Gloucester was as infirm of purpose as a weathercock. He was obstinate and overbearing and he brooked no opposition to his will.[10] He consistently refused to countenance any concessions to the French even to end the war, but his belligerent attitude did not endear him to the peace-loving young king. Henry came to resent Gloucester's overbearing personality and military propensities while Gloucester seriously underestimated his nephew's capacity for forming and retaining personal dislikes.

Gloucester's active political career had virtually ended in 1441 in a social and political scandal the like of which had not been seen in England since Henry V accused his stepmother Queen Joan of witchcraft. Sixteen years earlier Gloucester had abandoned his wife Jacqueline, Countess of Hainault, in favour of Eleanor Cobham, one of Jacqueline's ladies, who became Gloucester's mistress and then his wife. Eleanor was fascinated by astrology and equally enthralled by more dangerous studies. She persuaded Roger Bolingbroke, a member of the ducal household and his associate Thomas Southwell, to cast the King's horoscope and assess her chances of becoming Queen.[11] They predicted that King Henry would suffer a life-threatening illness in the summer of 1441. Rumours circulated that the pair had encompassed King Henry's death. Bolingbroke, Southwell, and John Humme, another member of the ducal household, were arrested. Bolingbroke was hauled before the Council and under vigorous interrogation he implicated the Duchess of Gloucester.

Necromancy was linked to heresy and came under the Church's jurisdiction. Bolingbroke was condemned as a heretic and put on public display at St Pauls Cross. The spectacle was witnessed by the Mayor, aldermen, and members of the King's Council and it sent a thrill of superstitious horror through the watching crowd. Seated on a chair painted with strange symbols, surrounded by his instruments, and dressed in the magic garments he wore to perform his incantations, Bolingbroke recanted his heresies. He was tried for treason at the Guildhall where he denied that he had threatened King Henry's life. He was hanged, drawn, and quartered at Tyburn, and his head was set on London Bridge. Thomas Southwell died in the Tower, probably by his own hand before a like punishment could be inflicted on him.

Duchess Eleanor took fright and sought sanctuary in Westminster Abbey, but sanctuary did not offer protection for spiritual sins. She was arrested and brought before a panel of bishops in St Stephen's chapel at Westminster, accused of heresy and treason. She maintained her innocence but damning testimony was elicited from Margery Jourdemain, known as the Witch of Eye. Margery said she had supplied Eleanor with magic potions to make Gloucester marry her, implying that the Duchess's suspect practices dated back over many years. Eleanor claimed pathetically that her dealings with Margery sprang from her desire to have a child by her husband and that the potions she purchased were for that purpose only. Eleanor admitted to five of the charges brought against her, she abjured her sins and threw herself on the mercy of the assembled ecclesiastics. Margery Jourdemain was burned at Smithfield as a witch.

Eleanor was confined to Leeds Castle in Kent until she was brought back to London to be sentenced. The proud duchess was ordered to face public humiliation. She was not popular with the women of London; they had sympathised with Gloucester's first wife and cried shame on him for setting aside his lawful marriage in favour of a lowborn mistress On three consecutive market days, when the populace could stare at and revile her, Eleanor walked through the streets of the City dressed in black, bareheaded, and carrying a candle weighing two pounds to be offered at the altar of one of London's churches.[12]

Eleanor never saw her husband again. King Henry had been frightened by the prediction of his death and although he spared her the extreme punishment for heresy, death by burning, he condemned her to prison for the rest of her life. She was placed in the custody of Sir Thomas Stanley, Lord of the Isle of Man, who was allowed a pittance of 100 marks a year for her upkeep. Henry ordered Stanley to escort her under heavy guard to Chester and not to listen to any excuses she might make to delay the journey. Stanley moved the luckless Eleanor to the remote Isle of Man in 1446 and from there to the bleak castle at Beaumaris in Wales where she died in 1452.[13] Gloucester's already waning influence suffered a permanent eclipse. Eleanor's foolish dabbling in sorcery tainted him with her guilt. He made no move to save her and stayed away from Westminster while she was examined and condemned, but the blow to his pride was incalculable.

In 1446 there were rumours, probably bruited by Suffolk's henchmen, that Gloucester was coming to Parliament to demand the release of Duchess Eleanor. King Henry had always been a little afraid of his domineering uncle and it was easy for Suffolk to suggest that if his plea went unheeded the embittered Gloucester would launch a full-scale rebellion and have himself proclaimed King.[14] Gloucester was justiciar of South Wales, a region known for its continual unrest. Most Englishmen regarded the Welsh with suspicion; the great rebellion of Owen Glyn Dŵr against King Henry IV was still a living memory and Suffolk could remind Henry that an earlier Duke of Gloucester, Thomas of Woodstock, had threatened his nephew, Richard II, with death if his demands were not met.

The tradition that Suffolk destroyed Gloucester because he remained implacably opposed to peace with France is of long standing. So too is the fiction that Gloucester stood up in Parliament in 1445 and denounced the Truce of Tours and the promise to cede Maine.[15] Gloucester was no fool; he had long since taken the measure of his nephew and he knew that the glory days of Henry V would never come again. He had raised no objection when Suffolk was sent to treat for peace and a marriage with a French princess, and he had congratulated Suffolk in Parliament on achieving a truce with France.[16] Gloucester's downfall had nothing to do with ceding Maine or peace with France, and everything to do with Suffolk's ambitions. Suffolk had no need to destroy Gloucester politically – Duchess Eleanor had accomplished that – but King Henry's dislike of his uncle

The Suffolk Years

played into Suffolk's hands and when Suffolk chose to attack him, Gloucester was as vulnerable as his wife had been. Gloucester had made more enemies than friends during his tempestuous life.

It was an anxious time. The main player did not arrive until a week after Parliament met. Gloucester finally rode into Bury with a small escort of about eighty men, including several Welshmen. Sir Thomas Stanley, who had custody of Duchess Eleanor, met him as he approached the south gate and gave him a message from King Henry: as it was so cold and he had ridden a long way Gloucester need not present himself to the King; he should go immediately to his dinner. All unsuspecting, Gloucester proceeded to his lodging in St Saviour's Hospital near the north gate. He was arrested that afternoon by Viscount Beaumont, the Constable of England, accompanied by the compliant Duke of Buckingham, the ambitious Earls of Somerset and Salisbury, and Lord Sudeley. The Duke of Exeter, Gloucester's former companion in arms, refused to join them.[17]

Gloucester was taken unawares; he had no idea why he had been arrested but he expected to be summoned to the King's presence and given the right to defend himself. He was mistaken. Parliament appealed him of treason *in absentia*. No voice was raised in his defence, he had no friends at court and some of his estates and offices had already been granted in reversion to members of the Commons. The Speaker, William Tresham, had been bribed with a promise of the reversion of the chancellorship of the Duchy of Lancaster, and a week before Parliament met he was rewarded for his (unspecified) labours in the King's interests. His son Thomas was a member of the royal household, and MP for Buckinghamshire.[18]

The allegation that Gloucester intended to raise a rebellion to rescue his wife was preposterous, but it was the sort of extravagant gesture that Gloucester might have made in his younger days. The seriousness of the charge lay not in Gloucester's guilt, but in the fact that King Henry upheld it. No one else could order the arrest of the heir to the throne and Parliament would not have attainted him without Henry's acquiescence. To add verisimilitude to the accusations against him some of Gloucester's servants, including all those with Welsh names, were arrested and sent to prisons throughout southern England charged with complicity in Gloucester's 'plot'.[19]

Attainder would automatically 'taint Gloucester's blood' so that he could be legally stripped of his possessions. It did not necessarily carry a death sentence (it would be awkward to execute the heir to the throne) but it had the advantage that although the accused could defend himself through counsel or witnesses, it was not mandatory to allow him to appear in person. King Henry was not eager to face his uncle – a sentiment shared by his lords. Gloucester could be kept in close but comfortable confinement where he could pursue his literary and more esoteric studies, but with no chance to recover his estates or his power.

Gloucester's death was an unexpected bonus. The shock of learning that the nephew whom he had served for so long had allowed him to be accused of plotting rebellion was more than Gloucester could endure. He suffered a massive stroke and for some days he lay unable to move or speak. On Thursday, 23 February, he died.[20] He was fifty-seven years old and had lived longer than any of his brothers, but his life ended in failure. Military glory had eluded him, political power had been wrested from him, and in his last years Gloucester had cultivated a new *persona,* that of a man of letters. It earned him the posthumous title of the 'Good Duke Humphrey'.

Gloucester's body was publicly displayed on the day following his death and his coffin was carried by his servants in slow procession to its burial in the tomb that he had prepared for himself at the Abbey of St Albans. The Commons made a show of accepting the accusations against him, but few believed in them. Legislation against the Welsh was strengthened. Duchess Eleanor was stripped of her right to inherit any of her husband's possessions and Gloucester was deemed to have died intestate.[21] The job done, Parliament was dissolved on 3 March, after sitting for only three weeks.

The Suffolk Years

King Henry had been in a state of extreme nervous tension during the week-long wait for Gloucester's arrival and his agitation manifested itself in his duplication of grants at a level of carelessness that was high even for him. He had granted the reversion of Gloucester's post of Constable of Dover Castle and Warden of the Cinque Ports to Suffolk, but on the day after Gloucester's death he granted them to his newly appointed chamberlain Sir James Fiennes, whom he raised to the peerage as Lord Saye and Sele.[22] Fiennes was appointed an executor to dispose of Gloucester's possessions and settle his debts, and Margaret approached Fiennes's wife Emmeline, asking her to use her influence with her husband on behalf of George Ashby, Margaret's clerk of the signet, who was owed wages for his former services to Gloucester.[23] John Noreys, the treasurer of Margaret's chamber, purchased some plate and jewels from Gloucester's estate but Margaret did not like them and they were sold off to a London goldsmith.[24]

Margaret too was a victim of Henry's erratic liberality. The Commons had agreed that any estates escheating to the crown should be granted to Margaret in lieu of the cash component of her dowry, which was proving impossible to collect from the Exchequer. Henry granted her twelve of Gloucester's estates, plus Gloucester's annuity of 500 marks, but she retained only five of them, and they were not confirmed to her for life until 1452.[25] Henry gave Colchester to John Hampton on the same day as he granted it to Margaret and he apparently forgot that he had previously granted Gloucester Castle in reversion to another favoured courtier, John Beauchamp, whom he had summoned to the Bury Parliament as Lord Beauchamp of Powick.[26] Unfortunately for Margaret's reputation, two stern Victorian historians castigated her for her eagerness to 'share in the spoils' of Gloucester's death.[27] But royal grants immediately following the death of a tenant in chief were not unusual. When King Henry's friend Henry Beauchamp, Duke of Warwick, died on 12 June 1446, King Henry made his first grant from the Beauchamp estates on the following day.

Destruction of a Duke

Henry betrayed his uncle with no qualms and no regrets, but his complicity in Gloucester's demise fatally weakened the Lancastrian dynasty. The reverberations rumbled on for the rest of the reign and eventually it was widely believed that Gloucester had been murdered. Whatever the faults of the maverick duke, Gloucester would never have rebelled against his nephew no matter what the provocation. If he had lived the forces of dissent would have been kept in check, but after his death the question of the succession cast a long shadow over English politics and over the Queen. Margaret was not well acquainted with Gloucester; she met him only on state occasions, and her gifts to him at New Year were formal expressions of respect from the Queen to the King's uncle and heir.[28]

Within two months of Gloucester's death his arch-enemy Cardinal Beaufort died at his palace of Wolvesey on 11 April 1447, leaving an estate conservatively estimated at over £50,000.[29] Margaret had met him only twice: when she stayed with him at Bishops Waltham on her bridal progress to London, and in 1446 when she made a pilgrimage to the shrine of St Thomas Becket at Canterbury and spent a day in Beaufort's company.[30] She charmed the ageing statesman and he remembered her fondly. Two days before he died, he added a second codicil to his will leaving her the set of hangings of blue damask cloth of gold and three tapestries that had adorned her chamber at Bishops Waltham.[31]

The Cardinal left few personal bequests. The richest man in England invested the bulk of his fortune in the redemption of his soul. He had purchased a place in the councils of power on earth and he sought to purchase an equally assured place in heaven. Cardinal Beaufort's death knocked a second prop from under the House of Lancaster. It removed the only certain source of major loans to underpin the increasingly shaky finances of the Lancastrian government.

7

Ceding Maine

The embassy that King Charles had promised to send to London to resume peace talks was due to arrive in June 1447. Maine would be on the agenda and Suffolk was afraid that he would be made a scapegoat for an unpopular policy. He requested an acknowledgement from a carefully selected cross-section of the Council, including the Duke of York, that ceding Maine was the collective responsibility of the Council and not his alone. Suffolk swore that he had never made any promises concerning Maine, either at Tours or to the French ambassadors in 1445. The lords obligingly confirmed that Suffolk had 'justified himself to the full satisfaction of the King and the said councillors', and Suffolk felt safe for the moment.[1]

The French embassy of 1447 led by John, Count of Dunois, Bastard of Orleans, the foremost soldier at the French court, was not as magnificent as that of 1445, but it was more formidable: they had come to settle the question of Maine.[2] Henry and Margaret welcomed them and entertained them lavishly.[3] Margaret required an additional £50 from the treasurer of her chamber during their visit.

Dunois and Suffolk were old friends. Dunois had captured Suffolk at the Battle of Jargeau in 1429 and released him on easy terms. Suffolk hoped to persuade Dunois to accept a truce of twenty years with King Charles to match the proposed alliance with René of Anjou.[4] But Dunois had clear instructions from the French king and the outcome was never in doubt. On 27 July he presented King Henry and the Council with Charles's terms: Henry's visit to France could be

Ceding Maine

postponed until May 1448 and the truce would remain in force until then, but only 'provided that the said high and mighty prince nephew delivers, or causes to be delivered, the cities towns and castles of Le Mans and other towns, castles, and fortified places ... in the County of Maine.'[5]

Dunois assured the Council that once Maine was in French hands the alliance with the House of Anjou would be formalised and the longed-for peace would follow. The Council accepted his word in the self-induced belief that by sacrificing Maine they would safeguard Normandy. The Duke of York, Edmund Beaufort, Suffolk, and 'many others of our blood and council' witnessed King Henry's signature honouring his injudicious promise to surrender his sovereignty over Maine to King Charles and to René and Charles of Anjou by the first of November, just three months away. His only stipulation was that English landowners in Maine should be compensated.[6] Henry innocently wrote to Charles that he had happily ceded Maine because of the affection Charles had frequently expressed for him, which he reciprocated.[7]

Probably at Edmund Beaufort's suggestion to buy time before Maine was finally ceded, King Henry entrusted two war captains, Matthew Gough and Fulk Eyton, with the delicate and distasteful task of fulfilling his promise. Henry and Margaret knew Gough, who sometimes acted as a royal messenger and whom Margaret described as 'our welbeloved squire', but it is doubtful if they had ever heard of Fulk Eyton, the captain of Caudebec. Eyton was a staunch proponent of the war. He had been in France almost continuously since 1437 and he had been with Edmund Beaufort at the Siege of Harfleur in 1440.[8] Gough had taken part in the capture of Le Mans in 1424 and served under Sir John Fastolf during Fastolf's tenure as governor of Maine. Gough had the dubious distinction of fighting with the French as well as against them. In 1444 the Duke of York had taken advantage of the Truce of Tours to get the worst of the rapacious English 'free lances' out of Normandy, sending contingent of them under Gough to join

The Suffolk Years

the Dauphin Louis's campaign against the German territories of the Emperor Frederick because King Charles had agreed to pay their wages.[9] The French respected Gough's war record, and their chroniclers call him 'Mathago'.

Gough had been sent to Brittany in 1446 to deliver Giles of Brittany's English annuity.[10] While he was there Gough stood surety for an old comrade in arms, Roger, Lord Camoys, who had been captured in an attack on the Breton town of La Guerche. Camoys still owed two thousand *saluts* in ransom.[11] It was common practice during the wars in France to release a prisoner who undertook to pay his ransom, provided he offered adequate securities. Camoys was a soldier of fortune; he had assumed his father's title without licence when his elder brother died with no male heir and he had few resources of his own, but he had wealthy relatives: the Earl of Northumberland was his half-brother. Northumberland had promised Gough that he would underwrite Camoys's debt, but he failed to honour his promise and Gough appealed to Margaret.

Failure to pay ransom was dishonourable. The defaulter could be labelled a 'false knight' and his arms could be displayed hanging upside down as a mark of contempt. Under the laws of chivalry not only the defaulter but his 'pledge' too faced disgrace.[12] Margaret reminded Northumberland that Gough could 'be dishonoured and rebuked for ever' and she urged him to pay up immediately.[13] Presumably Northumberland complied. Camoys was back in England by the autumn of 1446, and in October Northumberland was again called on to stand surety of £2,000 that Camoys would appear before the Council (for unspecified reasons).[14]

Gough and Eyton were professional soldiers. They had been fighting in France for over twenty years and were comrades-in-arms with the men whom they would have to order to surrender hard-won territory. Garter King of Arms carried the King's commission to them in Normandy. They could not refuse to obey King Henry's order, but they could delay it, and they did not reach Le Mans until 23

September. Their commission gave them 'full power, authority and express command' to order English captains and officials in Maine to hand over control of all 'cities, towns and fortresses' as quickly as possible.[15] Osbert Mundford, Edmund Beaufort's captain of Le Mans, flatly refused. He stated categorically that he could not deliver Le Mans to anyone without a direct order from Edmund Beaufort. Maine had been granted to Beaufort by King Henry, so where were the letters from the King negating the grant? Gough and Eyton admitted they had no such letters and Mundford opined that they should have presented their instructions, not to him, but to Beaufort (who was in England and had been present when they were issued). Mundford's demand for a personal discharge from the King and from Beaufort was spurious – King Henry's instruction to Gough and Eyton *was* his discharge. Mundford's rigmarole was not a spur of the moment invention; it was meant to delay the proceedings still further. Mundford offered to send to England at his own expense to obtain the King's authorisation.[16]

King Henry was surprised and angered that a captain under Beaufort's command should disobey his orders, in all probability with Beaufort's complicity. He addressed a sharply worded reproof to Beaufort expressing his 'bitter displeasure' at the behaviour of Beaufort's men and of Beaufort himself: 'we order command and as strictly as may be we charge you by these presents [to deliver Maine].' Even King Henry knew who had orchestrated the delay. He issued a second set of letters explicitly discharging Mundford and the other captains of any responsibility and empowering Gough and Eyton to receive Maine into their hands.[17] But instructions issued in England on 23 October could not possibly reach them by 1 November.

The Council in Rouen had issued letters in King Henry's name appointing three commissioners to negotiate compensation for English landowners, in accordance with King Henry's stipulation. Thomas Direhill was a nonentity, but Nicholas Molyneux had served in Maine under Sir John Fastolf, and Fastolf still held extensive land grants there.[18] The third commissioner was none other than Osbert Mundford. Molyneux arrived in Le Mans to complain loudly that the French were not there to meet him, which was hardly surprising since King Charles had not been apprised of their appointment.[19] He was in Bourges where Walter Lyhert, Bishop of Norwich, and Robert Botill, the Prior of St John of Jerusalem, had stopped off on their way home from an ecclesiastical conference, ostensibly to discuss Church unity with King Charles but actually to raise the question of extending the truce. Charles was in a benign mood; Guillaume Cousinot and Jean Havart were about to set out for Le Mans to receive the surrender of Maine. Charles graciously agreed to extend the truce to 1 January 1449 and to put off the date for King Henry's promised visit to France, provided Maine was in his hands by 1 November.[20]

Cousinot and Havart presented themselves in Le Mans on 31 October. The ineffectual nature of King Henry's foreign policy is poignantly illustrated by the sorry fiasco that followed. The English commissioners from Rouen had no authority to dispute the surrender of Maine, but Molyneux had come to quibble, and quibble he did. He insisted that compensation must take precedence over surrender. Cousinot replied that Maine must be delivered first. Molyneux demanded an adjournment until the following day, the fatal first of November.

The meeting in the chapter house of the cathedral of St Julien, presided over by the Bishop of Le Mans, was crowded and noisy. The citizens had come to learn the fate of their city, and representatives of English landowners were there to hear what compensation they might expect, or on what terms they might remain. Molyneux was intransigent. He declared that there could be no change in the *status quo* until he received further instructions from King Henry. He also claimed that he did not speak French very well! Cousinot replied with asperity that although Molyneux's rhetoric lacked polish, he did not doubt that the Englishman spoke French well enough to accomplish the business in hand. Molyneux fell back on Mundford's arguments: if

Ceding Maine

Cousinot could produce a letter from King Henry ordering him to surrender Maine, he would obey, but not otherwise. Cousinot was thoroughly exasperated. These English obviously did not know how to behave and they appeared to have scant respect for the authority of their own king. He replied that it was neither his duty nor his responsibility to see that King Henry issued appropriate letters to his subjects. The deadline for the surrender of Maine could not be extended and the conference was at an end.[21] Gough and Eyton took no part in the proceedings; they may not have been in Le Mans. They hoped they would not be forced to cede Maine after all.

King Henry's reprimand to Beaufort proved ineffectual. Beaufort wanted full compensation before Maine was surrendered and to avert a crisis the Council resorted to bribery. On 13 November, the Dukes of York and Buckingham, Cardinal Kemp, Suffolk, and Lord Cromwell offered Beaufort a generous deal. They promised him 10,000 *livres tournois* a year from the revenues of Normandy, well in excess of what he could expect to receive from Maine.[22] It satisfied Beaufort, but if he ordered his captains to capitulate they ignored him.

Cousinot and Havart reported the fiasco to King Charles. The winter season was too far advanced to launch a military campaign, so Charles elected to play a waiting game. He summoned Matthew Gough to Tours to explain why Maine had not been surrendered and what he meant to do about it. Gough faced the intimidating trio of Dunois, Pierre de Brezé, and Bertrand de Beauvau. Ominously they reminded him that the truce was about to expire: the extension promised by King Charles at Bourges was conditional on Maine's surrender. Gough was out of his depth. He doggedly confirmed that King Henry had commissioned him to surrender Maine, but that the order was proving difficult to implement and certain conditions still had to be met.

Dunois dealt expeditiously with the promises he had made in London that King Charles would authorise a twenty-year truce between King Henry and René of Anjou. He informed Gough that compensation to disposed dispossessed English landowners would be paid and the truce would be extended to 1449 but only provided that Le Mans be surrendered and Maine ceded immediately. On 30 December Gough signed a memorandum of agreement to this effect but he requested an extension of two weeks, to 15 January 1448, to obtain Fulk Eyton's agreement.[23] Eyton persuaded Gough to ask for a further delay until Candlemas, the second of February, on the grounds that they were awaiting instructions from England. Eyton did not intend to surrender Maine; he wanted time for more troops to cross the border from Normandy to reinforce Le Mans.

King Charles agreed to Gough and Eyton's request 'for the reverence of God and to demonstrate his affection for his nephew.'[24] At the same time he sent orders to his war captains to begin mobilisation. Reports of French troop movement flooded into Rouen and the Chancellor, Thomas Hoo, was panic stricken. He wrote frantically to Brezé urging caution.[25] Never mind what Fulk Eyton had said, indeed no matter what he had said: Maine would be surrendered. Brezé offered Hoo a new deadline of no later than 8 February 1448. Hoo asked for, and got, an extra two days, but he was warned that if Le Mans was not surrendered on time everyone who held the town, including Gough and Eyton, would be declared outlaws and excluded from the protection of the truce.[26]

On 9 February Dunois, Brezé, and Bertrand de Beauvau appeared before the walls of Le Mans and summoned the city to surrender. Fulk Eyton rode out to meet them and stoutly denied receiving any communication from the Chancellor in Rouen. He said he knew nothing of Hoo's commitment to surrender Maine by 10 February. This was disingenuous at best since he still held King Henry's commission to hand over Le Mans. Brezé agreed to meet Gough, Eyton, and Osbert Mundford, although he found their behaviour arrogant, especially Mundford's. They informed him that they had instructions from King Henry under his private signet not to surrender *any* town in Maine until the arrival of the English ambassadors, who were on their way to meet with King Charles. It was probably not true. Adam Moleyns and Sir Robert Roos had been commissioned at the end January to resume peace negotiations, or an extension of the truce, and the meeting between the two kings.[27] They did not leave England until February and by the middle of the month they were still at Honfleur.

King Charles instructed Dunois to arrange a temporary truce to await their arrival. Dunois and other royal commissioners rode into Le Mans and met Gough and Eyton in the market square in front of the church of St Nicholas. The meeting was dramatically interrupted by Osbert Mundford at the head of an armed force of about 600 men. The astonished French were unable to believe such foolhardiness – even Fulk Eyton was apprehensive, and he ordered Mundford to withdraw. Mundford ignored him. In the best traditions of chivalry Dunois instructed his pursuivant to ask the English what they wanted, and what they meant by appearing fully armed in time of truce. The intrepid Mundford is reported to have replied with one word: 'Combat'.[28] Dunois immediately broke off negotiations and withdrew to await King Charles's order to attack. He had a force of nearly 7,000 men surrounding the city, with artillery trained on its walls. The English could muster about 2,500 men, including men-at-arms from Normandy.

More in sorrow than in anger, King Charles wrote to inform King Henry of Mundford's flagrant disobedience and to express his doubts that Henry had any idea of what was actually going on.[29] Pierre de Brezé sent messages to the tardy English ambassadors to get a move on if they hoped to avert a war.[30] Moleyns and Roos arrived at the chateau of Lavardin in March, south-east of Le Mans where King Charles was in residence, and by that time even King Henry had been forced to acknowledge the seriousness of the situation, although he did not understand how it had come about: 'And now it is come to oure knowledge that a grete powere and a mightye seege is laide before oure towne of Maunte, and sharpe werre dayly made to oure subgettes being therin, the whiche is no signe of peas, but a likelyhode to the werre.'[31]

The Suffolk Years

King Charles had promised the citizens of Le Mans that he would recover the town without bloodshed. With a French army and heavy artillery surrounding the town, Moleyns was not in a position to negotiate. He met Charles's representatives and accepted the French king's terms. The Treaty of Lavardin was signed on 11 March 1448.[32] Charles agreed to extend the truce to 1 April 1450, and to resume peace negotiations later in the year. He offered compensation, for what it was worth: English residents of Maine would not be taxed for the next two years (giving them plenty of time to change their allegiance or get out) and the revenue that Charles had been receiving from Normandy under the Truce of Tours would be used to recompense dispossessed English landowners. In effect, English Normandy would foot the bill for the loss of English Maine.[33] But the promised Anglo–Angevin alliance that might have guaranteed a neutral state bordering Normandy was dead in the water. Charles never intended to allow Margaret's husband to conclude a twenty-year pact with her father. On 15 March Moleyns and Roos endorsed the terms that Matthew Gough had agreed to in the previous December and Moleyns ordered the English to evacuate Le Mans.[34]

The English captains in Le Mans upheld England's honour to the last. Gough, Eyton, and Mundford, publicly united for the first time, issued a statement. Le Mans was being surrendered in the cause of peace, not in the face of French military threats. It would not compromise King Henry's sovereignty and he was fully entitled to recover Maine by force of arms at any future date.[35] Mundford even had the temerity to insist that his town of Fresnay-le-Vicomte must be exempt from the surrender and he held on to it until the final defeat of the English in Normandy in 1449. After this brave show of defiance the garrison marched out of Le Mans under French safe conduct and retired to the Norman–Breton border.[36] As Chancellor Hoo had promised, the question of Maine was settled to the entire satisfaction of the French king.

Throughout the whole sorry affair opposition to the sacrifice of

Ceding Maine

Maine did not come from the magnates, or the merchants, or members of Parliament. It was maintained solely by English war captains who had made their careers in France for over a quarter of a century. Mundford and his fellow officers resisted with a tenacity that almost precipitated the war that Maine was being sacrificed to avoid. These men simply could not credit that the son of Henry V would surrender Maine without a fight, and they preferred war to the dishonourable capitulation of territory they considered theirs by right of conquest. With the appalling irony of which he alone was capable, King Henry commended Matthew Gough and Fulk Eyton for the excellent way in which they had fulfilled their commission. Chancellor Hoo became Lord Hoo, and Suffolk was made a duke![37]

Once the precious truce had been extended Suffolk lost interest in Maine. He had a plan to secure Normandy's western border and to boost his own popularity by bringing Duke Francis of Brittany into line as a vassal of England. Relations with Francis had been uneasy ever since the English Council had rejected his claim to the Earldom of Richmond in 1443. Francis had witnessed Suffolk's negotiations at Tours, and he doubted the value of an alliance with King Henry. After weighing his options Francis had done homage to King Charles in 1446.

Francis's brother Giles had other ideas. He had declared that 'he was the servant of the King of England and did not wish to be subject to the King of France', and he had refused to do homage for two fiefs he held in France.[38] In 1445 he had foolishly offered to place his castles and towns at King Henry's disposal. Giles's letter fell into the wrong hands and Duke Francis warned Giles to mend his ways. He strictly forbade him to hold further communication with the English and he took the precaution of informing King Charles of Giles's offers to England. Giles was incorrigible. He defied his brother's prohibition and continued to correspond with his English friends in Rouen. He took to boasting that he had only to lift a finger to have an English army cross the Norman–Breton border and he even appealed to Chancellor Hoo to send him a bodyguard. Hoo was far too cautious to

The Suffolk Years

risk a diplomatic incident and he urged Giles to flee from Brittany, but Giles left it too late. Duke Francis summoned him to explain his actions and when he failed to comply King Charles ordered his arrest. Giles was put on trial and kept in close confinement while the proceedings dragged on.[39] He might have been executed for treason but his other brother Peter, and his uncle, Arthur de Richemont, the Constable of France, interceded for him.

Duke Francis's repudiation of his English allegiance and Giles's imprisonment did not go down well in England or in Normandy. Matthew Gough was so indignant that he suggested mounting a rescue mission, which may have given Suffolk an idea. Twenty years earlier Francis's father, the vacillating Duke John of Brittany, had been bullied by his brother Arthur de Richemont into recognising the Dauphin Charles as King of France. The Regent Bedford had promptly sent an English force across the Breton border and Suffolk had followed up with reinforcements. That was all it took for Duke John to send a messenger to Suffolk to sue for a truce and a year later, to keep his duchy intact, Duke John renounced his French allegiance and returned to the English fold.[40]

Suffolk planned to repeat Bedford's tactics but first he needed an experienced campaigner and he knew just the man. François de Surienne, known as L'Aragonais, was a mercenary in English pay. He was a flamboyant character with exalted notions of his own worth. King Henry had granted him a pension of 100 marks a year in recompense for his surely inflated claim that he had lost an inheritance worth £100,000 in France through adhering to the English.[41] De Surienne habitually sent representatives to England to complain of unpaid wages, and Suffolk entrusted de Surienne's envoy, Jean de Rousselet, with a letter of credence outlining a scheme for de Surienne's consideration: was it feasible to mount a lightning raid into Brittany and capture a town on the Breton border? De Surienne cross-questioned Rousselet closely before he concluded that Suffolk was serious. The rich woollen manufacturing town of Fougères

Ceding Maine

seemed a likely prospect and when de Surienne was satisfied that Fougères could be taken without much risk he informed Suffolk.

Suffolk had invited de Surienne to London in late 1447 as an honoured guest. He chivvied the Exchequer into paying the arrears of de Surienne's pension and persuaded King Henry to make de Surienne a Knight of the Garter.[42] The Order of the Garter held a special chivalric significance for a professional solider and de Surienne would not treat it lightly or dishonour it easily. Indeed, it revived his doubts about the morality of an unprovoked attack on an unsuspecting town in time of truce. Suffolk assured him that he had King Henry's approval and Edmund Beaufort invited de Surienne to his lodging in Blackfriars to discuss the question as one soldier to another. He argued that the enterprise was justified because Duke Francis had not behaved honourably towards King Henry. De Surienne returned to Normandy believing that he had the blessing of the King of England, the King's principal minister, and the King's Lieutenant in France, while Suffolk sold the concept of a military sortie into Brittany to King Henry on the only grounds he knew the King would accept: to rescue Giles.

Only one obstacle remained to be overcome. In his eagerness to obtain the Truce of Tours Suffolk had committed a major blunder. He allowed King Charles to name the Duke of Brittany among France's adherents and Brittany was subsequently listed as Charles's vassal in all extensions of the truce, including the Treaty of Lavardin. Since the projected attack on Fougères was predicated on the claim that the Dukes of Brittany were vassals of England, Suffolk had to negate this impediment. On 29 March 1448, by sleight of hand and stroke of pen, the word *Britanniae* appeared in the official English version of the treaty, aligning the Duke of Brittany with the English dukes as signatories and vassals of the King of England.[43] The stage was set for the final phase of the war in Normandy to begin.

8
The King's Lieutenant in France

Edmund Beaufort, Earl of Somerset, had been extremely lucky in his career. He was serving in Normandy when, thanks to the financial backing of Cardinal Beaufort, he had been able to rush troops to rescue Calais when the Duke of Burgundy laid siege to it in 1436. Four years later he was at the siege of Harfleur and when it fell, he returned to England with a glowing, if undeserved, record of military achievement. He had the good fortune not to accompany his brother John Beaufort on the disastrous expedition to France in 1443 and so was not tainted by its failure.[1] But Edmund's greatest asset was the King's favour. Henry had known him since childhood and had taken one of his rare likings to him.

Edmund should have taken up his post as the King's Lieutenant in France at the beginning of March 1447, but a year later he was still in England. He had been promised a force of 300 men-at-arms and 900 archers, but the hard-pressed Exchequer could only pay their wages for six weeks and in Beaufort's opinion this was not enough.[2] He preferred to remain at court and look after his interests. Suffolk saw no reason to hurry his departure. The council in Rouen had carried on without a King's Lieutenant after the Duke of York came home in 1445 and it could continue to do so. Only when it was too late to defend Le Mans or to cede Maine with dignity did the Council decide that it was high time to send the King's Lieutenant to France.

The King's Lieutenant in France

Before he left, Beaufort angled for one final inducement, and on 31 March 1448 he got it. Henry created him Duke of Somerset and in April he sailed for Normandy with his wife and family. Duchess Eleanor was a daughter of Richard Beauchamp, Earl of Warwick, and the widow of Lord Roos who had been killed in France, leaving her with a young family. King Henry stood godfather to Edmund and Eleanor's first son, born in 1436 and named for the King. A second son, Edmund, was born in 1439 and John in 1441. The boys probably accompanied their parents to Rouen; it would be good training for their later careers.[3] Eleanor's younger son by her first marriage, Richard Roos, was also with the ducal party.

Somerset barely had time to take up residence before King Charles VII put him under pressure. The ubiquitous Guillaume Cousinot arrived to complain of infringements of the truce. To get rid of him, Somerset promised to send representatives to Tours.[4] He had worries enough without having to deal with French nit-picking. The administration of Normandy was in disarray and the shortage of cash was acute. The salaries of royal officials were in arrears and the garrisons scattered throughout Normandy were underpaid to a man. The Council in Rouen had continued to issue orders in the Duke of York's name, a name that was respected throughout Normandy. Somerset had to stamp his own authority on the duchy. He expected the costs of his administration to be met from taxation voted by the Norman estates, but the estates were increasingly reluctant to meet this obligation, pleading poverty from years of burdensome taxation and stagnant trade. Somerset's attempt to raise money was not propitious. He ordered a special audit of accounts and he dismissed local tax receivers and centred tax collection on Rouen and Caen. Norman and Englishmen alike suddenly found themselves without employment. It did not enhance Somerset's popularity, and it alienated the men who had served under York.

Such practices inevitably led to the widespread belief that the new King's Lieutenant was insatiably avaricious. Like many of his contemporaries, the chronicler Thomas Basin mistakenly believed that Somerset had inherited Cardinal Beaufort's vast wealth and was rich enough not to need extra taxes or extraordinary fines.[5] But Somerset's private income never matched his public persona. He did not have the resources to sustain a military following comparable to that of the Duke of York, whose extensive estates made him one of the richest men in England. Somerset had been allocated the same salary as York, £20,000, but unlike York he could claim it only in time of war.[6] The 10,000 *livres tournois* granted to him from the wine tax in Normandy as compensation for the loss of Maine had seemed a great deal at the time but the expense of maintaining himself in the state demanded by his position absorbed most of it. Somerset was also responsible for disbursing the money that King Charles had promised to dispossessed landholders in Maine. He may have made some small settlements but the only known recipient was Viscount Beaumont, the steward of Margaret's Leicestershire lands. King Henry wrote to Somerset on Beaumont's behalf, and Margaret followed up with a letter of her own.[7] Somerset paid up.

The military problems in Normandy were only slightly less worrying than the lack of money. The steady increase and training of French armies was matched by a steady decline in the preparedness of English garrisons. Starved of money and ignored by the government in London, their morale was low. Somerset gave the command of Lower Normandy, the area most vulnerable to French attack, to his brother-in-law, John Talbot, Earl of Shrewsbury.[8] Shrewsbury was the most famous, and the most feared, of the English war captains. The French called him *le Grand Talbot*. *The Bourgeois of Paris* goes so far as to say that he was the only Englishman left alive capable of defeating King Charles.[9] In between sieges and bouts of garrison duty Shrewsbury specialised in guerrilla warfare. He would turn up with a small force where he was least expected, strike a blow, and retire. Thomas Basin tells a story that in 1441 Shrewsbury led a raid on King Charles's headquarters at the monastery of Poissy and almost captured the King. Charles beat a hasty retreat and when Shrewsbury reached the royal bedchamber the bed was still warm![10]

It was not long before Guillaume Cousinot returned to Rouen to complain yet again of truce violations, and specifically of the refortification of St James de Beuvron, a small town on the Anglo–Breton border which had been re-occupied by an English garrison after Le Mans was evacuated. Under the laws of war, and the terms of the truce, any dismantled military stronghold could not be re-fortified. Somerset haughtily rejected Cousinot's demand for an explanation of the presence of English troops at St James de Beuvron and he wrote a peremptory reply to King Charles telling him that the question should be referred to Adam Moleyns and Sir Robert Roos, who were in Tours and better versed than he was in the finer points of the truce.

Whether by accident or design Somerset addressed his letter to 'the King's uncle *in* France'. The niceties of diplomatic exchange required the English to address Charles as 'the King's uncle *of* France', and this was how Somerset had addressed him previously. Cousinot warned Somerset that Charles would refuse to receive so discourteous a letter and he declined to deliver it. Somerset then compounded his error by sending none other than Osbert Mundford, who had strenuously resisted the surrender of Le Mans and had helped to refortify St James de Beuvron, to Tours.[11] Cousinot was right. King Charles was quick to exploit Somerset's gaffe. He labelled Somerset's letter, as *trop grande arrogance ou ignorance* and complained self-righteously that he could not be sure it was intended for him, since the Dukes of Orleans and Burgundy, as well as the Count of Maine, were all the English king's uncles *in* France.[12] It was the first of many mistakes that Somerset would make in his dealings with King Charles.

Moleyns and Roos had left Tours before Mundford arrived, and Charles suggested that Mundford should go after them and arrange a meeting to discuss St James de Beuvron, but incredibly Mundford refused. He said he had no orders to go to Brittany and was returning to Rouen. By allowing (and possibly encouraging) Mundford's churlishness, Somerset played into Charles's hands. Charles dispatched Valois Herald to England to complain of Somerset's disrespect and to point out to King Henry that, unlike Somerset, the Duke of York had always shown the French king the deference due to a Valois prince even in time of war. King Henry expressed his regret that differences had arisen over St James de Beuvron 'and other matters', but he was sure that Somerset would not imperil the truce. He wrote to his very dear uncle that he would always be willing to accommodate Charles in any way he could.[13]

Adam Moleyns and Robert Roos were in Brittany in pursuance of Suffolk's policy of bringing Brittany into line as a vassal of England. Moleyns reminded Duke Francis that he owed allegiance to England and demanded that he release his brother Giles. Moleyns was confounded when Duke Francis cheerfully informed him that Giles had been arrested on King Charles's orders and could not be released without the King's permission.[14]

In the following August Adam Moleyns led an English delegation to a conference at Louviers that was supposed to discuss peace terms now that Maine had been surrendered, but which did nothing of the sort.[15] King Charles's commissioners adroitly derailed the talks by deflecting attention on to Brittany and the question of Duke Francis's allegiance. Guillaume Cousinot began by accusing the English of illegally fortifying St James de Beuvron. Significantly, he added that the Duke of Brittany had requested the King of France to demand that English troops be withdrawn from along the Breton border. Moleyns retorted that if Duke Francis felt threatened, he should take his complaint to his rightful overlord, King Henry VI. The Breton representative, Michel de Parthenay, Constable of Rennes, promptly denied that his master owed allegiance to Henry.[16] After further wrangling Moleyns called time-out and went to Rouen to consult Somerset, but Somerset flatly refused to evacuate St James de Beuvron, so Moleyns sent Garter King of Arms to England for further instructions: what was he to say in the face of Breton insistence that their duke was King Charles's vassal, and Charles's insistence that peace talks would not begin as long as Somerset refused to withdraw the garrison from St James de Beuvron?[17]

Suffolk prevaricated; he expected to hear any day now that François de Surienne had successfully attacked Fougères and until then he could not allow any concessions on the status of Brittany. The answer Moleyns received was ludicrous: he was told that since he was the man on the spot, he was the best judge of what to say. Nevertheless, he must insist on the Duke of Brittany's allegiance to King Henry but at the same time he must not to allow the truce to founder. He could invoke the oaths of loyalty sworn to the King of England by the dead Duke John V and by Giles and he could claim that Duke Francis had sworn allegiance to King Henry, something he had never done. If that failed, Moleyns was to declare that Francis owed allegiance to Henry as King of France![18]

The conference resumed at Vaudreuil in November with the cards stacked against Moleyns. He knew that Henry's claim to the Duke of Brittany's allegiance was untenable, but he did his best to get the talks back on track. He declared that he and the other English representatives had authority to discuss truce terms with the French, but not negotiate with the Bretons since their duke owed allegiance to England. Once again, Michel de Parthenay denied this. The wrangling went on for two weeks until, with his back to the wall, Moleyns sensibly opted out. On 25 November he and Sir Robert Roos, Raoul Roussel, Archbishop of Rouen, and the veteran soldier William Neville, Lord Fauconberg, signed an agreement postponing the negotiations to resume in London before 15 May 1449.[19] Although he could not know it, this was Moleyns's last meeting with the French. He and Robert Roos came home in December 1448, and Roos died shortly afterwards.[20]

In the meanwhile, the 'enterprise of Fougères' hung in the balance. François de Surienne's doubts persisted. He had only word of mouth authority for what could turn out to be a very risky undertaking. He

The Suffolk Years

sent messengers to London with a gift of a French Bible for Suffolk and a demand for payment upfront: he wanted the arrears of his pension and the money and supplies promised to him. He also wanted Suffolk to commit himself in writing, but all he got, via his messenger, was an expression of surprise that he had not acted sooner, and a verbal order to hurry up.[21] In December, de Surienne went to meet Somerset in Rouen for further discussions.

Somerset was apprehensive. The Earl of Shrewsbury had warned him that occupying a town in Brittany would stretch their resources. De Surienne's men had speculated quite openly for months that something major was afoot – far too many people were 'in the know'. Somerset feared that the English might walk into a trap and the long wait had unnerved him further. He dispatched Mortain Herald to order de Surienne not to make any move without his authorisation. L'Aragonais was furious. He had been reproached by Suffolk for not moving fast enough and now Somerset had ordered him not to move at all. He sent his secretary Pierre Tuvache to remind Somerset of the numerous discussions they had held in Rouen and in London and to insist that no one in Fougères had the least suspicion of his plans.[22]

Inclement weather delayed de Surienne, but in February he ordered his advance guard to make for Condé sur Noireau, his base of operations close to the Breton border. Suffolk had persuaded the parsimonious (but patriotic) Sir John Fastolf to turn over his town of Condé sur Noireau to de Surienne for a fee.[23] At dawn on Monday, 24 March 1449, de Surienne's force of some 600 men surprised and took the castle in the valley below the town of Fougères. His troops then stormed uphill to scale the walls and batter down the unprotected town gates.[24] By eight o'clock it was all over, de Surienne was in possession of Fougères in the name of the King of England. In accordance with the laws of war the town was plundered but not sacked since it had offered no resistance, but there was booty aplenty and everyone including Somerset and Shrewsbury got a cut. Forgetting his earlier misgivings, Somerset was ecstatic. He sent a message by Mortain Herald to tell de Surienne that he was happier than if he had received 100,000 crowns.[25]

The Duke of Brittany's envoy, Michel de Parthenay, arrived in Fougères to demand who had authorised this unprovoked attack, and to insist on an immediate withdrawal. Secure in the knowledge, or so he thought, that the King of England stood behind him, de Surienne replied that it was sufficient for de Parthenay to know that his action was honourable – he was a Knight of the Garter. De Parthenay revealed that Duke Francis had heard of a plan to rescue his brother Giles and that if this were the reason for the attack Giles would be set free the moment Fougères was evacuated. If the English wanted Giles that badly they were welcome to him; Francis valued his people above his treacherous brother. According to de Surienne, Duke Francis offered him 50,000 gold crowns to withdraw but Suffolk had judged his man to a nicety. The mercenary captain put his honour as a Garter Knight above money. He replied grandiloquently *'J'ai pouvoir de prendre et non de rendre.'*[26] (I have the power to take but not to give.) He sent word to Suffolk that he had rejected Brittany's offers and asked what he should do next. Suffolk assured him that Sir Robert Vere would be sent to reinforce him, but to de Surienne's bitter indignation Vere got no further than Caen. Nevertheless, Suffolk had told L'Aragonais to hold on and that is precisely what he did.[27]

Duke Francis was made of sterner stuff than his father and he appealed to King Charles for military assistance. Charles had been waiting for an opportunity to begin the re-conquest of Normandy and Fougères was all he needed to justify breaking the truce. He expressed outrage (whether feigned or real) over the attack and demanded that Somerset restore Fougères to the Duke of Brittany immediately. Moreover, since Somerset was responsible for the offence he must make good the losses suffered by the townspeople.[28] In a foolish attempt to counter Charles's demands Somerset sent his representatives to the French court to complain of French raids on English territory and to exhort King Charles to put a stop to such aggressive behaviour. Somerset would then guarantee the safety of French territories and possessions. Charles's courtiers found this funny; they contemptuously advised the envoys to look to their own defence. The King of France was well able to protect his people, could the English duke say the same?[29]

Somerset hedged his bets. He sent Thomas Hoo, the Chancellor of Normandy, and Reginald Boulers, Abbot of Gloucester, to London with a plea for reinforcements.[30] Hoo had been frightened almost out of his wits by the threat of war during the negotiations over Maine and he could attest to the serious plight of the English garrisons in Normandy. Boulers presented a strong case to Parliament for immediate military and financial aid. King Charles could put 60,000 men into the field; Somerset could not counter a threat of this magnitude. English garrisons were under strength, their fortifications dilapidated, and their castles lacked artillery. Boulers reminded the Commons that the truce had only fourteen months to run and he appealed to English pride and patriotism: if Normandy was lost without putting up a fight it would be 'a everlastyng spite, and perpetuell denigration in the fame and renoune of this noble Reme.'[31]

The Commons were not impressed. The truce had been extended intermittently for the past four years and could be extended again. Somerset should make do with his salary and such sums as he could obtain from the estates of Normandy. As a sop to him, they authorised the repayment of a 'loan' of £1,666 13s 4d that he had made to the crown but as it was assigned on a tax to be collected in November 1450, it was not much use for his immediate relief.[32]

The opening salvo in the re-conquest of Normandy was fired in May before the truce expired. King Charles turned a blind eye to an assault on the strategically important town of Pont de l'Arche, situated on the Seine just east of Rouen. On the night of 15/16 May French troops led by Robert Floquet and Pierre de Brezé's brother Jean stormed into the town wearing Breton colours and shouting the war cry *Saint Yves et Bretaigne!* The capture of Pont de l'Arche demonstrated that the French had not been joking when they suggested that Somerset should look to his own defence, and it enhanced King Charles's claim that the Duke of Brittany had 'many friends' who were ready to take revenge for the attack on Fougères.[33]

William Neville, Lord Fauconberg, was in Pont de l'Arche almost by accident, having come to attend a previously scheduled round of truce talks. Fauconberg organised a stout resistance and only surrendered when he realised that the unprepared English garrison must be overrun. A messenger carried the news of Fauconberg's capture and the fall of Pont de l'Arche to Rouen within two hours. Somerset was thunderstruck. He flew into a towering rage and swore that he would recover the town immediately.[34] He dispatched a herald to the French court to declare Pont de l'Arche a violation of the truce (which it was) and to demand its return, only to be told that the terms of the truce no longer held: Somerset had set the precedent at Fougères. The Earl of Shrewsbury moved his forces up to Pont Audemer, thirty miles from Pont de l'Arche, but he did not attack, and the town remained in French hands. This should have warned Somerset, Suffolk, and the English Council that King Charles could go on the offensive with impunity whenever and wherever he chose.

At the end of May Guillaume Cousinot met Somerset's representatives, Jean L'Enfant and Osbert Mundford, for a further conference. Cousinot demanded the restoration of Fougères and refused to discuss anything else until his terms were met. Jean L'Enfant stoutly maintained that Fougères was none of King Charles's business; it was not a violation of the truce since the Duke of Brittany was a vassal of the King of England. Osbert Mundford, as combative as ever, went further. In a written statement with his name inscribed before Somerset's (an unusual proceeding) he denied Somerset's responsibility and blamed de Surienne. The attack on Fougères 'was done without his [Somerset's] consent and contrary to his will and against his wish; and immediately after the event occurred he sent a message to the said messier François and wrote to him very sharply,

The Suffolk Years

and did not thank him for the deed which he had done but blamed him for it and laid it to his charge very strongly, and that he should bear the consequences of what he had done.'[35] This was demonstrably untrue, as Cousinot immediately pointed out. Well-versed in English diplomatic prevarication, he replied politely but uncompromisingly that he didn't believe a word of it and he reiterated that Fougères must be evacuated and compensation paid. L'Enfant and Mundford rejected his demand and the charade of claim and counter-claim came to an end.[36]

King Charles was determined to demonstrate to his allies and to his enemies that he had been forced to *end*, not to *break* the truce. Jean Havart left for England in June to inform King Henry that François de Surienne, a Knight of the Garter, had perpetrated an unforgivable outrage by attacking Fougères and desecrating its churches, an accusation calculated to shock the pious king. Havart was to say that King Charles had done everything in his power to preserve the truce, but the Duke of Somerset had wantonly broken it and unless Somerset returned Fougères to the Duke of Brittany and paid full compensation, France and Brittany would declare war. Charles also suggested, as he had before Le Mans, that Henry was not fully conversant with the facts, and he may have been right: Henry was adept at ignoring what he did not wish to know.[37] The dire warnings in Havart's instructions were not echoed in the cordial personal letters Charles sent to Henry and to Margaret.[38] The letter to Margaret merely enquired after her health and glibly offered to do anything that might please her, but what Havart told Margaret privately is not known. Was Charles still trying to enlist her support, or did Havart warn her that war was inevitable? There is no record of her reply.

Charles sent Dunois, Bertrand de Beauvau, and Étienne Chevalier to conclude a formal alliance with Duke Francis. Somerset and King Henry would be given until 25 July to evacuate Fougères (and so implicitly acknowledge Charles's right to demand it). If they did not, war would be declared on 31 July.[39] Charles also sent an embassy to his most powerful and potentially hostile vassal, the Duke of Burgundy, to convey the gist of the negotiations with Somerset and the alliance with Brittany. Contrary to expectations, Duke Philip declared that Charles had acted honourably in coming to Brittany's aid, but he suggested delaying a declaration of war until Havart returned from England and the outcome of the negotiations with Somerset's envoys was known.[40]

Somerset had not grasped the perilous situation he had blundered into. He denied responsibility for taking Fougères, but he refused to give it back and he apparently expected the French to continue negotiating indefinitely. A mere five days after his delegates had rejected Cousinot's terms, he wrote to Charles to suggest a continuation of talks to settle truce violations, just as if Fougères had never happened.[41] Somerset had been indoctrinated in his youth with the English distain for the Dauphin Charles, and he looked back to the days when English forces held the upper hand. He had not been in France when Le Mans was surrendered and he did not appreciate the state of readiness of the French army, or the speed at which it could move. Nor did he fully comprehend that there was no money in the English Exchequer and that his former victories in France had been won through the financial backing of Cardinal Beaufort. Somerset believed that if King Charles declared war the English Council and Parliament would be forced to come to his aid.

Suffolk had miscalculated badly, and his plan had miscarried. Without clear direction English policy had shifted from a reasonable demand that the French honour their commitment to make peace following the surrender of Maine, to an unseemly wrangle over the status of the Duchy of Brittany. The folly of the attack on Fougères paled into insignificance beside Suffolk's monumental stupidity in challenging Charles's claim to be Duke Francis's overlord, something Charles would never concede. Fougères was the catalyst but not the cause for the renewal of the war. King Charles wanted an excuse to break the truce, Suffolk's inept diplomacy and Somerset's arrogance supplied it.

9

Losing Normandy

No one in England had grasped that Normandy was in imminent danger. Parliament was in session at Winchester and in response to Somerset's plea for reinforcements a special council in June debated in desultory fashion how best to raise money 'for the setting forthe of armyes' into Normandy *and* Gascony.[1] Suffolk read out de Surienne's account of the taking of Fougères, and the Lords demonstrated their ignorance by declaring that it was 'right nobly written'.

The household officers were firmly of the opinion that lawlessness at home would have to be tackled before an army could be sent overseas. They suggested that oyer and terminer commissioners should punish anyone guilty of breaking the king's peace, although whether this would reduce lawlessness or provoke more of it was a moot point. The bishops took an optimistic, if impractical view: surely royal justice could be enforced with just a little good will on all sides. They thought the tax grant might be used to raise an army of archers. Half of them could be sent to France while the other half remained at home to enforce the peace. Suffolk and Cardinal Kemp favoured precedents: loans for the war had been employed with varying degrees of success throughout King Henry's reign.

Margaret's chancellor, William Booth, made the only positive contribution to the debate: everyone holding lands in Normandy should donate a year's income to defend the duchy and everyone receiving grants or annuities from the King in England should donate a year's income to finance an army.[2] His radical solution was not welcomed and Treasurer Lumley summed up the situation: the only real option was to entreat the Commons to make an additional tax grant.

The Commons had voted a tax of a half tenth and fifteenth and extended tunnage and poundage (customs on imports and exports) for five years.[3] The money had been allocated to defending the Scottish border, to keeping the seas, and to maintain the garrison at Calais, but not the garrisons in Normandy. The Commons had also renewed the wool subsidy on condition that King Henry stopped issuing licences for favoured individuals to evade customs duties by shipping wool through ports other than Calais. All wool exported from England was supposed to pass through Calais and be subject to customs duties there. King Henry had granted Margaret a licence in 1448 to ship wool duty-free to make up the shortfall in her income and the Commons exempted her licence from their ban.[4]

Treasurer Lumley's urging was met with a half-hearted response. The Commons agreed to another half tenth and fifteenth to be collected over the next two and a half years, but the combined subsidies would still bring in only about £30,000.[5] Not nearly enough to finance a war. The Commons also voiced their indignation over royal insolvency. In their opinion it was high time for the King to look to financial resources other than taxation. They toyed with an idea that was even more unwelcome than William Booth's suggestion: nothing less than a wholesale resumption of all the grants from crown lands that King Henry had made indiscriminately since 1437. Resumption would affect almost everyone who had ever held a position at court or come to Henry's notice.[6] Rather than allow the Commons to pursue this line of argument, Henry dissolved Parliament and the question of how to finance a renewal of the war was left unresolved.

A Great Council met in September to reconsider the question. The first casualty of England's lack of preparedness was the Treasurer, Marmaduke Lumley; he resigned at the Council meeting.[7] It was his and Suffolk's misfortune that wool exports fell sharply in the later 1440s with a correspondingly adverse effect on revenue. Lumley had staved off disaster for three years by enforcing strict financial controls and freezing grants assigned on customs duties and at the Exchequer. The financial crisis eased in 1449 and Lumley had cautiously redeemed outstanding tallies, Margaret's among them. But he had made no provision for an outbreak of war and only £480 5s 3d was left in the Treasury in September.[8]

The war would have to be financed by loans. King Henry pledged crown jewels worth over £8,000 as security for commissioners to canvass the shires, but the response was meagre. The largest sum came from Cardinal's Beaufort's estate, since Cardinal Kemp and the Duke of Somerset were the Cardinal's executors.[9] Margaret's chamberlain, Sir John Wenlock, turned over a collection of her jewels to William Aiscough, Bishop of Salisbury, as security for a loan of 1,000 marks and Wenlock returned crown jewels valued at £1,033 6s 8d that he had held in pledge for the repayment of a loan from Lord Fanhope's estate towards the cost of bringing Margaret to England.[10] Repayment was assigned on taxation and on the Southampton customs, but the debt was never honoured.[11]

The Duke of York did not attend Parliament, although he was still in England. Henry had named him as the King's Lieutenant in Ireland two years earlier, in 1447. Ireland was not as prestigious as France, but York had inherited the Mortimer estates there and he was the greatest English landowner in Ireland. The Mortimer Earls of March had traditionally been the King's Lieutenants. York delayed his departure hoping that Somerset's appointment as the King's Lieutenant in France would be rescinded. This did not happen and when Somerset sailed for Rouen in 1448 York watched from the sidelines, waiting for Somerset to fail. York's loyal lieutenants in Normandy kept him informed of the developing chaos there and by the summer of 1449 he judged that the time was right to distance himself from impending disaster.[12] Suffolk, the Council, and the Duke of Somerset may have underestimated King Charles, but the Duke of York did not. He and Duchess Cecily, who was six months pregnant, slipped out of England and crossed to Dublin in June 1449.[13] In October Cecily gave birth to their ninth child, christened George.

King Charles summoned his magnates and councillors to a Great Council and invited English and Breton representatives to attend. Guillaume Cousinot informed the assembled company that despite lengthy negotiations the Duke of Somerset refused to surrender Fougères. Somerset's envoy, Jean L'Enfant, made a last-ditch effort to defend his master but, unfortunately, he chose to remind the councillors that the Duke of Brittany's first reaction to the news of Fougères had been to offer Somerset and de Surienne terms for its return. This made it clear that Brittany was a vassal of England. The Chancellor of France, Guillaume Juvenal des Ursins, who was every bit as longwinded as his brother the Archbishop, launched into a recapitulation of English perfidy, making Somerset the villain of the piece: the Duke of York had honoured the truce, but Somerset had violated it. Beginning with the fortifications at St James de Beuvron and culminating in the attack on Fougères, Somerset had consistently failed to settle truce violations even though he had been given full powers to do so by King Henry. He had impugned King Charles's honour by refusing to recognise French suzerainty over the Duchy of Brittany. Somerset was simply not to be trusted; any treaty he signed would not be worth the parchment it was written on, and he would break his word at will. King Charles asked his councillors for their opinion and naturally it was unanimous: the King had been too patient. He had done all he could to avert a war, but his first duty was to protect his people and his realm in the face of English aggression. The Duke of Brittany's envoys confirmed that Brittany would join France if war were declared. King Charles called on God and the world to witness that it was impossible to reach an honourable accommodation with Somerset – or the English. *They* had broken the truce and he had every right to declare war.[14]

The Suffolk Years

Charles sent word to those magnates who were not at the Great Council, including René of Anjou, to prepare for hostilities. Dunois was given overall command and appointed Lieutenant General of the area between the Seine, the Oise, and the sea –in other words the Duchy of Normandy. Dunois, Brezé, and Cousinot were authorised to accept the surrender of any English-held towns willing to open their gates and to guarantee full protection to the inhabitants.[15] Charles's captains did not wait for his official declaration. At dawn on the morning of 19 July, Pierre de Brezé and his men entered the town of Verneuil by climbing over an unguarded section of its walls. Verneuil's absentee captain was none other than François de Surienne, still valiantly holding out in Fougères, waiting in vain for the relief force that Suffolk had promised him. Dunois brought his army up in support of Brezé and after some fierce fighting the English defenders were beaten back inside *La Tour Grise,* a strongly fortified bastion that was considered impregnable.[16] The recovery of Verneuil far outweighed its military importance. The Regent Bedford's victory at the Battle of Verneuil in 1424 had been a triumph for English arms second only to Agincourt, and its loss struck a serious blow to English morale in Normandy.

The Earl of Shrewsbury, accompanied by Osbert Mundford, a less than skillful diplomat but an intrepid soldier who was spoiling for a fight, marched to relieve Verneuil. Dunois moved to intercept them and on the same day that King Charles declared war, Shrewsbury and Dunois faced each other somewhere between Harcourt and Beaumont-le-Roger.[17] Shrewsbury held a strong defensive position, but he decided that the risk was too great. His resources were thinly stretched, he could not afford heavy losses in a pitched battle, and an increasingly nervous Somerset had summoned him back to Rouen. Shrewsbury withdrew in good order under cover of darkness.[18] A second French army was skirmishing around Rouen and ironically it was commanded by Charles of Artois, Count of Eu, and Louis of Luxembourg, Count of St Pol. Artois had been captured at the Battle of Agincourt, and Edmund Beaufort, as he was then, had arranged to exchange Artois as part of the negotiations in 1438 to ransom his brother, John Beaufort.[19] The Count of St Pol was the Duchess of Bedford's brother and a nephew of Archbishop Louis of Luxembourg, a former chancellor of English Normandy. The Luxembourgs had been staunch allies of England until the Duke of Burgundy changed sides in 1435.

Somerset pressed Shrewsbury to remain at Rouen to protect him. He did not care that this would expose Shrewsbury's headquarters at Pont Audemer – he was all for abandoning it. But its captain, Fulk Eyton, insisted that with only a few reinforcements Pont Audemer could be held and the ever-belligerent Osbert Mundford supported Eyton, just as he had at Le Mans. Pierre de Brezé's initial attack was beaten back but Dunois's force, combined with Eu and St Pol, surrounded Pont Audemer and set the town on fire.[20] Eyton was forced to come to terms and Dunois allowed him and the garrison to march out and join Somerset in Rouen. Osbert Mundford was captured. He later claimed that he had refused to surrender and that when Dunois sent him word that he wished to parley, he sent back a reply worthy of de Surienne: *'Je ne veulx point parler à lui.'*[21] (I do not wish to talk to him.) Mundford was not released until the following March when his brother-in-law, the veteran soldier Andrew Trollope, surrendered Mundford's town of Fresnay-le-Vicomte to King Charles in return for Mundford's freedom.[22] Charles derived considerable satisfaction from the deal. Mundford had defied him and refused to surrender Fresnay-le-Vicomte in 1448 when the rest of Maine was handed over to the French.

Dunois's next objective was the rich agricultural town of Lisieux. Margaret had tried to obtain the bishopric of Lisieux for her chaplain, Michael Tregury, who had been a rector of the University of Caen, but the canons elected the future chronicler, Thomas Basin.[23] Basin had sworn allegiance to King Henry in 1447 but he did not hesitate to abjure his oath the moment Dunois's army encircled the town. He

The Suffolk Years

negotiated a guarantee of safety for its citizens and their property and for the liberties of Lisieux. The vainglorious bishop, writing thirty years later, claimed that he was the wisest as well as one of the most famous bishops in all France: despite the danger to himself, his sagacity and diplomacy had saved the town from sack.[24] Basin was sagacious only in recognising that resistance was pointless, and fortunate that purely by accident Lisieux was the first town in Normandy to offer unconditional surrender. The commander of Lisieux's small garrison, Thomas Kirkby, had asked Somerset in vain to send provisions and reinforcements. He held out until only three days supplies were left and after that surrender was inevitable.[25] The garrison was given a choice: they could march out with all their possessions or they could stay and swear allegiance to King Charles.

Charles consistently offered protection to any town returning to his obedience. He did not want lingering memories of pillage and plunder to sour people's perception of him and he did not begrudge spending money rather than munitions. It became the norm for an agreement to be reached whereby the captains of English garrisons opened their gates in return for payment. Several Englishmen owed their freedom to Charles's willingness to let them go in exchange for evacuating their command. Dunois was neither bloodthirsty nor revengeful; his task was to sweep the English out of Normandy with as little loss of French life and damage to French property as he could contrive.

From Lisieux, Dunois swung south-east towards Mantes and Vernon. The captain of Mantes, Thomas St Barbe, had driven off a French attack in the spring and he was still prepared to resist. But the townsfolk were not, and Mantes surrendered. The garrison was permitted to march out, leaving their artillery behind, after St Barbe agreed not to go to the relief of any town under siege by French armies.[26] Dunois ordered Robert Floquet to invest Vernon. Floquet was an enterprising war captain who had taken part in the capture of Pont de l'Arche and been with Brezé at the capture of Verneuil. John Butler, a younger son of the Earl of Ormond, held Vernon, and he

Losing Normandy

answered Floquet's demand that he should surrender by sending Floquet some very old keys. Floquet reported the insult to Dunois who promptly trained his artillery on the town's walls. The laws of war decreed that a town under siege must be allowed a reasonable period for a relieving force to arrive, and Dunois, who adhered meticulously to the dictates of his trade, agreed to wait for eight days. Butler's urgent plea to Somerset went unanswered and on 5 September he surrendered and retreated to Rouen with his 140 men.[27] His derisory gesture with the keys was to cost him dear.

Throughout the summer of 1449 the full force of three French armies was unleashed against the hapless towns and garrisons of Normandy. Town after town capitulated and the noose around Rouen tightened steadily. Despite repeated pleas for assistance Somerset stubbornly refused to detach men from Rouen. He was preparing to withstand a siege until an army from England could come to his rescue but efforts to raise an army had proved ineffective. Pride in military achievement had narrowed to the relatively few men who stoutly defended Normandy in the face of increasing disengagement by King Henry, the English Council, and Parliament. War came at a price that many Englishmen were no longer prepared to pay. Somerset sent his lieutenant, Sir William Peyto, to England to recruit a force of 100 men-at-arms and 1,200 archers for Somerset's personal retinue. Peyto managed to raise less than half that number and they did not muster until 31 July, the day that King Charles declared war. Suffolk loaned £1,000 towards a contingent of 100 men-at-arms and 300 archers under Sir Robert Vere that he had promised to send to de Surienne; they reached Caen in September and remained there, probably on Somerset's orders to defend the town. Caen was far more important to Somerset than Fougères.[28]

Dunois concentrated his troops for the final assault on Rouen early in October. The counts of Eu and St Pol were positioned to the east of the city with Dunois to the west. King Charles took up residence in Pont de l'Arche. He was accompanied by René of Anjou, Charles of

Maine, John of Calabria and Ferry de Vaudemont. All the male members of Margaret's family were in the ranks of England's enemies as the final conquest of Normandy began. Charles of Nevers, whom Margaret should have married, played a prominent part and King Charles knighted him during the siege.[29]

The French king did not lack partisans among the citizens of Rouen; he had been courting their favour for months. A group of townsmen sent word that the wall near the St Hilaire Gate would be left unguarded on the night of 16 October. Dunois led the assault, but the Earl of Shrewsbury had been warned of this piece of treachery. He launched a vigorous counterattack that inflicted heavy losses on the French and unfortunately included the death of some citizens. Raoul Rousel, Archbishop of Rouen, did not trust Somerset, who all too often ignored his advice, and he decided to follow the Bishop of Lisieux's example and welcome the French king. A delegation of townsmen led by Rousel presented themselves at Dunois's headquarters to open negotiations and Somerset sent two of his officers as witnesses, which made him complicit in the deliberations. Rousel and Dunois quickly reached agreement: Rouen would be surrendered in return for a promise, which King Charles had already proclaimed, that its ancient liberties and privileges would be respected. The English would be allowed to march out with the full honours of war including all their goods and artillery.[30] For King Charles it would be a victory that was cheap at the price.

Somerset hesitated. To surrender the capital of English Normandy without a fight while it was still capable of withstanding a siege was at best dishonourable and at worst treasonable. Although the English forces in Rouen were inferior in numbers to the French, they were by no means negligible, but Somerset had never taken part in a battle much less commanded one. He had enough provisions to hold out and many of his men, Shrewsbury among them, opposed surrender. Did Shrewsbury urge Somerset to fight? The Great Talbot's apathy at this critical time is in stark contrast to his earlier readiness to defend

Losing Normandy

Rouen. His lack of initiative is explicable only if Somerset gave him a direct order not to engage. Somerset was an administrator, not a soldier, and King Henry had sent him to govern Normandy and maintain the truce, not to fight the French. In a brief show of bravado Somerset rejected Dunois's terms.

Somerset's highhanded and tight-fisted policies came back to haunt him: he could not depend on the citizens' loyalty. The townsmen had little faith in his ability to defend their city and they were naturally fearful that it might be sacked if they resisted. They were incensed by Somerset's refusal of Dunois's offer and resentful that some of their number had been killed by Shrewsbury's men. On 19 October, the citizens of Rouen rose in rebellion. They opened their gates, Dunois accepted the keys to the city, and French soldiers set foot in the capital of English Normandy for the first time in thirty years. Pierre de Brezé and Robert Floquet were to have shared the honour of leading in 200 of the now famous French lances and 200 archers, but in the excitement Floquet suffered a kick from a horse which broke his leg and obliged him to retire to Pont de l'Arche.[31] Thomas Basin, who had attached himself to King Charles court, claimed that he was the first to enter Rouen at the head of 100 lances, but we have only his word for this piece of bravado.[32]

As soon as Rouen was safely in Dunois's hands King Charles moved his court into St Catherine's Abbey overlooking the city. The abbey was key to the city's defence, but it surrendered without a shot being fired. English soldiers still held the palace and the bastion in Rouen. Somerset retreated into its castle, but Dunois brought up his heavy artillery and opened fire on the castle's walls. Somerset's nerve was shaken by the ferocity of the bombardment and he withstood it for only twenty-four hours. He was unlikely to be killed, but he was afraid of being captured and he had his wife and family with him. He sent word to King Charles that he was ready to negotiate and he humbled himself by going in person to meet the French king.

Charles savoured his revenge for the belittling attitude Somerset had displayed towards him for so long. He received Somerset with his courtiers, including the Angevins, grouped around him. Somerset declared that he was willing to accept the terms offered by Dunois, but he had missed his opportunity – the terms were no longer on offer. After six days of hard bargaining an agreement was hammered out. Rouen would be surrendered; the towns of Caudebec, Honfleur, Arques, Montivilliers, and Harfleur would be evacuated within fifteen days.[33] Even in this extremity Somerset refused to surrender Harfleur. Henry V's great Normandy adventure had begun with its capture and Somerset's best hope for a relieving army from England lay in keeping the port open.

Somerset promised to pay 50,000 *écus* within a year as reparation, a commitment he would fail to honour. Charles did not trust him and he required hostages as a pledge of Somerset's good faith, among them the man whom the French prized most of all, John Talbot, Earl of Shrewsbury.[34] Charles received him and greeted him cordially but Shrewsbury replied, '*Sire, pardonnez-moi, je ne suis point encore conseillé à ce faire.*'[35] (Sire, forgive me, I did not consent to this.) Shrewsbury's passive acceptance of his fate was a measure of his humiliation.

The other hostages were young men chosen for their rank and as a deterrent to their fathers, who would be reluctant to endanger their sons' lives by joining an English attempt to recover Normandy: the sons of Lord Abergavenny, Lord Dacre, and, the Earl of Ormond who had defied Floquet at Vernon;[36] Sir Richard Frogenhall, who had opposed the surrender of Maine and plundered the French town of Neufbourg;[37] Richard Gower, the son of the captain of Cherbourg, which was still in English hands;[38] Henry Radford, the Duke of York's *bailli* of Rouen.[39] Somerset also sacrificed Richard Roos, the Duchess of Somerset's son by her previous marriage.[40]

On 4 November Somerset, with his wife and children, the English garrison, and English civilians who wished to leave, were escorted from Rouen to Harfleur where they took ship and sailed down the coast to Caen. On the following day François de Surienne, who had held out for longer than Somerset with far fewer resources, surrendered Fougères. De Surienne made his way to Naples, to the court of his overlord King Alfonso V of Aragon. From there he sent a scathing account of Fougères and English faithlessness to King Henry and in a stinging rebuke he returned his Order of the Garter.[41] Honour meant more to de Surienne than it did to Somerset.

King Charles's hour of triumph had come. It was the culmination of four years of patient diplomacy, detailed financial planning, and meticulous military organisation. He rode into Rouen on the afternoon of 10 November 1449 through Porte Beauvoisine, the same gate by which Henry V had entered thirty years before. The townsmen welcomed him with professions of loyalty and apologised for having put up with oppressive English rule for so long. Charles graciously held them excused! They demonstrated their loyalty to the 'real' King of France by lining his route to the cathedral with tableaux and images of submission. The procession through the city displayed the martial might of France with the King in full armour, his helmet encircled with a crown of golden fleur de lys. He was flanked by four pages carrying his lance, javelin, axe and jack (for bending a crossbow). The royal standard depicted St Michael with his flaming sword. Jean Havart carried the King's pennon of three fleur de lys on a blue background. The symbol of undying sovereignty, the mystical body of the earthly king, was represented by a riderless white horse with a richly bedecked coffer containing the seals of the kingdom strapped to its saddle. Behind it rode Guillaume Juvenal des Ursins, the Chancellor of France.

René of Anjou and Charles of Maine, fully armed, rode to the right and left of the King. Behind them came Dunois, Brezé, and Jacques Coeur, the King's treasurer, whose financial acumen had contributed so much to the success of French arms. The white cross of France was embroidered on the surcoats and horse trappings of the nobles and their retainers. René of Anjou's archers, wearing his colours of grey, white and black, marched with the royal archers. The rear of the procession was brought up by the French lances who formed the core of France's professional army. It was the most splendid procession yet staged by King Charles, far surpassing his entry into Paris in 1437.[42]

The English hostages watched from a window high above the street. It was a bitter sight. Did Shrewsbury remember another procession through these very streets, four years earlier when, riding beside Margaret's carriage, he had represented the military might of England while these same citizens welcomed her as their queen?

10
Suffolk Disgraced

The realisation that the loss of Rouen spelled the loss of Normandy sank in only slowly in England. The Council continued until the end of 1449 to authorise expenditure for the defence of what remained. The Exchequer was instructed to advance £545 for supplies to reinforce Somerset in Caen, but only £200 was available. A total of 1,000 bows and 2,000 sheaves of arrows should have been delivered to the city. William Cantelowe was paid 100 marks for 1,800 lbs of gunpowder and 200 lbs of saltpetre for the safekeeping of Cherbourg. Its captain was to receive 100 marks to shore up its defences. Wheat, barley, and malt were to be shipped to Honfleur and Harfleur in December.[1] It was too late. Dunois laid siege to Harfleur in November despite the atrocious winter weather. The chronicler Jean Chartier was at the siege and he described *endurant de grand froidures, et souffrant beaucoup de vexation.* (Enduring very cold weather and many frustrations.) The promised supplies failed to arrive, the town's lieutenant, Thomas Everingham, surrendered and the garrison marched out on New Year's Day.[2] Richard Curzon, the captain of Honfleur, refused to open his gates. Dunois besieged Honfleur and within a month Curzon sued for terms.[3] The war in Normandy, if war it can be called, was almost over.

Initial disbelief in England gave way to a rumbling anger. How could it have happened? How could Normandy have been lost so swiftly and so ignominiously? A chorus of protest swept through London: the country was being ruined by bad government and

The Suffolk Years

avaricious favourites. Satirical verses varying in ferocity were posted up all over the City. A ballad mourned the death or absence of the great lords of the land. King Henry was warned that unless he got rid of his evil councillors, he would lose the love of his people because he had become too poor to rule as he should.

'Be ware kinge Henre how thou doost
Loose not the love of alle the commynaltee.'[4]

Albeit couched in veiled language, the King, his government, and his court, were being advised to mend their ways.

Parliament assembled on 6 November 1449 and the Commons choice of Speaker reflected their mood. Sir John Popham had been returned to Parliament only once before, but he was a highly respected soldier who had fought at Agincourt and he stood for everything that many people believed Suffolk had betrayed.[5] His election came as a shock to Popham, and to the government. Whether he was put under pressure to refuse the appointment or whether his plea of age and infirmity was genuine, the old warrior asked to be excused. It was unprecedented but King Henry granted his request and the Commons fell back on the experienced William Tresham, who had been Suffolk's choice as Speaker in 1447. Tresham would play a very different role in this Parliament.

In December, Adam Moleyns, who was closely identified with Suffolk's administration as the principal negotiator with the French, decided that it was time to get out. He pleaded that he had neglected his duties as Bishop of Chichester for too long, that his eyesight was failing, and his health was uncertain. He petitioned to resign all his secular occupations and to absent himself from Parliament and Council meetings to prepare for a pilgrimage to Rome. King Henry granted the petition but he did not keep his word.[6] In January 1450 the Council pressed Moleyns into service once again, and not for the first time he was sent on a hopeless mission.

The army that had been painstakingly raised over the previous months was bivouacked along the south coast of England waiting to

Suffolk Disgraced

be paid. Moleyns travelled to Portsmouth to plead with the soldiers to accept what he could offer, but the money at his disposal was considerably less than their due. The sailors whose ships had been lying idle for months were in an ugly mood. The men were disaffected, their tempers frayed, and their patience exhausted: they simply did not believe Moleyns's promises of future payment. An angry crowd gathered and turned violent. Moleyns was set upon, beaten, and stabbed. Cuthbert Colville, a captain who had served under the Duke of York in Normandy, delivered the death blow. When men such as Colville could bring themselves to assault a bishop and the King's Privy Seal, army discipline had disintegrated to a dangerous degree. The mortally wounded Moleyns took some time to die and a garbled version of his death bed confession reached London. It was widely believed that Moleyns had confessed that he and Suffolk were traitors because they had surrendered Maine and Normandy to the French.[7]

It was all too much for Archbishop Stafford. He had been Chancellor for over twenty years, and he was worn out. Threats were swirling all around him, Moleyns had been murdered and Suffolk was being savaged. On the morning of 31 January 1450, in the Council chamber at Westminster, Stafford delivered his seals of office, the Great Seal of gold and the silver seals, into King Henry's hands. John Kemp, Cardinal Archbishop of York, took the Chancellor's oath of office and King Henry handed the seals to him.[8] If the mighty Cardinal Beaufort's mantle had fallen onto anyone's shoulders it was onto Cardinal Kemp's. He had lent weight and dignity to Suffolk's administration without identifying himself too closely with it.

Suffolk was painfully aware of the mudslinging that followed Moleyns's death and the 'odious and horrible language' being used to slander him. But he misjudged the extent of the Commons' hostility and of the Lords' self-interest. He petitioned King Henry to be allowed to refute his critics' allegations in full Parliament and to have his defence entered on the parliamentary roll. In an impassioned plea he recalled his own and his family's sacrifices for the crown: his father

The Suffolk Years

and three of his brothers had been killed in France and a fourth had died in captivity. He himself had been captured and his ransom had impoverished him to the tune of £20,000. He was not a traitor and he challenged any man to say when, where, or how he had betrayed his country. His assertion that he had spent seventeen years abroad without once returning home was an exaggeration but his claim that he had devoted his life to the King's service was true. Unfortunately, in his anxiety to exonerate himself, Suffolk alluded to Moleyns's death and 'a certain confession of the keper of youre prive seal'. This gave the Commons their opportunity. The knives were out, and the storm broke over Suffolk's head.

Speaking for the Commons, William Tresham informed Chancellor Kemp that since Suffolk admitted the widespread rumours of his culpability he must answer the charges, and demanded Suffolk's arrest. King Henry was aghast but so were his councillors. They were wary of putting Suffolk on trial, for who knew what damaging allegations he might make of their responsibility for surrendering Maine? The Lords referred the matter to the judges and Lord Chief Justice Fortescue opined that rumours and slanders *per se* were not sufficient grounds to commit Suffolk to prison. The Lords heaved a collective sigh of relief and concurred, but the Commons thought otherwise. Tresham retorted that it was well known that the French would follow up their victories in Normandy by invading England and that Suffolk was privy to their plans. Suffolk was Constable of Wallingford Castle and he had recently sought the King's permission to retire there. Tresham alleged that he had fortified the castle as a base from which the French could launch their conquest of England.[9]

King Henry now faced the most acute personal dilemma of his reign thus far. He could not dissolve Parliament even to save his minister until he secured a tax grant, which would not be forthcoming unless he bowed to the Commons' demands. Henry consoled himself with the thought that at least Suffolk would be safe in the Tower, where he could not be lynched by the London mob. He ordered Viscount

Beaumont to take Suffolk into custody. Only three years earlier Beaumont had performed the same office at Suffolk's instigation when he arrested the Duke of Gloucester, who was also innocent of the charges against him.

The Commons submitted two bills, one impeaching Suffolk of treason and another indicting him for corrupt practices. The first bill was highly emotive and very dangerous, for treason was a capital charge.[10] It opened with the most damning as well as the most preposterous accusation of all, that Suffolk was aiming at the crown! Margaret Beaufort was the only child of the dead John Beaufort, Duke of Somerset, whose kinship with King Henry gave him a tenuous claim to the throne. Henry had granted her wardship and marriage to Suffolk in 1444 when she was a year old and Suffolk had recently arranged her betrothal to his young son John. The Commons seized on this as 'proof' of Suffolk's treachery: he planned, with the help of the French, to put Margaret and John on the throne of England.

The Commons' bill further alleged that during his embassy to Tours Suffolk had secretly promised to cede Maine to René and Charles of Anjou in return for a substantial remuneration. He had kept his promise in 1447 when his friend Dunois led a French embassy to England and Suffolk had betrayed military and diplomatic secrets to him.[11] Suffolk would certainly have known of English military plans, but no one bothered to ask if they actually existed. Suffolk's statement during the peace talks with the French ambassadors in 1445 that he wished to serve the King of France came back to haunt him. The Commons accused him of informing the French ambassadors in advance of what the English negotiators had to offer. He had facilitated a private meeting between King Henry and the French to persuade Henry to visit France, which was not in the interests of the King or the country.

Suffolk had betrayed Normandy and Gascony by appointing venal men to captaincies in the English garrisons in Normandy (which were under the command of the Duke of York) and he had diverted military

The Suffolk Years

supplies into enemy hands. Large sums of money had been paid on Suffolk's orders to King Charles's councillors, including Dunois, Pierre de Brezé, and even to the French queen, although the Commons could not produce any evidence for this.[12] King Henry had become so poor he was humiliated in the eyes of the world, so was it any wonder that his Norman subjects looked elsewhere for good lordship? The army that had been mustered to defend Normandy in the previous October had not sailed because Suffolk had accepted bribes from the French to oppose sending troops to France. In fact, Suffolk had loaned more than any other councillor to outfit the army.[13]

Suffolk had wrecked the embassy sent to Gascony in 1442 to conclude a marriage for King Henry by forewarning King Charles of English intentions. The Count of Armagnac's allegiance and the wealth that the marriage to his daughter would have brought to England had been lost through Suffolk's machinations. Suffolk had little to do with that aborted marriage and Armagnac was not rich, but the accusation has survived to this day in the tradition of Suffolk's misdeeds.[14]

King Henry routinely appointed his favourites to lordships and lucrative offices in the Duchy of Gascony, but the Commons alleged that these were Suffolk's clients. They had depleted duchy revenues to such an extent that there was no money left for its defence.[15] Suffolk had persuaded the King to bestow the Earldom of Kendal with lands in England and castles in Gascony worth over £1,000 on the 'Comte de Foix' because his wife was Suffolk's niece. Foix had then helped the French king to take castles in Gascony. It was true that King Henry had created John de Foix Earl of Kendal in 1446 at a time when England was desperate to retain the allegiance of the southern French magnates, but John de Foix was not the Comte de Foix, as the Commons claimed. Gaston, Comte de Foix, was a vassal of the French king, while John de Foix was a vassal of England.[16]

The Commons claimed that the Duke of Orleans, captured at the Battle of Agincourt, had bribed Suffolk in 1440 to facilitate his release

Suffolk Disgraced

and that Suffolk had purloined pledges for the payment of Orleans' ransom from the Exchequer in return for a reduction of his own unpaid ransom. They claimed that after his release (nine years earlier) Orleans had assisted King Charles to overrun Normandy and take Lord Fauconberg and the Earl of Shrewsbury prisoner.[17] Suffolk had not been party to the negotiations for Orleans' release but he had negotiated the release of Orleans' brother, the Count of Angoulême, and received a fee for his pains. This was enough for the Commons.[18]

Further allegations and amalgamations of half-truths ranged over a wide field: Suffolk had supported the Dauphin Louis against England's ally, the Emperor Frederick, when in fact it was the Duke of York who had sent his unpaid troops to serve under the Dauphin in Alsace during the Truce of Tours. Suffolk had included the Duke of Brittany and the King of Aragon in the Truce of Tours as allies of France when everyone knew they were allies of England; he had alienated Duke Francis of Brittany and allowed Giles of Brittany to be imprisoned, which had precipitated the renewal of the war. If Suffolk had a sense of irony, he would have smiled.

The Commons were on surer grounds with their second bill. It contained a long list of Suffolk's misdeeds in domestic matters, based on public knowledge and information furnished by men who were not sorry to see popular fury deflected onto the unpopular duke. Some of the accusations were cleverly calculated to 'prove' Suffolk's guilt.[19] It was alleged that Suffolk had lived for years at King Henry's expense and exploited the King's trust. Grants of lands, offices, and money to Suffolk had so impoverished the King that even the wages for the royal household could not be met. As an example, the great Earldom of Pembroke, which should have reverted to the crown on the death of the Duke of Gloucester, had been granted to Suffolk. He had persuaded King Henry to make grants to those he favoured, many of whom paid handsomely for his good offices, so that he and his ilk had grown rich while the crown grew poorer every day.

Suffolk had perverted the course of justice and only those he

The Suffolk Years

favoured could get a fair hearing in court. Fines that should have come into the royal coffers drained away into the pockets of Suffolk and his henchmen. Probably thanks to Lord Cromwell's willingness to provide them with 'evidence', the Commons presented a specific example of Suffolk perverting the course of justice. Sir William Tailboys had violated Parliamentary privilege by attacking Lord Cromwell outside the Star Chamber at Westminster. Cromwell was unhurt but he was sure that Tailboys had intended to murder him. Tailboys was under arrest and the Commons petitioned to have him transferred to the Tower, claiming that he had escaped punishment in the past because he was Suffolk's man.[20]

Lord Cromwell and Tailboys were Lincolnshire men, heavily involved in the feuds besetting that county. Cromwell had forcibly removed one of Tailboy's servants from gaol and taken him to Cromwell's home at Tattersall, where Cromwell intended to try him in an illegal court and hang him out of hand. Tailboys had appealed for redress to Viscount Beaumont, the principal magnate in Lincolnshire.[21] Beaumont was almost as influential with King Henry as Suffolk; Henry had created him England's first viscount and a Knight of the Garter. He shared Henry's interest in theology and the King's orthodox piety, and he had his own chamber 'within the King's chamber' at Westminster Palace.[22] Suffolk held no lands in Lincolnshire, but it was easy for the Commons to substitute Suffolk for Beaumont.

The Commons alleged that Suffolk interfered in the appointment of sheriffs and through them he rode roughshod over local interests to protect his clients and enrich himself. Since Suffolk conducted the business of government in the King's name he was naturally involved in the choice of sheriffs. It was not unusual for local magnates to intimidate sheriffs to favour their own nominees for election to Parliament; the Duke of Norfolk made a habit of it.[23] How far Suffolk profited personally in the appointment of sheriffs is open to question.

The Commons protested that they had tried in vain to keep

Suffolk Disgraced

Suffolk's profligacy in check; they had loyally rescued the King by voting taxes they could ill afford, only to find that Suffolk had embezzled the money. They claimed that when Lord Sudeley resigned as Treasurer in 1446 there had been ample funds in the Exchequer to defend Normandy. But Suffolk had siphoned off so much of it that the Exchequer was now empty. Two former Treasurers, Lords Sudeley and Cromwell, who were listening to this indictment, knew that it was a blatant lie – possibly furnished by Cromwell. The Commons declared that Suffolk's motivation was obvious: he had betrayed his king and bankrupted his country for personal gain. Suffolk could not deny that in achieving his ambition to become a duke he had amassed considerable wealth along the way.

A lurid and embellished version of the Commons' accusations was put into circulation to add scurrilous details for public consumption. It apostrophised Suffolk as Antichrist and Judas; he had debauched a nun and had an illegitimate daughter by her while he was serving in France, he had displayed cowardice in the wars, and he had left his brother to die a prisoner in France rather than pay his ransom.[24]

The wording of the charges against Suffolk obscured the facts behind the loaded rhetoric, and the parts added up to a hefty whole. Suffolk was the most hated man in England and the accusations against him were widely believed. Suffolk had taken his share of rewards as the King's favourite minister and his handling of King Henry's peace policy had been inept, but he was not solely, or even principally, responsible for the loss of Normandy. Nevertheless, the Commons' venom outweighed the truth and the cumulative effect was an overwhelming presumption of Suffolk's guilt.

King Henry exercised his prerogative to reserve the Commons' bills without reply but the Lords cravenly advised the King that Suffolk must answer the charges. On 9 March Suffolk was escorted from the Tower to Parliament to hear the indictments read out. He was lodged in the Jewel Tower at Westminster in the custody of three jailors, who remained with him night and day. This sparked more unrest and a new crop of rumours. Margaret Paston in Norfolk heard that Suffolk had been pardoned and was 'right well at ease and merry and in the King's good grace and that of all the lords.'[25] It was not true. Suffolk was at the mercy of his peers as well as his enemies; his pre-eminence had come at a price.

On 13 March 1450, kneeling before King Henry and the Lords, Suffolk submitted his defence. He did not attempt to answer all the Commons' articles, he sensibly concentrated on the treason charges and he categorically denied the accusations. He declared that everything he had done had been with the consent of King Henry and the Council, and in some instances with the assent of Parliament itself. His actions could not be construed as treason since they were acts of collective responsibility.

He poured scorn on the allegation that he had aimed at the throne. The idea that Margaret Beaufort could inherit the crown was so fantastic that it had never crossed his mind. He had intended to marry his son to Anne Beauchamp, the daughter of Henry Beauchamp, Duke of Warwick, the richest heiress in England, but Anne died in 1449, and only then did he decide to betroth John to Margaret Beaufort.[26] Suffolk insisted that his words during the visit of the French ambassadors that he wished to serve King Charles had been taken out of context. He had never divulged any secrets to the French. As for Maine, the manner and timing of its surrender had been handled exclusively by Adam Moleyns as the King's ambassador.[27] This was the weakest point of Suffolk's defence, and the most cowardly, but Moleyns was safely dead and Suffolk could not lay the blame where it rightly belonged: on King Henry.

A week later, on 17 March, in the King's private chamber at Westminster, Chancellor Kemp addressed Suffolk in King Henry's name. The Lords had heard Suffolk's defence, but he had not requested trial by his peers. Did he request it now? Suffolk replied that he had said all he had to say. His career and his life lay in ruins, but he stood loyally by King Henry and faced disgrace rather than put Henry in the invidious position of presiding over a trial that, given the political imperatives, would result in a grave miscarriage of justice. His erstwhile colleagues sat in silence as Chancellor Kemp delivered the verdict. King Henry on his own authority, sitting as a King, not as a judge, and without the advice or consent of the Lords, declared that the charge of treason was unproven. Henry dared not exonerate his minister completely, but he protected him as best he could. He banished Suffolk for five years. Suffolk was not to remain in any of the King's domains and he could not take refuge in Normandy, Gascony, or Calais.

Viscount Beaumont, speaking for the Lords, declared that the King's judgement must not set a precedent. The Lords reserved the right to claim trial by their peers and not by royal authority alone and their declaration was to be entered on the parliamentary rolls.[28] They were not concerned with justice; they were protecting themselves from present opprobrium or future coercion. They did not acquit Suffolk but nor did they condemn him. Suffolk had profited personally just like everyone else at Henry's court, but his sins of omission and commission were largely due to Henry's inability to rule as well as to reign. The King could not be blamed for the disasters in France, or the lawlessness at home, so the opprobrium was deflected onto Suffolk.

King Henry judgement infuriated the London mob, who were eagerly anticipating the public execution of the execrated favourite. Howling with rage they marched through the streets chanting that by allowing Suffolk to 'escape' King Henry would lose London and his crown. Suffolk was smuggled out of the City under cover of darkness and, baulked of its prey, the mob vented its anger on Suffolk's servants. Several of them were taken up by the city watchmen and held in prison overnight for their own protection.[29] Suffolk reached his house at East Thorp near Bury St Edmunds in safety and prepared for his departure from England.

The night before he sailed Suffolk wrote a last letter to his son John. After reminding the boy of his duty to God, Suffolk enjoined him to

The Suffolk Years

remain loyal to King Henry no matter what. He was to honour and obey his mother in all things, to learn a lesson from his father's fate and avoid the company of proud and greedy men.[30] John was eight years old; he would still be only thirteen when the period of Suffolk's banishment ended, but Suffolk was fifty-four, an ageing man by the standards of his time, and he doubted that he would ever see his family again. He entrusted the letter to his wife to be held until the boy was old enough to need such weighty advice.

Suffolk's destination is unknown. He could not go to Blois, to his friend the Duke of Orleans, since England and France were at war. He might reasonably have expected to be welcomed by the Duke of Burgundy for his literary accomplishments, although he can hardly have hoped to spend five years at the Burgundian court. Suffolk probably intended to go first to Rome on pilgrimage as 1450 was a Jubilee Year but a visit to Rome would not take five years. The Holy Land was the ultimate goal of every pilgrim, but it was a difficult, sometimes dangerous, and always lengthy journey. Suffolk may have planned to go to Jerusalem to expiate his sins and redeem his soul.[31]

Power Struggle

11

Aftermath

The winter and spring of 1449/50 was an unhappy time for Margaret. King Charles, her 'uncle of France' had betrayed her and her husband; he had broken the truce and renewed the war. She had suffered the humiliation of witnessing her family's participation in his triumphal entry into Rouen. Suffolk's impeachment came as a shock; he was her friend and Margaret knew only the best of him. King Henry's inability to shield his minister from the Commons, and the London mob howling for Suffolk's blood, made her aware of just how dangerously violent the capital could be. Defeat in France and Suffolk's banishment dealt a double blow to her sense of security. The French chronicler, Mathieu d'Escouchy, has a story that Margaret was often in tears, but only in private; in public she remained stoically calm.[1] To add to her woes the palace at Eltham caught fire during a thunderstorm in March while she was staying there.[2]

After Suffolk's banishment King Henry prorogued Parliament to meet again at Leicester away from the menacing atmosphere of London, but the country was still unsettled. Henry's leisurely journey north in April was impeded by John Harris, a 'shipman' who stood in the centre of the road at Stony Stratford wielding a threshing flail and shouting that thus would the Duke of York winnow out traitors when he returned from Ireland. The unfortunate man did not know that Suffolk was no longer in the King's company. Harris was hanged, drawn, and quartered, and his head was set on the south gate of Northampton.[3]

Aftermath

The Commons petitioned for an Act of Resumption to remedy the King's 'grete and grevouse' level of indebtedness.[4] Henry had to accept it as the only way to obtain a desperately needed tax grant, but it would adversely affect Henry's courtiers, his councillors, and his household. The Commons demanded the resumption of all grants of crown lands made since Henry came to the throne in 1422, with fifteen exemptions.[5] The first was for the Queen, because she had not received her full dowry.[6] Margaret was not averse to the prospect of resumption; the Parliament of 1447 had enacted that crown lands could be granted to her in lieu of the cash components of her dower assigned on the Exchequer. Grants to the King's foundations at Eton and Cambridge, and Duchy of Lancaster lands set aside to meet the provisions of Henry's will were protected, but the Commons insisted that specific revenues from the duchy must be allocated to reducing royal debt and to correcting the long-held grievance of purveyance.[7] Royal purveyors either failed to pay market prices for the goods they took, or did not pay for them at all.

King Henry passed the act, but he added 186 exemptions.[8] Before coming to Leicester he had colluded with his officials and promised to authorise only partial resumptions for those closest to him.[9] He showed less concern for his magnates, although he exempted grants to the Duke of York as the King's Lieutenant in Ireland, because York was complaining from Dublin that he had not been paid. Henry also partially exempted some members of Margaret's household.[10] He got his tax grant. The Speaker, William Tresham (who had surrendered only £20 of the £100 he held in royal annuities) announced that there could be no general subsidy due to the impoverished state of the country, but the Commons would grant a graded tax on income from land as a one-off measure – it was not to set a precedent.[11]

While Parliament was still in session alarming news reached Leicester. The English army had been virtually wiped out at the Battle of Formigny. It had sailed for France in March under the command of Sir Thomas Kyriell, much to the relief of the population along the southern coasts. Kyriell was a professional soldier and a former lieutenant of Calais who had served in the wars in France for thirty years.[12] He had indented for service in the previous December and he was to contribute ninety-nine men-at-arms and 300 archers, but only twelve other captains, none of them above the rank of knight, had volunteered.[13] The army numbered about 2,600 men.[14]

Kyriell had planned to land at Honfleur and move west to link up with the Duke of Somerset at Caen and bring the French to battle. But Honfleur had fallen to Dunois and Kyriell was forced to land at Cherbourg, the only major port still in English hands. From there he would have to march down the Contentin peninsula and then eastward, crossing two rivers, to reach Caen via Bayeux. The lure of plunder was enticing and Kyriell elected to reduce the towns along his route to secure his rear and his supplies. He wasted three precious weeks in besieging the town of Valognes.

As soon as Kyriell landed King Charles sent for Arthur de Richemont, the Constable of France, who was in Brittany, and he ordered the Count of Clermont to shadow the English army. Clermont, the son of the Duke of Bourbon, had risen to prominence while still in his teens. He had married King Charles's daughter Jeanne and become a king's councillor, but he was a young and inexperienced commander and understandably he hesitated to engage an English army that outnumbered him.

The Duke of Somerset ordered his senior captains, Matthew Gough, Henry Norbury, and Sir Robert Vere to muster all available troops, about 1,000 men, and move west to join Kyriell, but Somerset did not go himself. There was no experienced high-ranking commander to inspire the army with confidence. Kyriell, Gough, Vere, and Norbury were accustomed to siege warfare, not to planning a battle. Their tactical thinking was muddled, and their command was divided. Gough felt himself at liberty to ride off to Bayeux, and he had to be recalled in a hurry when Kyriell realised that Clermont was closing in on the English rear.

Aftermath

Kyriell reached Formigny, ten miles west of Bayeux, on 14 April 1450 and bivouacked overnight. Clermont waited for reinforcements but when there was still no sign of them on the morning of 15 April, he decided to risk giving battle. Initially the English had the upper hand, capturing Clermont's two field guns, but Pierre de Brezé led a charge on foot to recover them. His action almost turned the tide in Clermont's favour, but it was still touch and go until, at the last minute, Richemont arrived with fresh troops and the battle became a rout. Most of the English men-at-arms and archers were slain and the rest were taken prisoner while the French suffered few causalities. Kyriell and Norbury were captured, Gough and Vere managed to fight their way clear. They fled headlong back to Bayeux and Caen.[15]

The Count of Clermont moved on Bayeux and Dunois joined him with his heavy artillery. Gough and the garrison repulsed two frontal assaults but the constant bombardment over the next fortnight forced him to surrender. Gough's military career ended at Bayeux. He and his men were permitted to leave with their personal possessions but without their arms. The wives and children of the garrison were loaded into carts for the long, slow, painful retreat along the coast to Cherbourg.[16]

In England, the news of the Battle of Formigny was eclipsed almost immediately by a more sensational report: the Duke of Suffolk had been murdered.[17] Suffolk had sailed from Ipswich on the last day of April, with two ships and a pinnace. His ship was intercepted in the Straits of Dover by the *Nicholas of the Tower* and boarded by a party of sailors. They ordered Suffolk to surrender. He showed them his safe conduct but offered no resistance; he knew he could not rely on the loyalty of his own sailors.

He and his servants were transferred to the *Nicholas,* and as he came aboard the captain hailed him with the ominous words, 'Welcome, traitor.' The crew gave Suffolk a mock trial and adjudged him guilty. They, and probably the crews of Suffolk's ships as well, believed he had betrayed his country and deserved to die. He was allowed a day to confess and prepare his soul. On 2 May he was lowered into a small boat and beheaded on its gunwale. It took six strokes of a rusty sword to complete the decapitation.[18] Suffolk's body was thrown onto the Dover sands and the Sheriff of Kent sent the news to King Henry at Leicester and asked where the Duke should be buried. On Henry's orders, Suffolk's corpse was taken to St Martin's church in Dover where it lay for nearly a month before being carried in procession through Canterbury and Rochester for burial at Wingfield.[19] Suffolk's servants were put ashore unharmed, although they were robbed. The Duchess of Suffolk received a first-hand account of her husband's grisly death from Jacques Blondel, Margaret's clerk avener, who had accompanied Suffolk into exile. From Dover he made his way to join Duchess Alice's household.[20]

Suffolk's death gave rise to the legend of a prophecy that he would live if he could escape 'the Tower'. It was said that when he heard the name of the ship, he knew he was doomed.[21] The *Nicholas* was not named for the Tower of London, but for the structure amidships designed to protect the men-at-arms aboard her in a sea fight. She was a privateer, sailing out of Bristol, and orders had been issued in April to arrest her and press into royal service, so she may have been avoiding the King's officers when she encountered Suffolk's flotilla. By the end of 1450 she was engaged in piracy in the Channel.[22]

At Leicester there was an unseemly scramble to grab what could be had from the detritus of Suffolk's career. Lord Beauchamp of Powick obtained a lease on the farm of the Earldom of Pembroke, despite a petition from the tenants that King Henry should keep it in his own hands or grant it to Queen Margaret.[23] Viscount Beaumont became Great Chamberlain of England and the Earl of Northumberland was appointed Constable of England in Beaumont's stead.[24] The Duchess of Suffolk made haste to protect her son's interests. King Henry had promised Suffolk that if anything happened to him John de la Pole's wardship and marriage would remain in Duchess Alice's hands. She petitioned for custody of Suffolk's lands during John's minority and

Aftermath

Henry granted them to her.[25] She also prudently applied to the Pope for a papal dispensation to validate her son's 'marriage' to Margaret Beaufort.[26] For the rest of her life Alice would channel her formidable energies into defending her only child's inheritance. It was no easy task; she was a wealthy woman in her own right, and without Suffolk's protection she was fair game for predatory land-grabbers.

Suffolk's murder was greeted with general rejoicing. Doggerel verses gleefully invited rapacious courtiers to sing *Placebo and Dirige* for 'Jac Napes' soule. Suffolk's badge was an ape and clog.[27] But men were fearful too. Rumours spread like wildfire: it was whispered that the King would lay waste to the whole of Kent in reprisal for the murder of his favourite minister.[28] The flames of insurrection were fanned by propaganda and Kentishmen prepared to defend themselves. The subsequent rising was not spontaneous, it was carefully planned, and considerable efforts behind the scenes went into assembling a sizeable force. Its leader was to be an experienced soldier, able to organise civilians into a disciplined unit, but not a man of high rank since this was to be a peoples' movement.

Jack Cade has all the hallmarks of a seasoned campaigner and a successful freebooter. Nothing is known of his antecedents, but he had the habit of command and was impressive enough to rally men of substance to his banner. He probably returned to England from France in 1450, perhaps as a fugitive from the Battle of Formigny. As well as the title 'Captain of Kent', Cade assumed the emotive name of John Mortimer. Twenty-five years earlier, during King Henry minority, a John Mortimer had been executed for claiming that the Mortimer Earls of March were the rightful kings of England.[29] The Duke of York's son Edward was Earl of March.

At Leicester King Henry issued commissions to his lieges 'of whatsoever estate, rank and condition, to go against the traitors and rebels in Kent and to punish and arrest the same.'[30] The Duke of Buckingham and Sir Richard Woodville left Leicester for London. The King and the court came south more slowly and reached the Priory of

Power Struggle

St John of Jerusalem at Clerkenwell on Saturday, 13 June. The next day, being a Sunday, Henry did nothing. Cade and his army were camped on Blackheath and Cade demanded to meet the King, but Henry's councillors were reluctant to take the risk. It was a tricky situation: on the one hand Henry was quite capable of granting whatever the rebels demanded without worrying about whether he could honour his promises. On the other, if he refused, it might precipitate the armed clash that he and his lords were anxious to avoid. The Earl of Northumberland, as Constable of England, rode out to assess the rebel strength and reported that their numbers were far greater than expected.

King Henry sent a delegation to persuade them to lay down their arms and seek his pardon, but he made a major mistake by not going himself. Cade did not threaten the King; he wanted to present his petition to Henry in person. The petition had been carefully prepared, but not by Cade alone: it was an amalgam of reasonable complaint and flights of fancy.[31] It opened with the traditional statement that Cade and his men were the King's true liegemen. It advised Henry not to tax his people but to 'live of his own' as a 'Kyng Riall' should. It raised local grievances, especially extortions by royal officials in Kent, and the prohibitive cost of dealings in the Exchequer and in the King's Bench. It recommended the King to take counsel from his great lords, the Dukes of Buckingham, Norfolk, and Exeter, and especially the Duke of York, who had been exiled by Suffolk to the detriment of the realm. Buckingham was a member of the Council, but Norfolk was the most violent of all Henry's lords, and the new young Duke of Exeter was an unknown quantity. The petition further alleged that Suffolk and his henchmen had encompassed the deaths of the Dukes of Somerset, Warwick, and Exeter, and of Cardinal Beaufort, and that Suffolk had falsely accused the Duke of Gloucester of being a traitor and had then murdered him. The belief that Gloucester had been murdered was due to his sudden death and it had gained currency by repetition, but no one had ever suggested that these men, King

Aftermath

Henry's close kin and friends, had died of anything but natural causes. These accusations reflected the universal loathing of Suffolk.

King Henry's envoys assured Cade that his petition would be carefully considered and that the King would answer it, but no answer came. Henry rode to Blackheath on 18 June backed by men and artillery only to find it deserted – Cade and his army had decamped during the night. Cade may have been unwilling to commit treason by facing Henry in the field, but it is more likely that the experienced 'captain' decided not to risk an encounter with a heavily armed force. King Henry's courtiers were elated; this was the way to treat a rebel horde. So confident were they that Cade had been routed that with a disdain amounting to foolhardiness they dispatched only a small contingent under Sir Humphrey Stafford and his brother to complete the job. But Cade knew a thing or two about orderly retreat and as the Staffords approached Sevenoaks they were ambushed and some of their men were killed. A more formidable force under Lord Dudley, Sir Richard Woodville, Sir Thomas Stanley, and Thomas Daniel, with soldiers from Normandy who were accustomed to plunder, pursued the rebels. Following a time-honoured practice, the soldiers looted whatever they could lay their hands on and the opprobrious term 'Cheshire men' was subsequently applied to them.[32] King Richard II's personal bodyguard of 'Cheshire men' were still remembered for their ruthlessness.

King Henry did not stay on Blackheath. He rode to Greenwich to join Margaret, leaving the Duke of Buckingham in command. The royal army was ill at ease: the King had quit the field. They were also confused: it was wrong for any man to come in arms against the King but that was precisely what Cade had *not* done. The rebels were not riffraff; some of them were known to the King's men. Cade wanted 'traitors' around the King punished and so did they. They threatened to go over to Cade unless decisive action was taken against these traitors. The soldiers' reaction unnerved Buckingham and he too left the field to carry the devastating news to Greenwich.[33]

Power Struggle

King Henry panicked. He issued a woolly proclamation declaring that traitors everywhere would be punished, but exactly who he had in mind was left conveniently vague.[34] Henry had appointed his chamberlain, James Fiennes, Lord Saye and Sele, to succeed Marmaduke Lumley as Treasurer of England. It was a disastrous choice, Saye was the most hated man in England now that Suffolk was dead. He was notorious as an extortioner, going far beyond what was acceptable even in a society where veniality was the norm. Saye, his wife, and the Sheriff of Kent, Stephen Slegge, had forced the exchange of a property close to Saye's principal seat at Knowle for far less than it was worth by threatening the owner with imprisonment and death if he failed to comply.[35] Henry ordered Saye's arrest and he was imprisoned in the Tower. The situation was bizarre. The Duke of Exeter was the hereditary Constable of the Tower but during his minority King Henry had granted the constableship to none other than Lord Saye, who was now both its constable and a prisoner within its walls.[36]

Another unpopular courtier, William Aiscough, Bishop of Salisbury, fearing for his life and property, left London in a hurry. He got as far as the monastery of the Bonhommes in Edington where he broke his journey to celebrate mass. A mob attacked him in the church, dragged him onto a hillside beyond the town and hacked him to death. They cut his body into pieces in a cruel mockery of the punishment of hanging, drawing, and quartering meted out to traitors. His attackers plundered his baggage and made off with jewels, ornaments, vestments, and no less than £3,000 in cash, considerably more than he should have possessed as Bishop of Salisbury.[37] Some of the jewels belonged to Margaret: she had pledged them as surety for a loan to the crown.[38] The murder of his confessor shocked King Henry and he dashed from Greenwich back to London. The Mayor and aldermen pleaded with him not to abandon the City. They even offered to pay the costs of maintaining the royal household for six months if only he would stay.[39] Henry ignored their entreaties. He entrusted the safe keeping of the Tower to Thomas, Lord Scales, and he left London precipitously for Kenilworth and the safety of the Midlands. It was his second major mistake.

Elated at the news that he had forced the King to abandon his capital, Jack Cade moved into Southwark and occupied the White Hart Inn. On 3 July he crossed London Bridge and rode along Fish Street, turning into Candlewick Street where he circled the ancient London Stone, striking it with his naked sword in token of his conquest of the City.[40] He met with little resistance as many Londoners were in sympathy with his declared aims and felt a certain measure of admiration for his daring. Nevertheless, it was a case of 'do as I say, not as I do'. Cade's followers, aided enthusiastically by the more turbulent inhabitants, pillaged the City throughout the night. The Captain of Kent was remarkably well informed for a solider with no known connections in London. His men ransacked the house of an unpopular wealthy alderman, Philip Malpas, who had left London in the wake of the court. They carried off cash, jewels, and goods worth a small fortune, of which Cade took his share.[41]

King Henry had left Chancellor Kemp, John Stafford, the Archbishop of Canterbury, and William Waynflete, the Bishop of Winchester, at Westminster hoping, despite Aiscough's grisly fate, that their calling would protect them from the worst of the rebels' violence. On 1 July Kemp commissioned Lord Scales, Mayor Chalton, several aldermen, and six justices to deal with the rebels.[42] They had the legal power but not the resources, and their best hope of averting continuing depredations would be to placate Cade. It just so happened that two men, Thomas Kent and Edward Grimston, who were closely associated with the Duke of Suffolk, were still in London. Kent had acted as Privy Seal after the murder of Adam Moleyns. Grimston was a client of Suffolk and a diplomat in King Henry's service. Grimston's wife, Alice, had been introduced into Margaret's household by the Duchess of Suffolk.[43] Kent and Grimston were arrested and accused of complicity in Suffolk's 'plot' to put Margaret Beaufort and his son

John on the throne.[44] Other court favourites – John Say, John Trevelian, and Thomas Daniel – were tried and condemned *in absentia*.[45] Lord Saye was detested by the men of Kent and if anything could appease Cade's hordes it would be Saye's execution. Lord Scales hauled him out of the Tower, and he was indicted at the Guildhall. To the glee of the mob, Saye was found guilty of treason and dragged off to the Standard in Cornhill, the usual place of execution for traitors, to await Cade's arrival.[46]

Cade was not at the Guildhall. Attired in all the finery of a blue velvet coat trimmed with fur, a straw hat, and gilt spurs, in a sartorial parody of aristocratic authority, he rode through the streets of London brandishing his naked sword.[47] He dined with a citizen (and incidentally robbed his host in the process) and made his way through Aldgate to Mile End where men from Essex, inspired by the news of Cade's triumph, had marched on London. William Crowmer, a Sheriff of Kent and Lord Saye's son-in-law, was beheaded at Mile End. Cade then returned to the Standard in Cornhill to supervise Lord Saye's execution. Saye's body, stripped naked, was tied to a horse's tail and dragged across London Bridge to St Thomas's Hospital in Southwark. Saye's and Crowmer's heads were set on London Bridge.[48]

After experiencing two days of the wide gulf between Cade's words and his actions the citizens of London had had enough. Even those who sympathised with Cade initially began to wonder where it would all end, and on 5 July London rallied to its own defence. Matthew Gough had come home from Cherbourg at about the same time as Jack Cade appeared in England and he was with Lord Scales in the Tower. Together they assembled a force to prevent Cade re-entering the City from his base in Southwark. But Cade had spies everywhere. He hastily recalled those of his followers who were pillaging south of the Thames and prepared to assault London. By evening he was ready, but the Londoners held London Bridge. The clash of arms was long and bloody, and it was not until early the following morning that the Battle of the Bridge, as it came to be known, was over. The dead were

Aftermath

strewn along its length, and among them was the valiant Matthew Gough. Cade failed to force his way into the City and his last act was to set fire to the drawbridge to cover his retreat.[49]

The Mayor and aldermen were of one mind. There had been enough bloodshed and it was high time to restore order. Chancellor Kemp, Archbishop Stafford, and the Bishop of Winchester bravely met Jack Cade at St Margaret's Church in Southwark. Kemp offered Cade (as John Mortimer) a pardon if he and his followers would retire peacefully to their homes. Extensive pardon rolls were drawn up with 'John Mortimer' heading the list and a general pardon was offered at the request of the Queen.[50] King Henry had left Margaret at Greenwich and Kemp turned to her as the only readily available source of royal authority. Margaret endorsed the pardon to quell the revolt and restore the King's subjects to their allegiance.

Cade had his booty loaded onto a barge and taken down to Rochester while he rode for the coast, leaving his followers to fend for themselves. Most of them made their way home but a few rallied and prepared to continue the fight. The centre of disturbance moved from London to Rochester in Cade's wake. Cade's only thought was for his own safety. He tried to gain entrance to Queenborough Castle, a favourite haunt of pirates, where he could arrange for a ship to take him and his loot out of the country. He hoped to find an ally in its constable, Roger Chamberlain, one of the Duke of Gloucester's servants who had been arrested in the aftermath of Gloucester's death and reprieved only at the foot of the gallows. But Chamberlain proved loyal. He barred the gates of the castle and Cade was forced to turn back towards Maidstone.[51]

Chancellor Kemp either knew all along that Cade was using an assumed name, or an informer made it known to him. He declared Cade's pardon invalid because it was issued in a false name and a bounty of 1,000 marks was set on Cade's head.[52] A lesser sum was set on the heads of his followers who had not dispersed as stipulated by their pardons. The hunt for Cade was up in earnest. He was cornered at Heathfield in Sussex by a small band of men led by Alexander Iden.[53] Cade put up a desperate fight, but he was badly wounded, and he died before nightfall. His body was carried to London in a cart, to be hanged, drawn, and quartered and his head set on London Bridge.

Chancellor Kemp began the mopping-up process centred on the town of Rochester. He sent two commissioners to impound Cade's booty and they recovered an impressive haul, including large quantities of silverware, precious stones, a gold salver embossed with a sapphire and pearls, gold cups, and a considerable sum of money.[54] Had Cade managed to escape, he would have lived comfortably ever after.

Among Cade's followers arrested at Rochester was one John Payn. In a letter to John Paston written in 1465, some fifteen years after the rebellion, Payn claimed that the Bishop of Rochester had denounced him to the Queen and that she had him thrown into prison. His story was that he had been in Sir John Fastolf's service and had taken part in Cade's rebellion against his will. Paston was the executor of Fastolf's estate and Payn was begging for a hand-out; he painted a pathetic picture of his sufferings: Fastolf had sent him to Blackheath to obtain a copy of Cade's petition, but Cade threatened to have him beheaded and he was only saved by the intervention of Cade's lieutenant, Robert Poynings who, incidentally, was John Paston's brother-in-law. Poynings was safely dead in 1465.

Cade had forced Payn to swear an oath of loyalty to him as Captain of Kent before allowing him to take a copy of the petition back to Fastolf. Subsequently, at Cade's headquarters in the White Hart Inn, Payn was stripped of his costly military harness and valuable items were stolen from a chest in his quarters. The rebels had forced Payn to join a raiding party into Kent or lose his head. His home in Kent had been despoiled, his wife and five children were threatened, and his wife was left with nothing but the clothes she stood up in. Payn claimed that he had taken part in the Battle of the Bridge under duress. He had been severely wounded but had managed to make his

Aftermath

way to Rochester. He was apprehended and sent to the Marshalsea where he was questioned about Fastolf. Although he strenuously denied that Fastolf had anything to do with the rebels, he was sent to Westminster for further questioning and only released thanks to the good offices of his wife and a cousin in royal service, who obtained the King's pardon. After that he never prospered.

Edward IV was on the throne and Margaret was in exile in 1465, making her an easy target for Payn's attempt to enlist sympathy for 'wrongs' done to him in 1450.[55] Payn's allegation that he was interrogated because the authorities suspected Sir John Fastolf of being implicated in Cade's rebellion is, quite simply, a pack of lies. Fastolf was with Lord Scales defending the Tower against the rebels, and he attended the Council meeting on 18 July when a warrant was issued to pay the expenses of Chancellor Kemp's commissioners.[56] How much of the rest of Payn's story is true is open to question.

Margaret lent her authority to the arrests at Rochester, but it is impossible to believe that the Bishop of Rochester, or Margaret, singled out Payn for special treatment. Margaret would never have heard of him. If he was arrested it was as one of a group, probably a large group, of other men. But Payn's accusation that Margaret was responsible for his arrest has been generally accepted since it adds very conveniently to the legend of the implacable foreign queen. In general, Margaret preferred pardon to punishment. In May 1451 she sued to the King to pardon one John Eve, a Franciscan friar, when he was accused of complicity in Cade's rebellion.[57]

12

Somerset or York

The Duke of Somerset was holed up in Caen. He had several thousand men under his command but the French armies surrounding the city far outnumbered anything he could muster, and he had no idea what to do. Dunois's heavy artillery again unnerved him, and after three weeks of bombardment he abandoned Caen without offering battle. In an embarrassing little ceremony, the King's Lieutenant in France surrendered the keys of Caen to Arthur de Richemont, the Constable of France, and Richemont escorted Somerset and his family to the ships waiting to take them to Calais. The garrison marched out on 1 July 1450, leaving their artillery behind, and Dunois took possession of the city. King Charles entered Caen a week later accompanied by the Angevins.[1] The great port of Cherbourg capitulated in August and with its surrender Normandy was lost. The King of England had taken six months to raise an army only to have it defeated. The King of France took twelve months to recover the whole of the Duchy of Normandy.

King Henry had returned to London at the end of July when the news of Cade's death reassured him that it was safe to do so. The Mayor and aldermen received him, and he attended a thanksgiving ceremony at St Pauls. The Londoners were more inclined to give thanks for their deliverance from the anarchy of Cade's rebellion than for the King's presence in their midst. Somerset arrived from Calais four days later. King Henry was unperturbed that his father's duchy had been overrun and he welcomed the man who had lost it. The bitter truth was that Henry did not want Normandy if he had to fight for it. Margaret's reaction is not known. Normandy had been conquered by Henry V within living memory and Margaret had been brought up to think of it as French. She may have shared her husband's sentiments, but if she did, she paid a heavy price. King Charles's triumph shattered the peace that her marriage was supposed to guarantee.

Somerset's charm did not fail him; he quickly filled the void left in Henry's life by Suffolk's death. Although Somerset never achieved the dominance enjoyed by Suffolk, Henry's favour meant that the royal household looked to him for leadership. Margaret acknowledged the new power in the land. She granted Somerset an annuity of 100 marks for his services and to secure his influence, but he and Duchess Eleanor did not become her friends as Suffolk and Alice had been, and she did not shower Somerset with gifts as she had Suffolk.[2]

Cade was dead, but the unrest remained. Word reached England in September that the Duke of York was on his way home from Ireland. York's chamberlain Sir William Oldhall may have crossed to Ireland to report the groundswell of opinion in York's favour during Cade's rebellion, which Oldhall had helped to manufacture. York did not instigate the Kentish uprising, but he knew a good deal more about it than he ever let on. York had expected to be recalled following Suffolk's disgrace, since the King would need a new chief minister and he was the obvious candidate, but the call had not come. His administration in Ireland was hampered by a lack of money and York wrote to his brother-in-law, the Earl of Salisbury, that he did not have the resources to suppress a rising in Meath and unless he received immediate relief he would resign and come home. He would not have it said that Ireland had been lost by his negligence, a snide reference to Somerset's failure in Normandy.[3]

King Henry was apprehensive. He knew York was coming but not why. Sir William Beauchamp, the constable of Beaumaris Castle, refused to admit York and Beauchamp's deputy told him that the order to prevent his landing came from the royal household, and so by implication from King Henry. York believed that Sir Thomas Stanley, the Justiciar of North Wales, was behind it.[4] York landed at Denbigh and pressed on to his castle at Ludlow. Here he received a visit from Lord Dudley and Reginald Boulers, the Bishop-elect of Hereford, who came out of a mixture of respect and curiosity to ascertain what York had in mind and to warn him that his sudden arrival had alarmed the court. Dudley and Boulers were too closely associated with Suffolk's regime for York's liking and he cold-shouldered them.[5]

York continued south, arrayed in eye-catching red velvet and escorted by a large retinue.[6] Lord Welles and Sir John Talbot monitored his movements. If their paths crossed, they could offer York a valid reason for seeking him out. Lord Welles as a former lieutenant of Ireland and Talbot as its absentee chancellor wanted the latest news from that troubled land.[7] York summoned William Tresham, the Speaker of the Commons, to meet him at Stony Stratford. If anyone could accurately assess the mood of the country it would be the Speaker, and York was anxious to know what support he might receive when he reached London. Tresham was understandably nervous. He had no idea what York wanted, but a summons from Richard of York could not be ignored and he set out ostentatiously wearing the Lancastrian collar of esses, accompanied by his son Thomas and a few servants. Tresham was ambushed and murdered before he reached Stony Stratford, and his son was wounded in the affray.[8]

York's arrival in London on Michaelmas Eve coincided with the annual change in the City's authorities when the sheriffs handed the keys of the City's prisons to the Mayor, to be entrusted to the sheriffs elect. The City officials were distracted by their official duties and the excitement caused by York's arrival led to a riot in Newgate. Newgate prison housed men (and women) accused of serious crimes, as well as general troublemakers. Hardened criminals were shut away in windowless basement cells, but the less serious offenders, and those who could afford to pay, had more agreeable accommodation and

Somerset or York

were allowed to walk on Newgate's flat roof for recreation.[9] Alexander Manning, the keeper of Newgate, unwisely allowed too many of his charges to leave their cells; they stormed up onto the roof and showered down stones and other missiles onto citizens in the streets below. It took the Mayor, his officers, and the sheriffs who were responsible for any prison escapes four hours of concerted effort to bring the prison under control.

Blame fell on the luckless Alexander Manning; he was imprisoned in his own gaol, dismissed from his post, and censured for 'his negligent custody of the prisoners.'[10] Manning was brought up before Mayor Nicholas Wyfold only a week after a company of armed soldiers had disrupted Wyfold's inaugural ride through the City. Wyfold was determined to take a firm stance against unrest and he expounded on Manning's 'manifold defaults' as a gaoler, and he decreed that as Manning was unable to maintain order in the prison he was not to be reinstated.

Manning appealed to his kinsman, Thomas Manning, one of King Henry's chaplains, and Thomas petitioned Margaret to intervene. The position of keeper of Newgate was in the gift of the incoming sheriffs, and Margaret asked them to reconsider Manning's dismissal, but the sheriffs, uncertain of what they should do, did not respond. Margaret wrote to them again expressing surprise that they had not acknowledged her request. A year later she urged Mayor Wyfold to instruct the new sheriffs to favour Manning, and she wrote to the sheriffs themselves, describing Manning as an experienced keeper and a sober and reliable man.[11] Nothing more is known of the fate of Alexander Manning except that he was not reinstated. In her early years as Queen, Margaret's influence was negligible.

The Duke of York had sought an audience with King Henry as soon as he reached London. He reported his hostile reception at Beaumaris and complained that men had been sent to spy on him. He averred that he had been traduced by rumours 'whiche should sounde to my dishonour', and that malicious and lying persons had advocated laying charges of treason against him, to 'undoe me, myn issue and corrupt my blode.' Jack Cade's use of the name Mortimer spelled potential disaster for York; York's father, the Earl of Cambridge, had been executed by Henry V in 1415 for complicity in a plot to put a Mortimer on the throne. As the Mortimer heir, York had a concomitant claim to the crown. If he were linked with Cade's rebellion, however tenuously, he could be appealed of treason and his attainder would, among other things, wipe out the crown's considerable debt to him. He was afraid that King Henry would allow him to be impeached on hearsay evidence as the Duke of Gloucester had been and he demanded that the King should bring whatever evidence there was into the open, for he would not let matters rest until his name had been cleared. York was thirty-nine years old and at a crossroads in his career. He tended to see conspiracies where none existed, and his suspicions were inflamed by exaggerated reports of the court's antipathy to him.

King Henry's response to York's invective was conciliatory. He said gently that ever since the beginning of the year there had been rumours that York planned to return from Ireland with an army at his back and he himself had been threatened with what would happen when York reached England, so was it any wonder that his officers had been alarmed by York's sudden arrival? If they had overreacted it was the Duke's fault for coming home without permission. Henry threw the onus of proof back onto York, he said that he knew of no attempt to have York indicted for treason but if York could name those responsible, they would fall under his severe displeasure. Henry ended the interview by declaring, with less-than-perfect truth, that he had never doubted his well-beloved cousin's loyalty and fidelity.

York next addressed a stinging criticism to 'the trewe lordes of the kinges counsele'. He lamented that Henry's magnates, especially those of royal blood, had been shamed and undermined because powers which should have been vested in men of high birth had fallen into the hands of low born carls. The 'glorious' realm of France, the 'commodious' Duchy of Normandy, and the 'defensible' Duchies of Anjou and Maine had been lost. York urged the Council not to allow this dishonourable state of affairs to continue. He accused the men around the King of greed and corruption and said that if the Council wished to retain the respect of the people, they should commission 'honorable knightes and juges' to arrest the guilty parties. York offered to do the job himself: he would apprehend and imprison anyone accused of malpractice regardless of their status or influence. In effect, York was threatening those closest to the King and it was a colossal mistake. He would have been wiser to placate the royal household, since their influence with King Henry was far greater than his could ever be. York's officiousness caused them to close ranks and rally around the Duke of Somerset.

Henry's reply to York was a master stroke. In a stunning about-face he thanked York for his offer but declared it to be superfluous. He said he did not intend to be advised by any one man or even a small group of councillors. Instead he would establish a broadly based Council under the leadership of Chancellor Kemp to deal with all matters of state and all decisions would be made on their authority.[12] Henry reportedly told York, 'When need demands or necessity compels we will invoke your aid.'[13] It was a comprehensive dismissal.

Henry's politically astute response was not his alone. York's bid for power was checkmated by Chancellor Kemp, who was not the man to stand aside while York usurped the King's authority. Kemp was stern, unbending, autocratic, often irascible, with a strong sense of his own importance, but he was a loyal servant of the crown. Kemp was not afraid of York and if York expected support from a council under Kemp's influence he was sadly out of touch. York's heavy-handed approach also alarmed some of his peers. York's predicament was as simple as it was insurmountable: King Henry did not like him, and he was not welcome at court.

York cast around for allies outside the court and found one in the erratic, violent, and self-interested John Mowbray, Duke of Norfolk.

Mowbray was fortunate to hold his title at all. His grandfather, Thomas Mowbray, Earl of Nottingham, became Duke of Norfolk under Richard II, but he fell out of favour and lost the dukedom. His elder son, another Thomas, was executed for treason by Henry IV and the Mowbray fortunes were only restored by his younger son, John, who recovered the dukedom through loyal support of Henry V. But John died suddenly in 1432 while his son, another John, was still a minor and the dispositions in his will had unfortunate consequences: in addition to her dower he left a life interest in his estates to his wife. Born Katherine Neville, she was every bit as acquisitive as any member of her acquisitive family and what she had she kept.[14] The young John Mowbray never had the same financial resources as the Dukes of York and Buckingham, and his pride was wounded when King Henry created John Beaufort Duke of Somerset in 1443 and gave him precedence over the Dukes of Norfolk. The Mowbrays were Earl Marshalls of England and their titles long predated those of the upstart Beauforts.

Norfolk had fiercely resented the Duke of Suffolk's hegemony in East Anglia and after Suffolk's death he issued a public proclamation declaring open season on Suffolk's affinity and he enjoined anyone with a complaint against them to come forward. Norfolk headed the oyer and terminer commission that brought exaggerated charges against Suffolk's henchman, Sir Thomas Tuddenham. They encompassed every crime in the book except treason but including murder.[15] Norfolk announced that he and he alone would wield power in what had been Suffolk's stronghold: 'we lete yow wete that nexst the Kynge our soverayn Lord, we woll have the princypall rewele and governance throwh all this schir, of whishe we ber our name whyls that we be lyvynge.'[16]

Norfolk's propensity for acquiring property by violent means had brought him to Margaret's attention. Sir Robert Wingfield had been one of Norfolk's staunchest adherents until Norfolk sent armed retainers to take possession of the manor of Hoo that Norfolk's father had granted to Wingfield. Wingfield reacted by seeking the protection of another 'good lord'. He transferred his allegiance to Suffolk and accompanied Suffolk to welcome Margaret in Rouen. In 1447 Norfolk resumed his feud with Wingfield; he had Wingfield's son imprisoned, claiming that the young Robert had threatened the Duke's chaplain. Wingfield sent retainers to rescue Robert and within three hours they had set him free. Norfolk appealed to King Henry to prohibit the young man from coming within seven miles of the ducal seat at Framlingham, but Norfolk alleged that the Wingfields defied the ban. They had raided Mowbray lands and perpetrated a series of outrages that included theft, assault, and poaching. Wingfield ended up before King's Bench but he had friends at court, including the Queen, and he was pardoned in 1448.[17] Norfolk then sent his retainers to pillage Wingfield's house at Letheringham, which earned him a short spell in the Tower.[18] Wingfield appealed to Margaret for help to end the feud and she requested Norfolk to meet with Wingfield and his sons to settle their differences; Norfolk took no notice.[19] Wingfield was too old to continue the struggle. He made his will in 1452 and died in 1454.[20]

Norfolk's antipathy to the court made him a natural ally for the Duke of York and they met in October to select suitable candidates for the upcoming Parliament.[21] It met at Westminster on 6 November 1450 and the Commons elected York's chamberlain, Sir William Oldhall, as their Speaker, even though Oldhall had never stood for Parliament before.[22] York was an excellent self-publicist and he made sure that his version of the reasons for his return from Ireland were widely disseminated. They included a claim that he had been banished to Ireland by Suffolk but recalled by the Commons! According to gossip current in London 'the king gave him all power in parliament and everything he does has the Lord King's agreement.'[23] Reinventing the truth was typical of Richard of York.

York's banner of the fetterlock was prominently displayed in various public places. It was torn down and the royal arms substituted, but the fetterlock reappeared. The Mayor anticipated trouble and the City officials were put on high alert; chains were drawn across the streets to impede rioters or men on horseback. York rode into London two weeks after Parliament assembled with his sword carried before him. The Duke of Norfolk arrived a day later with his rowdy followers blowing trumpets to announce the presence of the Earl Marshall of England.[24]

The Commons blamed Suffolk for engineering the estrangement between King Henry and the 'grete Lordes to you right nygh', a clear reference to the Duke of York.[25] On 30 November a carefully co-ordinated but apparently spontaneous demonstration in Westminster Hall was staged by York and Norfolk's retainers and disgruntled soldiers from Normandy. They raised a great shout against the traitors who had sold Normandy to the enemy. It was an unnerving moment for King Henry and for Somerset, but worse was to follow. The retainers and the soldiery went on the rampage and ransacked Somerset's lodging at the Black Friars. According to some reports they even threatened to kill the Duke, but Somerset escaped to the safety of the Tower thanks to the prompt intervention of the Mayor and city officers, who got him away by barge.[26] York's tenants ransacked Somerset's principal seat at Corfe Castle.[27] Lord Hoo, the former Chancellor of Normandy, was widely believed to be responsible for failing to pay the soldiers' wages, an accusation that had once been levelled at York equally without foundation.[28] Hoo's house was plundered and the lodgings of Suffolk's henchman, Sir Thomas Tuddenham, was broken into.[29]

As the self-proclaimed champion of law and order York could not allow these disorders to get out of hand. They had served his purpose, but he had to rein them in. He had one man hanged as a warning to others and he and his officers rode through the City to proclaim that the same fate awaited anyone who robbed, pillaged, or destroyed property.[30] Disorder in London always made King Henry nervous and he convened an oyer and terminer commission at the Guildhall to try malefactors. The Londoners were treated to the unique and impressive spectacle of their peace-loving King riding through the City arrayed as if for war. The Duke of Norfolk headed the cavalcade and the Duke of York rode beside the King in an impressive show of armed might, but one chronicler lamented that it was a pity they had not ridden thus into Normandy.[31] York had overawed King Henry for the moment but Somerset did not remain in the Tower for long; he was back in his lodging at Blackfriars by Christmas while York took up residence at Stratford-at-Bow to contemplate his next move.[32]

While York was trying to intimidate the King and take over the government, King Charles was threatening the Duchy of Gascony. Even before he had completed the recovery of Normandy King Charles had begun to probe weak spots in Gascony. Gaston of Foix, his lieutenant in the south-west, had captured the castle of Mauléon on the border with Navarre at the end of 1449.[33] King Henry had neglected Gascony for years. Apart from a brief flurry over his proposed marriage with a daughter of the Count of Armagnac in 1442, Henry had never shown any interest in Gascony. The duchy's last seneschal, William Bonville, left Bordeaux for Rouen in 1445 to welcome Margaret and did not return to Gascony. Sir Edward Hull, the Constable of Bordeaux, became one of Margaret's knights of the body and remained at court in England.

Two French armies marched into Gascony in October 1450 and carried out a swift campaign. The castles of Bergerac and Bazas surrendered, opening the road to Bordeaux. Bordeaux's mayor courageously raised a force of untrained Gascons, reinforced by some English men-at-arms, but his ill-equipped troops were defeated in what the Bordelais called *La Male Journade*.[34] Winter was closing in, the French did not follow up their victory, and Bordeaux was spared for the moment.

The Council decided to get rid of the unemployed soldiers infesting London and the south coast ports by sending them to defend Gascony. Their choice to lead the expedition fell on Sir Richard Woodville. King

Power Struggle

Henry had created him a Knight of the Garter for his services during Cade's rebellion. His military background and relative affluence thanks to his wife's dower made him the ideal candidate. Woodville had served in Normandy under the Regent Bedford and a year after Bedford's death he married Bedford's young widow. It was a mésalliance comparable to that of Queen Katherine and Owen Tudor, for Jacquetta was the daughter of Peter of Luxembourg, Count of St Pol, while Woodville was only a knight, but he was handsome and reputed to be best jouster in England. The chronicler Waurin, while deploring the inequality of the marriage, described Woodville as *moult bel chevalier et bien forme de tous membres*.[35] (The most handsome knight in form and features.) The couple were fined £1,000 for their clandestine marriage, but it was a love match.[36] Jacquetta bore her husband at least fifteen children, thirteen of whom survived. Woodville indented to serve as Seneschal of Gascony with 300 men-at-arms and 2,700 archers, but the Council's initial optimism that he could be dispatched immediately faded in the face of reality.[37] Loans would have to be raised and the campaign was postponed to 1451.[38]

Parliament reassembled in January just as alarming news reached the capital: a second Cade's rebellion was in the making. One Stephen Christmas had warned Kentishmen that the King was so angry with them that he intended to unleash wild 'northern' men from the Duchy of Lancaster on the hapless county, echoing the rumour that had sparked Cade's rebellion. Christmas urged them to join him and band together for mutual protection. He was not just another rabble-rouser but a man of substance whose name was known in court circles. Ominously he had accompanied York to Ireland in 1449. King Henry had entrusted York with an oyer and terminer commission to investigate misdeeds in Kent and Sussex but York had not set foot in either county.[39] His failure to execute his commission aroused a suspicion at court that he was not ignorant of Christmas's actions and it reinforced Henry's belief that York was not to be trusted.

Somerset or York

The shadow of Cade brooded darkly over King Henry. For the first time he accompanied his magnates and judges on a judicial progress to try rebels and repress rebellion.[40] Hearings took place in Canterbury, Rochester, and Faversham. Stephen Christmas was hauled before the court at Rochester on 17 February and a blacksmith calling himself the 'Second Captain of Kent' was apprehended. About thirty men were condemned to be hanged; some were granted Christian burial, but others had their heads set on London Bridge as a reminder to the volatile populace that rebellion reaped retribution. Well might one chronicler describe this period as 'a harvest of heads'.[41] Such harsh penalties might be necessary, but they distressed King Henry; he did not enjoy seeing his people suffer and he offered pardons whenever he could.[42]

Henry returned to Westminster to deal with unfinished parliamentary business. He conciliated the Commons by assenting to their petition for a second Act of Resumption. They complained that the previous act did not amount to anything approaching the King's needs because he had added too many exemptions. Henry passed the act with only forty-three exemptions, few of them in favour of individuals.[43] The Commons had also petitioned that twenty-eight men and one woman who had a pernicious influence over the King should forfeit their crown offices and be banished from court for life. If they came within twelve miles of the King their personal property should be confiscated. Alice, Duchess of Suffolk, and Edmund, Duke of Somerset, headed the list. The Commons had demanded that the de la Pole lands be forfeited and the family disinherited. King Henry put the custody of Suffolk's lands into the keeping of Lord Scales and Sir Miles Stapleton to safeguard the inheritance until John de la Pole should come of age.[44] But he rejected the banishment petition, declaring that he did not understand why it had been made.

He promised to dismiss some members of his household but for one year only and he added that in an emergency he would exercise his right to summon any of his subjects at any time.[45] Despite the Duke of York's best efforts, Somerset remained at the King's side. If York, acting through the Commons, had been able to force Henry to accept the banishment petition it would have ended Somerset's career in England before it began. York's besetting sin was to overreach himself and by demanding too much he gained too little. Only the King could decide who might or might not attend on him.

Margaret's household was only peripherally affected. Her Chancellor, William Booth, Bishop of Coventry and Lichfield, had steadily acquired an assortment of benefices and used their income to buy land.[46] Scurrilous anticlerical verses accused Booth of simony, usury, covetousness, and pride. In a pun on Booth's name he was told:

'Thow hast getyne gret goode, thou wost welle how.

By symoni and usure bilde is thy bothe.'[47]

Booth retired to his diocese and Margaret quietly replaced him with his half-brother Lawrence Booth, an equally able administrator. Sir Edmund Hampden, Margaret's knight of the body, was also a feoffee for the Duchess of Suffolk's lands in Oxfordshire,[48] and his wife, Lady Anne Moleyns, was one of Margaret's ladies.[49] Margaret retained him. Sir Robert Wingfield's inclusion in the banishment petition had less to do with his services to the Queen than to York's wish to gratify the Duke of Norfolk.

When Parliament reassembled for its final session in May 1451 the Duke of York made a last bid to establish his right to a place in government. His attorney, Thomas Young, the long serving MP for Bristol, raised a question that had loomed large ever since the Duke of Gloucester's death. Who was the legitimate heir to the throne? Henry and Margaret had been married for six years and there were mutterings about her childlessness. A farm labourer was imprisoned in 1448 for claiming that she was barren: 'Oure Quene was none abyl to be Quene of Inglond because that sche bereth no child, and because that we have no pryns in this land.'[50] Young petitioned that for the security of the realm until such time as the King had a son, the Duke of York should be named as Henry's heir presumptive.[51]

Somerset or York

York had a strong, but not exclusive claim. He was the grandson of King Edward III's fifth son, Edmund, Duke of York and he was descended through the female line from Lionel, Duke of Clarence, King Edward's second son. The Lancastrian line descended from King Edward's third son, John of Gaunt. King Henry's closest male relative was Henry Holand, Duke of Exeter, the grandson of Gaunt's daughter, Elizabeth. And then there were the Beauforts, Gaunt's sons by his mistress, whom he later married. Richard II legitimated them but after their half-brother seized the crown as Henry IV, the first Lancastrian king, he excluded them from the succession. There was nothing to prevent King Henry revoking his grandfather's letters patent and making a Beaufort his heir presumptive. Margaret Beaufort, the only child of the late John, Duke of Somerset, was the direct Beaufort heir and she could carry her claim to any son she might have. But John's brother, Edmund Beaufort, Duke of Somerset, was the only adult male in the Beaufort line and he might be preferred. King Henry never showed any inclination to name a Beaufort as his heir, but the possibility worried York –Edmund was the King's favourite.

King Henry's reaction to Thomas Young's petition left no one in any doubt that he found it intolerable. He dissolved Parliament and sent the impertinent member to the Tower. The Duke of York had gambled and lost. Margaret did not relish having her childlessness ruthlessly publicised, but she did not hold it against York; they remained on good terms and exchanged gifts at New Year.[52] Margaret was an Angevin princess – She recognised York's Plantagenet lineage as exalted as her own. She hoped to give England an heir but failing that, she may have preferred a Plantagenet rather than a legitimated Beaufort to inherit the throne.

13

Strife

King Henry and his magnates spent the summer of 1451 riding about the southern counties on oyer and terminer commissions to seek out suspected rebels. The severity of his earlier judicial progresses had stirred up resentment and fear and a series of uprisings had spread through Kent and Sussex. The wildest rumours passed from village to village; it was bruited that the King was so intent on punishing Kentishmen that he was prepared to ask the King of France for assistance.[1]

Sir Richard Woodville's expeditionary force had still not mustered. Henry had authorised him to pawn the royal jewel 'the George' to the canons of Exeter Cathedral for £1,000 to raise money but other than that he took no interest in Woodville's campaign.[2] As early as March the Council had demanded how many ships had been requisitioned and for how long. A date for Woodville's muster had been set for the beginning of April only to be postponed to the end of May and then to the middle of June.[3] In the meanwhile the Duchy of Gascony was being lost.[4]

Dunois, the hero of the re-conquest of Normandy, had sailed into the Gironde and laid siege to the fortress of Blaye. The Garonne was blockaded by a fleet of French and Spanish ships about equal in number to those lying idle at Plymouth. Blaye and then Bourg, only twenty miles north of Bordeaux, capitulated. The castle at Fronsac lying between Bourg and Bordeaux was believed to be impregnable, but its defences were in bad repair and it was under-equipped and under-manned. On 5 June its captain, Sir John Strangeways, agreed to surrender if relief from England did not reach him within ten days. If Fronsac fell the citizens of Bordeaux faced a stark choice: they could hold out and risk a sack or they could protect their city and its essential vineyards by surrendering before a formal siege was laid.

Dunois offered them generous terms: King Charles would confirm all land grants to incumbent land holders, and no one would be dispossessed, which further undermined Bordelais loyalty to the English. Any man electing to retain his English allegiance would be free to leave the duchy, but his estates would be parcelled out among French loyalists. Dunois chivalrously extended the deadline for Fronsac's relief. He agreed that if no English army appeared before Bordeaux by St John's day, 24 June 1451, the city would surrender, and English Gascony would become French. Needless to say, no English army appeared.[5] Dunois made his triumphal entry into Bordeaux at the end of June with all the pageantry that had marked King Charles's entry into Rouen. Dressed all in white, Dunois proudly displayed the banner of the fleur de lys; a richly caparisoned horse carried a casket containing King Charles's royal seal.[6] Pey Berland, the Archbishop of Bordeaux, took the oath of allegiance to King Charles under duress but he remained an Anglophile and resigned his bishopric in 1456.

News of the fall of Bordeaux shocked the English Council into a totally unrealistic response and they allocated over £29,000 to Woodville for his wages and expenses. The Exchequer could not possibly meet such a commitment and the money was assigned on taxes that were yet to come in.[7] Woodville's final muster was set for 9 August. Bayonne was the only city left in English hands and the Council ordered the Mayor and sheriffs of Bristol to arrest ships to transport Sir John Astley, the Mayor of Bayonne, and a contingent of men-at-arms and archers to Gascony 'with all speed'.[8] It was too late. Bayonne surrendered to Dunois on 20 August. Its capitulation was marked by an augury so beloved of the medieval mind. An extraordinary cloud formation of a white cross standing out dramatically in the centre of a dark thunder cloud hovered above the town for over an hour.

Woodville never left England. Bayonne fell, and the whole costly exercise of raising an army to defend Gascony was abandoned. Lack of money was the major factor, but the crux of the matter was lack of will. The possibility that King Henry now in his thirtieth year might take command was never even considered. No magnate offered his services. Where the King would not lead the lords would not follow. Somerset was consolidating his position with King Henry and the royal household and York had concentrated his energies on manipulating Parliament to outmanoeuvre Somerset.

The loss of Gascony intensified English fears for the safety of Calais and a rumour that Calais was King Charles's next objective worried Duke Philip of Burgundy. Relations between the King of France and his most powerful vassal were never cordial and King Charles in possession of Calais would threaten Burgundian security. Philip did not trust Charles any more than Charles trusted him and on balance he preferred Calais to remain in English hands. He wrote to King Henry to suggest that now was the time for Charles and Henry to make peace and join him in the crusade that the Pope had been urging on all Christian princes for years. Henry was stung by Burgundy's letter and for once he stood firm. He had not forgotten the last time Duke Philip offered to act as a peace broker, at Arras in 1435, when Philip deserted his alliance with England. Henry replied that it was impossible for him to make peace with the King of France who had broken the truce and it would be dishonourable to approach him so soon after the defeat in Gascony. In any case this was only temporary; with God's blessing Henry intended to recover what had been lost.[9]

Henry appointed Somerset as Captain of Calais, which may not have been wholly welcomed by its recipient,[10] and to everyone's surprise he announced that he would accompany an army into France.[11] The royal promise was widely believed. Osbert Mundford

Strife

was with the Calais garrison and during his absence the lawless courtier Thomas Daniel had seized Mundford's manor of Braydeston. The only hope of recovering it was for Mundford to return to England, but he wrote to John Paston refusing to come home because a French attack on Calais was expected to coincide with King Henry's arrival and he would not desert his post at so critical a time.[12]

Calais had distracted King Henry and the Council from war of a different kind that had flared up in the West Country. A feud between the disgruntled Thomas Courtenay, Earl of Devon, and William Bonville had been smouldering for years.[13] The Courtenay Earls of Devon had been the leading magnates in the south-west for generations but although Courtenay had been granted livery of his lands in 1435, he had little to offer in the way of local patronage. His mother retained her dower lands and other Courtenay estates until her death in 1441 while Bonville enhanced his local standing by marrying Courtenay's aunt, and Courtenay fiercely resented Bonville's growing wealth and influence.

Courtenay was Steward of England for Margaret's coronation and this had emboldened him to lay claim to precedence over William Fitzalan, the Earl of Arundel.[14] Precedence among the magnates was rigidly adhered to and jealously guarded.[15] The Lords in Parliament had deferred their decision in 1446, but in 1449 they dismissed Courtenay's claim and King Henry summoned William Bonville to Parliament as Lord Bonville in recognition of his services. Another threat to Courtenay's hegemony raised its ugly head when Henry created James Butler Earl of Wiltshire. It was an unusual honour since James's father, the Earl of Ormond, was still alive, but James's wife, Avice Stafford, held extensive estates in the West Country. James was one of Henry's favourite courtiers; he was only a year older than Henry and they had known each other since boyhood. James's father had sent him to join King Henry's coronation expedition to France in 1430 with his own 'retinue' of two men-at-arms and six archers.[16]

Courtenay found the elevation of Bonville and Butler intolerable and he sulked. He had a growing family and King Henry had done nothing for him, all the while rewarding his enemies. Courtenay's frustration boiled over in September 1451 and he found an ally in Edward Brook, Lord Cobham, who was also at odds with the Earl of Wiltshire. They raised an army from among their tenants and marched towards Wiltshire's estate at Lackham. Thomas Beckington, Bishop of Bath and Wells, and Dean Nicholas Caraunt, Margaret's secretary, courageously tried to persuade Courtenay to abandon his rash enterprise, but Courtenay scornfully rejected their overtures and said he would fight Wiltshire no matter what. He reached Lackham only to find that Wiltshire was not there. Baulked of his prey Courtenay turned his men loose on Wiltshire's lands, allowing them to pillage to their hearts' content. He then retreated to lay siege to his old enemy, Lord Bonville, in Taunton Castle.

King Henry and the Council did nothing to deter Courtenay, but the Duke of York was quick to exploit the situation. Three days after Courtenay laid siege to Taunton York arrived with a large retinue. He induced Courtenay to break off the siege and Bonville agreed to surrender the castle, but only to York.[17] Neither was so foolhardy as to risk a clash with Richard of York. The Duke defused an ugly situation, but it made King Henry angry. York had usurped the royal prerogative by going in force against the King's subjects and imposing a settlement without reference to the King. Henry summoned the participants to his presence, probably at Wallingford.[18] York and Courtenay failed to obey. Henry may have been relieved; he was reluctant to antagonise York by hauling him before the Council or accusing him of *lèse majesté*. The Duke of Somerset too preferred to avoid an open conflict with York, although he was not above playing on King Henry's mistrust.

In November, the Milanese ambassador at the Burgundian court informed his master that a French army, supported by a fleet of ships, was only waiting for clement spring weather to invest Calais. He also reported that King Henry would rather lose Calais than fight for it.[19]

Strife

Henry had ceded Maine, lost Normandy, and surrendered Gascony without any apparent regret or retaliation, so why would Calais be different? The Mayor of London imposed a levy on the City for an advance force to be sent to Calais under Gervase Clifton, the Treasurer of Calais.[20] Bordeaux's wine trade had been an economic asset but customs duties on wool at the staple in Calais were among the crown's most valuable resources and Calais's psychological value was priceless: it was the last vestige of English-held land in France, a symbol of English conquest and French humiliation. Margaret's attorney general, Robert Tanfield, loaned £720 towards foodstuffs.[21] Sir Richard Woodville was instructed to hold himself in readiness, but it was not until the end of 1451 that a loan from a wealthy London merchant, John Croke, enabled him to take reinforcements across the Channel.[22]

Henry called a Great Council to Coventry at the beginning of 1452 to discuss Calais. The Duke of York completely misread Henry's motivation and expected the worst. He had spent Christmas and New Year at Ludlow in one of his periodic quandaries, becoming more and more anxious at his estrangement from the King. Henry had made it clear that he did not recognise York as heir presumptive, giving York a cogent reason to fear Somerset's influence. Always prone to self-delusion, York cast Somerset in the role of the King's evil genius. He convinced himself that it was his duty to rescue Henry and save the country (as well as himself) from Somerset's pernicious influence. York's sense of self-righteousness never wavered. His enemies, now personified by Somerset, were the King's enemies and York considered he was justified morally and legally to take whatever action he saw fit.

Uncertainty and suspicion got the better of him and he issued a public statement declaring that he was being slandered by unnamed enemies who had poisoned King Henry's mind against him. York affirmed his loyalty in the strongest possible terms and he summoned the Earl of Shrewsbury and Reginald Boulers, Bishop of Hereford, to come to Ludlow and witness his oath on the sacraments that he was a 'trewe liege man to the king, my sovereigne lord, evur have bene and shalbe to my dyeng day.'[23] York undertook to repeat the oath in the presence of anyone Henry chose to send to him but for all its seeming submissiveness it was an arrogant stance: King Henry was to send mediators to the Duke; York did not offer to attend on King Henry in person.

Instead he launched a propaganda campaign against the government in general and Somerset in particular. He dispatched letter bills (the fifteenth-century equivalent of newspapers) to several towns calling on the King's subjects to support him and he appealed to English pride: while the King of England ruled France and Normandy Englishmen were renowned throughout Christendom, but through the cowardice of the pusillanimous Duke of Somerset everything that England had won was now lost. Somerset's baseness had encouraged the King's enemies to overrun Gascony, to threaten Calais, and even to plan an invasion of England. York claimed that he had left Ireland specifically to warn King Henry and advise him how best to proceed for his people's safety, but owing to the 'envy, malice and untruth' of Somerset, Henry had ignored his advice. York struck the note that was to become the theme of his opposition, he was constrained to act for the good of the realm and he had no choice but to remove Somerset, by force if need be, before England was ruined. York reiterated the accusations he had made in 1450: persons (now identified as Somerset) had 'laboured continually about the King's highness for my undoing, and to corrupt my blood and to disinherit me and my heirs.' York would 'proceed in all haste against them with the help of my kinsmen and friends.'[24] York's stance was disingenuous at best and verged on paranoia at worst. Somerset had never tried to have York impeached, imprisoned, or disinherited; it was not in his best interests to make a mortal enemy of Richard of York.

York put himself under arms. King Henry ordered the municipalities to ignore all communications from 'any person of what degree condition or astate that ever he be' unless they were issued

Strife

under the King's signet, and he instructed the Mayor of London not to receive York or allow him or his men to enter the City.[25] York came south confident that he could rouse the men of Kent as Jack Cade had done. He deluded himself that he represented the *vox populii* and was in a strong position to demand Somerset's imprisonment or exile, thus leaving the way open for reconciliation with King Henry and a reconstructed government with himself at its head. The first check to York's ambitious dream came when the Mayor of London, William Gregory, refused him entry to the City.[26] Kent did not rise, and the support York had so confidently anticipated failed to materialise. Only the Earl of Devon and Lord Cobham joined him, largely out of self-interest and a misplaced trust in York's authority. Devon thought he had found a powerful protector in York who would mend his family's fortunes.

York pulled back and crossed the Thames to Kingston where he waited for three days, expecting reinforcements and gathering news. King Henry reached London on 28 February and made straight for the safety of the Tower, but on the following day he was persuaded to move to the Bishop of Winchester's palace in Southwark since York's force was now south of the river. York established a fortified encampment with artillery at Dartford. The royal army halted about three miles away and York drew up his forces in battle array with himself in the centre and Devon and Cobham commanding the wings. York was prepared to fight but Henry was not, and nor were his magnates. They would not countenance anyone who came in arms against the King but the last thing they wanted was to engage England's premier peer in battle.[27]

Henry sent William Waynflete, Bishop of Winchester, York's relatives the Neville Earls of Salisbury and Warwick, and Thomas Bourgchier, Bishop of Ely, to reason with York.[28] They urged him not to wade any further into a morass of his own making and convinced him that his best bet was to accept Henry's promise to hear his complaints. The presence of so many lords in King Henry's camp gave

York pause; the military and political odds were against him. He agreed to submit to Henry's judgement, but he remained adamant that the Duke of Somerset must be dismissed, and he clung to his belief that the Council would acknowledge the justice of his demand.

On 3 March, York, Devon, and Cobham, with an escort of only forty men rode into the King's camp. Henry was seated in his pavilion with his lords, including the Duke of Somerset, grouped around him. York knelt to present his petition. He displayed an intimate knowledge of Somerset's administration in Normandy, as well he might since he had inside information. Despite being the King's Lieutenant in France, Somerset was not captain of Rouen. York was, *in absentia,* and York's lieutenant in Rouen had remained active on his behalf.[29]

York was convinced that Normandy had been lost by cowardice, even though he knew better than anyone that without adequate funds from England Normandy could not be held. He was sure that if he had been the King's Lieutenant he would not have handled relations with King Charles so ineptly or have surrendered to him so tamely. But York had left France without witnessing the build-up of Charles's formidable army and he was not disposed to make allowances for Somerset's difficulties. York alleged that Somerset had broken his oath to maintain the truce by fortifying disputed towns and that his culminating folly was to instigate the disastrous attack on Fougères, which induced King Charles to resume the war.[30] Somerset was a coward. He had negotiated with Charles to obtain a safe passage for himself and his family. He had behaved dishonourably by surrendering Rouen and Caen without a fight and by leaving the Earl of Shrewsbury as a hostage for the surrender of Norman towns that were not under attack. One wonders what Shrewsbury, who was standing behind the King, made of this.

York asserted that the appointment of Somerset as Captain of Calais had disheartened the garrison. Soldiers could not be expected to serve bravely under a defeated commander and Somerset would sell Calais as he had sold Normandy. Was the King aware that Somerset planned

Strife

to betray it to the Duke of Burgundy in return for the marriage of one of his daughters to Burgundy's son and heir?[31] This was York's interpretation of information supplied by one of his agents. Somerset had corresponded with Duke Philip, but it is equally possible that Burgundy was urging a reluctant Somerset to second his attempt to lure King Henry into a crusade.

In an unconvincing echo of the accusations that had been levelled against the Duke of Suffolk, York alluded to Somerset's avarice. He had received generous compensation for the surrender of Maine, yet he embezzled the money that should have been paid to dispossessed English landowners. He had over-taxed Normandy and then failed to pay his troops. York declared that the people of England hated Somerset for surrendering Normandy, and that this was the cause of widespread unrest. York ended by denouncing Somerset as a traitor and demanding that he be tried for treason under the laws of England.[32]

King Henry's councillors knew better. York had confronted the King in battle array and ignored a royal command to disband his force. This was treason. Fortunately for York no one wanted to carry the matter further and King Henry temporised.[33] He rejected York's petition, but he did not order York's arrest. He decreed that the dispute between York and Somerset was a private matter to be settled by arbitration and he ordered them to post bonds of £20,000 each to accept the arbitrators' judgement. If the arbitrators failed to agree, he would pass final judgement by midsummer.[34]

York got off lightly. He was escorted back to London and permitted to stay in his own residence at Baynard's Castle. His penance was to swear a heavy oath of allegiance to King Henry at St Pauls. Witnessed by the lords, the bishops, and a large congregation, York swore not to engage in any hostile act against King Henry, to resist anyone who might try to do so and never to summon armed men except by the King's express command. Should he break any part of his oath he would be 'disqualified from all worship, estate or dignity.'[35] York left

London for Ludlow, but he never forgot his humiliation until he broke his oath and became a forsworn man.

King Henry issued a general pardon, excluding those who were responsible for the murder of Adam Moleyns and William Aiscough, but including the Duke of York, the Earl of Devon, and all those who had supported York at Dartford. It was a magnanimous gesture but also a lucrative one: pardons had to be paid for. Henry then returned his attention to the defence of Calais and reiterated his promise to go in person, although he entrusted overall command to the Earl of Shrewsbury. He instructed Lord Clifford to assemble ships and men in the north to join the royal flagship the *Grace Dieu* and the rest of the fleet at Sandwich.[36] Preparations then stalled. Word reached England, probably in April, that Pope Nicholas's emissary, Cardinal d'Estouteville, had arrived at the French court to pressure King Charles into making peace with England.[37] Charles would not attack Calais while the papal envoy was in Paris on a peace mission; it would only invite papal condemnation and in any case Charles had other plans. He had deliberately confused the Milanese ambassador (and the English) by letting them think that he intended to attack Calais when he was in fact preparing for military intervention in Italy.[38] The crisis passed, the ships did not sail, King Henry did not leave England, and no more was heard of his promise to accompany his forces into France.

The Duke of Somerset remained uneasy. He had been exonerated, but the threat from York remained. Somerset convinced Henry that further action was necessary to enforce royal authority and punish malefactors. In July 1452 Henry commissioned thirteen lords and six justices to accompany him on progress into the West Country.[39] They went by way of Exeter and the civic dignitaries gave Henry a warm welcome to assure him of their loyalty. The Mayor presented him with a gift of £50 and Henry honoured Lord Bonville with a visit to Bonville's manor at Shute.[40]

The royal entourage crossed the Severn at Gloucester on 3 August and proceeded into Shropshire. Henry's ultimate destination was York's town of Ludlow. The Duke of York and Duchess Cecily, who was expecting her twelfth child, left Ludlow for Fotheringhay. James Butler, Earl of Wiltshire, went ahead to set up show trials to demonstrate that King Henry could demand obedience and meet out summary justice even in York's heartlands. Local men accused of inciting rebellion in London, Kent, and the Welsh Marches, and two men from Kent suspected of supporting York before and after Dartford, had been brought to Ludlow. 'Evidence' was presented that they and others had openly asserted that an incompetent King could be deposed by Parliament (as Richard II had been when Henry's grandfather took the throne). They were found guilty, but King Henry arrived on 13 August the day after the hearings ended and he pardoned most of them as an act of royal clemency.[41]

The choice of Wiltshire to conduct the hearings was politically motivated. He had accompanied York to Normandy in 1441 and York had appointed him steward for life of the ducal estates in Somerset and Dorset.[42] But after Dartford Wiltshire distanced himself from York and he was eager to preside at Ludlow to show that he was no longer York's man.

14

Triumph and Disaster

While King Henry and Somerset were on progress the Council decided to put the ships that had been assembled to defend Calais to good use. In July they commissioned Sir Edward Hull, Margaret's knight of the body, the absentee constable of Bordeaux, and Gervase Clifton, the Treasurer of Calais, to patrol the Channel for three months with 1,000 men each to keep the sea lanes open for English merchant shipping.[1] This sensible intention was subsumed by a far riskier enterprise, nothing less than the recovery of the Duchy of Gascony. Peter Tastar, the exiled Dean of St Seurin, had kept in touch with dissident elements in Bordeaux. He claimed that a fifth column inside the city was ready to throw off French rule provided King Henry sent a force strong enough to make the risk worthwhile.[2]

In September Henry appointed John Talbot, Earl of Shrewsbury, as Lieutenant of Gascony. Shrewsbury's retinue, estimated at 3,000 men, combined with those of Edward Hull and Gervase Clifton, would give him a notional army of about 5,000.[3] Margaret encouraged the expedition. Unlike Normandy, Gascony was the heritage of the Kings of England and of the son she still hoped to have. She gave Hull a parting gift of a gold rose.[4] Shrewsbury saw it as an opportunity to wipe out the disgrace of losing Normandy and his humiliation at the surrender of Rouen. The 'Great Talbot' was in his mid-sixties, an old man by the standards of his day but as active as ever.

The English flotilla arrived at the mouth of the Gironde on 17 October and the army reached the outskirts of Bordeaux five days later without encountering serious resistance.⁵ The conspirators inside Bordeaux opened an entry port on the river and Shrewsbury took the town unopposed. He set up his own administration and taxed the Bordelais to fund his campaign, since no money was forthcoming from England. Clifton and Hull enrolled Gaşcon mercenaries at their own expense. One after another, the towns opened their gates; resistance meant lawful plunder and Shrewsbury's troops had a reputation as looters, since without regular pay they were forced to live off the land. By the end of 1452 most of Gascony was again in English hands, although the key fortresses of Fronsac, Blaye, and Bourg held out.

The year closed on a high note for Margaret and for King Henry. The Earl of Shrewsbury's military triumphs abroad and the assertion of royal authority at home had restored confidence in Henry's government. Margaret devised lavish entertainments for the Christmas and New Year festivities at Greenwich. Richard Bulstrode, her master of revels, purchased silks and cloth of gold. Tailors made elaborate costumes and artists painted colourful backdrops for the play acting and mummings, called 'disguisings', of which the Queen was especially fond.⁶ The revels at Greenwich continued until the middle of January 1453 with King Henry in a relaxed and happy mood.

Henry celebrated in his own way. He created his half-brothers Edmund and Jasper Tudor as Earl of Richmond and Earl of Pembroke respectively and he knighted them at a special ceremony in the Tower of London on 5 January.⁷ They were Queen Katherine's sons by her morganatic marriage to Owen Tudor and after her death in 1437 they had been placed in the care of Katherine de la Pole, Abbess of Barking, the Duke of Suffolk's sister.⁸ Edmund was in his early twenties and Jasper was twenty-one. As grandsons of King Charles VI of France, they were of royal blood and legitimate. Henry's choice of their titles underlined their close kinship with the Lancastrian line. The Regent Bedford had been Earl of Richmond and Humphrey, Duke of Gloucester, had been Earl of Pembroke.

Power Struggle

Parliament met at Reading Abbey in March and confirmed Henry's grants to his half-brothers. The Commons' mood had changed dramatically.[9] Men of substance viewed rebellion as a threat to property and a first step towards anarchy, and the Duke of York's ill-advised foray at Dartford had triggered a backlash of loyalty to King Henry. The Commons petitioned that all royal grants held by York's supporters at Dartford should be resumed.[10] York was untouchable but his chamberlain, Sir William Oldhall, made a handy scapegoat. The Commons blamed the malign influence of their former Speaker and of Jack Cade for their petition to banish the King's 'true subjects', and they attainted Oldhall for his involvement in Cade's rebellion and for encouraging risings in favour of York in 1452.[11]

Parliamentary expectation ran high. Surely now King Henry would send a large army into France to follow up Shrewsbury's success. In an overgenerous gesture of encouragement, the Commons voted to finance 20,000 archers for six months' service. They granted a tax of a tenth and fifteenth and as a singular mark of their approval, tonnage and poundage and the wool subsidy to the King for life.[12] They confirmed Somerset's wages as Captain of Calais although payment to the Duke of Buckingham for his term as captain received priority.[13] But their most surprising *volte face* was their consent to King Henry's request that the de la Pole lands and the wardship of her son should be restored to the Duchess of Suffolk.[14] Suffolk was no longer the villain of the hour; the storm had blown itself out.

But Duchess Alice lost out in other ways. King Henry annulled the 'marriage' between John de la Pole and the ten-year-old Margaret Beaufort and granted her wardship and marriage to the Tudor brothers to link them with the Beauforts. Margaret's mother, the Dowager Duchess of Somerset, brought her to London, and she attended the festivities for the Feast of the Garter at Windsor. The sight of Queen Margaret, radiant in her garter robes, made a lasting impression on the child.[15] Henry gave the Duchess 100 marks 'for her arrayment', possibly as a contribution to Margaret Beaufort's wedding finery, and Edmund Tudor married Margaret Beaufort, probably in the summer of 1453.[16]

Just before Parliament recessed for Easter King Henry received stupendous news: the Queen was pregnant. Richard Tunstall, an esquire of the body, 'made unto us the first comfortable relation and notice that oure most entierly belovyd wyf the Quene was with child, to oure most singular consolation.'[17] Margaret had conceived during the festivities at Greenwich and a delighted Henry ordered a special gift of a 'demy ceynt' for her from a London goldsmith.[18] Margaret was twenty-three and at last after nearly eight years of marriage she was expecting a child. She shared King Henry's veneration for the Mother of God to whom she had prayed most earnestly for a child of her own and she set out on a pilgrimage of thanksgiving to Our Lady of Walsingham in Norfolk, one of the most famous shrines in England.

The Holy House at Walsingham was a wooden replica of the Holy House in Nazareth where Mary was visited by the Angel Gabriel.[19] It was a place of ancient worship, dating back to before the Norman Conquest. The small age-old wooden statue of the Virgin stood in a shrine of solid silver. Margaret knelt to lay her thanksgiving offering before the shrine: a tablet of gold with a decorative border containing ten circles of pearls, five sapphires, and five spinel rubies. In the centre an angel carved as a cameo and holding a crucifix garnished with a ruby and nine ornamental pearls hovered above a beautiful sapphire.[20]

Margaret also paid a visit to Norwich accompanied by one of the Tudor brothers, although we do not know which one. The royal entourage caused a flutter in the Paston family. Much to Margaret Paston's chagrin her kinswoman Elizabeth Clere made a great impression on the Queen, who said she had seen 'no jantylwomman syn she come into Norffolk that she lykyth better.' Margaret suggested to Elizabeth that she should marry again but the widowed Elizabeth was content with her lot and returned a diplomatic answer.[21] The Mayor of Norwich presented Margaret with 100 marks and she persuaded the rich merchant Robert Toppes to donate money for a stained-glass window in the fashionable church of St Peter Mancroft.[22]

On her way back to Windsor Margaret received an unexpected visit from Cecily, Duchess of York. Cecily had come to congratulate Margaret on her pregnancy and to plead with the Queen on her husband's behalf.[23] If Margaret's child turned out to be a boy the Duke of York could no longer claim be heir presumptive and the breach between him and King Henry might be healed. Cecily told Margaret that she was not in good health; her continuing anxiety over York's estrangement from King Henry had made her ill. She hoped that Margaret would intercede with Henry on York's behalf. Margaret sympathised but she made no promises.

Sometime later Cecily wrote to Margaret to excuse herself for not coming in person to attend on the Queen. Her health had worsened since their meeting and she was unfit to travel. Cecily reminded Margaret that she had received her visit 'full benignly' and she reiterated her defence of York as the King's true, humble, and obedient servant. He was suffering serious depression ('infinite sorrow') due to their estrangement and he was willing to do anything in his power to serve the King.[24] It is impossible not to see York's hand behind a plea that cost the proud duchess a considerable effort to make. The impetus for Cecily's letter was King Henry's appointment of the Earl of Wiltshire to replace York as the King's Lieutenant in Ireland, significantly backdated to 6 March 1452, the week of Dartford. York had left Ireland of his own volition, but his indenture did not expire until 1457. Wiltshire's father, the Earl of Ormond, had died in 1452 and Henry granted Wiltshire all the Ormond lands in Ireland still in the King's hands.[25] If York needed further confirmation that his loyalty was suspect, this was it. Cecily was not exaggerating York's anxiety and frustration. He had failed at Dartford and Henry's judicial progresses through his heartlands had implicated his retainers in breaches of the king's peace – if not worse. Margaret's response to Cecily's appeal is not known but York remained *persona non grata* at court.

Parliament reconvened in June with the Commons having second thoughts. The cost of funding 20,000 archers would be prohibitive, and they requested a reduction to 13,000. King Henry acquiesced and promised not to call on them for the next two years, a sure indication that he was not planning to send (or lead) an army into France. Instead he asked for an additional subsidy to reinforce the Earl of Shrewsbury and the grateful Commons granted him a half tenth and fifteenth.[26] A small force financed entirely by loans that the tax would help to repay had left England in April under the command of Shrewsbury's son, Lord Lisle. It included the veteran soldier Lord Camoys and Robert Hungerford, Lord Moleyns, the son of Margaret's former knight of the body.[27] Altogether Henry was well pleased. The Commons had been more generous than any of his earlier parliaments. He thanked the members in person and, advised by Chancellor Kemp, he prorogued Parliament to November rather than dissolving it. A compliant Parliament was infinitely preferable to new elections that might return a less sympathetic Commons.

Henry then spent a few days at Greenwich with Margaret, who was six months pregnant. He had been informed that Sir John Wenlock, Margaret's chamberlain, was a friend of Sir William Oldhall and Duchess Cecily's plea had planted the suspicion in Henry's mind that the Queen's immediate circle was being infiltrated by York's partisans. Henry was extremely sensitive to any suggestion of support for the Duke of York and he dismissed Wenlock from Margaret's service. Possibly with Margaret's encouragement Wenlock tried to appease the pious King by requesting permission to go on pilgrimage. Writing from Clarendon later in the summer Henry gave his consent, but he suggested to Wenlock that he should seriously reconsider his allegiances. He knew that Wenlock had sympathised with the Duke of York during the recent 'untrewe troubleouse tyme' and he made it clear that he and the Queen would have to be satisfied of Wenlock's loyalty before he could be reemployed in royal service.[28] Margaret accepted

Henry's decision but she did not share his opinion. Wenlock's full wage as chamberlain was paid in December 1453.²⁹

Henry left Greenwich for a Council meeting at Sheen. Perhaps to placate Margaret for his treatment of Wenlock, perhaps because she asked him to, or perhaps because she was about to present the kingdom with an heir, Henry granted Margaret autonomy over all her dower lands. They were to be administered entirely by her own officials and the King's officers would have no jurisdiction within them. The Council's approval may have been no more than an endorsement of King Henry's expressed wish but it is an indication that its members had more faith in Margaret's ability to get a better return from her lands than could be expected from the King's officials, as indeed she did.³⁰

The Duke of Somerset felt secure in Henry's favour, but he made the biggest mistake of his political career by arousing the enmity of his cousin Richard Neville, Earl of Warwick. Richard had acquired the title thanks to the matchmaking propensities of his father, the Earl of Salisbury, who had arranged a marriage for his daughter Cecily (named for her aunt the Duchess of York) with Henry Beauchamp, the son and heir of the Beauchamp Earl of Warwick. As part of the deal the young Richard Neville was betrothed to Henry Beauchamp's sister, Anne. Henry Beauchamp died in 1446 leaving his only child, another Anne, as his heir. This Anne died in 1449 and Richard Neville claimed the title and the vast Beauchamp estates on behalf of his wife, as Henry Beauchamp's only full sister.

Anne Beauchamp had three half-sisters from her father's previous marriage and King Henry initially recognised that they had a legitimate claim to part of the inheritance, but he granted the title of Earl and Countess of Warwick to Richard and Anne.³¹ Richard was not yet twenty-one, Anne was twenty-two. The new Earl used a mixture of bribery and coercion to influence the jurors in their extensive *inquisitions post-mortem* into the complicated Beauchamp inheritance and the jurors found that *all* the Beauchamp lands belonged with the Earldom of Warwick and should pass intact to the new countess. In upholding this decision and rejecting the claims of the half-sisters, King Henry put a powerful weapon into Richard Neville's hands.[32]

Not content with the Beauchamp estates, Richard claimed the Despenser lands of Anne's mother, Isabel Despenser. Isabel had another daughter, Elizabeth, by her previous marriage to Lord Abergavenny. Elizabeth was dead in 1449 but her husband, Edward Neville, had claimed the Despenser inheritance for their son George. Richard Neville counter-claimed that the Abergavenny *and* the Despenser lands should pass to his wife through her mother. King Henry compromised; he granted custody of the Despenser lands to Warwick until George came of age. Edward and George Neville were Warwick's uncle and cousin but that made no difference: Richard had no sense of family loyalty where property was concerned and, in a nutshell, he got the lot.

Somerset's mistake in 1453 was to persuade King Henry to transfer George Neville's lands to him, backdated to 1449.[33] It was a serious error of judgement. Warwick never gave up anything once he possessed it and was never satisfied until he had accumulated more. Yorkist tradition has so blacked Somerset's reputation that any motive other than greed is rarely attributed to him and it is accepted that he grabbed the Despenser lands from a compliant king out of self-interest, but he may have had a more altruistic motive. The meat in the sandwich was the unfortunate George Neville, whom Somerset had left as a hostage in Rouen. George would not be freed until his ransom was paid and the custodian of George's inheritance had a moral, if not a legal obligation, to put up the money. Warwick did not do so and there is no proof that Somerset intended to, but Somerset could have obtained any grant he wanted from King Henry and yet he chose the Despenser lands, which he would be obliged to surrender when George Neville came of age. He may have intended to use their income to raise George's ransom, since he was responsible for George's captivity.

Power Struggle

Warwick went in person to resist Somerset's officials when they tried to take over the Despenser lands. The Council received disquieting reports of fighting in South Wales and they sent for Sir William Herbert, Warwick's steward in Glamorgan, to explain what was going on. They commanded Warwick to disperse his force and summoned Warwick and Somerset to attend the Council at Sheen. Somerset obeyed, Warwick did not. Lord Dudley was commissioned to take possession of the disputed lands until the matter could be sorted out, but Warwick ignored the order just as he had ignored King Henry's grant to Somerset.[34] It was an ominous early indication that Richard Neville was a law unto himself.

King Henry and Somerset left Sheen for their summer progress. They were at Kingston-Lacy in Dorset when catastrophic news reached them: The Earl of Shrewsbury had been defeated and killed on 17 July at the Battle of Castillon. Shrewsbury's arrival in Gascony had taken King Charles by surprise; he had assumed that because Shrewsbury had never fought in Gascony the English would launch their attack against Normandy. Charles reacted swiftly; he raised men and money to go onto the offensive and by July he had three armies in the field.[35]

One of them was encamped before the small town of Castillon. In his heyday Shrewsbury had been renowned for the speed at which he could appear where the French least expected him, and he marched to relieve Castillon with an advance body of troops, leaving instructions for the main bulk of his infantry to follow. French troops occupied the Abbey of St Laurent on Castillon's north side; Shrewsbury's unexpected appearance terrified them, and they fled back to the main camp. Shrewsbury allowed his men to refresh themselves in the well-provisioned abbey after their night's march. (French chroniclers do not fail to point out that wine was among the refreshments issued to the English troops.) On the following day, as Shrewsbury prepared to hear mass, a messenger arrived post-haste from Castillon to report that men and horses had been seen leaving the town with clouds of dust covering their retreat – the French were in full flight. Despite warnings from his senior commanders that it would be madness to attack an entrenched position before the arrival of his infantry, Shrewsbury insisted on engaging the enemy.

The battle lasted for over an hour of heavy fighting and the English were caught in a murderous crossfire from French cannon. Breton troops, stationed on wooded ground high above the abbey, rode down from their concealed position and thundered into the English right flank. Shrewsbury's men were forced to retreat but the River Dordogne was at their backs and they could not escape. Shrewsbury's horse was killed in the mêlée and as Shrewsbury lay on the ground a savage blow to the back of his head ended his life. His son, Lord Lisle, fell with him. Sir Edward Hull died of his wounds and Robert Hungerford was captured.[36] Gervase Clifton was lucky to escape; he may have remained in Bordeaux with Lord Camoys, Shrewsbury's Seneschal of Gascony, who set about organising the city's defence.[37] Shrewsbury's decision to fight at Castillon was in sharp contrast to his cautious approach to Dunois in Normandy, when he had done his utmost to guard Rouen without giving battle. A combination of faulty intelligence and Talbot hubris was responsible for the defeat: Shrewsbury believed what he wanted to believe, that on the approach of 'the Great Talbot' the French had run away.

The devastating news caused King Henry to turn back towards London. At Clarendon he suffered a complete mental and physical collapse and retreated into a semi-conscious state from which nothing could rouse him. He could not speak, or walk unassisted, or understand what was being said to him. The surviving accounts are meagre and contradictory, but Henry appears to have gone into a state of profound shock.[38] He had been under severe psychological pressure ever since Cade's rebellion and the attempt by the Duke of York to take over the government. He had been persuaded by Somerset and his own fears to meet out retribution, but this went against his instinct for clemency. Henry had seen his subjects hanged for disloyalty, he had

Power Struggle

witnessed dissentions among his magnates that he was powerless to control, and he had heard the rumours that his 'uncle of France' planned to invade England.

The news of the defeat at Castillon is not enough to account for Henry's sudden breakdown – English armies had sustained defeats before. But if someone at Clarendon suggested that in the wake of this latest disaster King Henry had no alternative but to call out the promised archers and lead an army into France, such a proposal coming on top of his already overstretched nerves would have been too much. The Duke of Suffolk had shielded Henry from the unpleasant realities of kingship; the Duke of Somerset had thrust these realities upon him. Somerset did not understand the importance of taking pressure off the King and eventually the inevitable happened. Henry could not lead an army and he knew it. His only means of escape was to turn his back on an impossible situation and collapse into a complete withdrawal from an intolerable strain.

Somerset's initial reaction was understandable: he tried to prevent the news from becoming generally known. Chancellor Kemp continued to handle routine Council business while Somerset kept Henry in the relative seclusion of Clarendon. No one knew what ailed the King; he might recover at any minute or he might die, an eventuality that Somerset preferred not to contemplate. The situation was unprecedented. King Edward III became senile in his old age, but he had sons aplenty to deputise for him. Never before had an adult king lost his senses while on the throne and to make matters worse there was no direct heir to the Lancastrian line.

Inevitably rumours circulated. Illness, mental and physical, was universally accepted as a visitation of God. Was it a judgement on the King as unfit to rule? Had he fallen under divine displeasure? Was it God's retribution for the loss of Normandy that his father had won with God's blessing? Or were witchcraft and sorcery behind it? Roger Bolingbroke had cast Henry's horoscope in 1441 and predicted that a dangerous illness would strike him in the summer months. Suppose his calculations as to the year had been wrong but his prophecy had been right? An approver at Southwark claimed that Lord Cobham (who had been with York at Dartford) had a spell cast over a velvet cloak belonging to Henry, a muddled association with Eleanor Cobham, the Duchess of Gloucester, who had been accused of witchcraft. Another man laid the blame on a group of Bristol merchants: they had consulted books of necromancy to bring about the King's demise. Henry had imprisoned Thomas Young, the MP for Bristol, for declaring that the Duke of York should be named heir presumptive. Both informers harked back to Jack Cade: 'Would God that the captain of Kent had reigned, for the King is but a sheep and hath lost all that his father won.'[39]

For the next two months everyone waited, eagerly or anxiously, for Margaret to give birth. It is unlikely that she risked travelling to Clarendon at this late stage in her pregnancy. Somerset would have been reluctant to subject her to the shocking sight of her husband's condition and it was of paramount importance to Margaret not to do anything that might endanger her unborn child. She had planned to withdraw to Windsor where Henry had been born, but under the circumstances maximum publicity must attend the birth of a Lancastrian heir who might become King at an even earlier age than his father. The child would be born at Westminster and baptised in Westminster Abbey, where the Kings of England were crowned and buried.

15

Queen in Waiting

Tradition required a queen to withdraw from court life at least one month before giving birth. Margaret came by river from Greenwich and was received into the City by the Mayor and aldermen on 10 September 1453.[1] She was taken by barge to Westminster Palace and escorted to her great chamber to be seated in full view of the court. She was then conducted to her inner chamber where prayers were said for her safe delivery. All the men at court, including her household officials, withdrew; no man would be allowed to enter the inner chamber until after the birth. Food, water for bathing, fuel, candles, and any other domestic necessities were received at the door by the ladies who were permitted to attend on her.

Margaret remained in seclusion for over a month, enclosed in semi-darkness since fresh air and sunlight were deemed harmful. She had time to wonder if the child would be a boy, if it would be healthy, if she would survive its birth, if her husband would recover or die. She may also have thought of her mother. The joy of her pregnancy had been overshadowed by the death of Isabelle of Lorraine, who died in Angers at the end of February before her daughter's news could reach her. Margaret and her ladies had gone into mourning as custom dictated but Margaret can hardly have been grief stricken; she had spent little time in her mother's company. They had corresponded but how frequently or how intimately is unknown.[2]

On 13 October 1453, Margaret gave birth to a healthy boy. The omens were propitious, for this was St Edward the Confessor's day and the day on which King Henry's grandfather had been crowned as the first Lancastrian king. Margaret named the child Edward in recognition of Henry's veneration for the Confessor. Messengers carried the news far and wide and *Te Deums* echoed throughout the land. England had an heir.[3] Giles St Loo, Margaret's usher of chamber, was rewarded with ten marks for conveying the tidings to the Mayor and Common Council of London.[4]

The minutely regulated ceremonies for Prince Edward's christening were carried out to the letter. The great state cradle was a massive five and a half feet long by two and a half feet wide; it reflected the importance of the baby who would lie in it only twice, just before and just after his baptismal ceremony. The baptismal procession formed up in Westminster Hall. Officers of the King's household delivered the precious ceremonial vessels to 'worthy' knights; 200 squires and men-at-arms in royal livery carried unlit candles and were followed by the kings-of-arms and heralds carrying their surcoats.[5]

The Prince's linen christening robe had a mantle of ermine with a train of russet cloth of gold twenty yards long. The silver baptismal font brought specially from Christ Church, Canterbury, stood on a dais between the altar and the choir. It was lined with fine linen and draped with cloth of gold. Its red satin canopy of estate was embroidered with 'a great sun of gold'. The dean of the royal chapel filled it with warmed holy water and the infant was taken into a withdrawing room to be undressed. He was then placed in the arms of Bishop Waynflete of Winchester, who baptised him by immersing him in the font in the presence of his godparents, the Duke of Somerset, Cardinal Kemp, and Anne Neville, Duchess of Buckingham.[6] The candles carried by the squires were lit and the kings-at-arms and heralds donned their surcoats. The baby was wrapped in his chrisom cloth and carried to the high altar by his godfathers to be anointed with holy oil. A large candle was presented as his offering and he was then taken back to the withdrawing room to be redressed in his christening robes while his godparents washed their hands and wine and spices were offered to them. Margaret waited in her great chamber for the ceremony to end. Traditionally the child would now be presented to his parents, but King Henry was not there.

Margaret's ordeal did not end with the Prince's birth. She remained in seclusion for another month until the ceremony of her churching on 18 November when courtiers, nobles and peeresses, including the Duchess of York, gathered around her great state bed.[7] Margaret lay under a rich scarlet coverlet that was ceremoniously drawn back, she was helped to her feet, a lighted candle was placed in her hand, and she was conducted to Westminster Abbey to be blessed and sprinkled with holy water. Margaret knelt at the altar and offered her candle and the chrismal cloth that the Duchess of Buckingham, as the baby's godmother, carried in the procession.[8] The court returned to the Queen's chamber and a banquet followed with the men still segregated from the ladies. Margaret sat in solitary splendour under her canopy of estate and the feast marked her formal restoration into court life.

Rumours that Prince Edward was not King Henry's son did not circulate until several years after his birth.[9] It was Margaret's duty to produce a son, but King Henry had little or no sex drive and he was not physically attracted to women or to men. If Margaret decided that Henry was incapable of fathering a child, she faced the stark choice of remaining barren or taking an appalling risk. A surrogate father would have to be someone as nearly related to King Henry as possible and she would have to trust him implicitly. Her choice was limited. The Duke of Somerset was older than Margaret's father and he stood godfather to the child, a spiritual risk that Margaret would not have taken had he been the baby's father. Somerset's eldest son, Henry Beaufort, was younger than Margaret but old enough at seventeen to father a child. He never married, making him a favourite candidate for later romancers. Henry Holand, Duke of Exeter, was the same age as Margaret and he was King Henry's closest blood kin in the Lancastrian line. But Exeter was volatile and unpredictable; if he provided an heir whose paternity he could not acknowledge, it would cut him out of the direct line of succession.

If Margaret was looking for the closest possible kinship to King Henry then Edmund Tudor, Earl of Richmond, fitted the bill. He was about the same age as Margaret and she had welcomed him to Greenwich during the festivities when Prince Edward was conceived. Edmund Tudor has never been postulated as Prince Edward's father because from a dynastic point of view his paternity is wrong. He had no claim to the throne, but as the son of Katherine of Valois he had French royal blood in his veins. He may also have been the Duke of Somerset's son.[10] The attraction between Queen Katherine and Edmund Beaufort, five years her junior, had been obvious to everyone in the 1420s. They may have planned to marry but the Duke of Gloucester was jealous of Beaufort influence and he took steps to ensure that the charismatic Edmund Beaufort did not become the young king's stepfather. An Act of Parliament forbade Katherine to marry without King Henry's consent, which he could not give until he came of age, but this is precisely what she did when she married Owen Tudor, a mere Welsh squire.[11] There is no proof that Edmund Beaufort and Katherine had an affair that resulted in her pregnancy, but if they did it would have been imperative for her to marry quickly before they were both disgraced. If Edmund Tudor was the son of Edmund Beaufort, and the father of Prince Edward, then the Prince was exactly what he should have been dynastically speaking: part Plantagenet, part Valois, and part Angevin. It is an interesting speculation, but there is no evidence that Prince Edward was not King Henry's son and the legitimate Lancastrian heir.

The birth of an heir did not solve the problem of government. King Henry showed no signs of recovery and without royal authority Somerset's regime was invalid. A Great Council would have to be called and although Chancellor Kemp was sure that a broadly based council could govern without the Duke of York, even members of the royal household thought otherwise. York would not accept such a slight: he would challenge any provisional government that excluded him and without his acquiescence stable government would be impossible. On 23 October Sir Thomas Tyrell was deputed to deliver an invitation to York in King Henry's name. It was signed by the household officers, Lords Dudley and Sudeley, Robert Botill, Prior of St John of Jerusalem, and the bishops on the Council. Kemp and Somerset did not sign. Tyrell was to excuse the delay as an administrative error and to express the hope that York would agree to join a council that might include Somerset, since there was an urgent need to set 'rest and union' between the lords for the good of the country.[12] The question was not would Somerset agree to work with York, but would York agree to work with Somerset? York would not.

He came to London in an uncompromising mood and made it plain to the lords assembled in the Star Chamber at Westminster on 21 November that he would brook no opposition. He insisted that every action taken against him and his servants was unjust and must be abrogated by a declaration under the Great Seal. Chancellor Kemp complied unwillingly.[13] The lords were bewildered; King Henry was said to have lost his wits, but no one knew precisely what ailed him. It was all very unsettling.

York's old ally the Duke of Norfolk submitted a bill accusing Somerset of the same crimes that York had articulated at Dartford: *lèse majesté* and the loss of Normandy and Gascony. Norfolk demanded that Somerset be put on trial for treason. The words were Norfolk's, but the sentiments were York's.[14] No one doubted that York would resort to force if his demands were not met and only Chancellor Kemp risked voicing his opposition.[15] The lords bowed to force majeure and meekly ordered Somerset to surrender himself to the Lieutenant of the Tower and Somerset as meekly obeyed. The apprehensive lords swore a collective oath to maintain royal authority and uphold the rule of law while King Henry lay ill. Anyone who broke his oath would be dealt with severely regardless of his estate, blood ties, or any other consideration. This has been interpreted as unanimity when it was nothing of the sort. The oath was administered on York's orders to buttress his authority, and none of the lords present that day would have dared to refuse.[16]

York had no legal power to direct the government any more than Somerset had; rather less in fact, since Somerset was King Henry's chosen minister. The lords debated the advisability and the legality of placing royal authority in the hands of a council. Only fourteen men were prepared to endorse so drastic a step: Chancellor Kemp, the Dukes of York, Norfolk, and Buckingham, the Earls of Salisbury and Warwick, the Bourgchiers, and the bishops on the council. They agreed to act in King Henry's name but only in matters of grave importance that could not be delayed.[17] With the exception of Kemp these men would support York's bid to become Protector of England.

Whatever debates took place in Council, whatever decisions were taken from the time that King Henry fell ill, Margaret had no say in them. She was in seclusion during these crucial months and she emerged after her churching to find herself in a different world.[18] Her husband was incapacitated, Somerset was to be incarcerated in the Tower and York had complete control of the Council.

Margaret had not seen her husband since the previous July. King Henry had been moved from Clarendon to Windsor and in December the Duke of Buckingham escorted Margaret and Prince Edward to visit him. Buckingham carried the Prince into Henry's chamber and asked for his blessing on the child; he tried several times to elicit a response, but Henry remained impassive. Margaret had hoped that the sight of his son would rouse Henry from his apathy. She took the baby and showed him to the King but Henry did not recognise her, he glanced at the child and looked away again.[19] Margaret now knew that her husband was suffering a living death and she faced a serious decision: should she become Queen Regent?

Regency was a familiar concept to Margaret; her mother and grandmother had ruled successfully in their husbands' names, Isabelle while René was in captivity and Yolande while her husband and sons were campaigning in Italy. Queen Maria of Aragon was Regent for King Alphonso V while he was fighting Margaret's father in Naples. Queen Eleanor of Portugal, widow of King Durante, became co-regent with Durante's brother. But the concept was foreign in England and Englishmen were strongly prejudiced not only against women rulers, but against regency in general. The lords had refused to recognise the Duke of Gloucester as Regent in 1422 despite Henry V's dying wish and even the highly respected Duke of Bedford, Regent of France, was not accepted as Regent in England. Placing the powers of the crown in any hands except those of the anointed king went against every precept of inheritance, authority, and accountability that the lords understood. So why did Margaret decide to make a bid for a major political role? Queen Katherine had not done so, but Katherine had spent only fifteen months in England before Henry V died, and her son had powerful kinsmen to act in his name. Margaret was alone. Prince Edward's future was insecure and her own was uncertain. Margaret saw it as her duty to exercise royal authority in King Henry's name until such time as he recovered.

London was unsettled and uneasy. It was widely rumoured that there would be a trial of strength between the Duke of York and those opposed to him. In January 1454 one John Stodeley addressed a mildly hysterical letter to the Duke of Norfolk, warning of danger on all sides.[20] Much of Stodeley's information was inaccurate and based on London gossip, but it reflected the heightened tensions in the City. He reported that the Duke of Somerset had spies everywhere even though he was a prisoner in the Tower, where Norfolk had helped to consign him. Stodeley advised Norfolk to come to London heavily armed. Weaponry was being smuggled into the capital in carts.[21] The Duke of York was expected to be accompanied only by his household men, but his son, the Earl of March (who was only eleven), would follow him, bringing armed men and ordnance. One of Stodeley's informants had heard that Edmund and Jasper Tudor might come with York and that they would be arrested if they did so, although

Stodeley did not know by whom.[22] The Earl of Salisbury would bring 1,400 men and the Earl of Warwick 1,000 men. The Earl of Wiltshire and Lord Bonville in the south-west, Viscount Beaumont in Lincolnshire, the Earl of Northumberland and Lord Clifford in the north were gathering men and arms. They did not come.[23] The Duke of Buckingham had issued a livery of 2,000 badges of the Stafford knot 'to what entent men may construe as their wittes wole yeve theym.' Four royal household officials, Thomas Tresham, William Joseph, Thomas Daniel, and John Trevelian would petition Parliament for a permanent garrison to be stationed at Windsor to guard King Henry and Prince Edward while the Queen would demand the regency. The Speaker of the Commons, Thomas Thorpe, was preparing to challenge the legality of York's actions in Parliament.

Thorpe had been Speaker during the previous session of Parliament, which had proved sympathetic to Somerset and decidedly unsympathetic to York.[24] York was determined to get rid of him and he accused Thorpe of removing (stealing) some of York's (unspecified) possessions from the Bishop of Durham's house in London. Robert Neville, Bishop of Durham, was York's brother-in-law. Thorpe knew what would happen next. Two days after Somerset's arrest he enfeoffed all his possessions on Lawrence Booth, Margaret's chancellor, and other feoffees. A jury under York's influence found Thorpe guilty of theft and ordered him to pay £1,000 in damages and £10 in costs. Thorpe was a Baron of the Exchequer and a comparatively wealthy man, but he was unable to raise £1,000 and he was imprisoned in the Fleet before Parliament reconvened.[25]

Chancellor Kemp demanded to be told who would open Parliament, since a warrant must be issued under the Great Seal. Twenty-eight Lords authorised York to preside, and Parliament met on 14 February 1454.[26] The Commons lodged an immediate complaint that their Speaker had not been released to attend, which contravened their ancient liberties and privileges. York's spokesman argued that Thorpe had been found guilty by a jury under the laws of the land at a time when Parliament was not in session, and therefore the Commons' privileges had not been breached. The Lords referred the matter to the judges, who replied that they were not qualified to rule on a question of Parliamentary privilege, although they added that it was customary to release any member of the Lower House to attend Parliament except in cases of treason or rebellion. The Lords were wary of antagonising York; he interpreted impartial justice differently when it affected his interests, and they decreed that Thorpe's imprisonment had been lawful. The Commons too were wary and without further complaint they elected Thomas Charlton as their Speaker.[27]

Having overawed the Commons, York turned his attention to obtaining Parliamentary acknowledgement of his loyalty. York averred that the charges against Thomas Courtenay, Earl of Devon, who had been imprisoned for coming in arms against King Henry at Dartford were untrue and impugned his own honour.[28] In a fine piece of theatrical grandstanding, York insisted that Devon must be allowed trial by his peers and he challenged anyone who believed in Devon's guilt to come forward; of course no one did. The Lords hastily assured York that 'we knewe nevere, nor at any tyme cowed conceive' that he could be suspected of disloyalty and they solemnly avowed their faith in him. Devon's exoneration was a foregone conclusion, but just in case there should be any lingering doubts about his suitability to become Protector, York had the statement of his loyalty entered on the Parliamentary rolls.[29]

Margaret came to London towards the end of February and was received into the City by the Mayor and aldermen. It is a measure of how high York had risen in the political stakes that the civic dignitaries accorded him a like honour when he opened Parliament, although they had declined to do so when he came to London in the previous November.[30] The articles in Margaret's bid to become Regent had been prepared by Robert Tanfield, her attorney general, and her chancellor Lawrence Booth, in consultation with those members of the Great Council who had not subscribed to substituting Council authority for royal authority.[31] Margaret's bill may have been presented in the Commons by Robert Tanfield, but is it more likely to have been put to the Lords in Council while Parliament was sitting as a solution to the crisis in government.[32] It is not recorded on the Parliamentary roll.

The bill consisted of five articles, 'wherof the first is that she desireth to have the whol reul of this land'. She would appoint all the great officers of state and nominate to any vacant bishoprics. She wanted assurances of an adequate income to maintain herself, the Prince, and the royal household. Unfortunately for her subsequent reputation, John Stodeley pretended ignorance of her fifth and last article. Margaret was inexperienced politically and she can hardly have expected, or been advised, to attempt to rule alone. She probably undertook that if she was granted the powers she sought, she would rule with the advice of a regency council.[33] She was not seeking unlimited or unprecedented powers.

Margaret may have received more support that is commonly believed. She had the royal household behind her, and Chancellor Kemp favoured her for reasons of his own. He knew she would encounter stiff opposition, but he did not trust the Duke of York, and he was determined to use all the means at his disposal to have the authority of the crown vested in a permanent council under his leadership, to make decisions and formulate policy in King Henry's name. Margaret would be a suitable figurehead. But there were sound practical reasons for the Lords to reject Margaret. She could be Regent, but she could not be Protector and Defender of the Realm. The Duke of York could. Had he been prepared to become Protector with Margaret as Regent, the two might have worked together, but quite apart from York's lust for power, his prejudice against a woman ruler was genuine. He would not have accepted such terms even if they were offered to him. In the end prejudice and tradition won the day.

Margaret's reaction to the Lords rejection of her is not known, but

Power Struggle

there was nothing she could do. She had the consolation of knowing that the Lords and the Commons remained loyal to King Henry and the House of Lancaster. On 15 March Parliament created Prince Edward Prince of Wales and Earl of Chester, the hereditary titles of the heir to the throne, and they decreed that he would become Protector for his father when he reached his majority, should this be necessary.[34] York wisely endorsed the act, a display of his loyalty at this crucial stage made sound political sense and enhanced his chances of becoming Protector in the immediate future.

One week later, York had the greatest stroke of luck in his entire career. Cardinal Kemp, Archbishop of Canterbury and Chancellor, died at the age of seventy-four.[35] Kemp had endured months of continuous stress: he had armed his servants for his own protection as he struggled to resist York and protect the royal prerogative while King Henry was helpless. On 23 March he suffered a stroke or a heart attack and at four in the morning he died. There was no suggestion then or afterwards that his death was not due to natural causes, but the timing could not have been more fortunate for York. Kemp was the principal stumbling block to York's bid for power, and while York would not contemplate a physical attack on the primate of England the Duke of Norfolk might not be so restrained; he had urged the Council to relieve Kemp of the Chancellorship, which could only be done legally by King Henry. Kemp's death precipitated a political crisis even more acute than the collapse of the King. Only the Chancellor could use the Great Seals and without them no government could function. Only the King could appoint a Chancellor and nominate an Archbishop of Canterbury. King Henry would have to be consulted – there was no alternative.

The Council's delegation to Windsor was carefully selected by York. William Waynflete, Bishop of Winchester, was Henry's confessor. Lords Dudley and Sudeley were Henry's household officers. Viscount Beaumont and Robert Botill, Prior of St John of Jerusalem, were Henry's councillors. Viscount Bourgchier and Thomas Bourgchier,

Bishop of Ely, were York's brothers-in-law and Thomas was York's choice to succeed Kemp as Archbishop of Canterbury. Lord Fauconberg and the Earl of Warwick represented the Nevilles' interests. The articulate Reginald Boulers, Bishop of Coventry and Lichfield, was the group's spokesman. The Earl of Oxford and the new Earl of Shrewsbury completed the delegation. Somewhat surprisingly, the Duke of Buckingham and Jasper Tudor were not included, possibly because they were already with the sick king. The delegation travelled to Windsor on the morning of 24 March with precise instructions. If King Henry was well enough to listen, their questions could be put to him in any order, but if he was not then only the first items were to be raised.

The lords were ushered into Henry's presence while he sat at dinner and they waited until he had finished before addressing him. It is unlikely that Margaret was present since they were under strict instructions not to disclose their purpose to anyone but the King. Bishop Boulers assured Henry that the whole kingdom was anxiously awaiting his recovery. Receiving no response, Boulers pressed on to say that the lords had undertaken to govern in the King's absence, and they hoped that he would be pleased by what they had done to uphold his authority.

Boulers then got down to business: he informed Henry that Chancellor Kemp had died. He asked Henry to name a successor for the Chancellorship and for the Archbishopric of Canterbury. He assured Henry that the Great Seals had been locked away in a closed casket and entrusted to the chamberlains of the Exchequer for safe keeping. Boulers reminded Henry that he had promised the Commons that he would appoint a 'discrete and sadde [wise] council', but owing to the King's indisposition this had not been done, so a list of potential councillors had been drawn up for Henry's consideration. Of course, any name could be omitted, or others added as the King thought fit. Henry made no reply.

It was abundantly clear that King Henry was with them in body only. He did not acknowledge their presence or react to Boulers's speech. Each of the lords tried addressing him in turn, kneeling before him as he sat motionless. Bishop Waynflete finally called a halt and suggested that as they had not dined, they should adjourn. Perhaps Henry needed leisure to think over all they had said? On their return Henry was still seated at table and once again the lords entreated him to answer them. When Henry did not respond they suggested that he might be more comfortable if he removed to his bedchamber. Henry was raised gently and supported by two attendants, one on either side, but the change of room did him no good. He was asked a third time for his instructions, or for anything he wished to say to them, but he was unaware that he was being spoken to. Finally, they asked if they should stay or go. The interviews had lasted all day but it was hopeless, and with 'sorrowful hearts' they left Windsor for Westminster, where Bishop Waynflete reported the melancholy news. King Henry was totally incapable of the simplest action and was certainly in no fit state to govern.[36]

The royal physicians, Masters John Arundel, William Hatclyffe, John Faceby, Margaret's physician, and two surgeons had been made responsible for King Henry's care.[37] They were now instructed to apply all the remedies known to them to speed his recovery. These included shaving the head, gargles and baths, potions, syrups and confections, laxatives and suppositories, embrocation, ointments and plasters, and bleeding, with or without cutting the skin. It says much for Henry's strong physical constitution that he survived the pharmacopeia of cures he underwent.[38]

16

My Lord Protector

The Lords still had reservations about accepting York as Protector. They knew that if King Henry had been able to nominate someone to rule in his stead that person would not be Richard of York, but they had no one else to turn to. York's hour had come. On 27 March 1454, the Lords in Parliament nominated York as Protector and Defender of the Realm. On 3 April by an Act of Parliament modelled on that of 1422, when the Duke of Gloucester became Protector for the child king, York's appointment was confirmed. He was to guard England against enemies from without and rebellion from within, but the Lords added a caveat: York was the King's Chief Councillor but not his regent and he would hold the office only during the King's pleasure or until Prince Edward came of age. His wage was set at 2,000 marks per annum, but the act stipulated that whatever monies were allocated to the Protectorate, the Queen's grants were not to be affected.[1] Under the circumstances it was the best Margaret could hope for.

York made the customary declaration of his unworthiness before he outlined his terms: Parliament must enact that he had been chosen by the Lords of their own free will and not as a result of any coercion on his part. King Henry must be informed as soon as he recovered that York had accepted the appointment because he was the King's loyal liege man and for no other reason.[2] There was one more hurdle to overcome: the act had to be endorsed by the Chancellor under the Great Seal, but there was no Chancellor. On 2 April, the day before he officially became Protector, York created his brother-in-law Richard Neville, Earl of Salisbury as Chancellor of England, the first layman to hold the position in fifty years. York needed a Chancellor he could trust. Traditionally, the Chancellor was a bishop but with disorder at home and the threat of invasion from abroad it made sense to appoint a magnate with considerable financial and military resources. As Warden of the West March Salisbury was as powerful as the King within his jurisdiction and far more respected and feared. He could raise as many men as he saw fit to defend the border with Scotland at the crown's expense, but they were not the King's men: they were retainers of the Warden of the March, and they wore the Neville livery.

Richard Neville was fifty-four, the eldest son of Ralph, Earl of Westmorland, by his second wife, Joan Beaufort, King Henry IV's half-sister. Salisbury could not inherit his father's title since Ralph had sons by his first marriage, but that did not matter; Richard was Earl of Salisbury in right of his wife, Anne Montague, the daughter of Thomas Montague, Earl of Salisbury. Earl Ralph had endowed Joan with extensive estates in Yorkshire that should have passed to the senior Neville line, but Joan left them to her eldest son.[3] The bad blood between the two branches of the Neville family, while never as acrimonious as that between the Nevilles and the Percys for domination in the north, continued throughout King Henry's reign. Like all of Joan's children Salisbury was ambitious and acquisitive and he relished the prospect of becoming Chancellor. The Earl of Worcester, the Earl of Warwick, and Viscount Beaumont came into York's presence in the Parliament chamber at Westminster carrying the chest in which the Great Seals of England had been deposited after Chancellor Kemp's death. York administered the oath of office and unlocked the chest. He displayed the three Great Seals to the assembled Lords before handing them to Salisbury, who ceremoniously replaced them in their white leather bags. The bags were sealed with Salisbury's seal and replaced in the chest to be taken to Salisbury's town house.[4]

York dissolved Parliament in mid-April and scheduled his first Council meeting for 6 May.[5] He hoped to form a balanced but subservient Council to underpin his authority, since the validity of his rule depended on its acceptance by the lords, and he prudently included some powerful men whom he preferred to have inside his tent rather than outside it.[6] He had made it a condition of becoming Protector that councillors should attend meetings when summoned. Accepting a place on the Protectorate Council was a two-edged sword: in the short term it offered influence at the heart of government but in the long term there could be serious repercussions. When King Henry recovered, he might hold the Council responsible for York's actions or even for accepting him as Protector. On the other hand, it was difficult and possibly dangerous for anyone to refuse. The lords' response was hardly an overwhelming vote of confidence in York.

The Dukes of Norfolk and Buckingham and the Earl of Oxford reserved the right to be absent should they be overcome by the various ailments that suddenly and mysteriously afflicted them. Buckingham went so far as to declare that there were times when he was unable to sit a horse (did he suffer from gout?). The Earl of Worcester, as Treasurer, had an eye on costs and he requested an undertaking that Council members be reimbursed for any expenses that rightfully belonged to the crown. The Earl of Shrewsbury said he would serve on the same terms as any other earl. The Earl of Warwick modestly claimed that he was too young and inexperienced, but he did not mean it.

Lord Scales, whose wife was Margaret's senior lady, refused to commit himself. He said he was primarily a soldier and he doubted that he would be of much use, but he would attend occasionally.[7] Salisbury persuaded Viscount Bourgchier to overcome his scruples and the blunt Sir Thomas Stanley declared that he knew he had only been included to act as the Council's errand boy. In this he was being disingenuous; his estates in Lancashire, Cheshire, and the Marches of North Wales made him the most powerful man in that region and

York could not afford to ignore him. Stanley was King Henry's man and a seat on the Council would allow him to safeguard the King's (and his own) interests in the Duchy of Lancaster. John Say, chancellor of the duchy, agreed to serve, probably for the same reason. York also needed Viscount Beaumont, the chief steward of Margaret's lands. He held his first wife's extensive estates in Lincolnshire in trust for their son and his second wife was none other than Katherine Neville, the Dowager Duchess of Norfolk, who clung so tenaciously to her life interest in the Mowbray lands. Beaumont declared that he was the Queen's man and that his first allegiance was to Margaret, and he lived too far away to attend Council meetings regularly.

Peter Tastar, the Gascon Dean of St Seurin, fell back on poverty, declaring that as an exile he did not have the wherewithal to do a duty that he had been doing since he came to England in 1449. Robert Botill, Prior of St John of Jerusalem, said he could only attend if his presence was not required elsewhere, although his commitments had never interfered with his attendance at King Henry's councils. Safety was his primary concern and he asked for a guarantee that Council members could come and go without being molested. His request was seconded by the timid Lord Cromwell, who cited his great age, infirmities, and general feebleness as reasons for declining. Salisbury pleaded with him not to withhold his vast experience at this time.

The bishops' excuse was the heavy workload of their diocesan duties. Bishop Waynflete even suggested that they should attend meetings by rote! Only William Booth, Archbishop of York, promised unreservedly to support York.[8] Booth was qualified to succeed John Kemp as Archbishop of Canterbury, but Booth was not born into the magnate class and York passed him over in favour of Thomas Bourgchier, whom he nominated to succeed John Kemp as Archbishop of Canterbury.[9] The Bourgchiers were half-brothers of the Duke of Buckingham and descendants of King Edward III. Thomas Bourgchier had received preferment in the church because of his lineage, becoming Bishop of Worcester and then of Ely despite protests from the Pope that he was under-age. York relied on his kinship with the Bourgchiers as well as with the Nevilles; he had no brothers or uncles and his sons were still too young.

The defence of Calais was York's first test as Protector and Defender. York had been outraged by King Henry's appointment of the Duke of Somerset as Captain of Calais. The Calais garrison of about 2,000 men-at-arms and archers formed England's only standing army and York wanted it to be at his disposal should the need arise. He persuaded the Lords in Parliament to 'request' that he should take the captaincy, and he demanded virtual autonomy over the Pale of Calais with guarantees of men and money, and the right to dismiss all officers in post and replace them with his own men. Parliament was to foot the bill and ensure prompt payment.[10] York wanted the prestige but not the responsibility that the captaincy entailed. He never visited Calais and he did not indent formally as captain until July, after the crisis that convulsed the town in the spring had passed.[11]

The soldiers in Calais were restive over non-payment of their wages and they were not inclined to accept a new captain, even Richard of York, until their grievances were addressed. The garrison mutinied at the beginning of May and seized the staple's precious wool and all the foodstuffs in the warehouses, causing alarm in London as well as in Calais.[12] Rebellious soldiery heightened the danger of an attack on the town either by the Duke of Burgundy or by the French. York approached the merchants of the Calais Wool Staple for a loan, but the Staplers demanded that the 12,000 marks (£8,000) owed to them on tallies at the Exchequer that had expired should be made good. The Lords in Parliament gave the requisite assurances and the Staplers agreed to advance 10,000 marks.[13] York sent Viscount Bourgchier to Calais to face the angry soldiers and offer them a pardon in the King's name. Bourgchier quelled the mutiny by distributing some 7,000 marks in cash thanks to the Staplers loan.[14]

While Viscount Bourgchier faced the angry garrison, York went north to deal with a threat that was more chimerical than real. Henry

Power Struggle

Holand, Duke of Exeter, York's son-in-law, had met with the Earl of Northumberland's son Thomas Percy, Lord Egremont, in the north early in 1454.[15] The Percy Earls of Northumberland were Wardens of the East March towards Scotland. They had been the ruling magnates in the north before the rise of the Nevilles and they viewed the Earl of Salisbury and the whole Neville clan as encroaching upstarts. Egremont was the most unruly and pugnacious of Northumberland's sons and he was engaged in a private feud with John Neville, the youngest of Salisbury's sons, despite the Council's orders to him to keep the peace.[16]

The Duke of Exeter, like Egremont, was a hot-headed young man with a strong sense of grievance that made him a natural rebel, and he had good reason to resent the Duke of York. In 1446 York had been keen to marry his eldest daughter into the Lancastrian line. Exeter's father, John Holand, the son of King Henry IV's sister Elizabeth, was not wealthy enough to support his dukedom and John succumbed to the blandishments and the enormous dowry that York offered him to marry his heir to York's eldest daughter. Henry Holand was sixteen, Anne was still a child, and the marriage was not a happy one. When John Holand died in 1447 King Henry unwisely granted the young Henry's wardship to the Duke of York, who never paid even half of the sum he had offered as Anne's dowry.

Exeter came to London in the spring of 1454 and quarrelled with York. He may have protested that as King Henry's closest blood kin he should have been summoned to Council and included in York's government. Typically, York rebuked him for 'the arrogant behaviour and misconduct which has been habitual with you.'[17] Exeter promptly re-joined Egremont in the north and using Percy retainers they occupied the city of York and took the Mayor and the Recorder hostage, even though the city offered no resistance.[18] York seized the opportunity to demonstrate that he could maintain law and order anywhere in England and he marched north. The Protectorate Council under York's direction accused Exeter of 'usurping other power than was yeven to you by us' (i.e. behaving unlawfully), and they ordered Exeter to return to London.[19]

As soon as they heard that York was coming in person the foolish young men fled.[20] Egremont and his men retired to the Percy manor of Spofforth. Exeter, accompanied by a band of only thirty men including his bastard brothers Robert and William, and thirteen men from Lancashire, launched his 'rebellion'. He urged the Percy retainers to rally to the Lancastrian colours, and primed by excitement and by Exeter's promise that they would no longer be liable for taxation, they shouted their enthusiastic approval. Egremont then disappeared; he was reported to be in Cumberland and Westmorland on a recruiting drive. Exeter moved into Lancashire to whip up more support, but his bravado did not last long.[21]

York sent reports of the rumours he heard or concocted to the Council, claiming that Exeter and the Percys were in open rebellion, and he convened a commission of oyer and terminer to sit in judgement on them.[22] York accused Exeter of writing seditious letters to men in Lancashire and Cheshire, among them Lord Greystoke. By a striking coincidence Greystoke was one of York's commissioners and the only man identified as receiving these letters. York's proceedings were extremely unusual: the commissioners were presented with pre-prepared accusations originating from the Privy Seal Office in London alleging that Exeter was either trying to usurp the throne or take control of the government. Exeter was accused of unlawfully assembling armed men with banners unfurled – which he probably had, men customarily grouped themselves around their lords' banners – but Exeter had not faced York or anyone else in the field. It was alleged that Exeter claimed that while King Henry was incapacitated and Prince Edward was still a baby he was the rightful custodian of the Duchy of Lancaster.[23] He had a point: if either the King or the Prince died he was the next heir to the duchy, if not to the crown.

The remaining indictments beggar belief: that Exeter would invite King James of Scotland to invade England was preposterous, but

Power Struggle

James enjoyed meddling in English affairs. He had requested permission for his stepfather Sir James Stewart, romantically known as the Black Knight of Lorne, to visit the Duke of Somerset in the Tower. James's mother, Queen Joan, was Somerset's sister and James, through Stewart, offered to rescue 'his cousin'. Somerset cleverly demonstrated his loyalty and his innocence by refusing. He told Stewart that he was confined by order of the Council for his own safety, implying that his life was in danger and that as King Henry's subject he would not accept aid from any foreign prince, even a relative. Stewart reported Somerset's reply to the Council; they were indignant and stated emphatically that Somerset was in the Tower on charges of treason and if Somerset said otherwise, he 'disclaunderith and blasphemeth'.[24] The memory of King James's impertinence and Somerset's riposte was fresh in York's mind. It did not require much imagination for York to link King James's offer with Exeter's 'rebellion'. The final indictment against Exeter was the recurring political calumny of attempted assassination: Exeter planned to murder York and the other commissioners by luring them out of the city of York to a nearby village, although how this was to be accomplished was not explained. It is on these indictments that the story of Exeter's rebellion has been built.[25]

The Council ordered Sir Thomas Stanley to disperse Exeter's few followers. Stanley urged Exeter to stop making a nuisance of himself and obey the Council's summons, 'whereupon he, right sadly the premises considering, anon from thence gently departed.'[26] Exeter was afraid of York. As soon as he reached London, he took sanctuary in Westminster Abbey.[27] York returned to the capital in July and ordered Exeter's removal, despite the protests of the abbot and the monks, and the Council 'authorised' York to consign Exeter into the care of the Constable of Pontefract Castle, who just happened to be the Earl of Salisbury.[28] Thus King Henry's closest kin, the Dukes of Somerset and Exeter, were incarcerated throughout York's Protectorate. As often happens when political expediency demands the blackening of a man's character, contiguity rather than common sense formed the basis of the accusations. Exeter's 'rebellion' was little more than a tempest in a teacup exaggerated by York for his own purposes. Exeter did not have the resources, even with Percy backing, to threaten York or his Protectorate seriously.

Margaret had returned to Windsor after her bid for the regency was rejected. Contrary to popular legend she accepted York as Protector with a good grace. She did not attempt to undermine his authority or to interfere in the running of the country. Acting as 'good lady', she even joined him to defend certain London parishes in a long-running dispute over the tithes that each parish was required to pay. York wrote to Pope Nicholas on the parishioners' behalf and someone, possibly York himself, enlisted Margaret's support. She sent her chaplain, Thomas Winchecomb, all the way to Rome to plead the case and Pope Nicholas ordered York and Margaret to get together with the Bishops of Norwich and Hereford to find a solution before the volatile Londoners resorted to rioting.[29]

Margaret thanked the prior of Canterbury cathedral for his offer to send holy water as a curative for the sick king and for 'the grete zele, love and affeccion that ye have towards my lords helth.' Margaret was a conventionally pious woman and she put more faith in the efficacy of prayer and fasting than she did in the men around her. Many years later, in exile, she would confess that she had not fulfilled all her vows to fast and to undertake pilgrimages in the hope of divine intervention to restore King Henry's health.[30]

The investiture of Prince Edward as Prince of Wales had been delayed, probably by Cardinal Kemp's death. It took place at Windsor on 9 June. The Duke of Buckingham, who had deputised for the King at the Knights of the Garter feast in April, probably performed the ceremony. York was absent whether by accident or design, but the Earl of Salisbury as Chancellor and members of the court witnessed it.[31] Margaret watched as the baby prince was crowned with a gold circlet, a gold ring was slipped onto his tiny finger, and a gold rod was placed in the small hand. Another carefully stage-managed ceremony took place at Windsor and Margaret may have been among those who witnessed the charade. Thomas Bourgchier had not yet been installed as Archbishop of Canterbury. The situation was difficult: the kiss of homage to the King by a newly created primate of England was so important that it was only omitted in time of plague. It could not be delayed for much longer and despite King Henry's condition it took place in August. Henry was seated on his throne in full public view with a cross in his hand. Thomas Bourgchier knelt before him, took the cross, kissed the King's hand, and repeated the oath of allegiance, even though Henry was oblivious of everyone around him.[32] Once installed, the Archbishop could not be dismissed.

The vexed question of what to do with the Duke of Somerset remained unresolved. A Great Council meeting in June had proposed to release him on bail pending trial, but of the sixty-six lords summoned only twenty-four attended and York himself was absent.[33] York vetoed the idea when he heard of it; he objected that the number of councillors present was insufficient to overturn a decision taken by a majority. He suggested that the judges should be consulted, knowing full well that in a matter affecting a royal duke they were unable to pass judgement.[34] The Council tried to have their cake and eat it too: Somerset must be put on trial but the hearing would be postponed until a larger Council could be convened. The absent lords were ordered to attend on 21 October and the Duke of Norfolk was charged to come prepared to repeat the accusations he had made against Somerset in 1453.[35] York had no intention of allowing Somerset to leave the Tower, and if a Great Council met on 21 October no record of it survives. The Duke of Somerset was left to languish where he was.

Richard of York wanted to be Protector, but did he want to do the job? Throughout his Protectorate, York ignored the lawlessness that he had once deplored. He showed as much indifference to the law, and partiality to his adherents, as he had accused King Henry's ministers of doing.[36] He allowed the magnates the prescriptive liberty of disorder which they enjoyed, and he left them to get on with it. The Earl of Devon, believing that he had York's protection, felt free to pursue his feud with Lord Bonville. The best the Council could do was to bind both participants to keep the peace for a year.[37]

The Duke of Norfolk made good his proclamation that he would have the 'princypall rewele and governance' throughout the shire that bore his name. In 1453 he had sent men to intimidate the sheriff's officials at Ipswich into returning his chosen candidates to Parliament. The sheriff, Thomas Sharneborne, was Margaret's household esquire and he invalidated the return, citing threats of physical violence and the fact that Thomas Daniel was ineligible to stand in East Anglia because he held no lands in Suffolk. The case was heard in the King's Bench in 1454 and Norfolk, as a member of the Protectorate Council, obtained an acquittal for his men on a technicality. He claimed that they had attended the election peacefully, and that they were victims of Sharneborne's avarice because he had been bribed to rig the election.[38]

In Derbyshire, the feud between the Blount and Longford families saw the sack of Walter Blount's manor at Elvaston. Sir Nicholas Longford accused Blount, whom Margaret had appointed steward of High Peak, one of her dower lands, of being a traitor because he took service with York. Longford was summoned to answer for his actions, and he defied the Protectorate Council's authority, literally. He refused to receive the summons and his retainers attempted to force the unfortunate messenger who delivered it to eat the parchment and its seal. York put in a brief appearance for a hearing in Derbyshire, but Longford failed to attend, and no further action was taken against him.[39]

Lord Egremont reappeared in Yorkshire in October and before long the Percys and the Nevilles were again at each other's throats. Egremont and his brother Richard encountered Thomas and John Neville in a fierce fight near the Neville manor at Stamford Bridge. Egremont and Richard Percy were outnumbered and captured.

Power Struggle

Thomas Neville sent them to his father's stronghold at Middleham and an oyer and terminer session in York condemned the Earl of Northumberland, his wife, and his sons, to pay the enormous sum of 16,800 marks (£11,200) in damages to the Nevilles.[40] This was far beyond the Percys' means and in any case they had no intention of paying it. York had Egremont and Richard Percy imprisoned in Newgate where Egremont remained until the end of 1456 when he engineered his escape.[41] The 'battle' at Stamford Bridge ended the 'rebellion' in the north, but it was thanks to the Nevilles, not to the Duke of York.[42]

York did make an attempt to reform the size of the royal household. Successive parliaments had deplored the cost of King Henry's generosity throughout his reign. The King's stables had already been reduced, since he no longer moved around the country.[43] At a special meeting on 13 November 1454, twenty-eight 'councillors' endorsed an ordinance cutting the royal establishment to more affordable proportions.[44] York did not remove those closest to the King, but he required them to sign the ordinance. The 'below-stairs' staff was left largely intact but the number of king's knights and esquires was massively reduced and the yeomen of the King's chamber were slashed almost in half.[45] York had sound financial reasons for these cuts but they were outside his authority, and Lord Dudley resigned as Treasurer of the Household in protest. It was one of York's last acts as Protector before King Henry recovered his senses. Margaret was not affected. The ordinance fixed her household at 120 persons, on a par with her existing establishment, and Prince Edward was allowed a household of thirty-nine persons.[46]

The Duke of York was Protector for less than a year and he spent much of that time away from London leaving the routines of government in the Council's hands. Having used every means at his disposal to become Protector, York faced but failed to tackle the same difficulties that had beset the Duke of Somerset: a near bankrupt Exchequer, local feuds, threats from abroad and inadequate defences at Calais. There was little to choose between York's regime of 1454 and Somerset's of 1452.[47] Neither was in power long enough to establish a broadly based and widely accepted government. York had power without royal authority. He procured the Lords' support in Parliament and Council by making vague threats of the consequences if they opposed him, but he did not have the King's mandate, the only indisputable source of the right to rule. Despite his own and later Yorkist propaganda, Richard of York never achieved consensus or an unconditional acceptance of himself as the King's true liegeman and protector.

17

Fortune's Wheel

King Henry came to his senses almost as quickly as he had lost them. He had been moved from Windsor to Margaret's palace at Greenwich for the Christmas festivities of 1454 and perhaps the less formal but equally familiar surroundings aided his recovery. He suddenly knew who and where he was on Christmas Day. Two days later he ordered his almoner to ride to Canterbury and his secretary to Westminster with his customary Christmas offerings. Henry could not remember anything that had happened while he was ill, and Margaret waited five days to be sure that he was well enough to be told of the birth of his son. Henry was surprised but delighted. He thanked God and asked the child's name and the names of his godparents and said he was well pleased. Margaret was careful not to overburden him, since his recovery might still be fragile, but she ventured to tell him the most important piece of political news that Chancellor Kemp was dead. Henry was sorry but not distressed, since Kemp was an old man.

William Waynflete, Bishop of Winchester, and Robert Botill, the Prior of St John of Jerusalem, were Henry's first visitors and he held a rational conversation with them. They probably told him warily that the Duke of York had become Protector during his illness, but Henry declared that he was in charity with all the world and he wished that all his lords were too. They left him with tears of joy and relief in their eyes. The royal household held its collective breath for two weeks before Margaret's squire, Edmund Clere, thought it safe to send the joyful news to the Pastons: the King was fully recovered.[1] Processions through the streets of the capital gave thanks for what seemed to be a miracle.²

Henry expected the court to be precisely the same as it had been in 1453 and he soon noticed that the Duke of Somerset was not in attendance. No one dared to tell him that his favourite minister was a prisoner in the Tower. The Duke of Buckingham, possibly encouraged by Margaret, had Somerset secretly conveyed to Greenwich.³ Henry signed an order covering Somerset's release. Buckingham, with three other lords, stood surety to the Protectorate Council at Westminster in February that Somerset would appear before the King in Council to answer the charges against him.⁴ The councillors were relieved: Somerset had been imprisoned for treason on conciliar responsibility but he had not been brought to trial.

King Henry convened a Great Council at Greenwich in March and Somerset complained that he had never been told why he was kept in prison for 'one year, ten weeks and more', while his pleas for a hearing were ignored. He challenged 'eny Persone [who] wold Charge him with any thyng contraire to his Trouth or Ligeance' to speak out. York preferred not to take up Somerset's challenge, since he was uncertain of his own future. He expected Henry to acknowledge his services as Protector, but Henry did not remember the Protectorate and he treated York and Somerset's antagonism as a private matter, just as he had after Dartford. Henry did not understand that his illness had irrevocably altered the political scene in England and he ordered York and Somerset to put up bonds of 20,000 marks each to keep the peace until June of the following year, pending further arbitration by the lords.⁵ Henry declared Somerset to be his true subject and not guilty of the accusations against him, 'to the which noe Persone said contrarie.'⁶

York felt humiliated. He resigned as Captain of Calais and the Earl of Salisbury resigned as Chancellor.⁷ In the chapel over the gateway at Greenwich, Salisbury ceremoniously laid the three leather bags containing the Great Seals of England on a stool before the King.⁸ York and Salisbury then left Greenwich. Henry had not expected Salisbury's resignation and he hastily conferred the Chancellorship on its traditional holder, the Archbishop of Canterbury. Henry then re-established his Council as he remembered it and there is no reason to suppose that he was influenced by Somerset, Margaret, or anyone else. He revived his practice of naming a favoured member of his inner circle as Treasurer of England and James Butler, Earl of Wiltshire, replaced John Tiptoft, Earl of Worcester, who had been Treasurer since 1452. Perhaps Henry thought Worcester had been too closely associated with York during the Protectorate.

Henry had instructed the Earl of Salisbury to transfer the Duke of Exeter, who was still incarcerated in Pontefract Castle where he had been confined on York's orders, into the custody of the Duchess of Suffolk at Wallingford, but Salisbury had ignored the order.[9] Henry sent Buckingham's son, the Earl of Stafford to release Exeter and escort him to Wallingford where he could be kept comfortably until the King made up his mind what to do about him.[10] Henry was not yet sure how far the reports that Exeter had raised rebellion in the north were true: was he a rebel against the crown or against York?

Henry had a lot of catching up to do and he summoned a second Great Council to meet at Leicester in May. Knights of the shire as well as the lords were bidden to attend since it was important that the (landed) 'gentilmen' of England should see for themselves that Henry was fully recovered.[11] A Great Council suited this purpose better than Parliament and it would also be less stressful for the King. It is dangerous to impose modern medical knowledge on the fifteenth century, but Henry was barely three months into his recovery and common sense dictated that he should not be subjected to the violent public demonstrations that too often accompanied meetings of Parliament at Westminster. The tradition that the Duke of Somerset was so unpopular in the capital that he convinced Henry not to summon Parliament is based on Yorkist propaganda.[12] Somerset was nearing fifty. He had been in the Tower and politically impotent for over a year and imprisonment had taken its toll; like Henry, Somerset needed time to recover. Margaret and the Duke of Buckingham may have influenced Henry's decision to call a council at Leicester in the heart of the Duchy of Lancaster and Margaret's dower lands.

As soon as he received the summons the Duke of York jumped to the wrong conclusion, just as he had when Henry called a Great Council in 1452. York was convinced that the Leicester Council would be directed against him, that Somerset would poison Henry's mind and use royal authority to encompass his disgrace.[13] York boycotted the Feast of the Garter at Windsor, claiming that he was ill. The Earl of Salisbury and Viscount Bourgchier also excused themselves.[14] York's fixation on Somerset loomed so large in his mind that he was unable to see round it. He would not meet Somerset in Henry's presence, especially not at a gathering of a brotherhood like the Knights of the Garter. The Nevilles had their own concerns. Salisbury feared that the King's displeasure with him would undermine the prospects of his extensive family: the Nevilles were a power-hungry clan. Warwick did not trust the King. The Earls of Warwick had been premier earls in England until Henry gave precedence to his Tudor half-brothers. Warwick also suspected that Somerset would claim a share of the Beauchamp inheritance in right of his wife, Eleanor.

Imprecise reports reached King Henry that York and the Nevilles were mustering their retainers. Henry sent the Earl of Worcester, Robert Botill, the Prior of St John of Jerusalem, and Bishop Boulers of Hereford to reason with York and he waited in vain for a response; York detained them.[15] Somerset, as Constable of England belatedly decided to raise reinforcements and he sent the Earl of Shrewsbury, Lord Cromwell, and Sir Thomas Stanley to muster men in the Midlands and converge on Leicester. On 18 May, the Mayor of Coventry was ordered to send an armed force to join the King 'wheresoever he be'.[16] On 19 May Chancellor Bourgchier sent letters under the Great Seal to York, the Nevilles, and the Duke of Norfolk, who was believed to be with York, ordering them to come peacefully to the King at Leicester on pain of forfeiture. York was to be accompanied by no more than 200 men, and the others by no more than 160 men each.[17]

King Henry left London on 21 May, the day the Great Council was supposed to convene. The Duke of Buckingham and his Staffordshire retainers formed the King's escort. Somerset, his son Henry, and his stepson Lord Roos, John Bourgchier, Jasper Tudor, the Earls of Stafford, Wiltshire, Devon, and Northumberland, and William Percy, Bishop of Carlisle, and the northern Lord Clifford were with the King, but they had only their personal retinues.[18]

At Watford Henry learned that York and the Nevilles were nowhere near Leicester; they had concentrated their army at St Albans to block his path. At this critical juncture Henry turned to the Duke of Buckingham, as he so often did in times of crisis, and Buckingham replaced Somerset as Constable of England. Buckingham advised Henry to proceed to St Albans and invite York to negotiate.[19] Early on the morning of 22 May Henry took up residence in a private house in the centre of the city rather than in the abbey. Buckingham sent his herald and a pursuivant to issue a formal warning to York: he must disband his army or face forfeiture for coming in arms against the King.

York asked if this order came from Henry himself and was told that it came from Buckingham and Somerset, but on Henry's orders.[20] The Duke of Norfolk was rumoured to be in the vicinity at the head of a large force. He hedged his bets by sending Mowbray Herald to York, and York employed the herald to as his go-between to give the impression that Norfolk was in the Yorkist camp. Mowbray carried an ultimatum from York to King Henry: Somerset must be put on trial for treason, Henry's word alone was insufficient to exonerate him. York, Salisbury, and Warwick had come to demand justice as York had on previous occasions (York had not forgotten Dartford). They were the King's loyal subjects and Henry should receive them and publicly acknowledge them as such. If Henry refused York would not answer for the consequences. York made a mistake by trying to coerce King Henry. Henry refused to receive York's communication and he ordered Mowbray Herald to deal directly with Buckingham.

Buckingham believed he could talk York out of being so foolhardy and he mendaciously told Mowbray that the King did not know which earlier petitions York was referring to. Buckingham assured the herald that he was not there to defend the Duke of Somerset; all he wished to do was to escort King Henry peacefully to Leicester. He suggested that York should withdraw to Barnet or Hatfield to avoid the possibility of an unwanted encounter. If the Yorkist forces pulled back, he would receive any nobleman York cared to send to him for further discussions. He instructed the herald to remind the Duke of Norfolk of their kinship and promised the King's grace and future royal favour if Norfolk held aloof. For all his rhetoric Buckingham had nothing to offer York.

Mowbray Herald bravely pointed out that Buckingham's offer was not what York had demanded or what he was likely to accept. He delivered Buckingham's message to York and York sent him back to Buckingham to request a personal reply from King Henry. Buckingham prevaricated. He promised to send his herald with the King's answer, but he did not keep his word. York made one last effort. He sent Mowbray Herald a third time for the promised response. Mowbray was detained at a barricade and asked to state his business, just as if this was his first visit! Buckingham then refused to see him; he sent word by a third party that King Henry would not reply to York until he held further consultations with his lords.[21]

York's patience was exhausted. If force was the only way to remove Somerset, then force it would be. He gave the order to advance along the two roads guarded by barricades that led into St Albans. Salisbury advanced along one street and York along the other, leaving Warwick in the centre at the rear ready to throw his weight behind whichever wing looked likely to break through. Warwick seized the initiative. He sent some of his 'northern men' to take the market square while he led his troops through the gardens behind Holywell Street and fell on the Lancastrian lords grouped around the royal banner.[22] Warwick had planned all along to turn conflict into deadly combat. Somerset had to die and so did Henry Percy, Earl of Northumberland, the Nevilles' rival in the north. Both were killed in the mêlée. Salisbury's personal enemy Lord Clifford died defending the barricades at one end of St Peter's Street. Somerset fought bravely, sustaining several wounds before he was felled by a blow from an axe. His son Henry Beaufort, fighting beside him, had to be carried from the field and was reported to be dead. Buckingham's son, the Earl of Stafford, was seriously wounded. The Earl of Wiltshire either fled the field or made his escape after the battle. A hostile chronicler recorded that Wiltshire, one of the handsomest men in England, fled from St Albans for fear of marring his looks.[23]

King Henry stood beside his banner but took no part in the fighting. Buckingham, standing close to him, was wounded in the face and Henry was grazed in the neck by a stray arrow. Sir Philip Wentworth threw down the royal banner and the fighting ceased.[24] For the first but by no means the last time the Earl of Warwick used a battle to get rid of his enemies. Bodies were strewn along the narrow streets and among the dead was William Cotton, Margaret's receiver general, and Roger Morecroft, the keeper of her council chamber.[25] King Henry was alone, in pain, and in a state of shock. He had never seen men dead on a battlefield. York, Salisbury, and Warwick came and knelt before him in the street to protest that they were his loyal liegemen; all they had done that day was for his safety. Henry accepted York's submission, hardly understanding what was being said to him, and meekly allowed himself to be conducted into the abbey to have his wound dressed and to spend the night. John Whethamstede, Abbot of St Albans, reproved York for leaving the bodies of his enemies untended in the streets and he persuaded York to allow the monks to bury Somerset, Northumberland, and Clifford within the precincts of the abbey.[26]

Fortune's Wheel

Within hours of the battle Margaret received the news that Henry had been wounded and taken prisoner. She took refuge in the Tower of London with the baby prince.[27] Her anxiety was enhanced by her fears for Henry's safety and for his sanity. It was an anxious time for the Duchess of Somerset as well: two of her sons were engaged in the battle. Lord Roos was captured and Henry Beaufort, despite his wounds, became Warwick's prisoner. The Duke of Buckingham was detained at St Albans for 'safekeeping', ostensibly to prevent York's soldiers from killing him.[28] He was permitted to return to London only after he agreed to accommodate the new regime. The outspoken Lord Dudley was reported to have 'appeched many men', and he ended up in the Tower, but the Earl of Devon made his peace with York and accompanied him to London. The Earl of Wiltshire remained in hiding in Hampshire, uncertain whether it was safe for him to return to the capital. York's enmity towards him was well known.[29]

York escorted Henry back to London with all the honour due to a king, but significantly Henry was lodged at the Bishop of London's residence by St Pauls, not at Westminster. To celebrate the Feast of Pentecost on Whitsunday, York escorted Henry, in full regalia and wearing his crown, to St Pauls for a thanksgiving service so that the Londoners could see the King attended by his most loyal subject.[30] The Battle of St Albans has been dismissed as a skirmish in the streets, but it was more than that.[31] Despite York's show of deference King Henry was his prisoner. York was triumphant, Warwick was satisfied, Salisbury was relieved, but the lords were uneasy.

York had not forgotten his annoying son-in-law. He sent the Earl of Worcester to take the Duke of Exeter into custody in King Henry's name, but the redoubtable Alice, Duchess of Suffolk, Constable of Wallingford Castle, refused to surrender her 'prisoner'. Alice and Exeter thought it safer for him to stay where he was. Thwarted, York directed the Council to warn Alice of the consequences if Exeter escaped.[32]

York could not allow the question of responsibility (and guilt) for the battle to remain unresolved. It was vital to his political future to establish his loyalty in the highest court in the land. York might not be Protector, but he intended to become the King's Chief Councillor. Writs to summon Parliament were issued and York set about reconstructing the government. He retained Thomas Bourgchier, the Archbishop of Canterbury, as Chancellor and reinstated Viscount Bourgchier as Treasurer of England.[33] The constableship of Windsor Castle was entrusted jointly to William Neville, Lord Fauconberg, Salisbury's brother, and John Bourgchier, Lord Berners, Viscount Bourgchier's brother, the only Bourgchier who had been with King Henry at St Albans.[34] The richest prize, the Captaincy of Calais, went to the Earl of Warwick. York no longer coveted it now that Somerset was dead. Warwick was young, ambitious, energetic, rich, and it was what he wanted.[35] He had emerged from the shadow of his father at St Albans and burst onto the political stage. York recognised Warwick as potentially a far more valuable ally than the Earl of Salisbury, but in the years ahead the Houses of Lancaster and York would pay dearly for letting this particular genie out of the bottle.

King Henry was far from well. He sent for Gilbert Kymer, a well-known physician, 'for as moche as we be occupied and laboured, as ye knowe wel, with Sicknesse and Infirmitiees.'[36] Possibly on Kymer's advice Henry, Margaret, and Prince Edward moved from Windsor to her castle at Hertford, a favourite residence of Queen Katherine where Henry had spent time as a child. The air around Hertford was said to be salubrious for invalids.[37] York had intended to keep Henry in safe custody at Windsor until Parliament convened, but he could scarcely countermand the King's preference for another royal castle. York took up residence in the immediate vicinity at the Friary in Ware, Warwick moved to Hunsdon, and Salisbury to Rye House, so that they could seize the King and 'escort' him back to London should the need arise.[38]

Their fears were unfounded; King Henry came to London in July to open Parliament as planned. York had prohibited public discussion of St Albans but the question of who was to blame was still a hot topic. Tensions swirled around the court and a quarrel flared up between the Earl of Warwick and Henry's chamberlain, Lord Cromwell, who foolishly maintained that the battle had nothing to do with him since he had not been there. Warwick shouted at him that he was a liar and accused him in the King's presence of provoking the conflict. Warwick's scornful diatribe was directed as much at King Henry's advisors as at Cromwell: they were to blame for the exclusion of the Duke of York from the King's favour and it was their fault that York had been obliged to take the field to defend his honour. The ageing Cromwell was thoroughly frightened by Warwick's onslaught, he resigned as Chamberlain and took refuge in the nearby Hospital of St James under the protection of the Earl of Shrewsbury, although he recovered his nerve sufficiently by the end of the month to come to Parliament and take the oath of loyalty to the King.[39]

Parliament opened on 9 July in an atmosphere alive with menace. York and the Nevilles were escorted by heavily armed men and large contingents of their retainers gathered in and around Westminster. The Commons elected Sir John Wenlock as their Speaker. Henry had dismissed Wenlock as Margaret's chamberlain, and although he was reported to have fought for the King and been wounded at St Albans, he was known to have sympathy for York.[40] York faced the Lords in Parliament and put up a spirited, if specious, defence, although no one had accused him of anything. His position was simple: it was all a misunderstanding. York was an expert at self-justification and his choice of the guilty parties was masterly. He laid the blame for the Battle of St Albans squarely on the shoulders of three men: the Duke of Somerset, who was dead, Thomas Thorpe the ex-Speaker, whom York had imprisoned in 1453, and who, it was claimed, had fled at St Albans, and William Joseph, a clerk in the King's household who had had the temerity to suggest that King Henry stood in need of protection while he was ill. They and they alone were responsible.[41]

Power Struggle

York alleged that they had intercepted and withheld two vital letters that he had written before the battle. The first, addressed to Chancellor Bourgchier, informed him that York and the Nevilles had banded together to clear themselves of false allegations before these could be repeated to the Council at Leicester. Their army at St Albans was solely for their own (and the King's) protection since they stood in physical danger from the machinations of their enemies. The second letter, dated 21 May on the eve of the battle, should have been delivered to King Henry at Watford by the Earl of Devon at two o'clock in the morning! Conveniently, Devon could not confirm or deny this since he was not present in Parliament. This letter referred to 'oure Enemies of approved experience, such as abide and keep them under the wyng of your Mageste Roiall.' Their malicious slanders had prevented King Henry from accepting York and the Nevilles as his loyal liegemen.[42]

These letters conflicted with York's demand before the battle that the Duke of Somerset be handed over to him or imprisoned to stand trial for treason. Whether Henry saw the letters or if they even existed before the battle was immaterial.[43] They were a face-saving device for the King and the Duke. York maintained that if King Henry had seen the letters he would have taken their protestations at face value, but Henry had not seen them and so the unthinkable had happened: Henry had misunderstood York's position while York, not knowing of Henry's ignorance, had been forced to fight. Both contentions were spurious.[44]

A full pardon, ostensibly in King Henry's own words, was read out in Parliament. It exonerated York, the Nevilles, and all those who were with them at St Albans.[45] The Lords pledged their loyalty and allegiance to King Henry and the Duke of York was the first to reaffirm the oath he had already broken. King Henry's clemency confused and dismayed many of the men at Westminster. If any man, even the mightiest, could be pardoned for coming in arms against the King then royal justice was not just in abeyance, it was defunct. A Paston correspondent referred 'to the which bill mony a man groged full sore' and he urged the recipient to burn his communication because 'I am loth to write any thing of any lord.'[46] It was unwise for anyone to criticise Richard of York.

King Henry issued a general pardon and prorogued Parliament on 31 July. On the same day, presumably to reassure the Nevilles of his favour, Henry issued a Privy Seal order for valuable military equipment forfeited by Lord Camoys (who had surrendered Bordeaux and was therefore deemed a traitor) to be given to the Earl of Salisbury.[47] Henry remained at Westminster throughout August. His presence was needed to authenticate the changes that York made in the Council, but at the end of the month he returned thankfully to the tranquillity of Hertford. [48]

Henry's world had fallen apart at St Albans, but he was adept at passive resistance. Throughout the parliamentary proceedings he simply opted out. God had given York the victory and Henry bowed to His will. Henry did not collapse into complete withdrawal as he had in 1453 but he unable or unwilling to reconvene Parliament. The Council received word in November that the King was ill and would remain at Hertford,[49] and they authorised the Duke of York to open Parliament on 12 November 1455, as he had in 1454.[50]

Lawlessness was uppermost in the Commons' minds. The Earl of Devon had resumed his favourite pass time of attacking his neighbours. Assembling an army of his retainers and tenants was easy, but paying for it was not, and Devon needed a large sum of money – fast.[51] Just before midnight on 23 October, Devon's eldest son, Sir Thomas Courtenay, left the family seat at Tiverton with a band of men and rode the few miles to Upcott Manor, the home of Nicolas Radford, a wealthy and well-respected figure who was the recorder of the city of Exeter and the legal representative of Devon's enemy Lord Bonville. Courtenay lured Radford's servants out of the house with shouts of 'Fire!' and Radford came to his bedroom window to see what all the noise was about. Courtenay asked to have speech with him and forced his way into Radford's presence while his retainers looted the house from top to bottom; they even stole Radford's horses to carry away their rich pickings. Radford was outraged but powerless. Courtenay insisted that Radford should accompany him back to Tiverton, assuring him that he would not be harmed, but as soon as Radford was out in the open Courtenay rode away, leaving six of his men to strike Radford down. It was a heinous murder of an old man, but worse was to follow. Henry Courtenay, Thomas's brother and Radford's godson, returned four days later and desecrated Radford's corpse. The news of this outrage was carried to Chancellor Bourgchier in London and he sent messengers galloping to inform the Duke of York and King Henry.[52]

The murder of Nicholas Radford shocked the Commons to the core. If he could be murdered in cold blood, then none of them was safe. York and his advisors took full advantage of the Commons' mood. York's councillor, William Burley, a wily lawyer and an ex-Speaker, persuaded John Wenlock to relinquish his role as Speaker to allow Burley to lead a delegation from the Commons to demand an immediate meeting with the Lords.[53] Burley petitioned them that as King Henry was ill and 'myght not entende to the protection and defence of this lande', he should be urged to nominate a lieutenant 'such an able person, as should best attend to the defence and protection of the said land.' Burley did not actually nominate York, but the implication was obvious: the precedent set in 1454 should be followed and York should become Protector once again. Burley did not allow the Lords time to indulge in their usual slow deliberations; two days later he submitted a second petition and two days after that a third petition making it clear that the Commons would brook no delay.[54]

Chancellor Bourgchier put the question bluntly to the Lords: what was to be done? The Commons would not conduct any business until they received a satisfactory answer. They were loyal to King Henry but they wanted stable government, and if the King was too ill to provide it the Duke of York was an acceptable substitute. No one knew how ill the King was or how long his malady would last. Chancellor Bourgchier announced that King Henry had requested that the government be placed in the Council's hands, provided he was kept informed of any action touching his 'honour, worship and suerte', and he had endorsed York as Protector.[55] The Lords confirmed the decision at breakneck speed; what had taken months of meetings, discussions, and possible alternatives to empower York in 1454 took only two days in 1455, and his patent was issued on 19 November. York made his usual show of reluctance before agreeing to become Protector for a second time, but he had got what he wanted.

In the meanwhile, the Earl of Devon had occupied the city of Exeter and proceeded to terrorise its inhabitants. The Bishop of Exeter had died in September and Lord Bonville, the Constable of Exeter Castle, was not there, so authority in the city was in abeyance. Devon was bent on extracting every penny he could from all available sources, and he compelled the dean to return the pledges that Devon had made for repayment of a loan of £100 from the cathedral. Nicholas Radford had entrusted much of his personal property to the cathedral and Devon ordered the canons to hand over all of Radford's valuables, threatening that otherwise the cathedral would be ransacked, and the goods forcibly removed. He also had Radford's house in the city stripped bare. The Mayor courageously told Devon roundly that he and his council were not party to Devon's quarrels and would take no part in them; but they were powerless to prevent Devon's occupation of the city.[56]

Devon laid siege to Powderham Castle, belonging to Sir Philip Courtenay, a relative of the Earl but an ally of Lord Bonville. Philip sent an urgent plea to Bonville for assistance and Bonville gathered his retainers and advanced on Powderham. Two armies clashed in a mini civil war at the field of Clyst, and Bonville's men were routed.[57] Devon then attacked Bonville's principal seat at Shute. Bonville fled to King Henry at Hertford, but Henry had no idea of what was happening, and he sent Bonville back to Parliament and the protection of the Duke of York.[58] In the Commons' opinion, Devon and Bonville were equally guilty and they petitioned to have both men imprisoned.[59]

Chancellor Bourgchier had assured the Commons that, as Protector, York would deal with lawlessness and the Council commissioned a number of nobles, including Lord Bonville, to array themselves and support York in bringing Devon to heel.[60] York made no move until he prorogued Parliament for the Christmas recess. He then travelled south-west in a leisurely fashion, sending for Devon and his sons to attend him. York never reached the long-suffering city of Exeter, which Devon had vacated on 21 December. He and his son dutifully submitted to York as York knew they would; he had given them plenty of time.[61] He 'arrested' Devon and brought him back to London in the new year, but he also ensured that Devon was not summoned to answer in Parliament for his misdeeds.[62] York did not instigate the Courtenays' outrageous behaviour but it played into his hands and he did nothing to check it. The damage was done, and the conflict was over long before York intervened, although he claimed credit for resolving it.

Lancastrian Queen

18

Queen Consort

King Henry remained at Hertford. The Duke of York opened the third session of Parliament on 14 January 1456 under the impression that he would continue as Protector for some time to come. The burning issue in this session was not lawlessness but money. The Commons had introduced a bill for a Third Act of Resumption that was more far reaching than their previous acts and encroached on the King's prerogative. They demanded the resumption of Duchy of Lancaster lands that King Henry had set aside for the accomplishment of his will, as well as grants to his cherished foundations of Eton and King's College and the estates he had bestowed on his Tudor half-brothers.[1]

York believed that resumption was the only way to reduce royal debt. He needed money to conduct his government and the Lords had stipulated that his salary would not be increased (or even paid) until income at the Exchequer improved. York rarely saw any point of view other than his own and he made a disastrous mistake. He backed the Commons' bill and attempted to bulldoze it through the Lords. But an Act of Resumption passed in the King's name without his assent was simply not acceptable and it dismayed even York's own supporters. York was betraying his trust.[2] It also aroused the enmity of the royal household.

Opposition to resumption gathered momentum over the Christmas recess. Magnates who had not attended Parliament in November reappeared at Westminster in January.[3] The Earl of Wiltshire came out of hiding. The Duke of Exeter was still under house arrest at Wallingford and York intended to put him on trial in Parliament for his 'rebellion' of 1454,[4] but the Duke of Buckingham, the Earl of Oxford, Lord Berners, and Thomas, Lord Richemont-Grey (Exeter's cousin), stood surety that he would appear in chancery when summoned to answer the charges against him.[5] Exeter was set free to come to Parliament.

York was not impervious to the changed atmosphere. No one knew what to expect. Some said that York would be arrested, although who would have the courage to do so was uncertain. York's partisans countered with a piece of wishful thinking. They started a whispering campaign that King Henry would retain York as Chief Councillor in recognition of his services. York came to Parliament in February with armed men at his back, just as he had in July 1455. A blazing star appearing in the night sky added to the general unease. Celestial manifestations were believed to be to harbingers of great events and the Lords debated what it might mean. The strange phenomenon undoubtedly conveyed a warning, but a warning of what?[6]

It was imperative for King Henry to come to Westminster if only to relieve the heightened tensions, and this brought Margaret to the centre of the political stage. She mistrusted York's ambitions and resented his manipulating Parliament to make himself Protector while King Henry was ill but not incapacitated. Unexpectedly, she was offered the means to dislodge York, provided Henry could be persuaded to act. Margaret threw her weight behind the Lords' opposition. She rallied the royal household, and together they urged Henry to attend Parliament and remove York. This led inadvertently to the most famous contemporary description of Margaret, which has been taken to 'prove' that she meddled in politics for her own ends. 'The Quene is a grete and stronge laboured woman, for she spareth noo peyne to sue hire things to an entent and conclusion, to hir power.'[7] In the fifteenth century, the verb 'to labour' meant 'to importune'. The sentence, properly understood, reads: 'The queen is being importuned on all sides and is doing her utmost to meet the demands made on her with all the resources at her disposal.'

Margaret's part in bringing Henry to London was known well before they left Hertford. Propaganda against her began to circulate and one John Helton, an apprentice at law formerly of Gray's Inn in the Inns of Court, was hanged, drawn, and quartered for distributing bills claiming that Prince Edward was not Queen Margaret's son but a changeling. Helton admitted before his death that his information was false – one wonders who put him up to it.[8] The acidulous Thomas Gascoigne, viewing developments with a jaundiced eye from the safety of Oxford, did not doubt that Margaret played a major role in York's dismissal.[9] The tradition that Margaret intervened from motives of greed is untenable: she did not stand to lose in the resumption. The Commons exempted all Duchy of Lancaster lands held by the Queen and decreed that if any of them were subsequently assigned to Prince Edward she was to receive compensation, provided her total dower did not exceed the original 10,000 marks.[10]

York had made it a condition of accepting the Protectorate that King Henry could not dismiss him without the assent of the Lords in Parliament, but he was hoisted with his own petard, for this is precisely what happened. York's support had evaporated. Henry came to Westminster on 25 February and dismissed York as Protector, Defender, and Chief Councillor.[11] York acquiesced with dignity, and he continued to attend Council until Parliament was dissolved, probably to ensure payment of his outstanding wages. King Henry repudiated the Second Protectorate. He awarded the Duke only 1,000 marks for his 'personal labour in journeying and riding on the business of the realm', but not as Protector.[12]

Whoever or whatever persuaded King Henry to reassert his authority, he dealt with the Commons' contentious Act of Resumption adroitly. After the offensive clauses that touched him personally had been removed and he had added some exemptions of his own, he won the Commons' approval by assenting to the act.[13] He also achieved a shift in the Nevilles' allegiance by retaining the Earl of Salisbury as a councillor and confirming him in the lucrative post of Chief Steward for the Northern Parts of the Duchy of Lancaster.[14] Henry exempted the Earl of Warwick from the Act of Resumption, referring to him as 'oure welbelovyed and trewe cosyn', and he honoured York's promise to make Warwick Captain of Calais. York had negotiated unsuccessfully for another loan from the merchants of the Staple to pay the Calais garrison. It was the only way to persuade the soldiers to admit a new captain, but it took royal authority to induce the Staplers to agree to lend the money.[15]

Henry dissolved Parliament on 12 March and turned his attention to the problems of government that York had not resolved. The sheriffs of Devon and Cornwall were ordered to enforce the peace in the West Country and to proclaim that all unauthorised gatherings, large or small, were illegal. The Earls of Wiltshire and Arundel, and eleven judges, received a commission to sort out the mess left by the Earl of Devon's machinations.[16]

York had not risked his popularity by attempting to restrain the anti-alien phobia that was never far below the surface in London. It erupted in April when a skirmish between an apprentice of the Mercers Company and an Italian escalated into serious disorder. The civic authorities imprisoned the apprentice for assault and the enraged Londoners ransacked houses and shops belonging to the Italian community.[17] King Henry moved to the Bishop of London's palace in the City hoping that his presence would quiet the unrest, and he convened an oyer and terminer session at the Guildhall presided over by his magnates, the Mayor of London, and the judges.[18] A mob surrounded the Guildhall howling for the apprentice's release and threatening to ring the great Bow Bell, calling on the citizens to arm themselves. The Duke of Buckingham was so disturbed by their lawlessness that he retired to his home at Writal and King Henry left the City for his palace at Sheen. The city authorities appeased the mob by releasing the apprentice, while the Mayor and the judges saved face by condemning three men to hang for robbery before they terminated the judicial session.[19]

London was not a healthy place in the summer months. Margaret and Prince Edward left the capital in May for her dower lands at Tutbury and went on to the Prince's castle at Chester.[20] York retired to his castle at Sandal in Yorkshire. They eyed one another warily: a Paston correspondent reported that York 'waytith on the Quene and she vpon hym.'[21] York's quiescence made Margaret uneasy and York distrusted Margaret's growing influence with the King.

Margaret had a more important reason than her suspicions of York for leaving London. King Henry had returned to the political world and regained control of the government, but for how long? He had twice been ill, once for an extensive period of total collapse, once for a shorter period when he had been absent in body or spirit for much of the time. No one, including Henry himself, knew if or when he might collapse again. The Council needed an alternative source of royal authority to confer legitimacy on conciliar rule if the King fell ill. A unique situation required a unique solution; was there an alternative to the Duke of York? One other person had been crowned and anointed by God: the Queen.

The suggestion that Margaret might play a political role as Queen Mother may have been mooted by Margaret herself, or by King Henry, or others close to the King. Margaret could count on support from the royal household and less certainly on the lords who had enlisted her help in their opposition to the Duke of York. She had learned her lesson: she could not become Regent, but with royal authority vested in the Prince of Wales as a surrogate for his father she could act in her son's name on her husband's behalf. It would be years before Prince Edward was old enough to assume the role of Protector, but for such a scheme to succeed acceptance of him as a figurehead would be vital.

To this end Margaret established her court in the Prince's patrimony of Chester and put the baby prince on display.[22] She chose the white swan as Prince Edward's badge and distributed elegant swan brooches made of gold and white enamel to the local lords and gentry. The white swan had been the Duke of Gloucester's emblem; it identified the Prince with the 'good Duke Humphrey', who had been Protector of England during King Henry's minority and over whose memory time had cast a golden glow.[23]

Margaret sent out a circular letter summoning local men who had affiliations with the Duchy of Lancaster and with the Prince's lands. She flattered them by asking for their support and good will.

> Trusty and welbeloved: We wol and charge you that all excusacions cessing and other occupacions y-left, ye shape yow for to be with us in all haste possible for certeine causes that moven us, which shalbe declared unto yowe at your commyng. Yeven, etc.[24]

Henry spent the summer at Sheen with Jasper Tudor in attendance, returning to Westminster for Council meetings.[25] Trouble was brewing along the Scottish border and there were disturbances in Wales. King James of Scotland, known as 'James of the fiery face' from a birthmark that marred his features but reflected his temperament, had murdered William, Earl of Douglas, the head of the powerful Douglas clan, in a drunken rage in 1452. The Earl's younger brother and heir, fearing for his life, fled to England and swore fealty to King Henry in 1455.[26] In the summer of 1456 King James accused Henry of harbouring a fugitive from Scottish justice and he repudiated the Anglo–Scottish truce, alleging English perfidy and bad faith, and he launched a series of raids into Northumberland.[27] The Council considered declaring war but decided against it. Instead, a contumacious letter under the Great Seal was sent to remind James that he was a vassal of England and that 'rebellion' on his part could have serious consequences.[28]

The Earl of Salisbury may have suggested that since the Duke of York was in the north, he was ideally placed to take order to King James and the Council offered York a commission to chastise the

Scots. York was relieved to think that the government still needed him, and he accepted with alacrity. He called out his Yorkshire levies and moved north in August to hurl defiance at the Scottish king. He wrote to King James as to an equal, although he was careful to refer to King Henry as his 'sovereign lord'. York declared that he was coming against Scotland in force and he challenged James to meet him in the field and not to skulk behind cowardly border raiding.[29] The King and the Duke were sabre rattling; neither had the resources to mount an invasion. But James's raids had been successful and that was enough for him; he returned home in triumph.[30] York maintained his threatening stance at Durham, well over a hundred miles from the Scottish border, but he did not venture further north.

Fighting was reported from Wales in June.[31] York had named Edmund Tudor, Earl of Richmond as the King's representative in Wales. The appointment owed more to the Tudor name than Edmund's relationship to King Henry. A half-Welsh son of Owen Tudor would be more acceptable to his xenophobic countrymen than an Englishman. Richmond took up residence with his young bride, Margaret Beaufort, in the Bishop of St David's palace at Lamphey in Pembrokeshire. York and Duchess Cecily had named Bishop de la Bere, and Gruffydd ap Nicholas as feoffees for their lordship of Nerberth.[32] The Welsh warlord Gruffydd ap Nicholas was the real power in the region and de la Bere may have facilitated a reconciliation between Richmond, Gruffydd, and his sons, Thomas and Owain. They were ruthless, lawless, and dismissive of royal authority except when it suited them. Gruffydd favoured King Henry over York because the King showed less inclination than the Duke to interfere in Welsh affairs.[33] Richmond recognised that Gruffydd had the power to suppress lawlessness (other than his own) on behalf of the crown, and that he could become a valuable ally.

Gruffydd's rival for power in the region was Sir William Herbert of Raglan, York's steward of Caerleon and Usk. Herbert's father-in-law, Sir Walter Devereux, was steward of York's lands in the marches of

Wales and constable of York's castle at Wigmore. He was staunchly loyal to York.[34] In August 1456 Herbert and Devereux, possibly at York's instigation, more probably on their own initiative but in York's name, assembled an army reputed to be 2,000 strong.[35] They filched the Great Seal from Lord Audley, the Chamberlain of South Wales, and used it to hold illegal judicial sessions and free prisoners to swell their ranks.[36] This was perilously close to treason. York had appointed himself constable of the royal castles of Carmarthen and Aberystwyth after the Battle of St Albans.[37] Herbert and Devereux captured Carmarthen, and with it the Earl of Richmond. They soon had second thoughts about imprisoning the King's half-brother; they abandoned Carmarthen and went on to 'recover' Aberystwyth. Richmond made no move to stop them; he may already have been ill.

King Henry was disturbed by the news from Wales and he ordered ordnance to be sent to Kenilworth.[38] He left London for Kenilworth in August, but he was still uneasy at the continuing unrest in the capital. He wrote from Lichfield on 3 September to prohibit large gatherings in the City and he instructed the Mayor, the aldermen, and the sheriffs that no one was to enter London except peacefully and with a moderate following. The City officials were to keep the City loyal and obedient, 'as ye wol answere unto us at your peril.'[39] Henry had William Cantelowe, Master of the Mercers Company, whom he believed to be the instigator of the riots against the Italians, placed under house arrest in Lord Dudley's custody at Dudley Castle.[40]

Henry met Margaret at Lichfield and they spent a week together possibly as guests of Bishop Boulers.[41] They finalised their plans to confer a measure of political authority on Margaret, and Henry instructed the Mayor of Coventry to prepare pageants for a civic reception for the Queen and the Prince.[42] The Prince of Wales would be recognised along with his father as first among equals, and the symbolic authority that Margaret had received at her coronation would be vested in her as Queen Mother. The city of Coventry in the heart of the Midlands was the ideal setting for what Henry and

Margaret had in mind. It was the largest provincial city in England after Bristol and York, deriving its wealth from the cloth trade. Henry had received a warm welcome there in 1451 when he created its first sheriffs, and he called its citizens 'the best ruled pepull thenne within my Reame.'[43]

Henry arrived a few days before Margaret and the Mayor, Richard Braycroft, footed the bill for a tun of wine as a gift to the King.[44] On 14 September Braycroft welcomed Margaret and presented her with a silver gilt cup containing fifty marks. Prince Edward was to receive a like gift, but Margaret had not brought him with her. A four-year-old was too young to be put through the gruelling business of day-long pageantry. Unfortunately, we have no description of Margaret or of her attire. She was twenty-six, in perfect health, as far as is known, and was happier than she had been for some years. She had fulfilled her primary duty by producing a healthy male heir, she had weathered the storms of Henry's illnesses, and she was about to be given the security of political recognition.

The first pageant to greet her was a representation of the Tree of Jesse flanked by the prophets Isaiah and Jeremiah, who rejoiced in the Prince's birth. St Edward the Confessor and St John the Evangelist stood at the east gate of St John's church, where St Edward declared that he stood 'godfather' to the Prince ('my gostly chylde') thus supplying a spiritual link to England's saint-king. At the conduit in Smithfold Street Margaret was welcomed by the four Virtues: Righteousness, Temperance, Strength, and Prudence, who assured her that her son was destined to bring peace and tranquillity to the land. Angels swinging censors were mounted on the Cross in Cross Cheaping where a conduit ran with wine.

The main pageant depicted the nine worthies (conquerors): Hector of Troy echoed Prudence's allusion to the Prince. Alexander the Great welcomed Margaret as 'quene principall' and referred to King Henry as 'the nobilest prince þat is born, whome fortune hath famyd.' King David linked Margaret's name with Henry's, and Judas Maccabeus confirmed King Henry's presence. King Arthur and Charlemagne promised to serve Margaret, King Joshua promised to fight for her, Julius Caesar hailed her and prophesied that her son, 'the same blessyd blossom at spronge of your body', would be a greater conqueror than Caesar himself. Last in line, Godfrey of Bouillon, the first Christian King of Jerusalem, described Margaret as 'stedefast & trewe'.

The final pageant displayed St Margaret miraculously slaying a great dragon and when the deed was done St Margaret addressed her namesake as 'Dame Margarete, þe chefe myrth of þis empire', and promised Margaret the protection of her prayers.

The four Virtues had proclaimed Margaret as 'quene crowned of this lande' and hailed her son as the legitimate successor to a long line of kings; he would be as great and as fearless a ruler as the nine worthies who had declared Margaret to be the most virtuous and venerated of women and had pledged their allegiance and their protection to her, an allusion to the expectation that the current lords of the land should do likewise. St Margaret had promised heavenly protection and therefore heavenly approval of England's queen. Margaret would form part of a new trinity of royal authority – king, queen, and prince – which would unite the realm in peace and prosperity, just as the pageants for her coronation had promised. Margaret was both wife and mother, but she was revered and empowered as Queen Mother, for she had given England a prince who would be the future protector and defender of his people.[45]

This elaborate display was a calculated political statement to precede the Great Council that Henry summoned to meet in October.[46] On 24 September Margaret's chancellor, Lawrence Booth, replaced the ailing Thomas Lisieux as Keeper of the Privy Seal.[47] Booth may have been Margaret's choice but he was well qualified to fill the position. An able administrator like his half-brother William, Lawrence was chancellor of Cambridge University and a cleric trained in civil law.[48]

Lancastrian Queen

The Great Council met, and King Henry replaced Viscount Bourgchier as Treasurer of England with John Talbot, Earl of Shrewsbury, and granted him the same rights as the former Treasurer John Tiptoft, Earl of Worcester. Bourgchier was not mentioned.[49] Shrewsbury was not a military man like his father, the Great Talbot – his talent lay in administration. He had spent his life in his father's shadow, and he was not the Great Talbot's favourite son. After the death of his half-brother, Viscount Lisle, at the Battle of Castillon, Shrewsbury had recovered the Talbot lands that his father had settled on Lisle, making Shrewsbury a rich man. His principal recommendation as Treasurer was his loyalty to King Henry and his wealth, an important consideration for the impoverished government.[50]

On 11 October, the lords of the land gathered in the King's chamber in the priory of Coventry Cathedral to witness the ceremony as the greatest office in the land changed hands. Chancellor Thomas Bourgchier, the Archbishop of Canterbury, surrendered the three Great Seals to the King and Henry bestowed them on William Waynflete, Bishop of Winchester.[51] Margaret might have preferred her former chancellor, William Booth, Archbishop of York, who was younger than Waynflete, but she recognised the importance of appointing a Chancellor whom Henry knew well and with whom he could work comfortably. Thomas and Henry Bourgchier had been York's appointees and they were unlikely to accept Margaret in her new role. The Duke of Buckingham questioned the wisdom of dismissing his Bourgchier half-brothers and he suspected Margaret's influence, but the Bourgchiers were strongly affiliated to the Duke of York and there was a suspicion that Viscount Bourgchier, or one of his sons, had been in the Yorkist ranks at St Albans.[52]

If King Henry had been in his senses when Cardinal Kemp died, Waynflete would undoubtedly have succeeded him as Chancellor and as primate of England. Of all the bishops, Waynflete was closest to the King. He had been provost of Eton and after Cardinal Beaufort's death in 1447 Henry rewarded Waynflete with the richest see in England.

Waynflete was Henry's confessor and the chief executor of Henry's will. They shared an interest in education. Waynflete founded Magdalen Hall at Oxford and enlarged it at considerable expense to become Magdalen College.[53]

On the same day as Waynflete became Chancellor and the Great Council was about to adjourn, a brawl erupted in the streets between the Duke of York's retainers and the Duke of Somerset's men. Henry Beaufort hated York and resented his presence at Coventry. York had labelled Henry's father Edmund Beaufort a traitor, and the slur was intolerable to the young duke. The city's watch was called out and two watchmen were killed in the affray before Buckingham intervened to restrain Somerset. The incident precipitated York's departure, giving rise to the rumour that Somerset had attempted to have him murdered. York took his leave on cordial terms with King Henry, but not with Margaret. He had not forgotten her part in ending the Second Protectorate and she had not forgotten his part at St Albans.[54]

Towards the end of 1456, Henry and Margaret paid a visit to Prince Edward's lands in the north-west. This was as close as Henry ever came to the disturbances in Wales. Somewhat surprisingly William Herbert and Sir Walter Devereux had obeyed Henry's command to come to Coventry. Devereux hoped to mitigate the consequences to himself and his family of capturing the King's half-brother, and he pledged a recognisance of £1,000 to present himself to the constable at Windsor Castle, and to remain in custody until such time as it pleased the King to release him.[55] Herbert had second thoughts and he escaped from Coventry before he could be committed to the Tower. He fled back to Wales where he set about mustering men from Usk, Abergavenny, Caerleon, and Glamorgan.[56]

In what may have been the last effort of his life, Edmund Tudor, Earl of Richmond, sent word to King Henry advising him to come to terms with Gruffydd ap Nicholas as the only man in Wales capable of stopping William Herbert in his tracks. Margaret took Richmond's warning seriously and she encouraged Henry to issue a comprehensive pardon to Gruffydd and his sons.[57] Henry and Margaret were at Shrewsbury when they learned that Edmund had died at Carmarthen Castle on 1 November, at the age of twenty-six. Jasper Tudor left immediately to rescue his sister-in-law, Margaret Beaufort, who was awaiting the birth of her child. Jasper escorted her to his castle at Pembroke and there, on 28 January 1457, when she was still only fourteen, she gave birth to the future Tudor king, Henry VII. Jasper would devote the rest of his life to the interests of his nephews, first Prince Edward and then Henry, Earl of Richmond. King Henry did not venture any further into Wales; he returned to Kenilworth while Margaret went to Leicester to prepare for the Christmas festivities. Did Margaret grieve for Edmund Tudor? We do not know.

19

Royal Court in the Midlands

Margaret had taken an active role in politics in 1456 and the Duke of Norfolk had come to her attention once again. Norfolk did not attend the Great Council; he had been hauled before a Council meeting at Westminster in May for unspecified causes, probably for disturbing the peace, but possibly in relation to Richard Southwell, one of his servants.[1] In one of his periodic land-grabs in 1453 Norfolk had seized two manors belonged to the Duchess of Suffolk. Alice had vigorously defended her possession of them in court, they were restored to her, and Norfolk was bound over 'to do no hurt or harm to Alice, Duchess of Suffolk, or any of the people.'[2] Norfolk had cunningly enfeoffed the manors on his brothers-in-law, Thomas and Henry Bourgchier as Chancellor and Treasurer, and they had lodged a petition on Norfolk's behalf. The crown's lawyers argued that the manors should be taken into the King's hands.[3] During the Second Protectorate the Duke of York had appointed Richard Southwell as escheator in Norfolk, and Southwell had flagrantly flouted the law and used his position to recover the manors for the Duke of Norfolk. His action was brought to King Henry's and to Margaret's notice, possibly by Duchess Alice herself. Henry sent the Duke of Somerset to deliver a strongly worded reprimand and an order to Norfolk to dismiss Southwell from his service.

Eleanor, Duchess of Norfolk, was Thomas and Henry Bourgchier's sister, and she was not on close terms with the Queen. Margaret exchanged New Year's gifts with the other duchesses, but not with her. Duchess Eleanor resorted to the time-honoured custom of bribery. She sent Richard Southwell to Sir Philip Wentworth, King Henry's knight of the body and the steward of Margaret's manor of Feckenham,[4] and to Thomas Babham, Margaret's yeoman of the robes, a close associate of Margaret's treasurer,[5] to offer Wentworth £5 and Babham 5 marks as inducements for their 'good will', to advise her how best to reassure the King and the Queen that Norfolk was loyal, despite his previous connection to the Duke of York. Eleanor's choice of messenger was unfortunate as it reminded Margaret that Southwell was still in Norfolk's employ. Margaret warned Norfolk that he and his duchess risked losing royal favour if he continued to maintain a servant against the King's wishes, and one moreover who had ties to the Duke of York.[6]

The Great Council reconvened at Coventry in February 1457. King Henry arrived on the eleventh. Margaret and her ladies came unexpectedly a day later, riding pillion behind their male escorts, and Margaret sent her harbinger ahead to assure the Mayor that she wished to enter the city quietly.[7] Did she make a last-minute decision to join Henry or was it a put-up job between them? Margaret wanted to be present for the formal recognition of a separate council for Prince Edward.

King Henry had issued letters patent authorising the formation of a household and council for the Prince, but he left the selection of personnel entirely to Margaret. She chose hard-headed, experienced men to administer the Prince's estates and look after his interests in the years ahead. They were not chosen for their lineage or even for their loyalty but for their competence. The Prince's chancellor, John Morton, and his receiver general, Robert Whittingham, had been appointed in September 1456.[8] Morton was a graduate of Oxford University, a cleric and doctor of laws who had not previously been in Margaret's service. It is not known how he came to her attention, but no clearer indication of her ability to choose men of outstanding administrative, if ruthless, capabilities can be found than in her selection of John Morton. He went on to a spectacular career as Chancellor of England and Archbishop of Canterbury under the Tudor King Henry VII. Robert Whittingham was about the same age as Morton, in his mid-thirties. He had gone to Rouen with the Duke of Suffolk to welcome Margaret in 1445, and in 1448 he married Katherine Gatewyne, who had accompanied the Queen to England.[9] Whittingham was captain of Caen when the city surrendered to the French in 1450, and he may have entered Margaret's service as early as 1451; he became keeper of her great wardrobe as well as being Prince Edward's receiver general.[10] Viscount Beaumont became steward of Prince Edward's lands.[11] Margaret valued him highly for his loyalty and she relied on his wealth and his local influence.[12]

Thomas Throckmorton, the Prince's attorney general, was a Worcestershire man, a former client of the Earls of Warwick with extensive experience of conditions in the West Midlands. He was well known to Lord Sudeley, who may have recommended him to Margaret.[13] Throckmorton belonged to the kind of rising gentry family whose support Margaret was seeking. Sir Edmund Hampden, the Prince's chamberlain, was excused all official and civic duties required of a knight since he would be in daily attendance on the Prince.[14] Giles St Loo, an usher of the Queen's chamber, became keeper of the Prince's great wardrobe with wide powers of purveyance to maintain it. He had married Edith Burgh, another of Margaret's ladies, as his third wife in 1453.[15]

The magnates on the Prince's council included Reginald Boulers, Bishop of Coventry and Lichfield, and John Stanbury, Bishop of Hereford, whose dioceses lay in the heart of the Prince's lands. Lord Dudley was a former treasurer of the royal household, Lord Stanley was the King's chamberlain and Constable of Chester Castle. The Earl of Wiltshire, the Earl of Stafford, the great officers of state, and William, Archbishop of York, served largely *in absentia*.[16]

Lancastrian Queen

Edward was not yet four years old. He was Prince of Wales, Earl of Chester, and Duke of Cornwall, but the income from his hereditary lands was in the King's hands and was paid into the Exchequer.[17] In 1457 the Council settled these revenues on the Prince, vested in his council. They were to be paid to him directly, not via the Exchequer, as the chances of recovering them once they were swallowed by that bankrupt office were not great. Edward would continue to contribute £863 9s 7d annually to the royal coffers for his maintenance for as long as he resided in the King's household.[18]

The establishment of the Prince's council continued the policy of an alternative source of royal authority begun at Coventry a year earlier as a buffer against future political adversity. Margaret had no authority on her own but if Henry fell ill again the King's Council could merge with the Prince's, to form a government, with Prince Edward as its figurehead. At need it could resist any attempt by the Duke of York to become Protector for a third time. The Council decreed that writs and charters would be issued in the Prince's name, but his warrants required the assent of his mother and the overall direction of his affairs and control of his finances were put into Margaret's hands.[19]

This has been interpreted as an example of her greed and lust for power. The misogynist Thomas Gascoigne was outraged. In his opinion a queen should not meddle in politics and with typical exaggeration he enlarged on the facts: everything in the kingdom would now be done, for better or worse (and Gascoigne feared the worst) by the Queen's will.[20] But to whom, if not to Margaret, should the Prince's council have been made accountable? To King Henry, who was never Prince of Wales and took no interest in the principality, and whose neglect meant that these lands returned little revenue to the crown? To the officials at the Exchequer, who would dissipate it even further? The crown and Parliament would have done better financially if Margaret had been allowed to manage Edward's estates from the time that he became Prince of Wales in 1454.

Margaret's income had risen steadily since 1453 when her estates came under her sole control. She instituted the 'chamber system' of finance with revenue from her lands paid directly to her receiver general and to the treasurer of her household, to be assigned as she saw fit rather than passing through the sticky hands of royal officials.[21] 'Chamber finance' is deemed admirable in a king such as Edward IV, who practised it on a far more extensive scale, but it is condemned as avaricious and detrimental to good government when practised by a queen.[22] The Council recognised Margaret's financial acumen: they confirmed the grants made to her by Parliament in 1447 that endowed her with land rather than with (non-existent) cash from the Exchequer.[23]

Once the future of the Prince of Wales had been settled, Scotland, Wales, and the Duke of York claimed the Council's attention. They (and possibly Margaret) suspected that York was behind Devereux and Herbert's rebellion in Wales.[24] Chancellor Waynflete recalled York's previous opposition to the government and Duke Buckingham, who had never forgiven York for rejecting his overtures before the Battle at St Albans, reminded York that he had been pardoned only through the King's clemency. Buckingham knelt before King Henry and begged him not to pardon York, or any other magnate, who threatened the peace and stability of the realm.[25] Henry promised. The lords in council, including York, swore an oath on the Holy Evangelists that in future they would submit their quarrels to the King's judgement and would not take up arms except in the King's cause.

York surrendered the constableships of Carmarthen and Aberystwyth and King Henry compensated him with an annuity of £40. He also renewed York's commission as the King's Lieutenant in Ireland for a further ten years.[26] Henry had forgotten that he had named the Earl of Wiltshire as the King's Lieutenant of Ireland in 1453 before he fell ill, but York had recovered the position by order of the Council in February 1454 just before he became Protector.[27] No one believed that York would leave England or that Henry could or would force him to go. York wanted Ireland as he had once wanted the Captaincy of Calais, for its prestige, but not the duties or the isolation of returning to Ireland.

In Scotland, King James was again threatening the northern border. Henry Percy, Lord Poynings, the son of the Earl of Northumberland, had been Warden of the East March since the age of nineteen and in 1455, just after the Battle of St Albans, he had defended the great fortress of Berwick at his own expense against King James.[28] Now Earl of Northumberland, following his father's death at St Albans, Percy was England's real bulwark against the Scots. At Coventry King Henry granted him livery of his father's lands still in the King's hands without payment of the customary fees.[29] He authorised Northumberland to raise men at 'the King's wages,' and to arrest ships to bring in food and other necessities to defend Berwick, although where the money was to come from was not apparent.

King James then changed his mind. He sent a delegation to Coventry to renew the truce that he had abrogated a year earlier, and it may be at this time that Margaret intervened. She had an enduring faith in dynastic marriage as the best way to promote peace, and she suggested that two of King James's long unwed sisters, Annabelle and Joan, should marry the two younger Beaufort brothers, Edmund and John.[30] The princesses were not in Scotland and King James instructed his ambassador in France, Thomas Spens, the Bishop of Galloway, to arrange for the princesses to be sent home.[31] Sir William Moneypenny, a versatile Scot in the service of both the King of France and the King of Scotland, was to escort them.

Annabelle was at the court of Savoy. She had been betrothed as a child to the Duke of Savoy's brother, but King Charles opposed the marriage and it did not take place. Annabelle did not want to leave Savoy and the kindly Duke Louis refused to force her, but she could not disobey her brother's order and she joined her sister Joan at the French court.[32] Joan had her own household, paid for by King Charles. This was not altruism: royal princesses were assets to be used as diplomatic pawns in the marriage mart. Joan is described as 'the dumb lady', which may only mean that she was not as talkative as the other ladies at court, or that she did not speak their language well. Joan's sentiments are unknown, but it seems probable that she too would have preferred to remain in comfort in France rather than return to the bleaker living conditions of her homeland.

King Charles had an excellent spy service and if the story of the proposed Anglo–Scottish marriages had any substance the King undoubtedly got wind of it. The princesses' departure was delayed by a combination of bureaucratic hindrances and diplomatic niceties. They waited for weeks at Harfleur for a 'suitable' convoy to take them across the Channel and when a crossing was finally attempted luck favoured the French king. The ships were driven back to port by a storm and Charles's officials declared that it was too late in the year to risk the lives of the royal ladies in another attempt. Bishop Spens was comfortably ensconced at the French court and he forbade their crossing until the following spring.[33] By the time the princesses reached Scotland in 1458 the plan for their marriages, if it ever existed, had been dropped and the unfortunate ladies were married to Scottish noblemen. An Anglo–Scottish truce for two years was negotiated at Coventry without the ladies being mentioned.[34]

King Henry left Coventry in the traditional fashion, escorted beyond the city's bounds with his sword borne before him by the Mayor, carrying his mace, and the sheriffs displaying their white wands of office. Two days later, in stark contrast to her entry into the city, Margaret demanded to be escorted in the same way, except that no sword would be carried in front of her. The Mayor and aldermen were aghast; never before had a queen alone been accorded the same honours as the king. Margaret's officials were adamant: 'the Quene owed to be met yn lyke fourme as the kyng shold' and a refusal would incur her extreme displeasure.[35] Margaret had achieved a great deal at Coventry, her status and her abilities had been recognised and she expected appropriate honours to be shown to her as Queen Mother.

But her success had gone to her head and she over-stepped the mark.

The King and the court moved to Hereford. William Herbert was still on the loose in Wales. The Council had outlawed him and set a bounty of 500 marks on his head,[36] and Henry had issued a commission of oyer and terminer 'touching all treasons, insurrections, rebellions, etc.' in the counties of Gloucester, Hereford and Worcester.[37] The judicial hearings were to be conducted by the Duke of Buckingham, the Earls of Shrewsbury and Wiltshire, and Viscount Beaumont. The commission indicted Sir Walter Devereux, William Herbert and their retainers on numerous charges.[38] Some were true and some were contrived, including the standard accusation of a plot to kill the King at Kenilworth at a time when Henry was not there.[39] Nevertheless there was sufficient evidence for the judges to find Devereux and Herbert guilty. Devereux was in custody at Windsor,[40] and Henry offered to pardon Herbert provided he came in person and surrendered to the King.[41] Margaret did not approve of such leniency and nor did the leading citizens of Hereford. They knew Herbert of old and feared that as soon as the royal entourage departed, he would take reprisals against them. Margaret and members of the Prince's council (John Stanbury was Bishop of Hereford) protested that a pardon was an insufficient safeguard: Herbert and his unruly followers should be constrained and bound over to keep the peace.[42]

Jasper Tudor may have influenced Henry's leniency; he was shrewder in his approach to pacifying Wales than Margaret. Jasper was respected in Wales for his Welsh heritage and he understood the importance of good relations between the crown and men such as Devereux and Herbert. He met and made friends with Gruffydd ap Nicholas's sons and, less certainly, he established a relationship with William Herbert.[43] King Henry granted him Carmarthen and Aberystwyth and Jasper became the King's representative in Wales.

The Earl of Warwick did not come to Coventry for the Great Council. He was in Canterbury preparing to take up his post as Captain of Calais. He courted the citizens of Canterbury with that combination of charismatic charm and bonhomie that made him the darling of the people and he entertained the leading men of Canterbury and Sandwich to thank them for their good will in providing him with victuals and other necessities. In April he attended the marriage of his brother John Neville to Isabel Ingoldesthorpe, whose wardship and marriage had been granted to Margaret in 1456.[44] The marriage was arranged by Isabel's uncle, John Tiptoft, Earl of Worcester, who had married the Earl of Salisbury's daughter Cecily, the widowed Duchess of Warwick. Cecily had died in 1450 and Tiptoft was keen to maintain his links with the Nevilles. He was a childless widower and if he died without a direct heir Isabel would have a claim to the earldom through her mother, Joyce Tiptoft, Worcester's sister. It was an advantageous marriage for a younger son and John Neville had agreed to purchase it from Margaret. He issued ten recognisances of £100 each, to be met between November 1458 and November 1463.[45] The ceremony was performed by Thomas Bourgchier, the Archbishop of Canterbury, and the Earl of Salisbury probably witnessed it.[46] Warwick crossed to Calais in the summer of 1457, taking his wife with him. He planned to take up residence in Calais and make full use of the independence that the captaincy offered him.

Henry and Margaret returned to Coventry to celebrate the Feast of Pentecost with the traditional crown-wearing ceremony and procession to the cathedral on Whitsunday. The Duke of Buckingham walked at the King's right hand, and their son the Earl of Stafford carried the 'cap of astate'. Sir Richard Tunstall, Chamberlain of Chester, bore the royal sword and Viscount Beaumont carried the King's train. Margaret's train was carried by the Duchess of Buckingham. The Mayor of Coventry, fearful of giving offence after his recent dispute with the Queen, sent to ask if he should cancel the parade of the civic dignitaries because of the royal procession, but King Henry, mindful of the citizens of Coventry's loyalty, did not allow the presence of the court to upset local custom. He decreed that 'the Meyre & his brethern with the Cominalte shold keep theyre owen procession that day as they had vsed before-tyme yn his absence.'[47]

Ten days later Margaret witnessed the Corpus Christi pageants at Coventry in the company of the Duke and Duchess of Buckingham. She atoned for her previous blunder by lodging quietly at the house of Richard Wood of the Grocers' Guild, and one wonders if she realised her previous mistake or if King Henry had admonished her. Entertaining the Queen was a costly business: the Mayor and council made her a gift of 300 loaves of white bread, a pipe of red wine, twelve capons, twelve pike, a basket of peascods, a basket of apples and oranges, two baskets of comfits and a pot of green ginger. Corpus Christi was a long day. Margaret and her entourage watched all the pageants staged by the city's guilds, except for Doomsday, the Drapers' pageant, which had to be cancelled because of fading light.[48]

Despite their past differences over the dismissal of his Bourgchier half-brothers, the Duke of Buckingham had become Margaret's ally. It was a natural partnership. He was steward of the Duchy of Lancaster honour of Tutbury, the most valuable of Margaret's dower lands, and he had a fatherly affection for King Henry. Anne Neville, Duchess of Buckingham, was Prince Edward's godmother. She was older than Margaret, but she became a friend and confidant of the Queen much as the Duchess of Suffolk had once been. Like Alice, Anne was a book lover. When she died in 1480, she left her book collection to her daughter-in-law, Margaret Beaufort.[49]

The court had been in the Midlands for over a year and Henry showed no inclination to return to London. His decision to remove to Kenilworth and Coventry was not the administrative disaster that has sometimes been claimed, although it may have been a psychological one. The Council under Chancellor Waynflete functioned as it always had, whether Henry was present or not, and his absence did not unduly delay the business of government since in matters where his authority was required it could be obtained fairly quickly. There is no evidence that Margaret spirited Henry away to Coventry and kept him

Royal Court in the Midlands

out of London. Henry did not feel comfortable in the capital; Kenilworth and Coventry were where he wanted to be.

Nevertheless, Margaret had sound reasons for preferring to remain in the Midlands. She was better placed at Kenilworth and Leicester to strengthen royal ties with local affinities. Henry IV and Henry V had been active as Dukes of Lancaster, drawing the magnates and gentry of the region into their service by personal contact. Henry IV used the duchy's resources to reward the men who supported his bid for the crown, and Henry V harnessed the duchy as a source of men and money to fight his wars in France, considerably depleting the duchy's assets in the process. Henry VI preferred to farm out his responsibilities and leave local politics to his magnates and duchy officials. Years of royal neglect could not be rectified overnight; it would take time for Margaret to rebuild Henry's natural affinity as Duke of Lancaster. When she left Coventry after the Great Council, she paid a visit to Sir Edmund Mountford, a client of the Duke of Buckingham, at Coleshill.[50]

William Herbert's rebellion had distressed King Henry. Before he left Hereford, he commanded the sheriffs in every shire to enforce the statute of 1399 against the giving of livery. It was common practice for lords to issue liveries displaying their colours or devices to the men they recruited in pursuit of private feuds, whenever they felt inclined to attack their neighbours. Margaret had rebuked Lord Ferrers of Groby for his unlawful giving of liveries, and for the attacks on her tenants by his liveried retainers in Leicestershire.[51] King Henry decreed that in future only he and the Prince of Wales would be permitted to issue them.[52]

Henry's fears of 'thinsolence of evil disposed and misgoverned people' runs through his letters and orders. He delegated sweeping powers to the lords who had estates in the Midlands, most of whom were with him at court, to act with the sheriffs in stamping out disturbances wherever they occurred.[53] Margaret may have encouraged Henry to delegate this responsibility to shield him from the stress of going in person to meet out summary justice. She may also have suggested that John de la Pole, Duke of Suffolk, be named as a commissioner rather than the Duke of Norfolk, possibly as an inducement for the young duke to come to court. The Duchess of Suffolk was a power to be reckoned with in East Anglia, while the Duke of Norfolk was unreliable. In a fit of pique Norfolk requested permission to go on pilgrimage, as he had in 1450, although he was not sure where he wished to go. His licence, issued in August, covered Ireland, Rome, Jerusalem, or 'elsewhere'.[54] He probably never left England, since he was named to a commission of array in September and summoned in November to attend the Great Council of January 1458.

Margaret was an inveterate matchmaker and she facilitated several matrimonial alliances while the court was the Midlands. Marriage was an integral part of a society in which property and inheritance equated with status and dynastic marriages were very much a queen's concern. The widowed Margaret Beaufort, Countess of Richmond, was the richest prize in the marriage market and she embodied the Beaufort claim to the throne.[55] Her brother-in-law, Jasper Tudor, was eager to ensure protection for her, and two months after she gave birth to her only child, before her year of mourning was over, Jasper took her to visit the Duke of Buckingham to negotiate her marriage to Buckingham's younger son, the thirty-three year old Henry Stafford.[56] Only the Duke of York could rival the Staffords in wealth and social standing and they were Plantagenets, descended from King Edward III. The marriage took place in January 1458 when Margaret was just fifteen.[57]

The Earl of Shrewsbury's son John Talbot was about ten years old in 1457 and he was betrothed to Buckingham's youngest daughter, Katherine.[58] Betrothals of children who were too young to marry were commonplace and considered binding. Shrewsbury, as Treasurer of England, was a favoured courtier and rich enough for Buckingham to welcome his heir as a son-in-law while an alliance with the Staffords would enhance the Talbots' social standing. At about the same time a more incongruous marriage was arranged to put an end to a feud between the Talbots and the Berkeleys that dated back to 1451. At the age of over sixty, Lord Berkeley married Shrewsbury's eldest sister, Joan Talbot, who was over thirty but had never been married. Perhaps Shrewsbury was glad to get rid of her. Shrewsbury's stepmother, Margaret Beauchamp, Dowager Countess of Shrewsbury, the Great Talbot's second wife, had a claim to the Barony of Lisle which was held by Lord Berkeley. She wanted it as an inheritance for her son, yet another John, since the Earldom of Shrewsbury must pass to the eldest son by Talbot's first marriage. King Henry had obligingly created young John Viscount Lisle in recognition of Talbot's services to the crown. Countess Margaret was every bit as aggressive as her husband, and Lord Lisle took after his parents. In 1451 he attacked Berkeley Castle, capturing one of Berkeley's sons and holding him hostage. Lady Berkeley prepared to appeal their case to King Henry but Countess Margaret got wind of it and she had Lady Berkeley abducted and imprisoned in Gloucester Castle, where the unfortunate lady died in 1452.[59] Viscount Lisle was killed at the Battle of Castillon. One of Berkeley's sons also died in the battle, and another was captured. Perhaps Lord Berkeley had mellowed, perhaps pressure from Queen Margaret and the Earl of Shrewsbury, who wanted an end to the feud, made him amenable, but Berkeley did not sign a deed of reconciliation with Countess Margaret until a month before his death in 1463.[60]

Margaret enticed the perennial trouble-maker Thomas Courtenay, Earl of Devon, back into the royal fold by offering her niece, Marie of Maine, as a bride for Devon's heir. Marie was an illegitimate daughter of Margaret's uncle the Count of Maine and she had come to England with Margaret when she was still a child. The match was a considerable honour for Courtenay, and the King's great wardrobe supplied Marie's trousseau and her cream and gold wedding gown.[61] It has been suggested that Margaret arranged marriages exclusively for her own political interests, but who else was there? Only one of Salisbury's daughters was still unmarried. Margaret had probably sanctioned the marriage of Salisbury's daughter Eleanor to Lord Stanley's son, and she had agreed to John Neville's marriage with Isabel Ingoldesthorpe.

The most important marriage of all was arranged by the Duke of York, but it required royal assent and if Margaret did not have a hand in it, she certainly knew of it and did nothing to prevent it. York offered his daughter Elizabeth, with a substantial dowry, to John de la Pole, Duke of Suffolk. The proud and dynastically minded York would not marry his daughter to a man of lesser rank, and John was the only unmarried duke in England, except for Henry Beaufort, Duke of Somerset, who was out of the question. The Duchess of Suffolk could look no higher for her son than a daughter of Richard of York.[62]

Margaret also took a keen interest in the appointment of bishops. When Robert Neville, Bishop of Durham, died in July 1457, Henry and Margaret unwittingly and certainly unintentionally offended the Earl of Salisbury. Salisbury wanted Durham for his son, George, for whom he had successfully snatched the bishopric of Exeter in 1455. Robert Neville was Salisbury's youngest brother and Salisbury had dominated him for the past twenty years and subverted Durham's extensive patronage almost exclusively in Neville interests.[63] The bishopric of Durham was one of the wealthiest and most powerful sees in England; bishops of Durham were great magnates as well as princes of the Church and traditionally they served the crown as Keepers of the Privy Seal, although Robert Neville never did so. Salisbury looked on Durham as a Neville preserve, a source of men, money, and power. Any appointment to Durham outside the Neville family inevitably diminished the Neville sphere of influence and their resources in the north.

Probably at Margaret's instigation, Henry commended Lawrence Booth to Pope Callixtus for the vacant see. He then complicated matters by commending a second candidate, John Arundel, his chaplain and physician. The Pope concluded quite correctly that Booth was far better qualified than Arundel to become Bishop of Durham, and he reminded Henry that Booth's nomination had been endorsed by Margaret and by the Council, and he suggested that the King would be wise to accept him. Henry acquiesced.[64] Possibly on Margaret's advice, but more probably out of self-interest, Lawrence Booth adopted a conciliatory stance towards Salisbury and the Nevilles, but this did not reconcile Salisbury to the loss of the bishopric.[65]

20

Loveday

Henry and Margaret's life in the Midlands ended abruptly in August 1457 when a French fleet commanded by Pierre de Brezé raided Sandwich, Calais's main port of supply. Brezé sailed from Honfleur on King Charles's orders, to cruise the Channel and disrupt English shipping in retaliation for English piracy and to remind the new Captain of Calais that the King of France had a formidable navy.

Brezé's flotilla did not encounter any English ships so he went one better. At daybreak on Sunday, 28 August, his ships stood off the Downs and he landed three companies of soldiers with orders to march overland to Sandwich while he sailed round to attack the town by sea.[1] English archers aboard ships in the harbour launched a hail of arrows at the incoming French fleet. Brezé bombarded the town and threatened to set fire to the ships unless the English disembarked their archers. Sandwich was defended on the landward side by a strong wall fortified by two towers and the advancing French soldiers met with stout resistance. There were casualties on both sides but eventually weight of numbers forced the defenders to retreat into the town, and after some fierce fighting the French succeeded in raising their standard over the town's gates.

Chancellor Waynflete sent King Henry an urgent message to return to London and he issued commissions under the Great Seal for armed resistance. He instructed the Earl of Arundel and Lord de la Warr to array men in Sussex. Sir John Fastolf was appointed to defend Great

Yarmouth. The Bourgchiers, Sir Thomas Kyriell and Gervase Clifton were to call out the men of Kent.²

Kyriell reached Sandwich on 30 August with a relieving force.³ By late afternoon Brezé realised that he was fast becoming outnumbered. He was out for plunder, not for sack. He had ordered that the town was not to be burned, churches were to be respected, women were not to be raped, and non-combatants were not to be killed in cold blood, although he took some of the wealthier citizens prisoner for ransom. His men were tired: they had broken into the town's copious wine supplies and Brezé was anxious to get them, his booty, and his prisoners away before they became too drunk to be manageable. He took a few merchant ships as prizes and set fire to all the vessels that were of no use to him. He then led his ships back to sea, collected the soldiers who had retreated to their original landing point and returned in triumph to Honfleur.⁴ There was strong indignation in England that the French had been able to land – and escape – with impunity.

Chancellor Waynflete's message reached Henry at Coventry on 31 August and he left for Northampton on the following day. Margaret was not with him; she went to Leicester on her way to hunt in Rockingham forest as planned.⁵ Waynflete was convinced that Sandwich was the prelude to a full-scale invasion and his fears were shared by the Mayor and aldermen of London. The Common Council offered to equip ships lying in the Thames at their own cost to repel the French and Waynflete accepted gratefully. Alderman Thomas Cook rode to meet Henry at Northampton to assure him of London's support, and Henry told Cook that he had written to Hull and 'other places' to equip ships to join those in the Thames.⁶

As soon as Henry reached Westminster, England was put on a war footing. Commissions of array were issued in the shires.⁷ The Duke of Buckingham, as Warden of the Cinque Ports, was to arrest ships to carry Lord Welles and a contingent of men-at-arms and archers to reinforce the Earl of Warwick in Calais. Warwick was to put to sea and

Lancastrian Queen

engage the French fleet.[8] The Duke of Somerset was given custody of the Isle of Wight and Carisbrooke Castle to defend Southampton, and Sir Richard Woodville was appointed keeper of Rochester Castle; both were potential landing points for a French invasion.[9] Initially the Earls of Salisbury and Northumberland were to guard the north, since King James was not to be trusted. If the French invaded so would the Scots. But Henry wanted Salisbury to attend the Council and he sent Viscount Beaumont to meet Salisbury at Doncaster and bring him to London.[10]

Indignation at the raid on Sandwich fuelled mutterings against the royal family. In October John Atte Wode, a gentleman of Norfolk, reportedly uttered 'horrible treasons' and slanders 'against the king's person or majesty, and against the person and honour of Queen Margaret and Prince Edward', implying that the King was not a proper man and that the Queen was not virtuous. In November Robert Burnet stated publicly that King Henry had 'lost all his father had won', and it would have been better if he had been killed at St Albans. Burnet also alleged that Queen Margaret was raising troops for service overseas since the King was incapable of doing so.[11] Did Margaret rally support in the Duchy of Lancaster against the threat from France?

King Henry summoned a Great Council to meet in mid-October and Warwick came over from Calais. The chronicles tell a probably apocryphal story, one of the many legends of his own making that gathered round Warwick's name, that the excitable Dukes of Somerset and Exeter, and Lord Roos, planned to ambush Warwick as he approached London. Roos, like Somerset, had been captured at the Battle of St Albans. Exeter was Admiral of England and he resented Warwick being chosen to guard the Channel. Warwick reached Westminster unimpeded. The hotheads backed off because, according to one chronicler, Warwick was 'the most corageous and manliest knight lyvng' and no one dared to stand against him.[12] More probably, if the story is true, they were deterred by the size of Warwick's retinue. From the time King Henry granted him his title Warwick attended

Parliament and Council with a large escort of armed retainers. He was not afraid; it was part of a habitual display of his wealth as the rightful heir to the Beauchamp estates.

The Great Council was supposed to coordinate the defence of the realm, but mistrust divided the participants even in the face of a common enemy.[13] When King Charles resumed the war in 1449 the lords in council had been unanimous that domestic discord must be settled before an army could be sent into France. The divisions between Henry's magnates were far greater in 1457 than they had been in 1449. The rights and wrongs of the Battle of St Albans had not been resolved; King Henry had pushed it out of his mind rather than face up to its consequences, but the mutual hostilities it engendered had not abated. This did not bode well for the future, since dissension in England would serve French interests all too well.

The crown had no money to raise and equip an army. King Henry was dependent on his lords for men, money and field service. Someone providentially recollected that in 1453 the Commons had pledged to raise and pay for 13,000 archers. These could form the core of an army, but who would take command? The Duke of York was the obvious choice, but would Somerset and Exeter, not to mention the Percys, serve under him? The Duke of Buckingham may have doubted the wisdom of trusting York with an army. Henry favoured using the archers for defence, not for war with France. He failed to reconcile his lords and the question of what to do about the French threat, and who should do it, was not resolved. Henry declared that the difficulty of achieving unity of purpose had proved insurmountable; he dismissed the Council on 29 November and summoned the members to reconvene in January 1458.[14] It was now too late in the year for the French to invade, but preparations for a spring campaign or a spring invasion were put in hand. The Mayor and Common Council of London were instructed to prepare muster lists for their quota of archers. The lords and knights in every shire were to establish each county's capacity to return the number of archers allotted to them and their indentures were to be sent to the Exchequer by February 1458.[15]

The Earl of Warwick was the only man to get what he wanted from the Council by sheer force of personality. Henry confirmed him as Keeper of the Seas for three years and, to the disgust of the Duke of Exeter, he gave Warwick command of the royal flagship the *Grace Dieu*.[16] Sea-keeping, to defend the coasts and protect English merchant shipping, had been a hit-and-miss affair throughout King Henry's reign. His impecunious government routinely identified it with the defence of the realm in order to obtain tax grants from Parliament. There was no royal fleet. Privately owned vessels were pressed into service during invasion scares, whether perceived or real, and sea-keepers were appointed on an *ad hoc* basis for short periods, sometimes for less than three months. It was all the government could afford.

The Earl of Warwick struck a far better bargain with the Council than any of his predecessors. The Captain of Calais was the town's civil and military governor and autonomous within its bounds. The Pale of Calais stretched for twenty miles along the coast and six miles inland, with the fortresses of Oye, Marck, and Gravelines to the east, and Guines to the west. Calais was defended by its castle and by the Rysbank Tower at the entrance to its sheltered deep-water port. The captaincy had never been combined with keeping the seas, but Warwick obtained conciliar authority to hold both positions simultaneously.

He was empowered to recruit several thousand men, to supply their victuals, and acquire suitable ships to resist the King's enemies and do those enemies as much damage as he could by land and sea. He would receive tunnage and poundage from all the ports in England except Sandwich and Southampton, plus £1,000 a year from the Duchy of Lancaster. He could name his own custom officials and receive revenue directly from them, not via the Exchequer, and he had the right to resign if the promised payments were not forthcoming. He could capture territories belonging to 'the King's enemies' but would not be held responsible if they were subsequently lost, though he was not to attack the King's subjects, friends, or allies. He was to prevent piracy, although, in accordance with the laws of war, he could keep any merchandise lawfully seized and retain a third of the profits. Finally, and crucially, he was not required to account to the King or anyone else for any of his dealing.[17] If any Englishman benefited from the French raid on Sandwich it was the Earl of Warwick. With his appointment a new and potentially dangerous force entered English politics, one that was not yet recognised by King Henry or the Council.

Margaret and Henry went to Abingdon Abbey for the twelve days of Christmas.[18] The festivities did not pass without incident. Henry had pardoned the Earl of Devon and his sons for Nicholas Radford's murder, and Devon's heir had married Margaret's niece.[19] The Courtney family was with Margaret and Henry at Abingdon when Devon collapsed and died; he was only forty-four, and although his father too had died at an early age, unexpected deaths always gave rise to suspicions of foul play. It was rumoured that Devon had been poisoned. An ambiguous report in a strongly pro-Yorkist chronicle has added to the tradition of Margaret's iniquities: she was a poisoner![20] At some time during the Christmas festivities at Abingdon a grandiose plan was conceived. The idea may have originated with King Henry, who favoured arbitration, or with Chancellor Waynflete, or even with Margaret. A 'Loveday' was a traditional method of reconciliation, similar to a court of law, in which each side aired their grievances, submitted their justifications, and made their demands to a panel of arbitrators acceptable to both sides who sat in judgement and delivered their verdict.

The Great Council reconvened at Westminster on 28 January 1458. King Henry harangued his lords on the 'evils' arising from the 'rancours' among them. Did Margaret stiffen Henry's spine and persuade him to exercise his prerogative to demand his lords' obedience? He announced sternly that their divisions threatened the peace and stability of the realm and made it impossible to conduct Council business. It was high time for the Council to put an end to this sorry state of affairs. Henry announced a Loveday and ordered the Council to select arbitrators. He declared that whatever settlement was reached would be binding on them all.[21] After he outlined his requirements in an unusually forceful manner Henry left them to get on with it and retired to Chertsey Abbey. The Duke of York and the Earl of Salisbury had arrived early with their retinues. York took up residence at Baynard's Castle near the Black Friars and the Earl of Salisbury established himself at the Herber, to the east of Dowgate. A little later the Duke of Somerset and his men lodged just outside the City at Temple Bar, and the Duke of Exeter, Thomas Percy Lord Egremont, and Lord Clifford took lodgings in the vicinity.[22] The City was tense and overcrowded and the Mayor, the city officers, and the trained bands remained on alert day and night 'to keep the king's peace'.

Following King Henry's instruction, fifteen councillors and two chief justices, were selected as arbitrators. The Duke of York's and the Nevilles' partisans, the Bourgchier brothers, George Neville, Bishop of Exeter, and William Gray, Bishop of Ely, met in the mornings at the Blackfriars. Chancellor Waynflete, the Earl of Shrewsbury, Lawrence Booth, Viscount Beaumont, and four bishops met in the afternoons at the Whitefriars to represent the Lancastrian lords.[23] The principal negotiators, Archbishop Bourgchier and Chancellor Waynflete, practised shuttle diplomacy between the two venues, which fortunately, considering that it was midwinter, were only a few hundred yards apart.

King Henry returned to London in the middle of February and found that despite his explicit summons, some lords had still not come in. He sent a sharply worded letter to William Fitzalan, Earl of Arundel, and other absentees, ordering them to come to Westminster without delay. The final settlement had to be endorsed by all the lords. Henry informed Arundel somewhat optimistically that the negotiations were going well.²⁴ Arundel probably stayed away; he avoided political involvement whenever he could, and only a week later he was commissioned with others to keep watch on the Sussex coast against French incursions.²⁵

The Earl of Warwick was delayed by contrary winds and he did not reach London until 14 February. He was accompanied by 600 men arrayed in bright red tunics embroidered with his emblem – the bear and ragged staff – and he stayed at the Grey Friars.²⁶ According to one chronicler, Warwick was about to go to Westminster by barge when he was warned that the Duke of Somerset and the Earl of Northumberland planned to ambush him. Warwick evaded them but vowed he would attend Council on the following day come what may: 'he wolle to Westminster on the morrow maugre [despite] them all.'²⁷

Margaret came to Berkhamsted, where Henry joined her. Together they received the Dukes of Somerset and Exeter, Lord Clifford, and Lord Egremont. This was not necessarily a mark of royal favour. Henry had just come from Westminster where he may have heard of the threat to attack Warwick. He would have warned Somerset and the others that if any unruly behaviour on their part jeopardised the negotiations, they would fall under his severe displeasure. Henry Percy, Earl of Northumberland, came south reluctantly and paid a visit to the King.²⁸ As Warden of the East March he was more concerned with defending the border against the Scots than with the Council's deliberations. He had a duty to his father's memory, but unlike the Duke of Somerset, the dead Earl of Northumberland had never been named a traitor.

Somewhat surprisingly the Earl of Salisbury was among the arbitrators. King Henry trusted him, and the Council hoped he might bridge the gap between the contending parties since he was more moderate (and less forceful) than York or Warwick. Salisbury had his own worries. London was a hotbed of gossip and seditious talk was rife among the lords' retainers. John Bromley, the Prior of Arbury, warned Salisbury that such talk could jeopardise his standing at court and with Queen Margaret. Innuendoes about Prince Edward's birth had been in circulation for some time and York, Warwick, and Salisbury himself were suspected of spreading them. Salisbury replied to Bromley, vehemently refuting that the slander could ever have originated with him, and in great agitation he assured the prior that 'I nevere ymagined, thought ne saied eny suche matter' and nor had York or Warwick to the best of his knowledge, but they must answer for themselves.[29]

Prior Bromley was known to Margaret: he had interceded with her on Salisbury's behalf in the past and conveyed a promise from the Earl to her. What that promise was we do not know, possibly a pledge to recognise her new status and that of Prince Edward. Margaret had written to urge the Council to do their utmost to set 'rest (peace) and unitee' between the lords, and her political status, so carefully established over the past two years, lent weight to her intervention. Salisbury praised Margaret's letters to the Council and he asked Bromley to reassure Margaret that he would not go back on his word.[30]

The Council's deliberations dragged on. Sir John Fastolf reported to Archbishop Bourgchier that a French fleet was cruising in the Channel. It had sailed so close to the coast of Norfolk that Fastolf had ordered it to be fired upon, and he urgently needed more ordnance to defend Great Yarmouth. Bourgchier reminded the Council that the threat of invasion had not gone away. Lord Fauconberg, Warwick's second in command in Calais, had come over with Warwick, and he was at Southampton guarding Warwick's ships. He was ready to sail at a moment's notice if he received orders to put to sea.[31] The Council awarded Warwick a cash advance of £500 to equip ships to go in search of the French fleet, but Warwick was not anxious to encounter the French navy and he did not leave London.[32] Archbishop Bourgchier used the French threat to good effect: he suggested that it was time for the contending parties to sink their differences and look to the welfare of the realm. The scare brought matters to a head and the harassed arbitrators were finally able to report to the King that agreement had been reached. Henry returned to London, and on 17 March he and his lords attended a service of thanksgiving at St Pauls. On 24 March, the settlement was officially announced.[33]

Henry proclaimed that the Duke of York, the Earl of Salisbury, and the Earl of Warwick were his true liegemen, but so was the dead Duke of Somerset. York would pay compensation of 5,000 marks (£3,333 6s 8d) for the death of the Duke of Somerset at St Albans, half to the widowed Duchess Eleanor and her other children, and half to Somerset's heir. It sounded generous, but it was not. York was too experienced to burden himself with this level of debt, and to obtain his consent Henry licenced him to ship uncustomed wool to the value of 10,000 marks (the equivalent of Margaret's dowry for one year) assigned on his unpaid wages as the King's Lieutenant in Ireland (where he had not been since 1450). As usual, York never paid up.[34] It was Richard of York, not Henry of Somerset, who benefited financially from the arbitration.

The Earl of Warwick would pay Lord Clifford 1,000 marks (£666 6s 8d), but since this too was to be paid from assignments due to Warwick at the Exchequer, how much the impecunious Lord Clifford received is a matter of doubt. Warwick did not care – the settlement did him no harm, and he was anxious to return to Calais. Salisbury came off best; he was not required to pay anything. He agreed to forgo the punitive reparations against the Percys that had been awarded to him and his family during York's First Protectorate, although these had nothing to do with the Earl of Northumberland's death at St Albans and Salisbury knew that the Percys would not honour the debt.[35] York, Salisbury, and Warwick promised to contribute £45 yearly to the Abbey of St Albans for masses for the souls of those killed, which would have pleased Abbot Whethamstede.[36]

King Henry demanded hefty recognisances from all concerned that they would keep the peace, but this was a legal formality and not a realistic intent, since even Henry realised that if the peace was broken the money could never be collected.[37] The Loveday settlement extended well beyond reparations for St Albans. Salisbury's sons Thomas and John Neville, and Northumberland's sons Thomas, Lord Egremont, Richard and Ralph Percy, who had not been at the battle, were required to post bonds to keep the peace. Henry pardoned Egremont for escaping from Newgate in 1456, probably because Egremont made a vow to go on pilgrimage, and he granted Egremont the manor of Wressle, a Percy stronghold that the Nevilles had claimed.[38] The Duke of Exeter was obliged to accept Warwick's appointment as Keeper of the Seas. He was awarded £1,000 from the hanaper for past service, but this did little to appease the disgruntled duke.[39] No amount of money could obliterate the underlying causes of the enmity between those whom the King favoured and those he did not. This was the root cause of the 'rancour' between them and the Loveday settlement did nothing to resolve it. It produced a financial but not a political settlement and satisfied no one except Henry and Margaret.

Margaret had taken a keen interest in the Loveday and Abbot Whethamstede recorded her part in its inception: King Henry had ordered it 'at the oft repeated request and insistence of the queen, whose heartfelt wish was for us to do this; she has been, and still is, desirous of the said unity, love and accord, and wishes for it, as strongly as she possibly can.'[40] The settlement was received with public rejoicing in London and a poem in praise of those responsible included the verse:

> Oure soveraigne lord kynge God kepe alway,
> *The quene*, and the archebisshope of Canterbury,
> And the bisshop of Wynchestre, chancellor of Anglonde
> And other that han laboured to his love-day ...[41]

The Duke of Buckingham and the Earl of Stafford, neither of whom had taken part in the Loveday, escorted Margaret to London and the accord was 'sealed' on 25 March with a procession to St Pauls. King

Loveday

Henry walked alone, wearing his crown. Queen Margaret walked with the Duke of York as England's premier peer.[42] The Duke of Somerset walked with the Earl of Salisbury, which Somerset may have resented. The Duke of Exeter certainly resented walking with the Earl of Warwick.

21

An Uneasy Interlude

After the Loveday Henry and Margaret spent three weeks at St Albans as the guests of Abbot Whethamstede. The court moved back to London in May 1458 and Margaret celebrated Pentecost with a week of splendid festivities. Robert Whittingham, keeper of her great wardrobe, purchased silks, cloth of gold, linen, and wool for costumes. Embroiders, tailors, goldsmiths, painters, masons, carpenters 'and other workmen, artificers, and labourers', were hired with carts and carriages to transport all the materials necessary for a royal show.[1] Sir Richard Woodville's son, Anthony, and Henry, Duke of Somerset, displayed their prowess in jousts held at the Tower. The court went to Greenwich for the summer and the two young men challenged three of Margaret's squires to face them in the lists.[2]

Before the Earl of Warwick left London for Calais he had to deal with complaints by a Dutch shipmaster that two of his vessels had been unlawfully captured by English pirates sailing out of Calais.[3] The case was not unusual – piracy was endemic and English mariners were among the worst offenders. King Henry's government encouraged private ship owners in the risky but lucrative practice of preying on enemy shipping, and English ships sailing under the King's letters of marque rarely distinguished between friend, foe, or neutral; the dividing line between pirate and king's officer was so thin as to be non-existent. Ships' captains, royal officers, and the crown all stood to gain. Everyone condemned piracy, but everyone admired it provided it was English, even the merchants who bore the brunt of reprisals

An Uneasy Interlude

against them by foreign governments. Clays Stephen was a typical example. He had been a mariner abroad a ship escorting Margaret to England, but he was one of a band of sailors who seized a vessel with a rich cargo belonging to Margaret's aunt, Queen Marie of France. They sailed it into Fowey, a favourite pirate haunt, and disposed of the merchants and crew on board, wounding some and killing others.[4]

The Calais garrison were seafarers as well as soldiers and they regularly captured ships of all nations as prizes for personal profit. Lord Fauconberg had indulged in a little private buccaneering while he was guarding Warwick's ships at Southampton during the Loveday. He was accused of capturing *Le James*, a ship of Spain sailing to England under safe conduct loaded with valuable cargo. Warwick and Sir Thomas Neville, the Duke of Buckingham, as Warden of the Cinque Ports, Viscount Bourgchier, and Lord Fauconberg himself posted bonds that the latter would appear in chancery in the following autumn to answer the charges against him.[5]

Warwick was anxious to return to Calais. At the age of thirty he had found his metier and he intended to establish his reputation as a fearless and independent commander. He rode through the streets of London in May on his way to the south coast in full martial array, and he pulled off his first spectacular exploit at the end of May.[6] Warwick was a born pirate and soldier of fortune; all foreign shipping was fair game to him. King Henry had commissioned him to suppress piracy but this in effect meant disciplining himself and his men. Warwick's brief as Keeper of the Seas was open to wide interpretation and Warwick had made the most of it. He built a small fleet of his own and profited as a private ship owner.[7] The Captaincy of Calais was lucrative as well as prestigious.

Warwick put to sea before dawn, giving him the advantage of surprise, and attacked a large Castilian fleet sailing in convoy. The King of Castile was France's ally and he had supplied Spanish ships to the French fleet.[8] Warwick's small force of five warships, supported by three caravels and four pinnaces, came up against sixteen Spanish warships, out of a total fleet of twenty-eight sail. It was David against Goliath. Warwick captured six ships and dispersed the rest. One of Warwick's men, John Jerningham, was in the thick of the fight, and he sent home a graphic description of the encounter. He and his shipmates had attempted to board a Spanish ship but were beaten back, and the Spaniards boarded Jerningham's ship and captured him. When the encounter was over Warwick arranged an exchange of prisoners, including Jerningham, which naturally endeared Warwick to his men – and to Jerningham. The liberated seaman was loud in his praises of the intrepid Earl, and he wrote to Margaret Paston that Warwick had won the greatest sea battle in forty years![9]

An impressive English embassy joined Warwick in Calais, possibly at his request, to impress the Duke of Burgundy.[10] Jean Doucereau, Pierre de Brezé's secretary and King Charles's agent, was in Calais to learn all he could of Warwick's dealing with the Burgundians.[11] King Charles did not trust the English and he had spies everywhere, in England, in Flanders, and in Calais. Richard Beauchamp, Bishop of Salisbury, was with the English embassy as Henry and Margaret's undercover agent. Beauchamp's credentials for opening secret negotiations on King Henry's behalf were impeccable. His father, Sir Walter Beauchamp, was one of King Henry's first knights of the body and Lord Beauchamp of Powick was his uncle. When William Aiscough was murdered in 1450 Henry had nominated Richard Beauchamp to the vacant see of Salisbury.

England and France were still technically at war – a war England had lost. Margaret hoped that King Charles would welcome overtures to resume peace talks. She knew that Brezé fancied himself as a diplomat and that he stood high in King Charles's favour; if anyone could persuade Charles to listen to an appeal from King Henry it would be Brezé. Sir John Wenlock advised Beauchamp to make contact with Doucereau and he may even have introduced them. Beauchamp told Doucereau piously that God had guided their meeting, since Brezé was the one man in the whole world he most

An Uneasy Interlude

wished to meet. Brezé was said to be susceptible to flattery and the good bishop laid it on with a trowel: he compared Brezé's exploit in raiding Sandwich to that of William the Conqueror's descent on the English coast in 1066! He claimed that Brezé was highly esteemed in England for his considerate behaviour towards the prisoners taken in the raid – courteous treatment of captives was the mark of a chivalrous knight.

Beauchamp said he wished to confide certain secret matters, but only if Doucereau would promise not to reveal them to anyone other than Brezé and King Charles. Doucereau agreed, and Beauchamp took him into a private room and solemnly swore him to secrecy. The mealy mouthed bishop claimed that King Henry loved him more than anyone else at court, he assured Doucereau that he was privy to the King's innermost thoughts, and what he had to say came straight from the King.[12] After this piece of mendacious self-promotion, he assured Doucereau that dissention between King Henry and the Duke of York, the Earl of Salisbury, the Earl of Warwick and their kin, 'who formed the most numerous party', in England was at an end. They were unanimous in favouring peace with France while the merchants and the people were clamouring for it. Beauchamp promised that no commitments prejudicial to France would be made to the Duke of Burgundy.

King Henry had been uncertain of whom to approach at the French court until he thought of Brezé, the 'hero' of Sandwich! Margaret's hand can be seen in this and in Beauchamp's next question: would King Charles consider a marriage for his daughter with an English prince? He suggested that Doucereau should report this meeting and procure a safe conduct for him to meet Brezé. If Beauchamp could have only a short talk with Brezé it would benefit France, and he would return to England to obtain a commission from King Henry for direct negotiations. Beauchamp claimed that Warwick, whom he described as 'his nephew', would join in these negotiations, and he gave Doucereau a letter of credence for Brezé.[13] Brezé sent it on to

King Charles, urging him to act on it and 'to let me know what will be your pleasure.'[14] Charles did not take the bait.

In the meanwhile, Warwick was entertaining the Duke of Burgundy's ambassadors, John, Count of Étampes, Antony, Bastard of Burgundy, and fifteen other commissioners.[15] Warwick was not interested in trade talks or truce violations; discussion of these topics continued throughout the summer but they were conducted by English and Burgundian officials in London and Bruges.[16] Warwick concentrated on exploiting the Duke of Burgundy's fear of France. The hostility between King Charles and Duke Philip was of long standing but their immediate bone of contention was the Dauphin Louis, who had been at loggerheads with his father for most of his adult life. Louis had finally fled from France in 1456, claiming that he feared for his life, and he took refuge at the Burgundian court. King Charles repeatedly requested his return, but Duke Philip refused to give him up, and Louis remained under Burgundy's protection. Charles's councillors urged the King to invade Burgundy and recover the recalcitrant prince.[17] France and Burgundy hovered on the brink of war. From Duke Philip's perspective Warwick as Captain of Calais could be a valuable ally if King Charles opened hostilities. From Warwick's perspective, friendship with the magnificent duke would add enormously to his prestige as well as giving him a free hand in Calais. It remains unknown if anything of a political nature was agreed between the Burgundians and Warwick at this time.[18] The Burgundian envoys left Calais in July, and Warwick turned his attention to the sea once again.

Inspired by the success of his attack on the Spanish fleet, Warwick emulated the famous, or infamous, act of piracy committed by Robert Winnington nine years earlier. In 1449 King Henry had commissioned Winnington to keep the seas, and Winnington initially planned to prey on Breton shipping; he lurked across the mouth of the Channel between Guernsey and Portland. It so happened that the Bay Salt Fleet, a convoy of over a hundred sail belonging to the Hanseatic

An Uneasy Interlude

towns of Germany, together with some Burgundian ships, was making its regular run northward from the Bay of Bourgneuf. Winnington abandoned the Bretons for bigger game, even though the Hanse towns and Burgundy had truce and trade agreements with England. He later justified his action by claiming that when he ordered the admiral of the Hanse fleet to dip his sails in salute to the English flag, the order was refused. Winnington held the weather gauge and he forced the Hanse ships into port in the Isle of Wight. He wrote a triumphant account of the encounter to the courtier Thomas Daniel, to be shown to King Henry and the Council.[19]

While Winnington's exploit aroused admiration (and greed) in some quarters, it benefited no one in the long run. It was Fougères at sea, and it too backfired. The Duke of Burgundy imprisoned any English merchant he could lay his hands on, and Englishmen trading in Lubeck and Danzig were arrested, while Prussian authorities seized English goods of greater value than the cargoes they had lost.[20] Lubeck, the largest of the Hanse towns, steadfastly opposed all English efforts to restore trading relations with the Baltic and closed their sea lanes to English shipping whenever they could. The repercussions reverberated for years to the detriment of English trade.[21] Henry's government made strenuous efforts to mend fences with the Hanseatic League, but it took until 1456 for English diplomats to obtain a trade agreement with the Hanse, to last for eight years.[22]

Piracy against individual Hanse ships continued, but there had been no major breach of the treaty until Warwick undid years of careful diplomacy in just one day. He waylaid a Hanse fleet of seventeen ships and plundered them with relative ease.[23] The Hanse towns, and Lubeck in particular, lodged a formal complaint. This blatant act of piracy may have appealed to English pride, but it did not appeal to King Henry. The importance of foreign trade was one of the few imperatives of government that Henry understood; throughout his reign he had welcomed foreign merchants to England and protected them as best he could. Henry roundly condemned

Warwick's action and he instructed Sir Richard Woodville and Sir Thomas Kyriell to investigate Warwick's action and report back to the Council by the middle of August, and he summoned a Great Council to meet in October.[24] The Dukes of York and Norfolk, the Earls of Salisbury, Warwick, Shrewsbury, Oxford, and Wiltshire, together with the veteran soldiers Lords Fauconberg, Scales, Welles, and Richard Woodville, as well as officers of the royal household, were summoned.[25] The Dukes of Somerset and Exeter, the Earls of Devon, Northumberland, and Pembroke, who supposedly constituted the 'Lancastrian faction' at court favoured by Margaret, were not. Despite the Loveday Henry and his Council were not prepared to risk a repetition of the dissentions that had marred the Great Council a year earlier.

Chancellor Waynflete remained convinced that King Charles planned to launch further raids on English coastal towns – a spy in Normandy had warned him that Southampton, a major port for collecting customs duties, was a likely target.[26] The Duke of Somerset was ordered to defend Southampton and the Isle of Wight, and to provision Carisbrooke Castle to withstand a siege.[27] King Henry issued commissions of array in thirteen shires.[28]

Margaret looked back to the only period of political stability she had ever known: her first years in England when the Duke of Suffolk was Henry's chief minister and government had centred on the household. At her instigation changes in personnel were implemented during the Great Council. She understood, as Henry did not, that the crown's credit and the ability to raise loans was inextricably linked. The Exchequer barely survived on a hand to mouth basis and there was an understandable reluctance on everyone's part, including Margaret herself, to accept uncashable Exchequer tallies. She expected the Council to support her in tackling the problem of royal debt.

James Butler, Earl of Wiltshire, replaced the Earl of Shrewsbury as Treasurer of England. Shrewsbury's abilities and loyalty were never in doubt: Henry had showered him with royal offices and land grants.

An Uneasy Interlude

He had become joint keeper with Jasper Tudor of lands in the honour of Richmond until Margaret Beaufort's son should come of age. He was keeper of the King's mews and falcons, and he replaced Lord Sudeley as chief butler of the royal household, making him controller of all the wines purchased for the court.[29] Henry had created him a Knight of the Garter at Hereford in 1457 and commissioned him to deputise at the Knights of the Garter ceremony, 'Forasmuch as various Affairs press upon us, so that we are not able to be in Person at the next Feast of St George.'[30] Shrewsbury was forty-five, and he may have been glad to relinquish the Treasury; it was a thankless and expensive task. Wiltshire was a member of Prince Edward's Council and he was wealthy enough to support the office of Treasurer. As Earl of Ormond he held lands in Ireland and he had retained his first wife's extensive estates in the West Country.[31] In April 1458, just after the Loveday, he drew even closer to the royal circle by marrying Eleanor Beaufort, the Duke of Somerset's sister.

Wiltshire made a valiant effort to resolve the problem of household debt. He negotiated with the Calais Staplers for a loan of £4,000 a year over four years to be repaid by a special grant to the merchants of the Staple, allowing them to ship wool from the ports of London and Hull free of duties until they recovered the sums they loaned. The Staplers were authorised to negotiate directly and independently with the Four Members of Flanders, a powerful trading bloc, and other Burgundian representatives, to fix prices for all wool passing through the Staple to the Low Countries, an arrangement that benefited both parties. The *quid pro quo* was an undertaking by the Council that royal licences to ship uncustomed wool would be suspended.[32]

The merchant community in and out of Parliament had repeatedly demanded an end to King Henry's practice of granting of licenses to individuals to whom the crown owed money, or as a mark of favour, allowing them to evade customs duties by shipping wool without passing through the staple at Calais. Henry had granted Margaret this right in 1448 to recover unpaid portions of her dower and she knew it was unpopular.[33] One wonders who thought up the idea of approaching the Staplers –Wiltshire or Margaret? The agreement made economic sense; it would relieve pressure on the Exchequer and the concession on licences would be popular. But it also meant that less money was available from the Staplers for loans to pay the garrison at Calais and this did not suit the Earl of Warwick. His response was to raise money by renewing his attacks on foreign ships, especially those carrying wool.[34]

Margaret never attempted to persuade Henry to curb his generosity but she intended to implement tighter controls over household expenditure and to introduce the system of chamber finance that she practised in her dower lands, to bring crown revenues under direct royal control. Sir Thomas Tuddenham replaced John Breknok as treasurer of the royal household. Margaret was not impressed by Breknok, who owed his position to the Duke of York. When Lord Dudley resigned in protest at York's reduction of the royal household during the Protectorate in 1454, York had appointed Breknok.[35] He was also Receiver General for the Duchy of Cornwall; Margaret and Prince Edward drew part of their income from the duchy, but it had proved to be an unreliable source of revenue under Breknok's administration.[36]

Tuddenham had been Keeper of the Great Wardrobe during Suffolk's regime and Chief Steward of the Duchy of Lancaster jointly with Suffolk, but his connections with the duchy went back much further. He had been a duchy servant for over thirty years, ever since his father-in-law, John Woodhouse, resigned his stewardship of duchy lands to Tuddenham in 1425. Tuddenham purchased a knighthood in 1431, a sure indication that he planned a career in crown and duchy service.[37] After Suffolk's murder Tuddenham came in for his share of opprobrium. He resigned as Keeper of the Great Wardrobe and returned to his home in Norfolk. The citizens of Norwich had seized the opportunity of Suffolk's fall to revenge themselves for the punishment meted out to them for their riotous behaviour in the early

1440s, and their scapegoats were Suffolk's closest associates, John Heydon and Thomas Tuddenham.[38]

Tuddenham's posthumous reputation has been blackened by his association with John Heydon, Suffolk's most powerful henchman in East Anglia. Even more damaging is the hostility of the Paston family as reflected in their letters. Heydon was John Paston's chief adversary and *bête noir* in long-running property disputes in Norfolk. Tuddenham incurred Paston displeasure in a quarrel with the courtier Thomas Daniel, one of Suffolk's rivals at court to whom the Pastons looked for support. Daniel had forcibly seized the manor of Roydon, belonging to Henry Woodhouse, whose sister, Alice, was Tuddenham's wife.[39] Alice had an affair with Tuddenham's chamberlain, resulting in an illegitimate child, and Tuddenham divorced her, an unusual and humiliating procedure in the fifteenth century.[40] But he remained on good terms with her family and he supported Woodhouse's efforts to recover Roydon, thereby earning John Paston's displeasure. Paston continued his struggle against Heydon, but he revised his opinion of Tuddenham: 'he gaff me no cawse of late tyme to labour ageyns him, and ... I know non deffaut in hym.'[41]

Margaret also righted an old wrong in 1458. John Hals, one of Margaret's chaplains, was a prebendary of Exeter Cathedral. Towards the end of his life Bishop Lacy of Exeter often appointed Hals as his proxy in Parliament and Convocation when he was too ill to attend in person and Hals was probably Lacy's choice to succeed him.[42] King Henry had promised the bishopric to Hals, and when Lacy died in September 1455 the cannons duly elected him.[43] But during York's Protectorate the Earl of Salisbury had been promised the next vacant bishopric for his son George, and Salisbury insisted that the promise must be honoured even though George, 'in or about his twenty-fourth year', was too young to be consecrated as a bishop. Letters to Pope Callixtus in King Henry's name, signed by the Yorkist Council, requested that the bishopric of Exeter be given to Neville.[44] Callixtus was not pleased, but Hals very prudently declined the appointment, and early in 1456 the Pope compromised. He stipulated that Neville could be the bishop-elect, but he could not be consecrated until he was at least twenty-seven.[45] Neville, who was Chancellor of Oxford University, was content to draw the temporalities of his see without actually residing there and he remained in Oxford.[46]

Margaret could not recover the bishopric for Hals, but when the Dean of Exeter died in 1458, she was determined that Hals, who was now her Chancellor, should succeed him.[47] Henry ordered his election, but the canons hesitated. Possibly Bishop Neville objected. Henry wrote to them a second time at the end of October repeating his choice of Hals and Margaret added a strongly worded endorsement of her own.[48] The royal letters were delivered by Edward Ellesmere, Margaret's treasurer, and Margaret undoubtedly entrusted him with a verbal message to remind the canons of their duty to obey the King, and of her displeasure should they fail to do so.

Margaret also tried her hand at foreign policy once again. England had few allies and Bishop Beauchamp's overtures to King Charles had fizzled out. She came up with a somewhat muddle-headed approach to securing peace through a double alliance with France and with Burgundy, based on her favourite ploy of marriage. Sir John Wenlock and Louis Gallet, who had been with the English embassy at Calais in May, were entrusted with a semi-secret mission to secure an accord with the Duke of Burgundy while simultaneously seeking a truce with the King of France. Margaret's choice of envoys seemed sensible to her, but she did not know that her former chamberlain, like many of his contemporaries, had fallen under the Earl of Warwick's spell and become Warwick's man. The Duke of York had sent Louis Gallet as an envoy to Burgundy during both Protectorates, and Louis's son, Edmond, had been the Duke of Alençon's envoy to York in 1456.[49]

Wenlock and Gallet met first with Isabelle, Duchess of Burgundy, who often represented her husband in diplomatic talks with the English.[50] Wenlock suggested an Anglo–Burgundian alliance, to be cemented by the marriage of the three most eligible candidates

England had to offer: Edward, Prince of Wales, still only five years old; Edward, Earl of March, York's eldest son, now aged sixteen, and Henry, Duke of Somerset, who was twenty-three. Their brides were to be Mary, the Duke of Burgundy's only grandchild and heiress of Burgundy, a daughter of the late Duke of Bourbon, and a daughter of the Duke of Guelders.[51] Isabelle agreed to consider the proposal and she undertook to furnish Wenlock with letters of credence setting out what he had proposed and what she had replied. It is a measure of the impression that the Earl of Warwick made on the Burgundians that Isabelle agreed to Wenlock's request that she send copies of her credence to Warwick, although Wenlock's remit had nothing to do with Warwick.

Wenlock and Gallet met Duke Philip at Mons and repeated their proposal to him. Ever the courteous prince, Duke Philip received them graciously and rewarded them handsomely. He had no intention of allying himself with King Henry but the possibility of a revival of the old Anglo–Burgundian accord would cause King Charles serious anxiety. Sure enough, Burgundy's cordial reception of Wenlock and Gallet elicited a safe conduct from Charles for them to travel to Rouen, and it was delivered to them by none other than Jean Doucereau.[52] Louis de Harcourt, Archbishop of Narbonne, represented Charles and Pierre de Brezé was included in the talks. Charles wanted to know what Burgundy was up to and what the English had offered him. Ironically, Wenlock's proposal was the same as the one Charles made to the Duke of Suffolk in 1444: a short truce to end the war to be sealed by marriage to open the way for peace negotiations. The same three bridegrooms would marry three princesses of France: a daughter of King Charles, a daughter of the Duke of Orleans, and a daughter of Margaret's uncle, Charles, Count of Maine.[53] Louis de Harcourt piously, if mendaciously, assured Wenlock and Gallet that King Charles had always desired peace with his nephew of England. If King Henry cared to send ambassadors of sufficient rank with plenary powers to treat, he would receive them gladly. The King agreed whole-heartedly that marriage alliances were a sure way of furthering diplomatic accords but he could not entertain the idea until future peace talks had progressed sufficiently for such proposals to be valid.[54] It was a polite 'Thank you, but no thank you; there is nothing in it for France.'

Isabelle of Burgundy was a far more experienced diplomat than Margaret and when she learned of Wenlock's meeting with the French she backed off. She informed Wenlock that she was withholding her letters of credence and warned him that she would need more information and further confirmation of his offers from King Henry and from the Duke of York before she would proceed. To reassure her, Wenlock sent a confidential messenger to her and to the Duke, with copies of various documents clarifying exactly what had been said during his negotiations with the French and he undertook to keep them fully informed of Henry and Margaret's reaction to his embassy when he returned to England.[55]

It seems not to have occurred to Margaret that in the unlikely event that the Duke of Burgundy *and* the King of France accepted the marriage proposals, the outcome would be a diplomatic disaster, since the English princes could not marry both sets of ladies. If Margaret hoped to play France and Burgundy off against each other she was mistaken. All Wenlock accomplished was to breed suspicion of Henry's and Margaret's intentions and their lack of good faith, but Wenlock was acting in the Earl of Warwick's interests, so perhaps this was his intention all along.

The Yorkists' Challenge

22
The Earl of Warwick's War

The Earl of Warwick did not take part in the Great Council, although he had been in England since late September. He was in the north, meeting with his father and corresponding with the Duke of York.[1] Royal messengers summoned him several times before he finally appeared on 16 November.[2] Westminster Hall was thronged with men of the royal household and with the lords' retainers, and a few days after Warwick arrived one of his men, either accidently or deliberately, provoked a member of the King's household by treading on his foot. This led to blows and the King's man came off worst. Others hurried to his assistance, Warwick's men weighed in, and the fight escalated with injuries on both sides. The noise brought cooks from the kitchens to watch the fun, and maybe to join in the fray, some still carrying their implements. Warwick saw his people being attacked by men in the King's livery and he rushed to defend them. Members of the Council came out to see what was happening and the lords closest to Warwick hastily restrained him: to draw a sword in the precincts of Westminster with the King present was a punishable offence. They shepherded Warwick away and his men covered his retreat, but the skirmishing continued down to Westminster Wharf where Warwick reached his barge and escaped to his lodging at the Grey Friars.

A year later Warwick would claim that the fracas was a deliberate attempt to murder him;³ but it is not beyond the bounds of possibility that the whole shebang was one of Warwick's clever publicity stunts to give him an excuse to leave London before the Council could promulgate any formal order against him.⁴ Warwick considered himself to be above all other men, not in rank or in wealth, but in heroic stature; he was a law unto himself and he would not submit to censure from anyone, even from the King. Warwick alleged that he had been reprimanded and threatened with dismissal for not checking English piracy, his own and others. In a typically flamboyant gesture Warwick declared that if the Council attempted to replace him as Captain of Calais he would give up all his estates in England rather than surrender his captaincy.⁵ He did not mean it.

The Duke of York also boycotted the Council. He felt aggrieved by the Loveday settlement; he had expected a different outcome, believing that his high estate should place him above arbitration. King Henry had declared him to be a true liegeman, but so was the dead Duke of Somerset. If Somerset was not a traitor, then York's action at St Albans was not justified. This rankled, and so did the prominence of the Queen. York was a man of his time – he shared Thomas Gascoigne's view that women had no place in politics. He did not accept that Margaret, acting in Prince Edward's name, could be an alternative source of royal authority. She was the one person York could not remove from King Henry's side, either by accusation or by killing her in battle.

If Henry had offered York a permanent place in government, the Loveday settlement might have held. But Henry did not want York's autocratic personality on his Council and despite his numerous protestations of loyalty York never served the King except on his own terms. The Loveday was the catalyst that hardened York's opposition to the King. He no longer harboured any illusion that Henry would include him in his councils, and he was too proud to remain in the political wilderness. Only possession of the King's person could restore York to power; he would have to repeat his

The Yorkists' Challenge

coup of 1455 and capture, isolate, and coerce Henry, and for this he needed allies.

Warwick was determined that Henry should not dismiss him as Captain of Calais and his self-interest coincided with York's. Once York was restored to power the Nevilles could aspire to the resources and patronage which only those in government could offer. Warwick persuaded his father that it was high time to switch their allegiance back to the Duke of York. Salisbury summoned his council to an emergency meeting at Middleham in November and announced that he would place Neville resources at York's disposal, to 'take full parte with the ful noble prince the Duke of Yorke' in whatever enterprise York had in mind. Warwick was the driving force behind a decision that could only mean a military coup. Sir Thomas Harrington, one of Salisbury's retainers, had no doubts. On returning home from the meeting he enfeoffed his lands to safeguard his estates against possible forfeiture.[6]

No word of the decision taken at Middleham in November reached the Council. Salisbury continued to receive his salary as Warden of the West March and he remained Chief Steward of the North Parts of the Duchy of Lancaster.[7] Nevertheless, when Henry sent for him to attend Council in January 1459, Salisbury distanced himself; he informed his 'entierly wele bilovede brother' Viscount Beaumont that he was too ill to leave his home at Sheriff Hutton.[8]

The Council's fear of a French invasion revived when Sir John Wenlock and Louis Gallet came home early in 1459 to report on the failure of their mission. There would be no truce with France.[9] Henry issued commissions of array to counties along the southern and eastern coasts and for the first time the Duke of York was not named as a commissioner, although he and Salisbury remained as commissioners of the peace.[10] Despite Henry's displeasure over his piratical activities, Warwick's tenure as Captain of Calais was secure. He was England's first line of defence against the French. In March the Council ordered ships and provisions to be sent to him in Calais. In

April bows and arrows were stockpiled in the Tower to guard the King against his enemies 'as well upone the see as on lande' and repairs to royal manors and castles along the Thames were put in hand.[11]

There was a new Pope in Rome. Callixtus III died in 1458 and his successor, Pope Pius II, renewed the call for a crusade. His emissary, Franciulo Seruopolos, arrived in England in January to enquire what contribution England might make to a crusading venture and who King Henry planned to send to a papal conclave at Mantua. Only a few lords were at court so early in the new year and Henry postponed dealing with the question until after Easter.[12] He and Margaret again celebrated Easter at St Albans and on his return to London Henry convened his Council to discuss the question of a crusade.[13] London was as tumultuous as ever and a serious affray erupted in Fleet Street while the Council was in session. The inhabitants of Fleet Street despised the rowdy attorneys at the Inns of Court and they in turn looked down on the citizens as inferior and uneducated men. Fleet Street residents armed themselves with bows and arrows and rang the church bells of St Bride's and St Dunstan's 'awkward', i.e. backwards, as a distress signal, a kind of Mayday, to summon other citizens to their aid. The scrambling fight lasted for three hours, some men were wounded, a few were killed and one of Margaret's attorneys was among the casualties.[14] Clifford's Inn was looted, and the Inner Temple was damaged.[15]

Henry sent his bishops, accompanied by the Earl of Wiltshire, Viscount Beaumont, and Lord Sudeley to quell the riot. The bishops progressed along Fleet Street in full regalia, carrying their crosses with the sacrament raised on high.[16] Order was restored, and twenty-four Londoners were arrested. Henry summoned Alderman William Taylor, in whose ward Fleet Street lay, to explain the dereliction of his duty to keep the peace. Taylor and the ringleaders were committed to prison where they languished until the following November when the newly elected mayor, William Hulyn, obtained their release.[17] Henry issued a proclamation that any further 'insurrection, rout, riot, or

The Yorkists' Challenge

rumour' would mean the suspension of the City's franchises and liberties and further arrests of its magistrates and citizens.[18] Margaret may have encouraged Henry to take a firm stand but this draconian display of royal authority was a mistake. The London oligarchy was far too powerful and too wealthy for the King to risk alienating the City by threatening its Mayor, aldermen, and Common Council. Londoners had long memories.

The court removed to the Midlands in May. In June Francesco Coppini, Bishop of Terni, arrived at Coventry to enquire why no English delegates had been appointed to attend the papal conference at Mantua. Coppini was a self-important little man; his appearance was not impressive but what he lacked in stature he made up in eloquence. He expounded at tedious length on the importance of his mission: the Turks held Constantinople. If they crossed the Danube their next objective would be the Rhine, which would severely disrupt English trade. Coppini stressed the damage that had been done by the continuing dissensions between Christian princes when it was their duty to unite behind Pope Pius. Participation in a crusade was not high on the Council's or the King's agenda and Chancellor Waynflete stemmed the flow of Coppini's eloquence by promising that the Council would give full consideration to all that he had said.[19] To pacify the pushy bishop King Henry issued a warrant for five delegates to be sent to Mantua, although in the event only one of them went.[20]

King Henry called a Great Council to meet at Coventry in June. Like many of Henry's councils in the late 1450s, no official record of a June Council has survived. The only source for it is an entry in *John Benet's Chronicle*:

> And after the Feast of John the Baptist the king held a great council at Coventry at which the queen and prince were present. The Archbishop of Canterbury, the Duke of York, the Earls of Salisbury and Warwick, the Bishop of Ely, the Bishop of Exeter, the Earl of

Arundel, Lord Bourgchier and others were absent. And on the advice of the queen all the aforesaid were censured at this council of Coventry.[21]

The Duke of York and the Earl of Salisbury absented themselves in accordance with their pact of mutual support and opposition to the government. York may have encouraged his well-wishers to follow his example and stay away.[22] The Bourgchiers were York's appointees to high office. York had promoted William Gray to the bishopric of Ely when Thomas Bourgchier became Archbishop of Canterbury. The Bishop of Exeter was Salisbury's son, George Neville. The Earl of Arundel was Salisbury's son-in-law, although his absence had nothing to do with York – Arundel routinely avoided Council meetings. Warwick was in Kent (probably at Sandwich) preparing to continue his belligerence at sea. In July, possibly to embarrass the Council, he engaged with five ships of Genoa and Spain and captured three of them to the delight of some Englishmen. Even Abbot Whethamstede was impressed.[23]

It was not customary for a queen to attend Council meetings and Prince Edward was not yet six years old, but with hindsight the pro-Yorkist chronicler had no doubt that Margaret was behind the Council's censure – after all, she was there. It is far more likely that an accusation of flouting royal authority and a demand that they present themselves before the Council to explain their behaviour came from the Duke of Buckingham. He had pleaded with King Henry at another Coventry council in 1457 not to show leniency towards York.

Margaret was there for an entirely different reason. She was involved in discussions with the Council on the finances and future of the Prince of Wales. The Council had settled his estates on Prince Edward in 1457 and it had been agreed that he would pay £863 per annum to the treasurer of the King's household for his upkeep. The Council now estimated that the Prince's maintenance, at £4 a day, amounted to £1,473 (sic), but that only £876 was being paid, and the

The Yorkists' Challenge

King could not afford to make up the difference. The Council freely admitted that the money from Prince Edward had been diverted and used for other purposes so that household servants had not been paid. They proposed that Prince Edward should continue to contribute the £863 9s 7d, but that an additional £400, originally assigned on the Exchequer, would be met from Queen Margaret's Duchy of Lancaster annuity of £1,000.

The Council also suggested that it would be financially beneficial for all concerned if the Prince's household removed from court from time to time, (taking his household utensils with him) to live either in Wales, Cornwall, or Chester for whatever periods Margaret and the Prince's councillors saw fit, although he must continue to contribute the agreed sum to the King's coffers. Margaret naturally took part in these deliberations and she accepted the arrangement even though it diminished her income.[24] It was not unwelcome, since it gave her a free hand to decide where the Prince would reside as he grew older. King Henry took little interest in the child. He was content to allow his heir to grow up away from court, while the Council's only concern was to save money.

It was for this settlement, and not a pointless harassment of the Duke of York, that Margaret 'attended' the council at Coventry. And it was at this time that she acknowledged that Sir John Neville had so far fulfilled his obligation for his marriage to Isabel Ingoldesthorpe and she surrendered her rights in Isabel's wardship and marriage. John and Isabelle were granted Isabel's full inheritance 'without suing livery thereof', with the issues from the land backdated to the death of Isabelle's father in 1456.[25] This is not the action of a vindictive queen. The assumption that Margaret used the Council in her efforts to destroy her 'enemies' is false. Margaret was not preparing to make war on York; she was happy to be left to manage her estates and those of Prince Edward rather than to promote faction. She sent Robert Whittingham, Prince Edward's Receiver General and an experienced soldier, into Wales with other members of the Prince's council to hold judicial sessions in his name and see to the collection of the revenues of the principality.[26]

The Council's censure played into York's hands. It revived his 'fears' of the council meeting at Leicester in 1455 that precipitated the Battle of St Albans. Once again, he could claim that his life and his lands were in danger. His clients Sir William Oldhall and Thomas Vaughan met in London to expedite York's plans. They warned the Earl of Warwick to get ready for whatever move York might make.[27] York sent a similar message to the Earl of Salisbury, and in September Salisbury began the long march from Middleham. The memory of St Albans loomed large everyone's mind. Margaret was determined that there should be no repetition of that catastrophe. Salisbury must not be permitted to rendezvous with York. King Henry went north to the strongly fortified royal castle at Nottingham, calling on his lords to join him.

Margaret was at Chester Castle with Prince Edward when she learned that Salisbury had bypassed Nottingham and was nearing Newcastle under Lyme. She called out the local levies in Prince Edward's name as commissioner for his father to cross Salisbury's line of march and prevent his junction with York.[28] King Henry sent orders for the new young Lord Stanley to join them but he was not the stalwart adherent of the King and Queen that his father had been, and he was married to Eleanor Neville, Salisbury's daughter. Lord Stanley had been the mainstay of royal authority in the north-west all his life, but he had died unexpectedly early in 1459 and his son felt insulted that none of his father's offices had been bestowed on him. Stanley gathered his forces and sent word to Prince Edward at Chester that he had only just received the King's message and his forces were not yet fully equipped, but he promised to come and even requested the honour of commanding the vanguard. Margaret moved to Eccleshall Castle, the seat of John Hals, her chancellor, whom she had helped to make Bishop of Coventry and Lichfield, and she ordered Stanley, again in Prince Edward's name, to move up in support.[29] Stanley sent

The Yorkists' Challenge

his brother William to join Salisbury while he remained aloof, waiting to see what the outcome would be.[30]

An army under Lords Audley and Dudley barred Salisbury's route at Blore Heath, just north of the town of Market Drayton. Chronicle estimates of the numbers of troops involved vary widely but they all agree that Salisbury won the day with a smaller army.[31] The account in *Gregory's Chronicle* marvels that Salisbury could win a battle with only 500 men, but it was the Earl of Warwick, on his way from Calais, who had only 500 men.[32]

Lord Audley was killed, fifteen knights and gentlemen were taken or slain, many other Lancastrians were either killed or captured and the rest fled. The chroniclers refer to the men who answered Margaret's call as 'the Queen's gallants'. They were the gentlemen of Cheshire, Shropshire, Staffordshire, and Derbyshire, whose loyalty Margaret had been courting since 1456.[33] But they were raised in a hurry and their forces comprised largely untrained men, so they may not have been superior in numbers, especially as the 2,000 men Stanley was supposed to contribute failed to arrive.

The Battle of Blore Heath was an encounter of the veterans: Audley was sixty-one, Dudley and Salisbury were fifty-nine, but Salisbury was by far the more experienced commander, and he led the more seasoned troops. The chronicle accounts gloss over the fact that at Blore Heath Salisbury committed treason. He might claim that the King was not in the field and the royal banner was not displayed, but King Henry's banner had been unfurled at Nottingham against his advance, and Salisbury could have withdrawn honourably when faced by a royal army: he chose not to – he was determined to join York at all costs.[34] Blore Heath was a Pyrrhic victory. It cost York the element of surprise and it warned King Henry of what to expect. Capturing him would now be far more difficult.

Lord Stanley wrote to Margaret at Eccleshall after the battle to excuse his absence by claiming that he had received conflicting instructions. King Henry had ordered him to come to Nottingham but she had ordered him to join Audley so he had been uncertain of what he should do. But the duplicitous Stanley also wrote to congratulate Salisbury on his victory and to promise him covert assistance. Salisbury circulated the letter to his elated followers and Sir Thomas Harrington, who had been so pessimistic about the outcome of Salisbury's undertaking to support York, is reported to have boasted, 'Sirres be mery, for yet we have moo frendis.'[35] But Salisbury did not get off scot-free; his sons, John and Thomas Neville, were ambushed and captured while pursing the fleeing Lancastrians. They were sent to Chester Castle for safekeeping in Margaret's custody.[36]

Warwick crossed from Calais, timing his arrival as closely as he could to coincide with the junction of York's and Salisbury's forces, since reports that the Captain of Calais had arrived in England unexpectedly, accompanied by 500 hand-picked veterans from the Calais garrison, would cause instant alarm and word would be carried to King Henry. Warwick reached London on 20/21 September and headed for his Warwickshire lands.[37] The Duke of Somerset was mustering troops in the south-west and as Warwick marched north-west to join Salisbury, Somerset marched north-east to join King Henry. They missed each other by the narrowest of margins; as Warwick passed through Coleshill on his way to cross the Severn at Bridgnorth Somerset passed through Coleshill on his way to Nottingham.[38]

York, Salisbury, and Warwick met at Ludlow. York had prepared a manifesto outlining their complaints and justifying their position. It comprised a conveniently vague indictment of the King's councillors while exonerating Henry himself. The King was being kept in ignorance of the true state of the realm, he was in the hands of evil men (unspecified) who had misled and impoverished him, and he was so poor that his subjects had to be robbed by 'minesters of the kinges housolde' just to maintain him.[39] It was the duty of his loyal subjects, and of all 'lordis of like disposicion', to apprise him of the truth. Henry should be advised to rely on 'the grete lords of his blood' (such as the

The Yorkists' Challenge

Duke of York) and replace the men who had been 'broughte up from noughte' with men of noble blood. This would restore law and order, revitalise trade and refurbish England's standing in the eyes of foreign princes.[40] But the suggestion that the best way to serve the King was by rebelling against him made little appeal and no great 'lordis of like disposicion' joined York.

York and the Nevilles took their manifesto to Worcester Cathedral to obtain the blessing of the Church and give their grievances wide publicity. York entrusted a copy to the Prior of Worcester to be delivered to King Henry. It was all window dressing. Even York cannot have believed that the proclamation would influence the King and perhaps it was not intended to. York always felt a need to justify himself. John de la Bere, the Bishop of St David's, administered the sacrament.[41] York and the Nevilles swore an oath of loyalty to the King and solidarity with each other.

The royal army moved south via Walsall and Coleshill in an attempt to cut York off at Worcester while he was separated from his main force, but King Henry moved too slowly and the Yorkists crossed the Severn lower down.[42] They returned to Ludford to prepare for an encounter with King Henry on grounds of their choosing. Henry still hoped for a reconciliation; he sent Garter King of Arms with Richard Beauchamp, the ubiquitous Bishop of Salisbury, who claimed kinship with Warwick, to offer a pardon to York and Warwick if they would 'come in' and submit to the King's grace within six days.[43] Salisbury was another matter. He had fought against and killed the King's subjects, and for that he would have to be put on trial before the Lords in Parliament. The Earl of Warwick forcefully rejected King Henry's offer on the grounds that it was worthless.[44] He was speaking the literal truth. York and the Nevilles were far too committed to their enterprise to draw back, and they did not wish to do so. If they submitted, they could rely on King Henry's clemency, but they would not control him or be reinstated in government.

To maintain their high moral stance, they addressed a final appeal to Henry to accept the truth of their protestations of loyalty and not to believe the malice of their enemies. They insisted that they were not acting from motives of personal profit or revenge for past wrongs, and that the army at Ludlow was incidental. It was there solely to protect them as they sought an audience with the King, a repetition of the claim that York had made at St Albans. They wished to come into King Henry's presence and set out their fears, provided it was safe to do so. They had kept quiet until now from reverence for God and the King and to avoid bloodshed (apparently the blood shed at Blore Heath did not count), but if persuasion failed they would resort to force.

York's fears had surfaced again: he declared that everyone knew that their lives were in jeopardy from 'the impostune impacience and violence of such persones as entende of extreme malice to procede vnder the shadow of youre hyghe myghte and presence to oure destruccione.'[45] But King Henry had never denied them an audience. He had treated them as loyal subjects in the face of their earlier rebellion, and they had been summoned regularly to his Great Councils, which they had as regularly failed to attend. Their demand to be admitted to the King's presence was not physical but metaphorical. What York wanted was nothing less than control and direction of the government. He hoped, and Warwick believed, that Henry would not fight, that he would collapse under a threat of armed force and that York's administration, if not his Protectorate, would be restored. Warwick held Henry's pacifism in contempt; he was set on a trial by battle and he did not doubt the outcome.

King Henry issued writs to assemble Parliament, with York's, Warwick's, and Salisbury's names omitted from the summons.[46] Henry replaced Warwick as Captain of Calais with the Duke of Somerset. The King's six days grace expired on 12 October and the royal army moved north. An encounter finally took place at Ludford Bridge on the River Teme just outside Ludlow, where York's forces were established in an entrenched position.[47] His eldest sons, Edward, Earl of March, and Edmund, Earl of Rutland, were with him, but he

The Yorkists' Challenge

had few supporters other than the Nevilles. Given a choice between Richard of York and their anointed King to whom they had sworn allegiance, most men preferred to remain loyal to King Henry. Only Lord Clinton, York's annuitant, Lord Grey of Powis, Viscount Bourgchier's sons John and Edward, Sir Henry Radford, Sir John Wenlock, Walter Devereux, and a few other knights and gentlemen were with York. There is no obvious reason why Richard Grey, the young Lord of Powis, joined York. Perhaps he did so from a sense of adventure – he was only twenty-three. Viscount Bourgchier's sons were a pledge of the Bourgchier's future loyalty – if York won. Sir Henry Radford had been York's *bailli* in Rouen. Sir Walter Devereux was dead, but his son remained faithful to York.

King Henry took the field in person. The royal banner and the banners of the lords who swelled the ranks of the King's army was a daunting sight. The Nevilles' foes, Henry Percy, Earl of Northumberland, his brother Lord Egremont, and Salisbury's half-brother, the Earl of Westmorland, were with the King, together with at least twenty other lords.[48] There is no record that Margaret and Prince Edward were (or were not) present. Henry did his utmost to avoid bloodshed. At the last minute, before battle was joined, he undermined the Yorkists' morale by sending his heralds to offer a pardon to any man who would surrender.[49]

Warwick had arrogantly assumed that he needed no other troops than the 500 veterans from Calais led by the war captain Andrew Trollope. He believed that these men would follow him through thick and thin, but the Calais garrison were royal troops, owing allegiance to the King (even if they were not always paid). They were not Warwick's personal retinue like the men who marched with Salisbury as Warden of the West March. Warwick had hoodwinked them into believing that they were to fight for King Henry, since he had proclaimed all along that he was a loyal subject. When they realised that Warwick had misled them, Andrew Trollope and the men of the Calais garrison refused to fight. The chronicle accounts imply that

The Earl of Warwick's War

York, too, could not bring himself to oppose Henry in battle; but given his past record this is hard to believe.[50]

The defection of the Calais garrison dismayed York and shook even Warwick's confidence. York lost his nerve; he had his whole family with him. He knew that Henry would not harm his wife and younger children and he slipped away during the night with his son, Edmund of Rutland, and they took ship for Ireland. Deserting men whom they had led into rebellion was shameful and dishonourable, but Salisbury and Warwick too preferred flight to the possibility of capture. Warwick and Salisbury, with York's eldest son, Edward, Earl of March, and Sir John Wenlock made for Calais.

The leaderless Yorkists surrendered on the following day[51] and the royal army celebrated the 'victory' in the traditional manner: they broke into the town's wine cellars and got drunk, they looted and committed rape, but the town escaped destruction.[52] Two days later King Henry left Ludlow and disbanded his army. The Duchess of York was not harmed. She was sent to her sister the Duchess of Buckingham, probably at Margaret's instigation, but Duchess Anne was markedly unsympathetic to Cecily's plight.[53]

Was it just happenstance that York made for Ireland with his younger son, while his eldest son escaped to Calais with the Earl of Warwick? Edward of March was seventeen and showing promise of leadership. Did Warwick see in Edward, rather than in York, the way of the future, and did Edward elect to follow Warwick rather than his father at this critical and potentially fatal point in his career?

23

The Defence of the Realm

The fugitives were not pursued. Margaret was relieved that there was no repetition of St Albans and Henry was relieved that there had been no bloodshed. He returned to Coventry to await the opening of Parliament, which met in the chapter house of St Mary's Priory on 20 November. It was better attended than any of Henry's previous parliaments. The Yorkists' flight was rebellion and treason on a wider scale than anything yet experienced during King Henry's reign. The Lords rallied to their King and came together in a show of solidarity. So did the Commons.[1] They elected Thomas Tresham, a household official known for his loyalty, as their Speaker, and they rehearsed the Duke of York's past misdeeds in damning detail, from Cade in 1450 to Dartford in 1452, St Albans in 1455, and finally at Ludlow. York had sworn numerous oaths of fealty and obedience to the King and he had broken them all. The Commons alleged that York had planned to capture King Henry at Kenilworth.

York had enjoyed a brief popularity with the Commons on his return from Ireland when the country was in turmoil following the loss of Normandy, but after he confronted King Henry at Dartford the Commons' sentiment turned against him. Parliament endorsed him as Protector in 1454 only because the King was incapacitated, and only after establishing Prince Edward's right to become Protector for his father in the future. It was King Henry, not the Commons, who pardoned York after the Battle of St Albans in 1455, and many men at the time felt he had got off too lightly. Despite his support for their Act of Resumption during his second term as Protector, the Commons as well as the Lords had welcomed the return of their King.

The Commons introduced a bill to attaint York, the Nevilles and their adherents of treason under the 1352 statute of Edward III.[2] Their bill was drawn up with great care, probably by York's enemy Thomas Thorpe, by the astute John Morton, Prince Edward's chancellor, and by the chief justice, Sir John Fortescue, in consultation with the judges.[3] York, Salisbury, and Warwick, York's sons, the Earls of March and Rutland, Salisbury's sons, Sir John and Sir Thomas Neville, and Viscount Bourgchier's sons, John and Edward, were attainted along with Lord Clinton, Lord Stanley, John Wenlock, and others who had been at Ludford.[4] Wenlock's attainder would have pleased Margaret, who had trusted him too freely. Their estates and all their possession were forfeit to the crown, 'and in lyke wise their heires, and the heires of everyche of theym, to be disabled for ever to have or enjoye eny enheritaunce by theym or eny of theym.'

Property held by their wives was exempted except for Alice, Countess of Salisbury; she was accused of inciting her husband and son in their rebellion. Alice was at Middleham in November 1458 when the Nevilles pledged their support for York, and her attainder alleged that on 1 August 1459 at about the time Salisbury began to gather his troops, she concurred in the plot to capture and/or kill the King. The allegation was probably false, but it had to be made. Alice was in a unique position. The lands of the Earldom of Salisbury were hers by right of inheritance; her husband, Richard Neville, had been recognised by Parliament as Earl in her right after the death of her father, Thomas Montague, Earl of Salisbury. Unlike Warwick, whose earldom had been bestowed on him by King Henry, Salisbury's Montague lands would not be forfeit unless Alice was a traitor too. Sir William Oldhall and Thomas Vaughan were accused along with Countess Alice of plotting the King's death. Oldhall had been indicted as a traitor in 1453, for fermenting rebellion in York's favour, and he had forfeited his lands; he recovered them while York was Protector, only to forfeit them again.[5]

The Yorkists had committed treason, and the opportunity to return solid financial gains to the impoverished crown from estates confiscated on a wide scale was too good to miss. Forfeiture would enrich King Henry and deprive York and the Nevilles of the income necessary to return to England and raise a successful rebellion, or so it was believed, but was the punishment meted out to them right or just? Not only they, but their heirs were condemned to forfeit their lands and possessions in perpetuity. Thousands of words were spilled in Parliament on this issue and thousands more have been spilled since.

A political pamphlet, now known as the *Sominium Vigilantis*, possibly written by the same men who drafted the attainder legislation, set out the arguments.[6] The framework is in Latin, the final peroration is in French, but the debate is in English. An unnamed advocate for the Duke of York rehearsed the arguments that York himself had always used as self-justification: York was King Henry's loyal liegeman so royal clemency was not mercy, it was justice. Counter arguments by the King's advocate, also unnamed, paralleled the rolls of Parliament: Henry could not afford to show mercy because York was obdurate and would never change his ways. The King had pardoned him in the past, to the detriment of the realm. The conclusion of the debate in a Parliament hostile to York naturally came down on the side of justice and punishment.[7]

King Henry reserved his right to pardon: the King should not be 'put from his prerogatyf to shewe such mercy and grace as shall please his Highnes.'[8] Henry's stance was consistent with his firmly held beliefs. He was a Christian king and as God's anointed the supreme prerogative of mercy was bestowed by God on him alone. The Duke of York and all those with him were Henry's subjects and it was his duty, no matter what the provocation, to pardon those who had been disloyal, provided they came as penitents and submitted to his justice.[9]

The Defence of the Realm

But for York and the Nevilles it was war to the death; they had agreed that they would prevail or perish. York wanted the throne, or at least sole direction of the government; Salisbury wanted security, which meant royal patronage; and Warwick wanted freedom to pursue his self-aggrandisement in any way he chose.

Margaret's influence had increased over the years and she undoubtedly favoured the attainder, offering as it did the prospect of crown solvency. But were the Commons, not to mention the Lords and King Henry, so subservient to the Queen that she was able to coerce them into punishing the Yorkists so severely?[10] She wanted Lord Stanley penalised for failing to answer her summons before the Battle of Blore Heath, but Stanley had not committed treason and King Henry remembered the old Lord Stanley's long years of loyal service. He refused the Commons' request that his son should stand trial.[11] It was Henry, not Margaret, who made the final decision.

Margaret concentrated on her financial position and that of Prince Edward. She requested an exchange of her lordship of Having-at-Bower with King Henry's lordship of Corsham in Wiltshire, plus £20 yearly from the customs on cloth in the port of London.[12] At her instigation a petition was presented to the Commons on Prince Edward's behalf to grant him full livery of the Duchy of Cornwall and all its appurtenances outside Cornwall (which included Coventry). Margaret had set her lawyers, and probably John Morton, to unearth and record in exact and excruciating detail Edward III's grant of the duchy to his eldest son that set the legal precedent for Henry's grant to Prince Edward. The Commons stipulated that Prince Edward must now maintain himself and his household out of his income and not be a charge on the royal household. King Henry endorsed the petition but reserved the right to appoint to any great offices that fell vacant within the territorial holdings of the duchy. He exempted his grants to Margaret and the Tudor brothers (the Earl of Richmond's share was now held by Edmund's son, the future Henry VII). Henry also confirmed John Breknok as Receiver General for the Duchy of

The Yorkists' Challenge

Cornwall, provided he could assure Prince Edward of his good behaviour, which cannot have pleased Margaret.[13]

One chronicler claimed that John de la Pole, Duke of Suffolk, was degraded to the rank of earl in Parliament because he had married the Duke of York's daughter.[14] The chronicler had half the story. The grant to Prince Edward exempted income from lands in Cornwall held by royal servants who had not fought against the King at Blore Heath, *except* the Duchess and Duke of Suffolk.[15] Duchess Alice did not send her son or any of her tenants to join the King at Ludford, and Henry (and possibly Margaret) was not pleased. John de la Pole was not named to the commissions of array in late December 1459 or the spring of 1460. The de la Pole's loyalty was suspect.

Cecily, Duchess of York, came to Coventry in December and King Henry received her graciously. She pleaded that she was destitute now that her husband's lands were forfeit and Henry granted her 1,000 marks a year from York's estates for the maintenance of herself and her children 'that have not offended ageynst us.'[16] One wonders if Queen Margaret or the Duchess of Buckingham were present at the interview. Duchess Anne had received Warwick's manor of Colyweston in Northamptonshire as a reward for housing and guarding her sister Cecily after Ludford.[17] Eleanor, Duchess of Somerset, was slower to seize the initiative. In January 1460 she complained that York had failed to pay her any of the 2,500 marks awarded to her by the Loveday settlement. She was granted only 400 marks a year from York's estates in compensation and she received York's manor of Purbright at a nominal fee of 5 marks annually, but for ten years only.[18] Belatedly she and her sister, the Dowager Countess of Shrewsbury, successfully petitioned for the recovery of a quarter each of their father's Beauchamp estates that King Henry had granted to the Earl of Warwick in 1449.[19]

Parliament did not sit for long once its principal business had been accomplished. A week before it was dissolved, Chancellor Waynflete asked each lord individually to pledge their loyalty and obedience to

King Henry. Thomas Bourgchier, Viscount Bourgchier, the Earl of Arundel, William Gray, and George Neville, all of whom had supposedly been censured by Margaret, took the oath. An observer noted that King Henry was particularly pleased by the always pliant George Neville's submission.[20] Lord Stanley too took the oath. The Lords then swore to protect the 'wele [weal], surete [security] and preserving of the persone of the moos high and benigne princess Margaret ... and also the right high and mythy Prince Edward my right redoubted lord', and to accept Prince Edward as King Henry's heir.[21] The wording was a deliberate confirmation of the political initiative begun by Henry and Margaret in 1456 to identify her and Prince Edward with the authority of the crown.

Margaret, the Earl of Wiltshire as Treasurer, and presumably the Council, were determined that the windfall of the forfeited estates should not be frittered away by King Henry's profligacy. They would be integrated into the royal demesne to put government on a sound financial basis and as a reserve against any contingency.[22] The lords who had rallied to the King at Ludford were rewarded, but the pay-outs were small.[23] The only large payment, £16,985 5s 7¼d, made with the assent of Parliament, was to the Earl of Northumberland for defending Berwick against the Scots, and for his wages as Warden of the East March.[24] Now that the Warden of the West March was on the run, the Percys were the main defence against the King of Scots.

Trusted administrators, receivers, and stewards were appointed in all the forfeited lands during the early months of 1460. Some of York and Warwick's appointees were retained in office to maintain continuity of local administration and the collection of revenue.[25] Reorganisation on such a wide scale would take time and no income could be expected immediately; not all of York and the Nevilles' tenants would abandon their offices without protest.[26] Margaret was not given time. By allowing the Yorkists to escape, King Henry ensured that they would return and reclaim their own.

Calais was the obvious destination for Warwick and Henry sent orders to the garrison not to admit him. Sir Richard Woodville was commissioned to take possession of Warwick's ships lying in the port of Sandwich to prevent him from escaping to Calais. It was too late. Warwick was already there.[27]

The tardiness of Henry Beaufort, Duke of Somerset, the new Captain of Calais in leaving England was due to the usual delay at the Exchequer in raising money to pay his troops. The Exchequer had been instructed to pay wages for one thousand men to accompany him to Calais, while Richard Woodville was to defend Sandwich.[28] Somerset was confident that the King's commission would be accepted by the Calais garrison, not unreasonably, since Andrew Trollope and the men of the garrison who had defected to the King at Ludford formed part of Somerset's force. Thomas, Lord Roos, Somerset's half-brother, and John, Lord Audley, the son of the Lord Audley who had been killed at Blore Heath, were to accompany him.[29]

Somerset was still only twenty-three. He had no experience of war by land or sea except for being wounded at St Albans, and his only qualification as Captain of Calais was his lineage: his father and grandfather had been Calais captains, and he was a royal duke. Roos was in his early thirties, but despite the difference in their ages, he and Somerset appear to have been friends. Roos had fought at the Battle of St Albans and had colluded in Somerset's proposed attack on Warwick in 1457, but he was inexperienced in military matters. He had fitted out a small flotilla at his own expense to defend the East Anglian coasts in 1452, although it is doubtful if he put to sea himself.[30]

Somerset's flotilla came under fire from Calais's guns, forcing him to veer away. He, Lord Roos, and Andrew Trollope landed at Scales Cliff and took refuge in Guines Castle to the west of Calais.[31] Audley's ships were permitted to enter the port and he and his men were captured. Warwick gave short shrift to those who had deserted him at Ludford; he had them arrested and hanged.[32] Although King Henry had granted Audley livery of his father's lands and he was Lord Roos's nephew, he did not hesitate to change sides and throw in his lot with the Nevilles even though Salisbury was responsible for his father's death. Audley may have decided that discretion was the better part of valour after witnessing Warwick's harsh treatment of the garrison soldiers, or he may have intended to defect. He had not fought alongside his father at Blore Heath and in one sense Warwick was his overlord. His family held a land grant in Hereford from Warwick.[33]

At the beginning of 1460 Warwick appeared to be in complete control of Calais in defiance of King Henry, but was he still its captain? Duke Philip of Burgundy sent Jean de Lannoy, the Stadholder of Holland, and Thibault de Neuchatel, the Marshall of Burgundy, one of his principal trouble-shooters, to meet Warwick at Gravelines while Charolais Herald spent a month in Calais picking up as much information as he could. Warwick undoubtedly did his best to convince the Duke's envoys that it was in both their interests to maintain their friendly relationship. Burgundy admired Warwick but he did not sign a formal truce with him. A unilateral agreement between Burgundy and Warwick was out of the question. The mighty Duke of Burgundy would not ally himself with the Earl of Warwick who, for all his vaingloriousness, was a rebellious vassal of the King of England.[34] Trade between England and Burgundy's territories was as important to Philip as it was to King Henry. The trade truce had expired, but on 26 November King Henry had appointed eleven envoys to negotiate a new deal.[35] He may also have requested Burgundy not to give aid to Warwick.

Sir Richard Woodville guarded Sandwich and its precious ships. He and Gervase Clifton, the Treasurer of Calais, were ordered to muster men-at-arms and archers and put to sea to guard the Channel. In December William Scot was commissioned for one year to defend Winchelsea and the adjacent coasts with 200 men-at-arms, although he was not to requisition supplies that might be needed for the relief of Calais.[36] Woodville did not expect any action in the dead of winter; his wife and son were with him, possibly for the Christmas festivities. Woodville certainly did not anticipate any immediate threat from

The Yorkists' Challenge

Calais, but he should have known better. Warwick could easily obtain the inside information that Sandwich was not being carefully guarded. In the predawn hours of 15 January 1460 John Dynham, who had facilitated Warwick's and his companions escape from England, led a raiding party that took Woodville completely by surprise. He and his son Anthony were captured and, more disastrously, the ships riding at anchor were quietly cut out and sailed back to Calais. This raid on Sandwich was even more spectacularly successful than that of Pierre de Brezé in 1457.

Warwick and Salisbury were not just triumphant, they were vindictive. Richard Woodville was a former lieutenant of Calais and he had opposed Warwick's appointment as captain. Worse still, King Henry had named Woodville to the commission that investigated and censured Warwick's attack on the Hanse fleet in 1458. Woodville confronted Warwick and accused him, Salisbury, and the Earl of March of disloyalty, an accusation that was too close to the truth for comfort. All three took it in turn to berate their captive as a parvenu, a lowborn knave who had risen through royal favour and marriage. He had been ennobled as Lord Rivers only because he had married Jacquetta of Luxembourg, the Dowager Duchess of Bedford and first lady of the land after the Queen. This was true, but the Nevilles were not much better. Although Salisbury's mother was a Beaufort, the Nevilles owed their earldoms and their wealth to their wives, not to their lineage. Young Antony Woodville came in for his share of abuse with much less cause. He at least was the grandson of a Count of St Pol through his mother, whom Warwick's raiders had prudently left behind in Kent.[37]

The raid caused consternation at court, in Council, and at Guines. Somerset sent Lord Roos back to England to plead for reinforcements and possibly to ask for instructions.[38] It was rumoured in London that King Henry would return to the capital, raising levies on his way. It was not true. The confrontation at Ludford and the attainders in Parliament had been too much for him and Henry had withdrawn

The Defence of the Realm

into piety once again. He was at Leicester Abbey for Christmas and he stayed there until the end of January. Chancellor Waynflete believed that an invasion was imminent. He rode to Leicester and persuaded Henry to come south as far as Northampton. Henry issued commissions of array for the counties believed to be the mostly likely points of invasion, especially Kent, and Sussex. The Duke of Norfolk was ordered to remain at Caistor to guard the East Anglian coast and in the West Country the new Earl of Devon and Lord Bonville received the same commission. The mayors of Bristol and Kingston on Hull were also put on alert.[39]

Margaret feared that York rather than Warwick would spearhead the invasion since York could raise an army in Ireland. King Henry reappointed the Earl of Wiltshire as the King's Lieutenant in Ireland and ordered the seizure of all York's possessions there, but it was an empty gesture.[40] Henry had neither the troops, nor the money, nor the will to oppose York in Ireland. Wiltshire had his hands full as Treasurer, and he certainly would not venture against York.

York was expected to land in North Wales and Jasper Tudor was entrusted with the defence of the principality. Henry appointed him constable and steward of York's castle of Denbigh and master forester of the lordship, with extensive judicial and military powers throughout Wales.[41] York had returned from Ireland via Denbigh in 1450 and its garrison remained loyal to him. Jasper besieged Denbigh for several weeks before he managed to capture it. Jasper believed he had won the friendship of Sir William Herbert despite Herbert's connection to York and Warwick; he was sure that given the right inducements, Herbert would bring South Wales under royal control. Herbert was named steward of York and Warwick's lordships in South Wales and confirmed in the offices he had been granted by them and he became sheriff of Glamorgan and Constable of Usk Castle.[42] Jasper's trust would prove to be misplaced.

Prince Edward was six years old, and towards the end of March Margaret dismissed his governess, Lady Lovell, because 'he is now so

The Yorkists' Challenge

grown as to be committed to the rules and teachings of men wise and strenuous, to understand the acts and manners of a man befitting such a prince, rather than to stay further under the keeping and governance of women.'[43] Margaret may have wanted Edward to be placed under Jasper Tudor's tutelage, but it may also reflect her increasing concern for King Henry's mental state. Henry retreated north again in April and paid a three-day visit to the great abbey of Croyland during Lent. He took up residence as a guest of Abbot Richard Ashton at Peterborough Abbey, where he celebrated Easter.[44] If Henry collapsed again Prince Edward's role and status would be vital.[45]

Margaret saw to it that Prince Edward's name was associated with Jasper's activities. They were named jointly to a commission of oyer and terminer with powers to arrest rebels, or to pardon anyone who submitted to the King. They were each granted £1,000 to defray their costs in recovering Denbigh, and subduing rebellion, but as the money was to come from York's lands, it was unlikely to be collected quickly or easily.[46] The Prince was to take possession of York and Warwick's lordships in Wales, and to garrison them with reliable men. He and his councillors were to suppress rebellion and 'all unlawful gatherings' in Wales. He was granted 500 marks yearly to recruit knights and squires to his service, 'so far as the said sum will extend.'[47] It would not go far. Whether Margaret allowed the Prince to rough it in Wales with Jasper or kept him with her is not known.

Chancellor Waynflete and the Council were concerned by the threat from Warwick in Calais.[48] Warwick's successful cutting out expedition at Sandwich meant that few ships capable of waging war at sea remained in English hands and merchant ships had to be pressed into service. Sir Baldwin Fulford, the sheriff of Devon, volunteered to assemble ships and men provided the King paid for them. The Exchequer was ordered to make £1,000 available to Fulford to equip and victual the ships, although wages would not be paid until they put to sea.[49] But where was the money to come from? Waynflete had not requested a tax from the Coventry Parliament and the Council had to fall back on solicited loans. To raise £3,000 the Earl of Wiltshire, as Treasurer, pledged that anyone willing to lend would be repaid by the first call on future income from the forfeited estates, from crown revenues of wardships and marriages, or from the customs on tonnage and poundage. Income from the customs on wool shipments were already earmarked to repay loans from the Calais Staplers.[50] It was not the best security, but it was all he could offer. Lawrence Booth loaned £1,048 out of his income as Bishop of Durham.[51]

Warwick got tired of waiting on events; it was high time to plan a spring campaign. He sailed from Calais in March with a sizeable fleet bound not for England but for Ireland to meet with the Duke of York. On reaching Ireland after his flight from Ludlow, York had the temerity to claim the right to govern based on King Henry's re-appointment of him as the King's Lieutenant in 1457. He summoned the Irish Parliament and his son, Edmund of Rutland, became Chancellor. York adroitly bribed the members to recognise his authority by allowing them to endorse, not just accept, King Henry's warrant. It was a major constitutional concession that York had no right to make, but it bought him the support and the safeguards he needed. The Irish Parliament enacted that any attack on York as the King's representative was treason, just as it would be on the King. They got around the awkward business of Henry's Privy Seal letters ordering the seizure of York's assets by declaring that they did not come from the King. Furthermore, English Privy Seal letters were not valid without the assent of the Irish Parliament.[52] York was no more interested in governing Ireland in 1460 than he had been in 1450, but he needed a refuge until he could return to England and Ireland provided it.

Warwick sailed into the harbour at Waterford on 16 March 1460 with twenty-six ships, having captured at least two of them on his voyage.[53] Baldwin Fulford was not ready to put to sea, and the Council succumbed to an appeal from Henry Holand, Duke of Exeter, the Admiral of England, to appoint him to command a second fleet.[54]

Exeter had never fought at sea but he was a ship owner and a royal duke. The Council intended to combine Exeter's fleet with Fulford's and they were promised repayment of half the income from tunnage and poundage, the other half being reserved to repay the loans raised to send them to sea.[55] Henry Holand was a fantasist; he believed in his own prowess largely because he *was* the Duke of Exeter. With little idea of how to go about it, he was determined to defeat his hated rival whom the Council had once named as Keeper of the Seas in preference to him.

His preparations lasted throughout March and into April. Treasurer Wiltshire hired five Genoese carracks to supplement Exeter's fleet and Venetian galleys moored in Southampton were requisitioned. But the Venetians refused to get involved: it was not their quarrel and the promise of payment was dubious. The risk of losing one of their ships was too great – Warwick's reputation as a successful pirate was well known. The Venetian fleet put to sea to keep out of harm's way and this gave the Council an excuse to arrest Venetian merchants still in England and to demand 36,000 ducats for their release.[56] One wonders how much, if any, of the money ever reached King Henry's coffers.

The Duke of Exeter mustered with fourteen ships to intercept Warwick on his way back to Calais in May. Exeter sailed from Sandwich with fourteen ships. The fleets sighted each other off Dartmouth and Warwick formed his ships in line of battle, but he did not engage. He waited to see what Exeter would do when faced by an enemy fleet. Even if Warwick had left some of his twenty-six ships in Ireland with York, his was still the larger fleet. When the moment of truth arrived, Exeter proved unequal to the task. As soon as he sighted Warwick's fleet on a morning in late May he sailed for Dartmouth and safety. Baldwin Fulford went home in disgust.[57] Exeter escaped because Warwick still proclaimed that he was a loyal subject of King Henry and like Somerset, Exeter was Henry's closest kin.[58] Warwick had not permitted Somerset's ship to enter Calais, where he could have been captured, because the time was not yet right to engage Somerset or Exeter in battle.

Recognising that they had a war on their hands and in desperate need of money, the Council ordered that 'all wools, woolfells, tin, lead and other merchandise pertaining to the Staple and woollen cloths shipped in the ports of London, Southampton, or Sandwich until Michaelmas following *should be shipped in the king's name or otherwise for the king's benefit* as should seem good to the treasurer.' This order would affect repayment of the Staplers' loans which had been authorised by the Coventry Parliament in 1459.[59] There is no record that Parliament placed a total trade embargo on Calais, and it is extremely unlikely that the merchant interest in the Commons would have agreed to such a ban.[60] The Staplers had to accept Warwick's presence in Calais, but it is a matter for debate as to how much help they gave him or how much sympathy they felt for him. Warwick looked to them for financial assistance, he cajoled and flattered them, but they had the repayment of their loans to the crown to consider, as well as the crown's grant to them of favourable trading privileges with the Low Countries.[61]

24

The Yorkists' Revenge

While Warwick was in Ireland the Duke of Somerset made a final attempt to gain entry to Calais. He had remained pinned down in Guines Castle, but some of the Calais garrison had deserted and joined him, probably because Andrew Trollope was with him. On St George's day, 23 April 1460, a fierce encounter took place at Newnham Bridge halfway between Guines and Calais. Somerset's men were no match for the Calais garrison under the command of the experienced war captain Lord Fauconberg, one of the most competent soldiers of his time, and Somerset was driven back to Guines after suffering heavy losses.[1]

The Council belatedly decided to send reinforcements to Somerset, and Osbert Mundford, who had returned to England after Warwick became Captain of Calais, was ordered to assemble ships and 200 men for the relief of Guines.[2] Optimistically, King Henry issued letters patent empowering Somerset to pardon any man who submitted to him, excluding those attainted in Parliament, plus Lord Fauconberg, John Dynham, Louis Gallet, and four others.[3] The choice of Sandwich as Mundford's mustering point was remarkably short sighted since it was acutely vulnerable to attack from Calais and had twice been raided successfully.

Lord Fauconberg, Sir John Wenlock, and the resourceful John Dynham, who knew Sandwich like the back of his hand, sailed into the port to repeat Dynham's coup of the previous January. Mundford fought bravely but he was captured and taken back to Calais where

The Yorkists' Revenge

Warwick had him executed. It was a cruel and unnecessary fate for a brave soldier, a veteran of the war in France, whose only fault was to serve his King and country loyally over many years. But Mundford had also served Edmund, Duke of Somerset, and that was enough to condemn him.[4]

Lord Fauconberg remained in Sandwich until Warwick could join him. Warwick's spies and agents circulated propaganda in the southern counties in England, especially in the volatile county of Kent, where Warwick consistently courted popularity. A ballad nailed up on the gates at Canterbury was undoubtedly displayed in London and elsewhere. It lamented the sinful state of England for accepting a false heir to the throne, that had offended God. Only the return of the righteous Richard of York, the famed Earl of March, the prudent Earl of Salisbury, the highly esteemed 'little' Fauconberg, and the Earl of Warwick as the defender of the realm could save England. The ballad urged King Henry to recall them in all haste before the country was totally lost: 'Thay shall come agayne and rekene for the scoore.'[5]

During Warwick's stay in Ireland York had prepared yet another statement of their loyalty, their innocence, and their good intentions.[6] Addressed to the Archbishop of Canterbury the preamble was new: it expressed a deep concern for the safety of the Holy Church, but it then it rehearsed past grievances, enhanced by clauses from Jack Cade's petition of 1450 to remind Kentishmen of their tradition of resistance to 'traitors'. It outlined yet again the accusations that York had been making for the past ten years and added that the French king was rumoured to be preparing an invasion. If they were not checked, the evil men around the King would surrender England to his enemies. York, Salisbury, and Warwick were ready and waiting to rescue the King and the country, and York begged Henry not to allow any further oppression of his people.

The manifesto touched on York's personal grievances: he had gone in fear of his life ever since the Duke of Gloucester's 'murder' because he had royal blood in his veins and, as the rightful heir, he had the

The Yorkists' Challenge

good of the people at heart. Prince Edward was not the true heir and no allegiance was owed to him. Salisbury and Warwick had been threatened because they chose to uphold the justice of York's claims. King Henry had no resources *except* Calais and Ireland, but the King's councillors would rather lose Calais than allow it to remain in Warwick's care. Henry had been coerced into requesting England's enemies not to aid Warwick, and no supplies were being sent to Calais from England. King Henry had been forced to send letters into Ireland urging rebellion there, and the Irish chiefs were so taken aback that they had approached the Duke of York, 'the same Yrussh enemyes sent unto ME the Duke of York', to show him the letters. They simply could not believe that the letters came from the King.

York singled out three particularly heinous councillors, the Earl of Wiltshire, the Earl of Shrewsbury, and Viscount Beaumont. Wiltshire was anathema to York and the enmity between them made him a natural target for vilification. The Earl of Shrewsbury had replaced Salisbury, Warwick, and Sir Thomas Neville as steward of Pontefract Honour in the Duchy of Lancaster, and Viscount Beaumont had replaced the Earl of Salisbury as Chief Steward of the North Parts of the duchy.[7] They had long coveted the Yorkists' estates and they had persuaded King Henry to hold Parliament at Coventry and attaint them. They had robbed and hanged some of York's loyal tenants, which was not what King Henry wanted or intended, and they were even now enriching themselves from the forfeited estates. Finally, York appealed to the people to join him in ridding the realm of evil men. This piece of propaganda forced King Henry to deny that the Yorkists had been attainted without his consent. He issued a proclamation stating emphatically that rumours of his sympathy with the exiled lords were false: 'his highness will that it be known that he demeth them enemyes, rebels and traytors ... accordyning to the seid acte.'[8]

The stage was set, the time was right. On 26 June 1460, Warwick, Salisbury, the Earl of March, Lord Audley, and Sir John Wenlock joined Lord Fauconberg at Sandwich. Warwick did not make the same

The Yorkists' Revenge

mistake twice, he brought over most of the Calais garrison and he had an ace up his sleeve: Francesco Coppini, the papal legate.

On his way from Rome to London in 1459 Coppini had stopped off in Milan and offered his services to Francisco Sforza, Duke of Milan, who already had an excellent spy service. Sforza's ambassadors provided him with a steady stream of information and gossip, much of it inaccurate, but designed to please their suspicious master. Coppini joined their ranks, although he was not afforded official recognition. After he failed to persuade King Henry to commit England to Pope Pius's crusade, Coppini had left England for Bruges. He hoped to propitiate the Pope by reporting a more favourable reaction from the Duke of Burgundy. In Bruges Coppini heard that the Earl of Warwick was preparing to invade England and he hastened to Calais to ingratiate himself with Warwick. Coppini claimed with less-than-perfect truth that Pope Pius had instructed him to use his influence to reconcile King Henry with his rebellious lords. Warwick was delighted to welcome him; a papal legate would add a spiritual justification to his enterprise, and he went out of his way to flatter Coppini, which was easily done. Coppini crossed to Sandwich with Warwick and carried his cross before Warwick's army all the way from Canterbury to London.[9] It was an impressive spectacle.[10]

Warwick knew there was no royal army between him and London, but it was vital to reach the capital as quickly as possible. He halted his army outside the City's walls so as not to alarm the Londoners, and he sent a herald to the Mayor, to request permission to pass through the City. The aldermen and Common Council were split between those who thought Warwick and his host should be repelled at London Bridge, and those who were prepared to admit to him.[11] The Recorder and twelve aldermen rode out to meet Warwick and request him to bypass the City. Warwick did not threaten, he cajoled. He assured them that his stay would be short, and that no harm would come to the City, his army would pass through peacefully and bivouac at Smithfield and Clerkenwell, ready to march north. The aldermen

The Yorkists' Challenge

succumbed to his blandishments and permitted him and the lords with him to enter London. On 2 July they took up lodging at the Grey Friars, where Warwick habitually stayed in the capital.[12] Winning London was Warwick's first tactical success.

King Henry's relations with the London oligarchy had been uneasy for some time. London's merchants had rallied to the King when the country was threatened by a French invasion in 1457, but Mayor Hulyn and the Common Council had not forgotten that Henry had threatened the City's franchises in the wake of the disturbances in Fleet Street in 1459. London citizens had been imprisoned on Henry's orders, and Hulyn had only obtained their release when he took office as Mayor. Early in 1460 the City's recorder and an undersheriff had travelled to Northampton to protest to the King in person against a commission of array that he had issued for London and Henry had been forced to write to the Common Council to reassure them that this would in no way infringe the City's liberties.[13] Londoners resented Henry's preference for living in the Midlands. Even now he was in Coventry when he should have been in London. On the other hand, many Londoners admired Warwick. He preyed on foreign shipping and posed as a champion of merchants and trade. And he was successful; the Duke of Somerset had not taken Calais from him and the Duke of Exeter had not defeated him at sea.

Warwick and the Duke of York had been in touch with Thomas Bourgchier, the Archbishop of Canterbury, well before Warwick landed. Convocation was in session at St Pauls and when Warwick requested an audience to state his case, Bourgchier graciously agreed. As primate of England no harm would come to him whoever won the inevitable confrontation, but he and his brother, Viscount Bourgchier, stood to gain if Warwick won, as the Bourgchiers believed he would.

Warwick addressed the assembled clergy at St Pauls in the presence of the Mayor, the aldermen, and the populace. He said that he spoke on behalf of those who had come with him, and he declared their innocence of any wrongdoing. He rehearsed many of the complaints in the Yorkist manifesto and although he did not mention the Duke of York, he had the Duke's son, the young, handsome, and charismatic Edward of March standing beside him. Edward had far more going for him than his austere father. Warwick and the other lords swore on the Archbishop of Canterbury's cross that they would never harm King Henry. They were his loyal subjects and had come to seek an audience with him to clear their names. If this were denied to them, they would fight and die on the battlefield rather than endure further injuries and injustices. Warwick succeeded where York had failed – he won over the people.[14]

Then it was Coppini's turn. The legate was in his element, and he wasted no time in establishing his own importance. He threatened to excommunicate Shrewsbury, Wiltshire, and Beaumont.[15] He read out a verbose letter addressed to King Henry. Stripped of its rhetoric and self-justification it argues the Yorkist case in the same terms as Warwick but goes much further. Coppini more or less ordered King Henry to make peace with Warwick, claiming that as the Pope's representative he had the authority to demand the King's obedience. If the King ignored his efforts to bring about a just peace and reconciliation, the ensuing battle would be on the King's head. It was Henry's 'duty to prevent so much bloodshed now so imminent'. Coppini told the King 'You can prevent this if you will, and if you do not you will be guilty in the sight of God' – and Coppini himself would require the King to answer for it on the Day of Judgement![16] Coppini's motives were entirely selfish. He believed that Pope Pius would be so impressed by his contribution to peace in England that Pius would reward him with what Coppini craved most, a cardinal's hat.

King Henry and Margaret had lived for months under the threat of invasion by their own subjects – now it had come. The Council considered a retreat to the Isle of Ely where King Henry would be safe, at least temporarily, but when the appalling news that London had opened its gates to Warwick reached Coventry the court scattered.[17]

The Yorkists' Challenge

The Earl of Wiltshire had the good sense to save what he could of the King's treasure. There was no hope of retrieving what was in the Tower of London, but Wiltshire gathered the money, jewels, and plate held at Kenilworth and Coventry and rode to Southampton with an armed escort. The Genoese carracks he had hired for the Duke of Exeter's abortive expedition were still in port and Wiltshire had his men and money loaded aboard the ships and he put to sea. After cruising indecisively in the comparative safety of the Channel he made for Flanders where he had friends, thanks to his earlier dealing with the Four Members of Flanders.[18]

King Henry left Coventry for Northampton, the gateway to Warwick's estates in the Midlands, but he did not want to fight, and perhaps he did not expect to win. There is a story that before he left Margaret at Coventry Henry warned her not to believe any messengers who appeared to come from him unless they carried a secret token known only to himself and to her.[19]

At Northampton, the royal tent was pitched in an open field near the village of Hardingstone close to Delapré Abbey, but defeatism was in the air. Late in the afternoon of 7 July, William Waynflete came to King Henry in his tent and resigned as Chancellor. He handed over one Great Seal of silver (presumably the only one he had with him) and it was locked in a small chest to which Henry held the key. Waynflete had been a competent Chancellor but he had not used his wealth as Bishop of Winchester to underpin King Henry financially as Cardinal Beaufort had done. Waynflete had used the money, probably with Henry's blessing, to endow Magdalen College at Oxford. The pathetic ceremony was witnessed by Lawrence Booth, the Privy Seal, John Stanbury, Bishop of Hereford and the King's confessor, Thomas Manning, the King's secretary, and two king's esquires. Henry issued a general pardon to Waynflete, Booth, Stanbury, and his great officers, the *magnos computante*.[20] In effect he gave them the only protection he had to offer. The bishops returned to their dioceses to await an outcome on which their future still depended.

The Yorkists' Revenge

The Duke of Buckingham had charge of the few military preparations that had been made. Buckingham was no soldier, and he seriously underestimated Warwick and the support Warwick could command. Buckingham believed that the Duke of York posed the greater threat and he expected York and Warwick to join forces before they approached the King. He had no way of knowing that York was still in Ireland and he was desperate to defeat Warwick before York could join him. The outlook was bleak – Warwick had adherents everywhere. In June John Judde, master of the King's ordnance, had been killed just outside St Albans while escorting an artillery train north, but the ordnance got through.[21]

Lord Fauconberg left London on 5 July with the advance guard. Warwick, the Earl of March, and Lord Audley followed him the next day. Warwick's army had the trained men of the Calais garrison as its core and their numbers had been swelled by recruits from the home counties and retainers of the lords who had hastened to London to join Warwick. Warwick's army marched under the protection of Holy Church, and he had no difficulty in convincing the bishops that it was their duty as men of God to avert bloodshed by pleading his case with King Henry.[22]

Warwick's host reached the outskirts of Northampton on 9 July and the bishops went in a body to the royal encampment. The Duke of Buckingham would not permit them to enter Henry's presence: either he feared that the pious Henry would bow to their entreaties or Henry himself preferred not to face them. Buckingham berated them for appearing with a heavily armed escort. He said it looked as if they had come not as emissaries of peace but as men of war. Archbishop Bourgchier sent the Bishop of Salisbury alone to request an audience with the King, but it was an unfortunate choice. Richard Beauchamp had been King Henry's emissary to the Yorkists before Ludford and his espousal of Warwick's cause was seen as an especial betrayal. Buckingham treated him with the contempt he deserved and Beauchamp, abandoning both sides, fled to his diocese.[23]

The Yorkists' Challenge

Warwick sent his herald to Henry offering to come in person and unarmed if Henry would guarantee his safety. Buckingham foolishly threatened that if Warwick ventured into the royal enclosure, he would lose his head. This was all the provocation Warwick needed and he issued an ultimatum: King Henry must agree to receive him by no later than two o'clock that afternoon or he and those with him would fight to the death.[24] There was never any doubt that there would be a battle; Warwick had not come to negotiate, only victory could return the Duke of York to power. Warwick's request for an audience was to reassure everyone that he meant the King no harm. He had intended all along to repeat the victory at First Battle of St Albans, which he had facilitated, to capture the King and kill the lords.

Henry had fewer magnates in his company than he had at St Albans, although their retinues were larger. Many of his lords were away on oyer and terminer commissions to seek out suspected Yorkist sympathisers.[25] Henry did not call on them to join him at Northampton or anywhere else. Buckingham, the Earl of Shrewsbury, Viscount Beaumont, and Lord Egremont, were with Henry at Coventry when Warwick landed at Sandwich. They could put Stafford, Talbot, Bardolf, and Percy retainers into the field, but that did not constitute a royal army.[26]

Buckingham drew up his forces in low-lying waterlogged fields with the River Nene at their backs and artillery on the flanks. Warwick's army, directed by Lord Fauconberg, launched a frontal assault with Fauconberg on the left wing, the Earl of March on the right, and Warwick in the centre. The Battle of Northampton was fought on the afternoon of Thursday 10 July in heavy rain. The artillery that Buckingham relied on to compensate for his lack of numbers proved useless. The cannons were too wet to fire and the protective stockade was inadequate. The victory was hastened by the desertion of Lord Grey of Ruthvin's men. They were with the Lancastrian left wing, facing Edward, Earl of March, and they simply threw down their arms in the mud and helped the attacking Yorkists to clamber over the earthworks. Edward, in the forefront of the battle, cut an heroic figure, and he may have played a part in encouraging their desertion.[27] Warwick kept his word to fight to the death, but it was the Lancastrian lords who died. Buckingham, Shrewsbury, Beaumont, and Egremont were killed. The fighting lasted for less than an hour. More men drowned in the River Nene while fleeing the victorious Yorkists than were killed in the fighting. Warwick did not win the Battle of Northampton; the Duke of Buckingham lost it.

Warwick found King Henry in his tent and knelt to protest his loyalty. For the second time in his life Henry accepted defeat and offered no resistance as he was led into Delapré Abbey by his victorious subjects. Warwick allowed him three days to recover, and then, in a repeat of the charade after the Battle of St Albans, he brought King Henry back to London. They entered the City on 16 July and as before Henry was lodged not at Westminster but in the Bishop of London's palace. From there the captive King was escorted in procession to a thanksgiving service at St Pauls, that was marred by the sound of gunfire from the Tower of London.[28]

As soon as he realised that there was no hope of stopping Warwick in Kent, Lords Scales had raced to defend the Tower. He had held it ten years earlier against Jack Cade when Mayor Hulyn, as a sheriff of London, had fought alongside him at the Battle of the Bridge. Hulyn did not want a repeat of that bloodshed. He and the Common Council refused to cooperate with Scales or allow him to take command of the City's trained bands. A few Lancastrian stalwarts joined him.[29] By sheer coincidence two of them had been captured at Castillon in 1453 and had only recently returned to England: John de Foix, the Earl of Kendal, who had joined the Duke of Exeter's ill fated excursion against Warwick's ships,[30] and Robert, Lord Hungerford, who came home in 1459 after his father managed to raise the first instalment of the £6,000 that King Charles had set as his ransom, a sum that crippled his family's fortunes and his own.[31]

While Warwick marched to Northampton, the Earl of Salisbury,

The Yorkists' Challenge

Lord Cobham, and Sir John Wenlock laid siege to the Tower of London. The Tower was impregnable; it could not be taken by storm, but it had not been stocked to withstand a siege. Warwick's ships sailed round from Sandwich to blockade it, and Salisbury threw a cordon of soldiers around its landward sides and along its wharves. Using money 'borrowed' from the Common Council of London, he bribed the Thames watermen to patrol the river so that no provisions or reinforcements could reach the Tower's defenders.[32] The besieged addressed a letter to the Common Council to demand why rebels had been allowed to make war on the King's true subjects. The Council replied that it was Lord Scales who had declared war by firing on the City. He had turned the Tower's guns on the besiegers, setting houses on fire and inadvertently killing or wounding some of the citizens.[33]

The standoff continued until Warwick returned to London. Once the defenders learned that King Henry was Warwick's prisoner, they knew that further resistance was pointless: they were almost out food, and they could no longer hope for relief. They negotiated with Salisbury for their freedom and on 19 July they surrendered.[34] Lord Scales was not so lucky. He left the Tower by barge and was recognised by the watermen still patrolling the Thames. They were every bit as violent and dangerous as the London mob and they had orders not to allow anyone to escape by water. Scales was murdered, and his naked body was dumped on the steps of St Mary Overy in Southwark where he was found some hours later. It was a sad end to a loyal soldier's life. Scales had fought for King Henry in France before Margaret was born and he never wavered in his allegiance. His wife was Margaret's senior lady in waiting and he had served on the Queen's council. Even the *English Chronicle*, which rarely had a good word to say for any Lancastrian, recorded that 'a grete pyte it was that so noble and worshypfull a knyght and so well approued in the warrys of Normandy and Fraunce should dy so myscheuously.' His death was something of an embarrassment to Edward of March; Lord Scales was his godfather. Edward ordered that Scales be given honourable burial in St Mary Overy, and Warwick concurred, although he was probably not displeased by Scales's death – he preferred dead enemies to live ones.[35]

Warwick needed a scapegoat for the defence of the Tower in opposition to him. Sir Thomas Browne and five servants of the Duke of Exeter, the Constable of the Tower, were arrested and put on trial for treason in Warwick's presence at the Guildhall. Browne was accused of breaking into the Tower with a band of men (which is most unlikely), of encouraging the men holding the Tower to resist the King's loyal subjects, and of unleashing wildfire on the City. The prisoners were summarily executed.[36]

Warwick's control of London was now complete, but Chancellor Waynflete had resigned, and without a Chancellor there could be no government. Warwick fell back temporarily on the ex-Chancellor, Thomas Bourgchier. Two chancery clerks brought the two Great Seals, one of gold and one of silver, to the Bishop of London's palace and on 25 July surrendered them to Bourgchier, together with the third Great Seal of silver that had been recovered from King Henry's tent at Northampton. If Bourgchier hoped to be reinstated he was disappointed, Warwick was calling the shots. George Neville, Bishop of Exeter, Warwick's youngest brother, swore the Chancellor's oath and King Henry handed the seals to him. The ceremony was witnessed by the Neville family. Either Warwick or Salisbury had arranged for Thomas and John Neville to be released from Chester Castle where they had languished as Margaret's prisoners after Blore Heath nearly a year earlier.[37] George Neville returned the gold seal and one of the silver seals to King Henry while retaining the second silver seal for chancery business.[38] Did Warwick want to keep the seals in King Henry's hands until the Duke of York arrived?

Three days later Viscount Bourgchier became Treasurer of England for the second time, and a newcomer, the biddable Robert Stillington, Dean of St Martin le Grand in London, replaced Lawrence Booth as Keeper of the Privy Seal.[39] The most urgent piece of business was now

The Yorkists' Challenge

to recover the Nevilles' estates and writs to summon Parliament were issued on 30 July.

As soon as the great officers had been appointed in the King's presence, Warwick had the good sense to get King Henry out of London and into a more congenial atmosphere. At the beginning of August, Warwick, Salisbury, and the Earl of March escorted him to Canterbury where Archbishop Bourgchier waited to receive him. That evening Henry attended evensong in the cathedral and a series of religious services and processions over the next few days saw the King take part in thanksgiving ceremonies at the shrine of St Thomas Becket; he also joined the monks in a procession through the nave and cloisters to the monks' burial ground. Henry's physician, John Arundel, Bishop of Chichester, who probably knew Henry's temperament and mental condition better than anyone, was on hand to preach before the King.[40] Throughout this time and in the weeks that followed, King Henry remained passive. He may even have been grateful to Warwick, and he had always trusted Salisbury. They treated him with all the honour due to a King but demanded nothing of him. He did not have to make decisions, issue orders, argue with anyone, or deal with routine business. Apparently, although he authorised whatever documents were put before him, Henry did not attend the meetings of Warwick's Council.

While Henry was immersed in religious devotions the hastily constituted Council began putting all to rights, mostly in favour of the Nevilles. On 5 August a warrant commanded the Duke of Somerset to surrender Guines Castle and Warwick was authorised to receive it.[41] The Earl of Salisbury and Thomas Neville were jointly appointed as keepers of the King's falcons and the royal mews.[42] John Neville's possession of his wife Isabel's inheritance was confirmed without further payments to Queen Margaret, who was in no position to claim the debt.[43] John also became King Henry's chamberlain.[44]

25

The Westminster Accord

The Duke of York remained in Ireland while Warwick secured the Yorkists' hold on England. York had negotiated with King James of Scotland for Scottish neutrality while Warwick crossed from Calais, and true to form, James had tried to turn the uncertain political situation to his own advantage. He professed to recognise the justice of York's claim to the throne (a claim that York had yet to make publicly) and he encouraged the rumour that York had agreed to marry his eldest son to one of James's daughters.

James invited King Charles to join forces with him in an invasion of England, pointing out that such an opportunity would surely never come again, but his grandiose plan came to nothing.[1] Charles was far too wily to indulge James's hair-brained scheme and he had no sympathy for the Duke of York. Impatient as ever, James went ahead anyway and laid siege to Roxburgh Castle, an English stronghold on Scottish soil that his father had tried and failed to capture. It was hardly the best way to aid York's cause. James was fascinated by artillery, he had brought several heavy guns to the siege, and he was killed on 3 August 1460 when one them exploded right next to him.[2] The threat to England's northern border was eliminated.

King Charles was more interested in French expansion into Italy than he was in the conflict in England. Genoa was under French control, the Duke of Orleans had a claim to Milan through his mother, and it looked as if John of Calabria would recover Naples. Three days before Warwick's victory at Northampton, John and a French army

The Yorkists' Challenge

defeated King Ferdinand of Naples at the battle of Sarno.[3] Francesco Sforza, the Duke of Milan felt threatened, and he formed an alliance with King Ferdinand.

The self-important little Coppini was still in England and he was feeling neglected; he had not received his cardinal's hat. He assured his patron the Duke of Milan that Warwick had prevailed thus far only through his, Coppini's, agency and he proposed a grand scheme to Sforza that he claimed was of his making. Nothing less than an Anglo–Burgundian alliance against the King of France. According to Coppini, 'within a few days a marriage alliance will be concluded between the Duke of Burgundy and these lords here', presumably Edward of March as the only readily available unmarried 'lord'. These lords would invade France in alliance with Burgundy to recover England's lost territories. With a little help from Coppini the English could put 100,000 men into the field! Coppini was sure that this would distract King Charles from his Italian ambitions. The plan would, of course, stand a better chance of success if Sforza could obtain secret authorisation for it from Pope Pius and a cardinal's hat for Coppini. Coppini told Sforza that the lords and people of England felt this to be his due.[4] The Dauphin Louis consistently encouraged any threat to his father, and he had been intriguing with Sforza for months, but he was too farsighted to encourage an invasion of France. King Charles was in poor health and Louis knew he had only to wait for the throne to be his. Sforza was intrigued and in September he sent his ambassador to the Burgundian court to find out how far Burgundy was committed to the scheme.[5]

Philip of Burgundy would certainly have welcomed hostility towards King Charles from the new regime in England, but the suggestion, based solely on Warwick's posthumous reputation, that the Duke of Burgundy, the Dauphin Louis, the Duke of Milan, and even Pope Pius supported Warwick's coup is untenable. None of them could formally acknowledge the Earl of Warwick while Henry VI was still King of England, and it is inconceivable that Warwick was party to any of this. He would never have embroiled himself in a plan to invade France, even as a bluff, while the Duke of York was still in Ireland. Warwick's government was temporary, and York's authority had yet to be established.

Warwick paid a lightning visit to Calais to install Lord Fauconberg as his lieutenant there.[6] According to the chronicler Waurin, the Duke of Somerset was still in Guines when Warwick arrived. They met in Calais and negotiated a truce, with Somerset promising never to fight Warwick again.[7] One cannot help wondering if this meeting ever took place. It is difficult to believe that Somerset would promise not to fight Warwick unless he was under serious constraint, and if he came to Calais to meet Warwick, would Warwick have let him go? Somerset no longer expected relief from England, and he had received a safe conduct from King Charles to allow him to escape via France.[8]

Somerset was at Arques, not far from Calais on 12 August, where he met the Count of Charolais, Burgundy's heir, and they got on well together. They were two of a kind: ardent, impulsive, and politically inexperienced. Charolais entertained Somerset royally and, possibly fired by a sense of chivalry, but more probably because he knew it would irritate his father, Charolais promised Somerset his support.[9] Somerset and his companions reached France and were lodged at Montivilliers while they waited for a ship and a favourable wind to cross to England.[10] King Charles paid their expenses but he wanted them gone as soon as possible. John Butler, the Earl of Wiltshire's younger brother, Lord Roos, Robert Whittingham, and Andrew Trollope were later reported to be with Somerset.[11] They sailed from Harfleur and Somerset reached his home at Corfe Castle towards the end of September. His arrival was not immediately known in London; he was reported to be in Dieppe in early October.[12]

Warwick was not worried about Somerset, or interested in France, but he was concerned by the threat from Wales. Jasper Tudor held Denbigh Castle and other strongholds and he could raise an army in the principality. A letter in King Henry's name ordered Jasper to surrender Denbigh and informed him that the King had accepted the Duke of York as his true liege man.[13] Jasper did not believe a word of it. Sir William Herbert and Walter Devereux who, despite Jasper's overtures, had never wavered in their allegiance to the Duke of York, were instructed to dislodge Jasper if they could and in the meanwhile they were to exercise jurisdiction over strategic points in Wales and guard them in King Henry's name.[14]

Warwick had the business of government well in hand; all that was needed to consolidate the Yorkists' revenge, courtesy of the Earl of Warwick, was for the Duke of York to return from Ireland. He was the unknown factor and he had been expected for so long that no one was sure when he would arrive, or exactly what he meant to do. York was in no hurry. He did not set foot on English soil until September when he bypassed Denbigh and took up residence in the Prince of Wales's castle at Chester.[15] He moved south slowly, showing himself to the people, meting out justice, and summoning men to his banner, just as if he were the King. He sent word to Duchess Cecily, whom he had not seen since he abandoned her at Ludlow and who was anxiously awaiting his arrival, to join him and the Earl of Rutland at Hereford.[16] York's behaviour was possibly illegal. Among other things he no longer dated his letters and orders by King Henry's regnal year.

King Henry opened Parliament at Westminster on 7 October 1460 before York reached London. After the election of the Speaker the first order of business was to undo the acts of attainder against York and the Nevilles. Warwick's Council issued an order restoring the revenues of the family seat at Middleham to the Earl of Salisbury.[17] The Commons petitioned the King that all acts of the Coventry Parliament should be repealed and the Parliament itself declared unlawful because, it was claimed, its elections had been rigged and its statutes and ordnances were therefore invalid.[18] The past had been undone; the next act in the drama was still to unfold.

On the morning of 10 October, a fanfare of trumpets announced the arrival of the Duke of York.[19] He strode through Westminster Hall,

The Westminster Accord

past St Stephen's chapel and into the Painted Chamber where the Lords had assembled for the parliamentary session. He went straight to the dais with its canopy of estate and laid his hand on the empty throne. After a few initial gasps of surprise, the silence in the Chamber was absolute. York turned and stared around him, awaiting the applause and acclamation of his peers. It did not come, and he sustained a severe shock – this was not the reception he expected. Archbishop Bourgchier was the first to recover. He greeted York and asked him if he wished an audience with King Henry. York reportedly replied haughtily with the famous words, 'I know of no person in this realm whom it does not behove to come to me and see my person rather than that I should go and visit him.'[20] The allusion was clear: King Henry was not the rightful king. York then left the Chamber angrily and made his way to the royal apartments and ordered the doors to be unlocked.[21]

The deposition of King Henry had been agreed in secret between York and Warwick during their conference in Ireland; it was the only logical solution to ending their exile since their previous attempts to control Henry had failed.[22] Rumours of their accord had reached Bruges from London in early July, when it was reported 'that they will make a son of the Duke of York King, and that they will pass over the King's son, as they are beginning already to say that he is not the King's son. Similarly, the Queen also runs great danger.'[23] Warwick's propaganda that Prince Edward was a bastard implied that Margaret had committed adultery, and adultery was treason in a Queen.

York had proclaimed himself King long before he reached London or sought Parliament's approval. At Abingdon he had replaced his banner of the fetterlock with the royal arms and he had his unsheathed sword carried upright before him.[24] York acted under the illusion that he had Warwick's backing, but a great deal had changed since Warwick had met York in Ireland. Somewhere along the line in the hectic weeks after his return to England Warwick changed his mind. He had taken all the risks and he had captured King Henry and

The Yorkists' Challenge

successfully conducted the government in the King's name. Warwick realised that attempting to force the Lords to accept York as King would be a mistake: no one wanted York, and it was not necessary to depose Henry. The King was alone, the men he knew best were dead, and Margaret was not there to prod him into resistance.[25] Warwick had succeeded against the odds, but his coup was based on his repeated assertions of his loyalty to King Henry. If York supposed that Warwick had laid the groundwork for his claim to the throne, he was wrong.

The Lords removed to the safety of Black Friars. They had expected a declaration from York but not that he would confront them in such a dramatic and uncompromising manner. Had he submitted his case discreetly and not at the point of a sword he would have lessened their initial shock, but in his usual overbearing fashion York went about his business in the wrong way. His arrival had stirred up popular unrest. York's panoply and pomp had attracted great numbers of people to Westminster agog to see what would happen next. Did York mean to have himself crowned?[26]

Archbishop Bourgchier and Chancellor Neville, supported by the other bishops, met with York and reached a stalemate. York would not back down, the Lords would not depose their anointed king to whom they had sworn binding oaths of loyalty and whom everyone, including the Neville earls, acknowledged as a good – if ineffectual – king. Henry VI was not a tyrant. The Lords wondered uneasily what would happen if York became King. He was quite capable of ordering wide scale resumptions of the grants that King Henry had made to them over the years.

York eventually allowed himself to be persuaded to submit his claim to the judgement of Parliament, the highest law court in the land. Chancellor Neville presented York's argument, and it was masterly. Using the name Richard Plantagenet for the first time, York declared that he was the rightful King of England through his descent from Lionel, Duke of Clarence, the second son of King Edward III.

The Westminster Accord

Although he had not borne Clarence's arms, for good reasons as everyone knew, he had a right to them and to the arms of England. York claimed he was seeking justice; he had not come as a conqueror, like Henry IV, but to recover his lawful inheritance. It was a powerful plea: the King's person was sacrosanct, but so were the laws of inheritance. York dismissed Henry IV's claim to the throne as false: if he had inherited it by just descent, he would not have needed an Act of Parliament to make himself King. As for York's oaths of fealty, God's law was above man's law, and forced oaths falsely sworn were invalid. York waited for twenty-four hours before he demanded, through the Chancellor, that the Lords give him their answer.[27]

King Henry had to be informed and consulted. Did he know of any precedents for deciding the descent of the crown? Henry did not. He instructed the Lords to search for all the arguments that could be found. They referred the question to the judges and the sergeants-at-law, who replied that they could not sit in judgement as the King's regal status was above the law.[28]

The Lords deliberated for a week. It is not known who came up with the solution. The idea may have originated with Warwick, but it was probably a collective compromise born of self-interest: a claim to be the rightful heir to the throne was different from claiming to be the King. This was a proposition that Warwick and Edward of March could support. Edward was the dark horse in these proceedings.[29] Not once did he show support for his father: he did not go to meet him on his way to London, he did not greet or recognise him when York laid his hand on the throne, and he did not side with him in confronting the Lords. Warwick and Edward wanted the Lords to accept York as Henry's heir, because that would automatically make Edward next in line. York was ten years older than King Henry; Edward, was only eighteen – he could afford to wait.

York never came face to face with King Henry. How could he? Who would kneel to whom? On 25 October, to avoid 'great troubles' and the possibility of civil war, Parliament recognised York's claim, but only in

The Yorkists' Challenge

part. Henry would remain King for the term of his natural life, but York would be heir to the throne, with his sons the Earls of March and Rutland after him. Chancellor Neville asked hopefully if anyone had a better solution, but no one had. As Chancellor he faced the unenviable task of breaking the news to King Henry. The Lords agreed to stand by him no matter what Henry's reaction might be and help him to persuade the King to accept the compromise.[30]

The precaution was unnecessary. In the thirty-ninth year of his reign King Henry VI accepted a proposal that disinherited his only son and surrendered his country into the hands of the man who, despite his repeated protests of loyalty, had shown himself to be the King's most implacable enemy. York and some of the Lords hoped that Henry would abdicate, but in this they wrong. It was the one thing that Henry's conscience would not permit. He was a twice-anointed king, he had been chosen by God, and he simply could not go against God's will even if he wished to. But that aside, he was willing to accommodate his lords.

The Westminster Accord was sealed on 31 October 1460 by a minority of the Lords in Parliament.[31] They swore an oath to recognise York and his sons as heirs to the throne.[32] York, March, and Rutland swore to abide by the terms of the Accord, provided King Henry did not break his word at any time in the future. A further clause disinherited Prince Edward of Lancaster, although he was not actually named.[33] The Lords who remained loyal to King Henry did not attend Parliament; their assent was not sought, and nor would it be given. York's oft-repeated fear that his life was in danger was still with him. Uniquely, Parliament was required to declare that his person was sacrosanct, and that it would be high treason for anyone to attempt to harm him in any way. York had his revenge for that earlier 'Loveday' when he had been obliged to walk hand in hand with Queen Margaret. On 1 November King Henry, wearing his crown, was escorted by Richard of York, his sons, and the signatories to the Accord to St Pauls to give thanks for a settlement that in effect ended

The Westminster Accord

the Lancastrian dynasty as Kings of England. It was proclaimed publicly on 9 November, and Parliament was prorogued at the end of the month to meet again in January 1461.[34]

King Henry's repudiation of his only son was consistent with his personality. He was not dynastically minded, and he had not wanted to be King as his father and grandfather had. He had elevated his half-brothers to the peerage, but this was to buttress a shaky throne and fill the gap in the military requirements of a king that Henry could not bring himself to face. He could not remember Prince Edward's birth, and he had left the Prince's upbringing entirely to Margaret. Edward was still only seven years old and Henry's limited imagination could not picture him as a future King of England. And what good would it do Prince Edward, or anyone else, if he refused to recognise York, since this would almost certainly lead to civil war? 'Inspired with the grace of the Holy Spirit and to avoid the shedding of Christian blood', Henry accepted what he could not change.

York did not get all he wanted, but it was enough. The justice of his claim had been validated, and his heirs would be Kings of England. With four sons to his name, the future seemed secure. Henry granted him and his two eldest sons 10,000 marks a year, the equivalent of Margaret's dower, to sustain their new status. The money would come from the disinherited Prince of Wales's patrimony.[35] If York expected to receive so large a sum from the Prince's lands, he had Margaret's careful administration and collection of revenue since 1457 to thank for it. Warwick secured an even better deal for himself and his family. King Henry remained Duke of Lancaster, but Warwick ensured that the administration of the duchy's resources was transferred into Neville hands. Salisbury was reinstated as Chief Steward of the North Parts jointly with Warwick, and together they became Chief Stewards of the South Parts. The stewardship of Tutbury and Leicester, Queen Margaret's dower lands, was allotted to Warwick.[36] Richard of York might be heir to the throne but the Nevilles would be the power in the land.

The Yorkists' Challenge

The news of King Henry's defeat and capture at the Battle of Northampton had reached Margaret at Coventry. Her first care was for the safety of Prince Edward. She gathered up her jewels and with only a small escort she travelled to her dower castle of Leicester and then to Tutbury. She hoped to reach Chester Castle in safety, but at Malpas some miles south of Chester she encountered a band of men and was recognised by one John Cleger, a servant of Lord Stanley, who had formerly been employed in Prince Edward's household. They robbed her, but she escaped with the help a young esquire, John Combe.[37] She and Prince Edward crossed into Wales not long before the Duke of York landed from Ireland and took possession of Chester Castle.

Margaret's original intention had been to seek refuge in France. She sent a messenger to King Charles requesting a safe conduct for herself and Prince Edward and she made for Harlech Castle from where she could take ship to France. Charles complied with her request, but he entrusted his envoys with a message advising her not to leave England unless her situation became desperate, and he assured her that she had his full (if insubstantial) support; he had requested his allies, the Kings of Scotland and Spain, to espouse her cause.[38]

Margaret was at first incredulous and then furious when she learned of the Westminster Accord. She knew King Henry's weaknesses all too well, but it had never occurred to her that he could or would disinherit his son. She abandoned her plan to take refuge in France, and almost overnight she became the leader of the Lancastrian party. Whatever her earlier doubts about resisting the Duke of York she had none now. King Henry had become a liability, but it was imperative to recover his person. Only he could restore Prince Edward as the rightful heir to the throne.

The Duke of Exeter joined Margaret not long after York landed in England.[39] Exeter's whereabouts to this point is something of a mystery, he was not at Northampton and he did not take part in the defence of the Tower of London. York's arrival galvanised him into

The Westminster Accord

action, and Margaret sent him to link up with the Earl of Northumberland and the lords who were assembling an army in the north, Lord Roos, Lord Clifford, Lord Greystoke, and Lord John Neville, of the senior branch of the Neville family. Margaret urged Duchy of Lancaster servants, royal officers, and anyone else she could think of to answer her call with all speed.[40] Jasper Tudor was recruiting in Wales and the Earl of Devon was raising troops in the West Country. Margaret was heartened by the news that the Duke of Somerset was back in England and she instructed him and the Earl of Devon to bring as many men as they could to join Northumberland. Less certainly, she could count on support in East Anglia. Friar Brackley told John Paston that Walter Lyhert, Bishop of Norwich, and her old friend Alice, Duchess of Suffolk, were sympathetic to Margaret's plight.[41] Margaret and the men around her gathered a sizeable army from scratch in a remarkably short space of time.

26

Embattled Queen

The only hope of rescuing King Henry was for a Lancastrian army to march on London. Margaret wrote to Mayor Richard Lee and the Common Council to assure them that she had no quarrel with them. Her fight was with the Duke of York. She told them that she had every faith in their loyalty, and she intended no harm to them or to their City. She poured scorn on York's claim to be the rightful King of England: it was utterly false, born of envy and malice. Everyone knew that York had been scheming for years to depose King Henry and he would have succeeded had it not been for the King's loyal subjects. Margaret implied that York meant to put her and her son to death and that they had only escaped by the mercy and protection of God. York had slandered her and tried to turn the people against her. He had spread rumours that she and Prince Edward, who was King Henry's true son and heir, would come south with an army of 'strangers' (i.e. men from the north) and destroy the City. This was not so. She and Prince Edward were coming to London to rescue the King, as their duty was, and the men who accompanied her would do no harm to anyone. Margaret thanked the citizens of London for their loyalty and ended with a plea to them to keep King Henry safe from the malice of his enemies.[1]

Her sentiments were echoed in a second letter in Prince Edward's name. It referred to the Duke of York as a 'falsely forsworn traitor' who claimed to have the wellbeing of the people at heart, when in fact he was responsible for the deaths of many of the King's innocent subjects.

The Prince's letter expressed outrage that York's lies might be believed. He, not York, was the true heir to King Henry, and he would never allow an attack on London, the city 'that is my lordes grettest treasour and owres'. On the contrary, he would punish severely any man who dared to rob or pillage its citizens. He was sure that when he came to rescue his father he could count on the Londoners' loyalty. Until that time came, he relied on them to protect the King and prevent the Duke of York from doing him any harm.[2] These letters, and others in the same vein from Jasper Tudor and the Earl of Northumberland, made little impression on the Common Council while the threat of an army approaching London hung over their heads.[3]

The Duke of York set about raising a force to deal with the northern lords. He had parliamentary authority to call on the King's lieges to assist him, and his commission of oyer and terminer, issued on 8 December, included the Earl of Westmorland and Westmorland's brother, Lord John Neville.[4] York expected these lifelong adversaries of the Earl of Salisbury to join him simply *because* he was now heir to the throne. They did not. York discounted Somerset, Exeter, and Devon as young hotheads without military experience and he left London accompanied by his son Edmund, Earl of Rutland, the Earl of Salisbury, Salisbury's son Sir Thomas Neville, and some adherents who had been with him at Ludford. York believed that as soon as he appeared in the north men would rally to him. Salisbury's main concern was the power of the Percys. The Earl of Northumberland held Salisbury's castles of Wressle and Pontefract, and he had ignored the Council's order to hand them over. Salisbury wanted them back.[5]

After a slow and cumbersome journey through wet and cold weather, York, Salisbury, and their army reached Sandal Castle on 21 December. York chose Sandal because it was only nine miles from Pontefract. Sandal was perched high on a hill overlooking the land leading to the village of Wakefield about two miles to the north. Reinforcements from Salisbury's retainers and York's estates were unlikely to arrive until early in the new year. Late on the morning of 30

The Yorkists' Challenge

December 1460, to allow time for the light to strengthen, Somerset, Northumberland, Lord Clifford, Lord Roos, and Lord John Neville rode from Pontefract with a large body of men and positioned themselves between Sandal and Wakefield where they could be seen from the battlements of the castle. It was a deliberate provocation to York to come out and fight. And York did just that. His pride would not allow him to ignore a challenge from rebels who flouted his authority and he thought he was more than a match for Somerset, which he may have been, but York should have known better. The Earl of Northumberland was Warden of the East March, and he had experienced troops under his command.

An alternative explanation for York's foray is lack of supplies. The main Lancastrian army was centred on Hull, a thriving port from where an army could be supplied by land and water.[6] York was not so fortunate. Food was always scarce in midwinter and his stocks had been depleted by the Christmas festivities. York sent out foraging parties and the Lancastrians attacked them.[7] York was so enraged by their action that he rode helter-skelter to rescue his men and thus precipitated a battle he did not need to fight. A third explanation that Somerset sued to York for a truce for the duration of the twelve days of Christmas and then broke it is less convincing, but accords well with Yorkist propaganda.[8] Somerset had no need to request a truce, and it is difficult to believe he would have negotiated with York, or York with him.

The Battle of Wakefield was more of a mêlée than a set battle, but why York chose to fight remains contentious.[9] Whatever his reasons he seriously underestimated the size of the army gathered against him. York himself, the Earl of Rutland, Sir Thomas Neville, and most of the men with him were killed.[10] The Earl of Salisbury was captured by a man serving in Somerset's ranks under Andrew Trollope. He was taken back to Pontefract and murdered by the 'common people who hated him'.[11] The Percy retainers of the Earl of Northumberland are the most likely culprits: they had long memories and strong hatreds.

York, Salisbury, and the Earl of Rutland were beheaded, and their heads were sent to the city of York to be displayed on Micklegate Bar as traitors.[12] Only someone of the highest rank could have given such an order. To kill York and Rutland and capture Salisbury in fair fight was honourable, but to desecrate their corpses was not. The Duke of Exeter hated York – was he with Somerset at Pontefract?[13] They were both rash, quick tempered, and undisciplined, and Somerset was euphoric: he had just won his first battle. Did they overawe the rest of the lords into condoning an outrageous act for which there was no legal or moral authority?

York's mistake was to go north in the first place. If he had waited, he could have opposed the Lancastrian army anywhere between Hull and London on ground of his choosing and with an army matching it in size. Typically, York saw himself as the one man who could quell rebellion in the north and restore order out of chaos, even when there was no chaos. Throughout his political life, Richard of York's hubris had caused him to overreach himself; at Wakefield it cost him and his adherents their lives.

Margaret was in Scotland at the time. She and Prince Edward had made the hazardous winter journey through the Irish Sea from Harlech to Dumfries to meet the recently widowed Mary of Guelders, Queen of Scotland, at Lincluden Abbey.[14] King James II's unexpected death at Roxburgh the previous August had left Queen Mary with an eight-year-old son whom the Scottish nobles had hastily crowned as King James III. Mary was his guardian and she aspired to be Regent, but the power struggles in Scotland were just a deadly as those in England and she could take nothing for granted. James Kennedy, Bishop of St Andrews, was the dominant force in Scottish politics, and he intended to use Mary of Guelders as Regent much as Cardinal Kemp had once planned to use Margaret.[15]

Margaret was not seeking Scottish military aid; she was on a diplomatic mission.[16] The Earl of Northumberland and the other northern lords were reluctant to leave the north unguarded while they marched south. If there was fighting in England the Scots would cross the border. Margaret had tried to engineer a peace between England and Scotland once before, in 1457, and the offer she made to Queen Mary was typical of her: a permanent peace to be sealed by the betrothal of Prince Edward to Mary's eldest daughter.[17] Queen Mary was receptive. Peace with England would be advantageous, at least until her son reached manhood. For Margaret it would negate the threat of a Scottish invasion during her attempt to recover King Henry, and both women favoured the prospect of peace. They signed a memorandum of agreement on 5 January 1461 just as the amazing news that the Duke of York had been killed reached Lincluden.

Margaret left Scotland immediately. Queen Mary probably provided her with an escort of Scots guards, which would account for the reports that Scottish soldiers had joined the Lancastrian army. Margaret and Prince Edward rode into the city of York through the Bootham Bar and on 22 January Margaret convened a meeting of the Dukes of Somerset and Exeter, the Earl of Northumberland and his brother, William Percy, Bishop of Carlisle, the Courtenay Earl of Devon, Earl of Westmorland, and his brother Lord John Neville, Lord Roos, Lord Fitzhugh, Lord Scrope of Masham, and Lord Dacre of Gillesland. These men would form the core of Margaret's army.

Margaret did not have the authority to implement a permanent peace with Scotland without King Henry's assent and neither did the lords. There never had been peace with Scotland: successive truces had been made and broken throughout King Henry's reign and border warfare was a way of life. Margaret failed to appreciate just how difficult peace might be. The Earl of Northumberland doubted that a permanent peace could ever exist between the two countries, but the Duke of York's death had inspired the Lancastrian lords with confidence; they believed that with York out of the way they could easily rescue King Henry and re-establish his rule. They signed a round robin agreement at Margaret's request to do all they could to induce King Henry to make good Margaret's promise to promote peace with Scotland, provided it was safe to do so.[18]

In London, the Earl of Warwick stood alone to face the threat from the north. Edward of March was recruiting in Wales, Lord Fauconberg was in Calais, while Archbishop Bourgchier and Chancellor George Neville were at Canterbury. Only Warwick's youngest brother, John Neville, was with Warwick. But York's death was not as severe a blow to Warwick as it would have been to a lesser man. He was a master of propaganda and he reacted swiftly to retrieve the disaster of Wakefield by turning the Lancastrian army into bogeymen. His most potent weapon was fear and he exploited it for all it was worth. Men and women in the southern counties viewed northern men as barbarians and Warwick's propaganda confirmed what people already believed: all England south of the Trent was in imminent danger – an army coming from the north threatened them and their property with destruction. Clement Paston wrote from London to warn his brother in Norfolk that a northern army would soon be upon them.[19]

Somewhat belatedly Warwick realised that Margaret posed a serious threat. An early attempt to lure her to London by a summons in King Henry's name had failed.[20] This had not worried Warwick initially. Margaret had fled to Wales and what could one woman do, isolated from the courtiers on whom she was accustomed to rely? After Wakefield he saw things differently and he enlisted Coppini's help. Perhaps the papal legate's spiritual authority could entice Margaret to come to London. It was unlikely, but it was worth a try. Coppini still wanted that elusive cardinal's hat, and Warwick obliged him by writing to Pope Pius, and to Coppini's patron the Duke of Milan, to reassure them that York's death had not seriously affected the political situation in England. He and King Henry hoped to promote a peaceful reconciliation between the warring parties with Coppini's help and Pope Pius could assist this noble endeavour by conferring a cardinal's hat on his legate. Warwick's communication was tinged with his usual arrogance: 'if in accordance with your former letters you

The Yorkists' Challenge

value my allegiance and the allegiance of others aiding King Henry', then Pius should see fit to reward Coppini.[21]

Coppini did not risk venturing in search of the Queen; instead he wrote a long self-explanatory letter to Lorenzo of Florence, a friar whom he believed to be in Margaret's company.[22] With his usual assumption of his own importance, Coppini implied that Margaret knew him well enough to trust him. He admitted that the tone of her letter rejecting the Westminster Accord had been too angry. This was unfortunate, because if she would only listen to him and be guided by his wisdom, peace would prevail. King Henry wanted reconciliation and so by implication should she, as a dutiful wife. Coppini denied that he had excommunicated the Lancastrian lords at Northampton, but he was quite willing to excommunicate anyone who opposed the Queen, provided she followed his advice.

Coppini warned Margaret not to rely on the Duke of Somerset. Much as he had once threatened King Henry, Coppini now threatened Somerset. Resistance was futile and if war came Somerset would be responsible in the eyes of God. Did Somerset realise that the Earl of Warwick, who was loyal to King Henry, could put 200,000 men into the field (with Coppini's help) if he chose to do so? The possibility of war grieved King Henry, but the King trusted Warwick and would stand by him. Friar Lorenzo was to remind Somerset that his victory at Wakefield was a small and unimportant thing. Coppini then summed up Warwick's propaganda in a nutshell: the whole of the south of England was ready to resist the northern army because of 'the countless acts of cruelty *related* of them.' Margaret was most unlikely to respond favourably to such a letter.

Warwick controlled King Henry, but he did not control the country as a whole and he took steps to root out Lancastrian sympathisers in the southern counties. Sir John Wenlock and Sir Thomas Kyriell among others were commissioned to supress 'unlawful gatherings', to arrest anyone spreading false rumours, and 'evil doers' who might offer supplies to 'the enemy'. Richard Hotoft, the bailiff of Margaret's dower lands in Leicester, and the sheriff of Leicestershire were to arrest the Duke of Somerset on sight. The bailiffs of Shrewsbury were instructed to guard the town carefully since Somerset's army might try to join forces with Jasper Tudor coming from Wales. Somerset and all other Lancastrian lords were to be apprehended and no one in Shrewsbury was to offer the Lancastrians assistance on pain of forfeiture.[23]

Warwick's Council signed commissions in King Henry's name, putting the country on high alert. King's officers, knights of the shire, sheriffs, mayors, bailiffs, and justices of the peace in the southern counties and in Cambridgeshire, Staffordshire, Rutland, and East Anglia were to raise men ready to join the royal army at a moment's notice. King Henry would take the field in person! The summons included only five peers: the Earl of Arundel and Lord de la Warr, Lord Cobham, Lord Abergavenny and Richard Fiennes, Lord Dacre.[24] At the last minute, although he had not been summoned, the Duke of Norfolk decided to throw in his lot with Warwick. Norfolk knew that Margaret distrusted him, but King Henry was in Warwick's hands, and Warwick appeared to be the safer bet. Warwick also enhanced his own status and authority. On 22 January 1461 he replaced his dead father as Great Chamberlain of England and his brother John became Lord Montague.[25] Warwick had not been made a Knight of the Garter and King Henry was required to rectify this oversight. On 8 February, at the Bishop of London's palace, he invested Warwick, Lord Bonville, Sir John Wenlock, and Sir Thomas Kyriell with the coveted Order.[26]

Edward of March was recruiting in the Marches of Wales. He spent Christmas at Gloucester where he probably heard the news of Wakefield and he wasted no time in heading for Shrewsbury to get between Somerset and Jasper Tudor's forces. He did not know that Jasper was in Carmarthen and Pembrokeshire gathering reinforcements, or that the Earl of Wiltshire had landed on the south coast of Wales bringing a mixed force of French and Bretons and men from

The Yorkists' Challenge

his Irish estates to swell the Lancastrian ranks. There were always mercenaries for hire in Europe, provided they were paid, and Wiltshire had put the crown's money that he saved by 'fleeing' before Northampton to good use.

As soon as he learned of his enemies' disposition, Edward moved at high speed, making for his castle at Wigmore to cut across Jasper and Wiltshire's line of march. Sir William Herbert, Walter Devereux, and other gentlemen in Wales hastened to join him. The battle at Mortimer's Cross, fought on 2 February 1461, was a one-sided affair. Edward had the larger army of better trained troops, and his self-confidence inspired his men. Jasper Tudor was an inept soldier and certainly no match for Edward of March. Neither was the Earl of Wiltshire. They had not planned to fight on their own with their ill-assorted forces and although Gruffydd ap Nicholas's sons, Owain and Thomas, were with Jasper, the Welsh recruits crumbled. Lancastrian casualties were high. The Earl of Wiltshire quit the field early on and Jasper fled, leaving his father behind.[27] Owen Tudor was captured and beheaded at Hereford along with ten other men, and on Edward's orders his head was set on the cross in the town's market square.[28] It was a poor revenge and unworthy of Edward. Owen was old, helpless and useless; he should never have been anywhere near a battlefield. Three weeks later from the safety of Tenby Jasper described the encounter as a 'great dishonour and rebuke' that he vowed to avenge.[29] His vengeance would be a long time coming.

Margaret was preparing to march south when she learned of Jasper's defeat. It was a serious set-back. With the loss of the Welsh army the Lancastrians might have to fight Edward of March coming from Wales as well as Warwick in London. Margaret sent to King Charles to ask for his help, but the Milanese ambassador did not think Charles would respond favourably.[30] Margaret also appealed directly to Pierre de Brezé for immediate assistance. Jean Doucereau, Brezé's secretary, who had handled the clandestine correspondence between King Henry, Margaret and Brezé in 1458 had come to England in 1460 to keep Brezé informed of events as they unfolded, and he may have been an observer of the Battle of Northampton.[31]

Margaret sent Doucereau back to Normandy with an urgent appeal to Brezé to attack Warwick's ships and destroy them if he could, in the hope that this would distract Warwick's attention from her army in the north. Brezé was an adventurer and a gambler, not unlike Warwick, and he was eager to do all he could for Margaret, provided he had King Charles's approval. Brezé was uncertain what to do and he sent Doucereau to the King to ask for instructions. Brezé did not know the whereabouts of the envoys Margaret said she had sent to the King, or what they might have to say, so should he sit tight and wait for them, should he leave Rouen and go to meet them, or should he attack the ships at Calais as Margaret requested? He warned Charles to keep the correspondence secret. Margaret might be in danger if it became known in England that she had called on Brezé for help.[32]

In the meanwhile, the Lancastrian army began its march south.[33] It comprised Duchy of Lancaster tenants, Northumberland's Percy retainers, the retinues of the other northern lords, the levies of the Dukes of Somerset and Exeter, and the Earl of Devon. Lionel, Lord Welles, brought a contingent from Lincolnshire and Talbot retainers, accompanied by the thirteen-year-old John, Earl of Shrewsbury.[34] Margaret had sent out commissions of array in Prince Edward's name to muster the local levies.[35]

Perhaps the rugged living conditions in Wales and the uncomfortable journey to and from Scotland had inured Margaret to physical discomfort, but she would have experienced hardship in the cold and wet winter as well as the anxiety of not knowing what she would face when she finally reached London. Warwick's propaganda had succeeded all too well. The monks at Croyland Abbey were petrified; they had heard that the Lancastrian army was looting on a thirty-mile front 'like so many locusts', but although the army came within six miles of the abbey, it was not plundered.[36] Fear induced the Common Council of London to make a further loan to Warwick to

The Yorkists' Challenge

safeguard the City,[37] and London citizens painted the Beaufort portcullis on the doors of their houses as a protective measure.[38] Little Coppini was so alarmed at the thought of facing Margaret that he left England for the Netherlands well before the Lancastrian army came anywhere near London.[39] Their approach even frightened the usually courageous Cecily, Duchess of York. She had been appalled by the shameful way the bodies of her husband and son had been treated after Wakefield, and she was taking no chances. She sent her children to the Burgundian court for safekeeping.[40]

The Lancastrian army came south via Grantham, Stamford, Peterborough, Huntingdon, Melbourn, and Royston.[41] None of these towns suffered the long recovery period usually required by sacked towns.[42] Peterborough Abbey was not touched. Nevertheless, later accounts of the ravages committed by 'the Queen's army' lost nothing in the telling: a mixed rabble of wild Scots, Irish, Welsh and 'northern men' were reported to be worse than pagans; they looted, burned, and despoiled all the towns they passed through. Margaret's reasons for permitting this devastation have been variously interpreted: either she was unable to control her troops and was powerless to prevent their depredations, or (the preferred option) she hated the Duke of York and was so angered by the Westminster Accord that she *ordered* her men to do as much damage as they could to York's lands. Pillaging was inevitable: all armies foraged, but the towns the army passed through no longer belonged to York, they were forfeit to the crown, and so in one sense they were Margaret's possessions.[43] The Lancastrian army's avowed object was to rescue King Henry.[44] Margaret had an additional incentive: to restore Prince Edward to his rightful position as King Henry's heir. Devasting the country that was her son's birthright was hardly the way to go about it, but Yorkist propaganda did its work well – the stories of her atrocities are repeated to this day.

Warwick did not know exactly where the Lancastrians were, and he decided to make a stand at St Albans to cover the approach to London. The first contingent of 'royal' troops left for St Albans on 12

February.[45] After sending a commission to Edward of March to gather an army and join him immediately,[46] Warwick and his brother John, with the Duke of Norfolk, the Earl of Arundel, Viscount Bourgchier and Lord Berners set out with the main army, taking King Henry with them.[47] Over the next few days Warwick entrenched his forces with artillery and weapons of war ten miles north of St Albans, on a line between Luton and Ware, just north of Sandridge.

As the Lancastrians neared Royston their scouts reported the presence of Warwick's troops. To avoid a battle before they could reach London the Lancastrians turned west to Dunstable, intending to bypass Warwick's forces. Here they encountered their first check. The citizens of Dunstable, under the leadership of the local butcher, offered a stout resistance, but they were routed.[48] On 17 February, the Lancastrian vanguard moved towards St Albans from the north-west. Warwick had stationed professional archers in the town as part of his reserves and they repulsed the first Lancastrian attack, but they were too few to hold the town and the Lancastrians made their way through the narrow streets, sweeping out pockets of resistance as they went. The 'wild northern hoards' had become disciplined troops overnight and they were now poised to attack Warwick from the rear.

When Warwick realised what had happened, he had no choice but to swing his army round and take up a new position facing St Albans to encounter the enemy. It was a daunting and time-consuming manoeuvre and the result was confusion in the ranks. The Second Battle of St Albans took place to the east of the town and lasted from about midday until six in the evening when it was dark.[49] The superior discipline of the Lancastrians won the day, but they were lucky. Warwick's forces were in disarray and he fled the field, followed by his men.[50] For the rest of his life Warwick blamed his defeat on one Lovelace, described as 'a Captain of Kent', who supposedly took his men over to the enemy in the thick of the fight.[51] But the truth was that the Lancastrians did not need Lovelace's help. For the third time in his life King Henry was 'rescued' by the victors. He did not know what to expect; he had been taken from the contemplative life he enjoyed and required to accompany 'his' army to face a rebel army from the north. He had then been abandoned within sound, if not sight, of the battle.[52] Did he know that Queen Margaret was with the northern army, or did he learn this from the Lancastrian lords who found him in his tent?

Margaret had remained at Dunstable and she and King Henry were reunited there on the following day.[53] It was an uncomfortable meeting. Until he signed the Westminster Accord Margaret had upheld and enhanced King Henry's authority, but she would do so no longer. Henry had betrayed her and their son. Henry was pleased to see Margaret, but he did not realise what Margaret's victory meant. She still needed Henry to reverse the Westminster Accord, and she would act in his name and invoke his authority whenever it was necessary, but from now on the decisions would be hers.

Prince Edward, still only seven years old, was to be his father's surrogate. The Battle at St Albans was fought in the name of Edward of Lancaster, Prince of Wales. The Lancastrians rank and file wore their lords' liveries, but they also displayed the colours of the Prince, a band of crimson and black with white ostrich feathers. At Margaret's behest King Henry knighted the son he had disinherited and barely recognised, and Edward, arrayed in purple velvet laced with gold thread, knighted the men who had fought for him, among them the young Earl of Shrewsbury and the veteran Andrew Trollope, who by his own account had stood still and killed fifteen men after he became immobilised by catching his foot in an enemy caltrop.[54]

Warwick had left William Bonville and Thomas Kyriell, whom King Henry had recently created Knights of the Garter at Warwick's instigation, to guard the King. Margaret could not forgive them for siding with Warwick, or forgive Henry for making them Garter Knights. She could not punish Henry, so she made Bonville and Kyriell her scapegoats. She required Prince Edward to sit in judgement on them; meting out justice to traitors was a responsibility of kingship. Edward condemned them, but Margaret ordered their execution.⁵⁵ She probably regretted that Sir John Wenlock had not been captured as well. Bonville's death paid off old scores. The Earl of Devon was in the Lancastrian ranks and his father had been Bonville's lifelong enemy.

Margaret did not execute two far more valuable prisoners, a decision she would come to regret. John Neville, Lord Montague, and John Bourgchier, Lord Berners, were captured at St Albans, but they were not traitors in the same way as Bonville and Kyriell, who owed their careers to King Henry. Neville and Bourgchier were honourable foes, and Margaret understood the ties of family loyalty. Her leniency surprised contemporaries and had to be explained away. A Milanese correspondent reported from London that it was being said that John Neville was spared because the Duke of Somerset's brother, Edmund, was a prisoner in Calais and Somerset feared reprisals.⁵⁶ But in the aftermath of St Albans, Warwick was in no position to order anyone's execution.

Abbot Whethamstede did not witness the battle. He had left St Albans after he authorised the monks to do likewise if they wished to, and he took himself off to safety. The Lancastrian soldiers helped themselves to the abbey's stores – plundered them according to the abbot, who later claimed that King Henry had forbidden them to do so, but that the Queen had permitted it. She probably did; the men needed to be fed. Whethamstede later claimed that during her stay in the abbey Margaret helped herself to 'the finest jewel the abbey possessed', but the abbey's other treasurers were not looted.⁵⁷

Margaret had gambled and she appeared to have won, but she had not thought beyond the recovery of King Henry's person. To most Londoners the King and Queen were absentees. Margaret had never courted popularity in the City as Warwick had, and Londoners had been told time and again that Margaret's bloodthirsty 'northerners' were coming to sack the City. The City's gates were barred and guarded, shops were shut, and people stayed off the streets.

The Mayor, Richard Lee, played for time. A delegation of aldermen

The Yorkists' Challenge

went out to meet Margaret, accompanied by three ladies who were well known to her. Jacquetta, the Dowager Duchess of Bedford, Anne, the widowed Duchess of Buckingham, and Emma, Lady Scales, who had been Margaret's senior lady in waiting and whose husband had lost his life after defending the Tower of London for King Henry.[58] They pleaded with Margaret to restrain her troops and Margaret reassured them that she would not allow her army to enter the City, but she reserved the right to punish those who had fought against her. She had promised Mayor Lee in the previous November that London would not be harmed, and she kept her word. At no time during the tense few days that followed did the Lancastrian army come anywhere near the City; it had pulled back to Dunstable.

Mayor Lee undertook to send out much-needed provisions, but his attempt to placate Margaret was thwarted by the populace. Carts loaded with food prepared to leave via Cripplegate but they did not get far. Londoners overturned the carts, made off with the supplies, and stole the money intended for the Queen.[59] Margaret had vivid memories of how volatile and dangerous Londoners could be. She was not sure that she and Prince Edward would be safe in the City, or even at Westminster. The Mayor issued an edict that Margaret's representatives Sir Edmund Hampden, Sir John Heron, and Sir Robert Whittingham were not to be molested, but they were met with suspicion and hostility and they feared for their lives. Sir Baldwin Fulford and Sir Alexander Hody tried to reach Westminster with an armed escort but were set upon. The Duke of Somerset sent his retainers to see if it was safe for him to enter, but the Beaufort livery was easy to recognise and his men were put to flight. Even the official concession that four knights and 400 men could come in as an advance guard had to be abandoned as too dangerous. The City magistrates imposed a curfew and London was again quiet – for the moment.[60]

Margaret was fixated on negating the Westminster Accord and she failed to appreciate the importance of first securing London. Henry was King of England and the Mayor could not refuse him entry into the City if he demanded it, but Henry did not. Instead, on 22 February he signed a warrant which was sent to the Mayor, the Council, and the sheriffs. It denounced the Earl of March, who styled himself Duke of York and heir to the throne, as 'our great traitor and enemy' and ordered the Mayor 'on your faith and allegiance [to] publicly proclaim [this] in our City ... despite any of our writings, breves, or orders whatsoever that were made to the contrary before this time.' Henry declared his intention to pursue 'Edward, our enemy, wherever he may be within the kingdom.'[61]

It was an empty threat. The Mayor and Common Council had received letters from Edward of March and Warwick announcing that they would arrive shortly. The Earl had rallied his troops and joined Edward, and they were marching on London with a large army. The City authorities were mightily relieved; they had invested a lot of money and faith in Warwick. The Londoners were ecstatic. They demanded the keys to the City's gates and prepared to defend them until Warwick could arrive. Despite his recent defeat, Warwick was London's idol.

Margaret did not know the size or strength of the Yorkist army and the risk of fighting another battle just outside London, where the odds would be against her, was too great. She had run out of time. The northern lords were not interested in London. They had set out to rescue King Henry and they had succeeded. Their army was restless, the men had made a gruelling march through unfriendly country in bad weather and won a battle they did not fully understand; they wanted to go home and the news of the imminent return of the Earl of Warwick tipped the scale. Fatally, at this crucial moment, Margaret's courage deserted her. She had never understood the symbolic and economic importance of occupying and controlling the capital of England.[62] Her power base in the Midlands had been destroyed by the deaths of the Duke of Buckingham and Henry's other loyal lords at Northampton, and the knowledge that she would have to regroup her forces in the north if she meant to make good King Henry's promise to pursue the Earl of March may have influenced her decision to retire.

The Lancastrian army withdrew from Dunstable and began the long trek northward, taking Lord Montague and Lord Berners with them. The accusations of depredations and theft as the army headed home, although exaggerated, were undoubtedly true.[63] Looting after battle was the norm to men from the north.

Queen in Exile

27

Victory into Defeat

Edward of March met up with Warwick in the Cotswolds and learned that Warwick had lost the King. Without the King, or a king, Warwick's authority and his right to demand obedience ceased to exist. Edward convinced Warwick that Margaret's recovery of King Henry's person was not a disaster but a triumph: it changed everything and justified Edward's claim to the throne. Edward argued that King Henry had broken his oath to accept Edward as his heir and had declared him a traitor. This absolved all those, including Warwick, who had sworn oaths of allegiance to Henry.

Edward and Warwick entered London in triumph. Their army encamped at Clerkenwell, just as it had when they came from Calais less than a year earlier. Edward was only nineteen, but he was a commanding figure, half a head taller than most of the men around him. He wanted to be King and he knew exactly how to go about it. He took up residence at Baynard's Castle and summoned the Chancellor, George Neville, and Thomas Bourgchier, the Archbishop of Canterbury, to join him. On 1 March, he ordered the ranks of his army to be paraded in St John's Field where Chancellor Neville addressed them, expounding Edward Plantagenet's right to the throne through just descent and because King Henry had broken his solemn oath. The Chancellor demanded if Henry was fit to reign, and (as expected) the rank and file shouted: 'Nay! Nay!' Neville then asked if they would accept Edward as their king and they shouted 'Yea! Yea!'

Archbishop Bourgchier, Chancellor Neville, and of course the Earl

Victory into Defeat

of Warwick urged Edward to accept what the army was offering him. Edward issued a public proclamation to the people of London to assemble at St Pauls Cross on Wednesday, 4 March. Splendidly accoutred in martial array, Edward progressed through the City's streets to St Pauls where Chancellor Neville once again expounded Edward's just claim and asked for public acclamation. The shouts of 'Yea! Yea!' were deafening. If there were dissenting voices they were drowned out. Edward was far better at manipulating public opinion than his father had been, and he did not make York's mistake of appealing to the lords; his appeal was to the people who loved excitement and could be easily swayed by a young, handsome, and charming prince. What was not touched upon, then or ever, was that by claiming the throne Edward too had broken his oath. The Westminster Accord had guaranteed that Henry would remain King for the term of his natural life.

Edward staged a secular coronation at Westminster with the spiritual element omitted, he was not crowned or blessed with the holy oil that would make him God's anointed. He wore the King's coronation robe and cap of estate and, seated in full public view on the 'white throne', the symbol of justice in the court of King's Bench, he swore the traditional oath to be a true and a just king to his people and to maintain the peace and security of the realm.[1] Edward needed one more justification before he would he be crowned: an appeal to God to destroy his enemies. Victory in battle would consolidate his claim and rid him of the unwanted King Henry. Nevertheless, King Edward IV dated his reign from 4 March 1461.

Two days later he issued a proclamation to the sheriffs of the shires south of the Trent, and to the mayors of the principal cities, declaring himself King. No one was to give help of any kind to 'the late' King Henry. Edward offered to pardon anyone who submitted to him within ten days provided their income was less than 100 marks a year. This was not as magnanimous as it sounded – it precluded the Lancastrian lords and many of the barons and lesser gentry who had fought for Lancaster. He offered bounties of £100 to anyone who killed (not captured) Andrew Trollope, Thomas Tresham, Thomas Fitzharry, the Duke of Exeter's two bastard brothers who had fought against him at Mortimer's Cross, and Robert Whittingham and William Grimsby, who had fought at Wakefield.[2]

King Henry and Margaret were in York when they heard the appalling news of Edward's enthronement. It was worse than anything Margaret had imagined, but she was determined to fight on. Throughout March the whole country was mobilised, and polarised, by commissions of array issued in the name of King Henry VI and King Edward IV. The largest armies ever assembled on English soil prepared to fight a decisive battle.

The vanguard of Edward's army, commanded by Lord Fauconberg, left London on 11 March. Edward followed on 13 March.[3] He rendezvoused at Doncaster with Fauconberg and with Warwick, who had been recruiting in the Midlands.[4] The Lancastrian army, commanded by the Duke of Somerset, gathered at Tadcaster to the north of the town of Towton. The Lancastrian leadership was overconfident. They had defeated the Duke of York and the Earl of Warwick, so how hard could it be to defeat the young upstart Edward of March? Lord Clifford and his men were sent to guard the crossing of the River Aire at Ferrybridge and to watch for the appearance of Edward's army. Lord Fitzwalter and an advance Yorkist guard reconnoitred the bridge, Clifford attacked them and Fitzwalter was killed.[5] Clifford broke down the bridge as a defensive measure but he (and Somerset) foolishly left the other crossing of the Aire at Castleford unguarded. Lord Fauconberg crossed the river and fell on Clifford's flank. Clifford and most of his men were killed and Fauconberg moved on to the village of Saxton. Edward's main army followed him and bivouacked at Sherburn in Elmet to wait for the Duke of Norfolk to catch up.

On Palm Sunday, 29 March, two massive armies faced each other just south of Towton in a snowstorm. The wind blew the snow into

Victory into Defeat

the faces of the Lancastrian archers, blinding them. The Earl of Northumberland, Lord Dacre, Lord Fitzhugh, and Lord John Neville of Westmorland faced King Edward on the left flank. Somerset, Devon, Wiltshire, the Woodvilles, Lords Hungerford, Richemont-Grey, and de la Warr opposed Fauconberg on the right flank. The Duke of Exeter, Lord Welles and his son, and Lord Grey of Codnore were with him in the centre with the reserves, opposite Warwick.[6] The fight lasted for many hours and might have ended in stalemate, but for the Duke of Norfolk's men, who arrived late in the afternoon and reinforced King Edward's wing. Norfolk reaped no reward for his change of allegiance, he died in 1461, eight months after Towton.

The Lancastrian ranks broke first. Thousands of men died in the fighting, thousands more were pursued and killed by the victorious Yorkists.[7] Some were drowned trying to cross the River Wharfe, many more were cut down without mercy by Edward's cavalry. Chivalry died at Towton. Contemporary accounts of the victory naturally attribute it to Edward's superior generalship, but it was probably the more experienced Lord Fauconberg who directed the actual battle. The Earl of Northumberland's wing opposing Fauconberg took the main shock. Northumberland, Lords Dacre, Welles, and Neville of Westmorland were killed. So was Andrew Trollope. The Dukes of Somerset and Exeter, Lord Roos, and others escaped and carried news of the defeat to King Henry and Margaret at York. The royal party abandoned their prisoners and fled north to seek safety in Scotland.[8]

The relentless pursuit and slaughter of the Lancastrian army cleared the way for King Edward to ride to York on 31 March. John Neville and Lord Berners interceded with him on behalf of the city and the city officials begged Edward's pardon for harbouring their king! The Earl of Devon had remained in York. He was wounded and unfit to travel, but he cannot have expected his fate. Edward had him executed.[9] The Earl of Wiltshire was captured sometime later and brought before Edward at Newcastle. He too was beheaded, and

Queen in Exile

Edward ordered his head to be taken to London and displayed on London Bridge.[10] Edward could be charming to his friends, but he was ruthless to his enemies and in 1461 anyone with Lancastrian sympathies was his enemy.

The royal fugitives evaded capture at Newcastle and reached Edinburgh safely. Queen Mary, now Regent of Scotland, generously put her palace at Linlithgow at their disposal and later they moved to the Dominican Friary, which King Henry at least found more congenial.[11] Margaret sent two Dominican friars to King Charles to ask for his help. She instructed them to vary her offers depending on Charles's response, but she demanded a lot of him, and she still thought in terms of an alliance. She wanted a loan of 80,000 *écus* on promise of future repayment and for a French fleet to put to sea. She had no navy and no way of preventing reinforcements from Calais being sent to England. She asked Charles not to issue safe conducts to any ships sailing under Warwick's orders. She also asked for the return of certain Englishmen who had escaped from England in a ship loaded with treasure. They had been captured in the Channel and were now prisoners in France. It is a measure of just how much bullion and other valuables they had in their possession that Margaret was willing to pay to get them back. They were rebels, and if she could recover them she could lawfully seize their assets.[12]

Margaret was mindful of the importance of her reputation and the lies that Warwick had circulated about her. One of the friars was to request a safe conduct and letters of endorsement to allow him pass through France on his way to Rome where he would refute Warwick's allegations that Prince Edward was a bastard, and complain to Pope Pius of little Coppini's unwarranted intrusion into England affairs. Charles's reaction was at best lukewarm; he informed the friars that his heavy financial commitments made it impossible for him to loan money to Margaret. The English prisoners and their treasure could only be released with the consent of their captors after their ransom had been paid. He could not revoke safe conducts already issued, but

Victory into Defeat

he would instruct his admiral not to issue any more. He was willing to allow a flotilla to put to sea, but it would be time enough to talk of treaties of alliance when King Henry was safely back on the throne.[13]

In Edinburgh Queen Mary held all the cards, and the price of her assistance was high: possession of the castle and town of Berwick, the strategic key to the English defence of the East March. On 25 April, King Henry, Margaret, the Dukes of Somerset and Exeter, Lord Roos, and Lord Richemont-Grey accepted Mary's terms to surrender Berwick.[14] They were eager to raise an army in Scotland to exact revenge for their defeat at Towton. The Earl of Northumberland and Lord Clifford, who understood the importance of Berwick for the defence of the northern border, might have opposed its surrender, but they were dead. Margaret believed that once she was victorious there would be peace with Scotland and the danger of invasion from the north would cease. She ignored, or more probably never realised, the damage that surrendering Berwick would do to her reputation, but she had no choice. At Lincluden she had negotiated with Queen Mary as an equal; now she was a penniless suppliant. The surrender of Berwick formed a staple item in Yorkist propaganda for years and it has blackened Margaret's name ever since. In return for Berwick Mary offered the exiles asylum, loans, and military aid. As a sop to Margaret's pride she confirmed her former agreement for a marriage between Prince Edward and one of Mary's daughters, although she had no intention of honouring it. Prince Edward was no longer a prize in the dynastic marriage market.[15]

The Lancastrian approach to recovering what they had lost was piecemeal. The Duke of Exeter, Lord Richemont-Grey, Humphrey, Lord Dacre, Edmund Hampden, Henry Bellingham, and Richard Tunstall, accompanied by a small Scottish force, crossed the border and occupied Carlisle.[16] They may have expected to receive aid from within the city as William Percy was Bishop of Carlisle. Carlisle was the key to the defence of the West March and it was later claimed that Margaret had promised to cede it to the Scots, but if she did it was an empty promise.[17] The Nevilles were Wardens of the West March and John Neville, Lord Montague, who was a far better soldier and tactician than Warwick, promptly laid siege to Carlisle and the Lancastrians and the Scots retreated back across the border.[18]

Another group of Lancastrians gathered at Brancepeth, the seat of the Earl of Westmorland in county Durham. The Earl's brother, Thomas Neville, and Thomas's son Humphrey, with Lord Roos, John Fortescue, William Tailboys, and Edmund Mountford raised King Henry's banner but won no support.[19] Even Lawrence Booth, the Bishop of Durham, and Margaret's ex-chancellor, raised local levies to repel the 'invaders'.[20]

The Burgundian court was awash with rumour and the Milanese ambassador there gathered every scrap of information he could and speculated on all he heard. Even though he professed to disbelieve some of it, he gleefully reported to the Duke of Milan that Margaret and the Duke of Somerset had persuaded King Henry to abdicate in favour of Prince Edward and that King Henry had said Prince Edward must be the son of the Holy Spirit. Furthermore, 'they say here that the Queen of England, after the king had abdicated, gave the king poison' and she planned to marry the Duke of Somerset.[21]

Edward of March was crowned King Edward IV of England and France, and Lord of Ireland, on 28 June 1461, with all the pomp and ceremony that he could muster. It was a serious blow, but Margaret refused to accept that her status as Queen of England was in any way diminished by her defeat or by King Henry's loss of the crown. She dispatched Robert, Lord Hungerford, and Sir Robert Whittingham as her ambassadors to King Charles, and she sent Henry, Duke of Somerset to the Burgundian court to renew his friendship with the Count of Charolais, and to approach the Dauphin Louis on her behalf.[22]

Hungerford was to ask Charles to loan her 20,000 *écus* and to muster an army at Neufchatel to sail to Scotland from Dieppe. At the same time, she hedged her bets by asking for safe conducts for herself,

Victory into Defeat

her husband, and her son to take refuge in France. Margaret did not understand her uncle. King Charles had ruled successfully for thirty-two years and earned the sobriquet 'Charles the Well-Served'. Throughout that period he kept his own counsel and spread disinformation whenever it suited him. The report from the Milanese ambassadors at the Burgundian court that Charles was gathering an army and navy in Gascony to aid Margaret was false.[23] At no time during his long reign did Charles contemplate a French invasion of England, despite periodic scares after he threw the English out of Normandy. Charles might sympathise with his niece but not to the extent of wasting French troops and money to put her and her inept husband back on the throne. During the last months of his life all of Charles's energies were focused on two issues of paramount importance to him: reconciliation with the Dauphin Louis and the recovery of Genoa.[24] Charles's army was destined for Italy, not to aid Margaret.

The Genoese had recently revolted against French rule and King Charles had called on John of Calabria to help suppress the revolt. A correspondent informed the Duke of Milan that Margaret's father, René of Anjou, was gathering an army for Margaret, but this too was false.[25] René had raised a contingent of men and ships to go to his son's aid and he sailed for Genoa in June. On 17 July 1461, an army under René's command engaged the Genoese in battle only to be heavily defeated. The ill-assorted French troops (they were not France's famous lances) broke ranks. René retreated to his ships and returned to Provence.[26] King Charles never heard of the defeat; he was too ill to be told, even if the news had reached France before he died on 22 July.

Hungerford and Whittingham arrived in Dieppe to be greeted by the shattering news that King Charles was dead. They hastened to join Somerset at Eu. The suspicious and devious Dauphin Louis was now King Louis XI, and Somerset feared the worst. Margaret had not obtained a safe conduct for him to travel from France to the Burgundian court – she did not think he would need one. Somerset sent an urgent message to the Count of Charolais to ask if he should proceed without a safe conduct or remain where he was. Could Charolais help him? Before Charolais could reply, Louis's secretary, Jean de Reilhac, arrived at Eu with an armed escort. Louis suspected Margaret and Somerset of plotting with his father without his knowledge.

Reilhac demanded that Somerset hand over to him all the documents he carried. Somerset protested that he was on his way to meet the Count of Charolais with a letter from the Queen of England addressed to the Dauphin Louis, whom she had believed to be at the Burgundian court. Reilhac insisted that Hungerford and Whittingham must turn over their dispatches too. Hungerford objected that they were on embassy from Queen Margaret and he had safe conducts to the French court. Reilhac was not impressed. He confiscated all their papers.

The documents Hungerford carried amounted to a diplomatic bag; they make it clear that he was Henry and Margaret's accredited ambassador, sent to apprise King Charles of all that had happened since the Battle of Towton, including documents recounting Margaret's negotiations with the Queen of Scotland, her correspondence with Pierre de Brezé, and a letter from her to her uncle, the Count of Maine and his wife. These documents reveal just how naïve Margaret was. She assumed that Henry could continue to conduct foreign diplomacy as though he was still sat on the throne. Hungerford and Whittingham were to treat with the King of France for peace, and Hungerford was to approach the French nobles as well as King Charles to solicit substantial loans, promising repayment on the word of the King and Queen of England. Henry had made Hungerford his lieutenant to take charge of a French army and prepare it to invade England under Somerset's command. Assorted official documents carrying Henry's seal were blank authorisations to endorse whatever terms Hungerford could obtain from anyone who would offer to help, and personal letters from Henry to his 'bel oncle' of France, to Dunois, and to the *bailli* of Rouen.

Victory into Defeat

Reilhac transferred Somerset to detention in Arques, while Hungerford and Whittingham were escorted back to Dieppe and placed under house arrest. They wrote at once to tell Margaret of King Charles's death and to report their plight, and they followed up with two more letters, which probably never reached her. On 30 August they wrote a fourth time to warn Margaret not to risk herself or the Prince by coming to France. They strongly advised her not to allow King Henry to leave Scotland until they had seen King Louis and a had clearer idea of whether such a journey would be safe. They planned to return to Scotland as soon as they had seen the King, and they would bring the latest news.[27]

Hungerford and Whittingham, as accredited envoys from the King and Queen of England, expected that any day now they would be summoned to the French court to present their credentials. They still had a lot to learn about King Louis XI. He was crowned on 15 August 1461, but he kept Hungerford and Whittingham waiting for two months until, in October, he sent for them and for Somerset to join him at Tours. The Count of Charolais was at court. He pleaded for their release, and Louis graciously agreed to allow Somerset to accompany him back to Bruges.[28] Hungerford and Whittingham remained in France.

Jasper Tudor, Earl of Pembroke, still held the castles of Denbigh, Harlech, and Pembroke in Wales and the Duke of Exeter left Scotland to join him. William Herbert and Walter Devereux raised an army in Wales and the Marches to apprehend them, and the Earl of Warwick received a grant to increase his fleet and blockade the castles from the sea.[29] Pembroke Castle surrendered to Herbert in September. Jasper was not there, but his nephew, Henry Tudor, Earl of Richmond, was captured and as a reward for Herbert's loyal service, King Edward raised him to the peerage as Lord Herbert of Raglan and granted him custody of the young Henry.[30] A month later Herbert cornered Jasper and Exeter and brought them and their Welsh army to battle near Carnarvon. Jasper and Exeter fled, taking refuge in the mountains of

Queen in Exile

Wales.[31] Denbigh surrendered early in 1462, and only Harlech continued to hold out.

Queen Mary was willing to shelter the royal fugitives, but she was a shrewd politician and she also encouraged overtures from King Edward. Edward issued safe conducts in September for Scottish representatives to come to London to negotiate future Anglo-Scottish relations and he authorised Sir Robert Ogle, as deputy Warden of the West March, to arrange a border truce for one year to curtail border raiding and put a stop to incursions such as that into Carlisle.[32] Lancastrian prospects were dwindling.

Edward opened his first Parliament in November 1461. His right and title to the throne were rehearsed in excoriating detail. Parliament declared that Edward had inherited the crown through his murdered father, the Duke of York, from the last legitimate king, Richard II. King Henry VI, his father, and his grandfather were usurpers and not kings at all. Henry was attainted of high treason, not as a usurper but because he had made war against Edward of March, the rightful king. Queen Margaret 'and her son' were convicted of high treason for the same reason.[33] Insofar as it could, Parliament completed the destruction of all known adherents of Lancaster, the living and the dead; they were attainted and stripped of their estates for their loyalty to King Henry and Edward became Duke of Lancaster as well as King of England.[34]

King Henry gave no indication that he would attempt to recover his kingdom, or even that he was sorry he had lost it. He moved to the Grey Friars monastery at Kirkcudbright near Dumfries and settled there.[35] Margaret was left alone in Edinburgh to continue the fight. She had no money, no power base except for the three great fortresses in the north of England of Alnwick, Bamburgh, and Dunstanburgh that were still held precariously for King Henry and most important of all, no competent military commander. The Christmas and New Year festivities of 1461/62 cannot have been a happy time for Margaret. But early in the new year she received a communication from Sir Aubrey

Victory into Defeat

de Vere, the son and heir of the Earl of Oxford, telling her of his plan to restore King Henry. Margaret had singled out and favoured Aubrey at Coventry in 1460, partly because he was a personable young man with estates of his own in East Anglia and Essex, and partly because his wife Anne, who presumably was with him in Coventry, was the Duchess of Buckingham's daughter.[36]

Aubrey's plan was simple, but ill informed. King Edward would go north with an army in the spring to bring the Scots into line. Aubrey would raise a force and either accompany the King while plotting treachery or follow him and fall on Edward's army from the rear while a Scottish force would cross the border to confront him. Margaret did not know that Aubrey's messenger had been intercepted or (according to King Edward's official version) had suffered a crisis of conscience and revealed Aubrey's letter to the King. Edward had it copied and the original sent on, with instructions to the messenger to bring Margaret's reply directly to him, which the messenger did.[37] We do not know what Margaret's response was. She would certainly have encouraged Aubrey, but did she warn him that he could not count on help from the Scots, or did she hope that if Aubrey's plan succeeded Queen Mary would be more amenable to backing the Lancastrians? Aubrey probably never received Margaret's reply unless King Edward let it go through as a deliberate provocation to encourage Aubrey to betray himself. Whichever it was, Edward prepared to spring the trap long before Aubrey and his confederates were ready to move.

On 7 February 1462, Edward created John Tiptoft, Earl of Worcester, Constable of England.[38] Worcester had had the good sense to go abroad before the Loveday of 1458, on pilgrimage through Italy to the Holy Land. He remained abroad until the victorious Edward was crowned and he returned to England in time to attend Edward's first Parliament. He was warmly welcomed by the King, who made him Justiciar of North Wales, Constable of the Tower, and gave him a seat on the Council.[39] Worcester was a humanist scholar, but he was as ruthless as Edward and they suited one another. Five days after

Queen in Exile

Worcester became Constable of England Edward issued highpowered commissions of oyer and terminer in no less than twenty-five counties and eight large cities and towns to investigate treason and to arrest anyone who fell under suspicion.[40]

On the same day, 12 February, Edward sent Worcester and his faithful henchmen, William Herbert and Walter Devereux to arrest Aubrey and his father, John de Vere, Earl of Oxford.[41] Oxford may have been unaware of what Aubrey had been up to. He is unique among the magnates in that he stood aloof and did not take part in any of the political or military manoeuvring from the first Battle of St Albans in 1455, to Edward's accession in 1461. He did not attend the 1459 Parliament at Coventry or swear the oath of allegiance to King Henry and Margaret. Oxford was fifty-four in 1462 and he had been excused attendance at Parliament in 1460 on the grounds of ill health, so he had not signed the Westminster Accord. But he was in London in June and he attended Edward's Parliament in November.[42]

Sir Thomas Tuddenham, the former treasurer of Henry's household, and other East Anglian gentlemen were implicated in Aubrey's plot. They were arrested and Tuddenham knew he could expect no mercy. Edward had pardoned him a year earlier, but he had also made it abundantly clear that while he would receive into his grace any former Lancastrians who submitted to him, there would be no second chance.[43] If they offended again, they would face hanging or the axe.

The Earl of Worcester presided over the conspirators' trial for high treason in the Constable's court of chivalry. It was an irregular proceeding, but King Edward would not risk allowing Oxford or his son to be tried by their peers in Parliament. A high scaffold constructed on Tower Hill gave people a clear view of the fate that would be meted out to traitors. Aubrey was the first to die. On 20 February he was taken from Westminster to the Tower and beheaded. Sir Thomas Tuddenham, Sir William Tyrell, and John Montgomery were executed on 23 February.[44] Edward kept the best to last: on 26

Victory into Defeat

February, the Earl of Oxford was forced to walk through the streets of the City to the Tower for his execution.[45]

King Edward had swiftly and ruthlessly quashed incipient rebellion, if that is what it was, and his rumour mill was in full swing. Sixteen Frenchmen captured on a ship off the coast were brought into Sheringham in Norfolk and their evidence linked the Earl of Oxford to preparations for an invasion. They deposed that the Duke of Somerset and Lord Hungerford had returned to Scotland, and although they had not brought any troops with them, 200 ships from the King of Castile (whom King Charles had once asked to aid Margaret) and 300 ships from the Duke of Brittany (where Jasper Tudor was believed to have taken refuge), together with some French ships, were to sail for England, although they still had to be gathered and manned.[46] A Paston correspondent was told 'in right secrete wise' that the Duke of Somerset, King Henry, and Margaret planned to cross the Trent and launch an attack on London. Another army would converge on London from Wales, and a third French army would come from the Channel Islands. This contingent should have landed at the beginning of February but had been delayed by bad weather.[47] They never materialised.

An even more fantastic account was recorded by a monk-chronicler at the isolated monastery on the Isle of Ely. He picked up rumours and a tall tale told by a spy and embellished them.[48] All Europe, it seemed, was on the move against King Edward. An army under the Duke of Exeter and the Earl of Pembroke would land in North Wales. A Spanish army, led Margaret's brother, Duke Herry (sic) of Calabria, the Duke of Somerset, and Lord Hungerford would invade East Anglia, and a third army of Frenchmen and Spaniards sent by Herry (sic) the Dauphin of France, and led by Sir John Fortescue, King Henry's chancellor, would land at Sandwich. King Henry, Margaret, 'her son', and the Duke of Brittany would come south with a Scottish army, and if this was not enough, the Kings of France, Denmark, Aragon, Portugal, and Navarre, Edward (sic), Duke of Burgundy, and

Queen in Exile

Margaret's father were poised for a full-scale invasion. Did King Edward really have that many enemies, or King Henry that many friends?

Edward claimed to believe what would now be termed 'fake news', and he issued some of his own. He needed money, and he knew how to get it. In a letter to the London alderman Thomas Cook, written while he was staying in Stamford (a town that Margaret's army was supposed to have devastated) he painted a picture of imminent danger: England, and everything Englishmen held dear, was about to be destroyed. King Henry, with an army of Scots and Frenchmen, was poised to invade England at the instigation of 'the maliacious counseyle and excitation of Margaret, his wyfe, namynge hir selfe queene of England.' Henry had renounced his right to be King of England and Duke of Gascony to King Louis of France at Margaret's behest to obtain French support. He had ceded Berwick to the King of Scotland and promised to grant lands in the north of England to Scottish nobles, while Margaret's uncle, Charles of Maine, was to become governor of England.[49]

Edward assured Cook that the only way to prevent this catastrophe was for his loyal subjects to 'graunt unto us, of theire goodness and frewilll some certayne some of money', and that he would not ask this of them except out of dire necessity. He required Cook to set in motion the necessary steps to induce the wealthy citizens of London, not 'by way of ymposition, compulsion or of precedent ... but onely humantie and good will' to advance him the funds he needed. Edward was even more adept at scare tactics than his mentor the Earl of Warwick, and he set a pattern for 'borrowing' that he would follow for the rest of his life. Edward was supremely confident. He was not afraid of King James, or of King Louis, or indeed of anyone, except perhaps Margaret.

28

The Search for Allies

The Duke of Somerset, Lord Hungerford, and Robert Whittingham had returned to Scotland in March 1462 with little to show for their prolonged embassy, but at least they were free. King Louis had finally treated Margaret's envoys with respect, if not with kindness, and Margaret hoped that he might be persuaded to espouse her cause now that he was King of France and they had a common enemy in 'Edward of March'. She sent Sir Edmund Hampden to Louis, and Hampden caught up with him at Bordeaux where the King was on progress. Louis played his favourite game of keeping his adversaries (and to Louis all other rulers were adversaries) guessing. He received Hampden graciously and gave him 275 *livres tournois* for his expenses, a rare mark of favour.[1]

With the coming of better weather in the spring, Margaret decided that although Hungerford and Whittingham had warned her against it, she must go to France. She wrote to her uncle, the Count of Maine, to the Archbishop of Narbonne, and to Étienne Chevalier, King Louis's treasurer, to inform them of her intention.[2] Did she also ask them for advice on how best to approach King Louis? The Count of Maine, wishing to retain Louis's favour, hastily forwarded the correspondence to Louis. He referred to Margaret not as his niece, but only as the Queen of England.[3]

Queen Mary loaned Margaret £290, and King Henry issued her with a *carte blanche* authorisation to negotiate in his name and under his authority.[4] He addressed a letter to King Louis as his beloved *cousin germain de France,* thanking him for his good will and consistent support of Henry's attempts to recover his throne. Henry had no grasp of the difficulties facing Margaret. Louis had never espoused the Lancastrian cause; he consistently gave malicious encouragement to the Yorkists.[5] Margaret consigned Prince Edward to Queen Mary's care and took leave of King Henry. In April 1462 she sailed from Kirkcudbright to the Duchy of Brittany. Duke Francis I of Brittany had died in 1450, only a year after the attack on Fougères. He was succeeded by his brothers, Peter, and then Arthur de Richemont, the former Constable of France, none of whom had a son. There would have been no help for Margaret from that quarter, but Arthur died in 1458. The Count of Étampes (by French but not Burgundian reckoning) had married Francis I's daughter, and he became Duke Francis II of Brittany.[6] Margaret made only a short stay with him and Francis gave her 12,000 *écus* to speed her on her way.[7]

She went to meet her father at Angers, and one wonders how pleased René and his second wife, Jeanne de Laval, were to welcome her and what demands she made of him. She certainly expected René to entertain her in fine style, since he had to borrow 8,000 florins to foot the bill for her visit.[8] He was more concerned by John of Calabria's perilous position in Italy than he was in Margaret's plight.[9]

As soon as Louis learned that Margaret had crossed the border into France, he instructed Jean de Montauban, the Admiral of France, to send the *baillis* of Rouen and Caen to welcome her. With his usual black humour, Louis informed Montauban that Margaret's arrival was providential: she would provide him with a shield against King Edward of England, who would think twice about forming alliances with Louis's enemies while the threat of a Lancastrian resurgence, aided by France, hung over his head.[10]

Louis invited Margaret and her entourage to join him at Chinon in June.[11] He had not seen Margaret since that far off day in Tours when he had conducted the fourteen-year-old bride into the church of St Martin to be married by proxy to King Henry. Louis appointed

The Search for Allies

Georges Havart, Étienne Chevalier, and Pierre de Brezé as his negotiators. Brezé had been uncertain of his future during the first months of Louis's reign since Louis had long believed Brezé to be his enemy, and Brezé knew just how vengeful Louis could be. Brezé had gone into hiding, but he was either apprehended or eventually gave himself up, and Louis had him confined in the castle at Loches for interrogation.[12] The new king was avid to learn as much as he could of his father's dealings in the last few years of his reign, and Brezé, as Grand Seneschal of Normandy, and King Charles's confidant, would know all the details. The silver-tongued Brezé may have convinced his interlocutors that he would serve Louis loyally, or Louis may have realised just how useful Brezé could be.[13] Brezé was released and he was at Angers with René when Margaret arrived. Louis ordered Admiral Montauban to make friendly contact with him (*faites-lui bonne chere*) and listen carefully to whatever Brezé might tell him on how best to deal with Margaret.[14] Brezé was a recognised authority on English affairs; he had regularly sent agents into England and Margaret had appealed for his help before her victory at the Battle of St Albans.

Margaret expected Louis to meet her on equal terms and she made him a substantial offer. Her paramount need was for money, so in return for a loan of 20,000 *livres tournois* she mortgaged Calais to him. Calais was not hers to give – it was held by the Earl of Warwick – but that did not daunt Margaret. She undertook that as soon as King Henry recovered Calais, taking it for granted that this was a foregone conclusion, he would appoint a reliable Captain, either Jasper Tudor, Earl of Pembroke, or John de Foix, Earl of Kendal. Henry would then have a year to repay Louis the 20,000 pounds (which was feasible because the merchants of the Calais Staple could be relied on to raise most of it to keep Calais out of French hands). If, however, the money was not forthcoming at the end of that year, then the Captain of Calais would surrender the town and its environs to King Louis, and Louis would pay Henry an additional 40,000 *écus* before he took possession.

Queen in Exile

On 22 June 1462 Louis authorised his representatives to accept the offer and on 24 June Margaret signed a quittance for the receipt of the money.[15] She was careful not to antagonise Louis by using her full title of Queen of England and France, although she was careful to deny Louis his title. She addressed him as the 'most illustrious and serene prince, our cousin Louis of France', not as King of France. How far Louis believed that Henry (or Margaret) could recover the throne is anyone's guess. He risked losing 20,000 pounds and a few ships and men, but it was worth the gamble as a stick to beat King Edward with, and in the long term it would give him a quasi-legal claim to Calais.

Louis left Chinon for Amboise while Margaret and her entourage went to Tours, where they and Louis's representatives drew up the terms for a formal treaty.[16] A truce between France and England was to last for 100 years; the Emperor Frederick, the King of Portugal, who was related to the House of Lancaster, and the King of Aragon, whom Louis was courting, were included in the truce as allies. Louis would publicly recognise Henry VI as the rightful King of England, they would offer each other mutual aid against 'rebels', and Louis would forbid his subjects to give any aid to 'Edward of March'. No safe conducts would be issued to Englishmen by Louis, except for fishermen and prisoners, and only those authorised by Henry or Margaret would be recognised. Trade between England and France, especially with Gascony, was to be curtailed for as long as Edward remained on the throne, and any Englishmen wishing to land in Gascony must obtain a safe conduct from Louis as well as from Henry.

Margaret undertook to have a copy of the treaty sent to King Henry for ratification by a messenger of Louis's choice, and she optimistically promised that Henry would sign it, have it authorised by Parliament, and returned to Louis by the following Christmas. Henry's chancellor, Sir John Fortescue was to be a conservator of the truce, which was signed on 28 June by Margaret, Jasper Tudor as Earl of Pembroke, and John de Foix as Earl of Kendal (he had just promised to change his

The Search for Allies

allegiance and become King Louis's man in return for a substantial reward).[17]

Apart from the notional hundred years' truce that no one except Margaret believed in, the Treaty of Tours was primarily designed to cover the near future, until Henry (or Margaret) recovered the throne. She and her advisors were intent on crippling England's trading prospects to make Edward unpopular and restrict his ability to raise money to make war. Public recognition of Henry as an ally of France would help Margaret in her quest for other European allies and it would undermine Edward's credibility in diplomacy and foreign relations.

Margaret believed that since 'Edward of March' had no right to the throne it was only a matter of time and effort on her part before the rightful king would be restored. Those with her had perforce to believe it too: they had lost everything when Edward's Parliament attainted them, and self-interest as well as loyalty bound them to Henry and to Margaret. Without her, there would be no hope. King Louis of course, would abide by the treaty only so long as it suited him, and since its validity rested on its endorsement by Henry as King of England *and* by Parliament, it was at best an insubstantial agreement, but it satisfied Margaret. Louis stood to win whatever the outcome. He promised to furnish Margaret with an army under Brezé's command, and it was probably at Louis's instigation at this time that Margaret granted the lordship of the Channel Islands to Brezé as a reward (and an inducement) for his support.[18] Louis hoped to recover them for France.[19]

A garbled version of the agreement between Louis and Margaret over Calais soon reached England. King Edward feared that Margaret had given Calais to Louis outright, and that he might attempt to occupy it at any moment. A Paston correspondent reported that Margaret would return to Scotland with an army financed by the King of France, to invade England. He had heard that Margaret was at Boulogne with enough money to pay the Calais garrison, who might

Queen in Exile

then defect and throw off their allegiance to Warwick.[20] But using the precious 20,000 *livres tournois* that she needed to fund her invasion never formed part of Margaret's plans.

While Margaret was in France the Earl of Warwick led a delegation to meet Queen Mary in Dumfries, and rumour had it that Warwick offered Mary a marriage with King Edward, but this is unlikely.[21] Warwick would look higher for a bride for Edward IV than the Dowager Queen of Scotland, while Mary would not risk her son's future autonomy, or be willing to give up her position as Queen Regent of Scotland, to become the *parvenu* King of England's consort. Nothing came of the meeting and Warwick left Scotland in disgust.[22] Queen Mary kept her options open. She sent Scottish envoys to Carlisle in June to resume discussions. Warwick, accompanied by Henry Bourgchier, now Earl of Essex, Lord Hastings, King Edward's favourite courtier, Lawrence Booth, Bishop of Durham, and Sir John Wenlock, met the Scottish representatives, but all they managed to obtain was a temporary truce, to last from June to 24 August 1462.[23]

What King Edward really wanted, and what Warwick demanded and did not get, was the return of the royal fugitives and their adherents. This exasperated Edward and he wrote nominally to King James III, but actually to Queen Mary, to demand that the Scots give up the usurper called King Henry, his wife, 'her son', and all other traitors, unless they had become Scottish subjects. Ironically, since to the Scots Edward *was* a rebel and a traitor, he argued that kings, princes, and rulers formed a brotherhood and had a duty to support each other in suppressing rebels and traitors. He expressed surprise that King James did not acknowledge this, even though he had previously warned James that he was wrong to shelter Henry. Edward requested James to send a favourable reply to his legitimate demand, with a veiled threat that if James continued to refuse Edward would have to consider war with Scotland.[24]

Before she left Tours, Margaret received an unexpected invitation from Charles, Duke of Orleans, to visit him at Blois where his duchess had just given birth to a son after nearly twenty years of marriage.²⁵ The child would be named for King Louis, who was to be his godfather, and Orleans honoured Margaret as Queen of England by asking her become the baby's godmother.²⁶ Perhaps Orleans remembered that King Henry had released him from his long captivity in England before his full ransom was paid.

After the christening at Blois Margaret went to Rouen, once the capital of English Normandy, where she was received with the same honours as those accorded to a queen of France. She and her entourage were accompanied by the Archbishop of Narbonne (who happened to be Pierre de Brezé's brother-in-law) and as they approached the city on 13 July, the King's officials, the city's councillors, and representatives of the clergy rode out greet her. The Archbishop of Narbonne replied on Margaret's behalf to their formal welcome and she was conducted in procession to the cathedral, to pray for God's blessing on her enterprise. She lodged at the Hôtel of the Golden Lion where the Count of Charolais had stayed a year earlier, and her host presented her with a gift of red wine.²⁷ Louis may have intended the city's royal reception of her to convince King Edward of his support for Margaret, or it may be another example of Louis's black humour – an ironic reminder to Margaret that once before, under very different circumstances, she had been received into Rouen as England's queen. Margaret, of course, took her reception at face value as no more than her due.

She had to wait a month for Louis to make his state entry into Rouen on 12 August 1462,²⁸ and on 16 August he ordered Rouen's shipmasters to place as many vessels as she required at the Queen's disposal.²⁹ Louis had assigned 4,000 *livres tournois* to finance the expedition, and Brezé received an advance of 1,090 *livres* and then a further 500.³⁰ Margaret was still hard pressed for ready money and Brezé loaned her 800 *écus* for her private expenses and sent another 200 that did not reach her.³¹ She was at Harfleur on 1 September waiting to embark, but a number of factors delayed her sailing. Brezé was too canny to put to sea until he could be sure of the whereabouts of the English fleet, and he excused the delay as being due to contrary winds.

King Edward had requisitioned ships and men to assemble in the south ports.[32] The fleet, under the command of Lord Fauconberg, now the Earl of Kent, had sailed to Brittany on a marauding expedition early in August, where Fauconberg burned and pillaged the Breton enclave at Le Conquet.[33] Duke Francis assembled an army and prepared for war. He ordered repairs to the port of Brest and he had all English merchants travelling in his domains without safe conducts arrested.

Fauconberg turned his attention to the coast of southern France and harried Poitou. His men pillaged the Ile de Dieu and the Ile de Ré for several days, even burning part of its cathedral. King Louis sent reinforcements to the garrison at La Rochelle and had heavy artillery positioned on the hill overlooking the harbour. A Breton fleet was ready to sail in September, but Fauconberg was warned of the forces gathering against him; he broke off his campaign and returned to England before the autumn weather made seafaring too dangerous.[34] If Edward's intention in sending Fauconberg to sea was to intimidate Duke Francis and distract King Louis's attention from Calais, it was ill conceived and had the opposite effect. Louis turned the attacks to his advantage by suggesting to Margaret that she should ask Duke Francis to help finance her invasion against a common enemy, and Francis obliged to the tune of 1,000 *écus*.[35] All Edward accomplished was to strengthen French and Breton ill will towards him.

The widespread story in England that Fauconberg won a great victory at sea over a fleet of French, Breton, and Spanish ships was a pure fabrication, put about by Edward to disguise the ineffectiveness of Fauconberg's foray, which was largely a waste of men and money.[36] Edward may also have spread the rumour that Margaret was at Boulogne attempting to suborn the Calais garrison. Boulogne was in Burgundian territory. Edward employed his tried and tested scare

The Search for Allies

tactic of imminent invasion to appeal to the Common Council of London for a loan of £3,400 because Margaret and King Louis were about to invade Calais. The Common Council appears to have offered about £2,000, towards the garrison's wages, but this was not enough.[37]

Edward exploited the vested interests of the Calais Staplers. By their reckoning the crown owed them the enormous sum of £40,917 19s 2¼d in unredeemed loans, and they wanted a guarantee of repayment before they would advance any more money. Edward fell back on King Henry's practice of issuing licences to them to ship wool free of customs duties.[38] The Staplers believed Edward's story that failure to supply him with the money he needed would mean the inevitable loss of Calais, and they agreed to advance £6,872 7s 4d for half a years' pay for the garrison to keep the soldiers loyal.[39]

The intelligence that the English navy had returned to port at the beginning of October and been disbanded was sent to King Louis by Bertrand de Beauvau.[40] Shortly afterwards Margaret and her entourage sailed for England, with Pierre de Brezé, his son Jacques, a small number of French volunteers, and an army amounting to no more than 2,000 men.[41] They made landfall at Bamburgh on 25 October 1462. The Duke of Somerset and Sir Ralph Percy, the last surviving brother of the Earl of Northumberland, joined Margaret there. Bamburgh and Dunstanburgh were still in Lancastrian hands, but the Percy stronghold of Alnwick had been captured for King Edward. It had not been reinforced to withstand a siege and its garrison was short of supplies. It surrendered to Margaret's forces without putting up much resistance.

This small success encouraged Margaret. She had believed all along that she had only to appear in the north with the nucleus of an army, and enough money to fund a campaign, for loyal Lancastrians throughout England to flock to her banner as they had in York and Hull in 1461 after the Duke of York claimed the throne. Margaret suffered the first of a series of disappointments at Bamburgh: the north did not rise and the army she had hoped to raise did not

Queen in Exile

materialise. King Edward had reconciled former opponents to his rule and steadily tightened his grip on the throne. Most of the Lancastrians who had not died at Towton had made their peace with him and the few die-hards who remained stubbornly loyal to King Henry had been attainted and their estates forfeited to the crown. They were in exile or in hiding and they had no resources to offer the Queen.

Nevertheless, the news that Margaret was campaigning in England seriously alarmed King Edward and he summoned his lords and knights to follow him north.[42] He tapped the Common Council of London for another £2,000, promising to prevent the rebels from marching on London.[43] On 6 November he commissioned Warwick to undertake initial resistance and he set out for York.[44] Margaret had been at Bamburgh for only two weeks when she learned that Edward was on his way and she decided that rather than risk defeat she would withdraw to Scotland and negotiate for Scottish help.

She garrisoned Alnwick, Bamburgh, and Dunstanburgh with French soldiers, and on 13 November, Margaret, Brezé, and their few remaining followers sailed north. Her ships were caught in a ferocious storm off the coast of Scotland. Three 'great ships' foundered and a fourth, carrying a contingent of Frenchmen, made landfall on Lindisfarne, but it was not long before their presence became known and they were captured. Margaret and Brezé were lucky to escape drowning. They abandoned ship and were picked up by a fishing boat that put them ashore at Berwick, but the chests containing the precious money and Margaret's other valuables went down with her ship. She reached Scotland safely, but once again she was a penniless refugee.[45]

King Edward reached Durham by the end of November where he succumbed to a bout of the measles, and it was left to the Earl of Warwick to take change. Warwick had Sir John Wenlock, Henry Grey of Codnore, now firmly committed to King Edward, and Humphrey Bourgchier, Lord Cromwell, in his company.[46] From his base at Warkworth, a former Percy stronghold, Warwick supervised the siege

The Search for Allies

of the three northern fortresses. He was supplied with victuals and artillery from Newcastle.[47]

The Duke of Somerset was thoroughly disillusioned. He was the leader of the Lancastrians after Margaret herself and yet she appeared to have no use for him. She had not invited him to accompany her to France but left him to his own devices in Edinburgh, which for Somerset was not only dull but uncomfortable, after the opulence of the Burgundian court. He did not enjoy being in exile. Somerset was thirty-five and unmarried, and his title and estates had escheated to the crown following his attainder in 1461. His loyalty to King Henry was strong – he was Henry's godson – but the passive king had proved a disappointment to one of Somerset's ardent temperament. He was not the only prominent Lancastrian to question whether King Henry could ever recover the throne. Richard Woodville and his son Anthony, despite their humiliation by Warwick (and Edward) at Calais in 1460, had joined Edward because Woodville came to the conclusion that the Lancastrian cause was lost.[48]

In September, before Margaret left France, Somerset made contact with the Earl of Warwick. Somerset did not hate Edward in the way that he had hated Edward's father, and he was Warwick's cousin through their shared Beaufort blood. Could the Beaufort family fortunes be recovered from the wreckage? It was worth considering, and if any man could persuade Edward to offer an honourable settlement to the Beauforts, it would be Warwick. Warwick recognised a great propaganda coup when he saw one. What a triumph it would be for King Edward if the most prominent of the Lancastrians could be persuaded to turn his coat! He forwarded Somerset's letter to Edward in London.[49] But then Margaret landed in the north and Somerset wavered – perhaps there would be action after all. He joined Margaret but her hasty retreat at the first threat of danger completed his disillusion.

Before she sailed for Scotland Margaret had committed the defence of Bamburgh to Somerset, Lord Roos, Sir Ralph Percy, and Jasper Tudor. She expected Somerset to defend a bleak and inhospitable castle with few men and fewer supplies, and for what purpose? In December, the Earl of Worcester, John Neville, Lord Montague, and the deputy Warden of the East March Sir Robert Ogle besieged Bamburgh. Somerset conferred with Sir Ralph Percy, who also wondered what Margaret thought she was doing in retreating to Scotland, for no Percy would ever welcome a Scottish invasion. Somerset persuaded Percy that the only way to avoid capture and imprisonment was to change sides and surrender Bamburgh.

Just before Christmas Somerset sent word, probably through the constable, the Earl of Worcester, that he and Ralph Percy were prepared to offer their allegiance to King Edward, provided they and the other Lancastrians in Bamburgh were not punished and the garrison was allowed to go free. Warwick sent Somerset and Percy to Edward at Durham, where they took the oath of allegiance to him as King of England. Somerset hoped to recover his estates in the south, but Percy wished to return to the north, and under their terms for the surrender of Bamburgh Edward entrusted the constableship of Bamburgh and Dunstanburgh to Percy.[50] This was not altruism or foolhardiness on Edward's part, it was sound common sense. Warwick did not wish to remain in the north indefinitely, or to be called back at intervals to deal with sporadic unrest. The Percys no longer threatened Neville ascendancy – Warwick was too powerful for that – but he knew the fanatical devotion of Percy clients, tenants, and retainers to their lord, and that Edward's rule would only be accepted at the behest of a Percy, and Edward had insurance for Ralph's good behaviour. Ralph's nephew, Henry Percy, still only sixteen, had been stripped of his father's title as Earl of Northumberland and he was in Edward's custody.

Jasper Tudor and Lord Roos refused to sue to Edward for pardon or take the oath to him. They were permitted to leave Bamburgh unmolested and they returned to Scotland. Dunstanburgh was under

The Search for Allies

siege by Lord Fitzhugh, Lord Scrope of Bolton, Lord Powis, and Lord Greystoke, who had defected from his Lancastrian allegiance. As soon as Sir Richard Tunstall, Sir Philip Wentworth, and John Morton, who were defending Dunstanburgh, learned that Somerset had deserted Bamburgh, they submitted to Warwick on the same terms.

Warwick remained on the defensive throughout December. With Margaret back in Scotland, a Scottish army might cross the border at any time, although young John Paston, serving with the new Duke of Norfolk's men at Newcastle, doubted it. The Scots, he said, rarely kept their promises, and he expected to remain at Newcastle at least until Christmas.[51] At the end of the month King Edward seized the temporalities of the rich bishopric of Durham to augment his war chest. He accused Bishop Lawrence Booth of treachery, although there is no indication that Booth was disloyal, or that he intended to help Margaret. But Edward needed the money and to be on the safe side he packed Booth off to exile at Pembroke College, Cambridge, where Booth held a fellowship.[52]

In Scotland Margaret had found an ally in the Scottish Warden of the East March, George, Earl of Angus, the 'Red Douglas'. Unlike his cousin and bitter enemy James, Earl of Douglas, the 'Black Douglas', who had fled to King Henry's protection in England in 1455 and was now King Edward's pensioner, Angus was loyal to the Scottish crown. He was an experienced soldier who had been with King James II at the siege of Roxburgh when James was killed, and he was a member of the six-man regency council for King James III.[53]

Much to Angus's disgust, the Black Douglas was stirring up rebellion among the disaffected factions of the Scottish nobility at King Edward's behest (and cost). This made Angus willing to make common cause with Margaret. King Henry offered to grant him an English dukedom and an estate in the north of England worth 2,000 marks if Angus would raise a Scottish force to invade England. If war subsequently broke out between England and Scotland (after Henry had recovered his throne) Angus would be free to follow his first

Queen in Exile

loyalty to the King of Scots without forfeiting his title and estate. He could even send his own Scots representatives to administer his English lands in his absence.[54] This is typical of the unlikely agreements that Margaret was prepared to offer to anyone who would help her.

Alnwick, the last of the three fortresses, was under siege by Lord Fauconberg and Anthony Woodville. King Edward sent the Duke of Somerset to join them to demonstrate his good faith. The Earl of Angus and Pierre de Brezé prepared to march to its relief. Brezé had a personal as well as a professional interest in the foray; Alnwick was defended by Lord Hungerford, Sir Robert Whittingham, and Brezé's son Jacques. Warwick respected Angus's reputation as Warden of the March; he did not know the size or strength of the Scottish force and he did not have the resources to risk a battle with the Scots. At the approach of Angus's army Warwick sensibly ordered Lord Fauconberg, who was mortally ill, to raise the siege and retreat.

Angus and Brezé crossed the border on 5 January 1463 and the defenders of Alnwick, who were near starvation, thankfully opened their gates. The adventurer Brezé was all in favour of pressing on but Angus was wary. What was Warwick up to? Was it a trick to lure them into an ambush? Deep midwinter was not the best time for marching further into northern England, and Angus advised caution. Hungerford and Whittingham, not to mention Jacques de Brezé, had had enough of trying to hold an untenable position. Bamburgh and Dunstanburgh had fallen, so what use was Alnwick alone? They backed Angus and opted to return to Scotland.[55] Warwick took possession of Alnwick unopposed, but it was a bitter victory. His uncle, the gallant Lord Fauconberg, died at Durham on 9 January 1463. King Edward left Durham soon afterwards, taking the Duke of Somerset with him. Like Warwick, he fully appreciated the propaganda coup of the Lancastrian leader's defection, and he was anxious to show him off in London.

29

Into Exile

Somerset and Sir Ralph Percy's defection and the loss of the northern castles was a set-back, but there was more encouraging news in the spring of 1463. Percy had sworn allegiance to King Edward on condition that he be retained as Constable of Bamburgh and Dunstanburgh castles. Did Percy mean to keep his oath, or was it only a temporary expedient? As Earls of Northumberland, Percy's father and brothers had died fighting for King Henry. To a Percy, Henry was still the rightful king and his oath to the usurper Edward, given under duress, was invalid. Percy sent word to Henry and Margaret that he was willing to return to his obedience and he opened the gates of Bamburgh and Dunstanburgh to a contingent of French soldiers to reinforce their garrisons, while several French ships sailed for Bamburgh with relief supplies.[1]

The Northumbrian knight, Sir Ralph Grey, was Constable of Alnwick. Grey had been in King Henry's service since 1455 as deputy keeper of Roxburgh Castle and he had served on several commissions with the Earl of Northumberland in the later 1450s.[2] Grey had a personal connection to Margaret through his mother, Lady Elizabeth Grey, who had been one of Margaret's ladies in waiting. When her husband died in France in 1443, Elizabeth had purchased her son's wardship and marriage.[3] Ralph Grey was granted livery of his lands in 1449 and in 1452 his mother arranged his marriage to Jacquetta Stanlowe, the daughter of Margaret Stanlowe, one of Queen Margaret's damsels.[4] Ralph had submitted to King Edward after the

Earl of Northumberland was killed at Towton and Edward exempted Ralph from prosecution for his previous adherence to King Henry.[5] In July 1462 Lord Hastings and Ralph Gey forced the Lancastrian Sir William Tailboys to surrender the castle of Alnwick, and King Edward made Grey its constable.[6]

Grey was not at Alnwick when Margaret's forces besieged it; he was serving on an oyer and terminer commission with Warwick.[7] Alnwick fell to the Yorkists in December 1462 and King Edward reinstated Ralph as its constable, but in May 1463 Grey followed Percy's example and surrendered Alnwick to Lord Hungerford.[8] The chroniclers tell the story that Grey resented the appointment of Sir John Astley as captain of the garrison at Alnwick, and he took Astley prisoner by a trick (did he get him drunk?) and then surrendered the castle. This may be true, but it is more likely that for Grey, as for Percy, old loyalties died hard.

With the three northern castles again in Lancastrian hands, Scottish interest in Margaret's cause revived. Her stalwart ally the Earl of Angus died unexpectedly in March, but a self-interested faction at the Scottish court was ready to lend Margaret military aid for their own ends. Their immediate objective was the castle at Norham, a principal fortress on the English side of the River Tweed a few miles south-west of Berwick and a bulwark for the defence of the East March. Only John Neville, Lord Montague, the Warden of the March, stood between the Scots and Norham. The traitorous Earl of Douglas, financed by King Edward, had again attacked across the border into Galloway and defeated a Scottish force sent against him. He would have to be apprehended.[9]

The Scottish Council agreed to a course of action compounded of misplaced enthusiasm, widely divergent aims, and military ignorance. A combined force of Scots and Frenchmen would take Norham and then march south, gathering recruits along the way. Margaret believed that there were pockets of resistance to King Edward throughout England and this time she would bring King Henry with her to appeal

Into Exile

to their allegiance, but except for Pierre de Brezé, a Frenchman and therefore not entirely to be trusted, Margaret had no experienced war captain to coordinate her campaign. An already risky enterprise was further undermined by the extraordinary decision that both royal families, Henry VI and James III, Queens Mary and Margaret, and the Prince of Wales, should be present at the siege of Norham.[10] Perhaps Queen Mary hoped to strengthen her position as Regent by riding in triumph with her son to take possession of an English fortress.

Warwick arrived in the north in June and learned that a Scottish army had laid siege to Norham and that this was the prelude to a full-scale invasion. Warwick set about raising additional forces from his northern estates and he sent to Archbishop William Booth for reinforcements from the diocese of York.[11] The resources of the bishopric of Durham, which included Norham, were not available to Warwick as King Edward had impounded its temporalities and sent Bishop Lawrence Booth away to Cambridge.

Warwick warned King Edward of the danger and suggested that it would be as well if the King himself came north. Edward announced his intention to do so, and once again he turned the situation to his financial advantage. He assured the Common Council of London that he had perfect faith in their readiness to support him (with a loan) in the face of this new danger. He informed them that Margaret had made a bargain with the King of Scotland: she had promised to cede seven English shires in the north to King James and to leave her son Prince Edward in the care of James Kennedy, Bishop of St Andrews, who dominated the Scottish Council. The boy would remain in the Bishop's custody for seven years, to be brought up as a Scot, until he was old enough to marry James III's sister. Margaret had also promised to make Kennedy Archbishop of Canterbury; she would bestow other English bishoprics on (unnamed) Scottish prelates, and large tracts of land in England would be given to (unnamed) Scots and Frenchmen, thus putting all England under foreign domination. Edward claimed that Margaret hated the English – she was French after all – and she expected that the new lords of the land would show 'the greatest and largest cruelty' to Englishmen because of her 'insatiable malice towards them'. Finally, England would be forced to join the 'Auld Alliance' between Scotland and France (presumably against England).[12] Edward promised the Common Council that he would risk life and limb to prevent this farrago of nonsense from happening and they awarded him 500 marks to help victual a royal army for Scotland.[13]

Margaret was undoubtedly prepared to hand over Norham to the Scots (once they had taken it) as she had Berwick, but she would never have promised to surrender a large part of England. The northern shires were Prince Edward's inheritance and they were also for the most part Percy country. Margaret was looking to the Percys for support. Unless she intended to capture and execute Thomas Bourgchier, the Archbishop of Canterbury, his archbishopric was not hers to give, and the Pope would have had something to say about it, as Kennedy well knew.[14]

Sir Robert Ogle, now Lord Ogle, stoutly defended Norham and resisted the Scots demand that he should surrender it. The siege lasted eighteen days in July, until Warwick and John Neville rode to its relief and the Scots beat a hasty retreat.[15] They were not cowards, but their forces were not nearly as numerous as Warwick had been led to believe and the non-combatant royals in the field were a heavy liability: they could not be allowed to be captured. Warwick had not been pleased at having to go north once again, but he could not leave John Neville to face the Lancastrians and the Scots on his own. Warwick was angry. He had bigger fish to fry than suppressing a parcel of unruly Scots. He should have been at St Omer as King Edward's representative to a conference under the aegis of the Duke of Burgundy, to effect a reconciliation between England and France. Warwick's absence meant that the meeting had been postponed.[16] Uncharacteristically, since there was nothing to be gained by invading Scotland (as King Edward had several times threatened to do)

Warwick took reprisals. He pursued the Scots across the border and laid waste to the countryside for miles along the East March.[17]

In the meanwhile, King Edward, accompanied by the Duke of Somerset, came to Northampton. Edward had treated Somerset with exceptional generosity; his attainder was reversed in Parliament and his titles and estates were restored to him.[18] Edward had supplied Somerset with ready money and established him within the inner circle of his favoured courtiers; he had taken him hunting (a special mark of royal favour and trust) and encouraged Somerset to show himself off by engaging in a public display of jousting.[19] Edward also awarded annuities to Somerset's mother, the Dowager Duchess Eleanor, and just before leaving London he had ordered the release of Somerset's brother Edmund, who was imprisoned in the Tower of London.[20]

While he was in Northampton, possibly to celebrate Warwick's victory, Edward distributed largesse among the citizens and gave them a tun of wine. They promptly got drunk, and to show their loyalty and appreciation of their sovereign's generosity they took exception to Somerset and his retainers who wore the Beaufort livery: everyone knew that the Duke of Somerset was the King's enemy and a traitor.[21] King Edward's other favourites, such as Lord Hastings, resented the King's intimacy with a man that they too saw as an enemy, and they may have encouraged the citizens' belligerent attitude. Somerset escaped harm but the episode made him think again. He was proud of his Beaufort inheritance. He had acted on impulse and a sense of despair when he surrendered to Edward, but it was an impulse that he gradually came to regret. He might be Edward's boon companion, but he was also the King's lap dog and he would never be truly free. Was the recovery of his dukedom worth the sacrifice of being denied freedom of action? Somerset felt no loyalty towards Edward; his loyalties lay with King Henry and the incident at Northampton showed him that his position at Edward's court was at best ambivalent. Sometime between the end of July and the early autumn

Queen in Exile

of 1463 Somerset slipped away from court and headed for sanctuary in North Wales, where insurrection was never far below the surface.[22]

Back in Edinburgh after the ignominious retreat from Norham, Margaret decided on her next move. She was no longer welcome in Scotland and she left her hapless husband and set out to appeal to the one man who might still be persuaded to help her: Philip the Good, Duke of Burgundy. Margaret sailed for Sluys in Flanders, taking Prince Edward, Pierre de Brezé, and a few attendants with her, an indication that she did not intend to return to Scotland.[23] She took up residence in Bruges and sent Jean Carbonnel, a kinsman of Brezé's who had probably been with him in Scotland, to inform Duke Philip of their arrival. Philip was at Boulogne and Margaret's arrival took him by surprise. He had just welcomed King Edward's envoys, who were at Calais awaiting a Burgundian escort to take them to St Omer to initiate the truce talks between France and England that had been delayed by Warwick's absence. Burgundy hastened to reassure King Louis that Margaret presence would not derail the talks, although one of his councillors was sure that she had come for no other purpose![24]

Philip was too chivalrous to behave churlishly to Margaret, who was still Queen of England and King Louis's cousin, but he did his best to avoid meeting her. He sent his chamberlain, Phillipe Pot, to Bruges to find out from Brezé what Margaret wanted. Pot excused the Duke's failure to welcome her in person, explaining that Philip was detained by important state business requiring his presence, and he suggested that now was not the most propitious time for Margaret's visit. Margaret was not deterred. If Philip would not come to her then she would go to Philip no matter where he was.

This caused Philip further concern. Boulogne and St Omer were far too close to Calais for comfort, and once Margaret's presence became known King Edward (or Warwick) might well order the men of the Calais garrison to kidnap her. Philip increased patrols along the border with the Pale of Calais.[25] He was genuinely concerned for her safety and he was also honour bound to protect her. He could not allow her to fall into Edward's hands while she was on Burgundian soil. Since he could not stop her, Philip moved to St Pol on 25 August to await Margaret's arrival. She was aware of the risks she ran in travelling to St Pol, which was south of St Omer but still close to the border with Calais. She left Prince Edward safely in Bruges and set out with Brezé, three women attendants, and a small escort. They reached St Pol on 31 August 1463.[26]

Margaret was as naïve as ever in her approach to international relations; she thought only in dynastic terms. Throughout the years of her exile she would appeal to first one and then another of the kings and princes of Europe for help in restoring her husband to his throne. She was proud of her status as a queen and she expected to influence other potential allies either through kinship, marriage, or just *because* they were fellow monarchs and so should befriend a dispossessed king.

The first difficulty Margaret had to overcome in approaching Burgundy was King Henry. He had never disguised his dislike and mistrust of Duke Philip, who had deserted him, and England, at Arras nearly thirty years earlier. Margaret did her best to convince Philip that Henry's antipathy had been exaggerated by his enemies, and that she did not share it.[27] She appealed to Burgundy as the mightiest, the most magnanimous, and the most chivalrous prince in Europe, whom she was sure would understand her predicament. Philip was too wily to contradict her outright and he replied evasively that he never believed all that he was told. He tried to turn the conversation away from so touchy a subject by suggesting that they should talk of something else, it was not fit for ladies, even for queens, to dwell on unpleasant subjects, but only on joyous ones.

Margaret left it to the eloquent Brezé to plead King Henry's case, and Brezé rehearsed all the misfortunes that the peace-loving Henry had suffered through no fault of his own and who was now experiencing adversity in exile. Brezé repeated that the reports of King Henry's enmity had been exaggerated, and that Henry and Margaret recognised Burgundy as a glorious prince.[28] Margaret then tried to persuade Burgundy to become her advocate and protect her interests at the upcoming conference with the usurping Edward's ambassadors. She could not go to St Omer herself or send representatives, but as convener of the conference Burgundy could take a neutral stand and ensure that her position (which King Louis had recognised only a year earlier) would not be ignored. Burgundy temporised. He promised to do what he could, but he cautiously reminded Margaret that he could not answer for King Louis's intentions.

Burgundy favoured the Yorkists, although not to the extent that has sometimes been supposed, because he admired the Earl of Warwick. He had no special liking for King Edward but as long as Edward sat on the throne Burgundy would not jeopardise relations between England and the Low Countries by antagonising the belligerent and unpredictable Edward in the interests of Margaret and King Henry.

Philip spent only a day in Margaret's company, but he paid her all the honours due to a queen. He laid on a splendid banquet and he sent for his sister Agnes, the Dowager Duchess of Bourbon, her daughters, and one of her sons to join him at St Pol.[29] According to Georges Chastellain, Margaret poured her woes into Agnes's sympathetic ear and the Duchess suggested that Chastellain should write a consolation for Margaret.[30] Chastellain claimed to have known Margaret as a child and he was a friend and admirer of Pierre de Brezé. The romantic chronicler conceived the literary conceit of an imaginary temple dedicated to the long dead Boccaccio, whose works Margaret was believed to admire. In *Le Temple de Bocace,* Chastellain surveys the tombs and recounts the deaths, some deserved and some not, of kings, princes, and great men brought low by adversity far worse than Margaret's own. Margaret enters the temple and indulges in long self-accusatory conversations with Boccaccio, in which her present predicament is contrasted with, and blamed on, her former overweening pride (and opposition to the Duke of Burgundy). Designed to please a French and Burgundian audience, *Le Temple de Bocace,* if she ever saw it, can scarcely have consoled Margaret. She

Into Exile

would not have been pleased to be told that the Lancastrians dynasty had usurped the throne, waged an unjust war against the French, and that her husband had allowed Humphrey, Duke of Gloucester, to be murdered.[31]

In a final chivalrous gesture as he rode away from St Pol, Burgundy relieved Margaret's financial embarrassments by sending her a large diamond and 2,000 *écus*, with 500 to Brezé, 200 to Jean Carbonnel, and 100 each to Margaret's three women attendants.[32] Margaret read more into Burgundy's glib professions of admiration and sympathy than his response warranted. She was gratified by the deference shown to her at St Pol, but she appears not to have understood that it was courtesy without substance.

Margaret returned to Bruges escorted by Burgundian archers, and was royally received by Burgundy's son, the Count of Charolais, and the civic dignitaries, who gave her gifts of wine and candles. Charolais was as much of a showman as his father. He welcomed Margaret with an elaborate show of deference because, he said, she was a queen and Prince Edward was heir to a throne while he was only the son of a duke.[33] Margaret parted company with Pierre de Brezé for the last time in Bruges. Brezé was a loyal Frenchman, he had helped Margaret because he disliked the English, but his adventure in her service had ended in failure, and he had his own future to consider. Brezé went to Hesdin to join Louis and renew his allegiance. Late in 1463 he visited Jersey to make good, if he could, his lordship of the Channel Islands that Margaret had granted to him.[34]

Margaret and Prince Edward left Bruges on 5 September 1463 escorted by Burgundian archers. They made the journey of nearly 200 miles across Burgundian territory to her father's Duchy of Bar.[35] Margaret had nowhere else to go. She could not remain indefinitely as a guest of the Duke of Burgundy, she could not return to Scotland, she was too proud to set foot in France while King Louis was negotiating with her arch-enemy, and her presence in Anjou would embarrass René; but the Duchy of Bar was not French territory.

Duke Philip waited at Hesdin to greet Louis, who did not arrive until the end of September. Burgundy fancied himself as the arbiter of Europe and Louis encouraged him in his belief. If that meant acceding to Burgundy's attempt to foster peace between England and France, Louis was happy to go along – it would cost him nothing. His real aim was quite different. Louis was determined to recover the nine strategic towns along the River Somme that King Charles had ceded to Burgundy at the 'peace' conference at Arras in 1435 to persuade Burgundy to change his allegiance. It had been agreed then that King Charles could buy them back for 400,000 gold crowns, but Charles considered the price too high and they remained in Burgundy's hands. Louis thought differently and he was prepared to pay for them. Despite opposition from the Count of Charolais, who had a vested interest in retaining the towns as a strategic defence against France, Burgundy had agreed to sell them to Louis. At Hesdin, under cover of the peace conference, Louis made the final payment and the Somme towns passed into Louis's hands.[36]

Burgundy had been receptive to Louis's overtures partly because he wanted to be recognised as the man who ended the war between France and England, but more immediately because he was concerned with the salvation of his soul. He was sixty-seven and he had suffered a serious illness in 1462, so serious that his life was despaired of. It made him aware of his own mortality and of his spiritual shortcomings. He had vowed on several occasions to lead a crusade against the infidel, but he had never done so. He was now too old to go himself, but the money for the Somme towns might furnish the means to send someone in his stead and secure his place in heaven.[37]

King Louis refused to go to St Omer, so the English ambassadors had to come to Hesdin. Burgundy paid their expenses (and Louis's), and he laid on elaborate festivities and sumptuous banquets for their entertainment as well as distributing valuable gifts to the English.[38] King Edward wanted a temporary truce with France to counter Louis's designs on Calais and prevent him from giving further aid to

Into Exile

Margaret. The Earl of Warwick had been expected to lead the English mission, but he was not there. King Edward sent Warwick's brother George Neville, Henry Bourgchier, Earl of Essex, John Wenlock, now Lord Wenlock, and Louis Gallet, who had once been Margaret's envoys to Burgundy, in his stead.[39] Edward had created George Neville, the Bishop of Exeter, as Chancellor of England when he took the throne in 1461 at a time when nothing was too good for Warwick and his brothers. George did not have Warwick's status or personality, but as Chancellor he was the best substitute Edward could offer.

As so often happened at international 'peace' conferences, there was hypocrisy on both sides. The protagonists had differing aims and agendas. After a month of wrangling a truce was agreed on 8 October, to last for one year only, beginning on 20 October for France, and 5 November for England, ending on 1 October 1464.[40] Louis and Edward undertook not to make war against each other during that time. Louis would not give aid or sanctuary to King Henry, Queen Margaret, 'her son', or to any of Edward's other enemies, and Edward would not help Louis's enemies. Burgundy half kept his promise to Margaret: he was not included in the prohibition to give sanctuary to her or to other Lancastrians, although he looked after his own interests by concluding a separate pact with Edward to continue free trade between his lands and England.[41]

The truce secured Edward against one potential enemy but there were others. In late November, the Duke of Somerset left North Wales to join King Henry and bring him the news that Somerset had laid the groundwork for rebellion in Wales. According to *Gregory's Chronicle*, Somerset was making for Newcastle where King Edward had sent his Beaufort retainers; he got far as Durham before he was recognised and almost captured. He escaped and he fled with only the clothes he stood up in.[42] Somerset made his way north to safety at Bamburgh Castle where he unexpectedly found King Henry.

Unfortunately for King Henry, Queen Mary died on 1 December 1463, and her death cleared the way for Bishop Kennedy to open truce talks with King Edward. The power-hungry bishop had been struggling with the Queen for possession of the boy king, James III, and domination of the Scottish Council. According to Kennedy, King Henry, fearing for his safety, had put himself under Kennedy's protection and Kennedy had provided him with a refuge in his own palaces and had paid for his upkeep without recompense.[43] But it was Queen Mary who, while keeping on side with Edward IV, had extended aid and sanctuary to Henry, Margaret, and Prince Edward. Henry had been safe in Scotland until Queen Mary died and within a week of her death Kennedy sought an accommodation with Edward.[44]

The Scots had not been invited to attend the conference at St Omer. Nevertheless Kennedy told the Scottish Council that he knew what had been agreed there. King Louis had promised King Edward that if the King of Scotland refused to do homage to the King of England as he ought, Louis would abandon the 'Auld Alliance' and make common cause with the English king against the Scots.[45] This was a lie. The canny Louis would not have risked alienating his Scottish ally by promising to aid King Edward against King James.

On 5 December Edward issued a safe conduct for Kennedy and other Scottish envoys to meet him at York. Kennedy did not come in person, but Edward got what he wanted and conceded little in return. The Scots agreed to give no further aid to the Lancastrians once their current safe conducts expired and Edward would put a stop to the Earl of Douglas's raids across the Scottish border (by sending him to Ireland).[46] On 9 December the Scots signed a temporary truce to commence on 16 December on land and 1 February 1464 at sea, to last until 31 October 1464.[47] King Henry, who appears to have had little idea of what had happened, was forced to leave Scotland before the truce was signed, and he sought the protection of Sir Ralph Percy at Bamburgh Castle.[48]

30

Margaret in Exile

After she left Bruges, Margaret took up residence at Koeur near the town of St Mihiel in René's Duchy of Bar. René put the chateau at Koeur at Margaret's disposal and promised her an income of 6,000 écus a year.[1] Margaret was thirty-three, and for the next seven years Koeur would be her place of residence, if not her home. She maintained her status as Queen of England with a small court at Koeur. Here she was joined by John Courtenay, the self-styled Earl of Devon, and Thomas Butler, called Ormond, Doctor John Morton, Sir John Fortescue, the former chief justice and King Henry's chancellor in Scotland,[2] and Doctor Roger Mackerell.[3] Thomas Bird, Bishop of St Asaph, was one of the few bishops who remained loyal to King Henry. He came to Koeur after King Edward stripped him of his bishopric.[4]

Also at Koeur were Margaret's niece, Marie, the widowed Countess of Devon, Katherine Gatewyne, Sir Robert Whittingham's wife, and Katherine Penyson, who had married Sir William Vaux in 1456.[5] Edmund Hampden, Edmund Mountford, Robert Whittingham, Henry Roos and William Grimsby were Lancastrian servants of long standing; they had been in Tours with Margaret when she signed her treaty with King Louis in 1462.[6] Sir William Vaux probably entered Margaret's service following his marriage to Katherine Penyson.

The atmosphere was one of anxiety, alternating between hope and disappointment as the little band of exiles followed the shifts of political fortunes outside their control. What did the future hold, and would they ever see England again? Ever since the defeat at Towton

Margaret had been in denial. Through all her vicissitudes, and despite all her setbacks, she clung to her hope that somehow, in some way, Henry would recover his throne. She settled at Koeur and prepared to continue her search for allies. She was not unduly discouraged by the temporary truces between England and France, and England and Scotland – they would not last long. She was annoyed by the recognition of 'Edward of March' as King of England but knew how much Louis's word was worth; he would break his truce with Edward as soon as it suited him, just as he had with her.

The news that King Henry had been forced to leave Scotland was distressing. Margaret needed confirmation of the authorisation he had given her in 1462: she could not negotiate from a position of strength except in the King's name. She required an experienced diplomat, well-versed in foreign affairs, who could travel to Bamburgh in safety and for this an Englishman would not do. Fortunately for Margaret, King Louis wanted much the same thing from a different angle. He wanted to know how strong the resurgent Lancastrian party might be now that Henry was back on English soil and the Duke of Somerset had joined him. How many others might do so?

Louis offered Margaret the services of Guillaume Cousinot, the wily diplomat whom Margaret had first met during the abortive negotiations with King Charles for peace with France in the early years of her marriage. Cousinot left for England in January 1464 as Louis's emissary, possibly in the company of Jasper Tudor, who was at the French court.[7] Margaret sent her own messengers to tell Henry of her favourable reception by the Count of Charolais at Bruges, and the sympathy shown her by Duke Francis of Brittany. Cousinot's mission was to obtain information for King Louis, and to tell King Henry what Margaret wanted.[8] She believed that an alliance between Henry, the Count of Charolais, and the Duke of Brittany could restore Henry to the throne. It would enable Henry, or more probably Somerset, to put an army into the field. Henry instructed her to pursue the possibility and promised to endorse whatever bargain she might make.

Margaret in Exile

Somerset enthusiastically opted for military action. He told Cousinot that he knew of seventeen Welsh lords who could be counted on to raise rebellion in Wales, and that further support would come from other lords in the south and west of England.⁹ He thought he could raise enough men, but he needed artillery. Jasper Tudor wanted Margaret to send Cousinot, when he returned to France, to persuade the Duke of Brittany to furnish a small army – 1,000 or even 500 men would do – and presumably ships to transport them, so that Jasper could invade Wales. Simultaneous attacks from the north, the south-west, and Wales could turn the tide in Henry's favour. Henry told Cousinot that he had faith in his people: he was sure that they were loyal to him and would rise to accomplish his restoration.

Henry instructed Margaret to ask her father, René, to send culverins and cannoneers to Bamburgh, to request Charolais to supply victuals and artillery, and to persuade *anyone* she could think of to lend Henry money. Margaret also hoped that her father, together with Charolais and Brittany, would put pressure on other French nobles to prevent King Louis from following through on his commitment at Hesdin to reopen negotiations with King Edward for a longer truce or permanent peace. She seriously overestimated René's ability and his will to help her. He had little influence with King Louis, who had abandoned John of Calabria's effort to recover Naples.

Henry tried to bolster Margaret's endeavours by writing a fulsome and flattering letter for Cousinot to show to 'the King and Queen of Sicily', René and his wife, Jeanne de Laval. He thanked them for the good will they had shown him in the past (one wonders if Henry remembered that the Queen of Sicily was not Margaret's mother) and for René's 'kindness' to Margaret and Prince Edward. He hoped too that John of Calabria would 'continue' to favour him (although John is not known to have done so), and he repeated that the people of England wanted him back. He added that 'Edward of March' was now hated in England, and René must see that if he sent only a little help, *and persuaded King Louis to do likewise*, Edward would be prevented from launching the summer campaign against him that Henry feared he was planning!

In a second letter Henry instructed Cousinot to thank Duke Francis of Brittany for his courteous reception of Margaret and for his gifts to her. He acknowledged that Francis had helped him by sending a Breton supply ship to Kirkcudbright, and he promised Francis that if he recovered his kingdom by the mercy of God, he would repay Francis in whatever way Francis wished. The rest of Henry's letter is muddled and contradictory. Cousinot was to repeat the message sent to René – the people of England looked forward to Henry's return, but this could only be accomplished with the help of men and money that he was unable to obtain where he was. His life was in danger, and Francis, as a fellow prince, would surely understand his need for help. Henry listed the supplies he wanted, victuals (wheat, malt, wine, and salt) and some artillery, as well as hard cash, and he endorsed the request that Margaret was to make to Francis: if the Duke was unable to send ordnance to Bamburgh, he should entrust it to Jasper Tudor, together with men paid for a half year's service to invade Wales. Henry would repay Francis at some future date, and he would honour any agreement Margaret made with him.[10] Henry was out of touch with the real world. Did he write these instructions to Cousinot, or, as he had when he was in Warwick's custody, did he sign whatever was put before him by Somerset, Jasper, or other members of his entourage?

King Henry's court at Bamburgh, if such it can be called, was even smaller than Margaret's at Koeur. He had been joined by Lords Roos and Hungerford, Philip Wentworth, Richard Tunstall, Thomas Findhern, and William Tailboys. Henry Bellingham and Humphrey Neville of Westmorland had been pardoned by King Edward, but like Somerset they broke their oath and fled north as soon as they heard that Henry had left Scotland.[11] Somerset marshalled the forces at his disposal and led forays into the Tyne valley. He captured the small, largely undefended castle of Langley, the nearby tower at Hexham,

Bywell Castle, and possibly Skipton in Yorkshire.[12] These gains were of little strategic value and by the spring of 1464 Somerset had become impatient.

In April he got wind of a proposed conference between the Scots and King Edward and learned that John Neville, Lord Montague, would ride to Norham to meet the Scottish ambassadors and escort them south. Somerset sent Humphrey Neville with about eighty spearmen and archers to ambush Montague in a wooded area not far from Newcastle. Montague was far too seasoned a campaigner to travel through hostile country without a sizeable escort or without sending out scouts. He was warned and evaded the trap, but as he continued towards Norham Somerset's main force barred his way at Hedgeley Moor, about nine miles from Alnwick. Montague's seasoned retainers made short work of the Lancastrians. Somerset, Roos, Hungerford, Tunstall, and Findhern fled, but a Percy does not run away. Sir Ralph Percy died on the battlefield.[13]

Montague escorted the Scots from Norham to York without further incident, but he had had enough. It was time to teach Somerset a lesson. He returned to Newcastle to raise fresh troops and less than a month after the encounter at Hedgeley Moor Montague moved north once again. Somerset had fallen back towards Alnwick and his small army reached the tower at Hexham. His troops bivouacked in a low-lying meadow called Linnels, on the banks of the River Tyne. Montague caught up with them and the Battle of Hexham, fought on 15 May 1464, rapidly became a rout. Somerset was captured and Montague ordered his summary execution.

Henry Beaufort, Duke of Somerset, was only twenty-eight when he died. He was an indifferent soldier, with a poor grasp of strategy or tactics, but he had spent long periods of enforced inactivity in remote castles, first at Guines and then at Bamburgh. He was frustrated, he could see no future other than an endless wait for King Henry's fortunes to improve, and rather than endure the tedium any longer he unwisely chose to match himself against the far superior military skills of Lord Montague. In the end Somerset fell victim to his pride and his impetuosity. His decapitated body was buried in Hexham Priory.[14]

Lancastrian resistance to King Edward in the north was broken at Hexham and Montague showed no mercy. Lords Roos and Hungerford, Philip Wentworth, Thomas Findhern, and twenty-two others were beheaded on Montague's orders. The Earl of Worcester, Constable of England, tried and condemned the captives who were held at York, which threw a cloak of legality over the proceedings. William Tailboys was later discovered hiding in a coal pit not far from Newcastle with the Lancastrian war chest in his keeping, some 3,000 marks. Montague distributed the money among his soldiers and Tailboys was beheaded.[15] King Henry narrowly escaped capture. He had not been at Hexham, Somerset had left him at Bywell Castle, twelve miles from Newcastle, for safekeeping. When Montague and his men arrived at Bywell they discovered that Henry had been there, but he had fled, leaving his coroneted helmet and sword behind him.[16] There is no record of who rescued and hid him, and Montague had no idea where he was.

King Edward arrived at York in late May to greet the Scottish ambassadors and on 1 June they signed a truce to last for fifteen years. There was no longer any hope for the Lancastrians of further aid from Scotland. Edward granted the Percy title of Earl of Northumberland to Montague in recognition of his services, and he and the Earl of Warwick were named as conservators of the truce.[17] Warwick joined his brother and together they recovered two of the three remaining northern fortresses.[18]

Alnwick capitulated on 23 June, and Dunstanburgh a day later when Warwick offered terms. Warwick and Montague's force then appeared before Bamburgh and Warwick's heralds rode forward to offer a pardon and free passage to everyone within, except Ralph Grey and Humphrey Neville. Grey had escaped after Hexham and fled back to Bamburgh. Not surprisingly he refused Warwick's offer. He said he would rather die fighting, since that fate awaited him anyway if he

Margaret in Exile

surrendered. The heralds warned the defenders that Warwick and Montague were equipped to continue the siege indefinitely. They had three powerful cannons, but they wanted to avoid damaging Bamburgh's walls by firing heavy shot. If they were forced to use their artillery a member of the garrison would be hanged for every cannonball fired.

Grey ignored the threat, and Warwick ordered his cannoneers to open fire. Grey was injured in the bombardment, probably by falling masonry, and while he was unconscious Bamburgh surrendered. Grey was taken to Doncaster where the Earl of Worcester was on hand to try the 'disgraced' knight. Worcester castigated him for betraying the order of knighthood by repudiating his oath and turning traitor. He condemned Grey to the humiliation of being marched on foot to the edge of the town and from there dragged on a hurdle to his place of execution. King Edward had Grey's head set on London Bridge.[19]

Reports of these disasters reached Koeur by the autumn of 1464, and Margaret had the added anxiety of not knowing where King Henry was. She cast her net further afield and sent William Joseph on a mission to King Afonso V of Portugal.[20] England and Portugal had long been allies; Afonso and Henry VI were descendants of John of Gaunt, and Afonso was a Knight of the Garter.[21] Joseph was received courteously at the Portuguese court, and it was probably his visit that encouraged John Butler, the Earl of Ormond, to write to Margaret.

Ormond was no stranger to adversity. As a younger son he had been left as a hostage after Edmund Beaufort, Duke of Somerset, surrendered Rouen in 1449 and it was some years before his ransom was paid. He had joined Edmund's son, Henry Beaufort, in Guines Castle in 1460 and endured the long wait before he escaped to France and then to England with Beaufort. He fought at Towton and followed King Henry and Margaret into exile.[22] In 1462 he escaped to the Ormond estates in Ireland after he was attained by King Edward, and he foolishly resumed the clan warfare that was endemic there. Ormond was defeated at Pilltown by the Earl of Desmond, whom

Queen in Exile

Edward rewarded by appointing him Deputy Lieutenant of Ireland in 1463.[23] Ormond probably left Ireland after that and, with no resources left to him, he may have become a soldier of fortune and offered his sword and his services to King Afonso of Portugal, who was engaged in a war against the Muslims in North Africa.[24]

Ormond probably did not know that Margaret had established a court at Koeur until William Joseph's visit. He wrote to tell Margaret where he was, and how he had escaped to Portugal. He wanted to join Margaret and he asked her for a safe conduct to travel through France. Fortescue sent Margaret's safe conduct to him, but Fortescue was not sure that it would be honoured, as King Louis was not to be trusted. He suggested that Ormond's best bet was to get in touch with Pierre de Brezé, or failing him, to approach John de Foix, Earl of Kendal, who was now in King Louis's service, to obtain safe passage. Fortescue warned Ormond to bring whatever money he could with him since the court at Koeur was at subsistence level, but before he left Portugal Margaret wanted Ormond to approach King Afonso for military aid.

Fortescue drafted Margaret's instructions to Ormond and to Master Roger Tonge, who was with him at the Portuguese court. The eleven-year-old Prince Edward wrote a naïve letter to Ormond, 'written 'wᵗ myn awn hand, that ye may se how gode wrytare I am', although it was probably dictated by Fortescue. The boy prince thanked Ormond for his loyal support of King Henry in Ireland and asked him to do all he could to persuade the King of Portugal to help Henry recover this throne. Fortescue also composed a letter in Latin to Afonso for Prince Edward to sign. It flattered Afonso as a famous warrior who had enhanced the fame of the House of Lancaster. Edward said he planned to follow Afonso's example when he grew up. He also promised that when he reached his majority he would repay any services that King Afonso rendered to his family. He reminded Afonso of their close kinship and recounted the misfortunes that his father had suffered, despite being a virtuous king (a Fortescue touch),

Margaret in Exile

and he requested Afonso to give the Earl of Ormond an audience to learn more.[25]

Margaret's letter to Ormond has been lost, but her instructions reflect her thinking at this time.[26] Ormond was to thank the King of Portugal for his good will and for his favourable reception of William Joseph. She addressed Afonso as her cousin; she was sure that she could count on his aid in 'theire grettest and extreme necesssite' because he and King Henry were related and had long been allies. Margaret (or Fortescue) remembered that Afonso was a Knight of the Garter, although no one at Koeur could remember his name,[27] and she reminded Afonso that as a member of that select brotherhood, and because they were both Christian kings, they both had a duty to suppress rebellion (an argument that King Edward had used to James III). Margaret somewhat sententiously opined that rebellion threatened the security of the Church and was an affront to women (possibly because in war women were raped?).

Margaret was careful to emphasise that King Henry has not been captured: he was free and in good health. She claimed to have received letters from him and she repeated what Henry had said to Cousinot: the people of England wanted Henry back, but there was 'no grete lorde to be theire captayne' left in England who could rally the people to rise in Henry's favour. She needed to send Henry a force of about 3,000 well-equipped men, led by a competent captain who would find a welcome in certain parts of England where King Henry would join him. This would cost money, of course, but the Chancellor (Fortescue) held the Great Seal and could use it to bind Henry to repay all the expenses of an expedition, provided Margaret authorised it. After Henry was restored, England would become Portugal's ally and place the whole of the country's military resources at Afonso's disposal.

With her usual unfounded optimism Margaret asked Afonso to approach Frederick III, the Holy Roman Emperor, and King Enrique IV of Castile, both of whom were married to Afonso's sisters, to solicit

Queen in Exile

their aid for King Henry. She was aware that King Edward was trying to mend fences with Enrique and she wanted Afonso to put a stop to the negotiations.[28] She also hoped he would approach the Pope and the college of cardinals in Rome, as well as Spanish and French cardinals, for their support. Nor did she forget to include the Count of Charolais – Afonso should remind him of his kinship with the House of Lancaster.[29]

Margaret waxed lyrical: King Henry's restoration would guarantee perpetual peace between Spain, Portugal, and England, and they would present a united front against their enemies. It might even be possible for them collectively to conclude peace with France! How much of this pie in the sky came from Margaret and how much from Fortescue? They were both woefully out of touch with political realities outside their immediate circle, but the idea that restoring King Henry to the throne would result in perpetual peace and cooperation is simply ludicrous. If Margaret did indeed believe in these instructions, she was not just delusional, she was fantasising. We do not know what Ormond, or Afonso, would have made of them since they never reached Portugal. King Louis had spies everywhere and he kept a close eye on Margaret. Her messenger was intercepted by one of his agents and the correspondence ended up in French hands.[30]

Margaret may have been ignorant of politics outside her immediate orbit, but she was well informed of what was being said at the French and Burgundian courts. Astonishing news had reached France in October 1464: King Edward had made a clandestine marriage in May and managed to keep it secret from everyone, including the Earl of Warwick, until September.[31] Edward was the greatest prize in the marriage market, and Warwick had favoured a match with King Louis's sister-in-law, Bona of Savoy. But Edward had outgrown his mentor, if indeed he ever considered Warwick to be his mentor. It was not his marriage but his bride that astounded contemporaries in England and abroad.

Margaret in Exile

Elizabeth Woodville was the eldest daughter of Sir Richard Woodville and Jacquetta, Dowager Duchess of Bedford. She was older than Edward and a widow with two children. Her husband, Sir John Grey had been killed at St Albans in 1461 fighting for King Henry. Margaret was shocked, but she may have been pleased by Edward's mésalliance – he was obviously unworthy to be King of England. She could not know that in the years ahead Edward's marriage would upset the political balance of power in England to her advantage.[32] The gossips had a field day speculating on what might happen. King Louis declared that if there was a breach between Edward and Warwick, he would support the Earl.[33] But Louis had more pressing problems of his own.

The Count of Charolais and the Duke of Brittany had made common cause against him and called on other disaffected French nobles to join them.[34] Charolais was furious with Louis for taking advantage of the Duke of Burgundy's almost mystical devotion to the crown of France to induce him to surrender the Somme towns, and he feared further encroachments by Louis. Philip of Burgundy's ill health made it likely that Charolais would become duke sooner rather than later, and he was prepared to use every means at his disposal to thwart the French king. Louis had also attempted to intervene in Breton affairs: he claimed the right as King of France to appoint to ecclesiastical benefices in Brittany.[35] Duke Francis was fiercely protective of his duchy's independence and determined to defend it. They might not like the usurper Edward, but he was a better bet as a potential ally against Louis than Henry and Margaret.

Duke Francis wrote to King Edward that he wanted a truce, and while he would prefer to be able to offer asylum to Henry and Margaret, he would not to do so if that was a condition of achieving Edward's agreement.[36] Edward issued a safe conduct for a Breton envoy, William of Brittany, who was none other than the bastard son of the long dead Giles of Brittany, to visit England, ostensibly as a pilgrim to the shrine of St Thomas Becket at Canterbury. Edward also granted a safe conduct to an emissary from Charolais. Negotiations with Breton envoys continued in England throughout the summer of 1464, and in August Edward authorised the Earl of Worcester to conclude a one-year truce with Brittany, to begin on 1 October 1464.[37]

John of Calabria returned to Lorraine from Italy in 1464, and he and René visited Margaret at Koeur.[38] In December John set his seal to a treaty of alliance with Charolais and Brittany, and Margaret, who still believed them to be her allies, thought they would join forces and come to her aid. Margaret had construed Charolais's reception of her, and the admiration Duke Francis had expressed for her courage, to mean that they meant to assist her materially. It was all wishful thinking. Restoring King Henry was never a priority for anyone, even her own family. The pact with Charolais and Brittany had nothing to do with Margaret and everything to do with John's resentment of King Louis, who had abandoned John and his efforts to take Naples.[39] The Angevins were divided: René and his brother Charles, Count of Maine, were loyal to Louis.

Charolais and Brittany stirred up other French nobles who resented Louis's interference in what they saw as their prerogatives. Margaret would not have sympathised with rebellious nobles but with her usual single-mindedness she hoped to turn the situation to her advantage. In January 1465 she wrote to King Louis that with so many of his princes preparing for conflict, Louis should direct the rebels' attention towards England. If Louis refused, she would approach the dissidents herself without his endorsement, as she believed that they would be prepared to help her. Louis showed her letter to the Milanese ambassador with the comment 'Look how proudly she writes.'[40] This was not an expression of admiration but of exasperation. Louis faced the threat of a second Praguerie, the coalition of French princes who had opposed his father almost thirty years before. Did she really expect him to encourage them to come together under the pretext of invading England?

The Duke of Berry, Louis's younger brother and heir, joined the

Margaret in Exile

dissidents as their figurehead. On 13 March, the Duke of Bourbon issued a manifesto, the League of the Public Weal, declaring that the princes had taken up arms to curb King Louis and prevent him from becoming a tyrant.[41] Louis moved to René's town of Saumur and in April René joined him and swore a personal oath reaffirming his loyalty to King Louis against all comers. According to the Milanese ambassador Louis was sceptical.[42]

Louis planned to defeat the Leaguers one by one before they had time to join forces and work out a strategy. He failed. By July Charolais was at Étampes with an army and Edmund Beaufort, Duke of Somerset since Hexham, was among his recruits.[43] The two sides clashed at the Battle of Montlhéry on 16 July 1465, midway between Étampes and Paris.[44] René held aloof; he had been defeated too often in Italy to have any taste for battle. John of Calabria arrived too late, but the Count of Maine was with Louis on the battlefield.[45] At a critical moment, just as it looked as if the royal army had won, the Count of Maine quit the field.[46] The result was a stalemate. Pierre de Brezé, as feisty as ever, led the royal vanguard alongside his old comrade in arms, Robert Floquet. They were both killed.[47] Louis retreated to defend Paris while the Leaguers regrouped at Étampes and prepared to lay siege to him.

31

Years of Exile

Margaret was saddened by the death of her old friend Brezé but worse was to follow. King Henry had been in hiding in the north of England for over a year since the Battle of Hexham; he was probably passed from household to household and moved on each time it was rumoured that he might be in the area. He was under the protection of his chamberlain, Sir Richard Tunstall, who had fled with him to Scotland and remained with him for at least part of the time. As a king's esquire Tunstall had brought Henry the news of Margaret's pregnancy in 1453. John Bedon, a Doctor of Divinity, and Thomas Manning, Henry's secretary and Dean of Windsor, who had approached Margaret many years before on behalf of his brother Alexander, the keeper of Newgate, were Henry's companions in his wanderings.[1]

In July 1465 they were being sheltered by Sir Richard Tempest at Waddington Hall in Yorkshire. We do not know how long Henry had been there but long enough for word to spread through the family. Sir Richard's sister, Alice, had married the young Sir Thomas Talbot of Bashall, another local family. As Henry sat at dinner with his host, Talbot and his cousin forced their way into the house.[2] The chronicler Waurin has the story that Richard Tunstall drew his sword and held off the would-be captors long enough for Henry to escape to the stables and ride for safety into a wood near Clitheroe.[3] While he was attempting to cross the River Ribble, over a stepping-stone ford at Bungerly Hippingstones, Henry's pursuers caught up with him. He

Years of Exile

was captured on 13 July 1465. Bedon, Manning, and a squire named Elleston were captured with him. Sir James Harrington, whose father and brother had been killed at Wakefield fighting for York, escorted Henry and his party south.[4] As usual Henry offered no resistance.

The Earl of Warwick met them at Islington and took Henry into custody just as he had after the Battle of Northampton five years earlier, but this time he paraded the passive king through London via Newgate and Cheapside to the Tower, with his legs bound beneath his horse's girth in token of his captivity.[5] Henry was incarcerated in the Tower, but he was not ill-treated; anyone who wished could visit him. A delighted and relieved King Edward wanted the Londoners to witness that at long last Henry was his prisoner, but Edward was careful not to make Henry into a martyr or rouse the peoples' sympathy for him; while Prince Edward was alive it would be counterproductive to have him executed. Edward authorised enough money to keep Henry in comfort; he was attended by two squires and two yeomen as well as other servants, and Edward even paid 7½d a day for a priest to say mass for him.[6] Henry may have found his lodging in the Tower more congenial, and more comfortable, than being a fugitive in the north.

The news of his capture reached Margaret sometime in August. She was back on square one. She would have to rescue Henry before she could restore him to the throne. This posed a more daunting task than it had in 1461, but Margaret thought she saw an opportunity in the aftermath of the Battle of Montlhéry. King Louis held Paris. The Leaguers forces were gathered outside the capital, but they were at odds as to what to do next. For three months Louis cajoled them and undermined their commitment to each other by his preferred method of bribery. While Louis was engaged in these delicate and to him degrading negotiations, Margaret arrived in Paris. She suggested to Louis that now was the time for him to unite France by declaring war on England. The princes of the League were not interested, and Louis had no time or patience to waste on her. He was bribing everyone right and left, so he bribed her too. He promised her a pension of four or five thousand francs, provided she left Paris and returned to Koeur. He gave her 400 *livres tournois* for the expenses of her journey, and he had already given Sir John Fortescue 275 *livres* to enable him to visit England, possibly to ascertain details of King Henry's captivity.[7] There is no evidence that Fortescue went; the money could be put to better use at Koeur.

The War of the Public Weal had engendered mistrust on all sides. For King Louis the Count of Charolais was, and would remain, public enemy number one. Charolais looked around for potential allies against Louis, and although he was not keen on an alliance with England, he approached King Edward, who had so far held aloof from France's internal squabbles. Charolais was a widower and his major inducement to Edward was his offer to marry Edward's youngest sister, Margaret. A dynastic link with Burgundy would mean Burgundian acknowledgement of the House of York and of Edward as the rightful King of England. Furthermore, there would be no possibility that Charolais would aid Queen Margaret. King Henry was safely locked away in the Tower, but Edward still feared Margaret.

Edward commissioned Warwick, Lord Hastings, and Lord Wenlock to meet with the Burgundians and he instructed Warwick to get the best deal he could.[8] While negotiating for the marriage of Margaret of York, Warwick was to propose a marriage for Edward's brother and heir presumptive, George, Duke of Clarence, with Charolais's only child, Mary of Burgundy.[9] This was not to Warwick's liking: he had no son, and he had his eye on Clarence as a suitable husband for his daughter, Isabel. Warwick met Charolais in person at Boulogne in April 1466, but the talks broke down through their mutual antipathy.[10]

King Louis was not the only one who could play a double game; King Edward was good at it too. At the same time as he sent Warwick to meet the Burgundians, he invited King Louis to send representatives to Calais. Warwick broke off the talks with Burgundy and returned to Calais to meet King Louis's delegation. They were far more receptive, and they agreed to a temporary truce to last to the beginning of 1468.[11]

Edward and Warwick were seriously at odds over whether England should ally with Burgundy or with France. Warwick was the elder statesman, Edward was only twenty-four, and thus far Warwick had conducted England's foreign policy. Warwick favoured peace with France; war was expensive and unnecessary. Warwick had warned Edward against invading Scotland in 1462 and he advised against Edward's pet scheme of invading France for the same reason – England could not afford it. Pierre de Brezé had once warned King Louis that if he wished to be popular, he would not make friends with the English, and Edward understood that the reverse was true, something that Warwick failed to grasp. It was probably an impossibility anyway. Edward styled himself King of France and referred to Louis in his official correspondence as 'our adversary of France'. Louis would undoubtedly demand that Edward give up this claim in any peace negotiations (as indeed he did) but Edward would never do so. Edward enjoyed posing as a warrior king and he thought it more profitable and more enjoyable to threaten France. Peace with the ancient enemy would not go down well in England and he was working towards an alliance with Burgundy, Brittany, and Castile against Louis.[12] Edward ignored Warwick and renewed negotiations with Charolais in 1467.[13]

Although he had made up his mind, Edward kept his options open. He issued safe conducts for French ambassadors to come to England.[14] They carried proposals from King Louis designed to entice Edward to abandon all thought of an Anglo–Burgundian alliance and marriage. The big inducement was Louis's offer to pay Edward an annual pension of 4,000 *écus* to sustain their alliance and to open commercial avenues and markets in France to compensate for the loss of English trade with Burgundy. Louis would arrange a marriage for Margaret of York with Galeazzo Sforza, the new Duke of Milan, or with the French queen's brother, Philip of Savoy. Louis would furnish Margaret with a suitable dowry and pay the expenses of an elaborate wedding. It was a generous offer, designed to bribe the impecunious Edward, but it was not enough: Edward wanted the Burgundian alliance.[15] Louis did not recognise this. He claimed he had a secret understanding with Edward through the Earl of Warwick, who may have promised what he could not perform. Louis told the Milanese ambassador that Edward had written to him 'in his own hand, something he never does'. Tongue in cheek, Edward commissioned Warwick and John Wenlock to go to France to treat for peace, partly to get Warwick out of the way during the expected visit of a Burgundian embassy.[16]

King Louis always had more than one string to his bow and the first intimation that he might try to use the Earl of Warwick and the importunate Margaret as levers to undermine King Edward came in February 1467 through Margaret's brother, John of Calabria. John had sided with the Leaguers and although he missed the Battle of Montlhéry he had been loud in his demands that Louis supply him with an army to enable him to renew his war to recover Naples. Louis bought him off with a promise of money and certain territorial rights, but no army.[17] They settled their differences and in 1466 Louis welcomed John back to court. According to the Milanese ambassador, who may or may not have been present, John and Louis dined together early in 1467 and the devious Louis introduced Warwick's name into their conversation to gauge the Angevins' reaction.

Louis told John that he held Warwick in high esteem, but John called Warwick a traitor. Louis continued to praise Warwick and John lost his temper. He said roundly that rather than admiring Warwick, who was responsible for King Henry and Margaret losing their throne, Louis would do better to restore them. Louis replied that Warwick had advised him (and presumably King Edward) *against* making war with France, whereas King Henry had been his enemy and had waged war against him many times. (Surely a Milanese exaggeration?) Somewhat sarcastically John said that if Louis thought so highly of Warwick, but

Years of Exile

was not so sure of Edward, why not urge Warwick to restore Margaret? In that way Louis would be doubly sure of England as an ally. Louis pretended to be surprised. He asked what security the Angevins would give for such an enterprise. Would they, for example, agree to hand Prince Edward over to him as a hostage? And would they and the Prince (who was not yet fourteen) keep their promises? John replied heatedly that if his nephew gave his word, he would keep it or he would have him, John, to reckon with. John would 'fly at him and tear his eyes out!' (A piece of Milanese hyperbole?) As far as is known this was John of Calabria's one and only attempt to aid his sister.

The restoration of the House of Lancaster was an unimportant sideshow; John had his sights set on a far more glittering prize. He was about to leave for Barcelona, the capital of Catalonia. The independently minded Catalans had rebelled against King John II of Aragon and offered the Kingdom of Aragon, which was not theirs to give, to none other than the René of Anjou, whose mother Yolande had been the daughter of King John I of Aragon. Catalonia bordered René's County of Provence. René was too old to go himself, but he loved titles and he could not resist the lure of another one. He accepted the Catalan's offer and named his son John as his lieutenant general to go in his stead, just as he had once named his wife Isabelle to go to Naples in search of another ephemeral crown with about as much chance of long-term success. John would get a new title too: the heir to the throne of Aragon was known as the Prince of Gerona and he traditionally ruled Catalonia. John hoped to raise an army among the Catalans to pursue his dream of returning to Italy and conquering Naples. It took time to assemble an army and John did not reach Barcelona until the end of August 1467.[18]

Louis was looking forward to meeting Warwick, and while waiting for Warwick to arrive he followed up on the idea of involving Margaret in his schemes. It would be useful to test the waters. He sent Nicholas of Lorraine, John of Calabria's son and Margaret's nephew, to invite Margaret to join the court at Chartres. Her brother-in-law Ferry de Vaudemont was to escort her, but neither Nicholas nor Ferry told her the reason for the invitation. Louis wanted to discuss a reconciliation between Margaret and the Earl of Warwick before the Earl arrived. Ever since the defeat at Towton Margaret had striven by every means at her disposal to recover the throne, but there were lengths to which she would not go, and a reconciliation with Warwick was one of them. After the Duke of York's death at Wakefield, Warwick had become Margaret's bitterest enemy.

She refused Louis's invitation and sent Sir John Fortescue, who had no scruples, to find out exactly what Louis had in mind. It was probably at this time that Fortescue presented one of his many memoranda to Guillaume Juvenal des Ursins, the Chancellor of France, setting out the reasons why King Edward 'can in no way claim the said crowns of France and of England'. Fortescue averred that there would never be peace between the two countries as long as King Edward sat on the throne, but if King Henry was restored (and Edward was forced to accept this whether liked it or not) Louis could be sure of perpetual peace, which was more or less what Louis had in mind.[19]

Did Margaret know that Louis had suggested to John of Calabria that the Prince of Wales might become a hostage in such a scheme? Edward was the most important piece in Margaret's game of diplomatic chess and central to her plans. She had associated his name with all her political decisions and actions from the time she dismissed his governess in 1460. Margaret had groomed Edward to become Regent for his father, but she was not raising him to be a warrior prince. She entrusted his education to John Fortescue, the former chief justice of England and her legal advisor, who whiled away the tedium of his time at Koeur by writing and revising legal questions and answers on how England should be governed, while instructing the Prince in the intricacies of English law *ad nauseum*.[20] If Fortescue inflicted his work on the young prince it is no wonder that Edward

Years of Exile

occasionally rebelled against it. On the other hand, Fortescue's dialogue may be a literary conceit to air his pedantic views, with the Prince as a notional sounding board.

Fortescue was not Edward's only preceptor. The ageing George Ashby, Margaret's clerk of the signet from the time she came to England, had been arrested after Towton. While in prison he developed a facility for writing poetry and in 1463 he was among the small fry that King Edward released. He made his way to Margaret's court at Koeur and wrote a treatise, the *Active Policy of a Prince*, to supplement Fortescue's instructions. It advised Edward on how he should rule England and avoid his father's mistakes.[21] Ashby's theme reinforced Margaret's repeated assertion that the usurper occupying the English throne should be overthrown and the rightful heir restored.

All his life Edward had been instructed that he must never forget that he would succeed his father, whom he scarcely remembered, as King of England. He had been told that King Henry had lost his throne through the wiles of wicked men, who would someday be punished. From the age of seven Edward's life had been unsettled and insecure. He had fled with Margaret from England to Wales, from Wales to Scotland and then to the Netherlands and finally to a more settled, but boring, existence at Koeur. Unquestioning obedience to his mother was part of his life. It is not surprising that as a teenager he preferred military training to book-learning. Or that he boasted that when he was king he would have his revenge by cutting off the heads of all those who had rebelled against his father and driven his mother into exile, and he would become as renowned a warrior as the King of Portugal.[22] His model was probably his uncle John of Calabria, who told him stories of his exploits in Italy, and if John did not, the servants at Koeur surely would have.

Warwick arrived in Rouen in June 1467; Louis welcomed him with splendid gifts and elaborate banquets, as though he were indeed King of England.[23] It seems unlikely that Louis raised the possibility of an

Queen in Exile

alliance between Warwick and Margaret at this time, but with Louis one never knows. He may have suggested to Warwick that if the situation went from bad to worse in England there *was* an alternative. Warwick would certainly have heard gossip to this effect – the Milanese ambassador for one was agog at the idea. Warwick was far too shrewd to respond to what, even to him, would have seemed a staggering suggestion, but the seeds had been sown.

King Edward continued to court the Burgundians. Anthony, Bastard of Burgundy, one of Duke Philip's illegitimate sons, was renowned for his skill in jousting. King Edward invited him to England to take part in a tournament and pit himself against Anthony Woodville, whose father, Richard Woodville, had been a noted jouster in his day; he had been Queen Margaret's champion during the jousts to celebrate her coronation.[24] Anthony followed in his father's footsteps. It was supposed to be a purely social occasion but behind the pageantry and pomp secret talks with Charolais's envoys continued. The feasting in France and merry-making in England ended abruptly when Duke Philip of Burgundy died on 15 June 1467. He had been ill for some years and his death was often anticipated, but Duke Philip remained a powerful figure to the end. It was only after his death that the Count of Charolais, now Charles the Bold, Duke of Burgundy, could proceed unhindered with proposals for a marriage alliance with the House of York.

Warwick returned to England, accompanied by a French embassy to put Louis's second set of proposals to King Edward.[25] If Louis's terms, as outlined in his letter to Galeazzo Sforza, the new Duke of Milan, are an accurate reflection of Louis's expectations then the usually canny king was being wildly over-optimistic: King Edward would agree to give up his claim to the throne of France and Edward's younger brother the Duke of Gloucester (who was Warwick's ward) would marry Louis's daughter Jeanne, 'because the first (the Duke of Clarence) is married to the Earl of Warwick's daughter' (possibly 'is pledged to'?). As soon as the agreement was signed Louis and Edward would declare war on Burgundy and Jeanne's dowry would be Burgundy's territories of Holland, Zeeland, and Brabant. Philip of Savoy, the Queen of France's brother, would marry Margaret of York. Philip of Savoy was already collecting forces for the coming war, but Galeazzo was not to worry: Louis would continue to favour him and protect his interests. There was nothing in Louis's proposals to which Warwick might object. Louis's mistake was to believe that if Warwick accepted them so would King Edward.[26]

A great deal changed in England during Warwick's absence. The Nevilles were gradually being displaced at the centre of English politics. To his subsequent regret, Edward had created Chancellor George Neville as Archbishop of York after William Booth died in 1464, and the Nevilles were riding high. George had been enthroned in a magnificent and costly ceremony in September 1465, and Edward could not dismiss him. The Chancellorship was another matter. On 8 June in the midst of entertaining the Burgundians, Edward dismissed George as Chancellor of England and replaced him with Robert Stillington, Bishop of Bath and Wells, Keeper of the Privy Seal, and a member of Edward's negotiating team with Burgundy.[27]

Edward allotted the lodging that the Burgundians had just vacated to the French ambassadors, but he declined to discuss their proposals and he mendaciously promised to send another embassy to Louis with his reply. There was no point to their remaining and Warwick eventually escorted them back to their ships. They sailed for France to complain to King Louis that they had been ignored. Louis was angry and disappointed; Warwick had failed in his undertaking to persuade King Edward to make peace with France. Warwick was angry and humiliated. Edward's refusal to listen to the French proposals had caused him to lose face, and he had other reasons for his resentment. George Neville's dismissal as Chancellor would inevitably diminish Neville influence in council. Edward now favoured the Woodvilles, whom Warwick despised, and he had concluded a treaty with Burgundy behind Warwick's back. Most serious of all, Edward refused

Queen in Exile

to countenance what Warwick had taken for granted, the marriage of his daughter Isabel to Edward's brother and heir presumptive, George, Duke of Clarence.[28]

The news that an angry Warwick had left court delighted King Louis and he jumped to the conclusion that the breach with King Edward was permanent. Why else would Warwick have gone north except to raise troops? There might be war in England![29] Louis jubilantly revived the idea that Queen Margaret and the Lancastrian loyalists waiting in the wings at Koeur could be used in conjunction with Warwick to threaten King Edward and prevent him from finalising the Anglo-Burgundian marriage.

Margaret was still at Koeur. She followed the ebb and flow of these diplomatic exchanges apprehensively. None of them offered her any comfort, and the anxiety made her ill. She suffered under the constant strain of not knowing what might happen next. Pope Pius II, who had believed the lies about Margaret fed to him by the Earl of Warwick, was dead and Margaret looked to his successor, Pope Paul, for spiritual consolation and absolution. In a petition to the Pope she confessed that she had sought God's intervention and mercy during her many trials, and that she had vowed to fast four or five times a week but had been unable to keep her vow, due partly to the circumstances of her life and partly to ill health. She asked permission to eat 'milk meats', i.e. dairy food, on days when they were forbidden by the Church, because she could obtain the forbidden butter more easily than the scarce and expensive, but permitted, olive oil. Margaret's piety contributed to her sense of guilt. Failure to keep holy vows was a spiritual sin and during King Henry's first illness she had prayed for his recovery and vowed that if he lived, she would go on pilgrimage to holy shrines, but she had not fulfilled this vow either. If Margaret was fasting regularly, or starving herself by eating too little every day, it is no wonder she was not well.

The Vatican chancery issued an indult permitting her to relax her dietary regime even during Lent. A second indult catalogued standard 'crimes', most of which can hardly have applied to Margaret (including failure to go on crusade), for which plenary remission of sins and absolution could be given by a priest authorised by the Vatican, provided Margaret repented and demonstrated her penitence in tangible form. She must replace her broken vows and appease God by offering a suitable payment to the Church.[30] The authoritarian Pope Paul had no interest in an exiled queen – he would not have seen her letters – but presumably the indults eased Margaret's conscience if not her circumstances. It was probably as close to despair as Margaret ever came.

The chateau at Koeur underwent extensive renovations in the summer of 1467 to make its inhabitants more comfortable. Either René, or possibly King Louis with an eye to the future, footed the bill. Margaret had always loved large windows; the sixteen windows in the great hall were replaced, other windows were repaired, and the principal rooms were refurbished. The exterior stonework was strengthened. Fresh fish were released into the moat, which may have helped to supplement Margaret's diet.[31]

King Louis, exasperated by King Edward's conduct, gave Margaret some hope that he had not lost all interest in her. Louis decided to stir up trouble in Wales. William Herbert had subdued most of Wales in King Edward's name, but Harlech Castle was still held for Lancaster by its loyal constable, David ap Eynon.[32] At King Louis's instigation, Margaret sent a messenger to Harlech carrying letters from her to the garrison. The 'followers' that the Milanese ambassador reported Margaret would send to Harlech, if they existed, may have been promised to her by King Louis – she had few able-bodied men at Koeur, and no money to send them anywhere. Margaret's courier never made it. He was intercepted by the always-vigilant Lord Herbert, who sent him and his letters to King Edward in London. Under interrogation the terrified man professed to know that there was widespread treason in England, and he repeated what he had heard in France, that the Earl of Warwick was said to have sympathy for King Henry. Warwick did not deign to return to London to answer such a flimsy accusation but King Edward, perhaps to warn Warwick not to step out of line, sent the man to Warwick for further questioning. Warwick's presence alone was enough to make the wretched courier retract his statement and nothing more is heard of him.[33]

The diplomat spy, Sir William Moneypenny, now in Louis's service, came to England at the end of 1467 accompanied by Warwick's secretary, Robert Neville. In January 1468 Moneypenny reported to Louis that Warwick was still in the north and had refused to attend Council. He was consulting with his brother Lord Montague and he would defend himself if King Edward marched against him. It was not true, but it was precisely what Louis wanted to hear. Moneypenny also reported that Lord Wenlock had told him of the rumour that Prince Edward would marry one of Louis's daughters, and that this was causing alarm in London.[34] It is not improbable that it originated with something Louis himself had said to Wenlock, or even to Warwick. There is no evidence that Louis ever seriously considered this, or that he suggested it to Margaret. Louis was a past master at disinformation and Margaret was a pawn in Louis's diplomatic games.

The Last Years

32

Warwick's Apostacy

From the time he usurped the throne, King Edward had insisted on his title as King of France, and he had threatened periodically that one day he would recover the inheritance that King Henry had lost. By 1468 he felt secure enough to renew his threat. Chancellor Stillington's opening speech to Parliament on 17 May announced that the King had concluded truces with most of the princes of Europe except for the King of France. Impressed by these somewhat vainglorious claims, Parliament granted Edward a substantial war tax.[1]

Louis countered Edward's threat by encouraging Margaret, who did not need much urging, to make contact with wealthy men in London and solicit contributions to a Lancastrian war chest. He also offered to finance an expedition for an over-eager Jasper Tudor to return to Wales. No matter how many times William Herbert defeated him and forced him to flee, Jasper Tudor remained unshaken in his conviction that given sufficient men and money he could invade Wales and recover it for King Henry. Perhaps the periodic local revolts in that unruly country sustained his belief, just as it had the Duke of Somerset's, that the Welsh were King Henry's partisans.

Sir John Fortescue wrote a memorandum advising Louis on how best to threaten King Edward and he offered to demonstrate how easy it would be for Louis to dethrone Edward and re-establish King Henry. It would not even cost very much! Fortescue said he dared not put his advice in writing in case it fell into the wrong hands, but 'these things he will reveal to the King or to his deputies when it is his royal pleasure.'[2]

Fortescue may have heard that some London merchants were beginning to wonder if they had backed the wrong horse. Edward was proving to be more expensive than King Henry and with about as little to show for it. Hope revived for the exiles at Koeur and Sir Robert Whittingham sent a servant named Cornelius into England. Cornelius was searched when he landed and found to be carrying letters from Koeur, among them a letter from Whittingham himself.[3] Any suggestion of a conspiracy involving Margaret always alarmed King Edward. He had Cornelius arrested and sent to the Tower, where he was tortured by having red hot irons applied to his feet. The use of torture to extract confessions was almost unknown in England; it had never been used by the Lancastrian kings, but that did not bother Edward.[4] He needed to know urgently if there was a conspiracy, and if there was, just how widespread was it?[5] Cornelius accused several men, including a servant of Lord Wenlock's, of plotting treason. This was worrying, for Wenlock was Warwick's man and it was only a few months since Warwick had been suspected of looking favourably on King Henry. A flurry of arrests followed Cornelius's revelations and among those suspected was Sir Thomas Cook, the wealthiest merchant in London, a former mayor, and Edward's go-to man when the King wanted to raise loans in the City.

A jury refused to indict the accused for lack of evidence and a more compliant set of jurors was empanelled in early July. They too refused to convict Cook of anything more serious than misprision of treason, of having concealed knowledge of a conspiracy, which carried the penalty of a fine but not a death sentence.[6] Edward set Cook's fine at 8,000 marks, a welcome bonus for the cash-strapped king. It is unlikely that Edward wanted Cook convicted on a more serious charge – Cook was too useful – but he may have been more heavily involved with Lancastrian conspirators than could be proved.

King Louis hated to waste money and Jasper had to make do with only a small force of three ships and some fifty men.⁷ He landed at Barmouth, just south of Harlech, at the end of June. Harlech Castle was the last stronghold in Wales still being held for King Henry and Jasper did not attempt to relieve it; with only fifty men it would have been impossible. Instead, he marched north calling on disaffected local men to join him and proclaiming in King Henry's name that he had come to liberate Wales.⁸ Edward automatically associated Margaret's name with any invasion threat and in July he ordered Lord William Herbert and Walter Devereaux 'to array the men of the counties of Gloucester, Hereford and Salop, the marches of Wales and parts adjacent, against Margaret, wife of the late king, and Jasper, late Earl of Pembroke and other rebels.'⁹ Jasper sacked and burned the Yorkist town of Denbigh, which had given him trouble in the past, but revenging himself by destroying Denbigh was hardly the way to win Welshmen over to the House of Lancaster. Jasper's 'invasion' was short lived.

An army under Lord Herbert's brother defeated his motley force and once again Jasper fled the field. He went into hiding and escaped back to France. Edward added the final touch to Jasper's humiliation when he bestowed Jasper's Earldom of Pembroke on Herbert.¹⁰ David ap Eyron, the captain of the garrison who had held Harlech against the odds for so long, lost all hope of relief in the face of this latest broken promise and on 14 August 1468 Harlech surrendered. Sir Richard Tunstall, who had left King Henry in the north, was among those taken prisoner and William Herbert sent him and the other defenders to King Edward in London.¹¹

There was speculation at the French court that Margaret would come in person to urge Louis to send further aid to Jasper and that John of Calabria would help her to persuade the King.¹² John had been in Barcelona for less than a year, striving to establish his supremacy against the King of Aragon, but in the summer of 1468 Louis had ordered him to return to France. Louis was negotiating the tricky business of rescinding the grant of the Duchy of Normandy that he had made to his brother, the feckless Duke of Berry. Berry was under the protection of Duke Francis of Brittany and Francis was a tough nut to crack. He had stationed Breton troops in Norman towns in Berry's name, and Louis hoped to recover them by negotiation, but Francis refused to meet with any of Louis's representatives except John of Calabria.

Whether this was to frustrate Louis, since John was in Spain, or whether Francis trusted his former companion in arms was anyone's guess, including Louis's. Francis thought he could defy Louis or drive a harder bargain because the King of England was his ally, and under the terms of their agreement Edward was committed to sending troops to defend Brittany against French aggression.[13] It was the perfect opportunity for Edward to keep his promise to Parliament and declare war on France, but Edward was as slippery as Louis. Troops intended for France did not muster until mid-September and by that time Duke Francis, despairing of English aid, and knowing he was no match for King Louis if war came, had capitulated. Francis signed the truce of Ancenis with Louis on 10 September 1468.[14]

Louis informed the credulous Milanese ambassador that as a reward for John of Calabria's services he would equip seven ships in Rouen and put them at Margaret's disposal.[15] Louis was quite capable of making such a gesture, except that the ships would not sail. John of Calabria had no time or inclination to become involved in his sister's plight. During his absence in Catalonia a vicious local war over disputed territory had broken out with the Marshall of Burgundy and John had his hands full defending his Duchy of Lorraine.[16]

King Edward believed the rumour that Margaret and her son were at Harfleur assembling an army, just as Louis intended him to. The English army was under the command of Walter Blount, who had abandoned Margaret's service for of that of the Duke of York long before most men had been forced to take sides. Blount had risen steadily in Edward's service, and in 1465 he became Lord Mountjoy and married Margaret's old friend Anne, the Dowager Duchess of

Buckingham. Anthony Woodville, another defector from Lancaster, commanded the English fleet.[17] Edward ordered him and Lord Mountjoy to put to sea and intercept Margaret instead of invading France. They patrolled the Channel until the end of November looking for Margaret and her fictious flotilla, achieving nothing except a waste of money.[18]

The men in England suspected of Lancastrian sympathies were arrested. Henry Courtenay, the younger brother of the self-styled Earl of Devon who was with Margaret at Koeur, and Thomas Hungerford, the son of Robert Hungerford, killed at Hexham, were obvious targets and they were imprisoned at Salisbury to await the King's pleasure. They were condemned and executed early in 1469 for conspiring to assist Margaret to invade England. King Edward attended their trial.[19]

The young Earl of Oxford was incarcerated in the Tower. King Edward had treated him generously, restoring his estates and his title, but Oxford was unreconciled. Edward had executed his father and brother for plotting with Margaret in 1462. Oxford bought his freedom at the price of betraying others and he implicated another lifelong servant of King Henry, Thomas Tresham, whom Edward had attainted and then pardoned. Tresham was arrested and left to languish in prison. Richard Steres, a London merchant and a former client of the Duke of Exeter, was charged with conveying letters from Margaret to her friends in England. He and two others, said to have been in touch with the Duke of Somerset while they were in Bruges for Margaret of York's wedding, were executed without trial at the end of November 1468. Margaret probably was in touch with some if not all of them, but they were in no position to threaten Edward seriously or to offer tangible aid to Margaret – they were too few. Margaret's only real chance of invading England was with the backing of King Louis, and although she did not know it, this was about to become a reality.

Edward's fixation on Margaret and Lancastrian conspiracies distracted him from a real threat, his growing unpopularity. Perhaps he refused to see it; he was the Rose of Rouen, the handsome, charismatic king who had swept to the throne on a tidal wave of popularity. But by 1469 that tide had receded. Warwick on the other hand, remained popular with the people and he conceived the idea of threatening one brother with another. Edward's policy of courting the Duke of Burgundy, and marrying his sister Margaret of York to Burgundy, did not meet with Warwick's approval. Although he appeared to be serving the King he was looking to the future – his future.

Warwick had no son, and only two daughters. He always planned to marry his elder daughter, Isabel, to Edward's brother George, Duke of Clarence, an alliance that would bring him as close as possible to the throne. Edward prohibited the match, which added to Warwick's grievances, and Warwick worked in secret for months to obtain a papal dispensation. When it finally arrived Warwick crossed to Calais, taking his brother George Neville, the Archbishop of York, the Duke of Clarence, and Isabel with him. On 11 July 1469, the Archbishop performed the marriage ceremony.[20] Warwick had laid his plans with care. He suborned Clarence with a promise that he would capture Edward and take over the direction of the government. Clarence would be granted increased estates and given a more important role than his brother had ever allowed him. Warwick did not doubt that he could capture a king for a second time, but just to be sure he arranged for a 'spontaneous' rising of his retainers in the north to coincide with his return to England. He relied on his popularity, especially in Kent, to rally people to him. Warwick and Clarence issued a manifesto similar to the one the Yorkist lords had promulgated against King Henry in 1460. It drew the analogy of what happened to weak kings who surrounded themselves with evil councillors and oppressed the people with heavy taxation – they were deposed.[21]

Warwick and Clarence crossed from Calais to Canterbury and marched on London, just as Warwick had in 1460. King Edward was slow to move. He had not grasped, or he refused to believe, that Warwick could be behind the rising in the north, led by a captain

The Last Years

calling himself Robin of Redesdale. Unrest in Yorkshire earlier in the year had been put down by Warwick's brother John, now Earl of Northumberland, but this time John did not take the field. Edward went north and established his headquarters in the stronghold of Nottingham Castle, but instead of summoning his magnates and issuing commissions of array, he called on William Herbert, now Earl of Pembroke, and Humphrey Stafford, whom he had just created Earl of Devon, to raise an army in Wales and the West Country.[22] The northern rebels bypassed Nottingham and got as far south as Edgecote, near Bambury, when they unexpectedly encountered Herbert and Stafford's forces. Stafford withdrew with his men and Herbert's Welshmen were left to take the brunt of the battle. They were cut to pieces.[23] Had Edward been at Edgecote his presence might have turned the tide, but oddly neither the King nor Warwick, who was said to making for Coventry, took part in the battle.

Despite missing the encounter with Herbert, Warwick grasped the victory. Edward had only his household servants with him and he allowed George Neville, whom he had dismissed as Chancellor, to take him into custody and 'escort' him to Warwick Castle. From there Warwick had him transferred to the Neville stronghold at Middleham.[24] Warwick dealt with his enemies in his usual fashion and King Edward lost two of his most loyal subjects. William Herbert and his brother were summarily executed. It took a little longer to locate Sir Richard Woodville, who had gone into hiding with his younger son John; they were rounded up and executed at Coventry on 12 August.[25] The Woodvilles had usurped the Nevilles' place a court, and it was part of Warwick's overall strategy to rid himself of them. Humphrey Stafford, despite having avoided the battle of Edgecote, was beheaded at the end of August.[26] Reports of these bewildering events reached France.[27] It appeared that King Louis had been right in his surmise but wrong in his timing that the Earl of Warwick and King Edward would come to blows. Louis was not sure how much to believe or what use he could make of it, but there was little in the news to encourage Margaret. Edward, as Warwick's puppet, was no help to her.

Warwick had established control over the King but there was a world of difference between governing through a compliant King Henry, who did as he was told and signed whatever was put before him, and an uncompliant one, who resorted to passive resistance. Unwittingly, and to his cost, the Lancastrian die-hard Sir Humphrey Neville of Brancepeth was instrumental in 'restoring' King Edward. Humphrey had been lucky: he had escaped capture and death thus far, and as soon as he learned that Edward was Warwick's prisoner, he raised a revolt along the Scottish border in King Henry's name. Warwick issued commissions of array, but Edward's subjects refused to answer a summons not issued by the King and Edward refused to cooperate unless he was set free. Warwick allowed Edward to go to York to show himself to the citizens and Edward promptly issued orders to raise the necessary troops. Humphrey had few followers and his rising was easily quashed. Warwick captured him and his brother Charles and brought them back to York where they were beheaded in Edward's presence.[28]

Warwick soon realised that he could not hold Edward indefinitely and the King's 'captivity' did not last long. He returned to London in October accompanied by his loyal magnates to a splendid welcome from the Mayor and civic dignitaries.[29] Conciliation was the order of the day and Edward played his part to perfection. At a series of Council meetings lasting into 1470 Edward appeared to make peace with Warwick, but it is entirely possible that Edward deliberately gave Warwick enough rope to hang himself. Arresting Warwick, to say nothing of Clarence, would only provoke more unrest and uncertainty. Warwick thought that by ridding the realm of his enemies, the Herberts and the Woodvilles, he could come to terms with Edward and so regain the influence he had lost, but once Edward was free he made it clear that Neville dominance at court was at an end.[30]

The Last Years

To Warwick, power was a drug. He could no more relinquish it voluntarily then he could relinquish his life. There was only one way to recover his hegemony: he would have to defeat Edward in battle, just as he (and Edward) had defeated King Henry at Towton. Warwick did not recognise the sanctity of kingship unless it suited him. He would depose Edward and replace him with the Duke of Clarence. Warwick offered Clarence a glittering prize: he was Edward's male heir presumptive, and with Warwick's help he would replace his increasingly unpopular elder brother on the throne. Clarence succumbed to temptation, influenced by jealousy of his brother, resentment at Edward's treatment of him, and Warwick's overbearing personality.

Opportunity offered when a feud in Lincolnshire between Richard, Lord Welles, his son Robert, and Sir Thomas Burgh, master of the King's horse, erupted into a serious disturbance. King Edward raised a force to go to Burgh's aid and set out from London on 6 March 1470. This sparked a rumour (possibly spread by Warwick's agents) that the King's 'comyng thidre was to destroie the comons of the same shire.'[31] Richard's son, Robert Welles, issued a proclamation calling on the men of Lincolnshire to take up arms and oppose the King. There was not much time for Warwick to turn the insurrection to his advantage, but he believed he could raise an army in Kent and call out his retainers as well as the northern men who won the battle at Edgecote. The Duke of Clarence would summon men from the south-west, although his main role would be to dupe Edward into believing that he and Warwick were loyal, and to lull the King into a false sense of security. Edward played along, feigning ignorance of Warwick and Clarence's involvement with Welles, and even delayed his departure from London so that he could meet with Clarence.[32] He issued (limited) commissions of array to them after they promised to join him, but he was not fooled.[33] Edward had nothing to lose. If Warwick and Clarence remained loyal well and good; if they did not, he would have clear evidence of their treason.

Warwick's Apostacy

Warwick threw caution to the winds. He was overconfident: he misjudged Edwards' determination, and his preparation was slipshod. Unlike his rebellion a year earlier, Warwick did not allow sufficient time to coordinate his troop movements. He planned to allow Edward to move north unmolested, where he would be trapped between two rebel armies coming from the south and the north and be heavily defeated.

Edward suspected that the Lincolnshire gentry had Lancastrian sympathies, which made him react harshly. Lord Welles was with him at court. He had fought for King Henry at Towton and been pardoned. Edward had him executed. He then offered to pardon Robert Welles if he disbanded his army, but Robert refused, possibly because he had been promised protection (and victory) by the Duke of Clarence. In less than a week Edward scattered the Lincolnshire 'army' in a rout that came to be called Lose-cote Field. Warwick was not there. Robert Welles was captured and brought before the King. Before he suffered the same fate as his father, Robert accused Warwick and Clarence of fomenting the rebellion. Edward had the evidence he needed, and he ordered them to desist their unlawful activities and submit to him at once. They arrogantly demanded safe conducts for themselves and their followers, as well as a guarantee of pardon. Edward was furious. They would do as they were bid, or he would proceed to extreme measures against them.[34]

Warwick and Clarence moved north expecting reinforcements, but Lord Scope of Bolton, who had been Warwick's partisan in 1460, and Lord Stanley, always a weathercock, preferred to sue to King Edward for pardon.[35] With Edward in hot pursuit, and with nowhere to hide, Warwick accepted failure but not defeat. He and Clarence retreated south-west to the coastal ports where Warwick could commandeer ships and make for Calais with his remaining followers. He would recoup his fortunes and launch another better-prepared campaign from the safety of Calais. Warwick embarked at Dartmouth on 9 April 1470 and made for Calais with his wife, his daughters, and his

The Last Years

son-in-law. Once again Warwick had underestimated Edward, who knew where he was most likely to go. The King sent orders to the garrison to hold the town against Warwick and as his ship put into port it was fired upon. Lord Wenlock claimed that he would have admitted Warwick, but that the Marshall of Calais refused, and the garrison obeyed the King's orders.[36]

Warwick could not believe that 'his' town would refuse him entry. His ships lay off Calais out of range of its guns for several days. Warwick's natural element was the sea, but his family fared less well. His daughter Isabel was pregnant. She went into labour and lost the child. A squadron of the English navy, commanded by Warwick's cousin Thomas Neville, Bastard of Fauconberg, deserted Edward and joined Warwick. With his increased numbers Warwick resumed his old role as a pirate. His fleet attacked and captured a large Flemish and Breton mercantile convoy in the Channel. But even with his successful piracy to fund him, Warwick could not remain at sea indefinitely. There was only one man to whom he could turn: the King of France. On 1 May 1470 Warwick's fleet dropped anchor in the Seine estuary at Honfleur.[37]

False news of the fighting in England was reported in France: Warwick had won a great victory and King Edward was dead. King Louis was delighted, but not for long.[38] When it was learned that Edward was very much alive and that he had driven Warwick out of England it was Margaret's turn to be delighted. Divided, Edward and Warwick could be defeated. With Warwick preying on foreign shipping, Margaret saw a potential ally in the German merchants of the towns of the Hanseatic League. Technically, their ships would be fair game for Warwick since England was at war with the Hanse. King Edward had ill-advisedly followed Warwick's advice and declared war after the seizure of some English ships in 1468, and by 1470 Hanseatic trade with England was at a standstill, to the detriment of both economies.[39]

On 1 May, just as Warwick's ships took refuge at Honfleur, Margaret addressed an impassioned letter, signed by herself and Prince Edward, to the members of the Hanse gathered in Lubeck, the largest and most influential city of the consortium.[40] She labelled King Edward an avaricious usurper, but her invective was directed against Warwick as the Great Satan. Warwick was the instigator of all the injuries that the Hanse had suffered from the time of his attack on their fleet in 1458 and, in a bid for sympathy, Margaret cast herself as their natural ally: she too had suffered grievously from Warwick's machinations.

Margaret appealed to the Hanse merchants to take advantage of the dissentions in England. She quoted the Bible that a house divided against itself could not stand and God would favour a righteous cause. Margaret claimed she had powerful friends in England on whom she could rely and together with the Hanse they would prevail. She reminded the Hanse that they had enjoyed a preferential trade status under King Henry, and she guaranteed that she would restore and enhance it as soon as Henry was set free. Margaret's focus had shifted. The restoration of her husband was necessary but incidental, Prince Edward was growing up, and what was important to her now was the destruction of *her* enemies. She suggested that Hanse representatives in Bruges should meet her councillors there as soon as possible to coordinate their efforts.

Despite her passionate plea, Margaret's demands were unrealistic. The Hanse was to provide an army, but *her* followers (the Dukes of Somerset and Exeter?) should be given command. Margaret was clutching at straws; the Hanse's war with England was a naval engagement. Hanse ships harassed and captured English merchant ships whenever they could, but an invasion of England was too great a risk for the Hanse to contemplate and was probably beyond their resources. The merchants of the Hanse were hard-headed men; the offer of favourable trade privileges sometime in an uncertain future was insufficient to persuade them to get caught up in what seemed to most people to be a lost cause.

While Margaret was trying to persuade the Hanseatic League to

The Last Years

come to her aid, Warwick was persuading King Louis to do just that. After he was refused entry into Calais and before he reached Honfleur, Warwick had concluded that the Duke of Clarence was no longer any use to him. As along as King Edward was alive, no one in England would back a bid to put Clarence on the throne. Edward had once told Warwick that without *a* king Warwick had no authority to govern, and this had proved to be true. Warwick remembered King Louis's suggestion of an alternative: he had governed successfully through King Henry once before and he could do so again, but first he had to convince Louis that he could make it worth his while to back a Lancastrian restoration.

Louis had to weigh the risk of war with Burgundy, and possibly Francis of Brittany, against Warwick's offer. Warwick's attack on Burgundian shipping had angered the Duke of Burgundy and when he learned that Warwick was sheltering in a French port and selling Burgundian goods to maintain himself, he protested vehemently to Louis, and to the Parlement of Paris. He demanded that Louis should order Warwick to quit France immediately and he threatened that if Louis allowed Warwick's ships to remain in French ports, he might declare war.[41] Louis explained to Warwick that in view of Burgundy's hostility he could not receive him openly, and he kept up the pretence to his council, his courtiers, and foreign diplomats alike that he did not welcome Warwick and was doing all he could to make him leave, but that Warwick refused to budge.[42] The Earl took lodging for himself, his countess, his daughters, and the Duke of Clarence at Valognes not far from the port of Barfleur, where his ships now lay at anchor.

33

The Queen and the Earl

Louis and Warwick corresponded in secret and Warwick outlined his plans. The key to them was twofold: Edward of Lancaster, Prince of Wales, now nearly seventeen, would marry Warwick's younger daughter, the fourteen-year-old Lady Anne Neville, and return to England with Warwick at the head of an army supplied by Louis. The Prince would be the figurehead of the invasion: he would reprise the role that Edward of March had played in 1461 as the rightful heir to the throne who had come to reclaim his inheritance. Former Lancastrians would rally to him, King Henry would be restored, and Warwick would rule through the Prince. In return England would become France's ally and Warwick would commit English resources to an Anglo–French war against the Duke of Burgundy. Louis was impressed, the concept appealed to the gambler in him, just as Warwick intended it to.[1]

Louis feared that King Edward and the Duke of Burgundy planned to declare war on France. Warwick and a Lancastrian revival would negate this threat and keep Edward at home. Louis made up his mind. He met Warwick and Clarence at the beginning of June to arrange their public reception and a week later they were welcomed to Amboise by the King and his court; even Queen Charlotte, despite being heavily pregnant, stood ready to receive them at the gates of the castle. Louis entertained them lavishly and over the next four days of intensive negotiations an agreement was hammered out.[2]

Since Prince Edward was central to Warwick's plan, it was essential for Margaret to come to court with the Prince and give her consent. Jasper Tudor went to apprise Margaret of what had been decided and persuade her to come to Amboise.[3] It did not occur to Louis or to Warwick that Margaret might object. John of Calabria had told Louis that the Lancastrians would commit Prince Edward to any attempt to restore King Henry. Louis kept Margaret's earlier refusal to meet Warwick himself and Warwick expected Margaret to jump at the chance he was offering her to achieve what she had been seeking for years. Preparations for the invasion got underway. The parsimonious Louis wanted the expedition to be fitted out on the cheap, but Warwick would not risk failure through underfunding. His sailors had to be paid, his ships had to be provisioned and French troops had to be ready before he would launch the 'enterprise of England'. In the tussle of wills, Warwick won, but he did not sail.[4]

Warwick still needed Margaret's consent, but he preferred not to meet her until Louis had a chance to explain the situation to her and he left Amboise before she and the Prince arrived at the end of June. Margaret was in what the Milanese ambassador described as a 'hard and difficult' mood. The King of France had sent for her and she had obeyed his summons, but Louis had his work cut out to persuade her to meet Warwick, let alone endorse his plans.[5] Louis flattered and cajoled her, he invited Prince Edward to be godfather to his long-awaited son and heir, born on 30 June and christened Charles.[6] Nevertheless, it took almost a month for Margaret to agree to receive Warwick and during that time she advanced all the arguments she could think of. She even claimed to have received a better offer, no less than a letter from King Edward suggesting a marriage between Prince Edward and his eldest daughter Elizabeth.[7] Was Margaret lying or had Edward put out feelers? If he could entice her into believing his offer was genuine, it would delay her acceptance of whatever Warwick might offer her.

Margaret's instinct was to reject Warwick out of hand, but she was in a difficult position and under strong pressure from her own people

The Queen and the Earl

as well as from Louis. Warwick's reputation was such that few people doubted that he could make good his promise to put King Henry back on the throne. The court at Koeur had been in exile for a long time: they wanted to go home, it was all that mattered to them, and the means were incidental. Sir John Fortescue had being trying for years to interest King Louis in his unrealistic schemes to depose King Edward, and he wrote another of his naïve memoranda: the King's Council, i.e. Fortescue himself – and perhaps the Queen –favoured a marriage between Prince Edward and Warwick's daughter because it would ensure Warwick loyalty. Fortescue outlined in his muddled way the trade advantages for both countries once King Henry was restored, although Fortescue still wanted his plan kept secret in case things did not turn out as they should. His proposals were not unlike those that Margaret had offered to the Hanse, special trading concessions, although he appears to have forgotten that the wool staple at Calais was English, unless he meant to flatter Louis by implying that Calais itself was French since Margaret had mortgaged it to him. As he had earlier, Fortescue assured Louis that any costs he incurred could be recovered.[8]

Louis pulled out all the stops. He moved the court from Amboise to Angers and he summoned Margaret's father René from Provence to bring family pressure to bear on her. René was always short of money and as he was committed to helping John of Calabria in the conquest of *his* Kingdom of Aragon, he would certainly be glad to be relieved of maintaining Margaret and the court at Koeur. Warwick arrived in Angers on 22 July, the same day as Margaret and Prince Edward. Warwick's brother-in-law, the Earl of Oxford, had slipped out of England to join him. Margaret received Oxford graciously. She said she was glad to pardon him because she knew his father and brother had suffered death in her cause.

Warwick had last seen Margaret in 1458 when he walked in the Loveday procession behind her and the Duke of York. It would be his first meeting with the boy prince whom he had consistently labelled a bastard but whom he was now eager to marry to his daughter.⁹ Louis presented Warwick to Margaret and Prince Edward in the reception room of the castle at Angers in the presence of Louis's brother, the Duke of Berry, and the French nobility. Margaret refused Warwick's offer of reconciliation.¹⁰ She stated that it would be dishonourable for her to make peace with the man who had deposed her husband and accuse her of adultery. She added that she had other potential allies whom she would risk losing if she accepted Warwick's proposal. The men in England who had remained loyal to her, secretly or openly, would not trust Warwick any more than she did. She requested King Louis not to ask her to pardon Warwick or to press her further to make peace with him.

Margaret's refusal would wreck Warwick's plan. He had never bent his knee to anyone except a reigning sovereign and not always then. It cost him a supreme effort, but he went on his knees before the Queen and the Prince and humbly begged Margaret to pardon him for disseminating what he now admitted were untruths. He could not quite bring himself to acknowledge that his rebellion was treason; he said he had only done what any nobleman in his position who had been unfairly treated would have done to uphold his honour. It cost Margaret an equal effort to accept Warwick's protestations, but in the end against her better judgement she pardoned the man who more than any other had caused King Henry to lose his throne, and she accepted in principle a marriage between Prince Edward and Warwick's daughter. After all, in her search for allies she had offered the Prince in the dynastic marriage market on more than one occasion, but she refused point blank to risk the Prince's person. Warwick must depose King Edward before it would be safe to send the Prince to England.¹¹

A week later in the cathedral of St Maurice in Angers Warwick swore on the true cross to be faithful to Margaret, to her husband, and to her son.¹² Margaret swore to accept Warwick as her liege man and never to remind him or upbraid him for his past actions. But she drove a hard bargain. She agreed to the betrothal of Prince Edward, but no marriage would take place before a papal dispensation was obtained. Until then the Lady Anne would remain in Margaret's care. A betrothal was a binding contract, but it could be nullified if a dispensation were not forthcoming or if Warwick failed to keep his promises. The Prince would return to England only after Warwick had established King Henry securely on the throne and he would be Regent for his father under Warwick's guidance. It was Margaret's second serious mistake: the Prince's presence, as Warwick knew, was half the battle.

Margaret required King Louis, the Duke of Berry, and the French nobles who were present to pledge their unconditional support for the restoration of King Henry, herself, and the Prince of Wales, and to declare King Edward a usurper who must be driven out of England, with their help if necessary. He was not to be received or given shelter anywhere in France. Even then Margaret was wary. A clause in the agreement stated that if things went wrong in the future, she, King Henry, and Prince Edward could take refuge in France and be maintained by King Louis.[13] One suspects that King Louis's tongue was firmly in his cheek, since the agreement was signed by the Duke of Berry. The Earl of Warwick is not mentioned, and it is most unlikely that Louis would come to Margaret's rescue if he failed.

Warwick ruthlessly sacrificed the Duke of Clarence to his new ambition to see his second daughter become Queen of England. Clarence renounced his claim to the throne in favour of Prince Edward with the proviso that if the marriage of Edward and Anne produced no heir, he would be next in line. Once King Edward was deposed and in exile, or better still dead, it would increase Clarence's chances; in the meanwhile he would become of Duke of York.[14] It was a poor reward for the sacrifice Clarence had made, admittedly of his own accord, of his brother's trust and favour. By throwing in his lot with Warwick he had committed treason. Clarence was a far weaker personality than Warwick; he was a follower not a leader and he had

The Last Years

to accept his changed circumstances, otherwise he would be a penniless exile like the Lancastrians, since his brother was unlikely to forgive him and he could not go back to England without Warwick.

Warwick endured a month of frustration throughout August. The Duke of Burgundy's fleet was blocking his passage and the weather had turned stormy. His sailors were restive, they wanted their wages, and Warwick demanded additional funds from Louis.[15] He had hoped originally to return to England in July, but Margaret's recalcitrance upset his timetable and it was not until September that he finally sailed, accompanied by the Duke of Clarence, the Earl of Oxford, and Jasper Tudor. They landed in Devonshire on 13 September and as soon as they came ashore they issued a proclamation on the authority of Queen Margaret and the Prince of Wales. They had come to restore Henry VI to the throne as the rightful King of England and to depose the usurping Edward of March, styling himself King of England and Duke of York. A commission of array in King Henry's name summoned all able-bodied men between the ages of sixteen and sixty to join Warwick, who promised that his army would be disciplined, that law and order would be maintained, and that there was to be no looting or attacks on personal or Church property. A proclamation by the Duke of Clarence to the same effect went unheeded.[16] To celebrate Warwick's return the men of Kent unwisely ransacked London's suburbs south of the Thames.[17]

At first all went well. Warwick's popular appeal did not fail him and there was a surge of support for King Henry, but Warwick had yet to win the acceptance of the lords of the land. He marched north to Coventry gathering recruits along the way and he soon had a sizeable army.[18] The Earl of Shrewsbury and Lord Stanley, who a year earlier had deserted Warwick in favour of King Edward, joined Warwick's ranks.

Edward was in Yorkshire where he had just put down one of the periodic northern risings. He believed the exaggerated reports that people were flocking to Warwick and he moved south to Doncaster.

His first thought was to summon John Neville, Lord Montague, to join him with as many men as he could muster. Edward, like his father, was singularly obtuse when it came to understanding other men. Montague's loyalty had been cooling for some time, and he no longer trusted the King. Edward had released Henry Percy, heir to the Earldom of Northumberland, who had been stripped of his title and estates after his father died fighting for King Henry at the Battle of Towton. A Percy rising in the north in 1469 had demanded Percy's restoration but Edward had made John Neville Earl of Northumberland. Percy retainers and tenants were fanatically loyal to their lord and they refused to acknowledge a Neville as Earl of Northumberland. In 1470 Edward restored lands belonging to the earldom to Henry Percy and then the earldom itself. This gained him a valuable ally but lost him John Neville. Edward compensated John by making him Marquis of Montague and bestowing other lands on him, even going so far as to create John's son George Duke of Bedford and betroth him (for the time being) to Edward's eldest daughter Elizabeth.[19] John resented the loss of an ancient earldom for a newly created title. The Percys were the Nevilles' hereditary enemies and the reinstatement of Henry Percy was a direct challenge to Neville predominance in the north. Edward's treatment of Warwick by forcing him into exile had added to Montague's resentment and he declared he would join his brother and fall on the King's army from the rear.[20]

Montague's unexpected desertion and Warwick's threat to depose him caused Edward to panic. He had about 3,000 men with him, but he was uncertain of Warwick's exact strength and instead of continuing his march south he fled to Bishops Lynn on the east coast. From there, on 2 October he foolishly left the country with only a few followers to seek protection from the Duke of Burgundy.[21] News that Edward had halted his march reached Warwick and Queen Elizabeth Woodville almost simultaneously. The Queen, who was pregnant, was at the royal apartments specially prepared for her lying in at the Tower of London. She fled to sanctuary in Westminster Abbey and sent the

The Last Years

Abbot of Westminster to request the Mayor of London to take possession of the Tower. Richard Lee was in his second term of office. He had been the Mayor in 1461 when he welcomed Warwick (and Edward of March) following Margaret and the Lancastrian army's retreat. Possibly on Warwick's orders, Lee went in person to arrange the release of a bewildered King Henry and he moved Henry into the apartments vacated by Queen Elizabeth at the Tower. Lee and his fellow aldermen called out the London trained bands to guard the City against marauders from Kent.[22] Mayor Lee may have been relieved by Warwick's arrival.

Warwick understood from previous experience how best to handle King Henry. He chose William Waynflete, Bishop of Winchester, Henry's former confessor and Chancellor, who was in residence at his palace in Southwark, to go to the Tower.[23] Waynflete was the perfect choice to reassure King Henry that he was safe and to explain his changed circumstances. At the same time Warwick sent word to his brother, George Neville, the Archbishop of York, who was under house arrest close to London, to secure the capital. George arrived on 5 October with an armed escort and took charge of the Tower.

Warwick, Clarence, Oxford, and a number of other lords arrived on the following day and knelt before King Henry to proclaim their loyalty. Henry was fifty years old, he had been in the Tower for five years and he was almost the forgotten man. He was a poor substitute for a young Prince of Wales, but Warwick made the best of what he had. The King was dressed in a gown of blue velvet and escorted to St Pauls, probably at his own request so that he could make an offering after his long captivity. Warwick then lodged him in the Bishop of London's palace just as he had after the Battle of Northampton. Henry had no qualms in accepting Warwick's presence: Warwick had treated him with deference and expected nothing of him in 1460, and he did so again. Warwick also paid the expenses of re-establishing the King's household.[24] On 8 October a jubilant Warwick wrote to King Louis to report that Henry was securely re-established on his throne.[25]

The Queen and the Earl

Once Edward had left England those who might have rallied to him had no incentive to resist Warwick; they had their future to think of, and Warwick was not a merciful man. Nevertheless, Warwick had to tread carefully. He could not afford to alienate moderates who had accepted King Edward and were uncertain of what a Lancastrian restoration might mean for them. A general pardon was issued to everyone who had 'mistakenly' served King Edward, and there was only one major reprisal. Warwick allowed the Earl of Oxford to take revenge on King Edward's favourite, John Tiptoft, Earl of Worcester, who had overseen the execution of Oxford's father and brother and had carried out his duties as Constable of England with unprecedented cruelty. Oxford, now Constable of England in his turn, tried Tiptoft for treason and condemned him to death. Tiptoft had done King Edward's dirty work, but he had enjoyed doing it, and Warwick had his own axe to grind.

After Warwick escaped from England, Tiptoft had come to Southampton on King Edward's orders to arrest men who were believed to have aided Warwick's attempt to commandeer the royal ships at anchor there. Tiptoft had condemned twenty men to death and he treated them in a brutal and illegal way; they were impaled on stakes, 'for the whiche the people of the londe were gretely displesyd.' It was not an English way of meting out justice. Tiptoft's execution was a popular spectacle: crowds gathered to see him taken to the Tower and the press was so great that the sheriffs had trouble forcing their way through.[26]

Warwick had been a central figure in King Edward's government, and he meant to resume where he left off and make the transition to King Henry's 'rule' as smooth as possible. Government departments and the bureaucracy continued to function as they always had, and officials got round the awkward gap in Henry's regnal years since 1461 by dating warrants issued in his name 'the 49th year from the beginning of our reign and the first year of the readeption of our royal power'. Warwick resumed the offices of Great Chamberlain of

The Last Years

England, Captain of Calais, Warden of the West March (with his brother John as Warden of the East March) and declared himself to be King Henry's lieutenant. He reappointed George Neville, Archbishop of York, as Chancellor and to please Margaret, Warwick made John Hals, Bishop of Coventry and Lichfield, Keeper of the Privy Seal. John Langstrother, the newly elected Prior of St John of Jerusalem, had been Warwick's appointee as Treasurer of England during his brief control of the government after Richard Woodville's death in 1469, but Edward IV had promptly dismissed him. Langstrother became Treasurer once again in 1470. There were no other major changes in government personnel.

Despite Warwick's boast to Louis, King Henry's legal readeption had to wait until Parliament met. Henry had been attainted by the Commons in Parliament and only Parliament could reverse the attainder. Seven peers, including those who had fled with Edward, were omitted from the thirty-four writs of summons to Parliament issued as early as 15 October but we do not know how many attended.[27] Parliament convened on 26 November and Chancellor Neville made the opening speech, but apart from that no records of the proceedings have survived. The rolls were destroyed on Edward's orders when he regained the throne.[28] It is probable that King Henry was reinstated with Prince Edward as his heir, and King Edward was attainted once again, but it is impossible to be sure.[29]

The attainders of the Lancastrian lords may have been reversed to establish that they were now accepted as King Henry's loyal subjects, but this was not the same as the restoration of their confiscated estates, a far more complicated and potentially divisive issue that Warwick was in no hurry to tackle. Sir John Fortescue had warned in one of his lengthy, idealistic, and unrealistic memoranda that while rewards for loyal Lancastrians would be expected they should be subject to a review by an impartial council; reparation should not be made until it could be done equitably, and only after sufficient income to the crown had been assured.[30] Money would have to be found to re-establish

The Queen and the Earl

Queen Margaret's and Prince Edward's households and the reintegration of the exiles who would return with her. A final reconciliation could not be achieved until she and the Prince returned to England. Warwick would need Margaret's help. She could command, and indeed demand, the Lancastrian lords' cooperation.

King Louis instructed an embassy headed by Louis de Harcourt, Bishop of Bayeux and Patriarch of Jerusalem, and Sir William Moneypenny to congratulate King Henry on his readeption and to emphasise Warwick's part in it. Sir William Moneypenny was to test the waters and advise Louis on how best to win over the English mercantile community. Louis was aware that there would be opposition to a war with Burgundy and his ambassadors were to inform everyone they met in London that Louis had offered special trading privileges to English merchants in France and he would do much more for them in future so that they would not feel the loss of their markets in the Netherlands. Louis also asked Warwick to provide him with a list of 'great men' in England whom it would be necessary to influence, and how best to go about it. Louis had great faith in bribery.

The ambassadors were to assure Warwick that Louis considered him his best friend in all the world, that Louis would never desert him, and he would do whatever Warwick required. This was all flimflam. Louis wanted his informal agreement with Warwick confirmed by a treaty in King Henry's name and he spelled out his requirements in detail. He had already given orders to outfit a French fleet and arranged to send supplies to Calais. King Henry and Warwick should now declare war on the Duke of Burgundy, a war that would continue until all Burgundy's *pais, terres, et seigneuries,* had been conquered. Neither side was to make peace or a truce without the consent of the other. Warwick was to be rewarded with the counties of Holland and Zeeland, but Louis would keep the rest of the Netherlands for himself.

Louis and King Henry would finance the costs of their respective armies, but Louis wanted to know the projected size of the English army and the exact date at which it would engage. He outlined how the war should be fought, although he left it up to Warwick to decide which alternative was preferable. Basically, English troops should be sent into the *Pays de Caux* in Normandy and to Calais. Louis's army would advance into Picardy while the English would be joined at Calais by companies of French lances and advance to St Omer. Alternatively, Louis would send troops into Compiègne and Noyon and the *Pays de Caux* to link up with Warwick's march from Calais. Finally, Louis asked Warwick to supply him with proof from English government archives that the Duke of Burgundy had contravened the Treaty of Peronne by making an illegal truce with King Edward.[31]

Louis left nothing to chance. At the end of November, he persuaded the Prince of Wales to set his seal to an agreement in almost the same words as his instructions to his ambassadors. Prince Edward undertook to wage war on Burgundy and persuade his father to do the same.[32] Edward was just seventeen. He had grown up in the tiny isolated court at Koeur under the domination of his single-minded mother and he had no idea of the political and diplomatic consequences of declaring war on Burgundy. He knew he would shortly assume the role of Protector and perhaps Regent of England for his father, and he had trained himself to become proficient in combat skills and declared his intention of becoming a famous warrior when he grew up. He was probably looking forward to a chance to prove his military worth.

Louis's ambassadors sent glowing and grossly exaggerated reports of their welcome in England.[33] Warwick had, of course, received them courteously, and they were probably granted an audience with King Henry. Margaret believed them, and she kept her promise. The Prince of Wales married Anne Neville in the middle of December. It is not known who performed the ceremony, but Louis de Harcourt apparently sanctioned it, even though he had previously told King Louis that only the Pope had the authority to issue a dispensation. Perhaps it had arrived in the interim; the Vicar General of Bayeux blessed the nuptials.[34] What the young couple thought of each other and of their marriage we do not know, or what Margaret thought of the girl she would have to train to become Queen of England. It was a quiet wedding. Its exact date is not recorded, but it coincided with the death of John of Calabria, who died in Barcelona on 11 December 1470.

Margaret, Edward, Anne, and Anne's mother the Countess of Warwick, whom Warwick had left in France to make sure that the marriage took place, left Amboise for Paris and then Rouen. They were royally received in the capital. The civic dignitaries accorded Margaret her status as Queen of England on Louis's orders. He gave Margaret 20,000 (sic) *livres tournois* as a parting gift, 50 marks to her lady of honour, 50 marks to her almoner, 20 *écus* to a knight escort, and 49 marks to John Fortescue.[35] Louis had maintained their households at Amboise since the previous August,[36] and he continued to pay the costs of Margaret's household in Rouen.[37] The Earl of Ormond joined the royal entourage there,[38] and on 17 December a warrant in King Henry's name instructed the Earl of Warwick to sail with a fleet of ships to bring Margaret home.[39] But crossing the Channel in midwinter was hazardous, and the sailing was delayed to 1471.

34

The Final Throw

King Louis's declaration that he and Warwick would defeat the Duke of Burgundy and dismember his lands was a typical Louis exaggeration. Burgundian territories were extensive and disparate; it would be impossible for him to conquer them all and he did not intend to try. He had his eye on the rich counties of the Netherlands including the Somme towns that he been forced to mortgage to Burgundy after the Battle of Montlhéry in 1465. Louis was impatient and he was so sure that he had his English 'allies' exactly where he wanted them that on 3 December, even before Prince Edward's marriage, he repudiated his Treaty of Peronne with Burgundy and absolved the Duke's subjects from their allegiance. French troops crossed into Picardy and the Count of St Pol, Constable of France, recovered St Quentin in mid-January 1471. Amiens surrendered in February, Burgundy mobilised, and the war was on.[1]

Warwick appeared to be honouring his commitment. Louis de Harcourt reported that the English had agreed to an alliance against the Duke of Burgundy and would shortly sign a truce and trade agreement with France. Warwick was about to order the Calais garrison to begin hostilities and he was sending several thousand men as reinforcements. An army of 8,000 to 10,000 archers was also being assembled; Warwick would take command and lead them in person. Warwick also had a fine fleet ready to sail. De Harcourt admitted that there had been resistance in Parliament to some of the terms of the trade agreement, but these would soon be ironed out. A ten-year truce and trade treaty between King Henry and King Louis was signed on 16 February 1471.[2]

Warwick confirmed what he and de Harcourt knew to be misinformation.[3] Warwick might be able to raise three thousand men to send to Calais, but to field a much larger army of archers for service overseas was beyond his means, economically and politically. For a second time Warwick had promised Louis what he could not perform. Louis expected Warwick to commence hostilities at Calais without delay and Warwick wrote to him on 12 February that operations had already begun, two men at Gravelines had been killed. This was in fact no more than an incident in the constant skirmishes between the Calais garrison and the pickets guarding the Burgundian border that had been going on for years. Warwick promised to come *as soon as he could* to fight 'this accursed Burgundian' (*ce mauldit Bourgoignon*).[4] The adjective would have pleased Louis, but did Warwick mean what he said? He was certainly raising troops: the town of Coventry received a royal order to contribute men destined for Flanders but no English troops went to Calais or to join the French army.[5]

Warwick's promise to King Louis, so easily given when Louis seemed his only hope, was proving difficult to implement. No one in England, no matter what his dynastic sympathies, wanted war with Burgundy. The Calais Staplers and the London merchants were opposed to endangering England's vital trade with the Low Countries. Would Parliament vote taxes for a war? The truce with France would not be popular; there had always been anti-Burgundian sentiment in London but in most Englishmen's minds France was still the enemy.

At the back of Warwick's mind was a constant question, what was King Edward doing and what was he planning to do? Warwick had issued commissions in King Henry's name to himself, Clarence, and the Earl of Oxford to guard the east coast against Edward, and the Earl of Oxford had taken the defence of East Anglia in hand.[6] The Pastons were delighted to have Oxford as their overlord and they responded enthusiastically. He inspired them to fight for Lancaster.[7] The Bastard of Fauconberg was patrolling the Channel and committing piracy against ships of all nations to maintain himself and Warwick, but he did not take his ships to Calais.[8]

King Edward was in the Netherlands where the Duke of Burgundy had refused to receive him, although he dutifully allowed Edward a small pension. He could hardly allow his brother-in-law to starve or live on the charity of others, but he would have done his best to ignore Edward if Louis and Warwick had not provoked him. French troops invading Burgundian territory changed Duke Charles's mind and Warwick's continued piracy infuriated him (and incidentally the Duke of Brittany and the merchants of the Hanse as well). At the beginning of January 1471 Charles invited Edward to join him at Aire. They had a second meeting at St Pol and Charles promised Edward £20,000 to kickstart his return to England.[9] By the end of the month Edward was fundraising with Charles's backing and in February he left Bruges to join his fleet at Flushing. Warwick was worried; many Lancastrians in England did not trust him, and he could not be sure of their loyalty. Warwick needed Margaret and above all Prince Edward. On 22 February John Langstrother, the Treasurer, was authorised to equip ships to bring Margaret and her son home. Warwick went to Dover to meet them, but they did not come, and after waiting for several days and wasting time he could ill afford he returned to London.[10]

Lancastrian exiles drifted back to England. One of the first was the Duke of Exeter.[11] He hated his brother-in-law King Edward as much as he had once hated Edward's father, and he joined forces with the Earl of Oxford. Others were not so trusting or so forgiving, and they held aloof. Margaret remained in Rouen. She assumed that once King Henry was restored Lancastrian loyalists would support Warwick even if she were not there. It did not happen. Winter storms in the Channel provided her with a convenience excuse, but it is hard to believe that for three long months she had no opportunity to make the crossing. Returning exiles managed it, messengers sailed both ways, merchant ships piled their trade, and the Bastard of Fauconberg's fleet remained active. Margaret's overprotective attitude to her son made her hesitate, and her delay proved fatal.

King Edward sailed from Flushing in March with a mixed force of English and Flemish troops.[12] Unlike Margaret he was determined to reach England at all costs, despite the atrocious weather. His attempt to land along the east coast was repulsed by Oxford's brother, Thomas Vere, and his ships were driven north. Edward made landfall at Ravenspur in Yorkshire on 14 March 1471. He was by no means certain of his welcome and he sheltered behind a convenient fiction: he claimed he was loyal to King Henry and he had come home as Duke of York. Few believed him, but it allowed him to reach the city of York in safety.[13] Lord Montague was at Pontefract where he sat tight. He could ill afford to waste trained troops in a premature encounter with Edward and Warwick would need him in the decisive battles to come. Henry Percy, the other power in the north, did nothing. Perhaps he was grateful to Edward for restoring his Earldom of Northumberland, perhaps, despite Percy loyalty to Lancaster in the past, he knew his people would be reluctant to fight alongside the hated Nevilles.

Inexplicably, Warwick made the same fundamental mistake that Margaret made after she won the Battle of St Albans – he abandoned London. He believed that his popularity with the Londoners would keep the capital loyal to him. The French ambassadors were not so sure; they sailed precipitously for France.[14] Warwick had not anticipated the situation he found himself in. Margaret and Prince Edward should have been with him in London long before King Edward could return. Warwick established his headquarters at Coventry to cut off Edward's advance and he resorted to a desperate measure: on 27 March a warrant in King Henry's name appointed the absent Prince of Wales as lieutenant of the King's army.[15] It was no substitute for the presence of the Prince, but a promise of his imminent arrival might be enough to rally support for the Lancastrian dynasty.

The Last Years

Margaret, like Warwick, had not thought through the ramifications of a declaration of war against Burgundy. She had not foreseen that Burgundy, who had professed sympathy for her and for King Henry, would help her enemy, much less provide him with ships and an army. The reports of Edward's successful landing in England finally woke her to an appalling possibility. Edward had been accepted as King for ten years; would his return tip the balance in his favour and enable him to recover the throne? Warwick and Edward had once been great friends. Would Warwick reach an accommodation with Edward and desert her? Margaret had never entirely trusted Warwick and she decided she must return to England at once. She joined her ships at Honfleur on 24 March; in reasonable sailing conditions the Channel could be crossed in twelve hours, but the conditions were not reasonable. Her ships left port several times only to be blown back by contrary winds and it was three weeks before the weather abated sufficiently for her to sail.

King Edward had continued his march south. He was at Nottingham when he learned that Oxford, Exeter, and William Beaumont, the son of King Henry's favourite, John Beaumont, who had been killed at Northampton, had gathered an army at Newark and were on their way to join Warwick. Edward promptly diverged towards them but like Montague they preferred not to face him in the field.[16] The Duke of Clarence was recruiting in the south-west. He wrote to reassure Warwick, as he had once reassured his brother, that he would come as fast as he could. He urged Warwick to wait and not give battle until he could reach Coventry with reinforcements.[17] Clarence also had a commission with Jasper Tudor, Earl of Pembroke, to raise troops in Herefordshire.[18] Jasper had made for Wales as soon he landed with Warwick but he was more interested in the future prospects of his nephew, Henry Tudor, than he was in helping to establish and sustain Warwick's government.[19]

In a provocative move King Edward occupied Warwick's own town of Warwick. His army appeared before the walls of Coventry and in a

The Final Throw

theatrical gesture designed to impress and intimidate, Edward challenged Warwick to come out and fight. Montague's troops and Oxford's, Exeter's, and Beaumont's levies had joined Warwick, but Clarence's force had not arrived. Warwick could take up Edward's challenge or he could stay behind Coventry's walls and wait. He knew Edward would not turn his artillery on the town. Edward gambled that Warwick would not face him in the field, and he was right. Warwick refused to take the bait.[20]

By that time, it was clear that Clarence had decided to switch sides. He had been worked on ever since his return to England by his mother, the formidable Duchess Cecily, and his sister Elizabeth, married to John de la Pole, Duke of Suffolk, and his youngest sister, Margaret, writing to him from Burgundy. They promised him that King Edward would welcome him back and restore him to his rightful place as the King's brother. Clarence was easy to influence, but his change of heart is understandable. Warwick had used him for his own ends and then side-lined him. The confirmation of Clarence as the King's Lieutenant in Ireland amounted to little more than a prestigious title, he would be glad of the income, such as it was, but he had no wish to go there.[21] And Clarence knew he would be made to surrender estates granted to him by King Edward from Margaret's dower lands, despite having been promised at Angers that he would retain them.

Edward and Clarence met and were reconciled on 3 April.[22] Edward forgave his brother in order to deny Clarence's troops to Warwick, and two days later he abandoned Coventry for London. Edward sent orders to the magistrates to take King Henry into protective custody. Warwick appealed to the Mayor and aldermen not to allow Edward to enter the City. He had instructed his brother Archbishop Neville to hold London and keep Henry safe until he could arrive. As had happened in 1461 after the Battle of St Albans, both letters arrived and were read by the Common Council on the same day, 10 April.[23] Richard Lee was no longer Mayor and his replacement lacked Lee's courage. He opted out and took to his bed.

The Last Years

The alderman and Common Council declared for King Edward. He was at their gates while Warwick was nowhere to be seen. If Warwick were to arrive and dispute possession of London, they could always change their minds.

Archbishop Neville and the aged Lord Sudeley made a last desperate effort to hold the City. They escorted King Henry, wearing the same blue velvet gown he had worn when he was released from the Tower in October, on a circuit of the City streets in a vain attempt to rouse the Londoners' sympathy. Poor Henry was not very impressive: his appearance aroused more derision than commiseration.[24]

King Edward entered London unopposed on 11 April. After giving the customary thanks at St Pauls, and even before he sought out his queen, who was still in sanctuary at Westminster, Edward made his way to the Bishop of London's palace to secure King Henry. Archbishop Neville probably had to tell Henry who Edward was, but the Duchess of Burgundy recorded a touching story that she had been told of their encounter. Edward offered his hand (did he expect Henry to kiss it?) and Henry greeted Edward with the words, 'My cousin of York you are very welcome. I know that in your hands my life will not be in danger.' Edward reassured him; with the future still uncertain Henry alive was a valuable bargaining counter.[25] The story may be true. It was the kind of thing Henry would say, and he had no reason to fear Edward, who had kept him in the comfortable confinement that he may have preferred to the readeption, which he did not want.

Edmund Beaufort, Duke of Somerset, and his brother Lord John Beaufort had been in exile at the Burgundian court with the Duke of Exeter. They had tried and failed to dissuade the Duke of Burgundy from giving military aid to King Edward. They returned to England after the readeption made it safe for them, but they took different approaches to the Earl of Warwick. Exeter was prepared to fight for him – Somerset was not. He preferred to wait for Margaret, believing that she would set up a Lancastrian court to include him and other exiles but exclude Warwick. Somerset had been abroad for so long

The Final Throw

that he was as out of touch with political reality, as was Margaret herself. John Courtenay, Earl of Devon, returned from Koeur, and Margaret was expected to arrive any day now. Devon joined Somerset and they began to recruit troops in the south-west, but whether they planned to use them for Warwick is uncertain.[26] In the event they did not. As King Edward approached London, Somerset and Courtenay left the capital and made their way to the south coast to welcome Margaret.

Warwick was dogged by betrayal. He had counted on Margaret and she had let him down. An impatient King Louis decided to cut his losses. He announced that his campaign had been such a success that he no longer needed English help and he approached the Duke of Burgundy in secret. Burgundy, who had not sought the war, was happy to oblige and on 4 April they signed a three-month truce.[27] Edward's landing may have influenced Louis's thinking as it had Margaret's. Louis had made Warwick's 'enterprise of England' and the restoration of King Henry possible for his own ends, but opportunist that he was, Louis was not far sighted enough to see that by forcing Warwick to publicly declare war on Burgundy he doomed his scheme to failure. Nevertheless, it was the absence of the Prince of Wales and the defection of the Duke of Clarence that ultimately undermined Warwick, not his commitment, which he never honoured, to fight Burgundy.

After Clarence's defection Warwick realised that he had made a mistake; there was no point in waiting any longer for reinforcements. He left Coventry with his army and artillery and reached St Albans on 12 April. He had planned originally to defeat Edward in the Midlands before Edward could come anywhere near London, but Edward had out-jockeyed him, and Warwick counted on the Londoners to shut the City's gates so that he could crush Edward outside the City walls. But London too betrayed him, and King Edward took possession of the capital.

Recruits flocked to Edward from all sides. Prisoners in the Tower

The Last Years

overpowered their guards (who would not have offered much resistance) and broke free. The young Duke of Norfolk left for East Anglia to counter the Earl of Oxford's influence. The Bourgchiers joined Edward en masse. Bishop Stillington and the staunchly loyal William Gray, Bishop of Ely, came out of sanctuary. Edward ordered the arrest of Archbishop Neville, who promptly deserted Warwick, and incidentally King Henry, and sued to Edward for pardon. He, Lord Sudeley, and John Hals, Bishop of Coventry, Margaret's former Chancellor, were incarcerated in the Tower on Edward's orders.[28]

Edward was now supremely confident; he had secured London. On 13 April, only two days after he arrived, he assembled his army and marched out along on the road to St Albans to encounter Warwick. Both armies sent out scouts but neither side realised just how close they were to one another. Under cover of darkness they formed up in the traditional order of three battles or divisions and positioned themselves across the main London to St Albans road just north of Barnet.[29] At dawn on Easter Sunday, 14 April, in mist so thick that it was hard for the opponents to see each other, King Edward's army advanced. Edward's brother, Richard, Duke of Gloucester, who was only a year older than Edward of Lancaster, commanded the van of Edward's army opposite the Duke of Exeter. Both fought bravely but Exeter was wounded and left for dead on the field; he was only discovered and smuggled to safety after the battle.

King Edward held the centre facing Lord Montague. He had Clarence with him for safekeeping, and he had brought King Henry along for the same reason.[30] Henry's partisans might attempt to rescue him once Edward was out of the way and he was too valuable to be allowed to fall into enemy hands. Edward's first action as soon as he entered London had been to locate Henry and secure his person. Not for the first time the unhappy king was dragged to a battle he barely understood, and on Easter Sunday too, the most holy day of the year. Edward knew Henry would not fight, but his presence meant that, technically, Warwick was fighting against the Lancastrian king.

The Final Throw

Lord Montague was a far better soldier than his brother and Warwick gave him command of the centre of the Lancastrian line. The Earl of Oxford held the right flank, opposite Lord Hastings. Due to mist the opposing armies were not perfectly aligned and Oxford outflanked Hastings. His men charged into Hastings' left flank, which broke and fled. Oxford's men chased them back towards London and it was some time before Oxford managed to regroup them and return to the fray. It seemed at first that Montague would win the victory, but the fortunes of war changed when Oxford came up from the south. The battle lines had shifted, and his troops were face to face with Lord Montague's men, who mistook them for the enemy and fired on them. Oxford's men fell back with shouts of 'Treason!' and the Lancastrian line wavered.[31] Lord Montague, in the centre in the thick of the fight, was killed. Edward pressed his advantage and the leaderless Lancastrian line disintegrated.

Warwick was a superb pirate, but an indifferent general. He commanded the Lancastrian reserve and he should have thrown them in as soon as he learned that Montague was dead. Instead he left the field and tried to reach his horses, tethered at the rear. He was easy to recognise and was cut down by some of Edward's men, much to Edward's relief.[32] By noon it was all over and against the odds Edward had won the day. The Earl of Warwick did not die in battle but in flight. It was an ignominious end for the man who had been the leading figure in European politics for so long. Warwick was a legend in his own lifetime: he had dominated two kings, but in the end he could not rule successfully without reigning. He tried twice, and he failed twice. King Edward returned to London. To silence any doubt that his greatest supporter and greatest enemy had perished, Edward had Warwick's body and that of Lord Montague, whose loyalty to Edward had been sorely tested, laid side by side and displayed publicly at St Pauls.[33] The unfortunate King Henry was again lodged in the Tower; he was probably happy to settle back into the tranquillity of captivity.

The Last Years

On the very day that the Battle of Barnet was being fought, Margaret landed at Weymouth in Dorset. With her were Prince Edward, Anne Neville, now Princess of Wales, Sir John Langstrother, whom Warwick had sent to fetch her in February, and Lord Wenlock, who had deserted his post in Calais to join her. Wenlock had hoped that by crossing with the Queen he could link up with Warwick. Margaret trusted Wenlock, despite his services to the Duke of York and King Edward. John Fortescue, Edmund Hampden, Richard Whittington, William Vaux, his wife, the ever-faithful Katherine, and Marie, Countess of Devon, landed with Margaret, together with a small force whose size and composition is nowhere recorded. The Countess of Warwick had sailed separately. She made landfall at Portsmouth and journeyed to Southampton, intending to meet the Queen at their agreed rendezvous, but when she learned of her husband's death she took sanctuary at Beaulieu Abbey.[34] Separated from her mother, Anne Neville alone mourned the death of her magnificent father.

Margaret had landed further west than she intended. She found shelter in Cerne Abbey to the north of Weymouth and it was there that Somerset, his brother, and the Earl of Devon met her two days later. They broke the news that Warwick was dead, King Edward was in possession of London, and King Henry was once again Edward's prisoner. Margaret was stunned, but she soon rallied. Somerset, Devon, and Prince Edward persuaded her that Warwick's death could be turned to her advantage. Warwick had been a stumbling block. They were sure that with Warwick out of the way it would be easy to recruit an army large enough to defeat King Edward. Men such as themselves who would not fight for Warwick would fight for her and the Prince. Warwick had summoned men in the south-west in King Henry's name to resist King Edward and they could be put to good use.[35] Margaret allowed herself to be convinced.

Unfortunately, Margaret did not know the Duke of Somerset very well. His eldest brother, Henry, had been executed by King Edward after the Battle of Hexham in 1464, and Edmund had assumed the title Duke of Somerset. He had sought service with the Count of Charolais, receiving a generous pension, and he remained in Burgundian service when Charolais became Duke of Burgundy in 1467.[36] Somerset's presence had caused a slight embarrassment in July 1468 when Burgundy had married Edward IV's sister Margaret of York in a splendid ceremony at Damme, not far from Bruges.[37] The day before she reached Bruges, Edmund and his brother diplomatically left the city. It would not do for them to be on hand when Margaret of York arrived.[38] They were not absent for long. Somerset was at court in Brussels by the end of the year and he remained there until 1471.

An informal council of war was held at Cerne Abbey and Somerset argued that they should move into the south-west and make the city of Exeter their headquarters and rendezvous point. He and the Earl of Devon could raise a large army locally. Somerset had greater confidence in his military abilities than he deserved. His service under the Duke of Burgundy hardly qualified him to command an army no matter how large against the experienced King Edward. Neither Margaret nor the Duke (or for that matter the Prince) had any idea of strategy or tactics, and there was no one in their ranks to advise them, even if Somerset had been prepared to listen. His one thought was to defeat King Edward, but he would have done better to move back to Southampton where Margaret had planned to land. The Lancastrian army could have linked up with the Bastard of Fauconberg, who had ships and men at his disposal to continue the fight. But Somerset would not countenance serving alongside a Neville, let alone under one.

For two weeks Somerset and the Earl of Devon recruited in Dorset, Wiltshire, Devonshire, and Cornwall, but they probably failed to raise the numbers they anticipated. The city of Salisbury had promised Somerset forty men; they were sent to King Edward. Prince Edward appealed to the city of Coventry, but even his name evoked no enthusiasm. The civic leaders forwarded his appeal to King Edward.[39] It was not an auspicious beginning.

The Last Years

The Lancastrian army marched from Exeter to Glastonbury and on to Wells. The Bishop of Bath and Wells was none other than Robert Stillington, King Edward's chancellor, who had taken sanctuary when Warwick landed. A year later, in 1472, Stillington apparently claimed that when the Lancastrians passed through Wells, Margaret, Prince Edward, and the Duke of Somerset, the only names he knew since he was not there, 'with other adherents in great multitude and might arrayed in manner of war, riotously, with force and arms, entered and spoiled the palace of Wells and, among other great and detestable offences there brake up the gaol and prison' and freed the prisoners.[40] It was the Bishop's responsibility to secure his gaol and it was for his failure to do so that he received a general pardon in 1472. Yorkist propaganda that Margaret was unable to control her troops was alive and well, but in fact it was Somerset who ordered his men to break open the prison to swell his ranks; the canons gave him £30 to go away.[41]

King Edward had learned of Margaret's arrival on the same day as she met Somerset at Cerne Abbey.[42] If he had hoped that Warwick's death would keep her in France, he was disappointed. Margaret always made him apprehensive and he did not doubt that he would have to fight her. On 18 April he threw down the gauntlet and issued a proclamation to the sheriffs in every county reiterating at extreme length that *he* was the King of England and France, by right of title in the eyes of God. He had proved it in battle many times, most recently at Barnet. He declared that 'Margaret, calling her[self] Quiene which is a Frenshwoman bourne and daughter to hym that is extreme Adversarie and mortall enemye to all this our land ... and her son', were rebels and traitors. The Dukes of Exeter and Somerset, the Earls of Oxford and Devon, Lord John Beaufort and Lord Beaumont were proscribed along with six knight, two squires, and four clerics.[43] If this was the extent of Margaret's armigerous adherents she stood little chance of victory no matter where she or Somerset chose to make a stand.

The Final Throw

To allow time for a fresh army to muster and to demonstrate his indifference to the threat posed by the Lancastrians, Edward attended the Feast of the Garter at Windsor and ordered his men to meet him there. He left Windsor on 24 April and marched west in search of Margaret. He wanted to encounter her army as far as possible from the capital. He claimed later that his spies reported that Margaret sent advance parties towards Salisbury and Yeovill, as well as east along the south coast, to confuse him and make him think that London was her objective (which it should have been). It is unlikely that Somerset risked detaching men from his still small force and that the advance parties were outriders sent to recruit in these areas. Edward moved north through Abingdon and Cirencester and then to Malmesbury, which he reached on 1 May. Margaret and Somerset were at Bristol, where they were well received and supplied with men, money, and artillery.[44]

The armies were now close enough to each other to prepare for battle. For once Edward's intelligence was faulty. He took up a position at Sodbury Hill expecting Margaret and Somerset to move towards him.[45] Instead they pressed on to Gloucester, the closest crossing point of the River Severn for an army coming from Wales. Margaret had a misplaced faith in Jasper Tudor. The decision to march north-west rather than seeking out King Edward more directly had been influenced in part by her belief that Jasper had raised an army in Wales and would march to her aid. He did nothing of the sort. He was at Chepstow Castle in Monmouthshire and he stayed there. He did not cross into England with or without troops and he took no part in the battles to come. Jasper had had enough of defeats and he may have believed that Margaret's cause was already lost.

Edward sent orders post-haste to Richard Beauchamp, the constable of Gloucester Castle, to hold the castle and the causeway crossing the Severn at all costs. Margaret must not be allowed to escape into Wales and Jasper was not to be allowed into England. Did Margaret remember that King Henry had granted Gloucester Castle to her in 1447 but that she did not get it? Henry had already granted it to a favourite courtier, Lord Beauchamp of Powick and his son Richard, for life. Richard Beauchamp closed and manned the gates. The town was too strong to be taken by assault and with Edward's army so close, a siege was out of the question. The Lancastrians continued north along the banks of the River Severn over rough and difficult terrain to the next crossing point at Tewkesbury.[46] It did not have a bridge, only a ferry crossing which was not ideal, but the army was exhausted, it had been marching for days and it was imperative to give the men a rest. Had Somerset or anyone in his ranks known the countryside at all well they would not have come that way, but it was the shortest route and Somerset was in a hurry. He bivouacked on a ridge close to the river just south of Tewkesbury Abbey.

35

Captive Queen

Margaret marched with her troops, as she had in 1461, but without any clear long-term objective. The Duke of Somerset was in command of the army. Why he decided to turn and fight at Tewkesbury is not clear – perhaps he was afraid that Edward's army would fall on him from the rear if he continued his march. He formed his battle line on a ridge of high ground just south of Tewkesbury Abbey. Below the ridge the terrain was rough: it would not be easy to cross. King Edward halted at Tredington three miles from Tewkesbury. His scouts brought in reports of Somerset's disposition and Edward prepared his battle accordingly. He commanded the centre, again keeping Clarence with him, but this time he positioned the Duke of Gloucester to his left and Lord Hastings to his right. Hastings had fared badly at Barnet while Gloucester had done well, and Edward wanted Gloucester to face Somerset. Somerset had chosen to command the right of the Lancastrian line, not its centre. Edward of Lancaster held the centre because of his rank, with the Earl of Devon on his left. At first light on 4 May, just as he had at Barnet, Edward gave the order to engage.[1]

The Battle of Tewkesbury was a disaster waiting to happen. King Edward opened up with an artillery barrage and Gloucester's archers launched a murderous hail of arrows into Somerset's ranks. Somerset abandoned the high ground and led his men down from the ridge, using the wooded countryside as cover in an attempt to cut down the archers and capture Edward's guns. His circuitous route led him a

The Last Years

point between Gloucester's and the King's men and he ended up engaging part of Gloucester's division and part of King Edward's. Edward drove Somerset halfway back up the ridge and the spearmen that Edward had stationed out of sight several hundred yards west of the battle charged into Somerset's right flank at the far end of the battle line. Somerset's men broke and fled, the Duke with them. Edward of Lancaster had to take part in the battle or be accused of cowardice, because the Lancastrian army was supposedly fighting for him. But to place him in the centre was a disastrous, if inevitable, decision. Sir John Langstrother and Lord Wenlock were there to protect him, but Somerset's desertion of his position confused them and instead of following him down from the ridge they stayed where they were. King Edward threw the whole weight of his army against the Lancastrian centre. Their line disintegrated and men escaped in all directions, some back to Tewkesbury, some to sanctuary in local churches, some further afield. Many more died pursued by King Edward's victorious troops. No quarter was given.

Lord Wenlock died fighting and so did Prince Edward, if he fought at all.[2] King Edward had not intended Warwick to survive at Barnet and he did not intend Prince Edward to survive at Tewkesbury. Everyone in the King's ranks was on the lookout for the Prince of Wales' livery; he was the prime target and he stood no chance. All his life Prince Edward had heard stories of the glories of war and how someday he would go into battle to recover his kingdom, but Margaret had never allowed him to expose his person or learn how to conduct a battle or fight a war. He was seventeen, too old to start learning his trade, and once he returned to England there was no one to teach him. Tewkesbury was Prince Edward's first and last battle; left alone on the field he probably panicked and ran, although who cut him down and where is unknown. John Courtenay, Earl of Devon, commanding the left of the Lancastrian line against Lord Hastings, was killed. So was Somerset's brother, Lord John Beaufort. So were the men who had stayed with Margaret in exile and remained loyal to the end: Edmund Hampden, Robert Whittingham, and William Vaux.

King Edward showed no mercy to those who survived. He ordered his men to violate sanctuary and drag out the Lancastrian fugitives who had taken shelter in Tewkesbury Abbey: the Duke of Somerset, John Langstrother, who had deserted Prince Edward, Hugh and Walter Courtenay, Gervase Clifton, William Grimsby, Thomas and Henry Tresham among others.[3] They were tried on 6 May by the Duke of Gloucester as Constable of England and the young Duke of Norfolk (who is nowhere recorded as taking part in the battle) as Earl Marshall of England. They were beheaded on a scaffold in the centre of Tewkesbury and the streets ran red with their blood; they would have done better to stand and fight. King Edward permitted them and the unfortunate Prince Edward to be given decent burial in the abbey. The King pardoned some lesser men, including the ambivalent Dr Mackerell and the loquacious Sir John Fortescue. A lawyer first, last, and always, Fortescue obligingly adapted his arguments as to why King Henry VI was the rightful King of England and cheerfully demonstrated that in fact it had been King Edward all along.[4] Shortly after Tewkesbury Jasper Tudor sailed from Tenby in Wales taking his other nephew, Henry Tudor, to safety in Brittany. The wily Jasper had known both Edward of Lancaster and Henry Tudor all their lives and he had decided, even before the disaster at Tewkesbury, that the latter was his best bet for the future.

Prince Edward's death was the greatest misfortune that Margaret had ever suffered but she was given no time to grieve. Her ladies urged her to escape without delay. It was too dangerous to take sanctuary in Tewkesbury Abbey where she would be found and captured by King Edward's men. King Henry was still a prisoner in the Tower, and it was her duty as Queen to remain free. She and her ladies fled north with a small escort towards Worcester, hoping to find refuge and safety if they could reach Lancashire or cross into North Wales.

By coincidence, King Edward was headed the same way. News of a

The Last Years

fresh rebellion in the north prevented him from celebrating his victory. Edward was conditioned by past experience; trouble in the north could all too easily get out of hand and there was no Lord Montague to suppress it. Queen Margaret was still at large and might be headed that way. Victory at Tewkesbury had not, as he had hoped, crushed the Lancastrian menace after all. Edward left Tewkesbury on 7 May heading for Worcester and Coventry. As he neared Worcester his outriders reported that they had discovered Margaret's whereabouts. She had taken shelter at Little Malvern Priory north-west of Tewkesbury, not many miles from Worcester.[5] Edward ordered her and the ladies with her to be brought to him at Coventry, the town in which for so many years Margaret had dominated King Henry's court. Anne Neville, now a widow, was a far more valuable prize than Margaret. She was part heiress to the Neville and Beauchamp estates of her father and mother and they were now up for grabs. Edward sent her back to London to the custody of her sister Isabel, and Isabel's husband, the Duke of Clarence.

Edward reached Coventry on 11 May where he received his second piece of good news. Two days later Henry Percy, Earl of Northumberland, came in person to assure the King of his loyalty and of the loyalty of the northern lords and towns. Neville and Lancastrian power in the north was defunct and Percy gave Edward his word that there would be no future rebellions in that quarter.[6] A relieved King Edward turned south on 16 April, taking Margaret with him, to deal with another rebellion from an unexpected quarter.

Thomas Neville, Bastard of Fauconberg, Warwick's cousin, had commanded Warwick's ships ever since Warwick fled from England in 1469. Fauconberg was cruising in the Channel and so he missed the Battle of Barnet and the news of Warwick's death. As soon as he learned of it, Fauconberg decided to act. He sailed for Calais to recruit men from the garrison. Fauconberg was well known to them and he had no difficulty enlisting men in Warwick's name. Calais was Warwick's town, despite the refusal of Edward's officials to allow him to land there, and the garrison was probably as shocked as Fauconberg by Warwick's death.

Fauconberg returned to England in May just as the Battle of Tewkesbury was being fought. Warwick might be dead, but his name still had pulling power in Kent, especially in Canterbury. Edward had commissioned Anthony Woodville, Lord Abergavenny, the Sheriff of Kent and several local knights to keep an eye on the always tumultuous county of Kent while he was in the north.[7] Fauconberg called on Kentishmen to follow him and they turned out in large numbers.[8] He presented himself before the gates of London at the head of a large body of men. Calling himself 'Captain of King Henry's lieges of Kent', he demanded passage through the City and promised that there would be no looting. The Mayor and Common Council, always mistrustful of any army close to their city, did not believe him and they refused him entry. Fauconberg's men set fire to the gates at the southern end of London Bridge, and his ships at anchor in the Thames below the Tower turned their guns on the City while Kentishmen attacked the east gates. Anthony Woodville and Henry Bourgchier, Earl of Essex, organised the City's defence and eventually gained the upper hand. They chased the rebels as far as Stepney, killing many of them.[9] London was far too well defended for Fauconberg's assault to succeed and he withdrew his men to Blackheath. Then came the news that King Edward and his army were approaching London. Fauconberg retreated to Sandwich and the men of the garrison sailed back to Calais.[10]

This was the battle Margaret should have fought. There was never any chance that she could conquer London, but if instead of marching north she had returned to the south coast with the forces she had at her command and combined them with the resources of the Bastard of Fauconberg, an encounter with Edward might have turned out differently. She would then have been in a strong position to bargain with the Mayor and Common Council for the release of King Henry – and they would have bargained. The safety of their City was always of

The Last Years

more importance to the London oligarchy than which king sat on the throne. Margaret made the wrong choice and Fauconberg left it too late. A combination of distance and failure of communication was responsible for the missed opportunity. Fauconberg did not know where Margaret was, she failed to make contact with him, and her best chance to defeat Edward was lost.

King Edward and his lords rode into London on 21 May at the head of a splendid cavalcade with trumpets blaring and banners flying to be welcomed by the Mayor and aldermen. Queen Margaret was seated in a chariot surrounded by guards at the end of the triumphal procession. She was on public display as the King's prisoner, a symbol that Lancastrian power was broken once and for all and that King Edward IV, by the grace of God, was indeed master of the realm.[11] Did Margaret's pride enable her to remain impassive, or did her grief make her indifferent to Edward's cruel humiliation of the woman who had resisted him for longer than anyone else?

Margaret was conveyed to the Tower by the Duke of Gloucester as Constable of England and committed into the custody of Lord Dudley, Constable of the Tower. Dudley was a survivor. Margaret had known him since she first came to England. Margaret's arrival may have inadvertently caused King Henry's death; he died that same night.[12] To reach the inner ward Margaret and her escort had to pass the Wakefield Tower where Henry was confined. If he saw her, or learned that the wife who had been absent for so many years had been captured, the shock may have caused a catatonic seizure similar to the one he experienced in 1453. He fell and hit his head and the blow killed him. Henry's skull was unusually thin; it could have fractured in such a fall.[13] When his body was discovered Lord Dudley as Constable of the Tower was the first to be notified, but Margaret and the other prisoners would soon have learned of it. There was no keeping such sensational news quiet. Various reports of the manner of Henry's death circulated, and few doubted that he had been murdered on King Edward's orders. If his death was unexpected, an explanation had to be manufactured hastily and the official line was that he died from displeasure and melancholy.[14]

Henry's body was conveyed on an open bier to St Pauls and an overnight vigil was kept under heavy guard. He was given a royal burial: wax candles, fine linen, and costly spices were ordered for his internment.[15] The ceremony was held at Blackfriars and he was taken by barge up the Thames to Chertsey Abbey for burial.[16] It was said that his body bled at St Pauls and again at Blackfriars in mute protest of his having been done to death. For years afterwards people came to pray at his tomb and attest to miracles worked there through his intervention.[17]

If there was any fight left in Margaret it was extinguished by Henry's death. She had long since given up hope that Henry could become king again in fact as well as in name, but his death completed her devastation and she would have wondered what her ultimate fate would be. She did not remain in the Tower for long. Edward had her transferred first to Windsor and then in the autumn to Wallingford in the keeping of the de la Pole family.[18] Edward had granted custody of Wallingford to John, Duke of Suffolk, and his wife Elizabeth of York, Edward's sister.[19] Elizabeth was allowed eight marks a day (£5 8s) for the Queen's 'diets', which would have included feeding her attendants, among them the widowed Katherine Vaux.[20]

Alice, Dowager Duchess of Suffolk, lived nearby at Ewelme. It would be pleasant to think that Margaret visited her old friend there as she had done in King Henry company in the early days of her marriage, and that the two ladies resumed their friendship after years of estrangement. Alice would readily have sympathised with Margaret for the loss of Prince Edward. They each had one son to whom they had devoted their lives, but Alice's son had survived by not taking sides in the dynastic struggle. John of Suffolk was not numbered among the Lancastrian lords. He had obeyed his father's injunction to be guided by his mother and Alice had made it her life's work to protect him. She kept him away from national politics and

The Last Years

concentrated on retaining all the de la Pole lands. She had married him to the Duke of York's daughter, something of a risk in the late 1450s, but one which had paid off handsomely. John gave his allegiance to Edward when his brother-in-law grabbed the throne. He did not oppose King Henry's readeption, but he did not support it. He did not fight at Barnet or Tewkesbury, but he rode in the triumphal procession when Edward entered his capital. Edward created John a Knight of the Garter in 1472 while Margaret was at Wallingford. How much of what had happened in the long years of strife that followed John's father's death did the two ladies remember and discuss?

Unfortunately for Margaret, opposition to King Edward flared up again in the summer of 1473. The Earl of Oxford, as unrelenting as ever, menaced the English coasts with a small fleet of ships financed by King Louis. Oxford had fled to Scotland after the defeat at Barnet and the following year he sought support from King Louis, who was always happy to cause trouble for King Edward in any way he could. Oxford apparently turned pirate in emulation of the Earl of Warwick until, in 1473, he became more adventurous and attempted a landing on the Essex coast that was repulsed by the Earl of Essex. In September he captured St Michael's Mount in Cornwall only to be blockaded and starved out. Edward offered to pardon Oxford's men and he even pardoned Oxford himself, although he sent the Earl to prison in Hammes Castle where he remained for the next ten years.[21]

As a precaution against any attempt Oxford might make to rescue her, Edward had Margaret brought back to the Tower and placed under strict guard. There is no reason to suppose that the apartments allotted to her were any more uncomfortable than in most royal castles, albeit somewhat grimmer. Lord Dudley was allowed £5 a day for her food, and fabrics to replenish her wardrobe. William Dudley, Dean of the Chapel Royal and Lord Dudley's son, was paid for waiting on the Queen.[22] By 1473 Margaret was more concerned for her soul than for her body.

In May 1475, when memories of Tewkesbury and the death of

Prince Edward were particularly painful, Margaret was further saddened by the death of Alice of Suffolk at Ewelme. Alice's death severed Margaret's last links with a happier past. In July, Edward permitted her to join the Skinners' Company of the Fraternity of Our Lady of the Assumption of the Virgin, whose membership included Queen Elizabeth Woodville. Margaret had maintained her devotion to the Virgin and a miniature of her wearing a hooded brown cloak over a blue dress depicts her kneeling before a desk with a book of the Skinners' Company open before her and her crown and sceptre lying to one side of it, acknowledging her former status. The background is patterned with marguerites and gold roses and the caption reads 'sumptyme wyff and spowse to kyng harry the sexthe'. The attendant kneeling behind her may be Katherine Vaux, who was also admitted to the Fraternity. Eleanor Roos, now Eleanor Haute, who had been one of Margaret's damsels and was now in Queen Elizabeth's household, joined the Fraternity at the same time.[23] Edward's apparently generous gesture was part of his rehabilitation of Margaret, whom he was about to ransom to King Louis.

A momentous event determined the final chapter in Margaret life. In July 1475 King Edward launched the 'great enterprise of France' that he had been promising to undertake for years. Edward crossed to Calais with an army to recover, or so he claimed, the throne of France. He had an offensive alliance with his brother-in-law Duke Charles of Burgundy, King Louis's arch-enemy, although Charles was none too keen when it came to implementing it. Their treaty specified that Edward would be crowned at Rheims! King Louis, true to his policy of buying his way out of trouble whenever he could, offered to negotiate. Edward was not averse to the idea, since Burgundy was proving an uncertain and unreliable ally and Edward was ambivalent about war. Warwick had been right – it was very expensive. Edward had launched it to silence his critics in England who complained that he never kept his promises. He made a brief foray into Burgundian territory but at the same time he sent envoys to Louis offering terms,

The Last Years

provided they were his terms. Louis was to pay Edward 75,000 crowns (£15,000) within two weeks, and 50,000 crowns (£10,000) a year thereafter for the duration of their truce. In return Edward would take his army back to England.[24]

The two kings met informally at Picquigny in August and signed a treaty ratifying Edward's conditions. Louis was willing to pay highly to free himself from English interference and the agreement would make the King of England Louis's pensioner. In the light of this newfound amity other arrangements were discussed. Edward wanted to get rid of Margaret. Her continued presence in England was a liability and a nuisance, and he was obliged to pay for her upkeep. He floated the suggestion that Louis might be interested in investing in another piece of insurance, since Louis's declared objective was to become king of the whole of France. Louis agreed, and he offered to ransom Margaret for 50,000 crowns. Her value as a tradable commodity was thus set as equal to a year of Edward's pension money. On his way back to England Edward got rid of another incumbrance. Henry Holand, Duke of Exeter, had spent the last four years in the Tower, but Edward had taken him with the expedition to France for safekeeping. During the Channel crossing as the English fleet sailed for home, Exeter fell overboard and was drowned. It was a fortuitous accident, if accident it was: Exeter was the last remaining Lancastrian in the male line.

On 2 October 1475 King Louis signed the formal instrument for Margaret to exchange one jailor for another.[25] Edward was to receive 10,000 crowns on delivery of her person and 1,000 crowns a year thereafter until the ransom had been paid. It was not a bad deal from Louis's point of view, since it would take years to clear the debt; for Edward it meant an additional 1,000 crowns a year, which was not a bad deal either. Edward renounced whatever rights he had in the unfortunate queen and undertook that he would not support anyone laying counterclaims on her behalf against the French king. Margaret would be accompanied by Katherine Vaux and a small number of servants. Richard Haute, Queen Elizabeth's cousin, who had been lieutenant of the Tower when Margaret was first imprisoned there and so was a witness to King Henry's death, was to convey them from London to Sandwich.[26]

Margaret was not consulted about these arrangements, but she made no demur. In December she crossed the Channel to Calais in the custody of Thomas Montgomery. She knew Thomas from past associations. He had consistently espoused King Edward's cause while his elder brother, John, had upheld the family tradition of loyalty to Lancaster. John had been implicated in the Earl of Oxford's 'plot' in 1462 and executed as a traitor. Did Margaret remember that their mother, Elizabeth, Lady Say, had been a member of her court circle but had changed her allegiance when her godson, Edward, seized the throne? Lady Say had made no effort to use her influence with the King to save her eldest son.

Montgomery was travelling to France for a trade mission on behalf of English merchants at Bordeaux. He had handled the negotiations for Margaret's release into Louis XI's keeping and he could kill two birds with one stone by supervising her journey and her reception. He left Margaret in the care of the Treasurer of Calais while he brought his trade negotiations to a satisfactory conclusion.[27] Margaret had never visited Calais and she had never understood its importance.

Montgomery escorted Margaret from Calais to Rouen at the end of January 1476 and handed her over to the captain of Rouen and to Jean Raguier, the Receiver General of Normandy, who had paid her living expenses while she waited to cross to England in 1471. It was Margaret's third visit to the capital of Normandy, once as a bride, once as an exile, and now as a prisoner of state. Before Montgomery formally relinquished Margaret into French custody he received the first 10,000 crowns down payment and a bond for the remaining 40,000, and Margaret was made to sign letters formally renouncing her claim to the crown of England, to any dower as Queen of England, and to any other claims she might have against King Edward.[28] Margaret had been attainted and stripped of all her possessions in

The Last Years

England by the first Parliament of King Edward's reign, but Edward did not trust Louis not to stake a claim at some future date to an English inheritance through his kinship with Margaret.

Did Margaret wish to return to France? Probably. The men she had known who had formed her court were dead and there was nothing left for her in England. But the price of her homecoming was yet another humiliation: the Queen of England was being bought and sold like any other commodity. Margaret's ransom did not buy her freedom. King Louis's price was Margaret's disinheritance. The Milanese ambassador reported that it was Margaret's claim to Provence that Louis was after, but John Paston was closer to the truth when he wrote from Calais, 'The Duke of Bourgogne hath conquered Lorraine and Queen Margaret shall not now by likelihood have it; wherefore the French king cherisheth her but easily.'[29] Margaret's sister, Yolande had claimed Lorraine for her son after René's grandson, Nicholas died.[30] René II had declared war on Burgundy in the spring of 1475 after several years of hostilities, and in the autumn Duke Charles had invaded Lorraine and occupied the duchy.[31]

The document drawn up by Louis's notaries on 7 March 1476 required Margaret to make King Louis her heir. Long ago in her marriage treaty Margaret had renounced whatever claim she might have to her parent's heritage. That was forgotten – Louis wanted a more immediate guarantee. She was required to state that she made over to her cousin, voluntarily and unreservedly, all claims she might have to the Duchies of Lorraine, Anjou, Bar, and the County of Provence as an expression of her gratitude for the aid and comfort Louis had given her, for the expenses he had been put to in helping her husband and her son in their attempt to recover the English throne, and for Louis's generosity in paying a large sum to rescue her from her enemy King Edward, who had held her captive against her will.[32] Whatever she may have felt when faced with this travesty of the truth, Margaret accepted it. She had no choice. Louis was quite capable of keeping her in a captivity far more onerous than she had endured in

England if his terms were not met. Louis allowed her a pension of 6,000 *livres tournois* a year, but once she had renounced her rights in his favour, she was free to go wherever she wished; the King had no further interest in her.[33] René came to her rescue and provided her with a place to live at his manor of Reculée only a few miles from Angers, the home of her childhood.

Margaret spent the last seven years of her life in exile and isolation with a small staff of servants and Katherine Vaux as her companion. Few Queens of England have lived and died in such obscurity. She lived long enough to hear of the death early in 1477 of Charles, Duke of Burgundy, at the Battle of Nancy outside the town where she had been born. It was good news. Margaret's nephew, Duke René II was in command of the army that defeated the belligerent duke who had once promised her so much but done so little. A year later Margaret learned that King Edward had finally convicted his wayward brother, George, Duke of Clarence, of treason and had him executed. Clarence's desertion of Warwick had contributed to Edward's eventual victory and the ending of Margaret's hopes. If she still cared about anything in the past, she would not have mourned either death.

René of Anjou died in Aix en Provence in the summer of 1480 at the age of seventy. A year later his widow, Jeanne of Laval, fulfilled René's dying wish and brought his body back to Angers for a splendid funeral in the church of St Maurice that he had done so much to embellish.[34] The elaborate ceremony would have pleased René: it was exactly what he would have arranged for himself. It is not known if Margaret travelled the few miles from Reculée to Angers to witness her father's obsequies.

Uncertain of her future, Margaret wrote to King Louis's council indirectly asking what was to become of her. She was now entirely dependent on Louis's generosity, not a trait for which he was well known. Louis required her to reiterate her undertaking that whatever she might receive under the terms of her father's will would be vested in him.[35] It was not a great renunciation on Margaret's part, as she had

The Last Years

few expectations. Margaret was fifty-two years old when she died in 1482, only a year before her arch-enemy King Edward. In her will, drawn up on 2 August, she petitioned the King for her soul's sake and his, to pay her debts.[36] She had nothing to leave except her dogs, the last of her pitiful possessions, and Louis made sure he got his hands on them. He ordered an equerry to bring the dogs, every last one of them, on pain of his extreme displeasure if any were kept back.[37] But he granted Margaret's last request, and she was buried in the cathedral of St Maurice in Angers, where she had grown up the youngest daughter of a younger son, who had never expected to become a queen. Her tomb did not survive the French Revolution.

Appendix: Finances and Dower Lands

A.R. Myers published Margaret's only extant household account, 'The Household of Queen Margaret of Anjou for 1452-53', in 1957. It is reprinted in Myers, *Crown Household and Parliament,* pp. 135–209. All information in this appendix is taken from Myers except where noted.

In March 1446 Parliament confirmed Margaret's dowry of 10,000 marks or £6,666.13s 4d a year. It comprised Duchy of Lancaster estates valued at £2,000 plus an annuity of £1,000, and cash grants of £3,666 13s 4d. The cash grants were assigned on the Duchy of Cornwall: £1,008 15s 5d; the customs of Southampton: £1,000; and the Exchequer: £1,657.17s 11d.[1] Assignments on the cash-strapped Exchequer proved difficult to collect.

King Henry attempted to transfer a debt claimed by the English Exchequer against the Exchequer in Rouen for a transport tax collected by John, Duke of Somerset, in 1443 for his campaign of that year. The King maintained that these costs had been met by the English Exchequer so the money should be transferred from Rouen and assigned to Queen Margaret. It may be doubted that Margaret ever received it.[2]

Margaret struggled constantly, through her receivers, her auditors, and her lawyers, to collect her dowry and the debts owed to her.[3] She

Appendix: Finances and Dower Lands

complained to Marmaduke Lumley, Treasurer of England, that she had not received payment from the Southampton customs and that she needed the money urgently to pay her debts.[4] Her dowry was never fully met in any one year, and her expenses consistently outran her income. For this she has been harshly criticised. Myers depicts her 'as a woman eager for power and ever watchful to gain and keep all the income she could.' In 1452-53 income from Duchy of Lancaster estates, including arrears, amounted to £1,324 13s 0½d, not the £2,000 at which they were valued, although the annuity of £1,000 and the 500 marks (£333 6s 4d) granted to her in 1447 were paid in full. Her income should have totalled £7,000 but her household account records an income of £7,563 12s 1d because it includes arrears and £52 16s 2d from queen's gold. If all the arrears due by 1452-53 had been paid, her income in that year would have amounted to considerably more.

Late payment was the norm. The local receiver stated that the sums paid were for a given period, either current or arrears, and that was how they were recorded by Margaret's receiver general. When payments due from previous years came in, they were noted as arrears. The fee of £40 10s 10d from the shire of Essex, for example, was paid in full in the year of account, and there is a separate entry for the additional sum of £10 10s 10d as arrears for Anno 25 [1446-47], giving a total of £51 0s 20d. But the balance of £30 for Anno 25 was not received, and the full sum for Anno 28 [1449-50] was still outstanding. Outstanding sums were entered as *nec reddit* and carried over in the account.

Margaret spent over six months of the year in the King's household between 1446 and 1453, and she contributed the traditional per diem payments for the 'diets' of her servants when the King and Queen were together: £6 a day until 1453, and £7 a day thereafter. From 1446 to 1451 Margaret paid between £1,364 and £1,726 a year into the King's coffers. In 1448-49 the figure reached £2,000. In 1453 the account records a payment of £797 8s 11½d to the treasurer of the King's

Appendix: Finances and Dower Lands

household.[5] Margaret's wardrobe accounts have not survived. In 1452–53 she assigned £2,073 5s 8¼d to the keeper of her wardrobe in part payment of £2,098 9s 6d assigned earlier, leaving a deficit of £25 3s 10d. A note in the margin records that only £1,110 6s 8d was actually paid and that £962 19s 0¼d would be paid at a future date: *reddit anno future.*

Margaret's income was protected by successive parliaments. In 1447 the Commons acknowledged the difficulty of collecting Exchequer assignments and agreed that estates and fees reverting to the crown should be granted to Margaret in lieu of cash, provided that the value of these grants did not exceed the amounts assigned in cash.[6] The Commons exempted her dower lands from their three Acts of Resumption. In 1450 money from the Duchy of Lancaster was allocated to meet the costs of the King's household, but the Commons decreed that the Queen's annuities from the duchy must be met first. In 1451 the Commons assigned the whole revenue from customs to the defence of the realm, but they restored Margaret's £1,000 to her in 1453. In the same year they compensated Margaret for surrendering the Earldom of Pembroke to Jasper Tudor. In 1455 when they made grants to Prince Edward as Prince of Wales, Duke of Cornwall and Earl of Chester the Commons stipulated that any grants previously made to the Queen by King Henry or by Parliament were not to be affected. If they were, other assignments should be made so that she would continue to receive the 10,000 marks due to her.[7]

Queens's gold

Queen's gold was a traditional voluntary 'tax' of 10% on payments to the crown for a variety of fines, licenses, and pardons, the majority of which were for licences to found chantries. Margaret would have been better off if the tax had been mandatory. The account lists fifty-seven claims over a period of years. Forty-two were not paid; fifteen were paid from 1448 to 1452. The total received in 1452–53 was £52 16s 2d, and even this may have been £20 short. Though £20 is added into the total sum received, the entry opens with *nec reddit,* and the grant of the wardship, for which John Kemp, Archbishop of York, Gervase Clifton, and others paid £200, was revoked when King Henry took the wardship into his hands. Apart from that, the highest sum received was £6 13s 4d from a wardship and marriage for which 100 marks were paid; the lowest, 14s, from a payment of £7 for a feoffment to use.

Income from original dower lands granted 1446, Duchy of Lancaster

Estates	Value	Receipts 1452–53
Tutbury	£927 17s 4¼d	£526 9s 8¾d
Leicester	£250 7s 11¾d	£189 16s. 10½d.
Kenilworth	£15 4s 6¼d	£29 5s. 0d.

Essex, Hertfordshire, Middlesex & London comprising:
Pleshey and Hertford Castles towns and manors
Enfield Manor and Hackeys, a tenement (Middlesex)
Blancheappleton Hospital, Steward's Inn in the parish of St Olaf (London)
Walton Manor (Surrey)

	£555 16s 3d	£353 13s 5¼d
Weathersfield, Essex	£27 10s 7d	No record in account
Essex Shire Fee	£40 10s 10d	£51 0s 20d
South Parts comprising:		
Yarkhill [Hereford]	£6 13s 4d	
Crenden [Bucks]	£20 11s 4d	
Oxfordshire	£155 7s 9½d	
Total	£182 12. 5½d	£174 16s 4d

Appendix: Finances and Dower Lands

Duchy of Cornwall

Margaret's portion from the royal demesne of the Duchy of Cornwall was £1,008 15s 5d in cash. She received £886 19s 8½d in 1452–53, but no income from the duchy in 1451–52.[8] The unpaid balance, combined with the arrears, meant that Margaret was owed almost a full year's income from the Duchy of Cornwall by 1452–53. In 1457 the duchy was settled on Edward, Prince of Wales, as Duke of Cornwall.

Customs duties

£1,000 of Margaret's dowry was assigned on customs duties. In 1448 she surrendered £1,500 in uncashable tallies at the Exchequer and received a licence to ship uncustomed wool to recover this amount. Her £1,657 17s 11d in cash from the Exchequer was reassigned on the customs. King Henry granted her the right to appoint one of the two customs collectors for the ports of Southampton, London, and Hull.[9] In 1449 she surrendered £3,658 in dishonoured Exchequer tallies to be replaced by the same amount charged on the customs revenues from Southampton, with an additional sum of 1,000 marks, 'she having heretofore paid for the king divers sums amounting to 1,000 marks.'[10] Thomas Cooke and John Somerton, her collectors at Southampton recovered arrears of £220 7s 11d for 1449-50, but only £428 5s 5d for 1451–52, leaving a short fall of £571 14s 7d. The additional 1,000 marks granted to her in 1449 remained unpaid, but she received the full £1,000 of the original dower grant in 1450–1451 and 1452–53. A late payment of £13 6s 8d in January 1454 left £360 8s 11d unpaid. In 1456 the Council acknowledged that Margaret had received only part of the £4,324 10s 7d due, 'but cannot have payment of the residue because the said subsidies have expired.' She was granted a balance due of £1,722 7s 10d.[11]

Appendix: Finances and Dower Lands

Exchequer

£1,657 17s 11d in cash from the Exchequer in the original dower grant was reassigned on the customs in 1448. In 1452-53 the Exchequer paid Margaret £1,013 6s 8d in varying amounts as arrears dating back to 1446-47.

Grants from the Duke of Gloucester's estates, 1447

In February 1447 King Henry granted Margaret the Duke of Gloucester's annuity of 500 marks from the Duchy of Lancaster, plus crown lands and fees that Gloucester had held. Of the original twelve grants, six were confirmed to her for life in February 1452, backdated to 24 February 1447, for which arrears were to be paid.[12]

Estates	Value	Receipts 1452–53
Marlborough and Devizes (Wilts.)	Not given	£180
Middleton and Marden (Kent)	Not given	£80
Queenhythe	£50, £10 granted	£35 18s 11½d
Northampton Fee Farm	£120, £10 granted	£46 11s 3d
Oseney Convent	£20, £10 granted	£10
Scarborough Fee Farm with Waldegrave (Yorks.)	£27	Nil

Appendix: Finances and Dower Lands

Berkhamsted castle, lordship, and manor, 1448

Valued at 40 marks (£26 13s 4d) it returned £21 6s 10d as arrears, paid from February to June 1454. £6 13s 4d was assigned to Margaret's auditor, John Walsh, as his 'fee and reward'. Arrears amounted to £66 12s 6d when the account closed. Berkhamsted was held by the Duke of Exeter. Just before he died in 1447 King Henry granted the farm of the castle to Edmund Hungerford and Gilbert Parr, but Margaret sued for livery and it was granted to her in June 1448.[13] Berkhamsted was part of the Duchy of Cornwall. In 1459 Margaret surrendered it to Prince Edward as Duke of Cornwall.

Additional grants from 1451 to 1453

Following the Act of Resumption of 1451, Margaret received further grants of lands and income in lieu of her cash dowry. These were confirmed to her by Parliament in 1453 and by letters patent in 1457.[14]

Estates	Value	Receipts 1452–53
Haverford West[15]	£121 2s 9d	£125 10s 7d
Bristol Fee Farm[16]	£102 15s 6d	£154 3s 3d

To be paid in half-yearly parts. £51 7s 9d was paid as arrears in December 1453. The full amount for 1452–53 was paid, leaving an outstanding sum of £21 13s 1½d from Michaelmas, 1451.

Havering at Bower[17]	£92

Margaret exchanged Havering with King Henry for Corsham [Cosham] in Wiltshire, plus £20 from the customs on cloth in the port of London, in 1459. Corsham's value is not stated but if the combined income exceeded £92, Margaret was to pay Henry VI the balance. If

Appendix: Finances and Dower Lands

the income from Havering exceeded the income from Corsham plus £20, Margaret would receive the difference from the customs on cloth.

Hadleigh[18]   £14

The Duke of York lost Hadleigh in the Act of Resumption of 1450. The Duke of Exeter was granted a twenty-year lease on the manor only, valued at £14; this was resumed in the Act of Resumption of 1451. The manor, but not the castle of Hadleigh, was granted to Margaret in 1453.

Colchester[19]   £35

The castle, lordship, and fee farm of the town were granted to Sir John Hampton in 1447, on the same day that King Henry granted them to Margaret. They were recovered in the Resumption of 1451 and re-granted to Margaret in 1453.

Redewell[20]   £15
Combined   £156   Total £78 14s 11½d
Bradwell[21]   £72   £48 granted   Nil

Listed as a separate item. Margaret was granted £48 – two thirds of it. The remaining third belonged to Jacquetta, Duchess of Bedford.

Feckenham[22]   £25 6s 8d   Nil

Feckenham had been granted to successive queens: Eleanor (1272); Margaret (1299); Isabella (1327), and Philippa (1331), and in 1465 Edward IV granted it to his queen, Elizabeth Woodville. As so often happens in 'official' sources, *VCH Worcestershire,* British History Online, does not include the grant to Margaret.

Appendix: Finances and Dower Lands

Earldom of Pembroke

Valued at £400 2s 8d, Pembroke was held by the Duke of Gloucester. King Henry granted its reversion to the Duke of Suffolk, who held it from 1447 to 1450. Henry then granted the farm of Pembroke to Lord Beauchamp of Powick. He lost it in the Act of Resumption 1451, and it was granted to Margaret.[23] Margaret surrendered it to Jasper Tudor when he became Earl of Pembroke in 1453. Myers claimed that the arrears due to Margaret before Pembroke was granted to Jasper Tudor were paid, but assignments are not the same as payments. Margaret received no arrears from Pembroke. Parliament compensated Margaret for its loss with grants of other crown lands.

Grants in lieu of the Earldom of Pembroke, 1453.[24]

Estates	Value	Receipts 1452-53
Odiham		£20
Gillingham		£46
Rockingham[25]	£83 6s 8d	
Bridgestock	£20	
Kingscliff	£40?	
Kingsthorp	£10	
Combined value	£153 6s 8d	£153 6s 8d

The grant excluded any lands held therein by Jacquetta, Duchess of Bedford. King Henry had granted Sir Richard Roos the right to take £120 worth of fire and brushwood from Rockingham forest. He lost the right when the forest was granted to Margaret. She agreed to 'loan' him £60 in two parts, to be repaid when the King made him a compensatory grant. It appears that Roos repaid half, but that £30 was still outstanding in 1452–53.

Appendix: Finances and Dower Lands

Cash grants[26]

The cash grants to Margaret in compensation for the Earldom of Pembroke were made with the proviso that they had not previously been allocated to King's College, Cambridge, or for the performance of King Henry's will.

Cash.	Value	Receipts 1452-53
Southampton.	£100	£100
Norwich.	100 marks (£66 13s. 4d.)	100 marks
Ipswich	50 marks (£33 6s. 8d).	£20
Nottingham	£40	Nil
Derby	£26 13s 4d	£17 0s 8d
Queenhythe	£50, £30 granted 1453	Nil

Abbreviations

Annales	J. Stevenson ed., *Letters and Papers Illustrative of the Wars of the English in France,* II, ii. [Pseudo William Worcester]
Anstis, J.,	*The Register of the Most Noble Order of the Garter,* (1724)
Arrivall	K. Dockray, ed., 'The Historie of the Arrivall of King Edward IV, A.D. 1471' in *Three Chronicles of the Reign of Edward IV,* (Gloucester, Sutton, 1988)
Auchinleck Chron	T. Thomson, ed., *The Auchinleck Chronicle,* (Edinburgh, 1819)
Bale's Chron	R. Flenley, ed., *Six town chronicles of England,* (Oxford, 1911)
Benet's Chron	G.L.& M.A. Harriss, eds., *John Benet's Chronicle for the years 1400–1460,* Camden Miscellany XXIV, (Camden Soc., 4th ser. IX, 1972)
Berry Herald, *Chroniques*	H. Courteault, H., & L. Celier, eds., *Les chroniques du roi CharlesVII par Gilles Le Bouvier dit le Heraut Berry,* (Paris, 79)
Berry Herald,	J. Stevenson, ed., *Narratives of the expulsion of the English from Recouvrement Normandy,* (Rolls Series, 1863)
BIHR	*Bulletin of Historical Research*

Abbreviations

Bourgeois	Bourgeois of Paris, *A Parisian Journal,* trans. J. Shirley. (Oxford, 1968)
Brief Latin Chron	J. Gairdner, ed., *Three Fifteenth Century Chronicles,* (1880)
Brief Notes	J. Gairdner, ed., *Three Fifteenth Century Chronicles,* (1880)
Brut	F.W.D. Brie, ed., *The Brut, or the chronicles of England,* Part II, (1908)
Calmette et Pèrinelle	Calmette, J. & Pèrinelle, G., *Louis XI et l'Angleterre* (Paris, 1930)
Chastellain	G. Chastellain, *Oeuvres,* ed., Kervyn de Lettenhove, 7 vols. (Brussels, 1863–66)
Chron. London	N.H. Nicolas & E. Tyrell, eds., *A Chronicle of London from 1089 to 1483,* (1827)
Chronicon Angliae	J.A. Giles, ed., *Incerti scriptores Chronicon Angliae* ... (1848)
CLRO	Corporation of London Record Office
CPR	*Calendar of the patent rolls*
CClR	*Calendar of the close rolls*
CFR	*Calendar of the Fine Rolls*
Complete Peerage	G.E. Cokayne, *The Complete Peerage,* 12 vols in 13, ed. V. Gibbs, *et al.* (1910–59)
Croyland Chron	H.T. Riley, ed., *Ingulph's Chronicle of the Abbey of Croyland,* (1874)
Davis, *PL*	N. Davis, ed., *Paston letters and papers of the fifteenth century* 2 parts (Oxford, 1971–76)
Devon, *Exchequer*	F. Devon, ed., *Issues of the exchequer* ... *Henry III to Henry VI,* (Record Commission, 1837)
DNB	*Dictionary of National Biography*
EHL	C.L. Kingsford, ed., *English Historical literature in the Fifteenth Century*

Abbreviations

English Chron	W. Marx, ed., *An English Chronicle 1377–1461,* (Woodbridge, 2003)
Foedera	T. Rymer, ed., *Fœdera, Conventiones, Literæ, et … Acta Publica, inter Reges Angliæ …*, 20 vols., vol. XI, (1704–35)
Gairdner *PL*	J. Gairdner, ed., *The Paston Letters*, 6 vols (1904)
Gough London 10	R. Flenley, ed., *Six town chronicles of England,* (Oxford, 1911)
Great Chron	A.H. Thomas & I.D. Thornley, eds., *The Great Chronicle of London* (1938)
Gregory's Chron	J.A. Gairdner, ed., *The Historical London in the Fifteenth Century,* (Camden Society, new ser. 17, 1876)
HMC	*Historical Manuscripts Commission: Reports, Various*
John Vale's Book	M.L. Kekewich, *et al.*, eds., *The Politics of Fifteenth Century England: John Vale's Book,* (Stroud, 1995)
King's Works	R. Brown & H.M. Colvin, eds., *History of the King's Works: the Middle Ages,* 2 vols., (H.M.S.O., 1963)
Letters of Margaret	H. Maurer & B.M. Cron, eds., *The Letters of Margaret of Anjou,* (Woodbridge, 2019)
London Chrons	C.L. Kingsford, ed., *The Chronicles of London,* (1905)
Milanese Dispatches	P.M. Kendall & V. Ilardi, eds., *Dispatches with related documents of Milanese ambassadors in France and Burgundy, 1450–1461,* 2 vols., (Ohio University Press, 1970–1971)

Abbreviations

Milanese Papers	A. B. Hinds, ed., *Calendar of state papers and manuscripts existing in the archives and collections of Milan,* vol. I, (1912)
Monstrelet	*The Chronicles of Enguerrand de Monstrelet* translated by T. Johnes, 2 vols., (1877)
Myers, 'Household'	A.R. Myers, 'The Household of Queen Margaret of Anjou' in *Crown, Household and Parliament in Fifteenth Century England* (1985)
Myers, 'Jewels'	A.R. Myers, 'The Jewels of Queen Margaret of Anjou' in *Crown, Household and Parliament in Fifteenth Century England* (1985)
ODNB	*Oxford Dictionary of National Biography* (2001–2004)
Papal Letters	J.A. Twemlow. ed., *Calendar of Entries in the Papal Registers relating to Great Britain and Ireland,* vols X-XII (1915–1933)
PPC	N.H. Nicolas, ed., *Proceedings and Ordinances of the Privy Council of England, 22 Henry VI 1443 to 39 Henry VI 1461,* vol VI (1837)
PROME	A. Curry & R. Horrox, eds., *The Parliament Rolls of Medieval England,* vols X-XIII, (Boydell, 2005)
Ramsay	J.H. Ramsay, *Lancaster and York,* 2 vols, (Oxford, 1892)
Rawlinson B 355	R. Flenley, ed., *Six town chronicles of England,* (Oxford, 1911)
Rot. Parl.	*Rotuli Parliamentorum 1439–1468,* vol. V. (1832)
Scofield	C. L. Scofield, *The Life and Reign of Edward the Fourth,* 2 vols, (1923)

Abbreviations

Short English Chron	J. Gairdner, ed., *Three Fifteenth Century Chronicles,* (1880)
Somerville	R. Somerville, *History of the Duchy of Lancaster*, vol. I, 1265–1603, (1953)
Stevenson, *L&P*	J. Stevenson ed., *Letters and Papers Illustrative of the Wars of the English in France, during the Reign of Henry VI*, 2 vols in 3, Rolls Series (1861–64)
VCH	*Victoria History of the Counties of England*
Warkworth's Chron	J. Warkworth, *A Chronicle of the First Thirteen Years of the Reign of King Edward IV,* ed., J. O. Halliwell, (1839)
Waurin	J. de Waurin, *Recueil des croniques et anchiennes istories de la Grant Bretaigne, a present nomme Engleterre,* eds., W. & E.L.C.P. Hardy 5 vols., (1864–91)
Wavrin-Dupont	J. de Wavrin, *Anciennes chroniques d'Angleterre,* ed., Mlle. Dupont, 3 vols., (1858–1863)
Whethamstede	H.T. Riley, ed., *Registrum abbatiae Johannis Whethamstede,* 2 vols., (1872–73)

Notes

1 Woe to Thee O Land

1. R. Vaughan, *Philip the Good,* (2002), p. 5.
2. G. de Fresne de Beaucourt, *Histoire de Charles VII,* 6 vols (Paris, 1881--1891), I, p. 120.
3. G.L. Harriss, *Cardinal Beaufort,* (Oxford, 1988).
4. J.G. Dickinson, *The Congress of Arras,* (Oxford, 1955).
5. M.G.A. Vale, *Charles VII,* (1974), p. 161, citing BN. MS. fr 18441 fol. 112^{v}.
6. J. Blacman, *Henry the Sixth, a reprint of John Blacman's Memoir,* ed. M.R. James, (Cambridge, 1919). Roger Lovatt, 'A Collector of Apocryphal Anecdotes: John Blackman revisited,' in *Property and Politics,* ed. A. J. Pollard, (Gloucester, 1984), pp. 172-197.
7. S.E. Dicks, 'Henry VI and the daughters of Armagnac,' *Medieval and Renaissance Studies* Vol 15 No 4, (Emporia State Research Papers, 1967).
8. *Foedera conventiones litterae...,* ed. T. Rymer, vol. XI, pp. 7-8. *A Journal by the one of the suite of Thomas Beckington,* ed. N.H. Nicolas (1825).
9. T. Beckington, *Official Correspondence of Thomas Bekynton,* 2 vols., ed. G. Williams (1872), II, pp. 181 and 183-84.
10. Bekynton, *Correspondence* II, pp. 200-01.
11. Bekynton, *Correspondence* II, pp. 220-22, 228-29, 231-32, 234, 241 and 243 for a series of letters relating to Hans.
12. *The Brut, or the Chronicles of England,* ed. F.W.D. Brie, II, (Early English Text Society, 1908). *Brut F,* p. 485: 'And then the Kyng sent his ambassiatours ouer the see, which was the Markes of Suffolk, with other lordes, Clerkys, knyghtes and Squiers, out of England, to knowe of this worthy mariage, and for to make a finall peas betwene the Reames of England and Fraunce.'

13. *Brut G,* pp. 511--12: 'Se now what A mariage was þis, as to þe comparison of þat oþer mariage of Armynyke! for þer shold haue ben delyuered so many castels & townes in Gwyhen; And so moche gode shold haue bene yiffen with hir, þat al Englond shold haue bene enryched þer-by, but contrary-wise fell.' This version was printed by Caxton in his *Polychronicon.* It was utilised by Tudor historians and immortalised by Shakespeare (1 Henry VI, Act V Scene 5).
14. *Calendar of the Patent Rolls (CPR) 1441--46,* p. 424. M.G.A. Vale, *English Gascony 1399-1453,* (Oxford, 1970), pp. 125-26. Vale estimates that of the original 620 mustered, less than 370 arrived in Bordeaux.
15. *Proceedings and Ordinances of the Privy Council of England, (PPC),* ed. H. Nicolas, 7 vols (1834-37), V, pp. 226-27 and 229.
16. *PPC* V, pp. 303-04 and Appendix, pp. 409-14.
17. *John Benet's Chronicle for the years 1400 to 1462,* ed. G.L. and M.A. Harriss, Camden Miscellany XXIV, (Royal Historical Society, 1972), p. 190.
18. Beaucourt III, p. 265.
19. *PPC* VI, pp. 16-17. Foedera XI, p. 48-49. *Letters and Papers Illustrative of the Wars of the English in France during the reign of Henry VI,* ed. J. Stevenson, 2 vols in 3, Rolls Series, (1861--1864), I,, p. 440. When Giles returned to Brittany King Henry gave him a gold cup containing £100 as a parting gift.
20. *PPC* VI, pp. 7-9.

2 The House of Anjou

1. C. N. L. Brooke, 'The birth of Margaret of Anjou,' *Historical Research,* 61, (1988).
2. M.L. Kekewich, *The Good King: René of Anjou and Fifteenth Century Europe,* (2008).
3. The Duke of Lorraine's brother, Ferry, was killed at Agincourt. Antoine de Vaudemont was Ferry's son.
4. Vaughan, *Philip,* p. 120.
5. A. Lecoy de la Marche, *Le Roi René,* 2 vols. (Paris, 1875), I, p. 93
6. Lecoy I, pp. 101 and 105.

Notes

7. Lecoy I, pp. 104. Monstrelet, *The Chronicles of Enguerrand de Monstrelet*, 2 vols., trans. T. Johnes, (1877), I, pp. 612–13.
8. The Angevin claim to Naples is incredibly complicated. Disputes over it date back to the late thirteenth century. Charles, Count of Anjou, was King Louis IX of France's brother. He was also King of Jerusalem, and of Naples and Sicily, known as the Two Scillies. Charles lost Sicily in 1282 to the House of Aragon and died in 1285. His son, Charles the Lame, lost Jerusalem. He married Mary, daughter of the King of Hungary and claimed the title in her right. They had five sons and dynastic marriages with the House of Aragon produced rival claimants resulting in incessant internecine warfare. Charles the Lame's granddaughter became Queen Joanna I of Naples and chose Louis I of Anjou as her successor.
9. D. Abulafia, *The Western Mediterranean Kingdoms, 1220-1500*, (1997), pp. 195–98.
10. Monstrelet II, pp. 7–8. Kekewich, *Good King*, p. 56.
11. Abulafia, *Western Mediterranean*, p. 204
12. J. Harthan, *Books of Hours*, (1977), p. 93.
13. Lecoy I, pp. 117–18 makes this suggestion on the strength of an obscure sentence in the Milanese ambassador's letter: 'the Duke of Burgundy is considering abandoning a kinship tie to the King of France and becoming related to King René instead in order to make sure that he does get the Duchy. He is convinced he will succeed in his intention ...' There is no other source for this.
14. Lecoy I, p. 122–25. Kekewich, *Good King*, p. 31. The ransom for the Duke of Orleans, England's most valuable prisoner, was set at 200,000 crowns. The *écu* was worth approximately the same as an English crown, 3s 4d. Lecoy II, pp. 224–33 for the text of the treaty.
15. Lecoy I, p. 127. The suggestion is accepted by Strickland and by Hookham based on statements by the early French historians Quatrebarbes and Villeneuve-Bargement. A. Strickland, *Lives of the Queens of England*, II, (1851) p. 68. M.A. Hookham, *The Life and Times of Margaret of Anjou*, 2 vols (1872), I, p. 182.
16. The county of Provence was the only part of the Neapolitan inheritance that the Dukes of Anjou managed to retain, due to its geographical location in the south of France.

Notes

17 A. Ryder, *Alfonso the Magnanimous,* (Oxford, 1990) pp. 227–47 for René in Italy. In Ryder's words, 'Genoa and the Neapolitans were flabbergasted' by René's offer to bargain with Alfonso.

18 Kekewich, *Good King,* pp. 58–66. Kekewich believes that René's loss of Naples was not inevitable, but it is hard to see how he could have held it without the finances he so sadly lacked.

19 Strickland, pp. 167–168. Hookham, pp. 166 and 171. So enduring are the legends surrounding Margaret that popular historians continue to repeat the tale. See E. Hallam, *The Chronicles of the Wars of the Roses,* (1988), p. 200. A. Weir, *The Wars of the Roses,* (1995) p. 107.

20 Lecoy I, pp. 36–48. M.G.A. Vale, *Charles VII,* passim.

21 J.C. Sorley, *King's Daughters* (Cambridge, 1937), p. 89. J.J. Bagley, *Margaret of Anjou, Queen of England,* (1948) p. 25. Lecoy I, p. 6, for Tiphanie's epitaph. She was buried in the tomb René had built for her in the church at Saumur.

22 Beaucourt III, p. 305, suggests that the embassy came to negotiate a marriage between Margaret and Frederick, but he adduces no evidence to support it.

23 Geoffroy de la Tour-Landry, *The Book of the Knight of La Tour-Landry,* translated and edited by T. Wright (Early English Text Society, 1906).

24 C.C. Willard, *Christine de Pizan,* (New York, 1984). *A Medieval Woman's Mirror of Honor: the Treasury of the City of Ladies,* trans. Willard, (New York, 1989).

25 H. Maurer and B.M. Cron, eds., *The Letters of Margaret of Anjou,* (Woodbridge, 2019), pp. 158–70.

26 Lecoy I, pp. 226–27.

27 Beaucourt III, p. 260.

28 By one of those confusingly complicated relationships so common in the fifteenth century, Charles of Nevers was Burgundy's first cousin as well as his stepson. Nevers's mother had been Burgundy's second wife.

29 Dom A. Calmet, *L'Histoire de Lorraine,* 3 vols, (Nancy, 1728) II, p. 826.

30 C. A. J. Armstrong, 'La Politique Matrimoniale des ducs de Bourgogne de la Maison de Valois,' in *England, France, and Burgundy in the Fifteenth Century,* (1983), pp. 248–49.

31 Nevers married Marie, the daughter of the southern magnate Charles d'Albret.

3 The Truce of Tours

1. L. James, 'The Career and Political Influence of William de la Pole, 1st Duke of Suffolk,' University of Oxford, B.Litt. Thesis in Modern History, (1979). C.L. Kingsford, 'The Policy and Fall of Suffolk,' in *Prejudice and Promise in Fifteenth Century England*, (1925, reprint 1962) pp. 146–76, for a sympathetic portrayal.
2. *PPC* VI, pp. 32–35. Misdated to 1445.
3. *Foedera* XI, p. 53. J. Ferguson, *English Diplomacy*, (Oxford, 1972), pp 178–79 and 184. Exchequer warrants were also issued for Thomas Bird, Edward Chiltern, John Say, Lord Dudley, and Sir Thomas Hoo to accompany Suffolk, but it is not known if they went.
4. Stevenson, *L&P* I, pp. 67–76. Beaucourt III, pp. 272–73.
5. Beaucourt III, pp. 274–76. There is no contemporary account of the negotiations at Tours. Beaucourt's reconstruction is based on information contained in the French embassy's report of their negotiations in London in 1445. See below, Chapter 5.
6. Chastellain, *Oeuvres,* ed. Kervyn de Lettenhove, 8 vols. in 4, (Brussels 1863-1866), III, p. 452.
7. *Calendar of State Papers and Manuscripts existing in the Archives and Collections of Milan* I, ed. A. B. Hinds, (1912) p. 19.
8. Margaret Scott, *Late Gothic Europe, 1400-1500,* (1980), p. 41. The quotation is from Eustache Deschamps, writing in the fourteenth century.
9. T. Basin, *Histoire de Charles VII,* 2 vols, ed. C. Samaran, (Paris, 1934-1944), I, p. 292. Basin described her as pretty and well-formed, which at fourteen she probably was.
10. Beaucourt III, pp. 276–77
11. Lecoy II, pp. 254–57, 'Procès-verbal de la celebrations des fiançailles de Henri VI, roi d'Angleterre et de Marguerite d'Anjou'.
12. R.A. Griffiths, *The Reign of King Henry VI* (1981). p. 235.
13. A. Vallet de Viriville, *Histoire de Charles VII,* 3 vols (Paris, 1862-1865) II, p. 454, n. 3. A transcription of Bodley, MS Digby 196, f.151. Stevenson, *L&P* II, xxxvii. *Brut F,* pp. 485–86.
14. *Foedera* XI, pp. 59–67. S. Dicks, 'The Question of Peace: Anglo-French Diplomacy AD 1439-1449,' University of Oklahoma, PhD thesis (1966) pp. 127–29.

15 *Literae Cantuarienses* III, ed. J. Brigstocke Sheppard, (1889, reprint, 1966), pp. 176–83.
16 Beaucourt IV, p. 91 and n. 5. Margaret was escorted by Bertrand de Beauvau, Lord of Précigny, Guy de Laval, Alain le Queu, Archdeacon of Angers, and Etienne Bernard, the Angevin treasurer.
17 G. Leseur, *Histoire de* Gaston *IV, Comte de Foix* I, ed. H. Courteault, (Paris, 1983), pp. 151–52. M. d'Escouchy, *Chronique*, 3 vols, ed. G. du Fresne de Beaucourt, (Paris, 1863-64), I, pp. 40–42.
18 Calmet, *L'Histoire de Lorraine* III, *Preuves,* col. ccciij. B.M. Cron, 'The Duke of Suffolk, the Angevin Marriage, and the Ceding of Maine, 1445,' *Journal of Medieval History,* 20 (1994), pp. 79–92.
19 G. Le Bouvier, *Les chroniques du roi Charles VII par Gilles Le Bouvier dit le Héraut* Berry, ed. H. Courteault and L. Celier (Paris, 1979) pp. 269–70 and Appendix XVIII, p. 440. The herald's story that Charles and Margaret were in tears when they parted is repeated by French and English historians. The editors established that it is a later interpolation. Berry Herald, followed by Beaucourt, mistakenly listed Suffolk as being at Nancy. (Beaucourt IV, pp. 93–94).
20 M. Jones, 'Henry VII, Lady Margaret Beaufort and the Orleans Ransom,' in *Kings and Nobles in the Later Middle Ages,* ed. R.A. Griffiths and J. Sherborne, (1986), pp. 254–73. Angoulême had been a hostage in England for thirty-three years. His ransom was owed to Thomas, Duke of Clarence. Clarence's widow and his stepson John, Duke of Somerset, inherited the debt. In one of the last acts of his life, Somerset entrusted Suffolk with approaching Orleans to settle the matter. Suffolk and Orleans agreed on the enormous sum of £15,140 and Angoulême was released. Needless to say, the Orleans brothers did not honour the debt. They tacitly assumed that the renewal of the war in 1449 ended their commitment. It took the far more tenacious Margaret Beaufort, her son Henry VII, and her grandson Henry VIII, to keep the claim alive long after all the original protagonists were dead.
21 *Benet's Chron.,* p. 190.
22 C. Barron, 'London and the Crown,' in *Crown and Local Communities in England and France in the Fifteenth century,* eds. J.R.L. Highfield and R. Jeffs, (1981), p. 94. The exact sum was £1,766.6s 2d (*PPC* VI, pp. 322–25).

23 Stevenson, *L&P* I, pp. 443–64 and 467. BL Add. MS 23,938. Emma, Lady Scales, received £45 10s for the five-month period; her annual salary in Margaret's permanent establishment as Margaret's senior lady in waiting, was £40.
24 Stevenson, *L&P* I, p. 450. BL Add. MS 26,805-7, for Rouen's gifts to the queen.
25 Escouchy I, p. 89. Most accounts say the Countess of Shrewsbury, but this is a misreading of the text: *Auquel estoient la dessusdicte comtesse de Suffort, lesdictes dames de Talbot et de Salsbery; et estoit lacdicte comtesse en l'estat de la Royne, pareil que le jour qu'elle espousa.*
26 Stevenson, *L&P* I, p. 449.

4 England's Queen

1 *Brut F*, p. 488.
2 *PPC* VI, preface, p. xvi.
3 *Milanese Papers*, p. 18. This same gossipy ill-informed letter, written to entertain Bianca of Milan, contains the description of Margaret as 'somewhat dark'.
4 *Foedera* XI, pp. 76–77. Stevenson, *L&P* I, p. 450. The beast was conveyed to the Tower and its upkeep provided for.
5 KB 9/260/85, indictment of 11 January 1447. 'the said Bishop of Salisbury and othir mo that wer abowte our sayd sovrayn lord the kyng counselyd hym that he schuld not come nye her wyche is cause that schee is not consewyd and so the lond is desavid of a prince.'
6 Stevenson, *L&P* II, ii, p. 470. F. Devon, ed. *Issues of the Exchequer ... Henry III to Henry VI*, (1837), p. 451.
7 *Brut F*, p. 488–89.
8 *The History of the King's Works: The Middle Ages*, 2 vols. ed. H.M. Colvin, (1963), II, pp. 935–36.
9 Kingsford, 'London in the Fifteenth Century,' in *Prejudice and Promise*, pp. 107–45. C.M. Barron, *London in the later Middle Ages*, (Oxford, 2004).
10 *Foedera* XI, pp. 82–83
11 J. Stow, *A Survey of London*, 2 vols. ed. C.L. Kingsford, (Oxford, 1908), II, pp. 173–74.

Notes

12. C. Brown, 'Lydgate's verses on Queen Margaret's entry into London', *Modern Language Review,* VII (1912) pp. 225-234. R. Withington, 'Queen Margaret's entry into London, 1445', Modern *Philology,* (May 1915), pp. 53-57. G. Kipling, 'The London Pageants for Margaret of Anjou', *Medieval English Theatre* 4, (1982), pp. 5-27. G. Kipling, *Enter the King,* (Oxford, 1998), pp. 188-201.
13. *Foedera* XI, p. 84. *PPC* VI, pp. 39 and 99. The 'Iklyngton Collar' had been pledged as security for a loan of 500 marks. Henry 'requested' its return for Margaret's coronation. The 500 marks were not repaid until August 1450.
14. Quarterly of six pieces enclosed in a green border: eight horizontal stripes of alternating silver and red for the kingdom of Hungary; gold fleur de lys on a blue background and a gold bar with three points at the top of the blazon for Naples; a large silver cross enclosing four gold crosslets for Jerusalem; fleur de lys on a blue background with a red border for Anjou; crosslets on a blue background displaying two barbells (fish) with golden scales for Bar; and a diagonal red bend (stripe) adorned with three silver eaglets on a gold background for Lorraine.
15. Devon, *Exchequer,* p. 462.
16. No record of Margaret's coronation has survived. The following reconstruction is based on G. Smith, *The Coronation of Elizabeth Wydeville* (1935), pp. 14-25. A.F. Sutton, and P.W. Hammond, *The Coronation of Richard III* (Gloucester, 1983). pp. 41-43. See also *Brut F,* p. 445, and *Gregory's Chronicle* in *The Historical Collections of a Citizen of London in the Fifteenth Century,* ed. J. Gairdner, (Camden Society XVII, 1876) p. 139, for descriptions of Queen Katherine's coronation banquet.
17. C.A. Knudsen, 'Antoine de la Sale's voyage to England,' *Romance Philology* 2 (1948-49), pp. 90-94. Devon, *Exchequer* p. 542. De la Salle and John D'Escoce received 100 marks each. John de Surenceurt, Margaret's steward on her way to England, received 50 marks.
18. *Rotuli Parliamentorum* V, pp. 118-20. See Appendix.
19. *Letters of Margaret, passim.*
20. K.B. McFarlane, *The Nobility of Later Medieval England,* (1973), p. 290: 'Patronage and service were the essence of contemporary society.'
21. Myers, 'Household', pp. 192-94.

Notes

22 *CPR 1452-61*, pp. 114 and 149.
23 Myers, 'Household', pp. 196 and 204.
24 A. R. Myers, 'The Household of Queen Margaret of Anjou, 1452-53', in *Crown, Household and Parliament in Fifteenth Century England*, (1985), pp. 207–08. From 1453 Margaret contributed £7 a day to the king's household. See Appendix A.
25 Myers, 'Household', *passim*.
26 *Letters of Margaret,* pp. 69–71. Myers, 'Household', p. 185.
27 Devon, *Exchequer,* pp. 454–55.
28 Five of Margaret's jewel accounts are extant: E 101/409 /14 (1445-46); E 101/409/17 (1446-47); E 101/410 /2 (1448-49);E 101/410/8 (1451-52). A.R. Myers, 'The Jewels of Queen Margaret of Anjou', in *Crown, Household, and Parliament,* pp. 211–229.
29 *Letters of Margaret,* pp. 85–87. Hayford went on to become Mayor of London under Edward IV.
30 Cambridge, Fitzwilliam Museum MS 38 1950. It has John Stafford's arms and the royal arms, to which those of Anjou have been added. Stafford may have presented it to Margaret to welcome her to England or to celebrate her coronation.
31 BL MS Egerton 1070 f. 94v.
32 Oxford, Jesus College MS 124.
33 *Liber Regie Capelle,* ed. W. Ullman, (Henry Bradshaw Society XCII, 1961), p. 7.
34 Myers, 'Household,' p. 200. Margaret's offerings amounted to £7 11s. Myers remarks reprovingly that this number of feasts is greater than Edward IV authorised!
35 G.F. Warner and J.P. Gilson, *Catalogue of Western Manuscripts in the Old and Kings Collections,* vol.2, (1921), pp. 177–79. Michel-André Bossy, 'Arms and the Bride', in *Christine de Pizan and the Categories of Difference,* ed. Marilyn Desmond, (Minneapolis, 1998), pp. 236–256.
36 A.F. Sutton and L. Visser-Fuchs, *Richard III's Books* (Gloucester, 1977), pp. 144 and 289–90. The suggestion that it might have belonged to Margaret is my own.
37 *King's Works,* II, p. 949. Myers, 'Household,' p. 204 and pp. 194–95.
38 *CPR 1446-52,* p. 143.

Notes

[39] J. Twigg, *A History of Queens College, Cambridge, 1448-1986*, (Woodbridge, 1987), pp. 34–35.
W.G. Searle, *History of the Queens College of Saint Margaret and Saint Bernard in the University of Cambridge, 1445-1560*, (Cambridge, 1867), pp. 15–16. R.G.D. Laffan, 'Queens College'. in *The Victoria County History of Cambridgeshire* III, (1959) pp. 408–15.

[40] *CPR 1441–46*, pp. 442 and 447.

[41] *Register of Thomas Beckington*, 2 vols. ed. H.C. Maxwell-Lyte, Somerset Record Society XLIX, (1934-35), II, pp. xliv-xlvii.

[42] Myers, "Household', p. 147, n. 2, infers that Caraunt was less important than George Ashby, Margaret's clerk of the signet, because he received no wages. But Ashby was only in minor orders; he was not eligible for a cure of souls position. Caraunt was in full orders and beneficed so he was not paid a wage, although he was remunerated for his outlay on pens, paper, ink, etc. Caraunt, as secretary to the Queen's council, was more important than Ashby. It is wonderful how writing poetry (even bad poetry) enhances a man's reputation in the eyes of historians.

[43] *Calendar of Entries in the Papal Registers relating to Great Britain and Ireland, Papal Letters* vols X-XII, eds. J.A. Twemlow, and W.H. Bliss, (1915-1933) pp. 2–4.

[44] *Papal Letters* X, p. 116, and XI, p. 184. *Letters of Margaret*, pp. 32–34.

5 The Quest for Peace

[1] *The Parliament Rolls of Medieval England, 1275, 1504*, vols XI–XIII, ed. A. Curry (2005), XI, pp. 410–12. Hereafter *PROME*.

[2] Stevenson, *L&P* I, pp. 87–148. A detailed account of the month-long visit of the French ambassadors (2 July to 30 July) encompassing the diplomatic negotiations, and pp. 153–59 for a shorter version of their arrival and reception.

[3] *Foedera* XI, pp. 86–87. Beaucourt IV, p. 145. *Benet's Chron.*, p. 191. Louis of Bourbon, the Count of Vendôme; Guy, Count of Laval; the Archbishop of Rheims; Bertrand de Beauvau; Guillaume Cousinot and Etienne Chevalier. René of Anjou sent Baudoin de Champagne the Lord of Tucé, treasurer of Anjou, and his secretary Guillaume Gauquelin, called Sablé.

Guillaume de Malestrait the bishop of Nantes, the Seigneur de Guémenée chancellor of Brittany, and Henri de la Villeblanche represented the Duke of Brittany. Jean Gillain and Alençon Herald represented the Duke of Alençon, and Alphonse de Breçiano represented the King of Castile.

4. Stevenson, *L&P* I, pp. 90–113.
5. *Foedera* XI, pp. 94–95. *CPR 1441–46*, p. 359.
6. Stevenson, *L&P* I, pp. 128–41.
7. Stevenson, *L&P* I, p. 142.
8. Stevenson, *L&P* I, pp. 143–48.
9. Bedford took the title Duke of Anjou after his victory, but he never conquered the Duchy, an inconvenient fact the English preferred to ignore. Even today few English historians bother to distinguish Maine from Anjou in this context.
10. Lecoy II, pp. 258–60.
11. *Foedera* XI, pp.106–07.
12. Lecoy I, p. 131. In 1438 a truce between Edmund Beaufort, Count of Maine, and Charles of Anjou, Count of Maine, established which parts of the unfortunate county each might tax to sustain their respective war efforts (Harriss, *Beaufort*, p. 282).
13. Stevenson, *L&P* I, pp. 164–67.
14. E 101 /409 /14.
15. Stevenson, *L&P* II, ii, pp. 639–43. The original of this letter is not extant. It is known from a copy included in a French report of a meeting in Le Mans in 1447 contained in 'William Worcester's Collections'. On the same day Henry wrote another letter to Charles VII touching on the extension of the truce and his intention to visit France, which does not mention Maine. (Escouchy III, pp. 151–53). He wrote again on the same theme on 2 January 1446 without reference to Maine. (Stevenson *L&P* II, pp. 368–71).
16. *Foedera* XI, pp. 111–14.
17. *PROME* XI, pp. 471–72.
18. Stevenson, *L&P* I, pp. 183–86.
19. *PPC* VI, pp. 46-49. *CPR 1441–46*, pp. 430–31. The list of commissioners is impressive; men of rank in almost every county are named.
20. P.A. Johnson, *Duke Richard of York, 1411–1460* (Oxford, 1988), p. 57.

York was owed the enormous sum of over £38,000 for his wages and expenses.

21 B.L. Harleian MS. 543, printed in *The Politics of Fifteenth Century England: John Vale's Book,* ed. M.L. Kekewich *et. al.,* (Stroud, 1995) pp. 180–83.
22 Griffiths, *Henry VI,* p. 505, citing *HMC* IX part 2, p. 410. He establishes that it is misdated in *HMC* to 1456. Stevenson, *L&P* I, pp. 79–86, 160–63, and 168–70.
23 BN MS Fr 4054 fol. 79.
24 Beaucourt IV, p. 289.
25 BN MS Fr. 4054, fol. 94
26 R. Virgoe, 'The composition of the king's council 1437-61', in *East Anglian Society and the Political Community of late Medieval England* (1997), p. 276.
27 Edmund Beaufort held a bewildering array of titles: Count of Mortain and Count of Maine in France; Earl of Somerset and Marquess of Dorset in England until he became Duke of Somerset in 1448.
28 M. K. Jones, 'Somerset, York and the Wars of the Roses', in *EHR,* CCCCXI, (April 1989) p. 292.
29 Stevenson, *L&P,* ii, p. 449.
30 *Foedera* XI, pp. 151–55.

6 Destruction of a Duke

1 C. A. Metcalfe, 'Alice Chaucer, Duchess of Suffolk, c.1404-1475', University of Keele, BA dissertation, (1970) pp. 15–19.
2 Griffiths, *Henry VI,* p. 130: 'The bane of a landowner's life was more likely than not to be his neighbours or his tenants.'
3 MS Trinity College, Cambridge, R. 3.20. H.N. MacCracken, 'An English friend of Charles of Orleans', *Publications of the Modern Language Association of America,* 26, (1911), claims that Suffolk wrote poems in English and dedicated one to Margaret. His argument is not entirely convincing. John Shirley (1366-1456) was a friend of John Lydgate. He credits Suffolk with writing poems in French. (W.F. Schirmer, *John Lydgate,*(1961), pp. 251–52.

Notes

4. R.F. Green, *Poets and Princepleasers*, (Toronto, 1980), p. 96.
5. E 404/63/14. 8. Alice was paid £200 in January 1447.
6. E 101/409/17. In 1446-47 Alice and Suffolk received six large gold plates each, with a total value of £90. Their son, John, received 'an armlet like a horn, decorated with pearls' and three diamonds worth £12. He was three years old.
7. *CPR 1441–46*, p. 198.
8. B.P. Wolffe, *Henry VI*, (1981) p. 130, citing C 81/1370/41.
9. *Brief Notes* in *Three Fifteenth Century Chronicles*, ed. J. Gairdner (1880), pp. 149–50. *Bale's Chron.*, p. 121. *Benet's Chron.*, p. 192.
10. K.H. Vickers, *Humphrey, Duke of Gloucester* (1907), the only biography of the Duke, is outdated. See Harriss, *Cardinal Beaufort* for a modern analysis.
11. H.E. Carey, *Courting disaster*, (1992), pp. 138–41.
12. *Brut F*, p. 478–81. *Brut G*, pp. 508–09. *Benet's Chron.*, p. 188–89. *English Chron.*, pp. 61–64. *Gregory's Chron.*, pp. 18384. *Rawlinson B 355*, p. 102. *Bale's Chron.*, pp. 115–16A. *Chronicle of London from 1089 to 1483*, eds. N.H. Nicolas and E. Tyrell, (1827), pp. 128–30. *The Chronicles of London (Cleopatra C IV)* ed. C.L. Kingsford, (1905), pp. 148–49 and 154. *The Great Chronicle of London*, A.H. Thomas and I.D. Thornley, eds. (London, 1938), pp. 17–76 and 222. *Annales*, [Pseudo William Worcester], in Stevenson, *L&P* II, ii, pp. 762–63.
13. R.A. Griffiths, 'The Trial of Eleanor Cobham: an episode in the fall of Duke Humphrey of Gloucester', in *King and Country: England and Wales in the fifteenth century*, (1991) pp. 233–252.
14. *Foedera* XI, pp. 178–79. *CPR 1446-52*, p. 74. A pardon subsequently issued to one of Gloucester's servants stated that he 'and others' had conspired 'to slay the king, purposing to make the said duke king, and to deliver Eleanor his wife from the prison where she was detained for high treason.'
15. It is still cited as 'evidence' of Gloucester's opposition, but it originated with a Tudor historian, Polydore Vergil: *Three Books of Polydore Vergil's English History, comprising the reigns of Henry VI, Edward IV, and Richard III*, trans. H. Ellis (Camden Society, 1844) p. 69. Later historians' accounts of the responsibility for Maine have become inextricably

entwined with Humphrey's death. It is still seen as 'suspicious' because of its timing.

16 *PROME* XI, p. 411.
17 J. Watts, *Henry VI and the Politics of Kingship* (Cambridge, 1996), p. 230, n. 112, citing C 47/14/6 no. 48.
18 J.S. Roskell, *The Commons and their Speakers in English Parliaments 1376-1523* (1965), pp. 229-30.
19 *Original Letters Illustrative of English History,* Second Series I, ed. H. Ellis, (1827), pp. 108-09.
20 *An English Chronicle of the reigns of Richard II, Henry IV, Henry V, and VI... with an Appendix,* ed. J.S. Davies, (1856), pp, 116-118. The account by Richard Fox, a monk of St Albans, is the most nearly contemporaneous.
21 *PROME* XII, pp. 23 and 29.
22 *CPR 1446-52,* pp. 45 (Suffolk) and 87 (Fiennes). Fiennes had no legal claim to the title: his elder brother Roger, Treasurer of the household until 1446, was still alive.
23 *Letters of Margaret,* p. 140.
24 E101/409/17. '£432 7s 5d received from William Boston, goldsmith of London, for the price of various jewels bought by the queen's council from the administrators and occupiers of the goods and chattels of Humphrey, late Duke of Gloucester for the use of the same and afterwards sold to the same William.'
25 *PROME* XII, pp. 19-22. *Foedera* XI, p. 155 (original grants). *CPR 1446-52,* p. 559 (confirmation of grants). See Appendix.
26 *CPR 1446-52,* pp. 33 and 48. Summoned to Parliament as John, Lord Beauchamp, and created Baron Beauchamp of Powick, 2 May 1447, with an annuity of £115 for good service to Henry V.
27 T.F. Tout in *DNB.* J.H. Ramsay, *Lancaster and York,* 2 vols. (1892), II, p. 77.
28 E101/409/14 and 17. A gold tablet with an image of the Virgin, worth £40 in 1445. A gold cup with amethysts, worth £66 13s 4d, in 1446, one of the most expensive gifts Margaret ever gave. Gloucester reciprocated, but the jewel accounts do not record his gifts.
29 K.B. McFarlane, 'At the deathbed of Cardinal Beaufort', in *England in the Fifteenth Century,* (1981), p. 134.

30. Harriss, *Beaufort*, p. 368.
31. *A Collection of all the Wills... of the Kings and Queens of England...*, ed. J. Nichols, (1780), pp. 339–40.

7. Ceding Maine

1. *CPR 1446-52*, p. 78. *Foedera* XI, pp. 172–74.
2. *Foedera* XI, pp. 160–62.
3. James, 'Suffolk', p. 206, citing E 404/63/132 and E 403/767 m 9: 'The ambassadors received payments totalling £644 3s 4d for their expenses and a number of gifts. Dunois received a pair of parcel gilt flagons and a gold cup worth £101 2s 3d, plus £33 6s. Beauvau received two parcel gilt flasks and twelve cups worth £79 8s. 5d. Cousinot received a pair of parcel gilt flasks worth £40 4s. 6d. and Havart a pair of small flasks worth £25 6s. 8d. E 101/409/17 for Margaret's £50.'
4. *Foedera* XI, pp. 176–77. The Duke of Buckingham, Adam Moleyns, Lord Dudley, and the veteran Lord Scrope of Masham were the other English negotiators.
5. *Foedera* XI, pp. 182–84.
6. Stevenson, *L&P* II, ii, pp. 642–43.
7. T. Basin, *Histoire des règnes de Charles VII et de Louis XI*, ed. J.E.J. Quicherat, 4 vols (Paris, 1855-89), IV, pp. 287–88.
8. A. Marshall, 'The Role of English War Captains in England and Normandy, 1436-1461', University College, Swansea, MA thesis, (1974), p. 288. A.J. Pollard, *John Talbot and the War in France, 1427-1453* (1983), p. 79.
9. Beaucourt IV, pp. 24 and 38, n. 1. Gough received 2,750 *livres tournois* from Charles VII.
10. Escouchy III, p. 157. James, 'Suffolk', p. 172 n. 1, citing E 403/762 m.11. Gough collected £116 13s 4d from the exchequer as part of Giles's pension.
11. The date of Camoys's capture is uncertain. There were two attacks on La Guerche, one by Edmund Beaufort in 1438 and a second by John Beaufort in 1443. *London Chrons.* (*Cleopatra C IV*), p. 145, dates Camoys's capture to 1438, but a grant to Isabel Camoys, because of her

Notes

husband's capture, is dated October 1443 (*CPR 1441–46*, p. 219). Matthew Gough was with John Beaufort's expedition of 1443 (Jones, 'John Beaufort', pp. 93 and 95), but Jones does not mention Camoys.

12 M. H. Keen, *Chivalry*, (New Haven, 1984), p. 175.
13 *Letters of Margaret*, pp. 126–27.
14 *Calendar of the Close Rolls (CClR)*, 1441–47, p. 460. Watts, *Henry VI*, p. 238 n. 147 speculates that the summons was because Camoys had voiced criticisms of Edmund Beaufort, shortly to be appointed the King's lieutenant in France. This adds weight to the argument for 1438 as the date of Camoys's capture.
15 Stevenson, *L&P* II, ii, pp. 696–702.
16 Stevenson, *L&P* II, ii, pp. 704–10.
17 Stevenson, *L&P* II, ii, pp. 692–96 and 702–03.
18 K.B. McFarlane, 'A Business Partnership in War and Administration, 1421–45' in *England in the Fifteenth Century*, pp. 150–174, for Molyneux's career.
19 Stevenson, *L&P* II, ii, pp. 670–72.
20 *Foedera* XI, pp. 189–91 and 19--94. *CClR 1447-54*, pp. 37–38.
21 Stevenson, *L&P* II, ii, pp. 634–90. The chronology in this document is chaotic, interspersed with copies of letters and mandates from Charles VII and Henry VI dating back to 1445, including the various dates for the surrender of Maine.
22 Jones, 'Somerset, York', p. 293 and n. 5. Lecoy I, p. 131. René of Anjou had valued Charles of Anjou's 'share' of the county of Maine at 4,000 *livres tournois* when he settled the county on his brother in 1437.
23 Stevenson, *L&P* II, ii, pp. 710–18
24 Escouchy III, pp. 175–78.
25 Stevenson, *L&P* I, pp. 198–201. The letter is dated 20 January.
26 Beaucourt IV, p. 303 and n. 2. Escouchy III, p. 183.
27 *Foedera* XI, pp. 196–97.
28 Escouchy III, pp. 189–90.
29 Stevenson, *L&P* II, pp. 361–68, misdated to 1445.
30 Escouchy III, p. 186.
31 Stevenson, *L&P* I, p. 482.
32 *Foedera* XI, pp. 19--204.

33. Wolffe, *Henry VI*, p. 198.
34. Stevenson, *L&P* II, ii, pp. 718. Stevenson, *L&P* I, pp. 207–08.
35. *Foedera* XI, pp. 204–06. Twenty-four signatures, including that of Lord Camoys, are appended, and it was signed by 'many others'.
36. Escouchy I, pp. 12831, with Beaucourt's chronological notes for a summary of these events.
37. *Foedera* XI, pp. 215–16.
38. Lecoy I, p. 221. Champtocé in Anjou had belonged to Gilles de Rais. Duke John V of Brittany claimed that de Rais bequeathed it to him, and he gave it to his younger son, Giles. René of Anjou maintained that Champtocé reverted to him on de Rais's death, and he bestowed it on his wife Isabelle in 1442 as a token of his gratitude for her support in Naples.
39. M.H. Keen and M.J. Daniel, 'English Diplomacy and the Sack of Fougères in 1449', *History,* Vol. 59, No. 197 (October 1974), pp. 38–86.
40. E.C. Williams, *My Lord of Bedford, 1389-1435* (1463), pp 135-36.
41. *CPR 1436-41*, p. 543.
42. Stevenson, *L&P* I, pp. 473–76. Hugh E.L. Collins, *The Order of the Garter, 1348-1461,* (Oxford, 2000), p. 200.
43. *Foedera* XI, pp. 206–10. The explanation that Brittany's name was added belatedly is more acceptable than the fantastic story that representatives of the signatories climbed down into a ditch, in the dark, outside Le Mans to exchange copies of the document. This, it was claimed, led to the oversight of Brittany's status as a vassal of England! For this version see Keen and Daniel, 'Fougères', p. 387. It is rightly rejected by Wolffe, *Henry VI,* p. 203.

8 The King's Lieutenant in France

1. Harriss, *Beaufort*, p. 355 and *passim* for Edmund's early career.
2. Jones, 'Somerset, York', p. 291.
3. It is nowhere recorded how many of Somerset's children were in Rouen.
4. Stevenson, *L&P* I, pp. 241–42, misdated to April 1449.
5. Basin, *Charles VII* II, ed. Samaran, pp. 66–67.
6. Jones, 'Somerset, York', pp. 298–300.

7. *Letters of Margaret,* pp. 129–30. Jones, 'Somerset, York', p. 298. Beaumont received 3,000 *livres tournois.*
8. Shrewsbury's wife was Margaret Beauchamp, the eldest of the Beauchamp sisters, daughters of Richard Beauchamp, Earl of Warwick. Somerset's wife, Eleanor, was her younger sister.
9. Bourgeois of Paris, *A Parisian Journal,* trans. J. Shirley (Oxford, 1968), p. 341.
10. Basin, *Charles VII* I, (ed.) Samaran, p. 269.
11. *The New Oxford Dictionary of National Biography (ODNB),* A. Curry, 'Mundeford'. Mundford became treasurer of Normandy after the death of York's treasurer John Stanlowe whose wife, Margaret, was one of Queen Margaret's ladies. Curry credits Mundford with instituting the fiscal reforms introduced by Somerset.
12. Stevenson, *L&P* I, pp. 211–17.
13. Escouchy III, pp. 208–210.
14. Dom. H. Morice, *Mémoires pour server de preuves à l'histoire écclesiastique et civile de Bretagne,* 3 vols, (Paris, 1742-46), II, cols. 1429-30.
15. *Foedera* XI, pp. 223–24. Other ambassadors were named but it is not certain if they attended. They may have been there for part of the time since the conference continued into November.
16. Morice, *Mémoires* II, cols. 1430–37 is the only extant detailed account of these proceedings. It is a protocol, in Latin, by Michel de Parthenay and therefore open to bias. It is analysed by Dicks, 'Question of Peace', pp. 222–23.
17. Beaucourt IV, pp. 314–16.
18. *PPC* VI, pp. 62–64.
19. *Foedera* XI, pp. 223–25.
20. Sir Robert Roos left a young son and a daughter, Henry and Eleanor. King Henry granted Henry's wardship to Sir Robert's widow (*CPR 1446-1452,* pp. 217–18.) He was a page in Margaret's household, and became one of her squires. (Myers, 'Household, p. 185). Eleanor had become one of the Queen's damsels by 1451. (E 101/ 410/2).
21. Basin, *Charles VII et Louis XI* ed. Quicherat IV, pp. 299–300.
22. Basin, *Charles VII et Louis XI,* ed. Quicherat IV, p. 302. Keen and Daniel,

Fougères, pp. 380–81. Tuvache's evidence contradicts de Surienne. De Surienne claimed that Somerset urged him go to ahead and assured him of his support (Stevenson, *L&P* I, pp. 286–87).

23 Stevenson, *L&P* I, p. 283. Basin, *Charles VII et Louis XI*, ed. Quicherat IV, pp 323–24, 'et en oultre lui avoit accordé la place Condé-sur-Néreau en paiant certaine somme d'argent à messier Jehan Fastolfz, pour approuchier des marches de Bretaigne et logier ses gens, comme il que parle pense;'

24 Jean Chartier, *Chronique de Charles VII roi de France*, ed. A. Vallet de Viriville, 3 vols, (Paris, 1858), II, p. 61. Escouchy I, p. 154. J. Stevenson, ed., *Narratives of the Expulsion of the English from Normandy*, (Rolls Series, 1863), pp. 239–40. Berry Herald, *Chroniques*, ed. Courteault, p. 288.

25 Stevenson, *L&P* I, pp. 288–89.

26 Basin, *Charles VII et Louis XI*, ed. Quicherat IV, p. 326.

27 Stevenson, *L&P* I, pp. 278–98 for de Surienne's letter to Henry VI and his scathing account of Fougères. See also A. Bossuat, *Perrinet Gressart et François de Surienne, Agents de l'Angleterre*, Chapter XII 'La Prise de Fougères et la rupture des trèves', (Paris, 1936), pp. 301–335.

28 Stevenson, *Narratives*, 'Conferences', pp. 383–385.

29 Stevenson, *L&P* I, pp. 252–53. Escouchy III, p. 237.

30 James, 'Suffolk', p. 168, n. 2, citing BL Add. MS. 11,509 fols. 55–55d. Boulers received 500 and 900 *livres tournois* from the Norman Exchequer for shipping on 16 November 1448. Margaret gave Hoo a gold cup worth £30 at New Year, her only recorded gift to him. (E 101/410/2).

31 *PROME* XII, pp. 54–55.

32 *CPR 1446-52*, p. 219. Probably part of Somerset's unpaid wages that had been notionally loaned by him to the crown.

33 Stevenson, *L&P* II ii, p. 619, misdating its capture to 9 May. Beaucourt IV, p. 328. Chartier II, pp. 69–71. Fauconberg's ransom was set at 8,000 *écus*.

34 Stevenson, *Narratives*, (Blondel) 'De reductione Normandiae', pp. 26–27. Basin, *Charles VII* II, ed. Samaran, pp. 83 and 85. The story of Somerset's temper tantrum may be true; Basin claimed to have met the Duke in Rouen immediately after the fall of Pont de l'Arche.

35 Stevenson, *Narratives*, 'Conferences', pp. 416–17.

36 Stevenson, *Narratives*, 'Conferences', pp. 496–502 (English offers); pp. 502–12 (French offers).
37 Escouchy III, pp. 225–39.
38 Beaucourt IV, pp. 456–57.
39 Escouchy III, pp. 239–42.
40 Stevenson *L&P* I, pp. 264–73.
41 Escouchy III, pp. 243–44.

9 Losing Normandy

1 A.R. Myers, 'A Parliamentary Debate of the Mid-fifteenth Century', and 'A Parliamentary Debate of 1449', in *Crown, Household and Parliament,* pp. 69–92. If the debate was held in full Parliament it is incredible, unless part of the record of the debate has been lost, that not one of the lay magnates who might be expected to lead an army offered an opinion. It was not unusual for council meetings to take place while Parliament was in session.
2 R.A. Griffiths, 'The Winchester Session of the 1449 Parliament, a further commentary', in *King and Country*, pp. 258–59 points out the error in reading Bishop of Chichester (Moleyns) for Bishop of Chester. The Bishop of Coventry and Lichfield was commonly referred to as the Bishop of Chester.
3 *PROME* XII, pp. 42–43 and Appendix I, p. 66. Direct taxation, known as 'a tenth and a fifteenth' was a fixed sum levied on communities, not on individuals. It could be granted as a whole or as a fraction. It was not always easy to collect; the usual excuse offered was poverty in the regions.
4 *PROME* XII, pp. 46–53. 'that this Act extende not, ner be prejudicial unto the licence grauntled by yore Highnes, by youre Letters Patents berying date the xxiiii day of July the xxvi yere of youre full noble reigne, unto our sovereigne Lady the Quene for to shippe... [etc.]... wool, wollfell and Tyne …'. James Ramsay's statement (*Lancaster and York* II, p. 90) that 'Margaret had obtained unlimited leave to export wool and tin withersoever she pleased' is quite unjustified. See Appendix.
5 Roskell, *Commons and Speaker,* p. 233.

6. *Bale's Chron.*, p. 125. B.P. Wolffe, *The Royal Demesne in English History*, (1971), p. 116, n. 60.
7. *Benet's Chron.*, p. 196, calls this gathering a 'Great Council'. Watts, *Henry VI*, pp. 245–46, argues that it was at this council that the 'lords' took over the running of the government and ousted Suffolk. There is no evidence for this, but if they did, they made a worse job of it than Suffolk had. The lack of leadership at this crucial period is painful.
8. G.L. Harriss, 'Marmaduke Lumley and the exchequer crisis of 1446-1449', in *Aspects of late medieval government and society*, ed, J.G. Rowe, (Toronto, 1986), pp. 143–78. Lumley redeemed tallies for the £1,018 owed to him since 1443 as Warden of the West March.
9. Harriss, *Beaufort*, p. 382. Devon, *Exchequer*, p. 465. *CPR 1446-52*, pp. 297–98. M.K. Jones, 'The Beaufort Family and the War in France, 1421-1450', University of Bristol, PhD thesis, (1982), p. 263, and James, 'Suffolk' pp. 182–85, for detailed analyses of the sources of monies raised and disbursed. Jones claims that Somerset received £4,382 13s 4d before war broke out, and £13,763 12s 4d from loans after July 1449, making a total of £18,174 2s 1d between 1447 and 1450. James claims that Somerset's agent, Thomas Maunsel, received only £7,694 from loans collected in November and December 1449.
10. *CPR 1446-52*, pp. 311 and 452. Aiscough loaned the money in September at the start of the crisis; it was due for repayment on 2 February 1450, but Wenlock delivered the Queen's jewels on 22 January as the repayment could not be met.
11. *CPR 1441-46*, p. 273. J.S. Roskell, *Parliament and Politics*, 3 vols (1981–83), II, p. 244.
12. York's lieutenant in Rouen, Theobald Gorges, remained in post under Somerset.
13. The tradition that York was banished to Ireland at Suffolk's instigation is open to question.
14. Escouchy III, pp. 245–51, (protocol of the 31 July council meeting). Stevenson, *L&P*, I, pp. 243–54, misdated to April 1449.
15. Beaucourt IV, pp. 330–31.
16. Stevenson, *Narratives*, 'Berry Herald', pp. 257–59. Chartier II, pp. 80–82. Escouchy I, pp 189–90. Bossuat, pp. 339–40. Beaucourt V, pp. 5 and pp.

437–44. Guillaume Cousinot to Gaston de Foix, a detailed but heavily biased account of the taking of Verneuil.

17 Stevenson, *Narratives,* 'Berry Herald', pp. 260–61. Chartier II, pp. 82–83. Basin, *Charles VII* II, ed. Samaran, pp. 89–91.

18 Pollard, *Talbot,* p. 65.

19 Harriss, *Beaufort,* pp. 279–80.

20 Jones, 'Beaufort Family', pp. 360–61. Chartier II, pp. 85–87.

21 Escouchy III, p. 354–58. In his deposition to his French captors Mundford stated that Eyton bargained with Dunois and agreed to surrender the town in return for a cash payment to himself and his men.

22 Stevenson *L&P,* II, ii. p. 627. J. de Waurin, *Recueil des croniques et anchiennes istories de la Grant Bretaigne, a present nomme Engleterre,* 5 vols., ed. W. and E.L.C.P. Hardy, (1864-91), V, p. 150. Marshall, 'War Captains', p. 49.

23 *Letters of Margaret,* pp. 34–36.

24 Basin, *Charles VII* II, ed. Samaran, pp. 96–105. M. Spencer, *The History of Charles VII and Louis XI,* (Nieuwkoop, 1997), pp. 21–24.

25 Jones, 'Somerset, York', p, 302, n. 1.

26 Chartier II, pp. 97–101 for the terms of the surrender. Stevenson, *Narratives,* 'Berry Herald', p. 267, estimates that Mantes was garrisoned by 700 to 800 men, which makes Blondel's claim (pp. 89–90) that Mantes could have been defended plausible, although the figure is probably on the high side.

27 Chartier II, pp. 103–04. Berry Herald, *Chroniques,* ed. Courteault, p. 301. A variant in the MS in Stevenson, *Narratives,* 'Berry Herald', p. 270 gives xij[xx] or xxj[xx]. The lower figure is the more likely.

28 Jones, 'Somerset, York', p. 301. n. 3. *CPR 1446-52,* pp. 268.

29 Chartier II, p. 142.

30 Beaucourt V, pp. 11–12 and 15.

31 Stevenson, *Narratives,* 'Berry Herald', pp. 301–03. Chartier II, p. 151.

32 Beaucourt V, p. 17. Basin, *Charles VII* II, ed. Samaran, pp. 124–25. The other French chronicles do not mention Basin, according to them Brezé entered first. Monstrelet II, p. 168.

33 Escouchy III, pp. 358–64, for the best account of the terms. Stevenson, *L&P,* II, ii, pp. 608–17 is incomplete and inaccurate in places.

Notes

34 Stevenson, *L&P* II, ii, p. 628.
35 Escouchy I, p. 230.
36 Vale, *Charles VII*, pp. 135–36. Neville and Butler were apparently still in French hands in September 1456 when Charles VII's council had to settle a quarrel over their ransom. Butler appealed for help to meet the sum demanded for him. *The Complete Peerage of England ...* ed. G.E. Cokayne, 12 vols (1910-1959), X, p. 129, dates it to after his 'capture' at Vernon, but since he was allowed to go free from there it seems more likely the appeal was for his ransom as a hostage at Rouen.
37 Stevenson, *Narratives*, 'Conferences', p. 493.
38 Stevenson, *Narratives*, pp. 366–67. Richard Gower's release was stipulated by his father for Cherbourg's surrender in August 1450.
39 *PPC* VI, pp 109–10. In July 1451 King Henry ordered a payment of 6,000 *saluts* to Radford for his ransom. It is not clear if Radford was free by this time or still in France. As the money was assigned against the sureties lodged at the Exchequer for the Duke of Orleans's ransom, dating back to 1440, one wonders if Radford ever received his grant.
40 *Complete Peerage* XI, pp.105–06, states that Duchess Eleanor's eldest son, Thomas II, Lord Roos, was left in Rouen. But Thomas was summoned to Parliament in 1449. Stevenson, *L&P* II, ii, pp. 611 and 628 says 'master Roos', and 'son of the Lord Roos'. They are more likely to refer to Richard, who was Master Roos.
41 Stevenson, *L&P* I, pp. 293–95.
42 Vale, *Charles VII*, pp. 202–03. Beaucourt V, pp. 19–24. The chronicle accounts differ in detail, but all agree on the magnificence and martial display. Monstrelet II, pp. 170–72 summed it up: 'It is certain, that in the memory of man, never was king seen with so handsome a body of chivalry, so finely dressed, nor so great a number of men-at-arms as the King of France had with him on his regaining his good city of Rouen.'

10 Suffolk Disgraced

1 Stevenson, *L&P* I, pp. 501–02. *CPR 1446-52*, p. 301. There is a further order for ordnance for Caen in February 1450 (Stevenson, *L&P* I, p. 513).
2 Chartier II, pp. 178–79.

Notes

3. Beaucourt V, pp. 25–26. Chartier II, pp. 188–89. Stevenson, *Narratives* 'Berry Herald', p. 327.
4. *A Collection of Political Poems and Songs Relating to English History, from the Accession of Edward III to the reign of Henry VIII*, ed. T. Wright, 2 vols. (1859-1861), II, pp. 221–23 and 229–-31.
5. *PROME* XII, pp. 82. Roskell, *Parliament and Politics* III, pp. 353–65.
6. *CPR 1446-52*, p. 297.
7. *Annales*, p. 766. *Gregory's Chron.*, p. 189. *English Chron.*, p. 67. *Benet's Chron.*, p. 196.
8. *CClR*, 1447-54, p. 194.
9. *PROME* XII p. 94. *Bale's Chron.*, p. 129. *Benet's Chron.*, p. 196–97.
10. *PROME* XII, pp. 95–98.
11. T. Gascoigne, *Loci e Libro Veritatum*, ed. J.E.T. Rogers, (Oxford, 1881) p. 190. The accusation that Suffolk promised to surrender Maine (and Anjou) in 1444 in order to obtain Margaret's marriage to King Henry was recorded by Thomas Gascoigne writing in 1457. This accusation would be believed long after Suffolk was dead and is still accepted by some historians today.
12. *PROME* XII, p. 76. Curry mistakenly reads 'the French queen' as referring to Margaret. The Commons would never have referred to her in this way and the context of the accusation makes it clear that 'the French queen' is Marie of Anjou, King Charles VII's wife.
13. *PPC* VI, pp. 86–87.
14. The entry from *Brut G*, p. 510, printed in Caxton's *Polychronicon*, has rarely been questioned: 'In this same yere wer diuerse Embassatoures sent in to Guyan for A Mariage for þe King for þerles doughter of Arminak, which was concluded; but, by þe mean of þerle of Suthfolk, it was lett & put Aparte.'
15. Vale, *Gascony*, pp. 118–19 for a list of grants in Gascony. Sir Robert Roos was a king's knight of the body, Edward Hull became Queen Margaret's knight of the body, William Beauchamp was created Lord St Amand by Henry in 1449, John Blakeney was a clerk of the King's signet, and John St Loo was an esquire of the body. John Say, keeper of the palace at Westminster and Speaker in Parliament, had made his way in the household under Suffolk, but they all prospered at court long after Suffolk's death.

Notes

16   *Complete Peerage* VII, pp. 108–110 dates the creation to 1446. Vale, *Gascony*, p. 134 dates it to 1444. The name of Suffolk's niece is not recorded in the parliamentary roll. *Complete Peerage* identifies her as Margaret, daughter of Suffolk's brother, John de la Pole, who died in France; the evidence for this is suspect. The name 'Margaret' comes from the will of Jean de Foix, dated 1485, but this presumes that he married only once. See W. Adams Reitwiesner, 'Margaret de la Pole and her parentage', *The Genealogist*, 3, (Fall, 1982), pp. 171–74. A second, more tenable, theory is that she was the daughter of Suffolk's sister Elizabeth by her second husband, Sir Thomas Kerdeston. See Charles M. Hansen, 'Suffolk's niece', *Genealogists' Magazine*, vol. 22, no. 10, (June 1988), p. 373–377.

17   Fauconberg had petitioned this Parliament for payment of wages due to him as Constable of Roxburgh Castle because he was experiencing financial difficulties due to his services and capture in France. (*Rot. Parl.* V, pp. 205–06).

18   Jones, 'Orleans Ransom', p. 258.

19   *PROME XII*, pp. 99–104.

20   This distortion is still widely accepted. R. Virgoe, 'William Tailboys and Lord Cromwell: crime and politics in Lancastrian England', in *East Anglian Society*, pp. 287–307. Virgoe accepts Tailboys's guilt, Suffolk's complicity, and Cromwell's innocence. But Tailboys continued his feud with Cromwell long after Suffolk's death, and Beaumont remained influential at court. See also R.L. Storey, 'Lincolnshire and the Wars of the Roses', *Nottingham Medieval Studies*, XIV (1970) pp. 76–78, for a different interpretation, but the same conclusion.

21   *The Paston Letters, A.D. 1422-1509*, ed. J. Gairdner, 6 vols. (1904), II, pp. 118–20.

22   *CPR 1446-52*, p. 83.

23   Virgoe, 'Three Suffolk parliamentary elections of the mid-fifteenth century', in *East Anglian Society*, pp. 53–64.

24   *HMC, Appendix to the Third Report*, (1870), pp. 279–80. The MS is incomplete and in parts defective; it is far more virulent than the account in the Parliamentary rolls and it too has been cited by later historians as proof of Suffolk's guilt. It is printed in modern English in *PROME* XII, Appendix, pp. 154–56.

Notes

25   *Paston Letters and Papers of the Fifteenth Century,* 2 vols, ed. N. Davis, (1971–76), Part I, pp. 237–38.
26   Anne's custody, wardship, and marriage, had been granted to Queen Margaret in 1446, but Margaret was short of ready money and she sold it to Suffolk. (*CPR 1441–46,* p. 436).
27   *PROME* XII, pp. 104–05. Although the rolls state that Suffolk 'answered himself to each of the said articles of treason, which were eight in number' they do not record his replies to all eight.
28   *PROME* XII, pp. 105–06.
29   *Bale's Chron.,* pp. 128–29. *Annales,* p. 767.
30   Gairdner, *PL* II, pp. 142–43.
31   *The Chronicle of John Hardyng,* ed. H. Ellis, (1812), p. 400, is the only source to suggest this possibility: 'In Maye, the duke of Suffolke toke the sea, On pilgrimage to passe...' *Benet's Chron.,* p. 198, says he was headed for Brittany. *Bale's Chron.,* p. 129, says he was going to the Duke of Burgundy.

11 Aftermath

1   Escouchy, I, pp. 303–04. Escouchy never visited England, he wrote his *Chronique* after 1461, and his details are suspect. King Henry's court was not so impoverished that there was no money to put food on the table for the Feast of the Epiphany. Rumours that Edward, Prince of Wales, was not Henry's son were current in the late 1450s but Escouchy's claim that it was rumoured in England that Margaret was not the daughter of René of Anjou, is unique.
2   *Bale's Chron.,* p. 128. C.L. Kingsford, 'An Historical collection of the 15th century', *EHR* XXIX (1914), p. 514.
3   C. L. Kingsford, *English Historical Literature in the Fifteenth Century (EHL),* (Oxford, 1913), 'John Piggot's Memoranda', p. 371. *CPR 1446-52,* p. 383.
4   *PROME* XII, p. 107: '... that you were in debt £372,000 which is a great and grevious sum and that your annual income was only £5,000 ... your necessary expenses of your household, without all other ordinary charges, comes to £24,000 a year ...' *EHL,* 'Collections of a Yorkist

Partisan', p. 360.

5. *PROME* XII pp. 106-111. Commons exemptions.
6. *PROME* XII, p. 108. See Appendix A.
7. *PROME* XII, pp. 87–91.
8. *PROME* XII, pp. 112-45. Henry's exemptions.
9. Wolffe, *Royal Demesne*, p. 128. Roskell, *Commons*, p. 240.
10. *PROME* XII, p. 129. Sir Richard Roos, Henry Roos, Sir Edward Hull, Sir John Wenlock, Sir Edmund Hampden, and Thomas Burneby.
11. *PROME* XII, pp. 84–85. Griffiths, *Henry VI*, p. 381: 'The collection of this tax, like the inquisitions into what grants were to be to be resumed, was never efficiently implemented.'
12. Marshall, 'War Captains', pp. 291–93.
13. *Annales*, p. 765, names five captains 'and others'. Marshall, 'War Captains', pp. 148–49, lists twelve names.
14. A. Curry and M. Hughes, eds., *Arms, Armies, and Fortifications in the Hundred Years War*, (Woodbridge, 1994), p. 47. Actual figures: 255 men-at-arms / 2,380 archers = 2,635. Indented figures: 315 men-at-arms; 2,780 archers = 3,095.
15. Beaucourt V, pp. 27–34. Gairdner, *PL* II, p. 147. Stevenson, *Narratives*, 'Berry Herald', pp. 332–36. Chartier II, pp. 192–98. Escouchy I, pp. 282–85. Stevenson, L&P, II, ii, p. 630 estimates 2,300 killed and 900 taken prisoner. The English chronicles are silent on the Battle of Formigny. A.H. Burne, *The Agincourt War*, (1956) pp. 315–24 reconstructs the battle, but he relies on what he terms IMP (inherent military probability), and his understanding of the political landscape of 1450 leaves something to be desired. A. Curry, *Arms, Armies*, p. 19, believes the English lost because they departed from the tried and true tactics for winning battles established in earlier encounters in the Hundred Years' War.
16. Stevenson, *Narratives*, 'Berry Herald', pp. 340–43.
17. Gairdner, *PL* II, p. 146–47
18. R. Virgoe, 'The Death of William de la Pole, Duke of Suffolk' in *East Anglian Society*, pp. 247–57. Richard Lenard and Thomas Smith were indicted in King's Bench in 1451 for complicity in Suffolk's murder and Lenard was named as the executioner. The traditional story of Suffolk's death is contradicted by a letter from King Henry addressed to the master

of the ship, *Nicholas of the Tower*, that must date to between May and August 1450. The King says he knows of the crime but has been told that the master 'did not agree to this and did not allow it to be done aboard ship.' Henry recalled the services of the *Nicholas* and pardoned the master because he had undertaken to sail to Cherbourg with news of its projected relief, and to bring back word on the condition of its inhabitants. (*John Vale's Book*, pp. 168–69.) Cherbourg fell on 12 August (not 1 January as noted by the editors).

19 *Benet's Chron.*, p. 198.
20 D.A.L. Morgan, 'The King's Affinity in the Polity of Yorkist England', *Transactions of the Royal Historical Society*, 23 (1973), p. 14. Blondel later became avener to Queen Elizabeth Woodville and lived to make his will in 1492.
21 *English Chron.*, p. 70. Gascoigne, *Loci e Libro*, p. 7: *domine dux si poteritis evadere vivus ab ista turri Londoniarium sub poena capitis nostri exitis tunc securus ab occisione cujuscunque.*
22 *CPR 1446–52*, p. 380, and pp. 434–35.
23 Wolffe, *Royal Demesne*, pp. 100, 129.
24 *CPR 1446–52*, pp. 326 and 239. *Foedera* XI, p. 270.
25 *Calendar of the Fine Rolls 1445-52*, p. 154.
26 *Papal Letters* X, pp. 472–73. The papal dispensation to legitimise the marriage is dated 18 August 1450 and addressed to John, Duke of Suffolk and Margaret, daughter of the late John, Duke of Somerset, allowing the two children to remain married.
27 Wright, *Political Poems* II, pp. 232–34.
28 I.M.W. Harvey, *Jack Cade's Rebellion of 1450* (Oxford, 1991), p. 186.
29 *Great Chron.*, pp. 130–31.
30 *CPR 1446–52*, p. 385.
31 Harvey, *Cade*, pp. 186–191. *John Vale's Book*, pp. 204–05.
32 Harvey, *Cade*, p. 84, citing C 1/19/501.
33 *Gough London 10*, p. 154.
34 *Benet's Chron.*, p. 199.
35 Harvey, *Cade*, pp. 37–39 with references. The evidence against Saye is based on depositions made after his death but it is sufficiently circumstantial to paint a picture of continual chicanery and malfeasance.

Slegge is named as an extortioner in one version of Cade's petition (*John Vale's Book*, p. 206).

36 *CPR 1446-52*, p. 84. Two chroniclers record that the Duke of Exeter arrested Saye: *Gough London 10*, p. 154 and *Benet's Chron.*, p. 199. The latter claims that King Henry tried to have Lord Saye spirited out of the Tower on the night after his arrest, but Exeter refused to release him. It was probably the Earl of Northumberland, as Constable of England, who arrested Saye, which may account for the chroniclers' confusion.

37 *English Chron.*, p. 67. Griffiths, *Henry VI*, p. 644.

38 *CPR 1446-52*, p. 311

39 *Short English Chron.*, p. 67

40 *London Chrons. (Vitellius A XVI)*, p. 160.

41 *Bale's Chron.*, p. 133. *Gough London 10*, p. 155

42 *CPR 1446-52*, pp. 388. The commission would have been issued in King Henry's name by Chancellor Kemp since Henry had already left London.

43 James, 'Suffolk', p. 129. A.W. Franks, 'Notes on Edward Grimston, Esq., Ambassador to the Duchess of Burgundy, *Archaeologia* 40 (1866), pp. 452–470. Two of Grimston's petitions, printed in this article, indicate that Grimston was imprisoned and that he exercised his right of appeal to the King.

44 Harvey, *Cade*, p. 92.

45 *CPR 1446-52*, p. 443 (Say); p. 444 (Grimston); p. 445 (Trevellian); p. 532 (Daniel).

46 *Short English Chron.*, p. 67

47 *Bale's Chron.*, p. 132.

48 *Great Chron.*, p. 184 adds the grisly detail that the heads of Saye and Crowmer were carried aloft on poles and the men carrying them 'put theym to gider, cawsyng that oon to kysse that othir.'

49 *Bale's Chron.*, pp. 130-34. *Gough London 10*, pp. 153-57. *Benet's Chron.*, pp. 198-201. *Gregory's Chron.*, pp. 189-94. *Short English Chronicle*, pp. 66-68. *Great Chron.*, pp. 181-85. *London Chrons. (Vitellius A XVI)*, pp. 159-62. *English Chron.*, pp. 67-69. See also Griffiths, *Henry VI*, pp. 610-49.

50 *CPR 1446-52*, p. 338.

51 Griffiths, *Henry VI*, p. 616.

Notes

52 *Short English Chron.*, p. 68. *John Vale's Book*, pp. 207–8.
53 *Foedera* XI, p. 275. The bounty was paid to Alexander Iden.
54 *CPR 1446-52*, p. 387. *PPC* VI, pp. 96–98. Harvey, *Cade*, p.100, citing E101/336/5 and E 357/40.
55 Gairdner, *PL* II, pp. 153–56. More 'evidence' for the details of Cade's rebellion has been adduced from this letter than its actual content will bear.
56 *PPC* VI, p. 98.
57 *Foedera* XI, pp. 285–86.

12 Somerset or York

1 Stevenson, *L&P* II, ii, pp. 631–32. Stevenson, *Narratives* 'Berry Herald', pp. 345–57. Beaucourt V, pp. 36–37. Ramsay II, pp. 108–110.
2 Myers, 'Household', p. 196. Somerset's servant received the customary reward of 66s 8d for bringing a gift to the queen only in 1452-53. There is no record of what it was, or if Margaret reciprocated. (Myers, 'Jewels', p. 217).
3 J.R. Lander, *The Wars of the Roses*, (1965) pp. 62–63.
4 Griffiths, 'Richard, Duke of York and the royal household in Wales, 1449-1450', in *King and Country*, pp. 265–76.
5 *Benet's Chron.*, p. 202 suggests that they went to York for protection. Kingsford, *EHL*, 'A London Chronicle', p. 297 claims York imprisoned them at Ludlow.
6 Kingsford, *EHL*, 'John Piggott's Memorandum', p. 372.
7 *Annales*, p. 769 identifies Talbot as Lord Lisle but in his bill York says Sir John Talbot. He is more likely to have been Sir John Talbot, the eldest son of the Earl of Shrewsbury, who had served with his father in Ireland. Talbot and Lisle were both named John. Likewise, Welles may have been Sir William Welles, Lord Welles's brother, who had been Talbot's deputy in Ireland. (*CPR 1452-61*, p. 179).
8 Roskell, 'William Tresham of Sywell' in *Parliament and Politics* II, pp. 137–51. Tresham's widow petitioned Parliament for redress; she received some sympathy but no action. (*PROME* XII, pp. 177–79). Griffiths, 'Duke Richard of York's Intentions in 1450', in *King and Country*, p. 292.

Griffiths does not accept Isabella Tresham's claim that her husband was riding to meet York at his invitation.

9. M. Bassett, 'Newgate Prison in the Middle Ages'. *Speculum* 18 (1943), pp. 233–246.
10. CLRO Journal 5, fol. 48. *Bale's Chron.*, p. 135. *Benet's Chron.*, pp. 202–-03. The latter claims that Manning deliberately released the prisoners because he knew he was to be dismissed, but this is a gloss; it would not do for a Yorkist chronicler to suggest that York's arrival triggered a riot. Johnson, *York,* p. 84 n. 35, confuses John Gargrave, keeper of the King's Bench prison, with Alexander Manning, keeper of Newgate.
11. *Letters of Margaret*, pp. 48–51.
12. Griffiths, 'York's Intentions', pp. 299–304. *John Vale's Book,* pp. 185–90. M. Hicks, 'From Megaphone to Microscope: the correspondence of Richard Duke of York with Henry VI in 1450 revisited', *Journal of Medieval History,* vol. 25, No 1. (1999), pp. 243–256. Hicks offers a different interpretation of these documents.
13. *Incerti scriptoris chronicon Angliae* ... ed. J.A. Giles, (1848), p. 42. *Quum opus exigit, aut necessitas compellat, vestrum auxilium invocabimus.*
14. R. E. Archer, 'Rich Old Ladies: the problem of late medieval dowagers', in Pollard, *Property and Politics,* p. 24.
15. R.L. Storey, *The End of the House of Lancaster,* (1966, reprint 1986), pp. 56–57.
16. Gairdner, *PL* II, pp. 258-60, dated to 1452. Re-dated by Storey, *End of Lancaster,* p. 278 n. 20, to February 1451. H. Castor, *The King, the Crown and the Duchy of Lancaster,* (Oxford, 2000), pp.168–71, for an analysis of Norfolk's state of mind. She accepts the 1451 date, but it could date equally well to 1450. Norfolk was on an oyer and terminer commission in September of that year. (R. Beadle & C. Richmond, *Paston Letters and Papers of the Fifteenth Century,* Part III, (Oxford, 2005), p. 95.
17. *CPR 1446-52,* pp. 137 and 130.
18. *CPR 1446-52,* p. 236. *Bale's Chron.,* p. 123. Bale does not give the reason, but the attack on Letheringham is the most probable.
19. *Letters of Margaret*, pp. 108–10.
20. *Testamenta Vetusta,* ed. N.H. Nicolas, 2 vols (1826) I, p. 275. Wingfield's will is dated 6 October 1452, but probate is recorded in November 1454.

Wingfield's sons made their peace with Norfolk.
21. Gairdner, *PL* II, pp. 184–85.
22. *PROME* XII, p. 173.
23. *PROME* XII, Appendix, pp. 208–09. A letter from London to the Grand Master of the Teutonic Order in Prussia.
24. *Bale's Chron.*, pp. 136–37.
25. *Rot. Parl.* V, p. 226b.
26. *Benet's Chron.*, p. 203, and *Rawlinson B 355*, p. 106 credit the Earl of Devon with Somerset's rescue, on instructions from York, but both chroniclers are Yorkist partisans. *Bale's Chron.*, p. 137, attributes it to the Mayor and city officials, which is far more plausible.
27. Harvey, *Cade*, p. 158.
28. *CPR 1446-52*, p. 439.
29. Jones, 'Somerset and York', pp. 287–88.
30. *Gregory's Chron.*, p. 196
31. *CPR 1446-52*, p. 438. *Bale's Chron.*, pp. 137–38. *Benet's Chron.*, pp. 203–04 conflates the ride through London with the lords named as commissioners at the Guildhall.
32. *Benet's Chron.*, p. 201. Kingsford, *EHL*, 'John Piggot's Memorandum', p. 372.
33. Vale, *Gascony*, pp. 132–33. The loss of Mauléon was one of the Commons' charges against the Duke of Suffolk.
34. Beaucourt V, pp. 43–44.
35. Waurin III, p. 207.
36. *CPR 1436-41*, p. 53.
37. *PPC* VI, p. 101. Vale, *Gascony*, p. 136 and n. 4.
38. *CPR 1446-52*, p. 472 and pp. 456-7. Four London merchants and the Dean of St Martin le Grand loaned £1,246 13s 4d between them. Five bishops on the Council loaned £100 each; Viscount Beaumont loaned £40. Orders to arrest shipping went out in August 1450 (*CPR 1446-52*, p. 389.) A second order went out in December, and five more were issued between February and April 1451. (*CPR 1446-52*, pp. 437–39 and 444). Wages for the shipmasters of 86 ships were finally assigned on the customs of London in June 1451. (*CPR 1446-52,* pp. 447–50).
39. Griffiths, *Henry VI*, p. 642 and p. 663, n. 226. *CPR 1446-52* pp. 264 and

435. A John Christmas was an esquire in Queen Margaret's household. (E 101/ 410 /8).
40. *CPR 1446-52* p. 442.
41. Griffiths, *Henry VI*, p. 649 and 665 n. 281. *Benet's Chron.*, p. 205 says 31 men. *Gregory's Chron.*, pp. 196–97, says 'many men', of whom twenty-one had their heads set on London Bridge. Kingsford, *EHL,* 'John Pigott's Memorandum', p. 372, has thirty men whose heads were sent to London.
42. *CPR 1446-52*, pp. 453 and 505. It is an interesting corrective to the claim that King Henry broke his word to Cade's followers to note how many incidents of rebellion in Kent are known only through the pardons he issued. The description of Blackheath, too, comes from the *pardon* to one William Soly.
43. B.P. Wolffe, 'Acts of Resumption in the Lancastrian parliaments, 1399-1456', *EHR,* LXXIII, (1958), pp. 605–06. *PROME* XII, pp. 186–202. The Commons exempted Margaret, as they had in 1450, but they withheld her £1,000 from the customs, which was earmarked for the Calais garrison. See Appendix.
44. *Rot. Parl.* V p. 226. *Calendar of the Fine Rolls 1445-52, (CFR)* pp. 220–21.
45. *PROME* XII, pp. 184–86.
46. A.C. Reeves, 'William Booth, Bishop of Coventry & Lichfield 1447-52', *Midland History* III (1975-76), pp. 11–29. King Henry and Margaret had recommended Booth to the Pope to become Bishop of Coventry and Lichfield in 1447. (*Foedera* XI, p. 160. *CPR 1446-52*, p. 55. *Papal Letters* X, p. 296).
47. Wright, *Political Poems* II, pp. 225–29.
48. Usher of the chamber in Rouen, 1445. (BL Add MS 23,938). Knight of the body by 1450, exempted as such in the 1450–51 Act of Resumption. (*PROME* XII, pp. 142–43). He received a gold armlet worth £2 4s 6d in 1445–46, and a brooch worth 13s 5¾d in 1446-47 (E 101 /409 /14 and 17). He and his wife, Lady Anne Moleyns, were granted of four pipes of Gascon wine yearly 'for good service to the King and Queen', from 1446. (*CPR 1441-1446*, p. 415). *CClR 1447-54* pp. 212 and 214 for Hampden as feoffee.
49. L. Boatwright, 'The Buckingham Six at Bosworth', in *The Ricardian* XIII, (2003), p. 58. Anne Moleyns was the widow of William, Lord Moleyns,

killed at the siege of Orleans in 1429 and the sister of Emma, Lady Scales. She received a gold belt worth £2 4s 6d in 1445-46, a gold chain worth £7 10s in 1446-47, a silver gilt cup worth £3 13s 4d in 1448-49, and a silver gilt salt worth £2 10s 10d in 1451–52. (E 101/409/ 14 and 17. E 101/410/2 and 8).

50 *HMC* Fifth Report (1876), p. 455.

51 *Annales,* p. 770. There is no petition from Thomas Young on the parliamentary rolls for 1451. But in the Yorkist-dominated parliament of 1455 (to which he was again returned as MP for Bristol) he petitioned for compensation for wrongful imprisonment and referred to words spoken by him in Parliament in 1451 (*Rot. Parl.* V, p 337). York's biographer does not doubt that York was behind the petition (if there was a petition) but his assumption that the Commons tried to tack recognition of York's claim onto a bill of supply is an anachronism. (Johnson, *York,* p. 98). Young went on to a distinguished career as an attorney and judge under Edward IV.

52 York's servants received a money gift from Margaret for bringing York's gifts to the Queen in every year for which her accounts survive. Unfortunately, there is no record of what York sent to Margaret and only one record of Margaret's gifts to him. In 1451–52, she gave York a gold cup worth £35 8s 9d (E 101/ 410 / 8).

13 Strife

1 Harvey, *Cade*, p. 157.
2 *PPC* VI, p. 105. *CPR 1446-52*, pp. 446 and 476. Kingsford, *EHL*, 'John Piggot's Memoranda', p. 372. Vale, *Gascony,* p. 141. King Henry had purchased the jewel from William Estfeld for £1,333 6s 8d in 1445 (Devon, *Exchequer,* p. 451).
3 *CPR 1446-52*, p. 476.
4 Wolffe, *Henry VI*, p. 248. *Benet's Chron.,* p. 205. *CPR 1446-52*, p. 477.
5 Ramsay II, p. 144–45. Chartier II, pp. 269– 271 and 271–75 for terms of the surrender.
6 Escouchy I, pp. 356–58. The chronicler records that Dunois was escorted by representatives of the French nobility, royal councillors, and 7,320

troops.

7. Vale, *Gascony*, p. 234 gives £29,402 14s 0¾d, made up of £3,316 assigned on 18 July, and three other sums on 9 August: £66 13s 4d and £2,390. The third figure, £23,036 5s 4¾d, must be notional. Ramsay, II, p. 146 is more realistic: 'liabilities to the amount of £13,000 and upwards having been incurred and nothing done.' Even this sum was probably not raised in full.
8. *CPR 1446-52* dated 12 July 1451, pp. 477–78.
9. Stevenson, *L&P* II, pp. 471–73. Stevenson misdates the letter to 17 August 1449. *John Vale's Book,* pp. 140–41. The editors accept 17 August but correct the year to 1451. It may have been written somewhat later than August. Would Burgundy have suggested peace to Henry VI before the conquest of Gascony was a *fait accompli*? Chartier II, pp. 326–27, records Henry's reply as being made to the Pope's representative, although no papal representative is known to have been in England at this time.
10. *PPC* VI, Preface, p. xxxvii.
11. *CPR 1446-52*, pp. 512–13 and 537. Wolffe, *Henry VI*, p. 257, citing PRO E 28/82/5: 'for our crossing into our kingdom of France which, God willing we are disposed and determined to undertake with the greatest possible diligence and expedition.'
12. Gairdner, *PL* II, pp. 256–57.
13. *PPC* V, pp. 173–75. King Henry had unwittingly exacerbated the feud in 1437 during the first year of his personal rule when he appointed Bonville to the lucrative position of steward of the royal Duchy of Cornwall. Courtenay petitioned for a stewardship defined as 'Duchy of Cornwall lands in the possession of the crown' and Henry granted it. Since this was virtually the post held by Bonville the Council realised the seriousness of Henry's error and ordered Courtenay not to act in this capacity. Courtenay continued to behave as if the post was his.
14. M. Cherry, 'The struggle for power in mid-fifteenth century Devonshire', in *Patronage, Crown and Provinces,* ed. Griffiths, (1981), pp. 123–44. Devon was not appointed steward of England for Margaret's coronation because of Beaufort influence as Cherry, p. 125 suggests, but because he was Earl of Devon.
15. J.E. Powell and K. Wallis, *The House of Lords in the Middle Ages* (1968).

Notes

16 A. Curry, 'The Coronation Expedition and Henry VI's Court in France 1430 to 1432' in *The Lancastrian Court,* ed. J. Stratford, (Donington, Shaun Tyas, 2003), p. 33.

17 *Annales,* p. 770. Storey, *End of Lancaster,* pp. 89–92. Storey's reconstruction is considered definitive but such facts as we have do not bear the weight of his interpretation, which is heavily biased in York's favour.

18 In October 1451 King Henry travelled from Coventry to Windsor via Wallingford where he spent two days. *Benet's Chron,* p. 205 says that Lords Cobham and Robert Hungerford, Lord Moleyns, were imprisoned at Wallingford for supporting Courtenay. *Annales,* p. 770, claims that Hungerford was with York, but Lord Cobham was imprisoned at Berkhamsted (Cherry, 'Devonshire' p. 142, citing KB 9/268, m. 90). The chronicler also says that Bonville and Wiltshire were imprisoned in Berkhamsted, but Wiltshire does not appear to have taken part in the fracas although Benet claims that he had been raising troops. Wiltshire and Bonville received general pardons in February 1452 (*CPR 1446-52,* p. 525). What part, if any, Hungerford played in the affair is unclear.

19 P.M. Kendall and V. Ilardi, *Dispatches with Related Documents of Milanese Ambassadors in France and Burgundy, 1450-1483,* (Ohio University Press, 1970), pp. 44–46.

20 *Bale's Chron.,* p. 138. *Benet's Chron.,* p. 205. *CPR 1446-52,* pp. 479–80.

21 *CPR 1446-52,* p. 518 and 573.

22 *CPR 1446-52,* p. 515.

23 Gairdner, *PL* I, p. 96. *John Vale's Book,* p. 195.

24 Gairdner, *PL* I, pp. 97–98.

25 *PPC* VI, pp. 90–92 (misdated by the editor to 1450). The letter was addressed to the mayors of Canterbury, Maidstone, Colchester, Sandwich, Oxford, Winchelsea, and Sudbury.

26 *Benet's Chron.,* p. 206. There is no mention of this refusal in *Gregory's Chronicle,* which is ascribed to William Gregory, who was mayor at this time.

27 Kingsford, *EHL* pp. 297–98 (Arundel MS 19). The most detailed and probably the most accurate contemporary source for the encounter at Dartford.

28 Kingsford, *EHL* p. 373, 'John Piggot's Memoranda', and p. 368 'Yorkist

Partisan'.
29. Jones, 'Somerset, York', p. 297. York's lieutenant was Theobald Gorges. York's receiver general for his Norman estates also lived in Rouen and remained in contact with York throughout Somerset's tenure.
30. *Benet's Chron.*, p. 206 claims that York accused Chancellor Kemp as well as Somerset of responsibility for the loss of Normandy.
31. Jones, 'Somerset, York', p. 286, n. 5, citing Archives du Nord for 'letters close from the Duke of Burgundy to the Duke of Somerset, (6 June 1451).'
32. Gairdner, *PL* II, pp. 103–08.
33. There are two versions of the encounter at Dartford. The more reliable chroniclers report only that York presented articles against Somerset to the King: *Benet's Chron.*, p. 206–07, *Rawlinson B 355*, p. 107, *English Chron.*, p. 71, *Chronicon Angliae*, p. 43. Kingsford, *EHL*, 'John Piggot's Memoranda', p. 373. Later versions, heavily influenced by Yorkist propaganda, claim that King Henry betrayed York: he had promised to arrest Somerset and put him on trial. With this assurance York had disbanded his army and come into the King's presence only to find Somerset there: *Great Chron.*, p. 186, *London Chrons.*, (*Vitellius A XVI*). p.163, *Short English Chron.*, p. 69, Nicolas, *Chronicle of London*, p. 138. They all derive from the same source.
34. *CCIR 1447-54*, p. 327. The arbitrators were the Bishops of Winchester, Ely, and Hereford; the Duke of Buckingham; the Earls of Salisbury and Shrewsbury; Viscounts Bourgchier and Beaumont, and Robert Botill, Prior of St John of Jerusalem. Nothing more is heard of this arbitration.
35. *PROME* XII, p. 455.
36. *PPC* VI, pp. 119-23. It was hoped that Clifford could raise 1,000 men. They would be paid 12d a week. Their captains should be offered a reward of 10 marks or £10 at Clifford's discretion. He was to bring his own ship, plus three from the port of Hull, with any others he had requisitioned,
37. Beaucourt V, pp. 199–200 and 207–08.
38. Beaucourt V, pp. 154–68. Historians, including Beaucourt, have accepted Charles VII's intention to attack Calais early in 1452 largely on the strength of the Milanese ambassadors' letters. Those notorious gossips consistently exaggerated whatever they were told. Charles VII's plan to

attack Calais with Burgundian assistance dates to later in 1452 when the Duke of Burgundy was soliciting Charles's support in his war with the city of Ghent. His terms, printed in *John Vales Book*, pp. 139–40, dated by the editors to 1451, belong in 1452. Burgundy refused to accept them. (Vaughan, *Philip*, p. 325).

39 *CPR 1446-52*, pp. 580–81. The Dukes of Buckingham and Somerset, the Earls of Warwick, Wiltshire, and Worcester, Viscount Lisle, Robert Hungerford Lord Moleyns, Lords Cromwell, Sudeley, Beauchamp of Powick, Stourton, St Amand, Bonville, and Audley. The sources are too scanty for a detailed reconstruction but the implication (Watts, *Henry VI* p. 296 n. 156) that some of them did not take part in the judicial proceedings out of sympathy for York (or antipathy to Somerset) is a conclusion that cannot be drawn from such evidence as exists, namely indictments in King's Bench.

40 *CPR 1446-52*, p. 526. Wolffe, *Henry VI*, pp. 259–60. Lord Bonville also received a gift in Exeter.

41 Wolffe, *Henry VI*, p. 260, citing KB 9/103/2; 103/15 270/34.

42 Griffiths, *Henry VI*, p. 672. Johnson, *York*, p. 64.

14 Triumph and Disaster

1 *CPR 1452-61*, pp. 78 and 108.

2 M.G.A. Vale, 'The Last Years of English Gascony, 1451–1453', *TRHS*, XIX, (1969) pp 119–38. Escouchy II, pp. 28–29. Chartier II, pp. 330–31. Berry Herald, *Chronique*, p. 385. Basin, *Charles VII*, ed. Samaran, II, pp. 184–85).Vale postulates a small number of about 300 dissidents inside the city. The tradition, based Basin, that King Charles's heavy-handed treatment of Gascony led the inhabitants to send a delegation to London begging the English to return can be dismissed. Vale demonstrates that no high- ranking delegation came from Bordeaux in the summer of 1452 as Basin claimed.

3 *Foedera* XI, pp. 313–15. Vale, *English Gascony*, p. 142.

4 Myers, 'Household', pp. 181–82. Myers, 'Jewels', p. 225.

5 *Benet's Chron.*, p. 208: 'Shrewsbury captured 33 ships on the Garonne, took Bordeaux by storm, and went on to conquer 32 castles and towns.'

Notes

6. Myers, 'Household', pp. 200–01.
7. *Annales*, p. 770. *Benet's Chron.*, p. 208. *Great Chron.*, p. 186. *Calendar of the Charter Rolls*, VI, p. 122, gives the date of creation as 23 November 1452.
8. *Foedera* X, p. 828. R.A. Griffiths and R.S. Thomas, *The Making of the Tudor Dynasty*, (Gloucester: Sutton, 1985), p. 32.
9. Roskell, *Commons*, p. 248, estimates that 17% of the Commons in this Parliament were household men. It is a curious feature of traditional accounts that when Parliament favoured the government it was because Parliament had been packed, but when it was critical it reflected popular discontent, personified by the Duke of York.
10. *Rot. Parl.* V, p. 329a.
11. *PROME* XII, pp. 307–09. *CPR 1452-61*, pp. 103 and 111–12. Oldhall's principal seat at Hunsdon was granted to Somerset for the fee of a red rose at midsummer; his other lands went to Jasper Tudor.
12. *PROME* XII, pp. 230–34 and 236.
13. *PROME* XII, pp. 241–44.
14. *Rot. Parl.* V, p. 394a. *CFR, 1445-52*, pp. 220–21. Lord Scales and Miles Stapleton, who had the keeping of the lands, did not meet their commitment to pay £278 9s 4d per annum to the Exchequer.
15. M.K. Jones and M.G. Underwood, *The King's Mother, Lady Margaret Beaufort, Countess of Richmond and Derby*, (Cambridge University Press, 1992), p. 39.
16. E 404 / 69/ 145. Devon, *Exchequer*, p. 479.
17. *PROME* XII, p. 423. This statement was made two years later in the Parliament of 1455/56 when Tunstall was exempted from the resumption of that year.
18. Stevenson, *L&P*, II, ii, pp. 507–08. A demy ceynt was a girdle made of decorative gold work in front and tied behind with silk ribbons. It was valued at £250 and was not paid for until October 1456.
19. John Ashdown-Hill, 'Walsingham in 1469: The pilgrimage of Edward IV and Richard, Duke of Gloucester', *Ricardian*, XI, No. 136, (March 1997), pp. 2–16 for the description of the shrine.
20. Myers, 'Jewels', p. 222. The tablet was valued at £29.
21. Davis, *PL*, I, p. 248 dates Margaret's visit to 17–19 April.

Notes

22 C. Rawcliffe, 'Women, Childbirth and Religion', in *Women and Religion in Medieval England,* ed. D. Wood (Oxbow Books, 2003), p. 104.

23 BL Egerton Roll 8365. There is a claim for 3s 2d in the Hitchin bailiff's account, for Michaelmas 31 Henry VI to Michaelmas 32 Henry VI, for the expenses of York's treasurer staying one night at Hitchin when the Duchess of York *abmaneat* (visited, stayed with?) the Queen of England. I owe this reference to Miss Ann Kettle.

24 Huntington Library, Battle Abbey Collection, BA 937.

25 *CPR 1452-61*, pp. 75 and 102.

26 *PROME* XII, pp. 237–41.

27 Stevenson, *L&P* II, ii, pp. 479–80. *CPR 1452-61,* p. 61. *Benet's Chron.,* p. 209.

28 *John Vale's Book,* p. 173. The letter is not dated, but it is given under the King's signet 'at our manoir of Claryndon.'

29 Myers, 'Household', p. 181. There are no grants to Wenlock from King Henry after 1453. Roskell, *Parliament and Politics* II, p. 247 considered it 'remarkable' that there is no information about Wenlock in 1454.

30 *CPR 1452-61*, pp. 114-116. The signatories to the charter were Chancellor Kemp, William Booth, Archbishop of York, the Bishops of London and Worcester, the Duke of Somerset, the Earls of Wiltshire and Worcester, Lords Cromwell and Dudley, Thomas Lisieux, 'and others'. The Duke of Exeter, although still a minor, signed as Admiral of England.

31 *CPR 1446-52*, pp. 262–63, grant to all four Beauchamp daughters.

32 Hicks, *Warwick,* p. 82. The Beauchamp inheritance is incredibly complex; an outline cannot do it justice. It has been studied in detail by Storey, *End of Lancaster*, pp. 231–41 and Hicks, *Warwick,* pp. 39–53. See also A.J. Pollard, *Warwick the Kingmaker* (2007), pp. 17–23.

33 *CFR, 1452-61,* p. 34.

34 Hicks, *Warwick*, p. 84. Storey, *End of Lancaster,* p. 135. Both cite E 28 /83 /41–2 (27 July).

35 Beaucourt V, pp. 266–67.

36 There are no English chronicle accounts of the battle. *Benet's Chron.,* p. 209 notes the death of Shrewsbury, Lisle, and Edward Hull, and the capture of Hungerford. Accounts of the battle in the French chronicles vary: Escouchy II, pp 35–36. Chartier III, pp 3–7. Berry Herald,

Chronique, pp. 389-391. Basin, *Charles VII*, ed. Samaran II, pp. 197-199.
37 Beaucourt V, pp. 283-84. Lord Camoys and the remnants of the Earl of Shrewsbury's army surrendered Bordeaux to King Charles in person in October and the English garrison marched out with the honours of war. The end of the Hundred Years' War passed almost unnoticed in England.
38 *Chronicon Angliae* IV, p. 44. *Benet's Chron.*, p. 210. The exact date of Henry's collapse is disputed but 10 August, suggested by Gairdner, *PL* I, p. 130, n. 3, is probably the most accurate. See Wolffe, *Henry VI*, pp. 270-71 for a detailed analysis of the sources and dating. See also B. Clarke, *Mental Disorder in Earlier Britain*, Chapter 7 'Henry VI, his person and his grandfather' (1975). V. Green, *The Madness of Kings*, Chapter IV, 'The royal saint' (1993). C. Rawcliffe, 'The Insanity of Henry VI', *The Historian*, 50, (1996), pp. 8-12.
39 Wolffe, *Henry VI*, p. 18, citing KB 9/273/103. Storey, *End of Lancaster*, p. 136, citing KB 9/273/2 and 7. J. Hughes, *Arthurian Myths and Alchemy: the Kingship of Edward IV*, Chapter 3, 'The Legacy of Henry VI; the Fisher King', (2002), for a highly theoretical interpretation.

15 Queen in Waiting

1 CLRO Journal V, fol. 120.
2 *Letters of Margaret*, pp. 67-68. Arundel MS 26, fol. 29b (for the blue mourning robes).
3 *Bale's Chron.*, p. 140. Bale is the only nearly contemporary chronicle to record these rejoicings. The other chronicles mention what at the time was a momentous event in one short sentence, if at all. They have obviously been edited to play down its importance to suit Yorkist propaganda.
4 CLRO Journal V, fol. 125b.
5 E 101/410/12 (Wardrobe account). Devon. *Exchequer*, p. 478. Ullman, *Liber Regie Capelle*, pp. 67-72. Kay Staniland, 'Royal Entry into the World' in *England in the Fifteenth Century*, ed. D. Williams, (1987). J.L. Laynesmith, *The Last Medieval Queens*, (Oxford, 2004), pp. 113-119.
6 *Bale's Chron.*, p. 140-41.
7 Lincoln College. Hales MS 12.

Notes

8. Ullman, *Liber Regie Capelle,* pp. 72–73. Myers, 'Household', p. 203. In addition to the offerings she made at the time of her purification, Margaret sent the Dean of the royal chapel a drinking cup valued at 20 marks.
9. *Benet's Chron.,* p. 216. For the earliest known reference in 1456, claiming that Edward was a changeling. A later chronicler, Robert Fabyan, in *New Chronicles of England and France,* ed. H. Ellis, (Rolls Series, 1811) p. 628, noted that the 'noble mother susteynyd not a little dysclaunder and obsequye of the common people saying he was not the naturall sone of the Kinge Henry but changed in the cradell.'
10. Harriss, *Beaufort,* p. 178, n. 34.
11. Griffiths, 'Queen Katherine of Valois and a Missing Statute of the Realm', in *King and Country,* pp. 103–113.
12. *PPC* VI, pp. 163–64.
13. *CPR 1452-61* pp. 143–44.
14. Gairdner, *PL* II, pp. 290–93. This peculiar document is a later copy of Norfolk's peroration. If it had not been signed (J M Norff), historians would unhesitatingly ascribe it to York. If Norfolk had previously accused Somerset, and had tried to get action taken against him, no record of this survives. Likewise, if Norfolk was with York at Dartford the fact is not recorded elsewhere. *Benet's Chron.,* p. 210 confirms that the accusations were made by Norfolk.
15. *Chronicon Angliae,* p. 44. There may be an oblique reference in *Benet's Chron.,* p. 211; the chronicler says that Kemp was reputed to be a friend to Somerset.
16. Griffiths, 'The King's Council and the First Protectorate of the Duke of York, 1450-1454', in *King and Country,* pp. 315–16.
17. Griffiths, 'The King's Council ...' in *King and Country,* p. 317. The signature of the Earl of Worcester, as Treasurer, does not appear, but this may be an oversight.
18. Lincoln's Inn, Hale MS 12, Item 75.
19. Gairdner, *PL* II, pp. 295–96.
20. Gairdner, *PL* II, pp. 295–99.
21. *Benet's Chron,* p. 211 dates the lords' return to the beginning of February but says nothing about heavy armaments. Magnates coming to

Parliament heavily armed was not unusual. They had done so following York's return from Ireland in 1450.
22. Gairdner, *PL* II, p. 298. Stodeley's newsletter is the sole source for this information. There is no evidence that Edmund Tudor came to London; he did not attend the meeting of the Great Council on 30 November 1453. Jasper attended Parliament, but not the February council meetings that preceded it. Far too much credence has been given to this piece of gossip, which may have been garbled: it could equally well be that it was rumoured that York would have them arrested if they came to London.
23. None of them were at the Council meeting in London on 13 February, the day before Parliament convened.
24. *PROME* XII, p. 252. To buy time until the political situation became clearer, Chancellor Kemp had prorogued Parliament, which should have met in November 1453, to meet in February 1454.
25. *CClR 1447-54*, p. 484. Roskell, 'Thomas Thorpe' in *Parliament and Politics*, II, p. 216.
26. *Foedera* XI, p. 344. J.F. Baldwin, *The King's Council in England during the Middle Ages* (Oxford, 1913), p. 197, n. 3.
27. *PROME* XII, pp. 254–56
28. *PROME* XII, p. 229. Devon had been released and summoned to Parliament at Reading in 1453 where he was named a trier of petitions.
29. *PROME* XII, pp. 275–76.
30. C. M. Barron, 'London and the Crown, 1451-61', p. 94, citing CLRO Journal 5, fo. 150.
31. Griffiths, 'King's Council', in *King and Country*, p. 311 lists the council members who did not endorse conciliar rule, but he does not suggest that they endorsed Margaret.
32. A. Gross, *The Dissolution of the Lancastrian Kingship*, (Stamford, 1996), pp. 56–57 suggests that Thomas Thorpe, as Speaker of the Commons, was invited to contribute to the composition of these articles; but this is based on a false assumption. Setting aside that Thorpe was in prison while the articles were being prepared, the Commons could request the King to appoint a 'sad and wise' council, but not dictate its composition. The decision on how the government was to be constituted would be taken by the Lords and reported to the Commons. Gross claims that

Thorpe was not in prison at the time the Queen's articles were being prepared but the evidence suggests otherwise.

33 Gairdner, *PL* II, pp. 297. John Stodeley's newsletter is the only record of Margaret's 'bill'. If it had not survived, Margaret's bid for the regency would have remained unknown. English historians have made too much of the 'unprecedented' nature of Margaret's articles. R.L. Storey, *End of Lancaster,* p. 139 calls them 'alien … to all constitutional precedents', but in 1454 there was no precedent. Watts, *Henry VI,* p. 305, n.193 describes Margaret's proposed powers as 'awesomely wide', but they were the King's powers, which she was attempting to protect. Griffiths, *Henry VI,* p 724, says the Queen was 'bent on a course of breath-taking novelty.' And he is right, Margaret's situation was novel, but it was not of her making: it had been brought about by King Henry's collapse.

34 *PROME* XII, pp. 274–75. *CPR 1452-61*, p. 172.

35 Such is Kemp's posthumous reputation that one historian claims, with pardonable exaggeration, that the Wars of the Roses could not begin until Kemp died. R. C. Davies, 'The Church and the Wars of the Roses', p. 139, in *The Wars of the Roses,* ed. A.J. Pollard, (Macmillan, 1995).

36 *PROME* XII, pp. 257–59.

37 *PPC* VI, pp. 166–67. *Foedera* XI, p. 347. *CPR 1452-61*, p. 147. Master Robert Wareyn and John Marchall were the surgeons.

38 C. Rawcliffe, *Medicine and Society in Later Medieval England,* (Stroud, 1995), p. 63. Rawcliffe thinks the doctors were treating Henry primarily for 'acute lethargy.'

16 My Lord Protector

1 *PROME* XII, pp. 261–64.
2 *PROME* XII, pp. 259–61.
3 Storey, *End of Lancaster,* pp. 112–13, estimates that Salisbury's income at a minimum of £2,490 p.a.
4 *CClR 1447-54,* pp. 50–09. *Foedera* XI, p. 344–45. *PPC* VI, pp. 355–57.
5 *PPC* VI, p. 174.
6 Griffiths, 'The King's Council', in *King and Country*, pp. 317–20.
7 Thomas, Lord Scales, was a veteran of the wars in France. He was an

advisor to Margaret's council in 1453 and paid £10 for his attendance. (Myers, 'Household,' p. 203).

8. It is assumed by most historians that because Booth had been Margaret's chancellor, he was an opponent of York's regime. Such evidence as we have suggests the exact opposite.
9. *PPC* VI, pp. 168–69 and 170–71.
10. *PROME* XII, pp. 284–88.
11. *PPC* VI, pp. 199–206. Stevenson, *L&P* II, ii, pp. 501–2. *Foedera* XI, p. 351.
12. G.L. Harriss, 'The Struggle of Calais', *EHR* LXXV (1960), p. 36.
13. *PROME* XII, pp. 289–91. Stevenson, *L&P* II, ii, pp. 495–96 (misdated to July). Griffiths, *Henry VI*, pp. 731 and 763 n. 90 and n. 93.
14. Gairdner, *PL* II, p. 325.
15. Gairdner, *PL* II, p. 296. The ubiquitous John Stodeley's letter of 19 January 1454 is the only source for a meeting between Egremont and Exeter in January, but it fits reasonably well with subsequent events. It may also account for Stodeley's incorrect statement that Egremont and the Percys were assembling troops to march on London.
16. *PPC* VI, pp. 140–41.
17. T.B. Pugh, 'Richard Duke of York and the Rebellion of Henry Holand Duke of Exeter in May 1454', *Historical Research* vol. 63, no. 152 (October 1990), pp. 248–62. Pugh prints York's letter dated 8 May, which refers to a recent meeting with Exeter in London.
18. Storey, *End of Lancaster*, p. 144.
19. *PPC* VI, pp. 189–90. The letter is undated. The editor dates it to 3 June, but it could have been written in May, just after York went north. Garter King of Arms passed through Spofforth in May on his way to Scotland. (*Foedera* XI, p. 349). His reason for going via Spofforth was probably to deliver letters to Exeter.
20. *Benet's Chron.*, pp. 211–12.
21. Storey, *End of Lancaster*, Chapter X, 'The Duke of Exeter's Rebellion.'
22. Griffiths, 'Local Rivalries', pp. 321–364. Griffiths takes the view, based on the later indictments, that York was dealing with a serious political rebellion.
23. Hicks, *Warwick*, pp. 110–11, citing KB 9/149/4/27.
24. *John Vale's Book*, pp. 183–84.

25. Griffiths, 'Local rivalries', p. 344 n. 124, in *King and Country,* citing KB. Anc. Indict., 149/4/27 and 5/3/ 9/8. Plea Roll rex m.3d.
26. *PPC* VI, pp. 130-31. Misdated (as Pugh and Griffiths note) to 1453. Storey, *End of Lancaster,* p. 146.
27. Gairdner *PL* II, p. 321. 'It ys seyd the Duc of Exceter ys here covertlye'. The letter is dated 8 June.
28. *PPC* VI, pp. 218. *Great Chron.,* p. 187. *Benet's Chron.,* p. 212.
29. *Papal Letters* X, pp. 165-66.
30. Inner Temple Library, Petyt 538/47 f/409x. *Papal Letters 1458-71*, XII, pp. 373-74.
31. *CPR 1452-61*, pp. 171-72. Gairdner, *PL* III, pp. 320-21.
32. *PPC* VI, p. 168. *CPR 1452-61*, p. 151. *Foedera* XI, pp. 347 and 357. Gairdner, *PL* III, p. 2.
33. Virgoe, 'The Composition of the King's Council, 1437-1461' in *East Anglian Society*, pp. 278-79. York is recorded as present at twenty-eight meetings during the Protectorate; Salisbury, as chancellor, attended fifty-nine.
34. *PPC* VI, pp. 206-07:'And I in no wise will yeve myne assent to the said enlargement w^tout th'avis of the said juges knowlech and assent also of mo lordes y^t nowe be absent ...'
35. *PPC* VI, pp. 214-19.
36. Johnson, *York,* pp. 149-51.
37. *CClR,* 1447-52, p. 512.
38. *PPC* VI, p. 183-84. Castor, *Duchy of Lancaster,* pp. 172-74 and 178-79. Virgoe, 'Three Suffolk Parliamentary Elections ...' in *East Anglian Society*, pp 55-57.
39. H. Castor, 'Walter Blount was gone to serve traytors': the sack of Elvaston ... 1454', *Midlands History*, Vol 19, (1994), pp. 21-39. Storey, *End of Lancaster,* Chapter XI, 'The Sack of Elvaston.'
40. Griffiths, 'Local rivalries' in *King and Country,* pp. 354.
41. *Rawlinson B 355*, p. 109. *Gough London 10*, p. 158. *Chron. Angliae,* pp. 45-46. *Brut G,* pp. 523-24. *Brief Notes,* p. 149.
42. It is interesting that at the end of November 'the crown'. i.e. the Duke of York, leased several manors to Henry Percy, Lord Poynings. York was not being generous or even handed. The rent from the manors far

outweighed their income. (J.M.W. Bean, *The Estates of the Percy Family*, (Oxford, 1958), p. 75.)
43 *PPC* VI, pp. 210–14.
44 *PPC* VI, pp. 220–233.
45 Wolffe, *Henry VI*, p. 283. 'the knights, esquires, and gentlemen of the household, numbering 301 ... were reduced to 24, while the yeomen of the crown and chamber were reduced from 72 to 31.'
46 *PPC* VI p. 233. *CPR 1452-61*, p. 158–59.
47 Modern historians frequently refer, vaguely, to York's reforms or to his 'programme of reform'. But apart from his attempt to reduce the size of the royal household, what did he actually accomplish?

17 Fortune's Wheel

1 Gairdner, *PL* III, pp. 13-14. Edmund Clere of Ormsby. He is not to be conflated with his cousin Edmund Clere of Stokesby, who went on to serve Edward IV (as in Wedgwood *Biographies* p. 189). Clere joined Margaret's household in Rouen and he appears in all her surviving household and jewel accounts.
2 *Gough London 10*, p. 158. As with the celebrations for Prince Edward's birth, thanksgiving for Henry's recovery is omitted from most of the (Yorkist) chronicles.
3 *Bale's Chron.*, p. 141.
4 *CCIR 1454-61*, p. 9 (order for release), p. 144 (surety of bail). *Foedera* XI, p. 361. The other signatories were Thomas, Lord Roos Somerset's stepson, William Bourgchier Lord Fitzwarin, and the Earl of Wiltshire.
5 *Foedera* XI, p. 362–63. *CCIR 1454-61*, p. 49.
6 *CPR 1452-61*, p. 226. Yorkist propaganda later distorted the facts. The *English Chron.*, p. 178, claimed that Somerset was made to swear that he would take no further part in government or come within 20 miles of the King. Thomas Gascoigne, *Loci e Libro*, p. 203, asserted that Somerset's release was illegal because it did not have the assent of the Council. Both are obvious glosses, contradicting the actual proceedings.
7 Harriss, 'Struggle for Calais', p. 39. It is generally accepted, based on Harriss, that Henry immediately restored the captaincy to Somerset. All

Harriss says, however, is that Somerset *probably* resumed contacts with the officers in Calais, but he does not cite any source confirming that the captaincy was restored to Somerset. *Foedera* XI, p. 363, states that York was relieved of the post at his own request. It does not mention Somerset.

8   *PPC* VI, pp. 358–59. *Gough London 10*, p.158. *Chronicon Angliae*, p. 47 claims that Salisbury resigned over an order to release the Duke of Exeter but is mistaken in saying the Earl of Devon (who was not in prison) was also released. The order for Exeter's release was directed to Richard Neville as Chancellor, not as Earl of Salisbury, and he did not resign as Chancellor until a month after he received it

9   Wolffe, *Henry VI*, p, 285 citing E 28/86/1

10 *Foedera* XI, p. 365. *CClR 1454-61*, p. 13.

11 *PPC* VI, pp. 339–42.

12 *Benet's Chron.*, pp. 212–13. *Great Chron.*, p. 187. *Brut G*, p. 521. *Gregory's Chron.*, p. 198-99. *English Chron.*, p. 72. All the chronicles were written or revised under the Yorkist Edward IV and are hostile to Somerset.

13 This explanation has been accepted by historians ever since, even though there is no evidence that the King, or Somerset, intended to use the Leicester council for this purpose.

14 D. Dunn, 'Margaret of Anjou, Chivalry and the Order of the Garter', in *St George's Chapel, Windsor, in the late Middle Ages*, eds. C. Richmond and E. Scarff, (Windsor, 2001), p. 49.

15 *Chronicon Angliae*, p. 47. It is the only source for the King sending a delegation to York at this time.

16 *The Coventry Leet Book*, Part II, ed., M.D. Harris, (Early English Text Society, 1908), pp. 282–83. The letter is headed 'By the kyng'. One hundred armed men were to be assembled at the city's cost. They were never sent. By the time they were ready King Henry was no longer at St Albans; he had returned to London.

17 C.A.J., Armstrong, 'Politics and the Battle of St Albans', *BIHR*, XXXIII no 87 (May 1960), p. 19.

18 Armstrong, 'St Albans', *The Fastolf Relation*, pp. 65–66 is the only source to note the presence of William Neville, Lord Fauconberg, in King Henry's company. He did not attend the Garter Feast in April because he was 'outside the kingdom'. (D. Dunn, 'Margaret of Anjou,... Order of the

Garter', p. 49.) Fauconberg was Salisbury's brother. Would he have taken the field against his brother and his nephew?
19. *Chronicon Angliae*, pp. 47–48.
20. Armstrong, 'St Albans', p. 29 accepts the *Fastolf Relation's* claim (p. 65) that Somerset sent the Duke of Exeter's pursuivant to York separately with the same demand – couched as a threat – but Exeter was still under house arrest at Wallingford.
21. M.A. Hicks, 'Propaganda and the First Battle of St Albans, 1455', *Nottingham Medieval Studies*, 44, (2000), pp. 167–83. Hicks suggests that Henry rejected York's petition in the much the same way as he rejected petitions in Parliament: *le roi s'advisera*, but the consequences were potentially far more serious at St Albans than the rejection of a Parliamentary petition.
22. J. Whethamstede, *Registrum Abbatiae Johannis Whethamstede*, ed. H.T. Riley, 2 vols. (1872-73), I, p. 171. *Great Chron.*, p. 187. *Brut G*, p. 522. The chronicle entries are the same; they were written long after 1455 and derive from a common source. They claim that Warwick began the battle; he charged before negotiations had been broken off. If he did it was certainly in character.
23. *Benet's Chron.*, p. 214. *Gregory's Chron.*, p. 198, wrongly states that he was not yet Earl of Wiltshire and that he carried the King's banner: he 'sette the kyngys baner agayne an howse ende and fought manly with the helys, for he was a feryd of lesynge of beute, for he was namyd the fayryd knyght of thys londe.' Of such is tradition born: Storey, *End of Lancaster*, p. 91: 'Wiltshire was to distinguish himself in the Wars of the Roses by running away from every battle in which he took part.' *Bale's Chron.*, p. 142 and Gairdner, *PL* III, p. 28, record that Wiltshire 'fled' *after* the battle.
24. *English Chron.*, p. 73, records that Lord Sudeley carried the banner, but a letter to William Worcester, written in June 1455, names the more likely candidate: Sir Philip Wentworth, one of King Henry's knights of the body. (Gairdner *PL* III, p. 33).
25. Gairdner, *PL* III, p. 28.
26. Whethamstede I, pp. 175–178.
27. Watts, *Henry VI*, p. 317, n.146, citing E 159/232, comm., Mic., rot.3. Margaret was in the Tower on 23 May.

Notes

28 Armstrong, 'St Albans', *Dijon Relation*, p. 64.
29 Gairdner, *PL* III, p. 33.
30 *Rawlinson B 355*, p. 108. *Benet's Chron.*, p. 214 adds an unlikely detail: King Henry insisted on receiving the crown from York's hands!
31 Storey, *End of Lancaster*, p. 162, goes so far as to call it murder although he exonerates his hero, York.
32 *PPC* VI, pp. 245–46.
33 *CPR 1452-61*, p. 242.
34 *CPR 1452-61*, pp. 242–43.
35 Hicks, *Warwick*, p. 149, puts it succinctly: 'The captaincy of Calais was Warwick's share of the spoils of war.'
36 *Foedera* XI, p. 366.
37 *Kings Works* II, p. 680, citing DL 29/58/1103-1107 and DL 29/74/1477-78. Hertford was part of Margaret's original dower and 'her accounts show that the castle was regularly repaired during her tenure.'
38 Gairdner *PL* III, p. 32.
39 Gairdner, *PL III*, pp. 43–44.
40 Gairdner, *PL* III, p. 28.
41 Gairdner, *PL* III, pp. 28–29.
42 *PROME* XII, pp. 338–43.
43 M. Hicks, 'Propaganda', pp. 174–75 establishes their provenance, but not when they were written.
44 Armstrong, 'St Albans', p. 6: 'The document, [pardon] if not actually stained with blood and disgraced by plunder ... is none the less a prolongation of the battle into the parliament chamber.'
45 *PROME* XII, p. 343.
46 Gairdner, *PL* III, pp. 44–45.
47 *PPC* VI, pp. 251–52.
48 *PROME* XII, pp. 343–45.
49 J.R. Lander, 'Henry VI and the Duke of York's Second Protectorate', in *Crown and Nobility, 1450-1509*, (1976), pp. 74–93 discusses the question of Henry's health, and the situation in the West Country in detail.
50 *PPC* VI, p. 261-62. *Rot. Parl.* V, p. 453. This is not on the rolls of parliament. It is copied from Cotton MS Titus E VI f 336.
51 Cherry, 'Struggle for power', pp. 137–38.

52 A.R. Myers, *English Historical Documents,* (1969) pp. 1230–33. Gairdner, *PL* III, pp. 48–50. Storey, *End of Lancaster*, pp. 167–69.
53 York later rewarded Wenlock for his compliance by granting him £20 p.a. 'for good service and council.' (Johnson, *York*, p. 172 n. 108, citing SC6 /850/ 4).
54 *PROME* XII, pp. 348–50.
55 *PROME* XII, pp. 350–56. *Foedera* XI, p. 369. *CPR 1452-61*, p. 273.
56 Storey, *End of Lancaster,* pp. 169–72.
57 Myers, *English Historical Documents,* p. 1233.
58 *London Chrons,* (*Vitellius A* XVI) p. 166. According to *Benet's Chron.,* p. 216, Bonville was imprisoned in the Fleet.
59 *Rot. Parl.* V, p. 332b.
60 *PPC* VI, pp 267–70.
61 *Rawlinson B 355*, pp. 109–10.
62 Gairdner, *PL* III, p. 76. John Bocking's letter of 9 February makes it clear that York protected Devon: 'this day was myn lord Deuenshire at Westminster, and shuld haue apperid, but he was countermaunded.'

18 Queen Consort

1 *PROME* XII, pp. 381–82. Wolffe, *Royal Demesne*, pp. 138–40.
2 *Benet's Chron.*, p. 216. Watts, *Henry VI,* pp. 322.
3 *PPC* VI, p. 286.
4 Storey, *End of Lancaster*, p. 254 citing KB 9/149, no 5/3.
5 *CClR 1454-61*, p. 109. The recognizance was for £2,000.
6 Gairdner, *PL* III, p. 75. The inveterate rumour-monger, John Bocking, to Sir John Fastolf, recounting all the gossip he had heard.
7 Gairdner, *PL* III, p. 75.
8 *Benet's Chron.*, p. 216: *quod Edwardus princeps non fuit filius regine.* This is the first recorded suggestion of Prince Edward's bastardy; it would become a staple of Yorkist propaganda.
9 Gascoigne, *Loci e Libro,* p. 204.
10 *PROME* XII, p. 385. *Rot. Parl.* V, p. 330a. See Appendix A.
11 *PROME* XII, pp. 431–32. *Foedera* XI, p. 373.
12 Watts, *Henry VI,* p. 333, n. 301. *CPR 1452-61*, p. 278.

[13] *PROME* XII, pp. 386–428. The wording of the King's acceptance suggests that some exemptions could have been added after the initial act was passed: 'all such provisions and excepcions as been by his highnesse, by thadvice of the said lords ... made and agreed, *or to be agreed* ... be goode and effectuell, ye seid act notwithstondynge ...'

[14] R. Somerville, *History of the Duchy of Lancaster* 1265-1603, (1953), p. 421. Salisbury got off lightly in the resumption too, losing only £80 from the fee farm of Carlisle (*PROME* XII, p. 401).

[15] Harriss, 'Struggle for Calais', p. 46. Stevenson, *L&P,* II, ii, pp. 505–06. *PROME* XII, 374–81 (loans) and p. 401 (Warwick exempted).

[16] *CPR 1452-61*, pp. 304–05, 310, and 358. The Earl of Wiltshire received licence to go on pilgrimage to St James de Compostela on 9 March 1456. (*Foedera* XI, p. 375). He did not go, as his commissions date to March and May 1456.

[17] *Rawlinson B* 355, p. 110. *Brut G,* p. 522 and *Great Chron.,* p. 188. R. Flenley, 'London and Foreign Merchants in the Reign of Henry VI', *EHR* XXV (1910), pp. 650–61.

[18] *CPR 1452-61,* p. 306. The Dukes of Buckingham and Exeter, the Earls of Salisbury, Pembroke, Northumberland, Worcester, and Stafford.

[19] Gairdner *PL* III, p. 87. *Bale's Chron.,* p 143. The chroniclers' claim that these riots forced King Henry to leave London for the Midlands has been followed by some historians, but the lapse of time between early May and late August negates this.

[20] E101/410/15. Margaret's household left Westminster on 11 May. She was at Chester on 16 August. (*Letters of Margaret,* p. 62.)

[21] Gairdner, *PL* III, p. 92.

[22] D. Dunn, 'The Queen at War: the Role of Margaret of Anjou in the Wars of the Roses', in *War and Society in Medieval and Early Modern Britain,* ed. D. Dunn, (Liverpool, 2000), pp. 150–51.

[23] *English Chron.,* p. 78, recounts the distribution of the swan badges as taking place just before the Battle of Blore Heath in 1459. Margaret 'callyed vn to her alle the knyghtes and squyers of Chestreshyre for to haue theyre benyuolence, and helde open householde among theym [and she] 'made her sone called the Prince yeue a lyuery of Swannys to alle the gentilmenne of the contre, and to many other thoroughout the lande.' This

fits the circumstances of 1456 better than those of 1459.
24. BL, Add. MS 46,846, f. 33. The letter is undated, but it belongs to a time when Margaret was not in King Henry's company. There is no note of to whom it was addressed or from where it was written. Although it summoned the recipients urgently, it did not require them to come armed, as would surely have been the case had it been written later, during the military clashes of 1459–1461.
25. Gairdner, *PL* III, p. 92. The ubiquitous John Bocking was a master of half-fact and half-rumour. He reported that a 'great council' had been summoned for June 7 but was attended only by the Earl of Salisbury and the Bourgchiers, as Chancellor and Treasurer. His statement is misleading. Virgoe, 'Composition of the King's Council', p. 285, n. 97, accepted Bocking's statement but noted that a few days later, on 11 June, a warrant was signed by seven members of the continual council. King Henry was unlikely to call a Great Council to Westminster in the summer months; many of his magnates, judges, and gentry were employed on various commissions. Watts, *Henry VI*, p. 333 n. 303, and Griffiths, *Henry VI*, p. 823, n. 2, note the presence in council of Archbishop Booth, the Duke of Buckingham, Bishops Waynflete of Winchester, Gray of Ely, and Lyhert of Norwich.
26. Devon, *Exchequer*, pp. 479–80. *Foedera* XI, p. 367.
27. Beckington, *Correspondence* II, pp. 139–41.
28. Devon, *Exchequer*, p. 480–81. *Foedera* XI, p. 383. The copy in Beckington's *Correspondence* (p. 141) is misdated to 24 August.
29. Beckington, *Correspondence* II, p. 142–44. The misdating in Stevenson, *L&P* I, pp. 323–26, of a letter from King James to King Charles VII to 1456 instead of 1460 has added to the confusion and resulted in several muddled accounts of this episode.
30. *Benet's Chron.*, p. 217. *Auchinleck Chronicle* in C. McGladdery, *James II*, (Edinburgh, 1990), p. 169.
31. Gairdner, *PL* III, p. 92: 'þ'Erle of Richemond and Griffith Such ar at werre gretely in Wales.' It has been assumed that this was Gruffydd ap Nicholas for want of an alternative candidate. It may have been just another rumour gathered by John Bocking.
32. *CPR 1446-52*, pp. 234–35.

33. Griffiths, 'Gruffydd ap Nicholas ... and Lancaster', in *King and Country*, pp. 201–19.
34. Johnson, *York,* pp. 230–31. *CPR 1452-61,* p. 586. *Rot. Parl.* V, p. 342. Devereux had been indicted in 1452 for raising a force in Hereford for York before Dartford. In 1455 he petitioned to be declared a true man.
35. Herbert was the son of William ap Thomas but changed his name. He married Anne Devereux, daughter of Sir Walter Devereux and sister of Walter Devereux, making them Herbert's father-in-law and his brother-in-law.
36. Griffiths, *Henry VI*, p. 832, n. 56, citing KB 9/35/24 71. The reconstruction of these events is based on indictments in the King's Bench of April 1457.
37. *CPR 1452-61,* p. 245. They had previously been held by the Duke of Somerset.
38. Devon, *Exchequer,* pp. 481–82.
39. R.R. Sharpe, *London and the Kingdom,* 3 vols, (1895), III, p. 376–77.
40. *Short English Chron.,* p. 70.
41. Margaret would have passed through Lichfield on her way south from Chester. There seems no other reason for Henry to go north from Kenilworth if not to meet the Queen. The importance of this meeting has been largely overlooked.
42. *Coventry Leet Book,* II, pp. 285–292. The Mayor convened a meeting on 28 August to raise money for the Queen's visit.
43. *Coventry Leet Book,* II, pp. 262–65.
44. *Coventry Leet Book,* II, p, 292. The total cost to the city of the pageants was £21 13s 2d, including 25s for labour. The council also authorised a douceur of 20s to members of Henry's household. The Mayor paid £8 0s 4d for King Henry's wine, £10 10s 1d for two silver gilt cups, and 2s for rose water for Sir Richard Woodville. What Woodville did to deserve it is not recorded.
45. Laynesmith, *Last Medieval Queens,* pp. 14–43. Mauer, *Margaret of Anjou*, pp. 140–41. G. Kipling, *Enter the King,* pp. 315–16, should be taken with a grain of salt. Margaret did *not* regard herself as Regent of England in 1456.
46. Attendance at this council is not recorded; thirty-five lords, bishops

and abbots attended the second council at Coventry in February 1457. It is reasonable to assume that much the same number were present in 1456.

47 Lisieux was too ill to accompany Henry to Coventry. He died in October 1456. (*CPR 1452-61*, p. 326).

48 A. Compton Reeves, 'Lawrence Booth: Bishop of Durham (1457-76), Archbishop of York (1476-80) in Sharon D. Michalove and A. Compton Reeves, eds., *Estrangement, Enterprise and Education in Fifteenth Century England,* (1998), pp. 6–88.

49 *CPR 1452-61*, p. 324.

50 Griffiths, *Henry VI*, p. 788. Pollard, *Talbot,* p. 120. As Treasurer, Shrewsbury loaned over £3,000 to the crown.

51 *Foedera* XI, pp. 383–84. *CClR 1454-61*, pp. 211–12.

52 *Brief Notes,* pp. 151–52 ... *domino de Cromuel ... domino de Bowser comes de Hyu.* This chronicle was written under Edward IV when the Bourgchiers stood high in the King's favour, so it may be an afterthought. Viscount Bourgchier was styled Count of Eu, and his son, Humphrey Bourgchier, became Lord Cromwell in 1456 in right of his wife, Lord Cromwell's heir.

53 V. Davis, 'William Waynflete and the Wars of the Roses' *Southern History* 11, (1989), pp. 1–22.

54 Gairdner, *PL* III, pp. 108–09.'It is seid þat my lord of York hath be with þe Kyng and is departed ageyn in right good conceyt with þe Kyng but not in gret conceyt with þe Whene.' A Yorkist chronicler, writing with hindsight, included the Earl of Warwick in Margaret's chilly reception. 'They came and were received most graciously by the king, but not by the queen who held them in great dislike.' (*Benet's Chron.,* p. 217.)

55 *CClR 1454-61*, p. 174.

56 *CPR 1452-61*, p 158. Griffiths, *Henry VI*, p. 780.

57 *CPR 1452-61*, p. 326. H.T. Evans, *Wales and the Wars of the Roses,* (Cambridge, 1915), p. 96, suggests that Margaret handled the negotiations (unspecified), though how, or through whom, is not explained. The implication that she met Gruffydd in person is highly unlikely. This tradition has been followed by later historians, who claim that Margaret issued the pardon to Gruffydd as the price of his loyalty.

Notes

But the pardon does not refer to the Queen; it could have been issued at her request, but not on her orders.

19 Royal Court in the Midlands

1. Watts, *Henry VI*, p. 341, n. 338, citing BL Add. MS 18,612 fols. 63v-64r.
2. *CClR 1447-54* dated 11 December 1453, p. 476.
3. Castor, *King, Crown and Duchy*, p. 179 and n. 111.
4. *CPR 1446-52*, p. 283. *CClR 1447-52*, p. 392
5. *CPR 1452-61*, pp. 421 and 462.
6. Davis, *PL* II, p. 176. Gairdner, *PL* III, pp. 3–4. Dated by Gairdner to 1454. Dated by Davis to 1458. Although Southwell's letter was probably written in October 1458, it refers to incidents that occurred earlier, in 1456: 'within this ij yere we were in likewise laboured a-geyns to the Quene ...'
7. *Coventry Leet Book* II, p. 297, records the arrival (and departure) of King Henry and Margaret but does not mention Prince Edward.
8. *CPR 1452-61*, p. 323. The appointments were made two days after Lawrence Booth became Keeper of the Privy Seal. There is nothing sinister in this; Margaret was not overriding Henry's authority, as has been suggested. The writs could not be issued until then because Thomas Lisieux, Booth's predecessor, was too ill to accompany the King.
9. Myers, 'Household', p. 183. King Henry granted the couple 40 marks a year in survivorship (*CPR 1446-52*, p. 165) and Katherine received letters of denization in 1449 (*CPR 1446-52*, p. 240).
10. *CPR 1446-52*, p. 478. Whittingham was named to a commission for Hertford with four others who were in Margaret's service in July 1451. He was keeper of Margaret's great wardrobe in 1458, but it was not a new appointment. (*CPR 1452-61*, p. 429).
11. *CPR 1452-61* p. 338.
12. *CPR 1452-61* p. 338. Beaumont's fee of £66 13s 4d as steward of Margaret's lands was higher than that of any of her other officials. She gave him a silver gilt cup worth £8 10s in 1448–49, possibly because he contributed to Queens College. (E 101/410/2).
13. *CPR 1452-61*, p. 335. Griffiths, *Henry VI*, p. 782: 'Throckmorton knew the west Midlands like the back of his hand.'

Notes

14 *CPR 1452-61*, p. 336.
15 *CPR 1452-61* pp. 334 and 486. Edith shared a double wedding with another of Margaret's ladies, Isabel Dacre, whose husband is not named, and the Queen footed the bill for their wedding festivities. Myers, 'Household', p. 183, n. gives 1454, as the account reads *anno xxxij*, but Saturday and Sunday, the 4th and 5th of August, cited in the account, fell in 1453 not 1454. In 1455 Edith and Giles were granted an annuity of 20 marks for their services to the King and Queen (*CPR 1452-1461*, p. 243).
16 *Foedera* XI, pp. 385–86. *CPR 1452-61*, p. 359.
17 *PROME* XII, p. 367. He was allowed £1,000 a year to pay his servants until he was eight; from eight to fourteen he would receive an additional £333 6s 8d a year.
18 *CPR 1452-61*, pp. 357–58.
19 *Foedera* XI, p. 388. *CPR 1452-61*, p. 341.
20 Gascoigne, *Loco e Libri*, p. 205.
21 Griffiths, *Henry VI*, p. 787, citing DL29/212/3261-69 [1445-59]. Griffiths elucidated Margaret's later finances, although he pictures Margaret as avaricious.
22 Ross, *Edward IV*, (1974), p. 374. Edward IV's practices encompassed crown and duchy lands.
23 *CPR 1452-61*, pp. 339–40. See Appendix.
24 Most modern historians accept that York was behind the disturbances in Wales, but it is strangely unlike him not to be on hand, if only to show that he could quell the rebellion.
25 *PROME* XII, pp. 456–57. This incident, and the lords' oath that followed it, is known only through the record of the 1459 Parliament that attainted York and Warwick. It was a legal prevarication to claim that Warwick also swore the oath, but Warwick was not at Coventry in 1457. Warwick had sworn fealty to the King when he was granted his earldom and a general oath of allegiance with everyone else in Parliament after the Battle of St Albans, but he had never sworn an individual oath not to come against the King in arms, whereas York had. It was necessary for the legal proceedings against Warwick in 1459 to establish that he had done so –hence his inclusion in the account of the oath at Coventry.
26 *Foedera* XI, p. 388. *CPR 1452-61*, pp. 340–41.

Notes

27. *CPR 1452-61*, p. 102. *PPC* VI, pp. 172–73.
28. *PPC* VI, p. 248. Northumberland was excused attendance at Parliament in July 1455 so that he could continue to defend the north.
29. *CPR 1452-61*, pp. 346 and 356.
30. Escouchy II, p. 352, is the somewhat dubious source for this suggestion, but it fits with Margaret's penchant for diplomacy by marriage.
31. Stevenson, *L&P* I, p. 352.
32. A.I. Dunlop, *The Life and Times of James Kennedy, Bishop of St Andrews*, (Edinburgh, 1950), p. 61, n. 4.
33. Stevenson, *L&P* I, pp. 354–57.
34. *Foedera* XI, pp. 389–401.
35. *Coventry Leet Book*, II, pp. 298–99.
36. *CClR 1454-61*, p. 158.
37. *CPR 1452-61*, pp. 348–49.
38. A. Herbert, 'Herefordshire, 1413-61: some aspects of society and public order', in Griffiths, *Patronage, the Crown and the Provinces*, p. 115: '285 of the 397 men who were accused before the commissioners were associates of Devereux, Herbert, or of members of their affinities.'
39. Griffiths, *Henry VI*, p. 832 n. 56, citing KB 9/35/24, 71.
40. *Benet's Chron.*, p. 218 confused Herbert with Devereux.
41. William Herbert presented himself before the King at Coventry in June and was pardoned along with his supporters (*CPR 1452-61*, pp. 360 and 365).
42. Gairdner, *PL* III, p. 118. William Worcester sent a list of Herbert's supporters to John Paston because he found the Welsh names and their pedigrees so comical.
43. *CPR 1452-61*, p. 340. Griffiths, *Tudor Dynasty*, p. 50.
44. *CPR 1452-61*, p. 325 and 359.
45. *CClR 1454-61*, pp. 300–01.
46. Gairdner, *PL* III, p. 118.
47. *Coventry Leet Book* II, p. 299.
48. *Coventry Leet Book* II, p. 300.
49. Jones, *King's Mother*, p. 7.
50. *Coventry Leet Book* II, p. 298.
51. *Letters of Margaret*, pp. 77–78.

Notes

52. *CCLR 1454-61*, p. 205.
53. *CPR 1452-61*, pp. 370-71. The Duke of Suffolk, the Duke of Buckingham, the Earl of Stafford; the Earl of Shrewsbury and Viscount Beaumont; Lord Beauchamp of Powick. Lords Welles, Sudeley, Audley, Grey of Ruthven, Sir Richard Woodville, Sir John Barre, and Sir John Lovell.
54. *Foedera* XI, p. 405.
55. Henry VII claimed the throne by right of conquest, not by inheritance, but his claim would have been difficult to sustain had he not been Margaret Beaufort's son.
56. Confusingly, Buckingham's eldest son, Humphrey, Earl of Stafford, married Edmund Beaufort's daughter, also called Margaret.
57. Griffiths, *Henry VI*, pp. 802 and 841, n. 179, citing Lich RO B/A/ 1/11/f. 97d. Jones, *King's Mother*, pp. 40–41: 'The ceremony may have taken place at Buckingham's favourite residence of Maxstoke (Warks.) within the Coventry and Lichfield diocese, on 3 January 1458.'
58. C. Rawcliffe, *The Staffords, Earls of Stafford and Dukes of Buckingham* (Cambridge, 1978), p. 21, n. 45, dates the marriage to 1458, citing E 404/71/77. Another of Buckingham's daughters, Joan, had married Viscount Beaumont's son William in 1452.
59. Griffiths, *Henry VI*, pp. 572-73. Pollard, *Talbot*, pp. 131–33.
60. *Complete Peerage* II, p. 132.
61. *CPR 1446-52*, p 240. Marie figures in Margaret's early jewel accounts as 'Little Marion'. By 1452-53 she has become 'Magistre Marie, Domine'. She is described as Mary, bastard daughter Charles of Anjou, born in the Duchy of Touraine, in her grant of denization in 1449. She received a silver belt worth 6s 8d in 1445-46, a gold chain worth £6 4s 2½d, in 1446-47, a gold armlet 13s 7d in 1448-49 (E 101/409/14 and 17, E 101/410/2), and a wine flagon worth £2 1s 4d in 1452-53 (Myers, 'Jewels', p. 224).
62. J.A.F. Thomson, 'John de la Pole, Duke of Suffolk', *Speculum* 54 (1979), p. 529 citing *Catalogue of Ancient Deeds*, 4:260-27 Nos. A 6337-43. The dowry of £1,533 13s 4d was to be paid over four years. The contract was signed in February 1458.
63. R.B. Dobson, *Durham Priory 1440-1450*, (Cambridge, 1973), pp. 224-25. Salisbury drew an annuity of £100 p.a. from the bishopric as a 'retainer', for as long Robert Neville lived.

⁶⁴ *Foedera* XI, p. 404–05. *Margaretae Regine Anglie illustris consortis tuae & aliorum plurimorum dominorum ac nobilium tui Regni…*
⁶⁵ A.J. Pollard, *North Eastern England During the Wars of teh Roses,* (Oxford, 1990), p. 268.

20 Loveday

1. Beaucourt VI, pp. 146. P. Bernus, '*Le rôle politique de Pierre Brezé 1451-1461*', Bibliothèque de l'Ecole des Chartres, 69, (1908) pp. 326–28.
2. *CPR 1452-61*, p. 371.
3. *English Chron.*, p. 75. *Bale's Chron.*, pp. 144–45. *Brut G*, p. 524–25. *Rawlinson B 355*, p. 110. *Brief Notes*, p. 152. *Great Chron.*, p. 189. Their reports are sparse with no details, just a strong sense of indignation.
4. Berry Herald, *Chronique,* p. 404–11. Waurin V, pp. 385–88. Monstrelet II, pp. 448–49. The French chronicles are detailed and laudatory, although their claim that the plunder amounted to 200,000 to 300,000 *livres* is surely an exaggeration.
5. *Coventry Leet Book*, p. 301.
6. Sharpe, London and Kingdom III, pp. 380–84. CPR 1452-61, p. 405.
7. *CPR 1452-61*, pp. 401–410. The Duke of York and the Duke of Buckingham were named to several commissions. The Duke of Norfolk, who was supposed to be on pilgrimage, was named for Norfolk and Suffolk. The Duke of Exeter was named for Devonshire and the Duke of Somerset for Hampshire. The Earl of Shrewsbury (but not the Earl of Devon or Lord Bonville) was named for the South West. The Bourgchier brothers and the Earl of Oxford were named for Essex and Oxfordshire. Viscount Beaumont was named for Leicestershire and Lincolnshire.
8. *CPR 1452-61*, p. 390.
9. *CPR 1452-61*, pp. 355–56, 391, and 394.
10. *CPR 1452-61*, p. 428.
11. *CPR 1452-61*, p. 404. Devon, *Exchequer,* p. 482. Wolffe, *Henry VI*, p. 309, citing KB 9/287/53 for Burnet.
12. *Bale's Chron.*, p. 144. The date of this incident, if it ever took place, is disputed. Bale dated it to 5 November 1456, but he is probably off by a year; he confused the encounter between Somerset and Sir John Neville

in London in November 1456 with Somerset's proposed attack on Warwick in November 1457. See Pollard, *Warwick*, p. 201.
13   No record of this council has survived. The following inferences are based on past and subsequent events.
14   *PPC* VI, pp. 290–93.
15   *CPR 1452-61*, pp. 406–10. London was to supply the largest contingent; orders for the rest of the country followed on 17 December. The counties quotas were based on their relative affluence: Norfolk was highest (1012), then Lincoln (910), then Kent (575). The northern counties were lowest, Rutland (64), Northumberland (60), and Westmorland (56). Eight cities had to make returns – the highest was York (152), then Norwich (121) and Bristol (91).
16   The chronicle accounts of the attack on Warwick may date to Warwick leaving London after the council rather than entering it.
17   *CPR 1452-61*, p. 413. *Foedera* XI, p. 406. Hicks, *Warwick*, p. 145.
18   William Ashendon was Abbot of Abingdon. He sent a gift to Margaret for her first Christmas/New Year in England (E 101 /409 / 14). What it was is not recorded and he is not mentioned again in her jewel accounts.
19   *CPR 1452-61*, pp. 358. *Benet's Chron.*, p. 218. The guilt was conveniently devolved onto Nicholas Philip, a Courtenay retainer, who was hanged at Tyburn.
20   *English Chron.*, p. 75: 'The xxxvj yere of kyng Harry, in the month of January, dyed the erle of Deuynshire in the abbey of Abyndoun poysened, as men sayde, and beyng there at that tyme with quene Margarete.'
21   Whethamstede I, pp. 296–97.
22   Gairdner, *PL* III, p. 125. The numbers of their retainers vary in the chronicles, but the letter from William Worcester to Sir John Fastolf is probably the most reliable. York: 140 'horses'; Salisbury: 400 'horses', 80 knights and squires; Somerset: 200 'horses'; Exeter, 'a grete felyshyp and strong'.
23   Gairdner, *PL* III, p. 127. *CClR 1454-61*, pp. 281–82.
24   *PPC* VI, pp. 293–94.
25   *CPR 1452-61*, p. 436.
26   *Great Chron.*, p. 190. *Rawlinson B 355*, p. 111. The *Chronicle of the Grey*

Friars does not record Warwick's residence with them. He was licenced to bring twenty-four 'foreigners' with him from Calais. (*Foedera* XI, p. 408).

27 *Great Chron.*, pp 189–90. *Gough London 10*, pp. 159–60. If there is any substance in the story, the Duke of Somerset and Lord Egremont are the more likely protagonists. It is interesting that John Bocking does not mention the incident in the budget of news from the capital that he sent to Sir John Fastolf on 15 March.

28 Davis, *PL* II, p. 533.

29 Salisbury's letter does not necessarily imply that the correspondence was over a long distance. Arbury was a small priory just north of Kenilworth and it is unlikely that the slanders reached the prior's ears there. He may have been in or near London during the Great Council where written messages could pass between him and Salisbury. I doubt that Salisbury would have used Bromley as an intermediary in such a delicate matter unless the prior had direct verbal access to Margaret.

30 BL Cotton, Vespasian F xiii (i), art, 64. Maurer, *Margaret of Anjou*, pp. 220–21 for a transcript. The dating of Salisbury's letter is controversial. Maurer dates it to 1454. Kingsford, *EHL*, p. 213, to 1455. Pollard, *Warwick*, p. 205, to 1457. Hicks, *Warwick*, pp. 155–56, to 1459.

31 Gairdner, *PL* III, p. 127.

32 *PPC* VI, pp. 294–95. The authorisation is endorsed by seventeen councillors including the Duke of York, the Earl of Salisbury, and the three Bourgchier brothers.

33 Whethamstede I, pp. 301–08. Hicks, *Warwick,* p. 134.

34 *CPR 1452-61*, pp. 424 and 546. Johnson, *York,* p. 184.

35 Bean, *Percy Estates,* p. 99 n. 3.

36 *CClR 1454-61,* p. 369.

37 *CClR 1454-61*, pp. 292–93. Henry was even handed. The Duke of York, and the Duke and Dowager Duchess of Somerset, were assessed at £10,000 each, The Earls of Salisbury and Warwick, the Earl of Northumberland, and the Dowager Countess of Northumberland at 12,000 marks each. Lord Clifford at 10,000 marks.

38 *CPR 1452-61*, p. 428.

39 Gairdner, *PL* III, p. 127.

40 Whethamstede I, p. 301. *ac etiam, ad magnam instantiam, cordiale*

desidederium, et preces, nobis facta per nostram carissiman et amantissimam uxorem, Reginam, quae fuit, et est, ita desiderabilis dictarum, unitatis, dilectionis, et concordiae, prout sibi est possible.

41 Wright, *Political Poems* II pp. 254–56.
42 *Holinshed's Chronicles of England, Scotland, and Ireland,* 6 vols, (1808). Reprint (New York, 1965), III, p. 249. Only the Tudor chronicles give details of the line-up of those taking part in the procession. *Bale's Chron.*, p. 146 merely says: 'the King and Quene and the lordes yede a procession at powles [which] was a greet gladness and comfort to the people.'

21 An Uneasy Interlude

1 *CPR 1452-61*, p. 429.
2 *London Chrons.(Vitellius A XVI),* p. 168. *Rawlinson B 355,* p. 112.
3 *CPR 1452-61*, pp. 436–37.
4 BL Add. MS 23,938; *CPR 1441-46*, pp. 420–21.
5 *CPR 1452-61*, p. 438. *CClR 1454-61*, pp. 287–88. Recognisances of 500 marks from each of the guarantors and 1,000 from Fauconberg.
6 *Bale's Chron.*, p. 146.
7 Hicks, *Warwick*, pp. 147–48. Pollard, *Warwick*, p. 132.
8 Beaucourt VI, p. 132. Ferguson, *Diplomacy,* p. 58.
9 Gairdner, *PL* III, p. 130.
10 *Foedera* XI, pp. 410–11. The embassy included Warwick's brothers Thomas and John Neville, Viscount Bourgchier and his sons William and Humphrey, Richard Beauchamp, Bishop of Salisbury, Robert Botill, Prior of St John of Jerusalem, Sir John Wenlock, Louis Gallet, a Frenchman and a diplomat in King Henry's service, the papal collector Vincent Clement, the mayor of Calais, lawyers, and four of the King's squires.
11 Vallet de Viriville, *Charles VII,* III, p. 167 n.1, and 395 n. 2. Stevenson, *L&P* I p. 358. Doucereau's name is given as 'Jean' [or Jehan] in French sources, except for the order to carry a safe conduct to Wenlock, where it is Morice Doulcereau. The latter is either a clerk's error, or, possibly, there were two Doucereaus.
12 Perhaps Henry (or Margaret) chose him for his boastful mendacity. In 1461 he claimed to be deep in the councils of King Edward IV: '[he] has

chosen me to be the chief of the three to whose judgement all the most secret matters of the council are referred. From the king, his predecessor [Henry VI]… I could not presume such favour.' (*Milanese Papers*, p. 64).

13. Bernus, '*Pierre de Brezé*', pp. 330–31.
14. Beaucourt III, p. 289. Beaucourt had not seen Doucereau's report, so he misdated Brezé's letter to 8 June 1460.
15. Chastellain III, pp. 427–28 is the source for secret negotiations, although he gives no details: *avecques aucuns autres secrets entendemens qu'ils avoient ensemble sur autres grandes matères particulières …*
16. *Foedera* XI, pp. 412–14 and 417.
17. Vale, *Charles VII*, pp. 169–71. Vaughan, *Philip*, pp. 353–54.
18. The suggestion that Warwick was acting in the interests of the Duke of York in May 1458 is hindsight. C.L. Scofield, *The Life and Reign of Edward IV*, 2 vols. (1923). Scofield, vol. I, p. 28 and n. 2, assumed, on the strength of an entry in the account by Gaston de Foix of Charles VII's last years, written for Louis XI after his accession in 1461, that York made overtures to King Charles at this time since Charles is known to have been at Montichard on 23 May 1458. Beaucourt VI, p. 260 makes the same assumption. *Sauf que estant le Roy a Remorantin au partir de Montrichart le Duc d'Yorke fist faire ouverture au Roy par le moyen de ceux d'Escossse & autres qu'il luy pleust luy donner faveur & aide en sa querelle a l'encontre du Roy Henri & faisoir de grandes offres …* (P. de Comines, *Memoires de Philippe de Comines*, vol II, (ed.) Lenglet du Fresnoy, (Paris, 1747), p. 310). But York did not 'quarrel' with Henry VI until 1459. It is impossible to believe that York would have contemplated calling on French help at any time before he burnt his bridges at Ludford (and probably not even then). His appeal, if he ever made it, is more likely to date to 1460.
19. Gairdner, *PL* II, pp. 103–05.
20. Ferguson, *Diplomacy*, pp. 101–02. The Burgundian ships were allowed to purchase their release, though they forfeited their cargoes, but the Hanseatic ships and cargoes were declared legitimate prizes. This was typical of the ambivalent attitude of the government and English public opinion to piratical activities.
21. King Henry had to make reparations (*Foedera* XI, pp. 235–36). In 1451

he authorised a payment of £4,666 to Burgundy as compensation, more than double the amount allocated to sea-keeping. Ramsay, II, p. 102, n. 3.
22. *Foedera* XI, p. 374. E. Power and M.M. Postan, *Studies in English Trade in the Fifteenth Century* (1933) pp. 130–32. T.H. Lloyd, 'A Reconsideration of two Anglo-Hanseatic Treaties of the Fifteenth Century', *EHR* 102 (1987) pp. 919–23.
23. *Short English Chron.*, p. 71. *London Chrons. (Vitellius A XVI)*, pp.168–69.
24. *Foedera* XI, pp. 415–16.
25. *PPC* VI, p. 297.
26. Hicks, *Warwick*, p. 146.
27. *CPR 1452-61*, p. 488.
28. *CPR 1452-61*, pp. 489–90. The Duke of York and the Bourgchiers were commissioned for Essex. The Dukes of Somerset and Exeter and the Earl of Wiltshire for the South West, the Duke of Norfolk in East Anglia, and Viscount Beaumont in Lincolnshire.
29. *CPR 1452-61*, pp. 394, 433, 428
30. Dunn, 'Margaret ... and the Order of the Garter', pp. 50–51, citing J. Anstis, *The Register of the Most Noble Order of the Garter*, I, (1724) p. 159.
31. *Complete Peerage* X, p. 128.
32. *CPR 1452-61*, pp. 500–01.
33. See Appendix A.
34. Hicks, *Warwick*, pp. 147–48. Pollard, *Warwick*, p. 133.
35. *CPR 1461-67*, p. 289. Breknok was paid £10 13s 4d as his arrears of wages in 1459, but in 1463, under Edward IV, he claimed to have become so impoverished as treasurer, because he could not collect assignments on the Exchequer, that he was still heavily in debt. Apparently, he expended the best part of 10,000 marks out of his own pocket! (Devon, *Exchequer*, p. 484)
36. See Appendix for Cornwall.
37. Castor, *Duchy of Lancaster*, p. 80. Somerville, pp. 594 and 420. Tuddenham became Suffolk's deputy in East Anglia in the 1430s, and an MP for Norfolk; he retained his stewardship of some Duchy of Lancaster lands even after he lost the more prestigious post of Chief Steward of the Duchy.
38. Storey, *End of Lancaster*, pp. 224–25.

[39] Castor, *Duchy of Lancaster*, pp. 140–42.
[40] Virgoe, 'The divorce of Sir Thomas Tuddenham', in *East Anglian Society*, pp. 117–31.
[41] Gairdner, *PL* III, pp. 46–47, dated to July 1455.
[42] Emden, *Oxford*, II, pp. 856–7.
[43] M. Harvey, *England, Rome and the Papacy, 1417-1464*. (Manchester U.P., 1993) p. 189. *Papal Letters*, XI, p. 30.
[44] *Foedera*, XI, p. 367–68. *PPC*, VI, pp. 265–66. In the letter Henry claims to have 'forgotten' the promise regarding George Neville. This was nonsense as he was out of his senses at the time it was made, and he probably never knew about it.
[45] *Papal Letters* XI, p. 30–31. The letters to Henry and Margaret, undated, were probably written at this time, as the entry makes note of a separate letter having been sent to the King. See also *CPR 1452-61*, p. 281 and *Foedera*, XI, p. 376.
[46] Emden, *Oxford*, II, p. 1347. Neville became Chancellor of Oxford in 1453 in succession to Gilbert Kymer.
[47] Hals became Margaret's chancellor when Lawrence Booth was promoted to be Bishop of Durham. Hals figures in each of Margaret's extant New Years' gift lists, where, as chaplain, he is ranked with the Dean of the Chapel Royal and the King's almoner. He received a rosary worth 30s 8d in 1445–46; a parcel-gilt paxbread worth 15s 4d in 1446-47; a silver salt of uncertain, but undoubtedly greater, value in 1448-49; a rosary worth 30s in 1451–52; and a silver-gilt paxbread worth 43s 9d in 1452–53. (E 101 / 409 / 14 and 17; E 101 / 410 / 2 and 8; Myers, 'Jewels', p. 223)
[48] *HMC: Various*, IV, pp. 85–6; Myers, *English Historical Documents* IV, pp. 280–81. These letters are traditionally ascribed to 1457, but J.M. Horn, *Fasti Ecclesiae Anglicanae*, 1300–1451, IX, Exeter Diocese, (University of London, 1964) pp. 5 and 48, established that John Cobethorn, Dean of Exeter, did not die until sometime in 1458 and that Hals succeeded him in that year.
[49] Beaucourt VI, p. 53 and n. 4. Johnson, *York,* p, 151, citing E 404/70/1/83. In 1454 during York's Protectorate Gallet accompanied Sir Edward Mulso on a mission to Burgundy to negotiate for the return of English

merchandise seized in retaliation for English piracy; the mission ended in failure.
50 M. Sommé, *Isabelle de Portugal, duchesse de Bourgogne*, (Presses Universitaires de Septentrion, 1998), p. 449, n. 85.
51 Charles, Duke of Bourbon married Agnes of Burgundy. Their daughters, Margaret, Catherine, and Joanna were Burgundy's nieces. Guelders appears to have had only one unmarried daughter, Catherine, at this time.
52 Stevenson, *L&P* I, p. 358–60. Where Doucereau is called Morice.
53 Stevenson, *L&P* I, p. 373. The identities of the prospective brides do not appear in this document; they are taken from the newsletter to Charles VII. (Stevenson, *L&P* I, p. 363.)
54 Stevenson, *L&P* I, pp. 374–77.
55 Stevenson, *L&P* I, pp. 361–69. Stevenson misdated this document to November 1458. It is headed *Des Nouvelles* and is an account of Wenlock's embassy from his reception by the Duke of Burgundy in October 1458 to his return to England in February 1459, and of the events in England during that period. It was sent to Charles VII in the early months of 1459. The author is unknown. It has been suggested that he was Maine Herald who accompanied the ambassadors to England. (Wolffe, *Henry VI,* p 315). But Maine Herald would not have known of the communications that were conveyed by Wenlock to the Duke and Duchess of Burgundy. Wenlock sent someone he trusted to Burgundy and that person re-joined him before he returned to England. *Des Nouvelles* probably originated with one of the suite of twenty-six persons who accompanied the English embassy. It is just possible that the author was Louis Gallet. Gallet later threw in his lot with the Earl of Warwick, but this does not preclude his being an informant of King Charles at this time.

22 The Earl of Warwick's War

1 Ellis, *Original Letters, Second Series* I, pp. 126-27, misdated to 1455. A letter from York to Warwick on 15 October in reply to a letter from Warwick 'writen at your manour of Rolyweston' on 7 October. Hicks,

Notes

  Warwick, p. 142, re-dates this letter to 1458. Pollard, *Warwick*, p. 37.
2. *Bale's Chron.,* p. 146. The earlier date, 9 November, in *English Chron.,* p. 77, seems too early since messages were still being sent to Warwick on 6 November.
3. Whethamstede I, p. 340. The Abbot's version in tortuous Latin of Warwick's speech at Ludford in 1459. The gist of it is that when Warwick did his duty and came to Westminster in response to the royal summons, he was attacked and nearly lost his life.
4. *Bale's Chron.,* p.146. *English Chron.,* p. 77. *Brut G,* p. 526. *Rawlinson B 355,* p. 113. *Great Chron.,* p. 190. Hicks, *Warwick,* pp. 152–53. Pollard, *Warwick*, pp. 37–38. Much ink has been spilt over this incident. The chronicles differ in detail; modern historians differ in interpretation. For the best analysis of the evidence see Pollard, *Warwick,* Appendix, pp. 201–02.
5. Stevenson, *L&P,* I, p. 369. The writer of this newsletter was repeating gossip he had picked up at court in February. Warwick's public pronouncement caused quite a stir; it was still being repeated a month or so later.
6. Pollard, *North Eastern England,* pp. 269–70 and 276.
7. Hicks, *Warwick*, p. 155. Somerville, p. 421.
8. Gairdner, *PL* III, pp. 121–22.
9. Stevenson, *L&P* I, p. 367: *ilz* [the English] *ont tout esmeu la coste depuis le north jusques a west, disans que larmee de France se preparoit de y venir a puissance.* To interpret this as meaning that Wenlock reported that the French were preparing for war is to read information into it that is not there. Hicks, *Warwick,* p. 153–54, following Beaucourt VI, p. 263.
10. *CPR 1452-61,* pp. 494–95. Commissions of array in Sussex, Kent, Lincolnshire, Southampton (Hampshire) Norfolk, Essex, Devon, Cornwall, Suffolk and Dorset.
11. Stevenson, *L&P* II, ii, p. 511. *CPR 1452-61* p. 496. It has been suggested that these were defensive preparations against the Duke of York, or alternatively, offensive measures in preparation for an attack on York!
12. M. Harvey, *Papacy,* p. 194. Stevenson, *L&P I,* p. 368.
13. *PPC* VI, p. 298–99.
14. Margaret employed three attorneys in 1452-53: John Vailard, Thomas

Lloyd, and Simon Ellerington. (Myers, 'Household', pp. 193-94). I have been unable to establish which, if any of the three, was killed in 1459.

15 *Bale's Chron.*, p. 146. *Brut G*, p. 525. The *Great Chron.*, p. 190 and *London Chrons.* (*Vitellius A XVI*), p. 169 have identical entries at the end of Year 1457-58. They were probably tacked on to the wrong year.
16 *Benet's Chron.*, p. 223. Archbishops Bourgchier and Booth, the Bishop of London, Chancellor Waynflete, and Lawrence Booth. Benet includes Lord Fauconberg, but it is unlikely that he was in London, unless he came over from Calais to act as Warwick's eyes and ears.
17 *Bale's Chron.*, p. 146. *Rawlinson B 355*, p. 113. Gairdner, *Three 15th Century Chrons.*, preface p. ix and *Short English Chron.*, p. 71.
18 Griffiths, *Henry VI*, p. 796 and 839 n. 146, citing London Journal 6, f. 158; misdated by Scofield I, p. 63, to 1460.
19 Whethamstede I, pp. 331–36. The abbot entertained Coppini at St Albans. Harvey, *Papacy*, p. 195.
20 *PPC* VI, p. 302. The Bishop of Worcester, the Earl of Worcester, the Abbot of Peterborough, Lord Dudley, Sir Philip Wentworth, and Master John Lax, who was the only one to go to Italy. The Earl of Worcester was at Padua, but there is no evidence that he attended the Mantua sessions.
21 *Benet's Chron.*, p. 223: *Et propter hoc per consilium regine indicati sunt omnes predicti domini per consilium apud Coventriam*. Benet does not specify the charges.
22 One of the accusations against the Yorkists in the Parliament of November 1459 was that they had repeatedly failed to attend council meetings when summoned. (*PROME* XII, p. 458)
23 *Bale's Chron.*, p. 147. Whethamstede I, pp. 330–31.
24 *CPR 1452-61*, p. 515.
25 *CPR 1452-61*, p. 507. John Neville later reneged on the outstanding payments.
26 Griffiths, *Henry VI*, p. 783.
27 Griffiths, *Henry VI*, p. 847 n. 274 suggests that Oldhall and Vaughan sent word of the Council to Warwick, and they may have done so, but this alone would not be enough to warrant attainder; they were accused in Parliament of being participants in York's conspiracy and that on 4 July in London they plotted the King's death. (*PROME* XII, p. 461).

Notes

28 J.L. Gillespie, 'Cheshiremen at Blore Heath: a swan dive', in *People, Politics and Community in the later Middle Ages,* ed. J. Rosenthall and C. Richmond (1987), pp. 77–89.
29 *John Leland's Itinerary,* ed. J. Chandler (Stroud, 1993), p. 396.
30 *PROME* XII, pp. 504–05
31 *PROME* XII, p. 458. The rolls of parliament put Salisbury's numbers at 5,000, but this is probably an inflated figure
32 *Gregory's Chron.,* p. 204. *English Chron.,* p. 79. *Bale's Chron.,* p. 148. *Short English Chron.,* p. 72. *Great Chron.,* p. 191. *London Chrons.* (*Vitellius A XVI*) p. 169 and *Brut G,* p. 526 are the same as the *Great Chron.* There is no definitive source for Blore Heath. Modern historians' accounts rely on the Yorkist chronicles, but are not entirely credible. See also A.H. Burne, *The Battlefields of England,* (First published 1950, 2002 ed.) pp. 222–31.
33 Gillespie, pp. 78–79. D. Clayton, *The Administration of the County Palatine of Chester.* (Manchester, 1990), pp. 84-90, identifies the Cheshire men.
34 J.G. Bellamy, *The Law of Treason in England in the later Middle Ages* (Cambridge, 1970), p. 201. There is no record of what banners Lord Audley displayed – those of Edward, Prince of Wales, or Margaret's arms of Anjou? Both were royal banners. *Benet's Chron.,* p. 224, excuses Salisbury by claiming that he elected to fight only after he had tried and failed to negotiate a safe passage.
35 *PROME* XII, pp. 504–05.
36 *Gregory's Chron.,* pp. 204 and *English Chron.,* p. 79 say that Sir Thomas Harrington was captured with the Neville brothers, but he was at Market Drayton with Salisbury after the battle when Salisbury received Lord Stanley's letter. *Great Chron.,* p. 191, says that the brothers had been wounded and were 'goyng homeward' on the day after the battle when they were captured.
37 *Bale's Chron.,* p. 148 states that the King and Queen's men ravaged Warwick's estates and 'hadde done much hurt' but they were afraid to face Warwick himself. Warwick is Bale's hero; he does not explain how or why Lancastrian troops assembling at Nottingham came to be in and around Warwick. Pollard, *Warwick,* p. 40, and Hicks, *Warwick,* p. 163, claim that the presence of the King's men prevented Warwick from

recruiting reinforcements in his own lands 'or even passing through it safely'. But Warwick could have sent messengers ahead to order his clients and retainers to arm themselves and prepare to join him and to protect his lands; he did not need to recruit in person.

38 *Gregory's Chron.*, p. 205 is the only chronicle to record a possible encounter at Coleshill. *English Chron.*, p. 79, says that York and Warwick intended to come to King Henry at Coleshill.

39 Ironically, although King Henry's debts had been mounting throughout his reign, such money as there was had repeatedly been earmarked for the defence of Calais, where Warwick was captain, and to guard the Scottish border, where Warwick and Salisbury were Wardens of the West March. As Hicks, *Warwick,* p. 161, puts it: 'Nobody was grossly enriching themselves at the king's expense in 1459, except, perhaps, Warwick himself.'

40 *John Vale's Book*, pp. 208–210.

41 *English Chron.*, pp. 79–80. If the letter signed by York, Warwick, and Salisbury at Ludlow on 10 October referring to their manifesto is genuine, there is an odd mistake in it. William Lyndwood is named as the 'doctor of divinity' who administered the sacraments when they took their oath. But Lyndwood, Bishop of St David's, died in 1446. John de la Bere, King Henry's former almoner, was Bishop of St David's in 1459. The Bishop of Worcester was John Carpenter. Whethamstede I, pp. 341–42 records a letter from the Yorkists that is different from that in the *English Chronicle*. Whoever compiled the latter did not know the incumbent bishop's name: Lyndwood had been a high-profile bishop and Keeper of the Privy Seal; de la Bere was less well known.

42 *Benet's Chron.*, p. 224 is the only source for a confrontation at Worcester. This has led some historians to postulate that the Yorkist gathering point was Worcester, within easy reach of Kenilworth. But Warwick would not have gone north to Coleshill if he meant to meet York at Worcester. If proximity to Kenilworth was their objective his castle at Warwick would have made more sense. The pro-Yorkist Benet's gloss that York did not wish to fight the King is understandable, but if York's whole army met the King at Worcester and he was forced to retreat in the face of superior numbers, he would not have risked an encounter with Henry at Ludford

only a week later with the same number of men. If York had only a small number of retainers with him at Worcester he would naturally retreat.
43 *PROME* XII, p. 459. Whethamstede I, pp. 339.
44 Whethamstede I, pp. 339–41. This version of events is based on Abbot Whethamstede's account where he puts a long and convoluted speech into Warwick's mouth.
45 *English Chron.*, pp. 79–80.
46 *CClR 1454-61*, pp. 420–22. *Foedera* XI, p. 436.
47 *Gregory's Chron.*, p. 205: 'the Duke of Yorke lete make a grete depe dyche and fortefyde it with gonnys, cartys, and stakys'.
48 C. Richmond, 'The Nobility and the Wars of the Roses, 1459-61.' *Nottingham Medieval Studies*, 21, (1977), pp. 71–86, lists twenty lords as present at Ludford, basing his hypothesis on those who were rewarded by King Henry in 1459/1460. His list does not include the Duke of Somerset, or the Earl of Westmorland, who is recorded as having ridden to join the King. A. Goodman, *The Wars of the Roses* (1981, New York, 1996 reprint), p. 28, citing *Records of the Borough of Nottingham II, 1399-1485* (London, 1883 pp 368–69) for Westmorland. The Scottish Earl of Douglas should be included, although he only got a measly 20 marks. (*Foedera* XI, p. 437).
49 Whethamstede I, p. 342. The Yorkist flight from Ludford presented a problem for the Yorkist chroniclers. None of them mentions King Henry's offer of a pardon. *Gregory's Chron.*, p. 205. *Brut G*, p. 527. *Great Chron.*, p. 191 and *Benet's Chron.*, p. 224 record the desertion of the Calais garrison under Andrew Trollope and gloss it as a betrayal of York. *Ingulph's Chronicle of the Abbey of Croyland*, ed. H.T. Riley, (1874). p. 454, has the most straightforward account. The *English Chronicle* is silent.
50 *Bale's Chron.*, p.148 and *Short English Chron.*, p. 72.
51 Whethamstede I, pp. 342–44, for a highly rhetorical (and very unlikely) version of the surrender after King Henry's offer of a pardon. There is no reference to the men of the Calais garrison.
52 Whethamstede I, p. 345, states that Ludlow was sacked. Abbot Whethamstede was terrified of soldiery of any description and he naturally assumed that the Lancastrians would sack Ludlow. *Gregory's Chron.*, p. 207, records the more traditional drunkenness, looting and rape. The actual sacking of a town was a rare occurrence in England.

⁵³ *Gregory's Chron.*, p. 207, 'and she was kept full strayte and many a grete rebuke.' (*CPR 1452-61*. p. 542).

23 Defence of the Realm

¹ *PROME* XII, p. 488. Curry: 'In spite of Yorkist claims, echoed by many subsequent writers, that the house had been packed, it was not an aggressively partisan assembly … 156 members of the Commons have been identified.'
² *PROME* XII, pp. 454–59.
³ Scofield I, p. 38 made this suggestion. Friar Brackley in a letter to John Paston reported that he had been told at third hand that John Allen had been heard to name himself, Fortescue, Morton, Thorpe, and John Heydon as being responsible for preparing the attainder. Brackley is not a reliable witness, and he may have thrown in the names of Allen and Heydon because he knew they were antagonists of the Pastons. The other three names are plausible but not proven. (Gairdner, *PL* III, pp. 242–43).
⁴ *PROME* XII, p. 461 and 463. York's other followers included in the attainder were Thomas Harrington, James Pickering, John Conyers, Thomas Parr, Thomas Meryng, Thomas Colt, John Clay, Roger Eyton, and Robert Boulde. (Gairdner, *PL* III, p. 199).
⁵ *CPR 1452-61*, p. 535. In 1460 his possessions were granted to the Duke of Buckingham.
⁶ J.P. Gilson, 'A Defence of the Proscription of the Yorkists in 1459', *EHR* 26 (1911), pp. 512–525, prints the pamphlet. The author is unknown. Gilson tentatively suggests Sir John Fortescue.
⁷ Abbot Whethamstede, who was not at Coventry, later wrote his own version: a debate between Justice and Mercy in which York's condemnation is deemed just, although it is softened. King Henry offered a pardon because the kingly attribute of Mercy is superior to Justice (Whethamstede I, pp. 346–56).
⁸ *PROME* XII, p. 464.
⁹ Lord Grey of Powis, Walter Devereux, and Sir Henry Radford, had deserted the Yorkist ranks at Ludford. Henry pardoned them their lives, but they forfeited their estates. (*PROME* XII, pp. 461–62).

Notes

10. M.L. Kekewich, 'The Attainder of the Yorkists in 1459: two contemporary accounts', *BIHR* 55, (1982), pp. 25–34. Kekewich accepts without question the traditional view of Margaret: it was all her fault; she persecuted the Duke of York and was instrumental in the death of Duke Humphrey of Gloucester.
11. *PROME* XII, p. 505.
12. *PROME* XII pp. 467–68. If the income from Havering at Bower exceeded the income from Corsham and the £20, Margaret would receive the shortfall also from the customs. See Appendix. Margaret's servant Peter Marshall was compensated in June 1460 for the income he lost by this exchange. King Henry granted him 5 marks a year from another source in lieu. (*CPR 1452-61,* p. 588).
13. *PROME* XII pp. 489–92.
14. *Benet's Chron.*, p. 224.
15. *CPR 1452-61*, pp. 557–61 and 603.
16. *CPR 1452-61*. p. 542.
17. *CPR 1452-61*, p. 571. The rent was a rose at midsummer.
18. *CPR 1452-61*, p. 546. *CFR 1452-61.* p. 261.
19. CFR 1452-61, pp. 268 and 272. Eleanor was also granted the manors of Salwarpe and Droitwich in late May for a rental to the crown of £30, but it must be doubted if either lady received their grants.
20. Gairdner, *PL* III, p. 198.
21. *PROME* XII pp. 465–67. No less than sixty-five lords swore the oath: two archbishops, three dukes (Somerset and the Duke of Suffolk were not there); sixteen bishops; five earls; two viscounts; twenty-two barons; fourteen abbots and the priors of Coventry and St John of Jerusalem. Perhaps this was the reason why the Yorkists later dubbed it 'The Parliament of Devils'. Unfortunately, and untruthfully, the name stuck.
22. As would happen when Edward IV seized the throne, and with it the Duchy of Lancaster.
23. Most of the grants 'for good service against the rebels' were authorised on 19 December. (*CPR 1452-61*, pp. 532-59). The earls were to receive 100 marks yearly, Viscount Beaumont and the barons £40 yearly; others were awarded strictly limited incomes from a variety of Yorkist estates. A few short leases went to King Henry's favourites.

24 *CPR 1452-61*, pp. 578–79. It appears to have been agreed on before Parliament met. Payment was to begin after Whitsuntide, 13 April 1460. The grant ends 'provided that this grant prejudice not Queen Margaret.' Northumberland was also made justice of the King's forests north of the Trent and granted Scarborough Castle with an annual income of £20 (*CPR 1452-61*, pp. 594–95).

25 *CPR 1452-61* pp. 530–31. 533, 573, 588. *CClR 1447-54*, p. 442. Johnson, *York*, pp. 117–18 and 234.

26 Griffiths, *Henry VI*, p. 826. Professor Griffiths prefers to credit the 'Lancastrian government' and 'the court' for the changes in the financial regime.

27 *CPR 1452-61*, p. 555. *London Chrons. (Vitellius A XVI)* p. 170 dates Warwick's arrival in Calais to 2 November. But the commission of 30 October states that Warwick had been *allowed by certain persons having the keeping of the town and castle of Calais to enter contrary to the king's mandates.*

28 Stevenson *L&P*, II, ii, p. 512.

29 *English Chron.*, pp. 81–82 and *Benet's Chron.*, p. 224, include Audley in Somerset's initial force. Whethamstede I, p. 369, gives a later date, possibly March, and it may be that Audley did not sail until then. The outcome in either case was the same.

30 *CPR 1452-61*, p. 55.

31 Waurin V, p. 279–80 claims that Trollope negotiated with the captain of Guines to admit Somerset.

32 *Brut G*, 526. *London Chrons. (Vitellius A XVI)* p. 170. *Great Chron.*, p 191. All three accounts are the same. They claim that the ships put in of their own free will.

33 The Audley family may have been divided. John's younger brother Humphrey was made Constable of Snodell Castle in Hereford and keeper of its park, forfeited by Warwick, 'for good service about the king's person in his journey [i.e. Ludford] of late' (*CPR 1452-61*, pp. 546–47).

34 M-R Thielemans, *Bourgogne et Angleterre*, 3 vols, (Presses Universitaires de Bruxelles, 1966), III, p. 375 and n. 3. Scofield I, p. 45. Beaucourt VI, pp. 272–73. The legend of Warwick the Kingmaker continues to colour historical hindsight. Thielemans established that Scofield misread

Beaucourt's account of the recriminations between French and Burgundian representatives over truces with the English at a meeting in late 1459. The treaties and truces they referred to were for a much earlier period and were with King Henry, not with Warwick.

[35] Scofield I, p. 50, citing French Roll 38 Hen VI, m. 22.
[36] *CPR 1452-61*, pp. 555–56.
[37] Gairdner, *PL* III, p. 203. *Short English Chron.*, p. 72. *Great Chron.*, p. 192.
[38] Gairdner, *PL* III, p. 205. Roos was back in England before the end of January. The *English Chron.*, p. 82, says Roos 'fled' to Flanders. It is interesting how often cowardice is imputed to Lancastrian lords just because they were Lancastrians.
[39] *CPR 1452-61*, pp. 561, 605, 606, 611.
[40] *CCLR 1454-61*, p, 426. *CPR 1452-61*, p. 563
[41] Griffiths, *Henry VI,* p. 829. *CPR 1452-61*, p. 534.
[42] *CPR 1452-61*, pp. 549 and 545–46.
[43] *CPR 1452-61*, p. 567.
[44] *Croyland Chron.*, p. 420. *CPR 1452-61* p. 593.
[45] King Edward III had been summoned to Parliament by his father when he was only seven as a symbol of royal legitimacy. I. Mortimer, *The Perfect King,* (2006), p. 29.
[46] *CPR 1452-61*, pp. 574 and 578. This may be a clerical error and the grant was for £1,000 only. The grant to Prince Edward is recorded in *Foedera* XI, p. 445, but not the grant to Jasper.
[47] *CPR 1452-61*, pp. 576 and 550. Prince Edward was also granted York's lordships, from which he was already drawing the fees due to the crown – if in fact York paid them!
[48] There are no surviving records of meetings in *PPC,* but *Foedera* XI entries for February to May indicate the Council's activities.
[49] *CPR 1452-61*, p. 563. Stevenson, *L&P II*, ii, pp. 512–15.
[50] *CClR 1454-61,* p. 409. *CPR 1452-61*, p. 554.
[51] *CClR 1454-61,* pp. 410–11.
[52] Johnson, *York,* pp. 19–-99.
[53] Hicks, *Warwick*, p. 176.
[54] Scofield I, p. 45, says that Exeter indented to keep the seas for three years with 3,500 men, although it is not clear how he or the Council thought

such a force could be raised and paid for.
55. *CPR 1452-61*, p. 554. *CFR 1452-61*, p. 258.
56. *Cal. State Papers ... relating to English affairs ... collections of Venice,* Vol I, (1864) ed. R, Brown, Kruse Reprint (1970), p. 88.
57. *English Chron.,* p. 82.
58. *Benet's Chron.,* p. 225. *Brut G,* p. 529. *English Chron,* p. 82. Waurin V pp 287–89. Waurin's chronicle is the basis for Warwick's elaborate self-propaganda and cannot be taken at face value. Much of it is demonstrably false. His account of the encounter at sea is detailed, exciting, and unreliable.
59. *CClR 1454-61,* pp. 418–19, refers to the authorisation by the Coventry Parliament of 1459.
60. The source for the trade embargo appears to be Scofield, *Edward IV,* p. 48, writing in 1923 and Hayward in Postan and Power, *English Trade,* pp. 316–17, writing in 1933. They cite the Tudor historian Fabyan, *New Chronicles,* p. 636, as their source, although Fabyan does not say that the embargo was imposed by Parliament. Harriss, 'Struggle for Calais', p. 51, repeats it without attribution. The confusion arises because King Henry was *at* Coventry in May 1460 when the order to ship wool and other goods for his profit only was issued.
61. The whole question of trade relations between Calais and England and the part played by the Staplers requires further research. The sources for loans to Warwick date to Edward IV's reign. Warwick received £3,580 from Edward in 1463 ostensibly to cover his debts for his visit to Ireland. (M.K. Jones, 'Edward IV, the Earl of Warwick and the Yorkist claim to the throne' *Historical Research* vol 70 no 173, October 1997, pp. 342–352). There is nothing in the original grant, printed by Jones, to establish that this sum was borrowed from any one source. It could be from the Staplers, or the bankers in Flanders, or it could even be that part of it was by way of a reward to Warwick.

24. The Yorkists' Revenge

1. *Annales,* p. 772. More has been made by modern historians of this brief entry than perhaps it warrants.

Notes

2. *CPR 1452-61*, pp. 608–09.
3. *Foedera* XI, p. 454.
4. *Annales*, p. 772. *Short English Chron.*, p. 73. *Great Chron.*, p. 192. Warwick may have dismissed Mundford when he became captain, or the undiplomatic Mundford may have refused to serve under him.
5. *English Chron.*, pp. 86–88.
6. *English Chron.*, pp. 82–85.
7. Somerville, p. 514 (Shrewsbury); p. 421 (Beaumont).
8. *CClR 1454-61*, pp. 415–16.
9. *English Chron.*, p. 88, has the Archbishop of Canterbury welcoming Warwick at Canterbury and carrying his cross at the head of the army. This is probably a confusion with Coppini.
10. *Bale's Chron.*, p 149. *Annales* p. 772. The chronicles report that Warwick came to London with 'a multitude of people', but many of them would have been from the Calais garrison. Estimates of between 20,000 and 40,000 men are obviously exaggerations.
11. *English Chron.*, p. 88. Sharpe, *London and Kingdom* I, pp. 300–01.
12. *Bale's Chron.*, pp. 150–51.
13. Sharpe, *Letter Book K*, pp. 402–03.
14. *English Chron.*, p. 89.
15. *Benet's Chron.*, p. 225. The chronicler claims that Coppini had papal bulls authorising the excommunication, but Pope Pius had not committed himself to such an extreme measure. Coppini was acting on his own, without papal authority.
16. *Milanese Papers*, pp. 23–26
17. *Bale's Chron.*, p. 151.
18. *English Chron.*, p. 85. The pro-Yorkist chronicle puts the worst interpretation possible on Wiltshire's action. If he fled because he was afraid to take part in a battle, why did he return to England to take part in two more battles in 1461? A Milanese ambassador reported that Wiltshire had a safe conduct from the King of France with whom he had dealings. This is nonsense; the ambassador, who was often muddled, probably confused Wiltshire's 'flight' with that of the Duke of Somerset, who did have a French safe conduct (*Milanese Papers*, p. 28).
19. *Gregory's Chron.*, p. 209.

Notes

20. *PPC* VI, p. 361. *Foedera* XI, pp. 456–57. *CClR 1454-61*, p. 459.
21. *Short English Chron.*, p. 73. *Bale's Chron.*, 149. *Benet's Chron.*, p. 225 says the ordnance was for Kenilworth.
22. Whethamstede I, p. 372 includes the bishops of London and Lincoln, but not Rochester. The lords in Warwick's ranks included his uncle, Edward Neville, Lord Abergavenny, with whom Warwick had made his peace, although he held on to the Abergavenny inheritance; Lord Clinton, Viscount Bourgchier's two younger sons, the young Lord Scrope of Bolton, William Fiennes, Lord Saye and Sele, the impecunious son of King Henry's hated minister James Fiennes, who had not found favour at King Henry's court; Robert Botill, the Prior of St John of Jerusalem, a perennial councillor who would serve whichever party was in power; Thomas Bourgchier, the Archbishop of Canterbury, George Neville, the Bishop of Exeter, William Grey, the Bishop of Ely, Richard Beauchamp, the Bishop of Salisbury, and John Lowe, the Bishop of Rochester.
23. The bishop sent to King Henry is not named in the *English's Chronicle's* otherwise detailed account, p. 89. Whethamstede I, p. 373 identified him as Salisbury. Waurin's fanciful and inaccurate account, V, pp. 296–97, substitutes the Bishop of Rochester.
24. *English Chron.*, p. 90.
25. *CPR 1452-61*, pp. 613–14. *Benet's Chron.*, p. 225. *English Chron.*, p. 85. The treatment supposedly meted out by the oyer and terminer commission in York's town of Newbury was grist to Warwick's propaganda mill.
26. I can find no source for Scofield's statement, I, pp. 85–86, that 'Northumberland, Clifford, Lords Neville, Roos, Egremont, and Dacre of Gillesland ... were able to send the king a fairly large army.'
27. *English Chron.*, p. 91. Whethamstede I, p. 374. It has been plausibly argued that Warwick had suborned Lord Grey before the battle. But it is also possible that it was pure chance that Grey's men refused to fight in what was not their quarrel, and that Grey claimed the credit after the victory. The suggestion that Edward of March may have appealed to Grey's men to join him is my own, but it fits Edward's character.
28. *English Chron.*, p. 91. *Short English Chron.*, pp. 74–75
29. *English Chron.*, pp. 89–90. *Benet's Chron.*, pp. 226–27. *Short English*

Chron., p. 73. Lord Hungerford's brother-in-law, Lord de la Warr, Lord Lovell, the son of Prince Edward's governess, Alice, Lady Lovell. He had married Viscount Beaumont's daughter. Sir Edmund Hampden, Sir Thomas Tyrell, Gervase Clifton, and Henry Bromflete, Lord Vesci. Thomas Thorpe, the Duke of York's long time enemy, was keeper of the privy wardrobe in the Tower, and Sir Thomas Browne, a former treasury official, was the sheriff of Kent.

30   *Foedera* XI, p. 450. Beaucourt V, p. 464.
31   MacFarlane, *Nobility* p. 29 and 126. M.A. Hicks, 'Piety and Lineage: The Hungerford Experience', in Griffiths and Sherborne, *Kings and Nobles,* pp. 90–108.
32   Sharpe, *London and Kingdom* I, p. 302, n. 3. £100 was distributed to the watermen on 11 July.
33   Sharpe, *London and Kingdom* III, p. 384.
34   Sharpe, *London and Kingdom* III, p 385.
35   *English Chron.*, pp. 91–92. *Annales,* 773–74. *Gregory's Chron.*, p. 211.
36   *Short English Chron.*, p. 75. *Annales,* p. 773.
37   *CPR 1452-61*, p. 607. On 28 July 1460 Thomas and John were named to a commission to arrest malcontents in Yorkshire.
38   *PPC VI,* pp. 362–63. *Foedera* XI, p. 458. *CClR 1454-61* pp. 455–56.
39   *Handbook of British Chronology* (1961), pp.103 and 92.
40   *The Chronicle of John Stone, Monk of Christchurch 1315-1471,* ed. W.G. Searle, (Cambridge Antiquarian Society 34, 1902), pp. 80–81.
41   *Foedera* XI, p. 459.
42   *CPR 1452-61*, p. 589.
43   *PPC* VI, p. 306. John petitioned Parliament in October to overturn his settlement with Margaret and absolve him of the debt. He stated that he had sued for livery on the grounds that Isabel was entitled to possession of her father's lands without payment because she had been over fourteen at the time of his death, but his claim had been rejected by Chancellor Waynflete. John had taken his case to court and Margaret had agreed, through her attorneys, that if the judges found in John's favour, she would drop her claim, as the law demanded. But no date had been set for a hearing. Unsurprisingly, John's petition was granted: *Soit fait come is est desire.* (*PROME* XII, pp. 542–44)

Notes

44   Hicks, *Warwick*, pp. 182 and 190. He gives no source for the appointment of John Neville as chamberlain, dating it to July and then to November 1460. *Annales* p. 776, refers to 'Lord Montagu', a title John held later, as the King's chamberlain. The Earl of Salisbury become Great Chamberlain of England on 29 October. (*CPR 1452-61*, p. 627)

25 The Westminster Accord

1   Stevenson, *L&P* I, p. 332-34. Misdated to 1456. Translated in J.H. Fleming, *England under Lancastrians*, (1921), pp. 133-34. It may be to this period, during King James's malicious activities, that the suggestion of York's attempt to enlist King Charles VII's aid belongs. In his account of Charles VII's last years the Comte de Foix claimed that York, *par le moyen de ceux d'Ecosse et autres*, approached the French king for military support against King Henry. (Comines-Lenglet II, pp. 310-11). It is hard to believe that York would have risked whatever popularity he possessed by inviting in the French even in 1460.
2   *CPR 1452-61*, p. 589. *The Auchinleck Chronicle*, ed. T. Thomson (Edinburgh 1819), p. 57. *English Chron.*, p. 92.
3   Bénet, Jacques, *Jean d'Anjou, duc de Calabre et de Lorraine*, (Nancy, Société Thierry Alix, 1997), p. 83.
4   *Milanese Papers*, pp. 28-34. Owing to the paucity of source material for this period far too much credence has been placed on Coppini's letters simply because they have survived. They were a tissue of lies and pie in the sky. Coppini would make any claim, no matter how fantastic, to secure a cardinal's hat. Coppini was useful to the Warwick's regime, but he was never part of it.
5   Kendal, *Milanese Dispatches* II, p. xvi. Scofield I, p. 115, and P.M. Kendall, *Louis XI*, (1971), p. 99, state that the Dauphin sent Lord de la Barde to England in September, but they give no source. Louis may have done so, but if he did it was not to form an alliance to invade France!
6   Fauconberg had been Constable of Roxburgh and was the more experienced solider, but it was Salisbury who was ordered to go north. Was Fauconberg already in Calais?
7   Waurin V, pp. 306-07. *Annales,* p. 774, also recounted their meeting, but

Notes

this was written or compiled after 1468, by which time Warwick's version of the events of these years as chronicled by Waurin was well established.

8. Thielemans III, p. 376 n. 57, dates the issue of the safe conduct to 12 July, but it probably did not reach Guines until a later date.
9. Waurin V, p. 291–92. Waurin's story, that Somerset offered to 'give' Guines to the Count of Charolais to 'save' it from Warwick, but that the Duke of Burgundy forbade Charolais to accept it, is also suspect. Waurin dates it to Warwick's return from Ireland at a time when Somerset was still expecting a relief force from England. Making such an offer would have been treason and Guines in Burgundian hands was no use to Somerset. Somerset may have surrendered Guines to Warwick only in the sense that he was not there when Warwick arrived.
10. Beaucourt, VI p. 297 n. 1.
11. Gairdner, *PL* III, p, 234. Waurin claimed that Lord Roos was with Somerset as well.
12. *English Chron.*, p. 99. Gairdner, *PL* III, p. 234.
13. *PPC* VI, p. 303. 'to make peaceable delivery of the said castle to Edward Bou …' The name is missing, but possibly it was Edward Bourgchier, Viscount Bourgchier's son, who had been with the Yorkists at Ludford. The constables of castles in Wales were instructed to hold the castles for King Henry.
14. *PPC* V, p. 304.
15. *Annales*, p. 774.
16. Gairdner, *PL* III, p. 233. A report by the Paston correspondent that York was acting under a commission from King Henry is a piece of propaganda probably originating with Warwick to explain York's behaviour.
17. *CPR 1452-61*, p. 647.
18. *PROME* XII, p. 514. This claim is still repeated today. There is no suggestion in the tradition that *this* parliament was packed!
19. *Benet's Chron.*, pp. 227–28. Benet gives the date of York's arrival as the same day as the Speaker was elected. It may have been a day or two later.
20. Whethamstede I, pp. 376-78, Translated in Myers, *English Historical Documents*, pp. 283–84.
21. Whethamstede records that King Henry was occupying the Queen's

apartments close to the Painted Chamber. (The anonymous letter cited below says that York occupied the Queen's apartments.) *Gregory's Chronicle*, p. 208, has the story that after York claimed the throne King Henry was forcibly removed from Westminster to the Bishop of London's palace. But Henry had been lodged in the bishop's palace after his return from Northampton and it seems probable that this was his residence. Had he still been at Westminster he would surely have attended the Parliamentary session on 10 October and been in the Chamber when York arrived.

22 Griffiths, *Henry VI*, pp. 855–57.
23 *Milanese Letters*, p. 27.
24 *Gregory's Chron.*, p. 208.
25 York's claim was known in Norfolk by 21 October, but it was Warwick's regime (in King Henry's name) that was widely accepted if a snippet of gossip recorded by Margaret Paston is anything to go by: 'Ther is gret talking in thys contre of the desyir of my Lorde of Yorke. The pepyll reporte full worchepfully of my Lorde of Warwyk ...' (Gairdner, *PL* III, p. 239).
26 A contemporary anonymous letter recording these events is printed in Johnson, *York*, pp. 213–14.
27 *PROME* XII, pp. 519–21. It is no accident that in the skimpy and carefully edited account in the rolls of parliament York's arguments come through loud and clear.
28 *PROME* XII pp. 517–18.
29 M.K. Jones, 'Edward IV, the Earl of Warwick and the Yorkist Claim to the Throne', *Historical Research* 70 (1997) pp. 342–52.
30 *PROME* XII, p. 521.
31 *PROME* XII, pp. 522–24. *English Chron.*, pp. 92–96. *Benet's Chron.*, p. 228. *Brut G*, p. 530. *Great Chron.*, p. 193. *Gregory's Chron.*, p. 208. *London Chrons. (Vitellius A XVI)*, p. 172. Despite the assertions in the chronicles, there is nothing on the parliamentary rolls making York either Regent or Protector for the King.
32 G. Baskerville, 'A London Chronicle of 1460', *EHR* XXVIII (1913) pp. 124–127.
33 *PROME* XII, p. 525.

Notes

34. *Benet's Chron*, p. 228, *Great Chron.*, p. 193.
35. *PROME* XII, p. 524.
36. Somerville, pp. 421–22, 429, 540, 564.
37. *Annales,* p. 773. *English Chron.*, p. 92. *Gregory's Chron.*, p. 209. Chastellain, *Oeuvres* IV, pp. 300–07. The 'robber story' is repeated with variations by the Burgundian chronicler Chastellain who places it in a forest in the north of England in 1463 not 1460. He credits Margaret with a long and improbable speech imploring mercy from those would rob her and kill her son. Unless she was unlucky enough to be robbed twice, it seems probable that Margaret told the story while she was a guest of the Duke of Burgundy in 1463 and Chastellain adapted and improved on it for his own narrative. An heroic figure, lost or hiding in a forest, is one of Chastellain's favourite tropes. Comines-Lenglet II, p. 178, following Chastellain, puts the encounter in 1463. See also Monstrelet II, p. 290.
38. Commines-Lenglet II, p. 308. The Comte de Foix in his report to King Louis XI of 1461 states that it was at this time that King Charles VII sent an embassy to Scotland requesting *le Roy, la Reyne sa mere & les gens des trois Estates* to give all the aid they could to Queen Margaret.
39. Gairdner, *PL* III, p. 234. Exeter was reported to be in Wales in September.
40. *Gregory's Chron.*, pp. 209–10 for Margaret's summons to Duchy officials. Gregory is the only chronicler to include Lord Latimer among the Lancastrian lords. This George Neville was the Earl of Salisbury's brother, and Lord Latimer in right of his wife. Salisbury had been granted custody of the Latimer lands in 1451 because George was 'an idiot'. He seems an unlikely recruit to the Lancastrian forces, and he is not mentioned again in any account of subsequent events.
41. Gairdner, *PL* III, p. 228. It should be noted that this may have been a malicious invention by Friar Brackley, who was not the most truthful of Paston's correspondents. Lyhert attended the October Parliament. Goodman, *Wars of the Roses*, p. 45, suggests that Lancastrian resistance in Norfolk was led by the unscrupulous courtier Thomas Daniel.

26 Embattled Queen

[1] BL Harleian MS 543, f. 147. Margaret's letter was first transcribed and published by M.A.E. Wood, *Letters of Royal and Illustrious Ladies of Great Britain* I, (1846), pp. 95–97. Wood misdated it to February 1461and this dating is followed in *John Vales Book*, p. 142, where it is claimed that the letter had not previously been printed. The 'late duke' does not mean that York was dead, just that he was no longer Duke of York following his attainder in 1459. The similarity of the letters makes it clear that Margaret's letter dates to November 1460, the same time as the letter from Prince Edward.

[2] *John Vale's Book*, pp. 142–43.

[3] Letters from Jasper Tudor and the Earl of Northumberland were received by the Common Council on 2 December 1460. CLRO fo. 279 and 284 Journal 6. These letters are no longer extant.

[4] *CPR 1452-61*, pp. 652–53. It is probably on this commission that the *English Chronicle*, p. 97, based the story that Lord John Neville and his retainers came to join York and subsequently betrayed him.

[5] *CPR 1452-61*, pp. 610 and 651.

[6] *Gregory's Chron.*, p. 210.

[7] *Annales*, p. 775. Whethamstede I, p. 381. Abbot Whethamstede would of course have believed this and it is the explanation favoured by historians to this day.

[8] *Brief Notes*, p. 154.

[9] K. Dockray and R. Knowles, 'The Battle of Wakefield', in *The Ricardian*, vol IX, no. 117 (June 1992).

[10] *Annales* p. 775 records that Lord Clifford (whose father had been killed at St Albans) cut down the Earl of Rutland on Wakefield Bridge as he tried to flee. The story was embroidered by Tudor historians, especially Edward Hall, and immortalised by Shakespeare in *Henry VI*, Pt 3. It is probably not true but it makes great drama. In the Loveday settlement it was the Earl of Warwick, not the Duke of York, who tacitly acknowledged responsibility for Lord Clifford's death.

[11] *English Chron*, p. 97: 'the commune people of the cuntre whyce loued hym nat.' It is surprising to find an apparent criticism of Salisbury in this strongly pro-Yorkist chronicle. *Annales*, p 775 says that Salisbury was

killed at Pontefract by the Bastard of Exeter.
12. The story that York's head was adorned with a paper crown is found only in *Annales* p. 775. It is apocryphal. A paper crown would not have lasted long on Micklegate Bar.
13. *Gregory's Chron.*, p. 210, is the only chronicle other than the *Short English Chron.*, p. 76, to record Exeter's presence at Wakefield. But the chronicle also lists the Earl of Wiltshire, who was not there.
14. *The Exchequer Rolls of Scotland* VII, 1460-1469, ed. George Burnett (Edinburgh, 1884), pp. 8, 39, and 157. Dunlop, pp. 215–16. R. Nicholson, *Scotland: The Later Middle Ages,* (Edinburgh, 1974), p. 400.
15. Dunlop, p. 219.
16. The assumption that Margaret was seeking Scottish soldiers to join her army is still repeated as fact but had this been the case, she would have approached a Scottish noble, most probably George Douglas, Earl of Angus, not Mary of Guelders.
17. *Auchinleck Chronicle*, ed. T. Thomson, (Edinburgh, 1819), pp. 21 and 58.
18. M. Hicks, 'A Minute of the Lancastrian Council at York, 20 January 1461' *Northern History* 35 (1999) pp. 214–221. Hicks prints the document.
19. Gairdner, *PL* III, pp. 249–50.
20. *Gregory's Chron.*, p. 209.
21. *Milanese Papers*, p. 44. *State Papers of Venice* I, p. 97, for Warwick's letter to the Duke of Milan.
22. *Milanese Papers,* pp. 37–41.
23. *CPR 1452-61,* pp. 655 and 657–58.
24. *PPC* VI, pp. 307–09. Sir Richard Fiennes was created Lord Dacre in right of his wife by King Henry in 1458. He is not to be confused with Ralph, Lord Dacre of Gillesland, who was with the Lancastrians in the north.
25. *CPR 1452-61,* p. 641. *PPC* VI, p. 307.
26. J. Anstis, *Register ... Order of the Garter,* pp. 166–68.
27. *Brut G,* p. 531. *English Chron.,* p. 99. *Short English Chron.,* pp. 76–77.
28. *Annales,* p. 776. *Gregory's Chron.,* p. 211.
29. Griffiths, *Henry VI,* p. 871.
30. Kendall and Ilardi, *Milanese Dispatches* II, p. 98.
31. Comines-Lenglet II, p. 308.
32. Basin, *Charles VII et Louis XI,* ed. Quicherat IV, pp. 358–60.

Notes

33 B.M. Cron, 'Margaret of Anjou and the Lancastrian March on London, 1461', *The Ricardian,* vol. XI, No. 147 (December 1999).
34 *Annales,* p. 776.
35 BNF, MS Latin 1892, fol. 187. *Letters of Margaret,* pp. 227–28. The commission is to Yorkshire, but the same summons would have been sent to other shires. No record of them has survived, or of the support Margaret received.
36 *Croyland Chron.,* pp. 422–23.
37 Sharpe, *London and Kingdom* I, p. 305, n. 1.
38 Jones, *King's Mother,* p. 43.
39 *Milanese Papers,* p. 53.
40 *Brut G,* p. 532. *Great Chron.,* p. 195. *English Chron,* p. 99.
41 *Brief Notes* is riddled with inaccuracies and its anonymous compiler apparently did not know Prince Edward's name, but it is the only chronicle to record the route, p. 155. It is possible that the Lancastrians used an alternative route via Northampton as suggested in *Milanese Papers,* p. 48.
42 I am grateful to Richard W. E. Hillier, Local Studies Librarian of Peterborough Central Library, Philip Saunders, Deputy Archivist of the County Record Office in Huntington and Robert McInroy, Area Librarian, Kesteven, Lincolnshire, for answering my enquiries and informing me that as far as their records show the towns on the Lancastrian line of march were not sacked. Grantham petitioned Edward IV for a renewal of its charter destroyed by his enemies but did not claim damages. John Paston was with Edward IV at Stamford in March 1462. His letter makes no mention of damage. Edward IV granted Stanford to his mother, Duchess Cecily, who drew revenues from it until her death. (A. Rogers, 'Late Medieval Stamford: a study of the town council 1465–1492', in *Perspectives in English Urban History* (1971), pp. 21 and 30.) The fiercely pro-Yorkist *English Chronicle,* p. 97, accused the Lancastrian army of 'robbyng all the contre ... spoylyng abbeys and howese of relygyon and churches' but does not mention the towns.
43 R.H. Britnell, 'The Economic Context', in Pollard, *Wars of the Roses,* p. 46.
44 *Brut G,* p. 531. *London Chrons.* (*Vitellius A XVI*), p. 173.
45 The chronicles all refer to Warwick's army as 'the king's army.'

Notes

46. *Foedera* XI, p. 471.
47. *Milanese Papers*, p. 48. Despite the statement in *Brut K,* p. 602, Lord Fauconberg was not with Warwick. If he had been the outcome might have been different. It is also doubtful that the young Duke of Suffolk was at St Albans. Duchess Alice would not have risked sending him to Warwick with the future so uncertain.
48. *Annales* p. 776. *English Chron.*, p. 97. *Gregory's Chron.*, p. 212.
49. Burne, *Battlefields,* p. 85. Lt. Colonel Burne was so bemused by the varying accounts that he came up with a convoluted interpretation of the battle and credited Margaret with the tactics. Only a woman could have devised such an unorthodox approach!
50. *Gregory's Chron.*, pp. 211–14. Modern historians have tied themselves in knots trying to reconcile the deliberate obfuscations in 'contemporary' accounts. *Gregory's Chronicle* is scathing on the ineptitude of the strategy and tactics of Warwick's army, but vague on details of the actual fighting. The *Annales* might have provided a clearer picture, but the relevant pages have been torn out of the manuscript.
51. *English Chron*, p. 98. Waurin V, pp. 327, 329. The story of Lovelace's 'treachery' is found only in the *English Chronicle,* and much less plausibly in Waurin.
52. *Milanese Papers*, pp 54–55. The story that Henry was discovered a mile from the battle seated under a tree laughing and singing is a typical piece of unsubstantiated Milanese gossip, possibly based on Yorkist propaganda.
53. *Milanese Papers*, p. 55. King Henry was at Dunstable on 19 February.
54. *Gregory's Chron.*, p. 214. *Annales*, p. 776. Gregory includes Robert Whittingham and Thomas Tresham as being knighted, but there is a blank in the *Annales* where the list of knights should be. *Great Chron.*, p. 194 says thirty men were knighted.
55. *Gregory's Chron.*, p. 212, says Bonville was executed but Kyriell was slain. *English Chron.*, p. 98 is the most hostile: the Prince sat in judgement; they were executed on the Queen's orders even though King Henry had promised that they would be safe if they did not desert him during the battle. Waurin knew nothing of Bonville; in his dramatic account the Queen demanded of the Prince what death the insolent Kyriell should

die, and the Prince condemned him. (Waurin V, pp. 329–330).
56 *Milanese Papers*, p. 51.
57 Whethamstede I, pp. 394, 396, 399. VCH, *Hertfordshire* IV, p 396.
58 *Annales*, p. 776. *Brut G*, p. 531. *Great Chron*, p. 194. *Milanese Papers*, p. 50.
59 *London Chrons.* (*Vitellius A XVI*), p 173. *Gregory's Chron.*, p. 214 adds the interesting detail that the Londoners were organised to pillage the carts by Sir John Wenlock's cook.
60 *Milanese Papers*, p. 51. *English Chron.*, p. 99. *Annales*, p. 777. Barron, 'London and Kingdom', p, 108, n. 81. Sharpe, *London and Kingdom* I, 305 n. 1.
61 CLRO Journal 6, fol. 13.
62 *Gregory's Chron.*, p. 215. 'He that had London for sake, Wole no more to hem take.'
63 *Brut G*, p. 192. *Great Chron.*, p. 194. *English Chron.*, p. 99. The accusations that they took animals and carts is far more credible for the homeward march than the accusation that they ransacked churches.

27 Victory into Defeat

1 *Gough London 10*, pp. 161–62. *Great Chron.*, pp. 195–96. *Annales*, p. 777.
2 *CClR 1461–68*, pp. 54–56. Ross, *Edward IV*, p. 35.
3 *London Chrons.* (*Vitellius A XVI*), p. 175.
4 *Benet's Chron.*, p. 230.
5 *Gregory's Chron.*, p. 216, records that the Earl of Warwick was wounded in the leg at Ferrybridge, but this seems unlikely, since Fitzwalter was in command and Warwick fought at Towton.
6 But not the banner of the Dauphin Louis! Burgundian troops (supposedly led by the elusive Lord de la Barde) would not have fought under the Dauphin's banner. The claim is based solely on Basin, *Charles VII*, ed. Samaran, II, p. 259. Basin gets all the details wrong. Edward was not sent to Burgundy by his father, nor was he recalled by Warwick after York's death at Wakefield. The claim by Scofield that the Duke of Burgundy would send a contingent of troops to fight for Edward under Louis's banner is untenable; they would have fought under their own banner if there had been enough of them. (Scofield I, pp. 159–60)

Notes

7. Somewhat surprisingly, since Towton was a Yorkist victory, English chronicle accounts are meagre. Historians have had to fall back on the Tudor chronicler Edward Hall, writing seventy years later, who claimed that his ancestor had fought at Towton, and on Jean de Waurin, whose information was, at best, second hand. Chancellor George Neville's account has been accepted because it is contemporary, but Neville was not at Towton or even in the north. He did not know that Ferrybridge and Towton were two separate encounters. (*Milanese Papers*, p. 61) Military historians do not agree on reconstructing the battle, though they are at one in making it far more complicated than, in all probability, it was. Burne, *Battlefields*, pp. 245–56. A.W. Boardman, *The Battle of Towton* (Stroud, 1994), pp. 101–45. Goodman, *Wars of Roses,* p. 50–52. G. Goodwin, *Fatal Colours,* (2011), pp. 157–88. Goodwin (p. 189) believes that the weather won the battle. 'It was through an ill wind that the Lancastrians lost the battle. Without it they would almost inevitably have won.'
8. Gairdner, *PL* III, p. 307.
9. *Gregory's Chron.*, p. 217.
10. Gairdner, *PL* III, pp. 269 and 271.
11. *Exchequer Rolls of Scotland* VII, xxxv–xxxvii, pp. 49, 145.
12. *Brut G*, p. 532. *Great Chron.*, p. 195. *Letters of Margaret,* pp. 250–52. Philip Malpas, John Foster, and Thomas Vaughan had chartered a ship to take them, their wealth, and that of other London merchants out of England. (The chronicle accounts include Margaret's physician William Hatclyffe as being with Malpas.) Edward IV too wanted the money. He negotiated successfully for their return and they prospered under his rule.
13. Comines-Lenglet II, pp. 309–10.
14. *PROME* XIII, p. 45. Thomas, Lord-Richemont Grey, was Exeter's brother-in-law. He had fought at Towton.
15. Too much has been made of visits by the Burgundian envoy, Lord de Gruythuse, to the Scottish court, based on Waurin's unsubstantiated claim that he scotched the projected Anglo–Scottish marriage on Burgundy's orders. (Waurin V, pp. 355–56). Why is it assumed that the independent Queen Mary would obey instructions from Burgundy just

because she was his niece? Perhaps because she was a woman?
16. Ralph, Lord Dacre, was killed at Towton. His brother Humphrey inherited the title. The Bellinghams were a north country gentry family with a seat in Northumberland.
17. *PROME* XIII, p. 46. The rolls of parliament record Margaret and Prince Edward's presence at Carlisle, but this is unlikely to be literally true. It is based on the accusation that Margaret intended to cede Carlisle.
18. Gairdner, *PL* III, p. 276. The Paston correspondent reported that Lord Clifford's brother was killed at Carlisle.
19. *PROME* XIII, p. 45–46. The only detailed account of these 'raids' comes from Edward IV's Parliament in November 1461, in which King Henry and Margaret were attainted and accused of every crime imaginable. The rolls are a record of their 'guilt' rather than necessarily of their presence. It is possible, but unlikely, that Lord Richemont-Grey and Humphrey, Lord Dacre, took part in both raids, as recorded in the rolls.
20. Reeves, 'Lawrence Booth', p. 76. King Edward suborned Booth by making him his confessor.
21. *Milanese Papers*, pp. 55 and 58.
22. A.A.M.J. Reilhac, *Jean de Reilhac, secrétaire ... des rois Charles VII, Louis XI et Charles VIII* (Paris 1886), pp. 102–07. What follows is based on Reilhac's report to Louis XI. He lists the documents carried by Somerset and Hungerford. Somerset carried sixteen documents, most of them in English, some to unidentified recipients. Hungerford, whom the French knew as Lord Moleyns, carried twenty-two, plus seven that Reilhac appears to have thought were carried by 'Messire Robert Hutingan, serviteur de Monsieur de Molins.' (Reilhac may have meant Whittingham). One of the letters carried by Somerset is listed as a letter addressed by Hungerford to Moleyns.
23. Kendall and Ilardi, *Milanese Dispatches* II, p. 216.
24. Vale, *Charles VII*, p. 177. Beaucourt VI, pp 332–33.
25. *Milanese Papers*, p. 56.
26. Beaucourt VI, pp. 339–40. Lecoy I, pp. 327–28 (for a sympathetic interpretation of René's participation). Bénet, *Jean d'Anjou*, p. 85. Kendal and Ilardi, *Milanese Dispatches* II, pp. 451–52.
27. Gairdner, *PL* III, pp. 306 and 312. This letter is a copy of the original 'that

was taken uppon the see' and fell into the possession of Henry Windsor, a Paston correspondent. It presumably never reached Margaret.

28 Comines-Lenglet II, p. 175. Waurin V, p. 410.
29 *CPR 1461–67*, pp. 36 and 45. Scofield I, p. 187, n.2. It was probably this fleet that the Milanese ambassador mistakenly believed had encountered the French off Cornwall.
30 *CPR 1461–67*, p. 114.
31 Gairdner, *PL* III, p 312.
32 *Calendar of Documents Relating to Scotland* IV, 1357-1509, ed. J. Bain, (Edinburgh, 1888), p. 267 and 270. F*oedera* XI, p. 477.
33 *PROME* XIII, pp. 46–47.
34 *PROME* XIII, pp. 13–21 and pp. 42–48.
35 Gairdner, *PL* III, p. 307.
36 Gairdner, *PL* III, p. 218. William Paston's sentence is misleading: 'Myn Lord Awbry hathe wedddit the Duke if Bokyngham dowter ... and he is gret with the Qwene.' It should read 'is wedded to', the couple were married in 1443. Rawcliffe, *Staffords,* pp. 21 and 120.
37 *Milanese Papers* p. 107. *Brief Notes,* p.162.
38 *CPR 1461–67*, p. 74. The grant was 'during pleasure.' And, interestingly, *By K. by word of mouth.*
39 *CPR 1461–67*, pp. 61–62.
40 *CPR 1461–67*, p. 132.
41 *Annales*, p. 779. *Benet's Chron.*, p. 232. Benet is wrong that three of Oxford's sons were arrested. Aubrey's brother John became the next Earl of Oxford and, since his father was not attainted, his estates were not forfeit. See J. Ross, *John de Vere, Thirteenth Earl of Oxford, 1442-1513* (Woodbridge, 2011), pp. 38–47, for an analysis of the sources for the 'Oxford conspiracy'.
42 Ross, *John de Vere*, p. 36.
43 Gairdner, *PL* III, p 278.
44 Aubrey probably named them in his original letter, or they may have been betrayed locally. John Montgomery's involvement with Aubrey is an example of a family split by the war. His younger brother, Thomas, was in King Edward's household. William Tyrell was steward of Duchy of Lancaster lands in Essex (Somerville, p. 605).

Notes

45 *Short English Chron.*, p. 78. *Gregory's Chron.*, p. 218. *London Chrons. (Vitellius A XVI)*, p. 177. *Gough London 10*, p. 163. These accounts probably derived from a common source.
46 Gairdner, *PL* IV, pp. 35–36. This memorandum, addressed 'Right worshipful sir ...', has no addressee and no signature.
47 Gairdner, *PL* IV, p. 32.
48 *Brief Notes* p. 158. Either the spy or the monk was singularly ill informed as to the correct names of the foreign participants.
49 Ellis, *Original Letters*, Second Series I, pp. 127–31

28 The Search for Allies

1 J. Calmette and G. Pèrinelle, *Louis XI et l'Angleterre*, (Paris, 1930), p. 16, n. 4.
2 Antoine du Bec-Crespin, Archbishop of Narbonne from 1460.
3 Calmette and Pèrinelle, pp. 280–82.
4 *Exchequer Rolls of Scotland*, VII, 80. Comines-Lenglet, p. 368.
5 Waurin-Dupont, *Anciennes chroniques d'Angleterre*, 3 vols., (Paris, 1863), III, pp. 169–70. King Henry's letter of 27 March 1462 (misdated by Dupont to 1461) may be mendacious diplomatic speak (written by Sir John Fortescue?) to prepare for Margaret's journey to France.
6 Richard d'Étampes died in 1438 and Philip of Burgundy granted the county of Étampes to John of Nevers. But in 1442 King Charles had confirmed Richard's son Francis as Count of Étampes. John continued to the Burgundian Count of Étampes.
7 *Annales*, pp. 779–80. But see FN 32.
8 Lecoy I, p. 345, n. 1.
9 Bénet, *Jean d'Anjou*, p. 87.
10 J. Vaesen, *Lettres de Louis XI*, vol. II, (Paris 1885), pp. 46–47.
11 Calmette and Pèrinelle, p. 20 and n. 1, for the expense of entertaining the Queen from 5 June to 15 June. This may be a transcription error for 25 June, the day on which Margaret left Chinon.
12 Chastellain, *Oeuvres* IV, p. 184. His detailed account of Brezé hiding in the forests of Normandy and his encounter with Thomas Roos is pure fiction (Chastellain IV, pp. 175–83). See Basin, *Louis* XII, I, ed. Samaran,

p. 45 and n. 3 for a more realistic account.
13. P. Bernus, 'Louis XI et Pierre de Brezé', *Revue de l'Anjou*, LXIII (1911), pp. 265–66. In May 1462 Louis authorised the marriage of Brezé's son Jacques to Charlotte, the natural daughter of King Charles VII.
14. Vaesen, *Lettres de Louis* II, p. 47, n 2.
15. *Letters of Margaret* pp. 253–54.
16. Comines-Lenglet II, pp. 367–373. Calmette and Pèrinelle, pp. 20–21.
17. Scofield I, p 251, n. 4. The other signatories were Lord Hungerford, 'Roos', Edmund Mountford, and John Morton. 'Roos' more likely to have been Sir Henry Roos (who was with Margaret at Koeur in 1464) than Thomas, Lord Roos, who appears to have remained in Scotland with King Henry. Robert Whittingham, Thomas Findhern, Henry Lewes, and William Grimsby, all members of Margaret's court, were also with her although they were not required to sign the treaty. (Comines-Lenglet II, p. 372)
18. Chastellain IV, pp. 227–30 for a panegyric on Brezé.
19. In May 1461, a small French force, led by Pierre de Brezé's son-in-law, captured the Castle of Cornet on Guernsey, and Mont Orgueil on Jersey. Scofield I, p 161, 'it is probably safe to conclude', following Beaucourt VI, p. 328, 'It was undoubtedly at this time', claims that Margaret granted the Channel Islands to Pierre de Brezé in 1461. They cite P. Falle, *An Account of the Island of Jersey* (Jersey, 1837) p. 55, but Falle he states clearly that the grant was made in 1462 when Margaret was in France negotiating with King Louis for military aid to be led by Brezé, and Brezé did not visit the Islands in person until 1463. (Bernus, '*Pierre de Brezé*', p. 337). Falle suggests that this was King Louis's underhanded way of recovering Jersey and Guernsey.
20. Gairdner, *PL* IV, pp. 50–51 and 57–58.
21. Scofield I, p. 247.
22. Hicks, *Warwick*, pp. 240–41. Warwick was back at Middleham by the end of April 1462.
23. Gairdner, *PL* IV, pp. 44 and 50–51. The Paston correspondent had heard that Queen Mary came to Carlisle, but this may be questioned. Would the Queen have left Scotland in person? It is more likely that the Queen's delegates are meant.

Notes

24 *John Vale's Book,* pp.144–45.
25 Comines-Lenglet II, p. 176, misdated to March.
26 Monstrelet II, p. 283.
27 Calmette and Pèrinelle, pp. 24–25.
28 Chastellain IV, p. 230. Comines-Lenglet II, pp. 12–13, who does not say that Brezé accompanied Louis.
29 Comines-Lenglet II, p. 373.
30 Bernus, 'Louis XI et Brezé', p. 267.
31 Bernus, 'Louis XI et Brezé', p. 369.
32 *London Chrons.* (*Vitellius A XVI*) p 177. *Gough London 10,* p.163. The reference to 'certeyn Bisshoppis' in Fauconberg's company is obscure, and he did not to hold on to Le Conquet.
34 Calmette and Pèrinelle, pp. 26–28.
35 Morice, *Preuves* III, col. 66. Calmette and Pèrinelle, p. 23. Unless Duke Francis gave two gifts or loans to Margaret, this may be the same gift or loan as that in *Annales* p 779 (see FN 7 above), which the chronicler misplaced to the time of Margaret's arrival in Brittany.
36 Gairdner, *PL* IV, p. 57.
37 Scofield I, pp. 255–56, citing London Journal 7, ff 6-9.
38 Henry VI has been criticised by historians for indulging in this unpopular practice, but no such criticism of financial mismanagement has been levelled at King Edward, even though the sum of over £40,000 is far in excess of any money borrowed by King Henry, or in his name.
39 *CPR 1461–67,* p. 222. The Staplers were authorised to ship wool and woolfells to Calais from any ports in the realm, quit of 40s for each sack of wool and every 240 woolfells. In addition they would receive 6s 8d for each sack of wool and 240 woolfells shipped from Boston and Sandwich to Calais by merchants who were not members of the Staplers' society, plus 13s 4d from each sack of wool and 240 woolfells sent through the Calais Staple from all other ports, until the debt was paid.
40 Bernus 'Louis XI et Brezé', pp. 369–70.
41 The number of Margaret's troops is disputed. Chastellain IV, p, 230 puts the figure at 800 men, and claims that his hero Brezé financed Margaret's expedition out of his own pocket, relying on information from Brezé himself. They both preferred exaggerated stories to the exact truth, and

Brezé probably contributed to the expedition. Waurin V, p. 431, and *Annales* p. 780, put the total at 2,000 men, which may be nearer the mark if the figures given in Ellis, *Original Letters,* Second Series,, p. 131 for the garrisoning of the castles by Margaret are accurate.

42 *Brief Notes*, p. 157, lists two dukes, seven earls, thirty-one barons, and fifty-nine knights in his company. The majority of them, except for those engaged in the sieges, probably went no further north than Durham.

43 Scofield I, p. 262, citing London Journal 7, fol. 15.

44 *CPR 1461–67*, p. 231.

45 *Gregory's Chron.*, pp. 218–19. *London Chrons.* (*Vitellius A XVI*) pp. 177–78.

46 Ellis, *Original Letters,* Second Series, vol. I, p. 131, for the whereabouts of besieged and besiegers at the end of 1462.

47 Gairdner, *PL* IV, pp. 59–60.

48 *Milanese Papers*, p 102.

49 Gairdner, *PL* IV, p. 52.

50 *Gregory's Chron.*, p. 219. *Brief Latin Chron.*, p. 176.

51 Gairdner, *PL* IV, pp. 59–60.

52 *CPR 1461–67*, pp. 325 and 347. *Foedera* XI, pp. 518–19. R.L. Storey, 'North of England', in S.B. Chrimes, *et. al.*, *Fifteenth Century England, 1399-1509* (Manchester 1972, second ed. Stroud, 1995), p.141. Edward made amends only in 1464 when the temporalities were restored to Booth and he was excused attendance at Parliament and Council. By that time, the danger from Scotland was past.

53 Dunlop, *Kennedy*, p. 220.

54 Goodman, p. 131, citing W. Fraser, *The Douglas Book* III, (Edinburgh, 1885), pp. 92–93. This appears to be the only source for the agreement.

55 J. Warkworth, *A Chronicle of the first thirteen years of the reign of King Edward IV,* ed. J. O. Halliwell, (1839), p. 2. *Annales*, p. 781. The chroniclers credit King Edward with conducting the campaign; they assumed that Edward and his host, all the lords of England, were at Alnwick, and that if the Scots had pressed their advantage they could have destroyed the whole of the English leadership, but this was not so. Edward had ventured no further north than Durham and Warwick had only his own northern levies to oppose the Scots. It made no sense for either side to give battle in such adverse conditions.

29 Into Exile

1. *Gregory's Chron.*, p. 220. Calmette and Pèrinelle, p. 31 n. 5. These ships may have been part of Margaret's French flotilla sent from Scotland or, since one of them was reportedly a caravel belonging to the Count of Eu, Margaret may have received additional support from France.
2. *CPR 1452-61*, pp. 203, 220, 407, 428, 492, 609.
3. Lady Elizabeth Grey was the widow of Sir Ralph Grey, the Captain of Mantes who died in Normandy in 1443. Elizabeth purchased the wardship and marriage of her son Ralph for the sum of 400 marks, which she was to pay off at £40 annually; she was pardoned the payment for 1445 (*CPR 1441-46*, pp. 258 and 376. Devon, *Exchequer*, p. 447). She joined Margaret's household in Rouen and received wages of £20 a year. (BL Add MS 23, 938. Myers, 'Household', p. 182). Margaret gave her a gold belt worth £2 4s 6d in 1445-46; a gold chain worth £7 10s in 1446-47; a silver gilt cup worth £3 13s 4d in 1448-49; a silver gilt salt worth £2 10s 0d in 1451-52; and a wine flagon worth £2 2s. 4d. in 1452-53. (E 101 /409 / 14 and 71. E 101 / 410 / 2, 8, Myers, 'Jewels', p. 224.
4. E 101/ 410/ 8: 'Jacquetta Stanlowe to her marriage, 1 silver gilt cup, £8 2s 8d.'
5. As early as March 1461 Grey was serving on commissions of array for Edward IV (*CPR 1461-67*, pp. 32 and 33).
6. *Gough London 10,* p. 163. *Annales* p. 779.
7. *CPR 1461-67*, p. 233.
8. *Gregory's Chron.*, p. 220, *Annales,* pp. 781–82. *Warkworth's Chron.*, p 38.
9. Scofield I, p. 275 and n. 1. N. MacDougall, *James III,* (Edinburgh, 2009), p. 53.
10. *Gregory's Chron.*, p. 220.
11. Hicks, *Warwick,* p. 243.
12. Halliwell, *Letters of the Kings of England* I, pp. 123–25 misdated to 1461.
13. Scofield I, p. 293, citing London Journal 7, f. 37. Note the similarities between this and Edward's letter to Thomas Cook of 1462, pp. 519 above.
14. Edward's letters have survived, many of Margaret's have not, and historians have taken Edward's letter at face value, perhaps unsurprisingly – since it was written by King Edward it must be true!
15. *Gregory's Chron.*, p. 220.

Notes

16   Scofield I, p. 294 suggested that the siege of Norham was Margaret's ploy to prevent the meeting at St Omer, but Margaret was politically naïve. Her thinking was subjective; it was not subtle or devious enough to conceive such a scheme. Nor could she know in advance that Warwick would come north rather than go to St Omer.

17   Scofield II, Appendix I, p. 461–62 for Lord Hasting's exaggerated account of Warwick's triumph and his chastising the Scots while King Edward took his ease, going hunting in the south. The sources for this period are so scanty, and with a so heavy a Yorkist bias, that it is difficult to reconstruct the exact course of events.

18   M. Hicks, 'Edward IV, the Duke of Somerset and Lancastrian Loyalism in the North', in *Richard III and his Rivals,* (1991), pp. 162–63.

19   *Gregory's Chron.*, p. 219.

20   M.K. Jones, 'Edward IV and the Beaufort Family: Conciliation in Early Yorkist Politics', *The Ricardian,* 83 (1983), p. 260 and n. 22.

21   *Gregory's Chron*, pp 221–22. The chronicle account, although detailed, is muddled and implausible as it stands. Its strong bias is based on hindsight, a gloss on Edward IV's misjudgement of the man he believed he could win over. According to Gregory, Edward saved Somerset's life by spiriting him away to Wales, but if he wanted to protect Somerset why send him to Wales? A return to London would be a lot safer. And wasn't Edward's presence enough to prevent any citizen, no matter how loyal, attempting to kill a man under the King's protection and in Edward's very presence? What possible reason could Edward have had for sending Somerset's men to defend Newcastle, even if he did pay them well, except that it fits Gregory's narrative?

22   Evans, *Wales,* p. 143. Jones *King's Mother,* p. 45, n. 25 citing BL Add MS 46399A fol. 1, a letter from Somerset dated from Chirk Castle, 20 September 1463.

23   *Annales,* p. 781 says Margaret had 200 men in her company and lists the Duke of Exeter, John Fortescue, Edmund Mountford, Edmund Hampden, Henry Roos, Thomas Ormond, Robert Whittingham, and Doctors John Morton and Robert Mackerell, but is it more likely that most of these crossed independently and joined Margaret's court at Koeur later in 1463. There is no mention of the presence of the Duke of

Exeter in the sources during Margaret's short visit to the Burgundian court.
24. Calmette and Pèrinelle, pp. 293–94. Scofield I, p. 302 and n. 1.
25. Thielemans, *Bourgogne et Angleterre* III, p. 397.
26. Comines-Lenglet, pp. 177–78 records Philip leaving St Pol for Hesdin on 1 September but receiving Margaret on 2 September. 31 August for her arrival is to be preferred. (Chastellain IV, p. 285).
27. Modern historians still repeat the tradition that Margaret encouraged King Henry's antipathy to Burgundy because the vindictive queen cherished an undying hatred for the Duke, who had impoverished her family by demanding an enormous ransom before he would release her father, but René of Anjou never paid his ransom. The Duchess of Burgundy negotiated an agreement with Charles VII to release René from his obligation in 1446. (Vaughan, *Philip*, p. 118) In this, as in so much else, Margaret has been tarred with the brush of King Henry's prejudices.
28. Chastellain IV, pp. 277–99 for a wordy, colourful, but heavily embroidered and implausible account of Margaret's visit. Waurin V, pp. 435–37 for a different version; both chroniclers stress that *tout le monde* knew that Margaret hated Burgundy.
29. Thielemans, *Bourgogne et Angleterre* III, p 398, n. 179.
30. Chastellain IV, pp. 300–07.
31. Chastellain VII, *Le Temple de Bocace, remonstrances, par manière de consolation a une désolée reyne d'Angleterre,* pp. 75–143. It was not completed until 1465 when Margaret was in exile at Koeur.
32. Chastellain IV, p. 299.
33. Thielemans, *Bourgogne et Angleterre* III, p. 398, n. 180. Chastellain IV, 309–14. Charolais's show of deference may be one of Chastellain's exaggerations, but it reflects the concept of the importance of status and its recognition in international relations, a status that Margaret took for granted.
34. Chastellain IV, p. 356. Bernus, 'Pierre de Brezé', p. 337.
35. *Annales,* p. 781.
36. Calmette and Pèrinelle, *Louis XI et l'Angleterre,* pp. 43 and 45. Commines-Lenglet, p. 178. Vaughan, *Philip,* p. 355.
37. Vaughan, *Philip,* pp. 369–70.

38 Thielemans, *Bourgogne et Angleterre* III, pp. 400–02.
39 *Foedera* XI, p. 504.
40 *Foedera* XI, pp. 508–09. Louis is named as Edward's adversary, and Edward uses the title King of England and France.
41 *Foedera* XI pp 507-08.
42 *Gregory's Chron*, p. 223.
43 J. Wavrin de, *Anciennes chroniques d'Angleterre*, ed. Mlle. Dupont 3 vols (1858-1863) III, pp. 169-71.
44 MacDougall, *James III*, p. 56, for a balanced assessment of Queen Mary.
45 Scofield II, Appendix, pp. 469-70.
46 Dunlop, *Kennedy*, p. 293.
47 *Foedera* XI, pp. 510–11.
48 It is debatable as to whether Somerset or Henry reached Bamburgh first. Scofield I, p. 309 n. 3 citing *Archaeologia* XLVIII, p. 190, states that there is proof that Henry VI was there on 8 December 1463.

30 Margaret in Exile

1 Lecoy I, pp. 344–45.
2 C.J.M. McGovern, 'Lancastrian Diplomacy and Queen Margaret's Court in Exile, 1461–1471', B.A. dissertation, University of Keele, (1973), pp. 31–35.
3 M. L. Kekewich, 'The mysterious Doctor Mackerell', in *Much Heaving and Shoving: essays for Colin Richmond*, eds. M. Aston and R. Horrox, (2005), pp. 45–53. Roger Mackerell's presence is dubious. He is not in the list of exiles compiled by Fortescue in 1464. He was pardoned by Edward IV in 1469 (*CPR 1467-77*, p. 175) but he is named as Margaret's chancellor in January 1471 (*CPR 1467-71*, p 235). He entered Edward IV's service after the Battle of Tewkesbury. (*CPR 1467-77*, p. 495)
4 Emden, *Oxford* I, p. 191.
5 Katherine Gatewyne and Katherine Penyson had come to England with Margaret. Katherine Gatewyne was an Angevin, Katherine Penyson's letter of denization describes her as of Provence (*CPR 1452-61* p. 342). They married Robert Whittingham and William Vaux, respectively.
6 M.L. Kekewich, 'The Lancastrian Court in Exile', in *The Lancastrian*

Court, ed. J. Stratford, (Donnington, Shaun Tyas, 2003) pp. 98–99. Henry Roos appears to have made his peace with Edward IV after 1471 and survived into Henry VII's reign. He started life as a page in Margaret's household and fled to Scotland with her after Towton. William Grimsby had been a squire in the King's household. He fought at Wakefield (for which King Edward put a price of £100 on his head) and at Towton, and he too had fled to Scotland. William Joseph, a household official whom the Duke of York had accused of 'causing' the first Battle of St Albans, was also at Koeur.

7. S.B. Chrimes, *Henry VII,* (1972), p. 14, citing Morice, *Preuves* III, col. 87, pp. 266-67, claims that Louis acknowledged Jasper as his blood kin and made him a member of his household. Although it seems unlikely, Louis was quite capable of doing so because it meant that, technically, he was not violating his undertaking not to aid any 'Lancastrian.'

8. Waurin-Dupont, *Anciennes chroniques* pp. 178–81, III, dated to 1462. Re-dated by Scofield I, p. 316, n. 1, to 1464.

9. Edward IV thought so too. He sent the Duke of Norfolk to Denbighshire to deal with the Welsh insurgents. (Gairdner, *PL* IV, p. 96)

10. MS Français 6978, ff. 69-72, printed in Scofield II, Appendix II, pp. 463–66.

11. *PROME* XIII, p. 123

12. *Brief Latin Chron.,* pp. 178–79. The account is mistaken in including Norham in the list of captured castles. Skipton is doubtful too; it was a family seat of the Cliffords, and unless some members of the Clifford family managed to recover, it is too far south for Somerset's forces to have reached it.

13. *Gregory's Chron,* p. 224. Goodman, *Wars of Roses,* p. 54

14. *Annales,* p. 782.

15. *Gregory's Chron.,* pp. 225–26. *Warkworth's Chron.,* p. 4. *Brief Latin Chron.,* p. 179, says there were executions at Newcastle, Middleham, and York.

16. *Brief Latin Chron.,* p. 179. *London Chrons. (Vitellius A XVI),* p.178.

17. *Foedera* XI, pp 525 and 527. *CPR 1461-67,* p. 332.

18. *CPR 1461-67,* pp. 342–43.

19. *Warkworth's Chron.,* pp. 37–39. *Annales,* pp. 782–83.

Notes

20 Clermont, *Fortescue* I, p. 26.
21 Collins, *Garter,* p. 294.
22 Gairdner, *PL* III, p. 307.
23 Otway-Ruthven, *Medieval Ireland,* p. 389.
24 H.V. Livermore, *A New History of Portugal* (Cambridge, 1976), p. 120.
25 Clermont, *Fortescue* I, pp. 22–23. S. B. Chrimes, *Sir John Fortescue, De Laudibus Legum Anglie* (Cambridge, 1942), p. 145. The concluding portion of the letter is copied in Prince Edward's own hand.
26 Clermont, *Fortescue* I, pp. 25–28.
27 This may not be as odd as it sounds. Ferguson, *English Diplomacy,* p. 56, n. 5, notes that King Afonso's clerks did not know King Henry's name. Letters addressed to him in 1450 and 1452 call him Ludovico. The habit in diplomatic despatches of referring to 'the King of' or 'my lord of' without a first name may account for what appears to be an extraordinary oversight.
28 Scofield I, p. 320. Warwick had proposed a marriage for Edward with Enrique's half-sister, Isabella, who was only 13. Edward refused, and according to Scofield, Isabelle never forgot the insult. Ten years later she succeeded Enrique as Queen of Castile and became, with her husband, Ferdinand of Aragon, one of the most powerful monarchs in Europe. They drove the Muslims out of Spain. One wonders what would have happened in England if Edward IV had married her.
29 Isabella, Duchess of Burgundy, Charolais's mother, was a Portuguese princess. Her mother was John of Gaunt's daughter.
30 The instructions are now in the Bibliothèque Nationale. (Griffiths, *Henry VI,* p. 894, n. 24). It seems probable that Margaret wrote to other European leaders in the same vein and that these letters too have been lost – or were intercepted.
31 *Milanese Papers,* p. 113–14.
32 Lander, 'Marriage and Politics in the Fifteenth Century, in *Crown and Nobility,* pp. 120–22, Ross, *Edward IV,* pp. 90–92, and Hicks, *Warwick,* pp. 258–61, for varying views of the political impact of Edward's marriage.
33 B. de Mandrot, *Dépêches des ambassadeurs Milanais en France sous Louis Xi et François Sforza* 2 vols (Paris 1916-1919), II, pp. 237–38.

34 *Milanese Papers*, pp. 111–12.
35 Kendall, *Louis XI*, p. 130.
36 *Milanese Papers*, pp 112–13
37 *Foedera* XI, pp. 525 and 531–32. Scofield I, p. 349.
38 C.E. Dumont, *Histoire de la ville de Saint-Mihiel* I, (Nancy1860), p. 175 says that René was at St Mihiel on 24 January 1464, preparing for the arrival of John of Calabria, who was coming to visit Margaret. Lecoy I, p. 342 says John did not return to Lorraine until the spring of 1464, and Bénet, *Jean d'Anjou*, p. 89 is more specific: John did not return to Bar and Lorraine until early August 1464.
39 Comines-Lenglet, II, pp. 422–23.
40 *Milanese Papers*, p. 116.
41 Kendall, *Louis XI*, p. 143.
42 Kendall, *Louis XI*, p. 146. Lecoy I, p. 359 cites a letter from Louis to the Chancellor of France which appears to affirm René's loyalty.
43 *The Chronicles of the White Rose*, ed. J.A. Giles (1845), p. 18.
44 Kendall, *Louis XI*, pp. 159–69. Vaughan, *Philip*, pp. 385–88.
45 Bénet, *Jean d'Anjou*, pp. 98–100.
46 Basin, *Histoire de Louis XI*, ed. Samaran, (Paris 1963-1972), I, p. 195
47 Chastellain VII, pp. 67–73. Chastellain wrote an epitaph for Brezé: King Edward would rejoice at his death, *Roy Édouard, donnez vous feste et joye*, but King Henry and Margaret would weep: *Plorez Henry; plorez ô reyne angloise*. King Louis, René, the Duke of Brittany, and all the people of France should lament his loss. Brezé was given an honourable burial in Paris. (Waurin V, p. 487).

31 Years of Exile

1 J. Otway Ruthven, *King's Secretary*, pp. 174–75. *Gregory's Chron.*, pp. 323-33 mistakenly says Manning was Margaret's secretary. He is followed by Bagley, *Margaret of Anjou*, p. 159. Manning was with Henry before the Battle of Northampton in 1460 and may have remained with him thereafter.
2 *Warkworth's Chron*, p. 5, and notes pp. 40–42 is probably the most accurate account.

Notes

3. Waurin V, pp 344–45 misdated to 1461. The only other chronicle to name Tunstall is *Annales* p. 785, where a misplaced comma in the transcription corrupts the text and makes it read as though Tunstall was among Henry's captors. It is obvious that no one really knew who had betrayed Henry. Legends grew around his capture and the later story that Turnbull was with him was based on the grants of Turnbull's lands to Sir James Harrington. (*CPR 1461–1467*, pp. 445 and 460-61). Turnbull was at Harlech Castle when it surrendered to Lord Herbert in 1468.
4. *Warkworth's Chron.*, notes p. 42.
5. *Short English Chron.*, p. 80.
6. Devon, *Exchequer,* pp. 489-90. *Warkworth's Chron.*, p 5. *Croyland Chron.*, p. 439.
7. Calmette and Pèrinelle, pp. 69–70, and n. 3. The Milanese ambassador who reported Margaret's visit said that Louis authorised her to remain on French soil for five years, but the Duchy of Bar was not French territory (although Louis may have claimed it because it was René's patrimony). The ambassador was not sure of the sum Louis promised Margaret as a pension, and it may have been the pension that he authorised for five years.
8. Ross, *Edward IV*, p. 107.
9. *Foedera* XI, pp. 562–65.
10. Pollard, *Warwick*, p. 59.
11. *Foedera* XI, p. 568.
12. Calmette and Pèrinelle, p. 88. *Foedera* XI, p. 583.
13. *Foedera* XI, pp 576–77.
14. *Foedera* XI, p. 577.
15. Calmette and Pèrinelle, pp. 79–81.
16. *Foedera* XI, p, 578.
17. Kendall, *Louis XI,* pp. 185–86. Kekewich, *Good King,* p. 212.
18. Lecoy I, pp. 368–369. Bénet, *Jean d'Anjou,* pp. 113–121., Kekewich, *Good King,* p. 219.
19. Kekewich, *Lancastrian Court,* p. 109. A synopsis of Fortescue's memoranda survives on a single sheet of paper which the Abbé Legrand in the eighteenth century dated to 1470. He dated his transcript '1468.' Calmette and Pèrinelle, pp. 303–05 for the original French. Fortescue

presumably wrote them over several years, to deal with several situations while he was in exile.

20 Kekewich, 'Lancastrian Court', pp. 109–10. Chrimes, *De Laudibus*.
21 *George Ashby's Poems* ed. M. Bateson, (EETS, 1999).
22 *Milanese Papers*, p. 121.
23 Ross, *Edward IV*, p. 109.
24 It is a mistake to assume that the Woodvilles favoured a Burgundian alliance because Louis of Luxembourg, Count of St Pol, was Jacquetta's brother. Count Louis fought with Charolais at Montlhéry but then went over to King Louis, who made him Constable of France. In 1467 Count Louis was in the *French* camp.
25 *Foedera* XI, p. 580.
26 *Milanese Papers*, pp. 119–120.
27 *Annales*, pp. 786–87. Ross, *Edward IV*, p. 110.
28 Pollard, *Warwick*, pp. 60–61. Hicks, *Warwick*, p. 264.
29 *Milanese Papers*, p. 121.
30 *Papal Letters* XII, pp. 273–74
31 McGovern, 'Margaret's Court in Exile,' p. 42, citing Dumont, *Histoire de la ville de Saint-Mihiel* p. 176. McGovern suggests that King Louis paid for the repairs. Louis never spent money unnecessarily. If he did, he had a definite, and important, role for Margaret in mind.
32 Evans, *Wales*, p 167.
33 *Annales*, p. 788.
34 Waurin-Dupont III, pp. 190–95.

32 Warwick's Apostacy

1 Ross, *Edward IV*, pp. 111–12. *Annales*, p. 789.
2 Kekewich, 'Lancastrian Court', p. 109.
3 *Annales*, p. 788.
4 J.G. Bellamy, *Crime and Public Order in England in the later Middle Ages* (1973), p. 139: 'The earliest and perhaps the only official use of torture proper before the reign of Edward IV was in 1310.'
5 Ross, *Edward IV*, p. 402. *Annales*, pp. 789–90.
6 A. E. Sutton, 'Sir Thomas Cook and his 'troubles': an investigation',

Notes

Guildhall Studies in London History, Vol. III, no. 2, (April 1978), pp. 85–108, especially p. 97. See also M.A. Hicks, 'The case of Sir Thomas Cook, 1468', in *Richard III and his Rivals*, (1991, first published 1978), for a statistical analysis of the Cook affair.

7. Scofield I, p. 458 and n. 1, citing MS Français 20, 496, f. 91, for the payment of £293 5s 5d for victualling the ships at Honfleur.
8. *Gregory's Chron.*, p 237. Evans, *Wales*, pp. 165–66.
9. *CPR 1467-77*, p. 103.
10. *Complete Peerage* X, p. 401. Chrimes, *Henry VII*, pp. 15-16
11. *Annales*, p. 791.
12. *Milanese Papers*, p. 125.
13. *Foedera* XI, pp. 626, 628, and 630.
14. Ross, *Edward IV*, p. 113.
15. Calmette and Pèrinelle, p. 104, n. 3. *Milanese Papers*, p. 126.
16. Bénet, *Jean d'Anjou*, pp. 122–24.
17. Woodville had married Elizabeth, the daughter of Thomas, Lord Scales, who had been murdered after defending the Tower for King Henry, and his wife Emma, Margaret's senior lady in waiting. Elizabeth carried the title to Woodville.
18. *Annales,* p. 792, claiming that the expedition wasted £18,000.
19. Ross, *Edward IV,* pp. 122–23. Bellamy, *Law of Treason*, p. 165. J.R. Lander, *Government and Community: England 1450-1509,* (1980), pp. 248–49.
20. Hicks, *Warwick*, p. 276.
21. *Warkworth's Chron.*, p. 46–49.
22. Not to be confused with Humphrey Stafford, the Duke of Buckingham's son, or with Buckingham's grandson of the same name. This Humphrey was the son of Sir Humphrey Stafford killed at Sevenoaks in 1450 while chasing Cade's rebels. He fought for Edward at Towton.
23. Pollard, *North Eastern England,* pp. 304–05.
24. *Croyland Chron.*, p. 458, for Edward being taken 'at a certain village near Coventry.' In fact, it was in Honiley, just south of Coventry. *Warkworth's Chron.*, p. 7, for 'a village bysyde Northamptone'. John Stow identified this as Ulney, which was in turn transposed to Olney in Buckinghamshire by Warkworth's editor. *Warkworth Chron.*, p 46. Olney is too far south to be plausible.

25. Ross, *Edward IV*, p. 132.
26. *Compete Peerage* IV, pp. 327–28. He had been 'an Earl for three months and no more.'
27. *Milanese Papers*, pp. 131–32.
28. *Warkworth's Chron.*, p. 7
29. Gairdner, *PL* V, pp. 62–63.
30. *Croyland Chron.*, pp. 458–59.
31. *Chronicle of the Rebellion in Lincolnshire, 1470*, ed., J.G. Nichols, (Camden Miscellany I, 1847), variously interpreted by modern historians. See Ross, *Edward IV*, pp. 138–44 and 440–41. Goodman, *Wars of the Roses* pp. 70–73. P. Holland, 'The Lincolnshire Rebellion of March 1470', *EHR* CCCCIX (October 1988) pp 849–69. N. Bennett, 'The Road to Losecoat Field', *The Ricardian,* vol. XXX (2020), pp. 137–49. M.A. Hicks, *False, Fleeting, Perjur'd Clarence*, (Gloucester, rev. ed. 1992), pp. 55–58, and Hicks, *Warwick*, pp. 282–86.
32. *Great Chron.*, pp. 209–10.
33. *Foedera XI*, pp. 652–53.
34. Gairdner *PL* V, p. 71.
35. Pollard, *Warwick*, p. 67.
36. Commynes, P de, *Memoirs, the Reign of Louis XI 1461–83*, trans. M. Jones, 1973), p. 183. Commynes claims that Wenlock warned Warwick not to put into Calais because he would be arrested, but that he, Wenlock, would secure the port for Warwick at some future date.
37. Hicks, *Warwick*, pp. 286–87, although the numbers of ships cited seems excessive.
38. *Milanese Papers*, pp. 135–36.
39. Ross, *Edward IV*, pp. 365–66.
40. *Letters of Margaret*, pp. 270–73.
41. Comines-Lenglet II, p. 84.
42. *Milanese Papers*, p. 136.

33 The Queen and the Earl

1. Hicks, *Warwick*, pp. 288–89.
2. *Milanese Papers*, pp. 138–39.

Notes

3   Calmette and Pèrinelle, p. 115, n. 1.
4   *Milanese Papers*, p. 139. Calmette and Pèrinelle, pp. 116–17 and 313–14. Louis supplied 25,000 crowns and promised another 25,000 would be paid after Warwick reached England.
5   *Milanese Papers*, pp. 139–40.
6   Calmette and Pèrinelle, p. 113.
7   *John Vale's Book*, p. 217.
8   Stratford, *Lancastrian Court*, p. 110
9   Chastellain V, p. 464.
10 *John Vale's Book*, pp 215–18, *The maner and guyding bitwene queen Margarete … and thele of Warrewic ….,*
11 *Milanese Papers*, pp. 140–41.
12 Not St Mary's, as in Stow's transcript of the *Manner and Guiding*.
13 Champollion-Figeac, *Lettres de Rois, Reines et autre personnages*, vol II, (Paris, 1847) pp. 488–91.
14 M. Hicks, *False, Fleeting, Perjur'd Clarence*, rev. ed. (Gloucester, 1992), p. 71.
15 Calmette and Pèrinelle, pp. 315–16.
16 *John Vale's Book*, pp. 220–22.
17 *London Chrons.* (*Vitellius A XVI*), p. 181.
18 *Coventry Leet Book*, II, p. 358.
19 Ross, *Edward IV*, pp. 144–45. Hicks, *Clarence*, p. 46–47.
20 *Warkworth's Chron.*, pp. 10–11.
21 Ross, *Edward IV*, pp. 152–53, n. 1 and n. 5. *Croyland Chron.*, p. 462 says 2,000 men.
22 Sharpe, *London and Kingdom* III, pp. 385–87. Stow, *Survey* II, p 170. *Great Chron.*, pp 211–12.
23 Davis, 'William Waynflete', p. 13. *Warkworth' Chron.*, p. 11. Warkworth's description that Henry was 'not worshipfully arrayed as a Prynce and not so clenly kepte as schuld seme suche a prynce', is less than just to King Edward, who had kept Henry in relative, if not royal comfort, for five years.
24 Myers, *English Historical Documents*, p. 306.
25 Waurin-Dupont III, pp. 43–44.
26 *Warkworth's Chron.*, p. 9. *Great Chron.*, p. 212–13.
27 Ross, *Edward IV*, p. 155. The Duke of Gloucester, Anthony Woodville,

Lord Hastings, and Lord Saye (William Fiennes) had fled with King Edward. John Stafford, whom Edward had created Earl of Wiltshire in January 1470, Lord Dudley and John, Lord Dynham, were still in England.

28 Government records for the last years of King Henry's reign, are scanty, either because they were not kept or because they were subsequently lost or destroyed under Edward IV. Edward was adept at suppressing what did not suit him. The paucity of sources cannot be laid solely at his door, but the fact remains that the few that are extant have been re-worked with a Yorkist gloss.

29 *London Chrons. (Vitellius A XVI)*, p. 183.

30 *John Vale's Book*, pp. 222-25. It is most unlikely that Warwick, if he ever saw the memorandum, considered implementing it. His name is not mentioned.

31 Waurin-Dupont III, pp. 196–204, especially pp. 199–200.

32 Calmette and Pèrinelle p. 126, citing Bibl. Nat. f. fr. 20936 n 139, claim that Prince Edward gave Louis the title King of France, contrary to English usage. This does not appear in the version printed in Waurin V, pp. 608–610, which is a memorandum by King Louis of their agreement. Basin, *Louis XI*, II, ed. Samaran, pp. 24–29, says it was found among Prince Edward's papers after he was killed at Tewkesbury and King Edward sent it to the Duke of Burgundy. But why was it in Prince Edward's possession and not Louis's? Is it genuine, or did King Edward fake it? He was quite capable of doing so and it is odd that Margaret and Sir John Fortescue, who presumably vetted it, allowed Prince Edward to make a major error on the eve of his expected return to England.

33 *Milanese Papers*, p. 144.

34 Calmette and Pèrinelle, p. 133, n.5.

35 Calmette and Pèrinelle p. 134. The 20,000 *livres* is a misprint or mis-transcription. Louis would not have given Margaret so large a sum; 2,000 *livres* is far more likely. Her lady of honour may have been Katherine Vaux.

36 Calmette and Pèrinelle, p. 125, copied from Waurin-Dupont III, p. 45, n. 2. *A madame la royne d'Angleterre pour ses depens, du princes de Galles son fils, madame Anne, fille de monsieur de Warwick femme dudit prince,*

Notes

es mois d'aoust. Septembre et Octobre 1470, 2,550 livres; pour les mois de novembre et decembre pour le fait de leur arenterie 2,830 livres et de1,000 livres pour ses plaisirs.

37 *Letters of Margaret*, pp. 278–79. Louis's receiver general for Normandy paid 2,500 *livres tournois* for Margaret's 'estate and maintenance' during January and February and 400 livres for 'silver plate' for January, February, and March.'
38 Calmette and Pèrinelle, p. 321.
39 Myers, *English Historical Documents*, p. 306.

34 The Final Throw

1 Vaughan, *Charles the Bold*, pp. 66–69.
2 *Foedera* XI, pp. 683–690. Charles, Duke of Berry, was included in the truce as an afterthought, but there is no mention of war against the Duke of Burgundy.
3 Calmette and Pèrinelle, pp. 323–325. Ross, *Edward IV,* p. 158.
4 A.R. Myers, 'The Outbreak of War between England and Burgundy in February 1471', in *Crown, Household, and Parliament,* pp. 319–20, and *English Historical Documents*, p. 306.
5 *Coventry Leet Book*, p. 362
6 *Foedera* XI, p. 677.
7 Ross, J., *John de Vere*, p. 61. Gairdner, *PL* V, pp. 84–5.
8 Hicks, *Warwick*, p. 304. Ross, *Edward IV*, p 161.
9 Ross, *Edward IV*, p. 160.
10 *London Chrons. (Vitellius A XVI)*, p. 183.
11 Jones, *King's Mother*, p.54, n. 56.
12 Ross, *Edward IV*, p. 160, estimates that Edward had thirty-six ships and about 1,200 men.
13 *Warkworth's Chron*, p. 13. *The Historie of the Arrivall of King Edward IV, A.D. 1471,* in *Three Chronicles of the Reign of Edward IV*, ed. K. Dockray, (Gloucester, Sutton, 1988), pp. 2–6.
14 *Milanese Papers*, pp. 149–50.
15 *Foedera* XI, p. 706–07.
16 *Arrivall*, p. 8. H. Kleineke, 'Gerhard von Wesel's Newsletter from

England, 17 April 1471', *The Ricardian,* vol. XVI (2006), p. 66–83. The *Arrivall* says Oxford and Exeter fled at Edward's approach. Von Wesel says Edward 'killed many of the Earl of Oxford's people on the way.'
17. *Warkworth's Chron.*, p. 14.
18. *CPR 1467-77*, pp. 241–243. *Foedera* XI, pp. 700–705.
19. Jones, *King's Mother*, p. 52.
20. Hicks, *Warwick*, p. 308 attributes Warwick's refusal to excessive caution.
21. *Foedera* XI, p. 693.
22. Hicks, *Clarence*, pp. 93–94.
23. Scofield, p. 574 citing London Journals 7, f. 232b and 8, f. 4.
24. *London Chrons.*, (*Vitellius A XVI*) p. 184. *Great Chron.*, p. 215.
25. Waurin-Dupont III, p. 211.
26. The suggestion that Warwick left Edmund Beaufort to guard London is implausible. So little is known about Beaufort that it is impossible to be sure what he intended to do. He was an optimist, as events were to prove. It is just possible, but speculative, that he hoped Warwick and Edward would cancel each other out and that a Lancastrian government under King Henry and Prince Edward, guided by himself and Margaret, could be established.
27. Kendal, *Louis XI*, p. 240. *Milanese Papers*, p. 152.
28. Kleineke, 'Von Wesel', pp. 69–70 and 79–80.
29. P.W. Hammond, *The Battles of Barnet and Tewkesbury* (Gloucester, Sutton, 1990), pp. 72–78. Kleineke, 'Von Wesel', pp. 81–82. *Arrivall*, pp. 18–20. *London Chrons.* (*Vitellius A XVI*), p. 184.
30. *Arrivall*, p. 18.
31. Ross, J., *John de Vere*, pp. 66–67.
32. *Arrivall*, p. 20
33. *Great Chron.*, p. 217. *Warkworth's Chron.*, p. 17. Kleineke, 'Von Wesel' p. 82.
34. *Arrivall*, p. 22
35. *Arrivall*, p. 23
36. Jones, *King's Mother*, pp. 51–54 and 58.
37. Vaughan, *Charles the Bold*, (Woodbridge, 2002), p. 48.
38. Gairdner, *PL* IV, p. 229.
39. The *Arrivall* p. 23, says 'the hoole myghte of Cornwall and Devonshire', but this is unlikely. The purpose of the *Arrivall* was to make Edward IV

look good by exaggerating the size of the forces arrayed against him. Hammond, *Barnet and Tewkesbury*, p. 145 n. 3, 4, and 5, citing HMC various vol 4 (1970), p. 208 for 40 men. *Coventry Leet Book* II, p. 366, for Prince Edward's appeal.

40 Scofield I, citing Signed Bills, file 1503, 25th Feb., 11 Edw. IV. Scofield quotes a petition from Thomas Overary, canon of Wells, asking for a pardon for the Bishop of Bath and Wells. The account of the incident is accepted without question by modern historians, but it is open to question. Why only Wells? Because the Bishop needed a scapegoat for his dereliction of duty? *CPR 1467-77* p. 303 and *Foedera* XI, pp. 736-37 for a general pardon to the Bishop. It mentions the escape of felons but not the spoiling of the Bishop's palace. The petition and the pardon both date to 11 February 1472.

41 Jones, *The King's Mother* p. 56.
42 Gairdner, *PL* V, pp. 99–100.
43 *Foedera* XI, pp. 709–711.
44 *Arrivall*, p. 25.
45 *Arrivall*, p. 26.
46 *Arrivall*, pp 27–28. *The Arrivall*, despite being a propaganda piece, is the best contemporary account and its author may have been an eyewitness. See also Hammond, *Barnet and Tewkesbury*, pp. 80-92.

35 Captive Queen

1 *Arrivall*, pp. 28–29.
2 *Arrivall*, p. 30
3 *Warkworth's Chron.*, p. 18. *Benet's Chron.*, p. 233. Gairdner, *PL* V, pp 104–05. *EHL, A Chronicle of Tewkesbury Abbey*, pp. 377–78. The *Arrivall*, p. 31, says Tewkesbury Abbey did not have the right to afford sanctuary and so King Edward's action was lawful.
4 Chrimes, *De Laudibus*, p. lxxv: 'The reversal of Fortescue's attainder and the restoration of his estates were withheld until he had written in favour of the new king's title and had refuted his own arguments against it.' *CPR 1467-77*, p. 296.
5 Hammond, *Barnet and Tewkesbury*, p.101. Little Malvern Priory is nowhere mentioned in the sources, but it is the most likely guess. The

Arrivall, p, 31, says a poor religious place, which may have been an apt description. *Warkworth Chron*, p. 19

6 *Arrivall*, p. 32.
7 *CPR 1467-77*, p. 285.
8 C. Richmond, 'Fauconberg's Kentish Rising of May 1471', *EHR* CCCXXXVII (October 1970), pp. 673–690. See also Hammond, *Barnet and Tewkesbury*, pp. 103-11.
9 *Great Chron.*, pp. 218–20.
10 Fauconberg was captured, or he surrendered. He was beheaded in September 1471 and King Edward had his head set on London Bridge, 'lokyng in-to Kente warde' – a nice touch and typical pf Edward. (Davis, *PL* I, p. 443).
11 *EHL, Yorkist Notes*, pp. 374–75, lists 27 lords. *Arrivall*, p, 38. Ross, *Edward IV*, p. 175.
12 *Arrivall*, p. 38.
13 A skeleton believed to be that of Henry VI was exhumed in November 1910 and examined by Dr Alexander MacAlister, Professor of Anatomy at Cambridge University. He described the skull as 'unusually thin.' W.H. St John Hope, 'The Discovery of the Remains of King Henry VI in St George's Chapel, Windsor Castle', *Archaeologia* 62 (1911) pp 533–42, for a full report of the exhumation.
14 *Arrivall*, p. 38. The tradition that Henry was murdered on Edward's order is the obvious explanation, but why did Edward wait seventeen days after Tewksbury before giving it? It would have been safer for him to have the deed done before he returned to London.
15 Myers, *English Historical Documents*, pp. 318–19.
16 *EHL*, 'John Piggot's Memoranda', p. 370. *Warkworth's Chron* p. 21, which accuses the Duke of Gloucester of Henry's murder. *London Chrons*, (Vitellius A XVI), p 185).
17 W.J. White, 'The Death and Burial of Henry VI, a review of the facts and theories, Part I' *Ricardian* VI, No 78, (Sept 1982).
18 Gairdner, *PL* V, p 131.
19 *CPR 1461–67*, p. 45.
20 Scofield II, p. 23.
21 Ross, *Edward IV*, p 192. Ross, J., *John de Vere*, pp. 69–76 for a detailed

analysis of Oxford's movements and motivation.
22. E 405 /56, 57, 58, 59.
23. J.J. Lambert, *Record of the Skinners of London* (1933), pp. 83 and 88.
24. Ross, *Edward IV*, p.230.
25. Champollion-Figeac, *Lettres des rois,* pp. 493--94.
26. Devon, *Exchequer*, p. 498.
27. *CPR 1467-77*, p. 571.
28. Scofield II, p. 158.
29. Gairdner, *PL* V, p. 258.
30. John of Calabria died in 1470. He was succeeded as Duke of Lorraine by his son Nicholas. Nicholas died in 1473 and the claim to the Duchy passed to René II.
31. Vaughan, *Charles the Bold*, pp. 308-10.
32. Lecoy II, pp. 356–58.
33. Comines-Lenglet, III, p. 473.
34. Kekewich, *Good King*, pp. 242–44.
35. Comines-Lenglet III, p 479.
36. Lecoy II, pp. 395-97.
37. Scofield II, p. 159 for a translation of Louis's letter.

Appendix A: Finances and Dower Lands

1. *Rot. Parl.* V, pp. 118–20 and 133.
2. Luce, *Mont-Saint-Michel* II, p. 189. Jones, 'John Beaufort', p. 93.
3. Edward IV continued to chase debts owed to Margaret throughout the 1460s. (*CPR 1461–67*, pp. 411 and 505).
4. *Letters of Margaret*, p. 121.
5. Griffiths, *Henry VI*, p. 271, n. 133 and p. 318, n. 117, citing E101/409/16, 20 and E 101 /410/ 6, 9. B.P. Wolffe, *Royal Demesne*, p. 137, n. 49, citing E 101/409/20: 'Margaret ... contributed nearly £12,000 in the eight years from Michaelmas 1446 to Easter 1454.'
6. *PROME* XII, pp. 19–20.
7. *PROME* XII, pp. 91, 234, 300, 358–59 and 367-68. Wolffe, *Royal Demesne*, p. 136 n. 40.
8. Myers's figure of £386 19s 8½d in his introduction is a misprint, which

Notes

was not corrected in the reprint of his article (p. 140). Wolffe, *Royal Demesne*, pp. 254–55. Griffiths, *Henry VI*, p. 273, n. 160, notes a suit in the Exchequer of pleas against the Receiver General of the duchy in 1450, 'presumably for non-payment of her dower grant.'

9 *CPR 1446-52*, pp. 171–72. There is no record in the household account of customs money received from London or Hull.
10 *CPR 1446-52*, 10 April 1449, p. 267.
11 *CPR 1452-61*, p. 290.
12 *Foedera* XI, p. 155 (original grants). *CPR 1446-52*, p 559 (confirmation). The 1447 grant included the Manor of Hampsted Marshall (held by Edmund Hungerford) and the Constableship of Gloucester Castle (already granted in reversion to Lord Beauchamp of Powick). Neither was received by the Queen. The Hundred of Tendrying in Essex may be accounted for as part for the fee farm of Essex county in Margaret's original dower grant. Colchester, in two parts, was granted to Sir John Hampton on the same day as King Henry granted it to Margaret. It was recovered in 1451 and granted to Margaret in 1453.
13 *CClR 1447-52*, p. 13-14.
14 *PROME* XII, pp. 297-301. *CPR 1452-61*, pp. 339–340.
15 *Kings Works* II, pp. 670-71. *CClR 1447-54*, pp. 224-225. *CPR 1452-61*, p. 340.
16 *CClR 1447-54*, p. 222.
17 Wolffe, *Royal Demesne*, p. 256. *PROME* XII, p. 505.
18 *CPR 1446-52*, p. 66. *Foedera* XI, pp. 322-23. Wolffe, *Royal Demesne*, p. 256.
19 *CPR 1446-52*, pp. 33 and 242. *CClR 1447-52*, p. 391.
20 The heading in the account includes Bradwell, and Ridgewell (Redewell) is called 'Kiddeswell', but this error is corrected and Bradwell is crossed through.
21 *CClR 1447-54*, p. 391. *Rot. Parl.* V, p. 352. *CPR 1452-61*, p. 66.
22 *CPR 1452-61*, p. 340.
23 *CClR 1447-54*, pp. 223-24.
24 *Rot. Parl.* V, p. 261b (1453).
25 *PROME* XII, p. 300. *CPR 1452-61*, p. 340.
26 *PROME* XII, pp. 298--301.

Bibliography

Place of publication is London except where noted.

Unpublished primary sources

British Library
BL Add MS 23,938
BL Add MS 26,805–7
BL, Add MS 40,851
BL, Add MS 46, 846, f. 33 Circular letter 1456
BL, Add. MS 46,846, f. 44?
BL, Egerton Roll 8365

Bibliothèque Nationale
BNF, MS Latin 1892, fol. 187
College of Arms, Arundel MS 26
CLRO Journal V
Huntington Library, Battle Abbey Collection, BA 937
Lincoln's Inn Hale MS 12 item 75
The National Archives

Exchequer
E 403/747 m4
E 403/757 m6
E 404/63/14
E 101/ 409 / 14 and 17
E 101/410/ 2 and 8
E 405/56, 57, 58, 59

Bibliography

King's Bench
KB9 /260/ 40a
KB9 /260/85

Oxford Bodleian Library
Hatton MS 73 fol 121
Jesus College MS 124, 5

Original authorities, published

Annales [Pseudo William Worcester] in Stevenson, *Letters and Papers Illustrative of the Wars of the English in France*
Bain, J. ed., *Calendar of Documents Relating to Scotland 1347–1509*, vol. IV, (Edinburgh, 1888)
Basin, T., *Histoire de Charles VII*, ed., C. Samaran, 2 vols (Paris, 1933, 1944)
—— *Histoire de Louis XI*, ed., C. Samaran, 2 vols (Paris, 1963, 1966)
—— *Histoire des règnes de Charles VII et Louis de Louis XI*, ed., J. Quicherat, 4 vols., (Paris, 1855–59)
Bateman, M. ed., *George Ashby's Poems,* (Early English Text Society, 1999)
Beadle, R., & Richmond, C. eds., *Paston letters and Papers of the Fifteenth Century,* part III, (Oxford, 2005)
Beckington, T., *Official Correspondence of Thomas Bekynton,* 2 vols., ed., G. Williams, (Rolls Series, 1872)
Blacman, J., *Henry the Sixth, a reprint of John Blacman's Memoir,* ed., M.R. James, (Cambridge, 1919)
Bourgeois of Paris, *A Parisian Journal,* trans. J. Shirley (Oxford, 1968)
Brie, F.W.D., ed., *The Brut, or the Chronicles of England,* vol. 2, (Early English Text Society, 1908)
Brown, R., ed., *Calendar of State Papers and Manuscripts ... relating to English affairs ... collections of Venice,* vol I, (1864)
Burnett, G., ed., *The Exchequer Rolls of Scotland* VII, 1460–1469, (Edinburgh, 1884)
Calendar of the Close Rolls
Calendar of the Fine Rolls
Calendar of the Patent Rolls

Bibliography

Champollion-Figeac, *Lettres de Rois. Reines et Autre Personnages,* vol II, (Paris 1847)
Chartier, J., *Chronique de Charles VII roi de France,* 3 vols, ed., A. Vallet de Viriville, (Paris, 1858)
Chastellain, G., *Oeuvres,* ed., Kervyn de Lettenhove, 7 vols. (Brussels, 1863–66)
Chrimes, S.B., *Sir John Fortescue, De Laudibus Legum Anglie,* (Cambridge, 1942)
Clermont, Lord, ed., *The Works of Sir John Fortescue,* vol I, (1869),
Comines, P de, *Memoires de Philippe de Comines,* ed., N. Lenglet du Fresnoy, (Paris, 1747)
Commynes, P de, *Memoirs, the Reign of Louis XI 1461–83,* trans. M. Jones (1973)
Courteault, H. & Celier, L., eds., *Les chroniques du roi Charles VII par Gilles Le Bouvier dit le Heraut Berry,* (Paris, 1979)
Curry, A. & Horrox, R., eds., *The Parliament Rolls of Medieval England,* vols. X-XIII, (Boydell, 2005)
Davies, J.S. ed., *An English Chronicle of the Reigns of Richard II, Henry IV, Henry V and Henry VI,* (Camden Society, LXIV, 1856)
Davis, N., ed., *Paston Letters and Papers of the fifteenth century,* in 2 parts, (Oxford 1971, 1976)
Devon, F. ed., *Issues of the Exchequer ... Henry III to Henry VI,* (Record Commission, 1837)
Dockray, K. ed., 'The Historie of the Arrivall of King Edward IV, A.D. 1471', in *Three Chronicles of the Reign of Edward IV,* (Gloucester, Sutton, 1988).
Ellis, H. ed., *Original Letters Illustrative of English History,* Second series, vol. I (1827)
Escouchy, Mathieu d', *Chronique,* 3 vols. ed., G. du Fresne de Beaucourt, (Paris, 1863–64)
Fabyan, R., *New Chronicles of England and France,* ed., H. Ellis, (Rolls Series, 1811)
Flenley, R., ed., *Six Town Chronicles of England,* (Oxford, 1911)
Gairdner, J., ed., *The Historical Collections of a Citizen of London in the Fifteenth entury,* (Camden Society XVII, 1876)
—— *Three Fifteenth Century Chronicles* (1880)

Bibliography

—— *The Paston Letters, A.D. 1422–1509*, 6 vols (1904)
Gascoigne, T., *Loci e Libro Veritatum*, ed., J.E.T. Rogers (Oxford, 1881)
Giles, J.A. ed., *Incerti scriptores chronicon Angliae* ... (1848)
—— *Chronicles of the White Rose*, (1845)
Halliwell, J.O., ed., *Letters of the Kings of England* ... 2 vols., (1846)
Hardyng, J., *The Chronicle of John Hardyng*, ed., H. Ellis, (1812)
Harriss, G.L. & M.Z., eds., *John Benet's Chronicle for the years 1400–1460, Camden Miscellany* XXIV (Royal Historical Society, 1972)
Harris, M.D. ed., *The Coventry Leet Book*, part II, (Early English Text Society, 1908)
Hinds, A.B., ed., *Calendar of State Papers and Manuscripts existing in the Archives and Collections of Milan*, vol. I, (1912)
Historical Manuscripts Commission, Appendix, Third Report, (1870)
Holinshed, R., *Chronicles of England, Scotland, and Ireland*, vol. III, ed., H. Ellis, (1808). Reprint New York, 1965
Horn, J.M., *Fasti Ecclesiae Anglicanae*, 1300–1451, IX, (Exeter Diocese, University of London, 1964)
Kekewich, M.L. et al eds., *The Politics of Fifteenth Century England: John Vale's Book* (Stroud, 1995)
Kendall, P.M. and Ilardi, V., eds. *Dispatches with Related Documents of Milanese Ambassadors in France and Burgundy, 1450–1461*, 2 vols., (Ohio University Press, 1970–1971)
Kingsford, C.L., *English Historical literature in the 15th century*, (Oxford, 1913)
—— *Chronicles of London* (Oxford, 1905)
—— 'An Historical Collection of the 15th century', *EHR* XXIX, (1914)
Leland, J., *John Leland's Itinerary*, ed. J. Chandler (Stroud, 1993)
Leseur, G., *Histoire de Gaston IV, Come de Foix*, ed., H. Courteault, (Paris, 1982)
Luce, S. ed., *Chronique de Mont Saint Michel 1348–1468*, 2 vols. (Paris, 1883)
Mandrot, B. de, *Dépêches des ambassadeurs Milanais en France sous Louis Xi et François Sforza*, 2 vols, (Paris 1916–1919)
Marx, W. ed. *An English Chronicle 1377–1461* (Woodbridge, 2003)
Maurer, H.E. & Cron, B,M. eds., *The Letters of Margaret of Anjou*, (Woodbridge, 2019)

Bibliography

Maxwell-Lyte, H.C., ed., *Register of Thomas Beckington*, 2 vols., Somerset Record Society XLIX, L, (1934–35)

Monro, C., ed., *Letters of Margaret of Anjou* (Camden Soc. 1863)

Monstrelet, E de, *The Chronicles of Enguerrand de Monstrelet* trans. T. Johnes, 2 vols., (1877)

Morice, Dom H., *Mémoires pour server de preuves à l'histoire écclesiastique et civile de Bretagne*, 3 vols (Paris, 1742–46)

Myers, A,R., *Crown, Household and Parliament in Fifteenth Century England,* (1985)

—— 'The Household of Queen Margaret of Anjou', in *Crown, Household and Parliament*

—— 'The Jewels of Queen Margaret of Anjou', in *Crown, Household and Parliament*

—— 'A Parliamentary Debate of the mid-fifteenth century', (1938) in *Crown, Household and Parliament*

—— 'A Parliamentary debate of 1449', (1978) in *Crown, Household and Parliament*

—— 'The Outbreak of War between England and Burgundy in February 1471', in *Crown, Household and Parliament*

—— *English Historical Documents,* vol. IV, 1387–1485, (1969)

Nichols, J.G. ed., *Chronicle of the Rebellion in Lincolnshire, 1470*, Camden Miscellany I, (1847)

Nicolas, N. H. ed., *Journal by one of the suite of Thomas Beckington,* (1828)

—— *Proceedings and Ordinances of the Privy Council of England,* 6 vols., (Record Commission, 1834–37)

—— *Testamenta Vetusta,* 2 vols (1826)

Nicolas, N.H. & Tyrell, E., eds. *A Chronicle of London from 1089 to 1483,* (1827)

Pizan, Christine de., *The Book of the City of Ladies,* trans. E.J. Richards, (New York, 1982)

—— *The Treasury of the City of Ladies,* trans. C.C. Willard, (New York, 1989)

Reilhac, A.A.M.J., *Jean de Reilhac secrétaire ... des rois Charles VII, Louis XI et Charles VIII,* (Paris, 1886)

Rymer, T., ed. *Foedera, conventiones, literae ...* 20 vols., vol. XI, (1704–35)

Rotuli Parliamentorum, 6 vols.

Bibliography

Riley, H.T. ed. *Registrum abbatiae Johannis Whethamstede,* (2 vols., 1872-73)
—— *Ingulph's Chronicle of the Abbey of Croyland,* (1874)
Robbins, R.H., ed., *Historical Poems of the XIVth and XVth centuries* (New York, 1959)
Searle, W.G. ed. *The Chronicle of John Stone, Monk of Christchurch 1315-1471, itors* Cambridge Antiquarian Society 34, (1902)
Sharpe, R.R., ed., *Calendar of the Letter-Books of the City of London: Letter Book K,* (1911)
Sharpe, R.R., *London and the Kingdom,* 3 vols, (1895)
Sheppard, J.B., ed. *Literae Cantuarienses.* The Letter Books of the Monastery of Christchurch, Canterbury. vol. III, Rolls Series LXXXV (1889)
Smith, G. *The Coronation of Elizabeth Woodville* (1935)
Stevenson, J., ed., *Letters and Papers Illustrative of the Wars of the English in France during the reign of Henry V,.* Rolls Series, 2 vols in 3 (1861-1864)
—— *Narratives of the Expulsion of the English from Normandy* (Rolls Series, 1863)
Stow, J., *A Survey of London,* ed., C.L. Kingsford, 2 vols., (Oxford, 1908)
Sutton, A.F. & Hammond, P.W., *The Coronation of Richard III: the extant documents* (Gloucester, 1983)
Thomas, A.H. & Thornley, I.D., eds., *The Great Chronicle of London,* (1938)
Thomson, T. ed. *The Auchinleck Chronicle,* (Edinburgh, 1819)
Twemlow, J.A., & Bliss, W.H., eds. *Calendar of Entries in the Papal Registers relating to Great Britain and Ireland, Papal Letters* vols X-XII, (1915-1933)
Ullman, W., ed., *Liber Regie Capelle,* (Henry Bradshaw Society, 1961)
Vaesen, J., ed., *Lettres de Louis XI, roi de France,* (Paris, 1883-1909)
Vergil, P., *Three books of Polydore Vergil's English History, comprising the reign of Henry VI, Edward IV and Richard III,* trans. H. Ellis, (Camden Society, 1844)
Warkworth, J., *A Chronicle of the First Thirteen Years of the Reign of King Edward IV,* ed., J. O. Halliwell, (1839)
Waurin, J. de, *Recueil des croniques et anchiennes istories de la Grant Bretaigne, a present nomme Engleterre,* 5 vols., eds. W. & E.L.C.P. Hardy, (1864-91)
Wavrin, J. de, *Anciennes chroniques d;Angleterre,* 3 vols., ed. Mlle. Dupont (Paris, 1858-1863)

Whethamstede, J., *Registrum abbatiae Johannis Whethamstede,* ed. H.T. Riley, 2 vols. (1872–73)
Wright, T., ed., *A collection of political poems and songs relating to English history, or from the accession of Edward III to the reign of Henry VIII.* 2 vols. (Rolls Series, Longman Green, 1859–1861)

Secondary authorities

Abulafia, D., *The Western Mediterranean Kingdom 1220–1500,* (1997)
Archer, R.E. ed., *Crown Government and People,* (New York, 1995)
Archer, R.E. & Walker, S. eds., *Rulers and Ruled in late Medieval England,* (1995)
Archer, R.E., 'Rich old ladies: the problem of late medieval dowagers', in Pollard, *Property and Politics* (Gloucester, 1984)
Armstrong, C. A. J., 'La Politique Matrimoniale des ducs de Bourgogne de la Maison de Valois', in *England, France and Burgundy in the l5th Century,* (1983)
—— 'Politics and the Battle of St Albans, 1455', *BIHR* Vol. XXXIII, No. 87 (May 1960)
Ashdown-Hill, John, 'Walsingham in 1469: the pilgrimage of Edward IV and Richard Duke of Gloucester', *Ricardian,* vol. XI, No. 136, (March 1997)
Aston, M., & Horrox, R., eds., *Much Heaving and Shoving: essays for Colin Richmond,* (2005)
Bagley, J.J., *Margaret of Anjou, Queen of England,* (1948)
Barron, C.M., 'London and the crown 1451–1461', in Highfield & Jeffs, *Crown and Local Communities* (1981)
—— *London in the later Middle Ages,* (Oxford, 1994)
Bassett, M., 'Newgate Prison in the Middle Ages', *Speculum* 18 (1943)
Bean, J.M.W., *The Estates of the Percy Family 1416–1537,* (Oxford, 1958)
Beaucourt, G. du Fresne de, *Histoire de Charles VII,* 6 vols, (Paris, 1881–1891)
Bellamy, J.G., *Crime and Public Order in England in the later Middle Ages* (1973)
—— *The Law of Treason in England in the later Middle Ages,* (Cambridge, 1970)

Bibliography

Bénet, Jacques, *Jean d'Anjou, duc de Calabre et de Lorraine*, (Nancy, Société Thierry Alix, 1997)

Bernus, P., '*Louis XI et Pierre de Brezé*', *Revue de l'Anjou* LXIII, (1911)

—— 'Le Rôle politique de Pierre de Brezé (1451-1461)', Bibliothèque de l'École des Chartes, vol. 69 (1908)

Boardman, A.W., *The Battle of Towton*, (Stroud, 1994)

Boatwright, L.' 'The Buckingham six at Bosworth', *The Ricardian*, XIII, (2003)

Bossuat, André, *Perrinet Gressart et François de Surienne agents de l'Angleterre*, (Paris, 1936)

Bossy, M-A., 'Arms and the Bride', in *Christine de Pizan and the Categories of Difference*, ed. Marilyn Desmond, (Minneapolis, 1998)

Britnell, R.H., 'The Economic Context', in Pollard, *The Wars of the Roses*

Brooke, C.N.L. & Ortenberg, V., 'Birth of Margaret of Anjou', *Historical Research* LXI, (1988)

Brown, R. & Colvin, H.M., eds. *History of the King's Works: the Middle Ages*, 2 vols., (1963)

Burne, A.H., *The Agincourt War* (1956)

—— *The Battlefields of England* (2002 reprint)

Calmet, A., *L'histoire de Lorraine*, 3 vols. (Nancy, 1728)

Calmette, J. & Pèrinelle, G., *Louis XI et l'Angleterre* (Paris, 1930)

Carey, H.E., *Courting Disaster* (1992)

Castor, H., *The King, the Crown, and the Duchy of Lancaster* (Oxford, 2000)

—— 'Walter Blount was gone to serve traytours', *Midland History*, vol 19 (1994)

Cherry, M., 'The struggle for power in mid-fifteenth century Devonshire', in Griffiths, *Patronage, Crown and Provinces*

Chrimes, S.B. et. al., *Fifteenth Century England, 1399-1509*, 2nd ed., (Stroud, 1995)

Chrimes, S.B., *Henry VII*, (1972)

Clarke, B., *Mental disorder in Earlier Britain*, (1975).

Clayton, D., *The Administration of the County Palatine of Chester*. (Manchester, 1990)

Cokayne, G.E. ed., *Complete peerage of England* - 12 vols., (London, 1910-1959)

Bibliography

Collins, H.E.L, *The Order of the Garter, 1348–1461,* (Oxford, 2000)
Cron, B.M., 'The Duke of Suffolk, the Angevin Marriage and the Ceding of Maine', *Journal of Medieval History,* 20 (1994)
—— 'Margaret of Anjou and the Lancastrian March on London, 1461', *The Ricardian,* Vol. XI, No. 147 (December, 1999)
Curry, A. and Hughes, M., eds., *Arms, armies and fortifications in the Hundred Years War,* (Woodbridge, 1994)
Curry, A., 'The Coronation Expedition and Henry VI's Court in France 1430 to 1432', in Stratford, *Lancastrian Court*
Davies, R.C. 'The Church and the Wars of the Roses', in Pollard, *Wars of the Roses.*
Davis, V., 'William Waynflete and the Wars of the Roses', *Southern History* 11, (1989)
Desmond, M., ed., *Christine de Pizan and the Categories of Difference,* (Minneapolis, 1998)
Dickinson, J.G., *The Congress of Arras l435.* (Oxford, 1955)
Dicks, S.E., 'Henry VI and the daughters of Armagnac', in *Medieval and Renaissance Studies,* vol. 15, no. 4, (Emporia State Research Papers, 1967)
Dictionary of National Biography
Dobson, R. B., *Durham Priory 1440–1450,* (Cambridge, 1973)
Dumont, C.E., *Histoire de la ville de Saint-Mihiel,* vol I, (Nancy, 1860)
Dunlop, A.I., *The Life and Times of James Kennedy, Bishop of St Andrews,* (Edinburgh, 1950)
Dunn, D., 'Margaret of Anjou... a Reassessment of her role 1445–1453', in Archer, *Crown Government and People*
—— 'Margaret of Anjou, Chivalry and the Order of the Garter', in Richmond & Scarff, *St George's Chapel, Windsor*
—— 'The Queen at War, the Role of Margaret of Anjou in the Wars of the Roses', in *War and Society*
—— *War and Society in Medieval and Early Modern Britain,* (Liverpool, 2000)
—— 'Margaret of Anjou' in *The New Oxford Dictionary of Biography*
Emden, A.B., *A Biographical Register of the University of Oxford to A.D. 1500,* 2 vols., (1957–58)
Evans, H.T., *Wales and the Wars of the Roses,* (Cambridge, 1915)

Bibliography

Falle, P. *An account of the Island of Jersey* (Jersey, 1837)
Ferguson, J., *English diplomacy, 1422–1461,* (Oxford, 1972)
Fleming, J.H., *England under the Lancastrians* (London, 1921)
Flenley, R., 'London and foreign merchants in the reign of Henry VI', *EHR,* XXV (1910)
Franks, A.W., 'Notes on Edward Grimston, Esq., Ambassador to the Duchess of Burgundy', *Archaeologia,* (40, 1866)
Gillespie, J. L., 'Ladies of the Fraternity of Saint George and of the Society of the Garter', *Albion* vol. 17 (1985)
—— 'Cheshire men at Blore Heath', in Rosenthal & Richmond, *People, Politics and Community.*
Gilson, J.P., 'A Defence of the Proscription of the Yorkists in 1459', *EHR* 26 (1911)
Goodman, A., *The Wars of the Roses,* (New York, 1996 reprint)
Goodwin, G., *Fatal Colours,* (2011)
Green, R.F., *Poets and Princepleasers Literature and the English Court in the late Middle Ages,* (Toronto, 1980)
Green, V., *The madness of Kings,* (1993)
Griffiths, R.A., *The reign of King Henry VI* (1981)
—— *King and Country: England and Wales in the fifteenth century,* (1991)
—— 'The Winchester Session of the 1449 Parliament, a further commentary', in *King and Country*
—— 'Queen Katherine of Valois and a Missing Statute of the Realm', in *King and Country*
—— 'The Hazards of civil war: the Mountford family and the Wars of the Roses', in *King and Country*
—— 'Richard, Duke of York and the royal household in Wales, 1449–1450', in *King and Country*
—— 'Duke Richard of York's Intentions un 1450', in *King and Country*
—— 'Local Rivalries and National Politics', in *King and Country*
—— 'The King's Council and York's First Protectorate', in *King and Country*
—— 'Gruffydd ap Nicholas and the Fall of the House of Lancaster' in *King and Country*
—— 'The Trial of Eleanor Cobham: an episode in the fall of Duke Humphrey of Gloucester', in *King and Country*

Bibliography

Griffiths, R.A., ed., *Patronage, the Crown and the Provinces in later Medieval England,* (Gloucester, 1981)
Griffiths. R.A. & Sherborne, J eds, *Kings and Nobles in the Later Middle Ages* (1986)
Griffiths, R.A. & Thomas, R.S., *The Making of the Tudor Dynasty* (1985)
Gross, A., *The Dissolution of the Lancastrian Kingship,* (Stamford, 1996)
Hammond, P.W. *The Battles of Barnet and Tewkesbury* (Gloucester,1990)
Harriss, G.L., *Cardinal Beaufort,* (Oxford, 1988)
—— 'Marmaduke Lumley and the Exchequer Crisis of 1446-1449', in Rowe, *Aspects of late medieval government and society*
—— 'The Struggle for Calais', *English Historical Review,* LXXV (1960)
Harthan, J., *Books of Hours,* (1977)
Harvey, I.M.W., *Jack Cade's Rebellion of 1450,* (Oxford, 1991)
Harvey, M., *England Rome and the Papacy 1417-1464.* (Manchester U.P., 1993)
Herbert, A., *Herefordshire 1413-1461*,' in Griffiths, *Patronage, Crown and Provinces*
Hicks, M., *False, Fleeting, Perjur'd Clarence,* rev. ed. (Gloucester, 1992)
—— *Warwick the Kingmaker,* (Oxford, 1998)
—— 'Piety and Lineage: The Hungerford Experience' in Griffiths & Sherborne, *Kings and Nobles*
—— 'Propaganda and the First Battle of St Albans, 1455', *Nottingham Medieval Studies,* XLIV, (2000)
—— 'From megaphone to microscope: the correspondence of Richard Duke of York with Henry VI in 1450 revisited', *Journal of Medieval History,* vol. 25, No. 1, (1999)
—— 'A Minute of the Lancastrian Council at York, 20 January 1461', *Northern History* 35 (1999)
—— 'The Case of Sir Thomas Cook, 1468', in *Richard III and his Rivals,* (1991, first published 1978)
—— 'Edward IV, the Duke of Somerset and Lancastrian Loyalism in the North', in *Richard III and his Rivals,* (1991)
—— *Richard III and his Rivals,* (1991)
Highfield, J.R.L. & Jeffs, R. eds., *The Crown and Local Communities in England and France in the 15th century,* (Gloucester, 1981)

Bibliography

Holland, P., 'The Lincolnshire Rebellion of March 1470', *English Historical Review*, CCCCIX, (October 1988)

Hookham, M.A., *The Life and Times of Margaret of Anjou, Queen of England and France and of her Father Rene 'the Good' with Memoirs of the House of Anjou,* 2 vols, (1872)

Hope, W.H. St John, 'The discovery of the remains of King Henry VI in St George's Chapel, Windsor Castle', *Archaeologia* 62 (1911).

Hughes, J., *Arthurian Myths and Alchemy: the Kingship of Edward IV*, (2002)

Johnson, P.A., *Duke Richard of York 1411-1460,* (Oxford, 1988)

—— 'Henry VII Lady Margaret Beaufort and the Orleans Ransom', in Griffiths & Sherborne, *Kings and Nobles*

—— 'John Beaufort Duke of Somerset and the French expedition of 1443', in Griffiths, *Patronage, the Crown and the Provinces*

—— *The King's Mother, Lady Margaret Beaufort, Countess of Richmond and Derby,* (Cambridge, 1992)

Jones, M.K., 'Edward IV, the Earl of Warwick and the Yorkist Claim to the Throne', *Historical Research,* vol. 70, no. 173 (October 1997)

—— 'Somerset, York and the Wars of the Roses', *English Historical Review*, CCCCXI, (April, 1989)

—— 'Edward IV and the Beaufort Family: Conciliation in Early Yorkist Politics', *The Ricardian,* 83 (1983)

Keen, M.H., *Chivalry,* (New Haven, 1984)

Keen, M.H. & Daniel, M.J., 'English diplomacy and the sack of Fougères in 1449', *History,* Vol. 59, No. 197 (October, 1974)

Kekewich, M.L., *The Good King,* (2008)

—— 'The attainder of the Yorkists in 1459: two contemporary accounts', *BIHR* 55, (1982)

—— 'The mysterious Doctor Mackerell', in *Much Heaving and Shoving: essays for Colin Richmond,* eds., M. Aston and R. Horrox (2005)

—— 'The Lancastrian Court in Exile', in Stratford, *Lancastrian Court*

Kendall, P.M., *Louis XI,* (1971)

Kingsford, C.L., *Prejudice and Promise in Fifteenth Century England,* (1925)

Kipling, G., 'The London Pageants for Margaret of Anjou', *Medieval English Theatre,* 4 (1982)

—— *Enter the King,* (Oxford, 1998)

Bibliography

Kleineke, H., 'Gerhard von Wesel's Newsletter from England, 17 April 1471', *The Ricardian,* vol. XVI, (2002)

Knudson, C., 'Antoine de la Sale's voyage to England', *Romance Philology,* 2 (1948/49)

Laffan, R.G.D., 'Queens College', in *The Victoria County History of Cambridgeshire,* vol 3, (1959)

Lander, J.R., *Crown and Nobility 1450-1509,* (1976)

—— *Government and Community: England 1450-1509,* (1980)

—— *The Wars of the Roses.* (1965)

—— 'Henry VI and the Duke of York's Second Protectorate', in *Crown and Nobility*

—— 'Marriage and Politics in the Fifteenth Century', in *Crown and Nobility*

Laynesmith, J.L., *The Last Medieval Queens,* (Oxford, 2004).

Lecoy de la Marche, A., *Le Roi Rene,* 2 vols, (Paris, 1875)

Livermore, H.V., *A New History of Portugal,* (Cambridge, 1976)

Lloyd, T.H., 'A reconsideration of two Anglo-Hanseatic Treaties of the Fifteenth Century', *EHR* 102 (1987)

Lovatt, R., 'A collector of apocryphal anecdotes: John Blacman revisited', in Pollard, *Property and Politics*

MacCracken, H.N., 'An English friend of Charles of Orleans', *Publications of the Modern Language Assoc of America,* (XXVI, 1911)

McFarlane, K.B., *England in the Fifteenth Century,* (London, 1981)

—— *The Nobility of Later Medieval England* (Oxford, 1973)

McGladdery, C., *James II,* (Edinburgh, 1990)

MacDougall, N. *James III,* (Edinburgh, 2009)

Maurer, H.E. *Margaret of Anjou: Queenship and power in late Medieval England,* (Woodbridge, 2003)

Michalove, S.D., & Reeves, A.C. eds., *Estrangement, Enterprise, and Education in Fifteenth Century England,* (1998),

Morgan, D.A.L., 'The King's Affinity in the Polity of Yorkist England', *Transactions of the Royal Historical Society,* 23 (1973)

Myers, A.R., *Crown, Household and Parliament in the 15th Century* (1985)

The New Oxford Dictionary of National Biography

R. Nicholson, *Scotland: the Later Middle Ages,* (Edinburgh, 1974)

Otway-Ruthven, J., *The Kings Secretary and the Signet Office in the XV Century,* Cambridge, (1939)

Payling, S.J., 'The Ampthill Dispute', *EHR* CIV (1989).
Pollard, A.J., *John Talbot and the War in France, 1427-1453,* (1983)
—— *North Eastern England during the Wars of the Roses* (Oxford, 1990)
—— *Warwick the Kingmaker* (2007)
Pollard, A.J., ed. *The Wars of the Roses,* (1995)
—— *Property and Politics: Essays in Later Medieval History,* (Gloucester, 1984)
Powell, J.E. & Wallis, K., *The House of Lords in the Middle Ages* (1968)
Power, E. & Postan, M.M., *Studies in English Trade in the Fifteenth Century* (1933)
Pugh, T.B., 'Richard Plantagenet, Duke of York, as the King's Lieutenant in France and Ireland', in Rowe, *Aspects of Late Medieval Government*
—— 'Richard Duke of York and the Rebellion of Henry Holand, Duke of Exeter in May 1454' *Historical Research,* Vol 63, No. 152, (October 1990)
Ramsay, J.H., *Lancaster and York,* 2 vols, (Oxford, 1892)
Rawcliffe, C., *Medicine and Society in later Medieval England,* (Stroud, 1995)
—— 'Richard, Duke of York, the king's 'obeisant liegeman',' *Historical Research,* LX, (1987)
—— 'Women, Childbirth and Religion' in Wood, *Women and religion in Medieval England*
—— 'The Insanity of Henry VI', *The Historian,* 50, (1996)
—— *The Staffords, Earls of Stafford and Dukes of Buckingham* (Cambridge, 1978)
Reeves, A.C., *Lancastrian Englishmen,* (Washington D.C., 1981)
—— 'William Booth, Bishop of Coventry & Lichfield 1447-52', *Midland History* III, (1975-76)
—— 'Lawrence Booth: Bishop of Durham (1457-1476), Archbishop of York (1476-80)' in Michalove & Reeves, *Estrangement, Enterprise and Education*
Richmond, C. 'The Keeping of the Seas during the Hundred Years War, 1422-1440', *History,* 49 (1964)
—— 'Fauconberg's Kentish Rising of May 1471', *HER,* CCCXXXVII (October 1970)
—— 'The Nobility and the Wars of the Roses', *Nottingham Medieval Studies,* 21 (1977)

Bibliography

—— *The Paston Family: the First Phase,* (1990).
Richmond, C. & Scarff E., eds. *St George's Chapel, Windsor, in the late Middle Ages,* (Windsor, 2001)
Robin, F., *La cour d'Anjou-Provence: la vie artistique sous le regne de René* (Paris, 1985)
ROHAN Book of Hours, (1975)
Rosenthal, J. & Richmond, C., *People, Politics and Community in the Later Middle Ages* (1987)
Roskell, J.S., *Parliament and Politics in Late Medieval England,* 3 vols., (1981-83)
—— *The Commons and their Speakers in English Parliaments, 1376-1523,* (Manchester U.P., 1965)
Ross, C., *Edward IV* (1974)
Ross, J., *John de Vere Thirteenth Earl of Oxford, 1442-1513,* (Woodbridge, 2011)
Rowe, J.G. ed., *Aspects of late Medieval Government and Society,* (1986)
Rowney, I., 'Government and Patronage in 15th Century Staffordshire, 1439-1459', *Midland History* 8. (1983)
Ryder, A.F.C., *Alfonso the Magnanimous,* (Oxford, 1990)
Scofield, C. L., *The Life and Reign of Edward the Fourth,* 2 vols., (1923)
Scott, M., *Late Gothic Europe 1400-1500* (History of Dress Series, 1980)
Searle, W.G., *History of the Queens College of Saint Margaret and Saint Bernard in the University of Cambridge, 1445-1560,* (Cambridge, 1867)
Sharpe, R.R., *London and the Kingdom,* 3 vols., (1895)
Somerville, R., *History of the Duchy of Lancaster,* 1265-1603 (1953)
Sommé, M., *Isabelle de Portugal, Duchesse de Bourgogne,* (Presses Universitaires de Septentrion, 1998)
Sorley, J.C., *King's Daughters,* (Cambridge, 1937)
Spencer, M., *The History of Charles VII and Louis XI,* (Nieuwkoop, De Graaf, 1997)
Staniland, K.,'Royal entry into the world' in Williams, *England in the Fifteenth Century*
Steel, A., *The Receipt of the Exchequer 1377-1485,* (Cambridge, 1954)
Storey, R.L., *The End of the House of Lancaster,* (1966, reprint 1986)
—— 'Lincolnshire and the Wars of the Rose', *Nottingham Medieval Studies* 14, (1970)

Bibliography

Stratford, J., ed., *The Lancastrian Court*, (Donington, 2003)

Strickland, A., *Lives of Queens of England*, vol 2, rev. ed., (1851)

Sutton, A.F., 'Sir Thomas Cook and his 'troubles': an investigation', *Guildhall Studies in London History*, Vol. III, no. 2, (April 1978)

Sutton, A.F & Hammond, P.W., *The Coronation of Richard III*, (Gloucester, 1983)

Sutton, A.F. & Visser-Fuchs, L., *Richard III's Books*, (Gloucester, 1997)

Thiebaux, M., 'The Medieval Chase', *Speculum* 42, (1967)

Thielemans, M-R, *Bourgogne et Angleterre*, 3 vols, (Presses Universitaires de Bruxelles, 1966)

Thomson, J.A.F., 'John de la Pole, Duke of Suffolk, *Speculum* 54, (1979)

Tout, T.F., "Margaret of Anjou', in *Dictionary of National Biography*

Twigg, J., *A History of Queens College, Cambridge, 1448–1986*, (Woodbridge, 1987)

Vale, M.G.A., *Charles VII*, (1974)

—— *English Gascony 1399–1453*, (Oxford, 1970)

—— 'The last years of English Gascony', *Transactions of the Royal Historical Society*, 5th series, XIX, (1969)

Vallet De Viriville, A., *Histoire de Charles VII roi de France et de son époque 1403–1461*, 3 vols. (Paris, 1862–1865)

Vaughan, R., *Philip the Good*, (1970)

—— *Charles the Bold*, (Woodbridge, 2002)

Vickers, K.H., *Humphrey Duke of Gloucester*, (1907)

Victoria Histories of the Counties of England

Virgoe, R., 'The Composition of the King's Council 1437–61', in *East Anglian Society*

—— 'William Tailboys and Lord Cromwell: crime and politics in Lancastrian England', in *East Anglian Society*

—— 'Three Suffolk Parliamentary Elections of the Mid-fifteenth Century', in *East Anglian Society*

—— 'The Death of William de la Pole, Duke of Suffolk' in *East Anglian Society*

—— 'The Divorce of Sir Thomas Tuddenham', in *East Anglian Society*

—— *East Anglian Society and the Political Community of Late Medieval England*, (East Anglia, 1997)

Bibliography

Visser-Fuchs, L., *History as Pastime: Jean de Wavrin and his Collection of Chronicles of England,* (Donnington, Shaun Tyas, 2018)

Warner, G.F. & Gilson, J.P., *Catalogue of Western Manuscripts on the Old and Kings Collections,* vol. 2, (1921)

Watts, J., *Henry VI and the Politics of Kingship,* (Cambridge, 1996)

Wedgwood, J.C., *History of Parliament: Biographies of the Members of the Commons House 1439–1509,* (1936)

W.J. White, W.J., 'The Death and Burial of Henry VI, a review of the facts and theories, Part I' *Ricardian* VI, No 78, (Sept 1982)

Willard, C.C., *Christine de Pizan* (New York, 1984)

Williams, D. ed., *England in the fifteenth century,* (1987).

Williams, E. Carleton, *My Lord of Bedford,* (1963)

Wolffe, B.P., 'Acts of Resumption of Lancastrian Parliaments', *EHR* LXXIII (1958)

—— *The Royal Demesne in English history.* (1971)

—— *Henry VI,* (1981)

Wood, D. ed., *Women and Religion in Medieval England,* (2003)

Wylie, J.H. & Waugh, W.T., *The Reign of Henry the Fifth,* 3 vols. (Cambridge, 1914–1929)

Dissertations and theses

Dicks, S.E., 'The Question of Peace: Anglo-French diplomacy A.D. 1439–1449', PhD thesis, University of Oklahoma, (1966)

James, L., 'The career and political influence of William de la Pole, 1st Duke of Suffolk', B.Litt. Thesis in Modern History, University of Oxford, (1979)

Jones, M., 'The Beaufort Family and the War in France' PhD thesis, Bristol University, (1982)

Marshall, A., 'The Role of English War Captains in England and Normandy, 1436–1461', M,A dissertation, University College, Swansea, (1974)

Metcalfe, C. A., 'Alice Chaucer, Duchess of Suffolk, c1404–1475', BA dissertation, University of Keele, (1970)

McGovern, C.J.M., 'Lancastrian Diplomacy and Queen Margaret's Court in Exile, 1461–1471', B.A. dissertation, University of Keele, (1973)

Index

Aberystwyth, 221, 231, 234
Abingdon, 313, 445
Abingdon Abbey, 247, 536
Afonso V, King of Portugal, (d. 1481). 385–388, 577
Agincourt, battle of 1415, 2, 8, 20, 61, 98–99, 108, 112, 477
Aiscough, William, bishop of Salisbury (d. 1450), 32, 128, 129, 158, 256, 496
Alençon, John, duke of (d.1476), 25, 28, 264, 486
Alfonso V, king of Aragon (d. 1458), 12–13, 15–16, 105, 479
Alnwick Castle, 348, 361–362, 366, 367–368, 383–384, 571
Amboise, 356, 419–421, 431
Angers, capital of Anjou, 15, 17, 23, 28, 172, 354–355, 421–422, 437, 459–460
Angoulême, John, count of, (d.1467), 28, 113, 481
Angus, George Douglas, earl of (d. 1463), 413–414, 416, 607
Anjou, duchy of, 15–16, 18, 52, 53, 486, 492, 375
Anjou, Louis II, duke of (d. 1417), 12, 16
Anjou, Louis III, duke of (d.1434), 10–11, 16
See also Marie of Anjou, René of Anjou
Annabelle, princess of Scotland, 232

Aragon, king of, see Alfonso V, John II
Armagnac, John, count of (d. 1450), 5–7
Arques, 104, 311, 347
Arras, Congress of 1435, 4, 51, 150, 373, 376
Arundel, William Fitzalan, earl of (d. 1487), 151, 217, 242, 248, 249, 273, 287, 327, 331
Arundel, John, (d. 1477), 184, 240, 241, 308
Ashby, George, (d.1475), 68, 399, 485
Ashendon, William, abbot of Abingdon, 536
Astley, John, 368
Audley, James, Lord (d.1459), 221, 276–277, 513, 534, 545
Audley, John, Lord (d.1490), 288–289, 298, 303, 550

Babham, Thomas, 228
Bamburgh Castle, 348, 361–362, 364, 367, 377–378, 380–385, 575
Bar, duchy of, 10, 14, 19, 375, 379, 418, 579
Barcelona, 397, 408, 431
Barnet, battle of 1471, 440, 442, 444, 447–448, 450, 454
Basin, Thomas, bishop of Lisieux (d. 1491), 84, 99–100, 103, 497, 513, 564
Battle of the Bridge 1450, 130, 132, 305
Baugé, battle of 1421, 8, 17, 58
Bayeux, 122–123

Index

Baynard's Castle, 157, 248, 338
Bayonne, 149–150
Beauchamp, Anne (d. 1449), 116, 166
Beauchamp, Henry, duke of Warwick (d. 1446), 32, 68, 116, 166
　wife of Cecily Neville, duchess of Warwick, countess of Worcester (d.1450), 166, 235
Beauchamp Inheritance, 166–167, 201, 286, 450, 515
Beauchamp, John, of Powick (d.1475), 68, 124, 256, 469, 489, 513, 534, 590
Beauchamp, Richard, bishop of Salisbury (d. 1481), 256–257, 264, 278, 308, 538, 554
Beauchamp, Richard, earl of Warwick (d. 1439), 33, 83
Beauchamp, Richard of Powick, 445–446
Beauchamp, William, Lord St Amand (d.1457), 499, 513
Beaufort, Henry, cardinal bishop of Winchester (d. 1447) 3–4, 33–34, 59, 69, 82, 93, 96, 126, 302,
Beaufort, Joan, countess of Westmorland, 168, 290
Beaufort, John, Lord (d. 1471), 83, 201, 205, 253, 286, 371, 493, 537
Beaufort, Margaret, 111, 116, 125, 129, 147, 162, 220, 226, 236, 238, 481
　see also Somerset, dukes of
Beaumaris Castle, 65, 135, 137
Beaumont, John, Viscount, (d. 1460), 38, 66, 84, 111, 114, 117, 124, 179, 182, 186, 188, 229, 234, 235, 244, 248, 270, 271, 298, 301, 304, 305, 493, 500, 507, 512, 531, 534, 535, 540, 549, 553, 555
Beaumont, William, 346, 347, 444
Beauvau, Bertrand de, Lord of Precigny (d. 1471) 21, 51–52, 75–76, 92, 361, 485, 490
Beckington, Thomas, bishop of Bath and Wells (d. 1465), 5–7, 45, 152
Bedford, John, duke of (d. 1435), 4, 20, 29, 53, 55, 80, 98, 144, 161, 178
　wife of see, Jacquetta of Luxembourg
Bedon, John, 392–393
Bellingham, Henry, 343, 382, 566
Bere, John de la, 45–46, 220, 278, 546
Berkeley family, 239
Berkhamsted, 249, 467, 511
Berry, Charles, duke of, 390, 409, 422, 423, 858
Berwick, 232, 287, 343, 352, 362, 368, 370
Bird, Thomas, bishop of St Asaph, 379, 480
Blackfriars, 81, 143, 248, 453
Blackheath, 35, 126, 127, 132, 451, 508
Blaye, 148, 161
Blois, 21, 118, 358, 359
Blondel, Jacques, 124, 503
Blore Heath, battle of 1459, 276, 279, 285, 186, 288, 289, 307, 527
Blount, Walter, 195, 409
Boccaccio, Giovanni, 17–18, 374
Bolingbroke, Roger, 63, 170
Bonville, William, Lord (d. 1461), 7, 9, 30, 143, 151, 152, 158, 179, 195, 209, 211–212, 291, 327, 332, 333, 510, 511, 513, 526, 535, 563
Booth, Lawrence, bishop of Durham (d. 1480), 146, 179, 180, 223, 240–241, 293, 302, 307, 344, 358, 365, 369, 531, 541, 544, 566, 571
Booth, William, bishop of Coventry, archbishop of York (d. 1464), 40, 44, 94–95, 146, 188, 224, 369, 401, 515, 520, 528, 544

610

Index

Bordeaux, 6–7, 9, 143, 148–149, 153, 160–161, 169, 209, 353, 457, 477, 513, 516
Botill, Robert, Prior of St John of Jerusalem, 74, 176, 182, 188, 198, 201, 512, 538, 554
Botiller, *see* Sudeley
Boulers, Reginald, bishop of Hereford, bishop of Coventry-Lichfield (d. 1459), 57, 90, 136, 153, 183–184, 201, 229, 494
Bourbon, Agnes, duchess of Bourbon, 374, 542
Bourbon, John, duke of, *see* Clermont
Bourbon, Louis de *see* Vendôme
Bourgchier, Edward and John, 280, 283, 538, 554, 557
Bourgchier, Henry (d. 1483) 177, 182, 187–189, 201, 206, 224, 227, 243, 248, 255, 273, 287, 300, 307, 331, 358, 377, 440, 451, 512, 528, 535, 537–358, 540
Bourgchier, Humphrey, Lord Cromwell, 362, 530
Bourgchier, John, Lord Berners (d. 1471), 202, 206, 243, 333, 440, 535, 537, 540
Bourgchier, Thomas, bishop of Ely, archbishop of Canterbury (d. 1486), 155, 177, 182, 188, 206, 194, 201, 208, 210-212, 224, 227, 235, 248, 250, 273, 287, 300, 303, 307–308, 313–314, 325, 338, 370, 440, 528, 537, 544, 554
Bourges, 3, 74–75
Brackley, Friar, 319, 548, 559
Breknok, John, 262, 285, 540
Brezé, Jacques de, 361, 366, 569
Brezé, Jean de, 90
Brezé, Pierre de (d. 1465), 23–24, 27, 75–77, 98–100, 103, 105, 112, 123, 242–243, 256-257, 265, 290, 328–329, 436, 357, 359, 361–362, 366, 369, 372–375, 386, 391–392, 395, 497, 568–570, 578
Brittany, duchy of, 9, 80, 85–88, 93, 97, 122, 351, 354, 360, 389, 409, 449, 492, 501, 570
Brittany, Francis, duke of (d. 1450), 9, 22, 25, 79–81, 86–87, 89, 91–93, 113, 354, 486
Brittany, Francis, duke of (d. 1488), 351, 354, 360, 380–382, 389, 390, 395, 409, 418, 434, 568, 570
Brittany, Giles of (d. 1450), 9, 32, 72, 80–81, 86–87, 113, 389, 477, 490, 492
Brittany, John V, duke of (d. 1442), 80, 492
Bromley, John, Prior of Arbury, 249–250, 537
Browne, Thomas, 307, 555
Bruges, city of, 258, 299, 313, 347, 372–373, 375, 380, 410, 417, 434, 443
Bruges, William, Garter King of Arms (d. 1450), 28, 48, 72, 86
Buckingham, Humphrey Stafford, duke of (d.1460), 25, 40–50, 57, 66, 75, 126–127, 162. 177, 179, 183, 187-188, 193, 199, 201–205, 215, 217, 224–225, 231, 234–236, 238, 243, 245, 252, 273, 303–305, 335, 490, 512–513, 527–528, 534–535, 548
  wife of Anne Neville, 173–174, 235–236, 281, 286, 334, 410
Bulgnéville, battle of, 1431, 11–12
Bulstrode, Richard, 161
Burgh, Edith, 229
Burgh, Thomas, 414
Burgundian court, 14, 118, 152, 258,

310, 330, 344–346, 363, 388, 438, 574
Burgundian territories, 14, 360, 375, 432–434, 455
Burgundy, Anthony, Bastard of, 258, 400
Burgundy, Charles, duke of from 1467, (d. 1477) 400, 411, 418, 424–425, 429–430, 432–434, 436, 438,–439, 443, 455, 458–459, 584–585
   See also Charolais
Burgundy, Isabelle, duchess of (d. 1471), 264–266, 577
Burgundy, Mary of, 265, 394
Burgundy, Philip, duke of (d. 467), 2–4, 11–15, 19, 25, 82, 85, 93, 99, 108, 150–151, 189, 256–259, 264–266, 289, 299, 310, 351, 370, 372–377, 389, 400, 478–479, 501, 510, 513, 540, 542, 557, 559, 564–65, 568, 574
Burley, William, 48, 210
Bury St Edmunds Abbey, 62, 117
Butler *see* Ormond, Wiltshire
Bywell Castle, 383–384

Cade, Jack, 125–127
Cade's Rebellion, 129–135, 138, 144, 155, 162, 169, 171, 282, 297, 305, 505, 508, 581
Caen, 83, 89, 101, 105, 107, 122–123, 134, 156, 229, 354, 498
Calais, 22, 82, 95, 117, 122, 134, 150–154, 156, 158, 160, 189, 235, 242–244, 246, 250, 254–256, 258, 270, 276–277, 281, 287–289, 292–296, 298–299, 311, 425, 329, 333, 342, 355–357, 360–361, 372–373, 376, 394–395, 411, 455, 512–513, 438, 544, 546, 550, 558, 582
   captains of *see* Buckingham, Somerset, Edmund and Henry, Warwick

garrison, 95, 189, 117, 217, 255, 262, 277, 280–281, 288, 296, 299, 303, 357, 360, 432, 433, 450, 508, 547, 553
Pale of, 5, 22, 51, 189, 372
Staplers, 189, 217, 261–262, 293, 295, 355, 361, 433, 552, 570
Calabria, *see* John of,
Callixtus III, Pope (d.1458), 240, 263-264, 271
Camoys, Roger, 72, 165, 169, 209, 490–492, 516
Cantelowe, William, 107, 221
Canterbury, Kent, 69, 124, 145, 173, 193, 198, 234–235, 297, 299, 308, 325, 389, 411, 451, 553
Caraunt, Nicholas, 45–46, 152, 485
Carbonnel, Jean, 372, 375
Carlisle, town of, 57, 343–344, 348, 517, 566, 569
   bishops of *see* Lumley, Percy,
Carmarthen, 221, 226, 231, 234, 327
Castile, King of *see* Enrique IV
Castillon, battle of 1453, 168–170, 224, 239, 305
Catalonia, 397, 409
Caudebec, 71, 104
Cerne Abbey, 442–444
Chamberlain, Margaret, 33
Chamberlain, Roger, 131
Channel Islands, 351, 357, 375, 569
Charles VI, (d.1422), 2–3, 161
Charles VII (d. 1461), 4, 14, 16–17, 19, 26–27, 56, 72, 84–85, 93, 112, 116, 122–223, 233, 242, 309, 311, 344, 355, 376, 539, 556, 559, 569
and Brittany, 79, 80–81, 86-7, 89, 91–93
and Burgundy, 4, 258, 513
and Calais, 150, 158
character, 2, 345

Index

as Dauphin, 2–3, 80
death of, 345, 347
and Gascony, 5–6, 143, 168, 513, 516
and Henry VI, 52, 77, 86, 92, 486
and Maine, 53–54, 56–57, 71, 75, 76
and Margaret, 23, 53, 92, 120, 135, 318, 328–329, 342, 481
and Normandy 59, 90, 98-99, 101, 113, 134
and peace negotiations, 9, 20–24, 49, 51–52, 58, 70, 74, 77–78
relations with England, 97, 256–258, 260, 265, 310, 345–346
and Rouen, 102–106
and Somerset, 83, 85–86, 89–90, 93, 103–104, 156
Charlton, Thomas, 180
Charolais, Charles, count of (to 1467), 311, 344–347, 359, 375–376, 380–381, 388–391, 394–395, 400, 443, 557, 574, 577, 580
See also Burgundy, Charles, duke of
Chastellain Georges, 374, 559
Cherbourg, 104, 107, 122–123, 130, 134, 498, 503
Chester, 65, 218, 229, 235, 274, 277, 307, 312, 318, 527, 529
Chevalier, Etienne, 92, 353, 355, 485
Christmas, Stephen, 144–145
Clarence, George, duke of (d. 1478), 394, 400, 402, 411, 413–415, 418–419, 423–424, 426, 433, 436–437, 439, 440, 447, 450, 459
wife of Isabel Neville, 394, 402, 411, 416, 450
Clarence, Lionel, duke of, 147, 314, 315
Clarence, Thomas, duke of (d. 1421) 17, 481
Clarendon, 165, 169–171, 177
Clermont, John, count of, 27, 122–123
Clere, Edmund, 198, 522

Clere, Elizabeth, 163
Clifford, John, (d. 1461), 248–249, 251, 319, 322, 340, 343, 537, 554, 560, 566, 576
Clifford, Thomas (d. 455), 29, 158, 179, 202, 204, 512
Clifton, Gervase (d. 1471), 153, 160–161, 169, 243, 289, 448, 464, 555
Clinton, John, Lord (d.1464), 280, 283, 554
Cobham, Edward Brook, Lord (d.1464), 152, 155–156, 171, 306, 327, 511
Colchester, 68, 468, 590
Coleshill, 237, 277–278, 546
Colville, Cuthbert, 109
Cook, Thomas, 243, 352, 407, 572
Coppini, Francesco, bishop of Terni (d. 1464), 272, 279, 301, 310, 325–326, 330, 342, 544, 553, 556
Corfe Castle, 142, 311
Cornelius, 407
Cornwall, duchy of, 262, 274, 285–286, 461, 465, 467, 510
Cotton, William, 204
Courtenay, Henry (d.1469), 210, 410
Courtenay, John, earl of Devon (d. 1471), 379, 439, 442–443, 447–448,
Courtenay, Philip, 211
Courtenay, Thomas, earl of Devon (d. 1458), 38, 151–152, 155–156, 158, 180, 195, 202, 205, 208–209, 211–212, 239, 247, 507, 510–511, 518, 523, 526, 535
Courtenay, Thomas, earl of Devon (d. 1461), 209–210, 239, 260, 319, 321, 324, 329, 333, 341
Cousinot, Guillaume, 53–54, 56, 74–75, 83, 85–86, 91–93, 97–98 380–382, 387, 485, 490

Index

Coventry, 153, 201, 221, 224–225, 228–230, 232–233, 235–237, 243, 272–274, 282, 285–286, 298, 300–302, 304, 318, 349, 412, 424, 433, 435–437, 439, 443, 450, 530, 532–533, 552, 581
Cromwell, Ralph, Lord (d. 1456), 8, 56, 75, 114–115, 188, 201, 207, 500, 513, 515
  See also Bourgchier, Humphrey
Crowmer, William, 130, 504
Croyland Abbey, 292, 329
Curzon, Richard, 107

Dacre, Humphrey, 343, 566
Dacre, Ralph, of Gillesland, (d. 1461), 104, 324, 341, 554, 561, 566
  See also Fiennes, Richard
Daniel, Thomas, 127, 130, 151, 179, 195, 259, 263, 504, 559
Dartford, field of 1452, 155, 158, 159, 162, 164, 171, 176, 180, 199, 202, 282, 511–512, 517, 529
Delapré Abbey, 302, 305
Denbigh, 136, 291–292, 311–312, 347–438, 408
Despenser lands, 167–168
Devereux, Walter (d. 1459), 220–221, 225, 231, 234, 529, 533
Devereux, Walter, (d. 1485), 280, 312, 328, 347, 350, 548
Devon, earls of *see* Courtenay
Dieppe, 311, 344–345, 347
Dockett, Andrew, 43–44
Doncaster, 244, 340, 385, 424
Doucereau, Jean, 256–257, 265, 328–329, 542
Douglas, George, *see* Angus, earl of
Douglas, James, earl of, 219, 365, 368, 547
Dudley, John Sutton, Lord (d. 1487), 56–58, 127, 136, 168, 176, 182, 196, 205, 221, 229, 262, 276, 452, 454, 480, 490, 515, 544, 584
Dunois, John, count of, Bastard of Orleans (d. 1468), 20–21, 70–71, 75–77, 92, 98–105, 107, 111–112, 123, 134, 148–149, 169, 346, 490, 497, 509
Dunstable, 331–332, 334, 336, 563
Dunstanburgh, 348, 361–362, 364–367, 384
Durham, 220, 344, 362, 364, 366, 377, 571
  bishopric of, 240, 365, 369
Dynham, John, 290, 296, 584

East Anglia, 140, 195, 238, 263, 319, 349, 351, 433, 440, 540
Eccleshall Castle, 275–276
Edgecote Field, battle of 1470, 412, 414
Edinburgh, 243, 343, 348, 363, 372
Edward III, 23, 50, 55, 170, 188, 238, 283, 314, 551
Edward IV, 133, 231, 347, 349–352, 354, 361, 364–365, 367–370, 382–385, 407–408, 410, 418, 423, 427–248, 435–437, 439–400, 441, 443–444, 451, 454
  as Earl of March, 56, 125, 178, 265, 279, 281, 290, 297–298, 301, 303–306, 308, 310, 315, 325, 237–328, 331, 335–336, 419, 426, 554
  and Brittany, 360, 389–390, 409
  and Burgundy, 374, 394, 400, 434
  claims the throne, 338–339, 344, 348
  and Henry VI, 339, 348, 381, 393, 438, 440, 452
  and Louis XI, 356, 376–378. 394–396, 400, 406, 455–456, 458
  and Margaret, 348, 357, 362, 380, 407–410, 450

Index

and Scotland, 348, 358, 378, 384
and Somerset, 363–384, 366, 371, 377
at Tewkesbury, 445–449
at Towton, 340–342
and Warwick, 395, 401, 404, 411–416, 441,
Edward of Lancaster, Prince of Wales (d. 1471), 177–179, 196, 206, 218, 222, 226, 265, 269, 275, 318, 323–324, 334, 343, 354, 369, 372–373, 375, 386, 397, 404, 417, 419, 420–422, 424–425, 431, 435, 442
  badge of, 218
  bastardy, 174–175, 216, 244, 250, 398, 313, 342, 344
  birth and christening, 173, 236
  character of, 398–399, 430
  council of, 228–229, 261
  death at Tewkesbury, 448
  finances of, 230, 262, 273–74, 285–286, 463, 465, 467
  Lancastrian heir, 182, 185, 191, 193, 230, 282, 287, 291–292, 316–317, 320, 329, 330, 332
  marriage of, 421–423
  wife of, Anne Neville, 419, 430, 442, 450
Egremont *see* Percy
Elizabeth of York, Henry VII's queen, 420, 425
Ellesmere, Edward, 264
Eltham, 34, 43, 120
Elvaston, 195
Enrique IV, king of Castile (d. 1474), 387–388, 577
Escouchy, Mathieu d', 120, 501
Estfeld, William, 25, 509
Étampes, 391
Étampes, Counts of, 258, 354, 568

Eton College, 43, 121, 214, 224
Eve, John, 133
Eu, Charles of Artois, count of (d. 1472), 98–99, 101, 530, 572
Eugenius IV, Pope (d. 1447), 13, 21, 45
Ewelme, 62, 453, 455
Exeter, bishop of *see* Neville, George
Exeter, city of, 209, 211–212, 443
Exeter, Henry Holand, duke of (d. 1475), 126, 128, 147, 174, 190, 200, 205, 215, 246, 248, 252–253, 293–294, 300, 307, 318, 323, 341, 343, 347, 351, 410, 434, 438, 440, 456, 468, 504, 515, 523, 535, 573
  wife of Anne of York, 190
Exeter, John Holand, duke of (d. 1447), 58, 6, 467
Exeter, Robert and William, Bastards of, 191, 340, 561
Eynon, David ap, 403
Eyre, Simon, 35
Eyton, Fulk, 71–73, 75–79, 99, 497

Faceby, John, 184
Fastolf, John (d. 1459), 71, 73, 88, 132, 133, 242, 250, 494
Fauconberg, Thomas Neville, Bastard of Fauconberg, 416, 434, 443, 450–452
Fauconberg, William Lord Fauconberg (d. 1463), 87, 91, 183, 206, 250, 255, 260, 296–298, 303–304, 311, 325, 340–341, 360, 366, 523–524, 538, 544, 556, 563
Feckenham, 228, 468
Ferdinand, King of Naples, 310
Ferrybridge, 340, 564–565
Findhern, Thomas, 382–384
Fiennes, James *see* Saye and Sele
Fiennes, Richard, 327, 561
Fitzhugh, Henry (d. 1472), 324, 341, 365
Fitzwalter, John (d. 1461), 340, 564

Index

Flanders, 256, 302, 372, 433, 551–552
  Four Members of, 261, 302
Fleet Street, 271, 300
Floquet, Robert, (d. 1465), 90–101, 103–104, 391
Foix, Gaston IV, count of (d. 1472), 5, 27–28, 112, 143
Foix, John de, earl of Kendal (d. 1485), 112, 305, 355–356, 386, 500
Forest, John, 45
Forest, Thomas, 45
Formigny, battle of 1450, 121, 123, 125, 502
Fortescue, John, 110, 283, 344, 351, 356, 379, 386–388, 394, 398–399, 406–407, 421, 428, 431, 442, 449, 548, 568, 573, 584
Fougères, 80–81, 87–89, 91–94, 97–98, 101, 105, 156, 259, 354
Frederick III, Holy Roman Emperor (d. 1493), 21, 25, 72, 113, 356, 387, 479
Fresnay-le Vicomte, 78, 99
Frogenhall, Richard, 104
Fronsac, 148–149, 161
Fulford, Baldwin, 292–294, 334

Gallet, Louis, 264–265, 270, 296, 377, 538, 541–542
Garter, Feast of the, 31, 162, 201, 261, 445, 523
Garter, Order of the, 43, 81, 89, 92, 105, 114, 144, 193, 201, 261, 327, 332, 385, 387, 454
Garter King of Arms *see* Bruges, William, Smert, John
Gascoigne, Thomas (d. 1458), 216, 230, 499, 522
Gascony, duchy of, 5–9, 22, 30, 36, 51, 94, 111–112, 117, 143–144, 148–150, 153–154, 160–161, 168–169, 176, 345, 352, 356
Gatewyne, Katherine, 229, 379, 757
Genoa, 13, 15, 273, 294, 302, 309, 345, 479
Glamorgan, 168, 225, 291
Gloucester Castle, 68, 239, 445, 590
Gloucester, Humphrey, duke of (d. 1447), 3, 4, 33, 38, 41, 43, 48–50, 58, 62–169, 111, 113, 126, 138, 161, 175, 178, 184, 375, 466, 469, 489, 549
  wife of Eleanor Cobham, (d. 1452), 63–67, 171, 488
Gloucester, Richard, duke of, 400, 440, 447, 449, 452, 583, 588
Glyn Dyr, Owen, 65
Gough, Matthew, 71–73. 75–80, 122–123, 130–131, 490–491
Gray, William, bishop of Ely (d. 1478), 248, 273, 287, 440, 528, 554
Gravelines, 246, 289, 433
Great Councils, 95, 153, 175, 181, 194, 199, 200–202, 223–225, 228, 237–238, 244–245, 247, 260
Greenwich, 43, 127–128, 131, 161, 163, 165–166, 172, 175, 198–200, 254, 268, 272, 496, 518, 528, 537
Gregory, William, mayor of London, 155, 511
Grey, Edward, Lord Ferrers of Groby, (d. 1457), 237
Grey, Elizabeth, 29, 367, 572
Grey, Henry of Codnore, 341, 362
Grey, John, 389
Grey, Ralph, 367–368, 384–385, 572
Grey, Richard, of Powis (d. 1466), 280, 548
Grey Edmund, Lord of Ruthin (d. 1490), 304, 534, 554
Greystoke, Ralph, Lord (d. 1487) 30, 191, 319, 365

Index

Grimsby, William, 340, 379, 449, 569, 576
Grimston, Edward, 129, 504
Gruffyd ap Nicholas, 220, 225–226, 234, 328, 528, 530
Guelders, duke of, 265, 542
Guildhall, 63, 130, 142, 217, 307, 507
Guines, 246, 288, 290, 296, 308, 311, 383, 385, 550, 557

Hals, John (d. 1490), 263–264, 275, 428, 440, 541
Hampden, Edmund (d. 1471), 146, 229, 334, 343, 353, 379, 442, 449, 502, 508, 555, 573
  Wife of Anne Moleyns, (d. 1486), 146, 508
Hampton, John (d. 1472), 68, 468, 490
Hanseatic League, 34, 259, 290, 416–417, 421, 434
Harcourt, Louis de, 265, 429–430, 432–433
Harfleur, 21, 31, 71, 82, 104, 107, 233, 311, 39, 409
Harlech Castle, 318, 323, 347–348, 403, 408, 579
Harrington, James, 393, 570
Harrington, Thomas, 270, 277, 545, 548
Hastings, William, 538, 368, 371, 394, 441, 447–448, 584
Hatclyffe, William, 184, 565
Havart, Georges, 355
Havart, Jean, 53, 56, 74–75, 92–93, 105, 490
Havering at Bower, 467–468, 549
Hayford, Humphrey, 42, 489
Hedgeley Moor battle of 1464, 383
Henry IV, 140, 147, 159, 173, 237, 315, 348
Henry V (d. 1422), 2–4, 22–23, 42, 51, 60, 63, 104–105, 138, 140, 178, 237, 348

Henry VI, (1421–1471), 3, 9, 20, 21, 28, 35–37, 45-46, 48, 56–57, 63–64, 81, 84, 99, 105, 108, 112, 114, 120, 141, 151, 175, 185, 187–188, 190–192, 200, 206, 211, 231, 239–241, 261, 264, 270, 272, 274–275, 279, 299, 301, 307, 310, 320, 324, 326, 376, 353–354, 406, 510, 557–558
  Armagnac marriage, 5–7
  attainted, 348, 428, 566
  and Blore Heath, 275–276
  and Brittany, 79, 86–87, 389
  and Burgundy 4, 150, 265–266, 289, 373, 551
  and Cade's Rebellion, 125–128, 504, 508
  and Calais, 152-53, 158, 288, 355–356, 522–523
  character, 4-5, 8, 25, 32-33, 150, 174, 209
  and Charles VII, 22, 50, 71, 78, 86, 92, 265, 343, 346, 486
  coronations of, 3, 23, 28, 32
  at Coventry, 221–223, 233, 235–236
  death of, 452–453, 588
  deposition, 313–317, 338
  diplomacy of, 256, 265–266, 346, 381–382
  finances and loans, 28, 96, 148, 483, 570
  fugitive in the north, 380, 382, 384, 392, 573, 579
  and Edward IV, 335, 338–339, 358, 377, 393–394, 435, 437, 440, 442, 449
  and Gascony, 143, 148, 150, 160, 499
  and Gloucester, 62–63, 65–67, 69
  government of, 61, 151–152, 224, 237, 244-245, 247, 260, 270, 272
    see also Great Councils
  household, 196, 262, 350, 522

617

Index

illness, 169–171, 175–177, 179, 182–184, 194, 206, 209–210, 214, 519
   recovers from, 198, 200
judicial progresses, 145, 148, 158–159, 168, 234
and London, 117, 128–129, 142–143, 217, 221, 245, 271–272, 300, 334–335, 527
and Louis XI, 353, 356–357, 396, 406, 418, 423, 429, 433, 439
Loveday, 247–249, 251–253, 537
at Ludford, 278–281
and Maine, 53–54, 58, 70–79
and Margaret, 23, 25–26, 31, 31–34, 43–45, 68, 95, 122, 131, 163, 165–166, 177, 215, 218, 221, 228, 230, 236, 240, 363, 287, 302, 318, 325, 333, 353–354, 380–381, 446, 461, 529, 549
minority of, 4
at Northampton, 302–304
and Normandy, 101,135, 341–342, 422
and papacy, 140–241, 263, 271–272, 325, 541
and Parliament, 95, 108, 121, 141, 145, 162, 165, 182, 207, 210, 216–217, 282, 286–287, 312,
   see also resumptions
and peace negotiations, 9, 22, 49–52, 54, 68–69, 70, 72, 75, 153
and Prince Edward, 174, 228, 230, 274, 316–317, 344,
prisoner in the Tower, 293–394, 426, 441, 449, 583
public perception of, 108, 117, 244
raid on Sandwich, 242–243
Readeption, 428–430
resistance to Yorkists, 290–292, 296, 301

St Albans, battle of 1455, 201–204, 208, 245, 524
St Albans, battle of 1461, 331–333, 563
Scotland, 219, 232, 325
   exile in, 342–343, 348, 358, 365, 369, 377–378
and sea keeping, 246, 258–259
and Somerset, Edmund, 59, 73, 82-83, 86, 103, 116, 134–135, 150, 199; Henry, 363, 371, 377, 381
and Suffolk, 60, 62, 109, 111, 113, 115–118, 124
and Towton, 349–341
and trade, 259, 261, 417, 539–540, 552
and Tudors, 161, 228
and Wales, 220, 225, 234,
and Warwick, 166–168, 201, 217, 246–247, 255, 260, 270, 305–308, 325–327, 404, 407, 419, 422, 424, 426
and York, 55, 96, 135–139, 144, 146–147, 152–157, 159, 164, 185, 199, 202–203, 205, 208, 215–216, 225, 231, 251, 269–270, 273, 277, 278, 284–286, 512, 525
and Yorkist propaganda, 277–278, 297–298, 351–352
Henry VII (d. 1509), 226, 229, 285, 481
Herbert, William (d. 1469), 168, 220–221, 225, 231, 234, 291, 312, 327–328, 347, 350,403, 406, 408, 412, 533, 579
Hereford, 234, 261, 289, 312, 328, 408, 529, 550
   bishop of, *see* Stanbury
Hertford, 206, 209, 211, 214, 216, 464, 525
Hesdin, 375–376, 381, 574

Index

Hexham, battle of 1464, 382–384, 391, 392, 410, 443
Heydon, John, 263, 548
Honfleur, 77, 204, 207, 122, 242–243, 416, 418, 436
Hoo, Thomas (d. 1455), 21, 76, 78–79, 90, 142, 480, 494
Hull, port of, 243, 261, 291, 322–323, 361, 465, 512, 590
Hull, Edward (d. 1453), 6, 30, 143, 160–161, 169, 499, 502, 515
Hulyn, William, mayor of London, 271, 300, 305
Hundred Years War, 2, 8, 502, 516
Hungerford, Robert, Lord Moleyns (d. 1464), 165, 169, 305, 341, 344–347, 351, 353, 366, 368, 382–384, 410, 511, 513, 515, 566, 569

Iden, Alexander, 132, 505
Ingoldesthorpe, Isabel, 235, 240, 274, 308
Ireland, 96, 120, 135–136, 138, 141, 144, 154, 164, 231–232, 238, 261, 281, 291, 293–294, 296–298, 303, 309, 311–313, 318, 378, 385–386, 437, 496, 505, 552, 557
Isabelle, duchess of Lorraine (d. 1453), 10–11, 13, 15–16, 19, 24, 26, 172, 177, 492,

Jacquetta of Luxembourg, duchess of Bedford, 38-39, 144, 290, 334, 367, 389, 468-469
James II, King of Scotland (d. 1460), 191–192, 219–220, 232, 244, 309, 323, 365
wife of see Mary of Guelders
James III, King of Scotland (d. 1488), 323, 352, 358, 365, 369, 378, 387
Jeanne of France (d. 1482), 23, 122
Jerningham, John, 256

Joan of Arc, 4, 17, 20, 28
Joan, princess of Scotland, 232–233
Joanna II, queen of Naples (d. 1433), 12
John II, King of Aragon (d. 1479), 356, 397, 408
John of Calabria (d.1470), 15–16, 28, 102, 309, 345, 354, 381, 390–391, 396–399, 408–409, 420–421, 431, 578
wife of Marie of Bourbon, 14–15, 24, 26
John of Gaunt, 147, 385, 577
Joseph, William, 179, 207, 385–387, 576
Jourdemain, Margery, 64
Juvenel des Ursins, Guillaume, chancellor of France, 97, 105, 398
Juvenel des Ursins, Jacques, archbishop of Rheims, (d. 1457), 49–52

Katherine, queen of England (d. 1437), 3, 23, 42, 144, 161, 175, 178, 206
Kemp, John, cardinal archbishop of York and Canterbury, chancellor (d. 1454), 51–52, 57, 75, 94, 96, 109–110, 116–117, 129, 131–132, 139, 165, 170, 173, 175, 177, 179, 181–183, 188, 198, 224, 323, 464, 504, 512, 515, 517–519
Kennedy, James, bishop of St Andrews (d. 1465), 323, 369–370, 377–378
Kenilworth, 129, 221, 226, 234, 236–237, 282, 302, 464, 529, 537, 546, 554
Kent, county of, 64, 124–128, 128, 130, 132, 144, 148, 155, 159, 243, 290–291, 297, 305, 411, 414, 424, 426, 451, 508, 536, 555
Kent, Thomas, 129
King's College, Cambridge, 43, 214, 470
Kirkcudbright, 248, 354, 382

Koeur, 379–380, 382, 385–87, 390, 394, 398–399, 401–403, 407, 410, 421, 430, 439, 569, 573–574, 576
Kymer, Gilbert, 206, 541
Kyriell, Thomas (d. 1461), 121–123, 243, 260, 326–327, 332–333, 563

La Guerche, 72, 490
Lancaster, duchy of, 39, 66, 121, 144, 188, 191, 201, 214, 216–217, 219, 236, 244, 246, 262, 270, 274, 298, 313, 329, 461, 462–44, 466, 540, 549, 567
Lancaster, house of, 69, 182, 356, 386, 397, 408
Langstrother, John, 428, 434, 442, 448–449
Laval, Jeanne de, 354, 381, 459
Lavardin, Treaty of 1448, 78, 81
lawlessness, 61, 94, 117, 194, 209, 212, 214, 217, 220
Leicester, 120–121, 124–125, 200–203, 226, 237, 243, 291, 317–318, 327, 464
Lee, Richard, mayor of London, 320, 333–334, 426, 437
Le Mans, 71–78, 82, 85, 92–93, 99, 492
L'Enfant, Jean, 91–92, 97
Letheringham, 141, 506
Lichfield, 221, 529
Lille, Treaty of 1437, 14–15
Lincluden Abbey, 323–324, 343
Lincolnshire, 114, 179, 188, 329, 414–415, 535, 540
Lisieux, town of, 99–100
Lisieux, Thomas (d. 1456), 223, 515, 531
Lisle, John, Viscount *see* Talbot
Little Malvern Priory, 450, 587
Longford, Nicholas, 195
London, 34–35, 64, 129–130, 134, 153, 189, 193, 249, 252, 300–301, 305, 320–321, 330, 351, 451, 464–465, 518, 520, 536, 586
  bishop of London's palace, 205, 217, 305, 307, 327, 426, 438, 558
  Common Council, 28, 173, 243, 245, 272, 299–300, 305–306, 320–321, 329, 335, 361–362, 369, 370, 437–438, 451, 560
  London Bridge, 35, 49, 64, 129–130, 132, 145, 299, 342, 385, 451, 588
  mayors of, 35–36, 39, 49, 63, 128–129, 131, 134, 136–137, 142, 153, 155, 172–173, 180, 190, 217, 221, 243, 245, 248, 271–272, 299–300, 305, 320, 333, 334–335, 413, 426, 437, 451, 452, 484, 507, *see also* Frowyk, Henry; Gregory, William; Hulyn, William; Lee, Richard; Wyfold, Nicholas
  merchants of, 5, 11, 34–35, 42, 79, 153, 407, 410, 433, 452, 489, 507, 565
  unrest in, 107, 109, 110, 117, 120, 142, 178, 217, 271, 306, 334, 426, 527
  Tower of *see* Tower of London
Lorenzo of Florence, 326
Lorraine, Charles II, duke of (d. 1431) 10
Lorraine, duchy of, 10–11, 19, 26, 390, 409, 458, 578, 589
  see also Isabelle of Lorraine
Lose-cote Field, battle of 1470, 415
Louis, cardinal duke of Bar (d. 1430), 10
Louis, marquis of Pont (d. 1443), 13–14
Louis XI (d. 1483), 345–347, 352, 355, 375–376, 378, 389, 391, 393–394, 396–397
  as Dauphin, 24–26, 49, 113, 258, 310, 344–345, 564
  and Edward IV, 377, 395, 409, 435–436

and Margaret, 353–357, 359–361,
372, 375, 380–381, 388, 390,
393–394, 398, 403–404, 406, 408,
410, 420–423, 431, 436, 458–460,
579, 580
and Warwick, 397, 399, 401,
418–419, 430, 432–433, 439,
Loveday 1458, 247–248, 251–253, 260,
269, 286, 316, 421, 560
Lovell, Alice, 291, 555
Lovell, John (d. 1465), 534, 555
Lovelace, 331, 563
Low Countries, 261, 295, 374, 433
see also Flanders, Netherlands,
Lowe, John, bishop of Rochester
(d. 1467), 132–133, 554
Lubeck, 259, 417
Ludford, 278–279, 283, 286–288, 290,
303, 321, 539, 543, 546–548, 550,
557
Ludlow, 136, 153, 158–159, 277, 279,
281–282, 293, 312, 505, 546–547
Lumley, Marmaduke, bishop of Carlisle
(d. 1450), 44, 57, 95–96, 128, 462,
496
Luxembourg, Jacques of (d. 1487), 11,
27
Luxembourg, John of, count of Ligny
(d. 1441), 11
Luxembourg, Louis of, count of St Pol
(d. 1475), 11, 27–28, 98, 580
see also Jacquetta of Luxembourg
Lydgate, John (d.1451), 62, 42, 487
Lyhert, Walter, bishop of Norwich, 74,
319, 528, 559

Mackerell, Roger, 379, 449, 573
Maine, Charles count of, 19, 21, 23,
25–26, 53–54, 71, 85, 101, 105, 111,
239, 265, 346, 352–353, 390–391,
486

Maine, county of, 5, 9, 51, 53–54, 56–58,
65, 70–71, 73–76, 78–79, 82, 84, 86,
90, 93, 99, 104, 109–110, 116, 139,
153, 157, 486, 488, 491, 499
Malpas, Philip, 129, 565
Manning, Alexander, 137, 506, 578
Manning, Thomas, 137, 302, 392–393
Mantes, 100, 497, 572
March, Edward earl of see Edward IV
Margaret of Anjou, (d. 1482), 15, 19, 26,
31, 34, 48, 50, 52, 56, 62, 69, 70, 71,
84, 96, 124, 127, 160, 162, 177, 183,
193–194, 200, 205–206, 226,
235–236, 247, 255, 263–264, 271,
280–283, 285–286, 308, 314,
324–325, 327, 344, 349, 358, 377,
389, 392, 396–397, 399, 408–409,
428, 445, 447, 451–452, 478, 501,
505, 519, 536, 559, 570
appearance, 23–25
attainted, 348, 566
Armagnac marriage, 7
betrothals, 11, 14, 15, 19, 23
birth 10,
and Blore Heath, 275–277, 527, 545
and Brittany, 359, 380–382, 389, 390,
570
and Buckingham, 177, 199, 201, 224,
236
and Burgundy, 372–375, 377
and Cade's Rebellion, 131–133
and Calais, 355, 357–358, 361
and Charolais, 344, 375, 380–381,
388, 390, 574
campaigns in the north, 361–362,
367–369, 566, 570–572
character, 68, 120, 147, 215, 230, 285
and Charles VII, 56, 92, 318, 342, 481
childlessness, 32, 146–147
coronation, 33, 35–39, 151, 483, 510,
council, 40, 44, 153, 188, 204, 306, 543

Index

daily life, 42–43
diplomatic activity, 256–257, 264–266, 344–347, 353–354, 357, 380–381, 386–388, 390, 417, 490, 538
dower lands, 39, 40, 84, 166, 195, 201, 236, 317, 437, 525, 590
early life and education, 16–18
and Edward IV, 344, 349, 353, 357, 368, 369, 380, 388–389, 413, 420, 436, 442, 451–456
entertainments, 161, 254
exile and death, 459–460
finances, 95–96, 121, 185, 216, 230–231, 261–262, 274, 285, 461–470, 495, 508, 532, 589, 549–550
gifts of, 41, 54, 62, 135, 147, 160, 228, 484, 489, 494, 505, 509, 531, 534, 541, 572
as good lady, 42, 44–45, 68, 72, 137, 485
and Henry VI, 31–32, 68, 165–166, 177, 198, 237, 302, 332, 380, 452, 529
household, 41, 68, 99, 129, 143, 146, 187, 195–196, 482, 493, 508, 520, 522, 531–352, 572
at Koeur, 375, 379, 385, 403, 573, 575–576, 578, 569
Lancastrian march on London, 319, 324, 329–330, 332, 333–334, 560–563
and London, 137, 272, 320, 333, 335
and Louis XI, 353–356, 393–394, 398, 403–404, 413, 455, 459, 579–580, 584–585
Loveday, 348, 350–351, 355
and Maine, 53–54
marriage, 23–28
as marriage broker, 232, 235, 238, 239, 240, 533, 555
and Norfolk, 140–141, 227–228
and Normandy, 102, 106, 120, 135
pageants for, 35-37 (**1445**), 221–223, 529 (**1456**)
piety, 42, 163, 193, 402–403, 455, 484–485
political activity, 215–216, 218–219, 221–224, 233–234, 240–241, 260–262, 274, 287, 528, 531
pregnancy and childbirth, 163, 171–175
and Prince Edward, 291–92, 317–318, 398, 423, 435, 448
and Prince Edward's council, 228–230, 273–274
Queens College, 43–44
raid on Sandwich, 243–244
ransomed, 455–459
Regency, 177–178, 180–181, 518
returns to England, 436–438, 442, 444–445
in Rouen, 28–30, 359, 431
and Salisbury, 250, 537,
in Scotland, 323–234, 343, 348, 365–366, 573
and Suffolk, 61, 120, 487, 500–501,
and Somerset, Edmund I, 135
and Somerset, Edmund II, 442–444, 447
and Somerset, Henry, 344–345, 364
and Wales, 225, 234, 530
and Warwick, 313, 420–422, 424, 429–430, 435, 439, 530
and York, 164, 193, 218, 225, 269, 291, 316
Yorkist propaganda, 216, 313, 320, 351–352, 360, 369–370, 444, 549
Margaret of Scotland, Dauphine, 21–22, 24–26

Index

Margaret of York, 394–395, 401, 411, 443, 438
Marie of Anjou, queen of France, (d. 1463), 14, 16, 21–22, 24–26, 28, 255, 499
Marie of Maine, 239, 379, 442, 534
Market Drayton, 276, 545
Mary of Guelders, Queen of Scotland (d.1463), 323–324, 342–343, 348–349, 353, 358, 369, 377–378, 561, 656, 569, 575
Middleham, 196, 270, 275, 183, 312, 412, 569, 576
Milan, dukes of *see* Sforza
Milanese ambassadors, 14, 24, 31, 152, 158, 328, 344–345, 390–391, 396–397, 400, 403, 409, 420, 458, 478, 512, 553, 567, 579
Moleyns, Adam, bishop of Chichester (d. 1450), 21, 55–58, 77–78, 85–87, 108–109, 116, 129, 158, 490, 495
Moleyns, Lord *see* Hungerford
Molyneux, Nicholas, 73–74
Montague, Lord *see* Neville, John
Monte, Piero da, bishop of Brescia, 25
Montgomery, Thomas, 457
Montlhéry, battle of 1465, 391, 393, 396, 432, 580
Morecroft, Roger, 204
Mortimer's Cross, battle of 1461, 328, 340
Morton, John, 228–229, 283, 285, 365, 379, 548, 569, 573
Mountford, Edmund, 237, 344, 379, 569, 573
Mowbray *see* Norfolk, dukes of
Mowbray Herald, 202–203
Mundford, Osbert (d. 1460), 73–74, 76–79, 85, 91–92, 98–99, 150–151, 296–297, 493, 497, 553

Nancy, city of, 11, 26, 28
Naples, Kingdom of, 1–16, 105, 309–310, 381, 396–397, 478–479
Netherlands, 330, 399, 429, 432, 434
  See also Low Countries
Nevers, Charles, count of (d. 1464), 19, 23, 102, 479
Neville, Edward, Lord Abergavenny (d. 1476), 104, 167, 327, 451, 554
Neville, George (d. 1492), 167, 498
Neville, George, bishop of Exeter, chancellor (d. 1476), 248, 263–264, 273, 287, 303, 314, 316, 325, 338–339, 377, 401, 411–412, 426, 428, 437–438, 541, 554, 565
Neville, George, Lord Latimer, 559
Neville, John, Lord Montague (d. 1471), 190, 195, 235, 240, 252, 274, 277, 283, 307–308, 325, 333, 341, 344, 364, 368, 370, 383, 425, 535, 538, 544, 556
Neville, Katherine, dowager duchess of Norfolk, 140, 188
Neville, Robert, bishop of Durham (d. 1457), 179, 240
Neville, Thomas (d. 1460), 195–196, 252, 255, 277, 283, 307–308, 321–322, 538
  See also Salisbury, Warwick, Westmorland, earls of
Newcastle, 341–342, 363, 365, 377, 383–384, 573, 576
Newgate, 136–137, 196, 252, 392–393, 506
Newnham Bridge, encounter at 1460, 296
Nicholas V, Pope (d. 1455), 45, 150, 158
Nicholas, duke of Lorraine, 589
Nicholas of the Tower, 123, 503
Norbury, Henry, 122–123
Norfolk, county of, 116, 163, 244, 250, 262–263, 325, 351, 536, 540

Index

Norfolk, John, Mowbray, duke of (d. 1461), 38, 114, 126, 139–143, 146, 176–178, 182, 197, 194–195, 201–203, 227–228, 238, 260, 327, 331, 340–341, 506, 517, 535, 540
   Wife of Eleanor Bourgchier, 227–228
Norfolk, John Mowbray, duke of (d. 1475), 440, 449, 576
Norham, 368–369, 370, 372, 383, 573, 576
Normandy, duchy of, 3, 5, 22–23, 36, 48, 51–53, 55, 58–59, 75, 77, 81, 94, 96, 110, 117, 143–144, 148, 156, 169, 329, 345, 355, 408, 430
   finances of, 78, 83–84, 493
   garrisons in, 4, 8, 48, 84, 90, 95, 111
   loss of, 78, 90, 98, 100–104, 107, 109, 112–113, 115, 134–135, 139, 142, 153–154, 157, 160, 170, 176, 282, 512
Northampton, 120, 243, 291, 300, 302, 371, 466, 562
Northampton, battle of 1460, 303–305, 307, 309, 318, 326, 328–329, 335, 393, 426, 436, 558, 578
Northumberland, Henry Percy, earl of (d. 1455), 57, 72, 124, 126, 179, 196, 202, 204, 504
Northumberland, Henry Percy, earl of (d. 1461), 232, 244, 249, 260, 280, 287, 319, 321–324, 341, 343, 367–368, 521, 527, 533, 537, 550, 554, 560
Northumberland, Henry Percy, earl of (d. 1489), 364, 425, 435, 450, 540
   See also Percy
Norwich, 163, 262, 470, 536
Nottingham, 275–277, 412, 436, 470, 545

Ogle, Robert, 348, 364, 370
Oldhall, William (d. 1460), 135, 141, 162, 165, 275, 283, 544
Olney, 581
Orleans, Bastard of, *see* Dunois
Orleans, Charles, duke of (d. 1465), 20–22, 25, 28, 61, 85, 112–113, 265, 309, 358–359, 478, 481
Ormond, James Butler, earl of (d. 1452), 151, 164
Ormond, John Butler, earl of Ormond (d. 1476/78), 100, 104, 311, 385–388, 451
Ormond, Thomas, 379, 573
Oxford, earls of, *see* Vere

Panizonus, Francisco, 30
Paris, 32, 106, 158, 391, 393–394, 431
Parliament, **1445-46**, 39, 48, 54–55, 65, 461. **1447,** 62, 66–68, 231. **1449,** 50, 90, 94–95, 151, 495, 498. **1449–50,** 108–110, 115, 120–121, 505. **1450–1451.** 141–142, 144, 146–147, 150. **1453–54,** 162–163, 165, 179–182, 185, 187, 189, 195, 197, 282, 467, 469, 518. **1455–56,** 206–209, 212, 214–217, 509. **1459,** 279, 282, 284, 286–287, 290, 292, 295–296, 298, 350, 532, 544, 549, 552. **1460–61,** 308. 312, 314–317, 550, 555, 557–559, **1461,** 348–350, 458, 566. **1468,** 406, 409. **1470,** 428, 432, 443
Parthenay, Michel de, 86–89, 493
Paston, John I, 132, 151, 263, 319
Paston, John II, 325, 365, 458, 562
Paston, Margaret, 116, 163, 256, 558
Paul II, Pope, 401–403
Payn, John, 132–133
Pembroke Castle, 226, 347
Pembroke, earl of *see* Tudor, Jasper
Pembroke, earldom of, 62, 113, 124, 408, 463, 469, 470

Index

Percy family, 186, 190–191, 195–196, 245, 251, 287, 321, 364, 3167, 370, 520
Percy, Ralph, 252, 361, 364, 367, 378, 383
Percy, Richard, 195–196, 252
Percy, Thomas, Lord Egremont (d. 1460), 190–191, 195–196, 248, 252, 280
Percy, William, bishop of Carlisle (d. 1462), 202, 324, 343
  see also Northumberland, earls of
Peterborough Abbey, 292, 330
Philip of Savoy, 396, 401
piracy, 124, 242, 247, 254–255, 258–259, 269, 416, 434, 542
Pius II, Pope (d.1464), 271–272, 299, 201, 310, 325, 342, 402, 553
Pizan, Christine de, 17, 43
Pleasaunce see Greenwich
Pole, Katherine de la, abbess of Barking, 223
Pole, see Suffolk, dukes of
Pont Audemer, 91, 99
Pont de l'Arche, 90–91, 100–101, 103, 494
Pontefract, 192, 200, 298, 321–323, 435, 561
Popham, John, 108
Powderham Castle, 211
Poynings, Robert, 132
Protectorate Council, 187, 190, 195, 199
  See also York, First Protectorate, Second Protectorate
Provence, county of, 15–16, 19, 345, 397, 421, 458–459, 478, 575

Queens College, 43–44

Radford, Henry (d. 1460), 104, 280, 498, 548

Radford, Nicholas, 209, 210, 211
Raguier, Jean, 457
Reculée, 459
Reilhac, Jean de, 346–347, 566
René, duke of Anjou (d. 1480), 10–17, 19, 21, 24–28, 38, 42–43, 53–54, 70–71, 75, 98, 101, 105, 111, 177, 345, 354–355, 375, 379, 381–382, 390–391, 397, 403, 421, 459, 478–479, 491–492, 501, 574, 578–579
René, duke of Lorraine (d. 1508) 458–459, 589
Resumptions, First Act of **1450**, 121, 165, 463, 468, 508. Second Act of **1451**, 145, 463, 467–469. Third Act of **1456**, 214, 216–217, 283, 514, 527
Richard II, 60, 65, 140, 147, 159, 348
Richemont, Arthur de, Constable of France, 80, 122–123, 134, 354
Richemont-Grey, Thomas, Lord, 215, 341, 343, 565–566
Richmond, earl of, see Tudor, Edmund
Richmond, earldom of, 9, 79, 261
Robin of Redesdale, 412
Rochester, 48, 124, 131–133, 145, 244
Rochester, bishop of, see Lowe, John
Roos, Eleanor, 455, 493
Roos, Henry, 379, 493, 502, 569, 573, 576
Roos, Richard (d. c.1482), 83, 104, 469, 498, 502
Roos, Robert (d. 1448), 5–7, 21, 77–78, 85–87, 493, 499
Roos, Thomas, Lord (d. 1464), 202, 205, 244, 288, 290, 311, 319, 322, 324, 341, 343–344, 364, 382–384, 522, 551, 554, 557, 568–569
Rouen, 4, 21, 26, 28–29, 76, 79, 85–86. 88, 90, 98, 101, 156, 265, 329, 346,

354, 359, 399, 409, 431, 434, 457, 494, 496, 512
Council in, 73–74, 82–83, 461
surrender of, 102–105, 107, 120, 156, 160, 167, 385, 498
Rousel, Raoul, archbishop of Rouen, 87, 102,
Rousselet, Jean de, 80
Roxburgh Castle, 309, 323, 365, 367, 500, 556
Rutland, Edmund, earl of (d. 1460), 279, 281, 283, 293, 312, 316, 321–323

St Albans, 439–440
St Albans Abbey, 67, 254, 271, 333, 489, 544
St Albans, first battle of 1455, 202–209, 221, 224–225, 231–232, 244–245, 251–252, 269, 275, 279, 282–283, 288, 304, 350, 524, 532, 560, 576
St Albans, second battle of 1461, 330–333, 355, 389, 437, 563
St James de Beuvron, 85–87, 97
St Loo, Giles, 173, 229
St Michael's Mount, 454
St Omer, 370, 372–374, 376, 378, 430, 573
St Pauls, 37, 63, 134, 157, 205, 251–252, 300, 305, 316, 339, 426, 438–441, 453
St Pol, counts of, *see* Luxembourg
Salisbury, Richard Neville, earl of (d. 1460), 29, 49, 66, 135, 166, 177, 186, 190, 206, 209, 219, 235, 240–241, 257, 260, 263, 270, 278, 281, 283, 285, 289–290, 305–307, 527–528, 534, 556, 559
attainted, 283
at Blore Heath, 275–277, 545
as Chancellor, 186–188, 193, 199, 521, 523

death, 322–232, 560
and Henry VI, 200–201, 217, 244, 308, 527
Loveday, 248–249, 251, 153, 536–537
at Ludlow, 280–281, 546
and Margaret, 249–250, 272, 537
at St Albans 1455, 202–205
Warden of West March, 57, 186, 280, 546
with Warwick, 298, 306–308, 312, 317, 556
and York, 155, 179, 186, 192, 273, 277, 283, 297–298, 512, 546
wife of Alice Montague (d.1462), 29, 186, 283
Sandal Castle, 218, 32–322
Sandwich, town of, 158, 235, 246, 273, 288–290, 294, 296–299, 304, 306, 351, 451, 457, 570
raid on 1457, 242–244, 247, 257
Saumur, 18, 391, 479
Savoy, Philip of, 396, 401
Say, Elizabeth, 457
Say, John, 130, 188, 480, 499
Saye and Sele, James Fiennes, Lord (d. 1450), 68, 128, 130, 503–504
wife of, Emmeline Fiennes, 68
Saye and Sele, William Fiennes, Lord, 554, 584
Scales, Emma, 29, 187, 334, 482, 509
Scales, Thomas (d. 1461), 129–130, 133, 145, 137, 260, 305–306, 514, 519–520, 581
see also Woodville, Anthony
Scotland, 186, 190, 220, 231–233, 323, 329, 341, 343–344, 347, 351, 353, 357–358, 362, 364–366, 370, 372, 378–379, 380, 384, 395, 454, 530, 559, 571–572, 576
Scrope of Bolton, John, 365, 490
Scrope of Masham, John, 324, 554

Index

Sforza, Francesco, 299, 310, 325, 345
Sforza, Galeazzo, 395, 400
Sharneborne, Thomas, 195
Sheen, 43, 56, 166, 168, 217, 219
Shrewsbury, earls of *see* Talbot
Slegge, Stephen, 128, 504
Smert, John, Garter King of Arms, 278, 520
Somerset, Edmund Beaufort, duke of
    (d. 1455), 49, 58–59, 66, 71, 73. 81, 96, 99, 142–143, 173, 179, 201, 225, 269, 297, 487, 491, 493, 507, 514, 523, 529
    Captain of Calais, 150, 162, 189, 206
    character, 93, 105, 167
    and Charles VII, 85–87, 89–90, 103, 494
    claim to the throne, 14
    death, 204, 524
    and Fougères, 81, 88, 91, 97, 494
    government of, 175, 177, 196–197
    and Henry VI, 134–135, 145, 147, 150, 158, 160, 169, 170, 199, 200–201
    imprisoned by York, 176–178, 192, 194, 276–277
    King's Lieutenant in France, 59, 82–84, 90, 97, 99, 101, 122, 134, 496, 521
    and Maine, 58, 71, 73, 75, 486
    and Margaret, 84, 171, 174, 505, 15
    and Queen Katherine, 175
    and Rouen, 100, 102–104, 385
    at St Albans, 1455, 201, 207–208
    and Warwick, 166, 168
    and York, 152-157, 176, 199, 202–203, 512, 513, 517, 522
    wife of Eleanor Beauchamp (d. 1467), 83, 201, 205, 253, 286, 371, 493
Somerset, Edmund Beaufort, duke of
    (d. 1471), 232, 371, 391, 410, 438–439, 443–449. 586
Somerset, Henry Beaufort, duke of
    (d. 1464), 97, 174, 204–205, 225, 227, 240, 244, 245, 254, 260–261, 265, 288, 324, 326–327, 329, 333–334, 343, 351, 353, 363, 371, 367, 377, 383, 385, 406, 535, 540, 547, 549, 553
    campaigns in the north, 361, 365, 382–383, 576
    captain of Calais, 259, 288, 290, 296, 308, 311, 385, 550, 557
    character, 288, 323, 363, 383–384
    and Edward IV, 364, 366, 371–72, 377, 444, 573
    in France, 345–347, 566
    and Henry VI, 377, 380–381, 575
    Loveday, 248, 251, 253, 536
    and Margaret, 84, 171, 174, 505, 515
    at Towton, 340-341
    and Warwick, 244, 249, 277, 294, 311, 535–356, 537
    and York, 321–323
Somerset, John Beaufort, duke of
    (d. 1444), 8–9, 25, 82, 99, 111, 140, 147, 444, 448, 481, 490, 491
Southampton, 31–32, 244, 250, 255, 260, 294, 302, 427, 442–443
    customs duties, 96, 246, 295, 461–462, 465, 470
Southwark, 129–131, 155, 171, 206, 426
Southwell, Richard, 227–228
Southwell, Thomas, 63–64
Stafford, Henry, 238
Stafford, Humphrey, earl of (d. 1458), 200, 202, 204, 229, 235, 252, 527, 534
Stafford, Humphrey, Yorkist Earl of Devon, 412, 581

Index

Stafford, John, archbishop of
  Canterbury, chancellor (d. 1452),
  21, 31, 34, 37–38, 42, 45, 49, 50, 54,
  57, 62, 109, 129, 131, 484
Stamford Bridge, 195–196
Stanbury, John, bishop of Hereford
  (d. 1474), 229, 234, 302
Stanley, Thomas (d. 1459), 25, 64–66,
  127, 136, 187–188, 192, 201, 229,
  275
Stanley, Thomas (d. 1503), 275–277,
  283, 285, 287, 318, 415, 424
Stanlowe, Jacquetta, 367, 572
Stanlowe, Margaret, 367, 493
Stapleton, Miles, 145, 514
Stewart, James, 192
Stillington, Robert, 307, 401, 440, 444
Stodeley, John, 178–179, 181, 518, 520
Stony Stratford, 120, 136
Stourton, John, Lord (d. 1462), 571, 513
Sudeley, Ralph Botiller (d. 1473), 51–52,
  57, 66, 115, 176, 182, 229, 261, 271,
  440
Suffolk, John de la Pole, duke of
  (d. 1492), 60, 118, 145, 162, 238,
  240, 286, 347, 453, 488, 503, 535,
  5459, 563
  wife of, Elizabeth of York, 240, 437,
  453
Suffolk, William de la Pole, earl,
  marquess, duke of (d. 1450), 20–21,
  26, 28–29, 48, 55, 57, 62, 86,
  93–94, 96, 101, 108–109, 117–118,
  140–141, 162, 260, 262, 469, 481,
  496, 499–500, 534
  attainder of, 109–116, 501, 507
  character, 60–61
  and Charles VII, 21, 59, 91, 93, 97
  death of, 123–125, 502–503
  and Fougères, 80–81, 87–89, 98
  and Gloucester, 62, 65–66, 68

and Henry VI, 60–61, 82, 110,
  116–117, 135, 170
and Maine, 54, 57–58, 71, 75, 79, 499
and Margaret, 31, 45, 61, 487–488,
  501
and peace negotiations, 49–52, 70
at Tours, 22–23, 25
unpopularity of, 108, 126–127, 129,
  136, 141–142
    wife of Alice Chaucer (d. 1475),
    29, 60–62, 124–125, 129,
    135, 145, 162, 200, 205, 227,
    236, 238, 240, 286, 319, 453,
    455, 488, 563
Surienne, François de, 80–81, 87–89,
  91–92, 94, 97–98, 101, 105, 494

Tailboys, William, 114, 344, 368,
  383–384, 500
Talbot, Joan, 239
Talbot, John, earl of Shrewsbury
  (d. 1453), 26, 29, 42, 49, 84–85, 88,
  91, 98–99, 102–104, 106, 113, 153,
  156, 158, 160–161, 165, 168–169,
  512–513, 515
  Wife of Margaret Beauchamp, 29,
  239, 286, 482, 493
Talbot, John, earl of Shrewsbury
  (d. 1460), 136, 187, 201, 207, 224,
  234, 238–239, 248, 260–261, 298,
  301, 304–305, 505, 530, 534, 555
Talbot, John, earl of Shrewsbury
  (d. 1473), 238–239, 332, 424
Talbot, John, Viscount Lisle (d. 1453),
  165, 169, 224, 239, 505, 513, 515
Talbot, Thomas of Bashall, 392
Tanfield, Robert, 40, 153, 180–181
Tastar, Peter, dean of St Seurin, 160, 188
taxation, 90, 94–95, 114–115, 121, 126,
  149, 162, 165, 191, 433, 246, 292,
  406, 411, 461, 463, 486, 495, 502

Index

Tempest, Richard, 392
Tewkesbury, 446–447, 449–450
Tewkesbury Abbey, 446, 449, 587
Tewkesbury, battle of 1471, 447–448, 450, 454, 575, 584
Thorpe, Thomas, 179, 207, 283, 518–519, 548, 555
Throckmorton, Thomas, 229, 531
Tiptoft, John, earl of Worcester (d. 1470), 186–187, 200–201, 205, 224, 235, 349–350, 364, 384–385, 390, 427, 513, 515, 517, 527, 544
Tiphanie la Maigne, 17
Tours city of, 21–22, 30, 50, 70, 75, 79, 83, 85, 111, 347, 356, 358, 379, 480
Tours, Treaty of 1462, 357
Tours, Truce of, 1444, 25–26, 28–29, 48, 57, 65, 71, 78, 82, 113
Tower of London, 35, 64, 110, 114–115, 124, 128–130, 133, 141–143, 147, 155, 161, 176–178, 192, 194, 199–200, 205, 254, 271, 302, 305–307, 318, 334, 349–351, 371, 393–394, 407, 410, 425–426, 438–441, 449, 451–545, 456–457, 504, 524, 555
Towton, battle of 1461, 340–341, 343, 362, 368, 379, 385, 398, 399, 414–415, 425, 564–566, 576, 581
Tregury, Michael, 39, 99
Tresham, Thomas, 179, 282, 340, 410, 449, 563
Tresham, William (d. 1450), 66, 108, 110, 121, 136
Trevelian, John, 130, 179
Trollope, Andrew, 99, 280, 288, 296, 311, 322, 332, 340–341, 547, 550
Troyes, Treaty of 1420, 3, 51, 54
Tuddenham, Thomas (d. 1462), 140, 142, 262–263, 350, 540

Tudor, Edmund, earl of Richmond d. 1456), 161, 163, 175, 178, 201, 214, 220, 225–226, 285, 518
Tudor, Jasper, earl of Pembroke (d. 1495), 161–162, 178, 183, 201–202, 214, 219, 226, 234, 238, 261, 285, 291, 311, 319, 321, 327–328, 347, 351, 355–356, 364, 380–382, 406, 420, 424, 436, 445, 449, 463, 469, 514
Tudor, Owen (d. 1461), 32, 144, 161–162, 175
Tunstall, Richard, 163, 235, 343, 365, 382–383, 392, 408, 514, 579
Tutbury, 218, 236, 317–318, 464
Tuvache, Pierre, 88, 494
Tyrell, Thomas, 176, 555
Tyrell, William, 550, 567

Valognes, 122, 418
Vaudemont, Antoine de, 10–11, 477
Vaudemont, Ferry de, count of, 27, 102, 398
  wife of Yolande of Anjou, (d. 1483) 11, 19, 26, 458
Vaughan, Thomas, 275, 283, 544, 565
Vaux, Katherine, 379, 442, 453, 455–456, 459, 584
Vaux, William, 379, 442, 449, 575
Vendôme, Louis of Bourbon, count of (d. 1446), 22, 49–50, 485
Vere, Aubrey de (d. 1462), 348–350, 567
Vere, John de, earl of Oxford (d. 1462), 38–39, 183, 215, 260, 350–351, 535
Vere, John de, earl of Oxford (d. 1513), 410, 421, 424, 426–427, 433–434, 438, 441, 444, 454, 567, 586
Vere, Robert, 89, 101, 122–123
Verneuil, 53, 98, 100, 497
Vernon, 100, 104, 498

Index

Wakefield, battle of 1460, 321–323, 325–327, 330, 340, 393, 560, 561, 564, 576
Wales, 65, 136, 168, 187, 219–221, 225–226, 231, 234, 274, 291–292, 311–312, 318–319, 325, 327–329, 347–349, 351, 372, 377, 381–382, 403, 406, 408, 412, 436, 445, 449, 532, 557, 559, 573
Wallingford Castle, 110, 152, 220, 205, 215, 453–454, 511, 524
Walsingham, Shrine of Our Lady, 163
Warr de la, Richard, 242, 327, 341, 555
Warwick, Richard Neville, earl of (d. 1471), 168, 177, 179, 183, 186, 207, 244, 247, 249–250, 257, 275–276, 269, 296–298, 307, 309, 311, 317, 325, 355, 423, 431, 438–440, 451 513, 524, 527, 530, 532, 539, 452–546, 550, 551
   alleged attacks on, 244, 249, 268–269, 536
   attainted, 283
   and Burgundy, Philip, 256–258, 265, 289, 324; Charles, 394, 418
   Captain of Calais, 206, 234–235, 243, 246, 270, 287–290, 292, 297, 357, 415–416
   and Calais Staplers, 262, 295, 552
   campaigns in the north, 362, 364–366, 368–371, 384–385
   character, 167, 206, 255, 358
   death at Barnet, 441–442,
   and Edward IV, 281, 338, 247, 352, 377, 388–389, 395, 401, 404, 407, 424–425
      rebels against, 411–415
   and Henry VI, 201, 229, 269, 278–279, 304–305, 308, 326–327, 393, 426
   invades and rules England 1460, 298–301, 307–308, 310, 312, 329
   and London, 335, 435, 437–439
   and Louis XI, 396–397, 399–401, 418–419, 429–430, 432–433
   Loveday, 251–253, 537
   at Ludlow, 277–278, 280
   and Margaret, 272, 325, 342, 398, 402, 420–422, 428–429, 434–435
   naval exploits, 254–256, 258–259, 273, 294, 416
   at Northampton 1460, 303–305
   Readeption, 424, 426–428
   at St Albans 1455, 203–205
   at St Albans 1461, 330–333
   and Somerset, Edmund, 167, Henry, 363–364
   at Towton, 340–341
   and York, 187, 206, 270, 293, 313–315
   wife of Anne Beauchamp, (d. 1492/5), 134, 166–167, 235, 415
   see also Beauchamp Inheritance
Waurin, Jean de, 144, 311, 392, 557, 563
Waynflete, William, bishop of Winchester (d. 1486), 129, 155, 173, 182, 184, 188, 198, 224–225, 231, 236, 242–243, 247–248, 260, 272, 286, 291–292, 302, 307, 426, 528, 544, 555
Welles, Lionel, (d.1461) 136, 243, 260, 329, 341, 505, 534
Welles, Richard, 414–415
Welles, Robert, 341, 415
Wenlock, Sir John (d. 1471), 21, 44, 96, 165, 207, 210, 256, 264–266, 270, 280–281, 283, 296, 298, 306, 326–327, 333, 358, 362, 377, 394, 396, 404, 407, 416, 442, 448, 496, 502, 515, 526, 538, 542–543, 582
Wentworth, Philip, 204, 228, 365, 382, 384, 524, 544

Index

Westminster Accord 1460, 316, 318, 326, 330, 332, 334, 339, 350
Westmorland, Humphrey Neville of Brancepeth, 382–384, 413
Westmorland, Lord John Neville (d. 1461), 319, 321–322, 324, 341, 554, 560
Westmorland, Ralph, earl of, (d. 1484), 280, 321, 324, 244, 547
Weymouth, 442
Whethamstede, John, abbot of St Albans, 204, 251–252, 254, 273, 333, 547–548, 560
Whittingham, Robert, 228–229, 254, 274, 311, 334, 340, 344–347, 353, 366, 379, 407, 449, 531, 563, 566, 569, 573, 575
  wife of see Gatewyne, Katherine
Wiltshire, James Butler, earl of (d. 1461), 30, 151–152, 159, 164, 179, 200, 202, 204–205, 214, 217, 229, 231, 234, 260, 262, 271, 287, 291, 293–294, 298, 301–302, 327–328, 341, 443, 511, 513, 515, 522, 524, 527, 540, 554, 561
Winchecomb, Thomas, 193
Windsor Castle, 43, 50–51, 164, 171, 177, 179, 183–184, 193–194, 198, 206, 225, 234, 445, 453
Wingfield, Robert, 30, 140–141, 146, 506
Winnington, Robert, 258–259
Woodhouse family, 262–263
Woodville, Anthony, Lord Scales (d. 1483), 290, 341, 363, 366, 400, 410, 451, 581, 583
Woodville, Elizabeth, Edward IV's queen, 44, 389, 425, 455, 468, 503
Woodville, Richard, Lord Rivers (d. 1469), 39, 125, 127, 143–144, 149–150, 153, 244, 260, 288–290, 363, 400, 412, 529, 534
Worcester, city of, 278, 449, 450, 546–547
Worcester, earl of, *see* Tiptoft
Wyfold, Nicholas, mayor of London, 137

Yolande of Aragon (d. 1442), 10, 14, 16–18, 51, 177, 397
York, city of, 190, 196, 222, 323–324, 340–341, 362, 378, 383–384, 413, 455, 536
York, Richard, duke of (d. 1460), 55–56, 58, 70–71, 75, 86, 120, 126, 142, 152, 158–159, 162, 165, 169, 171, 201, 209, 220, 225, 240, 245, 250, 260, 262, 264, 266, 270, 275–276, 286, 303, 320, 468, 487, 496, 505, 509, 517–518, 539, 543, 546, 556, 560
  attainder of, 283–284, 287, 292
  and Calais, 189, 523
  character, 55, 138, 141, 153, 323
  claim to the throne, 146–147, 312–317
  at Dartford, 155–156, 512
  death at Wakefield, 321–323
  and Exeter, 190–193, 205, 520
  exile in Ireland, 291, 293, 297–298, 309, 312
  First Protectorate, 185–188, 194–197, 521
  and Henry VI, 135, 137–139, 143–144, 152. 154, 196, 199, 205–206, 216, 231, 269, 281, 588
  King's lieutenant in France, 8, 21, 48, 59, 82–84, 111, 113
  King's lieutenant in Ireland, 96–97, 121, 231
  Loveday, 248, 251, 253, 536–537
  at Ludford, 279–281

Index

and Margaret, 28–29, 147, 164, 193,
  218, 225, 250, 269, 272, 274, 317,
  509, 530, 549
oaths of, 157, 208, 231, 282
and Parliament, 142, 146, 179, 180,
  207–208, 282
political ambitions, 136, 175–178,
  181–182, 206, 269–270, 273
and Scotland, 306–307
Second Protectorate, 209–212,
  214–215, 217, 227
at St Albans 1455, 201–205, 208, 525
and Somerset, 96, 150, 152–154,
  156–157, 176, 194, 225
and Wales, 220–221, 231
and Warwick, 206, 268, 270, 314, 532
wife of Cecily Neville, 97, 159, 164,
  174, 220, 281, 286, 312, 330, 437,
  515, 562
Yorkist manifestos, 277–279, 297–298
Yorkist propaganda, 167, 197, 200, 247,
  273, 297, 301, 322, 330, 343, 444,
  506–507, 512, 516, 522–523, 526,
  530, 546–548, 553, 562–563, 573,
  584
Young, Thomas (d. 1477), 146–147, 171,
  509

www.ingramcontent.com/pod-product-compliance
Lightning Source LLC
Chambersburg PA
CBHW030344190426
43201CB00042B/232